GERMA

A LINGUISTIC HIS

CW00957638

GERMAN:
A LINGUISTIC HISTORY
TO 1945

By
C. J. WELLS

OXFORD
AT THE CLARENDON PRESS
1987

Oxford University Press, Walton Street, Oxford OX2 6DP
Oxford New York Toronto
Delhi Bombay Calcutta Madras Karachi
Petaling Jaya Singapore Hong Kong Tokyo
Nairobi Dar es Salaam Cape Town
Melbourne Auckland
and associated companies in
Beirut Berlin Ibadan Nicosia

Oxford is a trade mark of Oxford University Press

Published in the United States by
Oxford University Press, New York

© C. J. Wells 1985

First published 1985
Paperback edition first published 1987

British Library Cataloguing in Publication Data
Wells, C. J.
German: a linguistic history to 1945.
1. German language—History
I. Title
430'.9   PF3075
ISBN 0–19–815795–9
ISBN 0–19–815809–2 Pbk

Library of Congress Cataloging in Publication Data
Wells, C. J.
German: a linguistic history to 1945.
Bibliography: p.
Includes index.
1. German language—History.   I. Title
PF3075.W43   1987   430'.9   87–5783
ISBN 0–19–815795–9
ISBN 0–19–815809–2 (pbk.)

Printed in Great Britain
at the University Printing House, Oxford
by David Stanford
Printer to the University

I dedicate this book to my family,
Rainhild, Imogen, and Carl,
who bore the brunt . . .

PREFACE

For out of olde feldes, as men seyth,
Cometh al this newe corn from yer to yere,
And out of olde bokes, in good feyth,
Cometh al this newe science that men lere.

(Chaucer, *The Parliament of Fowles*, 22–5)

THE late Robert Auty asked me to write an introductory history of the German language for a series of which he was then editor. I very much regret that neither he nor my former tutor Ruth Harvey lived to see it in print.

The book has been written primarily for undergraduates in their final year, and it presupposes a fair acquaintance with modern German, so that I have commented only on early or recondite examples. I have attempted to treat the formal historical grammar of German in conjunction with the social and historical developments in the speech-community without committing myself to any one socio-linguistic school or orthodoxy. Naturally, the problems and methods of writing linguistic history and of identifying and analysing the individual levels of language needed discussing, so as to enable students to follow articles in journals with some inkling of the issues in dispute. In offering this guidance, I have mostly avoided the more ephemeral or idiosyncratic terminology in the interests of comprehensibility.

To cope with the complementary but burdensome demands of methodology and material, I have limited my study in three main ways. First, I have cut down the pre-German background, since this has often been treated before, both skilfully and comprehensively. Secondly, I have closed my history at 1945, which I see as marking the dawn of a new era, not as the end of German civilization and culture—despite a collection of articles which appeared some twenty years ago under the pessimistic title *Deutsch — Gefrorene Sprache in einem gefrorenen Land* (ed. Friedrich Handt, 1964). Instead, as the Nazi regime recedes into the past, in both the German Democratic Republic and in the Federal Republic of Germany 'new beginnings' are being linked up once again to their cultural, political, and therefore also, inevitably, their linguistic heritage: a process clearly shown in the recent jubilees of Goethe (1982) and Luther (1983). Consequently, the collapse in 1945 increasingly appears as a subdivision but not a break in the German cultural and linguistic continuum.[1] Thirdly, in my presentation I have interlocked formal grammatical chapters with 'socio-linguistic' ones, using a different linguistic level to represent each historical period down to the seventeenth century, by which time the statements of contemporary grammarians and authors permit discussion of stylistic and lexical developments in their literary and social setting.

The artificial structure of this book is, however, less radical and new than might appear, for it only exploits changes in perspective forced upon any linguistic historian of German by the lack of suitable or comparable evidence from all levels and periods. Indeed, the scheme brings out into the open shifts of emphasis inherent in other histories of German from Adelung onwards. At the same time I have attempted, perhaps not always successfully, to break away from a rigorously descriptive presentation of my 'data' in order to explore and interpret through different linguistic levels the varying relationships between the speakers' history and that of their language.

Some account of how language works is obviously a sensible, if idealistic, starting-point for trying to understand the historical development of any language. The very complexity of language probably itself contributes to linguistic change. In particular, I am convinced that studying the interplay of linguistic varieties in a speech-community can provide insights both into how language works and also into how—and perhaps even why—it changes. The many fascinating sources for the recent history of German would repay much fuller treatment than I could give them here and from working on them we shall learn much about German today. Thus, I

---

[1] For me personally the Second World War was a turning-point: I had my fourth birthday on a ship bound for Germany in 1946 and first learned German as a child of the Occupation from children of the occupied. Although I subsequently forgot the language almost entirely, it has fascinated me ever since.

make no apology for devoting two of my eleven chapters to the language since 1800.

I hope this book presents a coherent, single view of the history of the German language, for that would be its main, possibly sole, advantage over more detailed collective studies.[2] On the debit side, many errors and inadequacies have crept in, and these would have been more numerous still, but for the vigilance of friends and colleagues.

First of all, I have to thank my colleague Peter Ganz, without whose encouragement I might not have finished the book, and without whose criticism it would have been the poorer. To David McLintock also I am indebted for his critical reading of the early chapters and for his loyalty and friendship. From generations of pupils I learned more than they may have been aware of and more than I dare to acknowledge. I naturally owe a great deal to other people who read parts of the book, or who were patient enough to have chunks of it tried out on them by way of conversation: I have so afflicted Jonathan Bartlett, Helmut Birkhan, Herbert Blume, Theodora Bynon, Dieter Cherubim, Denys Dyer, Kurt Gärtner, Helmut Henne, Fritz Hermanns, Magdalena Heuser, Fred Hodcroft, Maria von Katte, Mansur Lalljee, Francis Lamport, Elisabeth Lang, Bruce Mitchell, Kurt Ostberg, Brian Pickering, Uwe Pörksen, and Rainer and Marianne Vasel. I thank them all, and anyone I may have inadvertently missed out. The staff of the Taylor Institution Library, the Modern Languages Faculty Library, Oxford, and the Herzog August Bibliothek, Wolfenbüttel, provided most of my material, and here I am particularly grateful to Catherine Hilliard and to Ulrich Kopp. Claire L'Enfant gave me much encouragement and help with the preparation of the book for publishing over more years than I care to remember. My German relatives, especially Dr Hildegard Hanewald and Dr Iselind Hanewald, patiently answered many curious questions about their language. At bad moments, my companions at St Edmund Hall, especially Richard Fargher and Ken Segar, were unfailing sources of inspiration and advice and constant examples of the highest standards of scholarship and teaching. The River Windrush and its trout kept me sane.

[2] The most recent collective enterprise, a work of nearly 2,000 pages, contains 177 articles by some 135 scholars: Werner Besch, Oskar Reichmann, and Stefan Sonderegger, *Sprachgeschichte: Ein Handbuch zur Geschichte der deutschen Sprache und ihrer Erforschung*, 2 vols. (de Gruyter: Berlin and New York, 1984, 1985).

Finally, I am greatly indebted to the German Academic Exchange Service, to Oxford University, and to the Leverhulme Trust for grants of money which enabled me to spend sabbatical leave at Freiburg, Vienna, and Wolfenbüttel while working on various chapters and on related topics from which the book profited. The British Academy made me a generous grant to help with the costs of setting, and this was kindly supplemented by the Curators of the Taylor Institution, Oxford, from the Fiedler Memorial Fund. Various German publishers gave permission to reproduce diagrams or tables: these have been acknowledged in the appropriate place, but I am very grateful to them. The efficiency and charm of the staff of the Clarendon Press have made the final stages of publishing bearable, and my particular thanks are due to John Waś for his patient and careful editing of some very difficult copy.

C.J.W.

St Edmund Hall,
24 April 1985

CONTENTS

LIST OF MAPS

ABBREVIATIONS AND SYMBOLS

Forms in parentheses are alternatives.

LANGUAGES

Alem.	Alemannic
Bav.	Bavarian
EFrk.	East Frankish (~ Franconian) (*Ostfränkisch*)
EGmc.	East Germanic
EMG	East Middle German (= ECG, East Central German)
ENHG	Early New High German (*Frühneuhochdeutsch, fnhd.*)
EUG	East Upper German (*Ostoberdeutsch*)
Fr.	French
Fris.	Frisian
Frk.	Frankish (Franconian)
Gk.	Greek
Gmc.	Germanic
HG	High German (*Hochdeutsch, hochdt.*)
IE	Indo-European
It.	Italian
Lat.	Latin
LFrk.	Low Frankish (~ Franconian) (*Niederfränkisch, nfrk.*)
LG	Low German (*Niederdeutsch, nd.*; also *Plattdeutsch*)
Lgb.	Langobardic
MFrk.	Middle Frankish (~ Franconian) (*Mittelfränkisch, mfrk.*)
MG	Middle German (= CG, Central German) (*Mitteldeutsch, md.*)
MHG	Middle High German (*Mittelhochdeutsch, mhd.*)
MLat.	Medieval Latin
MNeth.	Middle Netherlandish (~ Dutch)
Neth.	Netherlandish (Dutch) (*Niederländisch*)
NGmc.	North Germanic
NHG	New High German (*Neuhochdeutsch, nhd.*)
NWGmc.	North-West Germanic
OE	Old English
OFr.	Old French
OFris.	Old Frisian
OHG	Old High German (*Althochdeutsch, ahd.*)
OIr.	Old Irish

OLFrk.	Old Low Frankish ($\sim$ $\sim$ Franconian) (*Altniederfränkisch, anfrk.*)
OLG	Old Low German (*Altniederdeutsch, and.*)
ON	Old Norse
OS	Old Saxon (*Altsächsisch, as.*)
PGmc.	Proto-Germanic (Primitive Germanic) (*Urgermanisch, urg.*)
PIE	Proto-Indo-European
Platt	*Plattdeutsch* (Low German)
Rh.Frk.	Rhenish Frankish ($\sim$ Franconian) (*Rheinfränkisch, rh.frk.*)
SFrk.	South Frankish ($\sim$ Franconian) (*Südfränkisch, sfrk.*)
Skr.	Sanskrit
SRh.Frk.	South Rhenish Frankish ($\sim$ $\sim$ Franconian) (*Südrheinfränkisch, srh.frk.*)
UG	Upper German (*Oberdeutsch, oberd.*)
US	Upper Saxon (*Obersächsisch, obers.*)
V.Lat.	Vulgar Latin
WFrk.	West Frankish ($\sim$ Franconian) (*Westfränkisch, wfrk.*)
WGmc.	West Germanic
WMG	West Middle German (= WCG, West Central German)
WUG	West Upper German

PERIODICAL and other titles

AdWdDDR	Akademie der Wissenschaften der Deutschen Demokratischen Republik.
ATB	Altdeutsche Textbibliothek.
BES	*Beiträge zur Erforschung der deutschen Sprache.*
BLVS	Bibliothek des Litterarischen Vereins Stuttgart.
BMZ	Benecke, Müller, and Zarncke, *Mittelhochdeutsches Wörterbuch* (see the General Bibliography).
CLG	F. de Saussure, *Cours de linguistique générale* (see the General Bibliography).
DAdWB	Deutsche Akademie der Wissenschaften zu Berlin.
DSA	*Deutscher Sprachatlas.*
DTM	Deutsche Texte des Mittelalters.
Dt. Wg.	*Deutsche Wortgeschichte.*
DVLG	*Deutsche Vierteljahresschrift für Literaturwissenschaft und Geistesgeschichte.*
DWA	*Deutscher Wortatlas.*
DWB	*Deutsches Wörterbuch* (started by Jacob and Wilhelm Grimm in 1854, completed Leipzig, 1960).
FMSt	*Jahrbuch des Instituts für Frühmittelalterforschung der Universität Münster.*
GAG	Göppinger Arbeiten zur Germanistik.
GLL	*German Life and Letters.*
GRM	*Germanisch–Romanische Monatsschrift.*
HAB	Herzog-August-Bibliothek.
IDS	Institut für Deutsche Sprache.

JEGP	*Journal of English and Germanic Philology.*
LGL	*Lexikon der germanistischen Linguistik* (see the General Bibliography).
MLR	*Modern Language Review.*
NDL	Neudrucke deutscher Litteraturwerke des XVI. und XVII. Jahrhunderts.
OGS	*Oxford German Studies.*
PBB	*Beiträge zur Geschichte der deutschen Sprache und Literatur* (after 1955 produced separately both at Halle (= H) and Tübingen (= T)).
PMLA	*Publications of the Modern Language Association of America.*
Rh. Archiv	*Rheinisches Archiv.*
TPS	*Transactions of the Philological Society.*
VdIfdSuL	Veröffentlichungen des Instituts für deutsche Sprache und Literatur.
VdSK	Veröffentlichungen der Sprachwissenschaftlichen Kommission.
VEB	Volkseigener Betrieb.
VMzR	*Vom Mittelalter zur Reformation* (see the General Bibliography s.v. Burdach *et al.* (1893–1934)).
WA	Weimarer Ausgabe (of Martin Luther's works).
WBG	Wissenschaftliche Buchgesellschaft.
WDA	*Wörterbuch der Deutschen Aussprache* (see the General Bibliography).
WW	*Wirkendes Wort.*
ZADS	*Zeitschrift des Allgemeinen Deutschen Sprachvereins* (now known as *Muttersprache*).
ZDL	*Zeitschrift für Dialektologie und Linguistik.*
ZfdA	*Zeitschrift für deutsches Altertum.*
ZfdPh	*Zeitschrift für deutsche Philologie.*
ZfdS	*Zeitschrift für deutsche Sprache.*
ZfdW	*Zeitschrift für deutsche Wortforschung.*
ZIfS	Zentralinstitut für Sprachwissenschaft.
ZMF	*Zeitschrift für Mundartforschung.*

PARTS OF SPEECH

abl.	ablative
acc.	accusative
adj.	adjective
adv.	adverb
cogn.	cognate
dat.	dative
dem.	demonstrative
fem.	feminine
gen.	genitive
ind.	indicative
instr.	instrumental

intrans.	intransitive
masc.	masculine
mod.	modern
neut.	neuter
nom.	nominative
part.	participle
pl.	plural
pres.	present
pret.	preterite
sg.	singular
subj.	subjunctive
trans.	transitive
voc.	vocative

SYMBOLS

/ /	denotes phonemic transcription.
⟨ ⟩	denotes spelling or grapheme.
[ ]	denotes sound or phonetic transcription.
≠	denotes an opposition or difference between forms.
~	indicates variation or alternation of forms.
*	denotes a reconstructed form, sometimes also an incorrect/ unacceptable form.
>	develops into, becomes.
<	derives from.
ā, â, etc.	macron or circumflex over vowels denotes length.
Ø	zero, absence of a sound or form.
′	acute accent indicates a stressed vowel except where otherwise stated.
╪	means 'is not'.
þ	thorn, phonetically a voiceless spirant, as in English 'think'.
ð	eth, phonetically a voiced spirant as in English 'then'.
ʒʒ	voiceless dental spirant in MHG, generally developing into modern German voiceless /s/ but originally phonetically distinct from it, perhaps in intensity.

INTRODUCTION

'Why,' said the Dodo, 'the best way to explain it is to do it.'
(Lewis Carroll)

LANGUAGE

LANGUAGE is the main means by which people communicate and interact with each other, and it involves the systematic use of conventional signs in either speech or writing. However, language is not a closed system separate from other social behaviour, nor are the individual human languages, such as German, closed systems either: their boundaries are sometimes difficult to determine, they may comprise several stylistic or regional varieties, and they are influenced by other languages. The linguistic conventions must also be acquired by native speakers without formal rules, by observation and imitation, and in this way they resemble social conventions.

The term 'language' can be used in several senses, more or less technical, and we have just met two of these—the general capacity of human beings to communicate by verbal signs, and the specific forms of such communication, as 'the German language', 'the English language', and so forth. We may also speak of group languages, technical, regional, and class languages, although other terms, like 'sociolect', 'register', 'technolect', 'dialect', and 'style' are sometimes more helpful. One reason for the wide range of meanings 'language' has lies in its complexity, since it has psychological, physiological, and physical aspects. Language is psychological in two ways: first, humans have a presumably genetically transmitted ability to acquire language (this has been held to distinguish them from animals, though the matter has yet to be finally demonstrated); secondly, humans must construct their patterns or models of the particular language they acquire from the speech of those around them, and this results in a linguistic competence which varies from individual to individual and which permits a person to understand and to form utterances in their language. Language is physiological because the anatomy of lungs, throat, and mouth responds to signals from the central nervous system resulting, finally, in the physical substance through which speakers perceive language, namely sound, or speech. It will presently appear that important distinctions are to be drawn between language and speech. We are conscious of speech primarily as linear, an impression reinforced, if not actually created, by the other medium through which language manifests itself, namely writing. Writing is often felt to be inferior or secondary, inadequate for the task of representing speech 'graphically', since it cannot cope with all phonetic nuances, intonational curves, and emphases.[1] However, writing can distinguish homonyms (words and forms which sound the same),[2] it is far more regular than speech, and in German even marks grammatical categories, since nouns are at present usually written with capital letters. Writing, then, is not simply notation for what is (to be) spoken, but an alternative vehicle for language—nevertheless, it can provide clues regarding features of speech, and historians of language spend much time puzzling over them. For, inevitably, the study of a language's history often depends almost exclusively on written evidence, and any knowledge of earlier speech comes only indirectly through the spellings, through rhyme, and, less commonly, through the (not always accurate or reliable) observations made by contemporaries about their language. Unfortunately, writing tends also to be more conservative than speech and denies us immediate access to the linguistic changes taking place in the spoken language; in any case, early colloquial language has seldom been preserved. By way of compensation—for German at least—spellings in the earlier periods are less fixed and consequently more informative about pronunciation, and, moreover, many old texts were written in verse. However, of pitch, stress, and intonation, which can be stylistically important, together with tempo and volume, we know little.[3]

Four factors especially affect language, namely time, place, function, and the relationship of the speakers.[4] The historian of any particular language will naturally be much concerned with describing and accounting for those changes and developments which appear in the course of time to alter the forms in which it has been preserved. But to see such changes clearly, the other variables ought strictly to be controlled, so that the history would ideally treat shifts in the language of a particular social group of speakers from a particular dialect area using their language for a specific range of purposes over some defined period of time. In practice the data, especially from the earlier periods, do not permit such a rigorous approach, and change of perspective is inevitable. What is more, the four factors can interact stylistically, so that a feature which has virtually died out in everyday discourse in the main urban centres may be retained in poetry as an archaism, or continue in use in one or more dialects. Indeed, sometimes what may have been chronological changes can persist as dialectal (i.e. spatial) distinctions, for example, the changes to the early German consonantal system known as the Second or High German Consonant Shift (see Chapter I and Appendix A). While chronological and geographical specimens of language are relatively easily identifiable and analysable, technical and social types pose problems: in particular, a stylistic approach to any language requires an awareness of the acceptable norms of communication in a range of situations and contexts, but for the past such norms are hard to establish, especially where no standard language existed. In the case of German, for example, as with other European languages, many centuries elapsed before the emergence of an accepted literary and written (printed) standard language, and in the pre-standard phase even the extent to which the early regional, functional, and social varieties of 'German' actually belong to any such hypothetical entity as *the* German language is open to debate and may depend upon the approach adopted by the observer. For instance, a phonological study of early German documents would naturally separate Low German dialect forms from High German ones,[5] whereas a syntactic or stylistic study might ignore such differences and concentrate on the common characteristics of medieval vernacular administrative language. But even at the other end of the history of German, in the modern and contemporary periods (from 1800 to the present), where a standard language does indeed exist, the ideal and artificial nature of that standard is evident, so that for most people it cannot represent *the* German language but exists only as a prestige-variant for formal purposes, taught in schools and learned by foreigners. The standard language also functions as a

symbol of national cohesion, which explains why attempts to reform the spelling of standard German today are bound up with
politics—for German is currently spoken in the Federal Republic
of Germany, the German Democratic Republic, Austria, parts of
Switzerland, Liechtenstein, and Luxemburg, and by minorities in
France, Italy, and other parts of the world, for instance in Romania
and Pennsylvania. The standard German language (with some
modifications) extends its hegemony over most of these varieties of
German, and they can be recognized as 'German' and probably easily
enough understood by German-speakers from the Federal and
Democratic Republics and from Austria.

So, all languages vary according to the speakers using them and the
purposes to which they are put. But we must consider that, in recent
times at least, most speakers have available several varieties of
language for their individual circumstances—these linguistic varieties
are not closed systems either, nor are they consistently kept apart in
the usage of any individual—who may indeed deliberately mix
varieties for stylistic effect.

Individual varieties of a particular language alter over periods of
time, both in themselves and in their relationship to each other:
examining the interplay between language variation and language
change, and interpreting these against the background of the social
and cultural development of the speakers, constitutes one approach
to linguistic history. Before developing this idea further, it will be
necessary to examine ways of looking at language and its varieties,
since the approach adopted and aims in view condition to some
extent the object of study.

APPROACHES TO LANGUAGE AND TO LANGUAGE CHANGE

The following outline of nineteenth- and twentieth-century approaches to the study of language considers only their main
implications for linguistic history, since our view of how human
language works inevitably affects how we look upon historical
changes which have occurred in a particular language.[6] The
individual schools and movements in linguistics are most easily
distinguished by their treatment of specific problems, for example,
pre-structuralist, structuralist, and generative approaches to prehistoric and early medieval vowel and consonant systems relating to

the history of German are presented in Chapter II and Appendix A, while other chapters, notably Chapter IX, deal with socio-linguistic issues in language variability.

A. 'PRE-STRUCTURALIST' THEORIES

Despite the great advances made in the nineteenth century in the comparative and historical study of Indo-European (IE) languages,[7] the comparative method itself is not necessarily tied to any chronological framework and provides only limited historical information. The reconstructed IE and Germanic 'ancestors' or 'parent languages' (*Ursprachen*) are actually linguistic archetypes or prototypes which stand outside time, and so may be termed 'metachronic'—they have, moreover, been established by the comparison of related dialects whose evidence has come down to us from widely differing periods. Nevertheless, the comparativist's family-tree model of genetic language relationships, the so-called *Stammbaumtheorie*, reinforced the view of languages and dialects as not merely interrelated but as dependants, which inevitably implied chronological development, reflected especially in their phonology.

1. The 'genealogical tree' model (Stammbaumtheorie)

The genetic and organic approach implicit in this metaphor treated linguistic development in terms of individual dialects splitting off from a main stem and further bifurcating and ramifying. Such growth was sometimes associated with the idea of decay promoted by changes in the sounds of language. A more restrained view held that the tree model presented equivalence relationships for sounds and forms across related languages and dialects, and this approach treated the tree much as the stemma in textual criticism—as a means of constructing prototypes against which the actually occurring evidence might be measured and classified (see Chapter I). Either way, changes to sounds and forms, whether viewed organically or 'mechanistically', remained outside the sphere of influence of the speakers, and the method was over-rigid, concerned especially with the 'prehistoric' prototypes and concentrating on differences which distinguished dialects, rather than their retention of shared forms; moreover, it ignored communication among various branches of the language tree, e.g. linguistic borrowing.

The comparative work on phonology and morphology naturally formed the basis for such genetic study, which was not much concerned with the political, social, and cultural life of the speakers but treated historical grammar in isolation from them. Admittedly, studies of the vocabulary sometimes speculated about the circumstances of speakers from prehistoric periods where direct evidence was lacking, but this presupposes some fairly simple correlation between language and social reality. Jacob Grimm (1785–1863), August Schleicher (1821–68), and Wilhelm Scherer (1841–86) all wrote on the history of German, but they concentrated on its earlier 'sounds' and grammar and did not attempt any serious presentation of changes in the language in relation to changes in the social circumstances of its speakers: above all, none of them treated the more recent history of the language, which provided ample material for such investigation. A younger group of linguists working at Leipzig, known at first somewhat contemptuously as the 'Neogrammarians' (*Junggrammatiker*), introduced a scientific rigour and precision into their study of language, whether in reconstructing earlier stages or making detailed phonetic observations. Hermann Osthoff (1847–1909) and Karl Brugmann (1849–1919) taught that sound-laws brooked no exceptions; Hermann Paul (1846–1921), Wilhelm Braune (1850–1926), and (Georg) Eduard Sievers (1850–1932) were above all responsible for standard historical grammars of Gothic, Old and Middle High German, and of Anglo-Saxon which set forth clearly the phonological and morphological regularities behind the heterogeneous textual evidence.[8] The Neogrammarians were very well aware of the systematic regularity found in language, and sought to isolate factors such as analogy and foreign borrowing which distorted the operation of sound-laws: Paul devotes considerable attention to analogy, which itself emerges as a complex but systematic syntactic mechanism of considerable importance, not merely as a means of reshaping morphology (see Chapter IV). Nevertheless, the Neogrammarians were perhaps 'atomistic' in working on individual grammatical problems rather than in providing coherent interpretations of particular stages of language as a whole; they remained positivistically tied to the limited evidence of the early texts, several of which they edited. Not surprisingly, perhaps, they left the writing of linguistic histories of German to others of a less rigorous cast of thought whose idealistic sociocultural accounts sometimes made up in patriotism and nationalism for their lack of any consistent discussion of the problems of relating linguistic developments to the history of the speakers.[9] By the close of the nineteenth century—and long after—the 'internal' and 'external' linguistic history of German were presented separately.[10] But the speakers were not eliminated from all linguistic study at this period. To counteract the rigidity of the *Stammbaumtheorie*, a pupil of Schleicher's, Johannes Schmidt, proposed a new theory, the *Wellentheorie* or 'wave theory', which played a big part in the study of dialects.[11]

2. *The wave model (Wellentheorie) and dialect geography*

Schmidt's wave theory emphasized the original geographical continuity of the IE dialects and attributed the spread of some forms at the expense of others to the political, religious, social, or other (technological, for instance) supremacy of the speakers of one dialect over their immediate neighbours. Prestige varieties of language might be borrowed or imposed through language contact but decreased in intensity as they spread, much like ripples moving outwards from some centre. This view lies behind several interpretations of the Second or High German Consonant Shift, which seems also to have decreased from south to north as it affected the West Middle German (WMG) dialects along the river Rhine (see Appendix A).

Dialect geography was developed in France in the late nineteenth century by Jules Gilliéron (1854–1926) and in Germany by Georg Wenker (see Chapter IX). Linguistic features (phonological, morphological, lexical, and syntactic) are plotted on maps to show their geographical distribution, which is then interpreted in terms of movement, spread, or loss. Loans from other languages can be similarly mapped to reveal mixed or bilingual zones of language contact and interference. While it cannot 'explain' linguistic changes, dialect geography can invoke both the structure of the language and the social and political reality of the speakers in order to account for the date and rate of their spread. For example, Theodor Frings, having interpreted some features of the Second Sound Shift in their relation to late medieval political territorial boundaries, turned his attention to the East Middle German (EMG) area, where since the twelfth century the intermixing of settlers from different areas of Germany seemed to have created a 'new' colonial language with a mixture of dialectal features, the basis, perhaps, for the modern standard German language (see Chapter III).

B. STRUCTURALIST THEORIES

Several schools of structuralist linguistic theory have sprung up in the twentieth century, but we shall here be concerned only with certain historical implications of a slightly elaborated Saussurean structuralism, following the views of the Swiss linguist Ferdinand de Saussure (1857-1913). Saussure's *Cours de linguistique générale* (*CLG*), published in 1916,[12] provided the first comprehensive account of the structuralist view of language as a system of relations holding between signs whose physical nature, whether spoken or written, was unimportant. Saussure regarded this language system, which he called 'la langue', as the proper and autonomous object of linguistic study, and he distinguished it on the one hand from an innate faculty for language, which he referred to as 'le langage', and on the other hand from actual language behaviour or 'speech', which he called 'la parole'.[13] *Le langage* will not be discussed here: apparently it refers both to the capacity to acquire languages and to the phenomenon of language in general, and as such it embraces both *langue* and *parole*, which relate to the structure of particular languages and to their use by individual speakers.

The Saussurean language system (*langue*) is social and collective since it constitutes the totality of linguistic structures and patterns known to, and used by, the members of a given speech-community. Consequently, no single speaker has a complete mastery of this language system. Nor can an individual change it without being misunderstood, for the native speaker has to acquire the structures of his language from other speakers in childhood. Moreover, the linguistic sign is itself largely arbitrary in relation to the 'real world'[14]—even forms once perhaps based on naturally occurring sounds (i.e. by onomatopoeia) quickly lose their original motivation—and this arbitrariness also restricts the speaker's ability to innovate on his own. But the overall linguistic system is not directly available for analysis either: both Neogrammarians and structuralists agree that the regular features of language can be established only by observing and describing actual speech or 'output'—indeed, Hermann Paul had already distinguished between *sprechtätigkeit* covering the activity of individuals in their multifarious daily communication, and the *sprachusus* ('usage') which governs that activity, and these concepts come close to Saussure's *parole* and *langue*.[15] But, whereas the Neogrammarians were preoccupied with the varying stylistic, geographical, and above all chronological manifestations of the data or output, the structuralists preferred to theorize about the inner regularities of the system *per se*, since, after all, the speakers need know nothing about the history of their language in order to be able to discourse with one another (*CLG* 171). As Antoine Meillet (1866–1936) put it, each language is 'a rigorously articulated system where everything holds together'.[16] Saussure contrasted the descriptive, or 'static', synchronic approach to the language system with the historical, 'evolutive', diachronic approach which was complementary with it and yet unnecessary for the speakers in their linguistic interaction: in a famous analogy, he compared language activity ('le jeu de la langue') with a game of chess (*CLG* 185ff.) where all the pieces on the board at any time relate to each other. A single move alters the relations between the pieces, so playing the game involves a succession of different states of play which might then be compared with one another to produce a history of the game in its successive phases. Similarly, successive descriptions of states of a language system at different periods would permit a linguistic history (or more properly historical grammar) in terms of 'diachronic synchrony'—although Saussure himself was not much interested in this. Once again, Hermann Paul had already seen the limitations of a historical treatment of such chronologically separated grammatical states of language (*sprachzustände*): as abstractions they are beyond the direct influence of actual language use, and one abstract synchronic stage cannot develop into another since they lack any causal connection:

Die descriptive grammatik verzeichnet, was von grammatischen formen und verhältnissen innerhalb einer sprachgenossenschaft zu einer gewissen zeit üblich ist . . . Ihr inhalt sind nicht tatsachen, sondern nur eine abstraction aus den beobachteten tatsachen. Macht man solche abstractionen innerhalb der selben sprachgenossenschaft zu verschiedenen zeiten, so werden sie verschieden ausfallen . . . aber über das eigentliche wesen der vollzogenen umwälzungen wird man auf diese weise nicht aufgeklärt. Der causalzusammenhang bleibt verschlossen, so lange man nur mit abstractionen rechnet, als wäre eine wirklich aus der andern entstanden. Denn zwischen abstractionen gibt es überhaupt keinen causalnexus, sondern nur zwischen realen objecten und tatsachen (Paul (1880/1968), 2nd edn. (1886), 22).

Two, more banal, problems for the historian are, (1) the difficulty of giving even a simplified account of the total and interlocking structure of the various phonological, morphological, syntactic, and semantic components of language, a difficulty compounded by the incomplete data available from periods in the past; and (2) the difficulty of identifying suitable texts to represent 'successive outputs' of the 'same' speech-community and to reflect linguistic continuity. In purifying the data to cope with the second problem, philological methods (such as palaeography, archive research, textual criticism), and literary and stylistic analysis, are necessary in order to date, localize and assess stylistically texts from the past—this relates partly to external factors conditioning the way the language system is used by speakers, and it is here that linguistic changes occur or, as Paul (1880/1968), 2nd edn. (1886), 29, put it, 'Die eigentliche ursache für die veränderung des usus ist nichts anderes als die gewöhnliche sprechtätigkeit'. Saussure too relegated such changes to *parole* as outside his focus of interest (*CLG* 77–81, 197 f.). The chess analogy appropriate to the language system breaks down at this point, for it takes no account of new pieces imported into the game, by linguistic borrowing, say, nor of the taking over by one structure of the functions of another by analogical change (but pawns *can* become queens).

An inherent weakness of the structuralist position lies in this view of the language system as utterly coherent, all variation being attributable to *parole*. Subsequently, structuralists of the 'Prague School' have questioned this assumption, e.g. its founder Nikolay Trubetskoy (1890–1938), for whom language was 'a whole composed of several partial systems'.[17] Again, the language system itself has been seen as susceptible to shifts for purely structural reasons, e.g. when its vowel or consonant systems become 'unbalanced' in some way. Although such shifts may still be triggered off by external factors like borrowing, they may be partly conditioned by the nature of the system itself (see Chapter II). At another level, the apparently straightforward matter of lexical borrowing implies gaps in the vocabulary (see Chapter VII), i.e. in the lexical structure.

The structuralist approach provides insights into the relationships of elements within the language system and has particularly favoured the study of abstract units such as phonemes and morphemes (see Chapters II and IV); furthermore, the Saussurean approach to the linguistic sign stimulated the study of meaning (see Chapter X). Nevertheless, partly because it represented a reaction against the comparative and historical positivism of the Neogrammarians, structuralism has tended to treat the language system and its individual levels of phonology, morphology, and so forth as complete and closed in themselves and, above all, separated from the speakers whose communication provides the basis for historical study. For the linguistic historian, to present a crude account of the developments in the output (*parole*) of a speech-community over a period of time seems possible: assessing the extent to which the language system (*langue*) changes is controversial and depends also upon how that system is described. While the structuralist approach allows for language change via the *parole* and assumes that innovations are adopted from there into the language system and become part of it, when and how this occurs remains unclear. For instance, borrowing from other languages can result in alternative forms and words entering particular sub-communities where their use fluctuates for a considerable time according to purpose, formality, and other stylistic factors. Here again the notion of a single homogeneous system seems too simple—and we have already mentioned the many varieties of German (above, pp. 3–4). Finally, the language system might be understood as virtually unchanging, while, instead, different structures from it become accessible or more or less prominent in speech at different periods. Such a view would remove the language system from the effects of time altogether, and this is surely implausible with respect to loan-words, many of which remain stylistically and formally identifiable as 'foreign' in the language for centuries.

C. GENERATIVE THEORIES

Generative grammar has undergone many developments since its initiation by Noam Chomsky in the late 1950s,[18] but central to all approaches which can loosely be termed 'generative' is the individual's linguistic creativity, which exploits the familiar dichotomy between the underlying language system (the 'grammar') and the realization or manifestation of this system in the actually occurring utterance. This linguistic creativity specifically involves the speaker–hearer's ability to produce acceptable sentences in his language which he has neither heard nor produced before, and to interpret sentences produced by other speakers which he has never heard before: this he achieves thanks to his intrinsic and more or less unconscious knowledge of his own language, his grammar of it. Ideally, generativists would like to know how the mind organizes linguistic data in that grammar, since this naturally has implications for how language is acquired and how linguistic structures are produced and perceived, i.e. understood. In practice, we are unable to determine how this part of the mind works—nor can physiological studies of the brain as yet provide a key to this immensely complex issue. However, although we cannot study the individual's own grammar of his language (which generativists call his 'competence'), linguists can still construct models to represent this competence, and such are the grammars whose formal properties are discussed by generative theories.[19] The relationship between the model and the speaker's 'real' grammar cannot be determined, and more than one model grammar can be devised—which explains much of the theoretical debate within the various generative approaches. Nevertheless, the competing model grammars for a particular language can be evaluated, since each grammar must conform to certain criteria, such as simplicity, adequacy, and generality. Briefly: simplicity requires the simplest grammar which can (1) account not merely for some given set of data but also for new sentences acceptable to speakers of the language (i.e. meet the adequacy requirement); and (2) which can embody a linguistic theory applicable to languages other than the one under analysis (i.e. meet the generality requirement).[20]

Note further that in the more modest aim of looking for the best model grammar to account for linguistic behaviour the term 'generate' is used in a special sense to mean 'attribute a structural description to': 'When we speak of a grammar as generating a sentence with a certain structural description, we mean simply that the grammar assigns this structural description to the sentence' (Chomsky (1965), 9); and this is akin to its use as a technical term in mathematical logic. Linguists postulate grammatical rules to relate the underlying syntactic 'deep structures' of the model grammar to its 'surface structures'. The surface structures themselves are not necessarily the utterances, but are rather 'subcutaneous' and need a physical interpretation by the application of phonological rules, just as the syntactic deep structures require a full semantic interpretation. The rules mediating between deep and surface structures represent encoding and decoding processes in the model grammars which are known as 'transformations'.[21] Consequently, generative theory reflects a dynamic conception of human language as system and process, rather than as a static store of systematic elements which the Saussurean view implies.

The dynamic approach to language as activity had already been proposed by Wilhelm von Humboldt (1767–1835):[22]

Die S p r a c h e, in ihrem wirklichen Wesen aufgefaßt, ist etwas beständig und in jedem Augenblicke V o r ü b e r g e h e n d e s . . . Sie selbst ist kein Werk (*Ergon*), sondern eine Thätigkeit (*Energia*). Ihre wahre Definition kann daher nur eine genetische sein. Sie ist nämlich die sich ewig wiederholende A r b e i t   d e s   G e i s t e s, den a r t i c u l i r t e n   L a u t   zum Ausdruck des G e d a n k e n fähig zu machen.[23]

Humboldt also realized that language makes 'an infinite use of finite means', which generativists interpret as the operation of recursive rules, permitting certain structures to be repeated or combined indefinitely.[24]

Chomsky replaces the Saussurean distinction between *langue* and *parole* by one between 'competence' and 'performance', where competence is the individual's grammar or knowledge of the language constructed in childhood by every speaker, and performance is the actual output produced by this internalized grammar in particular circumstances. Notice that, whereas *langue* is collective and social, competence is individual—although it is also idealized: 'Linguistic theory is concerned primarily with an ideal speaker-listener, in a completely homogeneous speech-community, who knows its language perfectly . . .' (Chomsky (1965), 3). But the linguist's model of competence also includes sets of combinatorial and recursive rules to account for the syntactic structures of the output: in this respect, part of the Saussurean *parole* seems to have been incorporated into the ideal individual's grammar. Performance, on the other hand, is characterized by memory limitations, errors, etc., not by socio-linguistic factors such as stylistic or regional variation—and here lies a weakness of generative theory, especially in respect of linguistic history which shows how the interaction of varieties of a language can shape its grammar.

Inevitably, a diachronic generative study of a language which disregards the dialectal and sociological influences by postulating a homogeneous speech-community will result in an idealized historical grammar, not in a linguistic history which interprets linguistic change against the background of changes in the speech-community. Thus, the historical generativist constructs a grammar, G1, for some earlier stage of a language and then compares it with a grammar, G2, which he has constructed for some later, possibly modern, stage of the same language: he must then account for the differences between the two grammars—usually in terms of changes to the rules applying to the base syntactic structures. As Calvert Watkins puts it:

A historical sequence of texts is a series of outputs of successive *synchronic* grammars—grammars, in other words, which were complete at a particular point in time. The problem of the linguistic historian, however, is to determine how one grammar actually changes into a succeeding one.[25]

However, several problems arise. First, in constructing models of the competence of earlier speakers we cannot call upon the native speakers to test the acceptability of the structures they generate—and only relatively late in German's history do we begin to find explicit comments from contemporary grammarians (late sixteenth century). Secondly, the historical texts or data usually reflect the interaction of several individuals, not *one* competence, for in monastery and chancery texts are translated, transferred from one dialect to another, copied and emended by scribes, and are often poorly datable or localizable; early printings reflect the combined effort of printers, compositors, and correctors, who may, like the monks and chancery scribes, all come from different regions and backgrounds. But even if we *can* draw up G1 and G2, establishing any relationship between them poses a third, more serious, difficulty: no true continuity connects the grammars, for, like Paul's abstract *sprachzustände* (see above, p. 9), they cannot, *qua* abstractions, relate to each other directly, but only via their output. Treating performance in isolation from competence is not possible either, for one individual's output cannot relate to or influence another individual's output except indirectly, via the competences of their users. Obviously, where data from different historical periods are concerned these outputs are clearly unconnected—except in the linguistic historian's comparison. Moreover, performances chosen for analysis from different periods may not even be attributable to any hypothetical succession of grammars at all: for example, the modern German standard language can only be traced back so far, until the elements which have come to make it up disappear in a mass of competing linguistic varieties in periods where no standard language existed and hence all language was 'dialectal'. So the exercise of comparing individual grammars across the centuries is a highly notional one. These objections do not discredit the generative approach in itself but merely show its limitations in historical linguistics. Without necessarily providing convincing models of the particular changes which have occurred, the formal presentation does at least identify those areas of a language which are, or have been, unstable and those which have remained virtually unaltered. Effectively, G2 is interpreted as the result of several kinds of changes which would have to have affected the earlier G1 to achieve the output from which G2 has been constructed. The differences may be of various kinds, including (1) rule addition—to account for traditional sound changes, for example see Chapter II and Appendix A; (2) rule loss; (3) rule reordering;[26] and (4) rule simplification. The last three types of rule change are often linked, are most easily observable in their effects on morphological systems (see Chapter IV), and are perhaps typical of changes taking place from one generation to another.[27]

A generative model of language acquisition has been applied to the question of language change,[28] again, formulating an old idea clearly. The child (C) is assumed to construct a grammar (competence) from the output (performance) of the adult (A). However, the child's analysis does not result in a grammar exactly like that of the parent: in other words, GA and GC are not isomorphic. From the linguist's viewpoint, the child has simplified or otherwise restructured the parental grammar and then constructs forms and sentences which can differ from those of the parent's performance, e.g. in overgeneralized forms like the preterites: English *goed (for 'went'); German *schlafte (for 'schlief'). A simplified model would be that shown in Fig. 1. The generative theory holds that the children

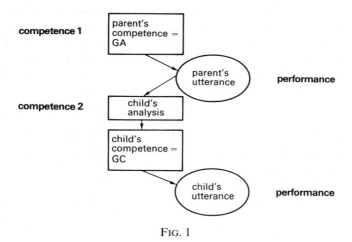

FIG. 1

grow up with slightly different grammars from their parents', and then in turn become the older generation whose performance again forms the basis for their children's grammars, which also differ: so language evolves from generation to generation. Obviously, this is all speculative. Among the objections[29] we should note that the child is subject to the performance of a whole series of adults, some of it idiosyncratic ('baby-talk'). More seriously, the over-simplified forms *goed and *schlafte are purified out of the grammar by *social* constraints, since the child's analysis, and consequently grammar, seem to be revised.[30] Social factors also account for the existence of groups of young people with 'languages' of their own—e.g. 'student slang', which has a considerable history within the German language.[31] As for children's language, this tends to be linked to institutions, notably school, where it remains sur-prisingly conservative, passed on as lore to successive generations at a particular phase of their development, not carried on into adult life. Consequently, language acquisition can have little obvious influence on the speech-community at large, and only very recently— since 1945—do we find an influential 'youth culture' which is both promoted and exploited commercially (and which has, indeed, become international).

D. SOCIO-LINGUISTIC APPROACHES

Studying language in relation to the users acknowledges both its 'conventional' nature[32] and its various social functions, including (1) to communicate information, attitudes, and opinions; (2) to inte-grate speakers into social classes and groups, which enables them to fulfil social roles; and (3) to influence and control individuals and communities. Indeed, it has been questioned whether any other than a 'socio-linguistic' approach to language is possible, making the use of that adjective otiose.[33] However, some defining term is probably necessary to mark attempts to bridge the gap which has opened up since the late nineteenth century between studies of language abstracted from the speech-community and the more pragmatic approaches of dialectology and, recently, of sociology. Perhaps 'integrational linguistics' is accurate and unexceptionable:

First and foremost, an integrational linguistics must recognise that human beings inhabit a communicational space which is not neatly compart-mentalised into language and non-language.[34]

From the diachronic standpoint which interests us here, such an approach would seek to overcome the distinction drawn between *internal* (structural and grammatical) linguistic history and *external* linguistic history relating changes in language (usually in vocabulary) to changes in the speech-community. Naturally, the simple juxtaposition of grammar and history proves unsatisfactory—the links between the two must be established and interpreted and this process of interpretation makes linguistic history fascinating and tantalizing.

Furthermore, historical linguistics suddenly assumes a greater importance than of late, for its whole conception of language must accommodate variability and change, and if a successful model can be devised it may yet have a bearing upon how language works. For, if variability can be shown to have influenced the development of a language, we can interpret it as an important factor in language use. Historical case-studies over long periods of time can complement and perhaps corroborate short-term but more sophisticated statistical examination of language use at the present day. While treating language as a rule-based activity, we need not postulate an underlying homogeneous system which is self-regulating (*homeostatic*). As Uriel Weinreich and others have put it:

It seems to us quite pointless to construct a theory of change which accepts as its input unnecessarily idealized and counterfactual descriptions of language states. Long before predictive theories of language change can be attempted, it will be necessary to learn to see language—whether from a diachronic *or* a synchronic routage—as an object possessing orderly heterogeneity.[35]

So, language is regarded by these scholars as a 'systemoid', comprising sub-systems or varieties determined by rules of which the speakers are aware. Any individual has at his disposal differing social and dialectal varieties which are not homogeneous, invariant systems, but themselves contain variables, such as archaisms or innovations which can survive as peripheral features for some time. The concept of a structural variable makes possible the interpretation of fluctuations in usage as 'systematic' themselves, since control of and perception of such variation are actually part of the linguistic competence of the members of the speech-community.

How individuals live and communicate accounts also for the varieties of their language and the purposes for which they use it. Consequently, changes in social structure and in the speakers' communicative needs are bound to affect their language, as are new forms of transport and travel which will bring them together, and

new media for communication which allow them to address each
other separated by time and space—writing, then printing, the
telephone, radio, and television, tape- and video-recorders, etc.
While the historian admittedly does not have access to all the
linguistically relevant social phenomena from the past, he can
observe the effects of the most important of them—after all, not all
historical events need be of great social and linguistic import, not
even military victories or the deaths of kings. Instead, the communicative needs and the media for transmitting them influence the kind
of data which will survive. For instance, in the earliest periods for
which we have texts, primarily religious, legal, and poetic varieties of
German are preserved—we catch only glimpses of a fourth variety of
language which must have existed, namely the everyday colloquial
language, and we are poorly informed regarding early technical
German for, say, medicine, agriculture, or fishing (except in glosses of
Latin texts). This picture is generally confirmed by the evidence from
other Germanic languages; indeed, religion, law, and poetry are often
linked in other early societies. The limited surviving functional
varieties of early German appear in 'dialectal' forms: and the absence
of any standard written language confirms a lack of cultural and
political cohesion, since the texts show strongly regional features
and differ in consistency and in their conformity to local written
traditions (see Chapter I). By comparison the indefinite number of
nineteenth-century linguistic varieties of German show considerable
standardization: most religious, legal, and poetic writing is firmly
linked to a standard and literary language—as are many of the
administrative technical and scientific forms of German. Although
political centralization was not achieved until late in the century, the
evolving standard language had long acquired sufficient prestige and
symbolic status to overcome geographical differences (but to maintain social ones) (see Chapter IX). Moreover, each technical variety
has functionally and formally varying types, some of which are close
to the spoken colloquial, which is no longer narrowly identifiable
with any particular dialect. Comparing German around 850 with
German around 1850, then, we find a massive increase in the
available data, new varieties of technical and social usage not
hitherto preserved on parchment or in print, a general loss in prestige
of dialectal and regional forms, and a corresponding concern with a
standard German for literary and all other intellectual, administrative, and representative purposes—a form of language, moreover,

which is almost exclusively the one with which grammarians and lexicographers are preoccupied.[36] This standard also symbolized the idea of German political unity—it provided an ostensibly unifying bond for all German-speakers, at least of the middle and upper social strata.

The prestige of certain forms of language can be used for social as well as political control. In the terminology of feudalism, the whole range of expressions for service and reward, dependency and respect naturally reflects the structure of feudal society. But, at another level, the *inappropriateness* of such language is crucial to its use for politeness: noblemen of equal status address each other in terms of vassalage which do not reflect their relationship, or again, a superior will verbally abase himself in a gesture which cannot possibly be taken at face value—for the discrepancy between the lord's rank and his public protestations of service is too great. At the same time, the use of such terms invests the station of vassal with positive value and contributes perhaps to the stability of the social system.

Marxist scholars of German also argue that the distinction between linguistic changes that are external (*sprachextern*) and those which are internal (*sprachintern*) should be discarded, since language ought to be integrated into the total system of social relationships.[37] However, the theories of socio-economic societal development and of the class struggle are perhaps too general in nature to be convincingly related to the linguistic details of any particular language. Nor would it be appropriate that they should be, since the processes involved are not limited to any particular society either. In other words, 'tribal', 'feudal', and 'bourgeois'/'capitalist' social systems need to be broken down further into their manifold characteristics in terms of classes, mobility, cohesion, and historical roles before specific linguistic features can properly be attributed to them. If not, they provide merely an alternative ideologically orientated periodization, as for example in a recent history of German by Joachim Schildt,[38] where a prehistoric phase of Indo-European and Germanic tribalism extends from the fifth millenium BC to the fifth century AD, followed by a feudal period from the fifth century to 1789, and then succeeded by a bourgeois/imperialist period from 1789 to 1945. To be fair, Schildt further subdivides these unwieldy chunks of time and discusses the socio-linguistic factors treated in 'bourgeois' linguistic histories. We shall return to the important and vexed matter of an adequate periodization for German below. In the mean while it will be useful to identify some of the possible sources of linguistic change implicit in a theory of language—whether we call it 'socio-linguistic', 'integrational', or 'Marxist–Leninist'—where language is not viewed as a determinate and monolithic system but rather as systematic activity within changing social circumstances.

VARIABILITY AND CHANGE

Once we accept the existence of linguistic varieties within a society we have a potential source of innovation, as forms from one variety spread and are adopted into the generally spoken colloquial and perhaps even into the prestige standard form of the language. Case-studies of changes under way in contemporary social and urban environments suggest that the generalization or spread of some already extant linguistic variant is involved, rather than the spontaneous emergence of 'new' forms.[39] The socially and geographically conditioned varieties of language are thus interacting among themselves and influencing each other.

But the individual varieties of language are themselves subject to change, since they too are not determinate systems. It has long been recognized, for example, that contiguous dialects are not sharply distinguished but tend to shade into each other, as do the LG and Neth. dialects: consequently the delimitation of a dialect area may depend upon the criteria applied, not on any 'natural break'. Technical and scientific varieties are open to influence from a different quarter, namely from the corresponding registers in other language communities. The modern international norms of scientific units and nomenclature break down cross-language barriers and erect new barriers within a given speech-community between specialist and non-specialist. These international influences on technical forms of German also occurred in the past, on a smaller scale and at a slower pace but nevertheless evident—for instance, the international military terminology for ranks, formations, and warfare in the sixteenth and seventeenth centuries (see Chapter VII).

Borrowing from other languages represents a major source of innovation and development in the vocabulary and to a lesser extent also in morphology and other levels of language. The reasons and routes of such innovation are many, but adoption into one of the linguistic varieties and spread into the others seems the obvious way in which one language is influenced by another. However, some isolated loans become current without establishing themselves within a particular specialist register or in the usage of a social group: nowadays, the press and radio and television provide the mechanisms for instant and general diffusion of a foreign loan, while the increasing economic and political interdependence of countries accounts for the linguistic interaction (for the types of borrowing, see Chapter VII).

The individual levels of language—phonology, morphology, syntax, and vocabulary—are not determinate, autonomous systems, for they interlock. In particular, phonology and morphology blend, as do morphology and syntax: indeed, some generative theories actually dispense with a separate morphological level altogether. But the linguist must also establish the units of each level in order to carry out his analysis, and these units are not predetermined and invariant either. For example, at the phonological level sound appears to be a continuum which must be organized into discrete units in terms of what is important for linguistic perception: the phonemes, or functional sound-units, of a language do not correspond to naturally occurring divisions of 'phonetic or acoustic space', they are established by several criteria, including their ability to differentiate forms. The actual phonetic realization of these basic sound-units varies considerably from speaker to speaker and also in the same speaker— no writing system can do more than suggest the phonetic richness of speech, and playwrights sometimes instruct actors to adopt a particular pronunciation without providing a consistent notation for it.[40] Indeed, all levels of language are affected by style, although this variability is most obvious in the differing pronunciation and choice of vocabulary employed by the same speaker, more or less consciously, in his varied everyday communication. Herein clearly lies a source of language change which has become increasingly important as greater geographical and social mobility and the availability of the mass media have brought speakers in modern societies into contact with a very wide range of styles.

So, when we consider possible mechanisms for the changes which have affected the German language we shall have to bear in mind the variability and indeterminacy of all forms of language and the versatility of the speakers in adapting their usage.

PERIODIZATION OF THE GERMAN LANGUAGE

The six periods into which German will be divided in what follows relate closely to the structure of the book, and some discussion of them is necessary here, although the details will be reserved for the appropriate chapters. German, like other languages, does not fall naturally and neatly into periods, and competing schemes for its chronological dissection reflect the differing criteria and aims of its historians.[41] Firstly, any periodization should facilitate the analysis and presentation of the data, whether the periods are based on linguistic, socio-linguistic, cultural, literary, or political criteria, or on combinations of these. Secondly, the scheme adopted cannot ignore the already well-established traditional periodizations, so some reconciliation and compromise with them is essential. The individual periods here proposed overlap to avoid undue subservience to fixed points in time, and the criteria for periodizing also change, partly because of the limitations imposed by the surviving evidence and partly because the traditional histories of German shift their perspective. By deliberately emphasizing this shift in perspective a selective and economical approach to the data is made possible, while the artificial way in which they are presented emphasizes the interpretative rather than purely descriptive approach. Wherever possible linguistic and socio-linguistic criteria have established the periodization, but for the modern periods since the mid-seventeenth century opinions about the importance of individual periodizing factors diverge.

Jacob Grimm proposed the famous division into three stages: Old High German[42] ('Althochdeutsch'), c.750–1100; Middle High German ('Mittelhochdeutsch'), c.1100–1500; and New High German ('Neuhochdeutsch'), from 1500 to the present (i.e. nineteenth century). This elegant tripartite scheme had a consistent terminology, was linked to extant historical periods, and was suitable for a large-scale comparison of stages from all Germanic dialects to show their progressive deviation from old, reconstructable 'proto-forms'. Subsequently, historical grammarians adopted Grimm's terminology and periodization, producing more or less complete grammars of 'OHG', 'MHG', and 'NHG'. However, this pattern proves inadequate for the detailed, small-scale examination of the whole span of German's linguistic history, which Grimm did not himself undertake systematically. First, another period, called Early New High German ('Frühneuhochdeutsch') is now generally intercalated between MHG and NHG, although its chronological boundaries remain disputed: 1350–1650, as proposed by its first exponent, Wilhelm Scherer,[43] seems the most widely accepted dating. This period, which cuts across Grimm's MHG period, is characterized by a multiplicity of texts in different dialect forms and a variety of registers, making its chronological extent difficult to establish on linguistic grounds alone; for the same reason, no full grammar of ENHG has yet been written.[44] While the texts of this tantalizing period are increasingly studied for their own sake, linguistic historians have persistently justified the starting-point at 1350[45] with the spurious argument that certain phonological developments characteristic of the modern standard language—notably diphthongizations and monophthongizations of some stressed syllables—are present in the orthography of documents from the imperial chancery at Prague, in an eastern area colonized by German-speakers since medieval times. Such 'colonial' German ('East Middle German'— EMG) has long been regarded as the source of the modern standard for precisely these phonological reasons, but the links between it and the immediately preceding MHG and the later periods of German's history are tenuous, as we shall see (pp. 134–7). At the least, there has occurred a multiple change of perspective from the MHG data: whereas 'MHG' in its typical form (as codified in grammars) is based on literature written for aristocratic circles mainly in the south or south-western parts of the German-speaking lands, the ENHG period begins in administrative documents in the eastern central regions. Geographically we have moved to new, 'colonial' areas, stylistically to a different kind of language, and 'teleologically' to the search for the origins of a standard German.

Another serious objection to both tripartite and quadripartite schemes is the need to subdivide the time-span from 1650 to the present. This 'NHG' period is characterized by the existence of a recognizable, if not at first generally recognized, 'book-language' which was progressively codified and successfully imposed on educated sectors of the population in schools. At the same time, no 'sound changes' or other radical alterations to the structure of the language are observed—instead, change occurs piecemeal by the selection and generalization of what are held by grammarians and authors to be desirable linguistic features—whole generations of grammarians constitute a formidable epistemological array. But in a sense the grammarians as arbiters of change and printing as its vehicle may be simply refinements of processes of 'variable generalization' akin to earlier 'sound change': what has made changes after about 1650 seem *qualitatively* different from earlier changes is the new medium of printing (see especially Chapter V). Printing and the grammatical activity stimulated by it allow us to examine the generalization of variables in the written traditions of German: this process seems 'messy' precisely because we can observe it more fully than the earlier changes, where we can only register the successful adoption of what may once have been phonological 'variables' as fully integrated 'constants'. However, an increasingly monolithic printed language constituted a barrier to actual spoken forms—indeed, the discussions about standard German were conducted in terms of variables in regional written (or printed) traditions. We can see this in the eighteenth-century grammatical controversy over the dialectal basis of the standard language—an issue which had by that time been out of date for nearly two centuries. These problems will be pursued later, here we note simply that preoccupation with the standard language obscures many interesting developments in other varieties of German during recent centuries which persist in dialectal, informal colloquial, or technical usage. Ironically, the standard language has apparently lost ground since its codification in spelling and pronunciation in the late nineteenth century: for new inventions—the telephone, phonograph, and radio—heralded the end of the monopoly of written language in public life, even though it symbolized German political unity and links with other states, like Austria-Hungary and Switzerland. Simultaneously, serious social drama began to explore the possibilities of non-standard speech on the stage (see Chapter IX).

The need to subdivide the later centuries of German raises terminological problems too, since the obvious modifiers like 'Early' or 'Late' are already in use. Moreover, because some formal topics of historical grammar will be treated in this book, replacing the traditional labels *OHG*, *MHG*, *(E)NHG* throughout would be difficult, and indeed misleading. Consequently, the old terms will be used for simplicity's sake in citing examples, discussing grammatical features, and so forth, while more differentiated labels will be reserved for the socio-linguistic developments. The term 'Prehistoric German' covers the centuries from which only isolated German words or inscriptions have been preserved—the pre-textual phase;

then follows the Early German period from the early eighth century until 1100, overlapped by the Medieval period from 1050 to 1500, which is in turn succeeded and overlapped by a Transitional period from 1450 to 1650 in which the effects of printing are increasingly felt. An Early Modern period comprising roughly the seventeenth and eighteenth centuries again overlaps the Transitional period and shows the civilizing of the literary language—and grammar subservient to literary taste, not empirical observation. The Modern period runs from about 1800 to 1950 and reflects above all the changed political circumstances of the speakers—the dates 1789 (French Revolution), 1805 (end of the Holy Roman Empire), and 1815 (defeat of Napoleon) might each have formed a starting-point, so here, too, 1800 is a convenient rather than compelling date. After 1950 another period begins which may be labelled the Contemporary German period, and it falls outside the scope of this book: in fact, no linguistic developments after 1945 will be discussed, partly because very little work has been done on the immediate post-war German language. The cataclysmic effects of the Second World War altered the whole geographical, social, cultural, and political life of Germany and to a lesser extent of Austria also. The political split into the Federal Republic and the Democratic Republic of Germany is perhaps the most striking political and social change. However, the dialectal foundations of German were shaken in many areas because of the migration, flight, and resettlement of the speakers; other regions, especially in their industrial and urban centres, were affected by an influx of refugees from different areas. However, the full effects of these upheavals were not felt until the 1950s, and immediately after the war there seems to have been a brief interlude of literary, linguistic, and 'social' reversion to the pre-1933 era. Fig. 2 (overleaf) illustrates the relationship of the two schemes.

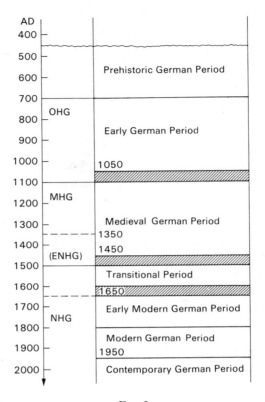

FIG. 2

PRESENTATION AND PERSPECTIVES

The limitations imposed by the available evidence and the existing
studies of it make shifts in perspective like those already mentioned
(p. 23) difficult to avoid when writing German linguistic history.
Other problems involve presentation—how to avoid repetitiveness.

Starting with a series of chronological stages becomes cumbersome if the aim is to survey changes occurring at all levels of language from spellings to style and meaning. On the other hand, treating individual levels separately permits a more thorough discussion of the best ways of analysing them, but at the expense of further repetition in the historical framework of reference, resulting in a series of discrete 'histories'—a history of the phonology, a history of the morphology, and so forth. Moreover, conflicting aims affect the actual selection of data to be presented: is the intention to trace the evolution of linguistic features which remain in the modern standard language or some other linguistic variety of German today? Or should the individual periods be illustrated by features typical of the language at the time and of the purposes to which it was put? If the first of these approaches is adopted, we might actually choose to start with contemporary German and trace its features back until they peter out in archetypal reconstructions;[46] in practice most histories of German tacitly select for discussion those developments which survive into modern times, and they may also concentrate too much on innovations instead of presenting the more constant linguistic elements which vouchsafe the language's continuity.

Here the problems of perspective-shift and presentation are tackled by adopting the deliberately artificial scheme of choosing a different level of language to illustrate each period. Surprisingly, the material lends itself to this simple approach, which avoids repetition and gains space for discussion and analysis of the individual levels of language. At the same time, the relationship between varieties of German and their users in a given historical period can perhaps be more readily interpreted by limiting observation to a particular linguistic level. Two premises are: (1) that the relationship between any linguistic level and the users will vary from period to period; and (2) that the examination of the relationship is interpretative rather than descriptive, since the selection of data necessarily involves commitment to a theory of language which in turn provides criteria for determining the 'facts' on which the investigation will be based. Perhaps criticism of this attempt to integrate internal and external linguistic history will contribute to the current debate on the role and limitations of diachronic linguistics.

Chapter I deals with both the Prehistoric and Early German periods and with the problems of linguistic reconstruction, identifying speakers and tribes, and distinguishing the main linguistic varieties. The IE, PGmc., and WGmc. background receives only limited attention. Chapter II illustrates pre-structuralist, structuralist, and generative approaches to OHG phonology, setting it off against the reconstructed or proto-languages. Chapter III discusses the main facets of the Medieval period—the geographical expansion, growth of towns, social mobility, and use of written language for new administrative and technical purposes. Chapter IV treats developments in the MHG morphology of the same time-span, looking both at functional interaction of competing grammatical systems within paradigms and at geographical variation, which reflects both the continuing lack of a standard language and other factors, including the mixed composition of chancery staffs and the peripatetic nature of government. The Transitional period of Chapter V is marked by the effects of printing, Humanism, and the Reformation, which can be illustrated from the vernacular writings of Martin Luther. At the same time, the early grammatical treatises on German and the importance of German in schools were eventually to lead, thanks to printing, to a standard language by narrowing down the degree of variation in most kinds of printed German, firstly in favour of a HG form, then in specific instances of spelling, phonology, and morphology. Chapter VI discusses syntactic developments in ENHG, relating them where possible to Luther and contemporaries and to statements by early grammarians. The next two chapters are devoted to the Early Modern period: Chapter VII brings external and internal history together in examining the vocabulary of the seventeenth century (but not its semantics) from the viewpoint of linguistic borrowing and the purist reaction against it. Chapter VIII moves 'outside' the language to consider the interaction of grammarians and authors in the eighteenth century, focusing on Gottsched, Klopstock, and Adelung and their opinions on the best form of German. The last two chapters attempt a closer scrutiny of sociolinguistic and semantic shifts in the Modern period from 1800 to 1945: Chapter IX sets forth a subdivision for the period and examines some of the available varieties of German, starting with the final stages of standardization in pronunciation and spelling, then assessing the relative importance and main characteristics of dialect, the colloquial language, technical and group languages. Finally, Chapter X treats in turn the more recent purism and its nationalistic inspiration, the linguistic effects of the political emancipation of the population in the nineteenth century, and of the National Socialist regime. These topics are looked at also from the semantic point of view, especially as regards the complex relationships between language and thought and language and reality. The 'language-and-reality' problem is, of course, the basic one for the historian of any language; attempts to define it more narrowly, the selection of data, and strategies for their interpretation are the stuff out of which we produce linguistic history.

SELECT BIBLIOGRAPHY

In addition to the works referred to in this Introduction, further bibliography on general theoretical issues and on German in particular can be found in the following:

Cherubim and Objartel (1981).
Grosse (1981) [not accessible
  before completion of the
  manuscript].
Kohlhase (1981) [not accessible
  before completion of the
  manuscript].

*Lexikon der Germanistischen
  Linguistik* [= *LGL*].
Sitta (1980).

OTHER HISTORIES OF THE GERMAN LANGUAGE

The principal linguistic histories of German consulted for this book are:

Adelung (1781*b*).
Bach (1965, 1970).
Becker (1944) [to be used with
  caution].
Behaghel (1968).
Chambers and Wilkie (1970).
Eggers (1963–77).
Feist (1933).
Frings (1957).
Grimm (1848).
Guchmann (1964–9).
Henzen (1954).
Hirt (1925).
Jungandreas (1947, 1949).
Keller (1978).
Kirk (1923).
Kleine Enzyklopädie (1969–70).
Kleine Enzyklopädie (1983).

Kluge (1918).
Kluge (1920).
Lichtenberger (1895).
Lockwood (1965).
Moser (1968).
Moser (1969).
Polenz (1978).
Priebsch and Collinson (1968).
Rückert (1875).
Scherer (1878).
Schildt (1976).
Schleicher (1869).
Schmidt *et al.* (1969).
Socin (1888).
Sonderegger (1979).
Sperber and Fleischhauer (1963).
Strong and Meyer (1886).
Tonnelat (1962).

Tschirch (1966–9, 1971–5).   Waterman (1966, 1976).
Van Raad and Voorwinden (1973).   Weithase (1961).

Addenda (not used here):

Besch, Reichmann, and   Coletsos Bosco (1977–80).
  Sonderegger (edd.) (1984, 1985):   Raynaud (1982).
  for details see p. ix n. 2.   Wolf (1981).

FORTHCOMING

Germanistische Lehrbuchsammlung (ed. Hans-Gert Roloff), a comprehensive
  collection of books on German language and literature, including
  Reiffenstein (below).

Moser, Wellmann, and Wolf   Reiffenstein (forthcoming).
  (in progress).

CHAPTER I

THE BEGINNINGS OF 'GERMAN'

As with other Germanic languages, the evidence for early German is heterogeneous and fragmentary. Grammarians must juggle chronological, geographical, and stylistic variables to create the illusion of coherent linguistic development. Their cosily regular abstractions are all the harder to relate to the history of the speakers in a period where so much history remains obscure. In fact, there is not just one form of 'German' which engages our attention in the earliest periods: instead we find separate, though related, dialects, some of which gave rise eventually to the modern German standard language by complex historical processes. This lack of a single starting-point bedevils the linguistic historian, forcing him to change his perspectives as evidence from different periods or regions dictates, but it accounts also for the lack of a generally accepted label for 'German' in the early texts themselves, and for the several competing designations in modern European languages: Fr. *allemand* preserves the tribal name *Al(l)emanni*; the English term *German* was once the name of a Celtic people; the German name *deutsch* is an adjective that may once have meant 'popular', 'vulgar', 'heathen', 'non-Latin'—Scandinavian *tysk* derives from an equivalent form, and Italian *tedesco* comes from the Latinized *theodiscus*, as does Fr. *tudesque*. On the vexed questions of the origin and meanings of *deutsch* and its cognates[1] we merely note here that the word derives from a Gmc. adj. **þiudisk* from the fem. noun **þeudō-* 'people', 'folk', OHG *deot, deota*. Apart from a Gothic adverb *piudisko* 'like a heathen', the earliest attestation is the learned Latinate form *theotisce* 'in the vernacular', 'not *latine*', found in a letter of 786 where the term actually applies to Anglo-Saxon. Other occurrences suggest meanings 'non-Latin', 'popular', or 'heathen', depending on whether the word is a loan-translation of Lat. *vulgaris* or *gentilis*. Certainly, in the ninth century it could also apply to the vernacular language in its Frk. form,[2] for the monk Otfrid of Weissenburg (present-day Wissembourg in Alsace) prefaces his translation of the Gospel harmony into SRh. Frk. verse (*c*.865) with a section entitled *Cur scriptor hunc librum theotisce dictaverit* ('Why the writer has composed this book in the popular tongue'). In the text itself Otfrid used the more political term *frenkisg, in frenkisga zungun*, which recurs in Latin form (*francice*) in a letter he wrote to Liutbert, archbishop of Mainz. Not until the tenth century do we find native German forms *diutisk* beside the learned *theotiscus*, and even then they and the later forms *diutsch, dietsch, dutsch, tiutsch* retain a wide range of meanings. With the gradual emergence of the Romance languages and the growth of linguistic and eventually political borders *diutisk/theotiscus* acquires the new task of distinguishing Germans of all types from Romance speakers, who in turn are known by the equally nebulous terms *Walh*,[3] *wälhisk* (= mod. German *welsch*, a derogatory name that applies equally to Frenchmen, Italians, and other 'Latins'). Following a patriotic tradition going back at least to the sixteenth century, Jacob Grimm used *deutsch* in a very broad sense to cover all Germanic languages, for example, in his *Deutsche Grammatik* (1819/22–37) and the *Geschichte der deutschen Sprache* (1848). Unfortunately, the vague nature of the word *deutsch* pandered to the nationalistic feelings of some less critical scholars who sought to project into the past a national unity and a national language which never existed. Nor, as we shall see, was there any homogeneous ethnic basis.

There is, then, no single source for the modern German standard language: instead, separate but related streams of dialect have been tapped in differing degrees and at different times to feed the main course of the standard. The dialects contributing most to the development of modern German fall into two groups, a northern group called *Low German* (LG) and a central and southern group called *High German* (HG). The earliest texts are labelled Old Low German (OLG)[4] and Old High German (OHG) respectively, and both come under the heading *Early German* (Hugo Moser's

Frühdeutsch), covering the period from 700 to 1100 (for the details see below). While we shall focus on material of HG type, the relationships between LG and HG dialects are complex and prominent throughout German linguistic history. Moreover, the HG dialects do not all differ from LG ones to the same extent, there are mixed texts from all periods, and today the hegemony of modern standard German extends over regions where the remains of LG dialects are still used in some situations.

PERIODIZATION: PRE-GERMAN AND EARLY GERMAN
(OHG AND OLG) 700-1100

On historical grounds the history of German begins with the emergence of the Frankish Empire, which extended its influence over the other important tribes—Alemanni, Bavarians, and Saxons. Linguistically, the HG or Second Sound Shift gives the *terminus post quem*—say, *c*.AD 500. But a literary view starts with the first recognizably HG texts, a handful of MFrk. glosses written in the early eighth century into Gospels from Echternach, the *Maihinger Evangeliar*,[5] which also contains OE glosses, underlining the Rhineland's importance for the history of German at the very beginning of Anglo-Saxon missionary activity—Echternach is one of the earliest Anglo-Saxon foundations[6]. Only from the late eighth/early ninth centuries do we have texts in continuous German of sufficient length to make linguistic analysis of morphology, syntax, and semantics feasible. Combining the three criteria based on history, language, and texts, we can distinguish between the onset of the Early German or OHG period in 700 and the pre-literary, pre-textual period in which we look for the linguistic foundations of the earliest evidence and for the social conditions that preserved it. The runic inscriptions, personal names, and isolated legal and political terms in latinized forms of the Merovingian period (late fifth century to mid-eighth) can conveniently be relegated to this pre-German period; they are in any case hard to identify dialectally.

The end of the early period is less easily determined: suggestions vary from 1050 to 1100 or 1150. After the writings of the great teacher Notker III (Labeo) of St Gall in Switzerland (d. 1022), there is, admittedly, a dearth of continuous texts in German for about a century, and those which do exist seem to look forward in form and style to later medieval writings, e.g. the commentary on the *Song of Songs* produced by Williram, abbot of the Bavarian monastery of Ebersberg *c*.1065. But the gap in the record is only apparent, for many of our early glosses derive from just this time, late tenth to twelfth centuries, testifying perhaps to the high level of learning in the Ottonian period since the aim is not so much to preserve German as to acquire Latinity. Many classical texts have been preserved by Ottonian monks, and the *Waltharius*, a Latin version of a Germanic 'lay' written down in the tenth century, and the *Ruodlieb*, a Latin poem of the eleventh century with affinities with later courtly epics, hint at the considerable sophistication of the audiences they were produced for. Not until the late twelfth century do we find vernacular secular poetry of outstanding quality, produced perhaps for a lower aristocracy or patriciate with taste but lacking a thorough Latin education. Beside these literary or socio-historical criteria, an important linguistic criterion helps to mark the end of the early German period—the apparent weakening of unstressed syllables in inflexional endings. Whereas the OHG evidence is characterized by widely differentiated inflexional syllables, most later texts tend, with a few exceptions, notably those in southern Swiss dialects,[7] to show uniform endings with *e*, which was probably an unstressed, lax, mid vowel with the approximate phonetic value [ə]. The weakening of inflexional syllables has important implications:

1. *Morphological syncretism.* Forms within the same declensional and conjugational sub-classes become indistinguishable, e.g.

> *Tatian* 82.1: 'man *thera* steti' = 'viri loci illius' (gen.).
>
> 92.7: 'fon *theru* ziti' = 'ex illa hora' (dat.).
>
> MHG would be: 'man *dere* stete'/'von *dere* zîte'.

The syncretism also affects the forms of verbs belonging originally to different classes,[8] e.g.

> *leiden* (1) 'make hated'
> *leidēn* (3) 'be hated'
> *leidōn* (2) 'accuse'.

All three verbs (attested in Notker) fell together in MHG in the homonymous form *leiden*.

2. *Phonemicization of umlaut* (see pp. 89-91). The loss of vowel quality and quantity in unstressed syllables has led to the phonemicization of mutated allophones, a process which begins with short

a > e even in the early period. The new mutated phonemes then serve a morphological purpose, distinguishing sg. ≠ pl. oppositions, ind. ≠ subj. oppositions, etc. In this restructuring of the morphology endings become purely facultative, i.e. dependent to a greater or lesser degree on the presence of other elements in the phrases like particles, or word order. This involves:

3. *Syntactic reshaping of the language.* Phonological weakening of unstressed syllables is probably inseparable from the loss of grammatical function of those syllables, and the resulting syncretism has important implications for OHG syntax: increasingly, 'analytic constructions' are used in OHG times to convey relationships between elements in the sentence that could otherwise be indicated morphologically. Word order was already grammatical to some extent in early OHG because in most sub-classes of the nominal paradigm nominative and accusative case-forms are homonymous and distinguished only by word order or particles. Among analytic syntactic features are the use of the definite article/dem. pronoun, and the use of the past participle + auxiliary instead of the preterite verb form (see Chapter VI).

4. *Increase in the rhyme inventory.* While the loss of flexible word order inevitably makes rhyming more difficult, the merging of inflexions increases the number of homonyms and actually facilitates rhyme. The rich and rhythmical verse of the thirteenth century depends in part on the many uninflected syllables.

The linguistic criterion, despite its importance in periodizing, is not an abrupt one. Even ninth-century texts show instability in their unstressed syllables, the OHG *Tatian* translation for instance, or Otfrid of Weissenburg, who sometimes sacrifices grammaticality to rhyme, which suggests some latitude in the use of inflexions.[9]

In order to relate the HG of this early period to other Germanic languages and dialects, we shall now consider pre-German conditions and the problems of analysing them.

GERMAN AND THE GERMANIC LANGUAGES

German and the Germanic languages belong to the IE family of languages but are recognizable as a group primarily because their consonantal systems underwent changes known as the *First* or

Germanic Sound Shift. The IE languages and the astounding intellectual achievements of their study and comparison will not concern us here,[10] nor will the reconstructed German parent language, except as a convenient reference point. However, it should be borne in mind that this reconstruction, called Primitive Germanic or Proto-Germanic (PGmc.), is an archetypal language, not a 'real' one: i.e. it contains all the features necessary to account for the forms occurring in the 'types' which derive from it, and in this respect the proto-language corresponds to the archetype in textual criticism, which is quite distinct from the original.[11] As a model, then, PGmc. differs from any spoken language, and is indeed of such abstract quality that attempts to date it are irrelevant, since it stands outside time. Caution is necessary here, however, since scholars do not agree about certain features of the reconstructed model and hence they speak of different chronological stages and argue that the proto-language must have contained dialectal and social variables. In effect, then, PGmc. is a notional model to which we can ascribe, albeit crudely, features that apply to natural languages, namely variations according to time, place, society, and function. The reasons for this curious mixture of abstract and real emerge from an examination of the relationships between the individual representatives of the Germanic group. Again, since we are here concerned with ascertaining the position occupied by 'German', we shall concentrate on the so-called 'West Germanic' dialects, without, however, attempting any detailed reconstruction of a WGmc. proto-language.

Unfortunately, we are handicapped in our attempts to establish non-controversial relationships between the earliest attested forms of the Germanic dialects because the evidence is insufficient and stems from widely differing periods. Handbooks regularly distinguish three main subgroupings: (1) *North Germanic* (NGmc.), designating the earliest forms of Scandinavian dialects which are traditionally sub-divided into *East Norse* (Danish and Swedish) and *West Norse* (Norwegian, Icelandic, and Faroese); (2) *East Germanic* (EGmc.), comprising Gothic, represented by the translation of (parts of?) the Bible attributed to the fourth-century West Gothic, or Visigothic, bishop Wulfila but preserved in sixth-century mainly East Gothic, or Ostrogothic, manuscripts, as well as other extremely exiguous linguistic remains, like Burgundian, Vandal, and Gepidian; (3) *West Germanic* (WGmc.)—also called South Germanic—(see Fig. 3,

p. 39), subsuming Old English (OE); Old Frisian (OFris.); Old Saxon (OS), which is held to be the forerunner of the modern LG dialects[12]; certain Frk. dialects, including a northern variety (called Old Low Frankish (OLFrk.) and regarded as the main source of modern Dutch and Flemish) and a southern variety, which, together with Alem., Bav., and the now extinct Lgb., we call Old High German (OHG) because of certain innovations to the consonants (see pp. 40–2). We shall treat this tripartite scheme merely as taxonomic, i.e. as convenient for classification, *not* as a model of actual 'genetic' relationships. The NGmc. dialect group does indeed show a relative cohesion over a long period and splits up late, but the EGmc. group is characterized by fairly early migration and extinction; moreover, evidence for the dialects it subsumes, other than Gothic, consists largely of names, which inhibits any definitive classification. If we subtract both NGmc. and EGmc. from PGmc. we are left with 'WGmc.', and controversy has raged about the nature and unity of this grouping. On the one hand, several linguistic features are apparently shared by WGmc. dialects, three of the most striking being:

1. A tendency to develop diphthongs[13] from PGmc. semi-vowels when these were doubled:

(*a*) PGmc. -*i̯i̯*- > Gothic. -*ddj*-, NGmc. -*ggj*- vs. 'WGmc.' diphthong, e.g.

> PGmc. **twaiio(n)* (gen. pl.) 'of two' > Gothic *twaddje*, ON *tveggja* vs. 'WGmc.'—OE *tweg(e)a*, OS *tweio*, OHG *zweio*.

(*b*) PGmc. -*u̯u̯*- > Gothic and ON -*ggw*- vs. 'WGmc.' diphthong, e.g.

> PGmc. **treuu-* / *triuui* (adj. 'loyal', 'true' > Gothic *triggwana* (acc. sg.), ON *tryggvan* (acc. sg.), vs. 'WGmc.' '—OE (*ge*)*trēowe* / (*ge*)*trīewe*,[14] OS *triuwi*, OHG (*gi*)*triuwi*.

The supra-segmental, accentual factors conditioning this strengthened articulation of semi-vowels known as 'Holtzmann's Law' (or *Verschärfung*) remain disputed.

2. Consonants (except /r/) preceding /j/ and certain other phonemes in PGmc. appear lengthened, i.e. doubled ('WGmc. Gemination'). Cf.

> OE *tellaþ*, OS *telleat*, OHG *zellent* vs. ON *telja*, all deriving < PGmc. *taljanþi / *taljandi 'they tell'.

Traces of this gemination are also found in ON in the case of velars /g/ and /k/: *liggja*, *hyggja*[15]

3. In WGmc., the second person sg. pret. ind. of strong verbs (see pp. 161–5) shows the root of the pret. pl. and reflexes of an ending -*i*, which causes mutation where possible,[16] while ON and Gothic forms have the root vowel of pret. sg. and end in -*t*. Cf.

> OE *bære*, OS *bāri* (= [bɛːri]?), OHG *bāri* (= [bɛːri]?) vs. ON *bart*,
> Gothic *bart* 'you (sg.) bore'.

So two underlying forms may be constructed for PGmc., namely **bērez/*barta*.

On the other hand, the proposed WGmc. group is split geographically by migration—Angles, Saxons, and others colonize Britain from the mid-fifth century on—and also linguistically, by the consonantal changes known as the Second or High German Consonant Shift (see p. 40) which affect only some dialects, and those in differing degrees. F. Maurer[17] postulated close relationships between the Alem. and NGmc. languages and cultures, rejecting the notion of any WGmc. linguistic unity for which we might construct a proto-language, and assuming instead that the individual dialects must once have been sufficiently in contact to acquire from each other their common features. This seems plausible, but whereas Maurer attributes the spread of shared features to the Merovingian 'hegemony' (*c*.496–750), they may instead originate in tribal contact during the first two or three centuries AD, when Germanic tribes were expanding, migrating, and intermixing. This would conveniently antedate the Anglo-Saxon colonization of the British Isles. However, the colonization process must have continued for some time and contact with the Continent will not have been lost, since seas unite as well as separate: consequently post-colonization linguistic links between OE and Fris. or OE and OS are still plausible, regardless of one's view of the WGmc. grouping. The remaining continental Germanic dialects can then be distinguished as to whether or not they are affected by the Second Consonant Shift. Other divisions taken from Tacitus' *Germania*,[18] namely *Ingvaeonic*, *Istvaeonic*, and (*H*)*Erminonic*, really reflect a classification according to the cult of the sons of a god, Mannus. Archaeological groupings based on the locations of certain 'cultures' yield the labels 'North Sea Germani', 'Weser–Rhine Germani', and 'Elbe Germani'. However, the three linguistic, religious, and archaeological subgroupings need

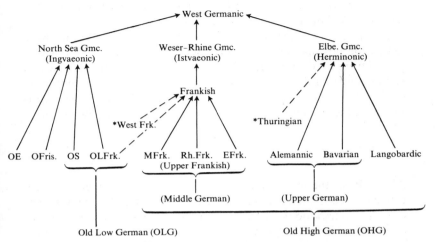

FIG. 3. A taxonomic model of 'West Germanic'
showing possible 'genetic' relationships

Note. The direction of the arrows emphasizes that the nodes of this diagram are derived from the extant linguistic forms; they are then given historical/geographical labels. The term LG applies to some 'Ingvaeonic' and some 'Istvaeonic' dialects: the mixture is more radical, however, since the literary OS of the *Hēliand* and *Genesis* apparently shows Frk. influences and cannot be the true linguistic ancestor of modern LG dialects: for that we must look to other, sparser OS evidence from glosses and personal names. HG comprises the 'Herminonic' dialects and the remaining Frk. ('Istvaeonic') ones. Thuringian is poorly attested and Langobardic does not show the HG Consonant Shift in entirety and is not preserved in any continuous vernacular text. Most problematic of all is WFrk., which is here regarded as the language of the early Frankish conquerors/settlers of Gaul (see pp. 49–50). The language died out when the speakers became Romanized, but later infusions of Rh.Frk.-speakers, i.e. HG-speakers, kept the knowledge of Frk. alive in the western parts of the empire for some time. Probably it was moribund by AD 850. Speculations concerning a Carolingian court language or attempts to claim the essentially Rh.Frk. *Ludwigslied* (881–2) as 'WFrk.' lack material foundation. For a rough map of OHG literary ('monastery') dialects see p. 43; for examples of these dialects and for discussion of the HG Consonant Shift, see Appendices A and B.

not coincide, and there is no proof that they do so. Given the long period of interaction and intermixture of Germanic tribes which we can only guess at rather than discern, we cannot expect any groupings, tidy or not, to be other than temporary. Consequently, we are unlikely ever to succeed in establishing a 'genetic' matrix for the Germanic dialects—which is tantamount to admitting that we cannot identify precisely the groups of people whose languages are the 'ancestors' of any modern Germanic language attributed to the so-called WGmc. group, and this holds true for German also.

Recently, linguistic features common to NGmc. and WGmc. have led to the postulation of a 'North-West Germanic' community or period from which individual dialects subsequently split off, or which subsequently broke down into NGmc. and WGmc., depending on one's view.[19] This 'NWGmc.' accords well with the known extra-linguistic fact of the early south-eastward migration of the Goths.

HIGH GERMAN

Alem., Bav., the main subdivisions of Frk., and fragmentary Lgb. evidence—consisting of names and isolated words in Latin texts—are classified in handbooks under the heading *High German*. They share consonantal innovations that developed some time in the pre-literary period as a result of the 'HG Consonant Shift'.[20] By the shift, pre-HG voiceless stops p, t, and k developed affricate and spirant allophones pf, ts, $k\chi$ and ff, zz, $\chi\chi$[21] and these series later became independent phonemes. The salient features of this consonant shift have entered the modern German standard language by processes we shall consider later (especially Chapter III), so that the sound shift has a synchronic as well as a diachronic value: diachronically it splits the HG dialects off from the PGmc. ancestor and enables us to recognize early loan-words with shifted consonants in those dialects; synchronically it distinguishes the consonants of the modern German standard language from those of other Gmc. standard languages and dialects: cf.

English *pound, open*		German *Pfund, offen*
tide, water	$\neq$	*Zeit, Wasser*
make		*machen*

It also has what may be termed a 'diatopic' value, since it distinguishes dialects—especially the sub-dialects of Frk. which show it in varying degrees. But the HG Consonant Shift is not the only feature separating HG from WGmc. dialects, as the following examples show:

1. *Phonological*

(*a*) HG retains nasals before voiceless spirants; LG dialects, especially 'Ingvaeonic' dialects, show loss of nasal with compensatory lengthening of the preceding vowel:

OHG *fimf* (NHG *fünf*) ≠ OE, OS *fīf*, LFrk. **fīf* (mod. Neth. *vijf*)

But LFrk. also retains most nasals:

OHG *mund, uns* (NHG *Mund, uns*), mod. Neth. *mond, ons* ≠ OE *mūð, ūs*, OS, OFris. *mūth, ūs*

(*b*) Despite general vowel weakening in unstressed syllables, some late OHG forms seem to show long vowel in this position, e.g. in Notker:

zungûn, lêrtôst, machôn (NHG *Zungen, lehrtest, machen*)[22]

2. Morphological

(*a*) Third person sg. masc. pronoun OHG *er/her* ≠ LG *hē/hi*— OS *hē*, OE *he*. This distinction is one of degree, for there are isolated *he-* forms in OHG texts: *Tatian, Ludwigslied*, and the *Second Merseburg Charm*.[23]

(*b*) OHG and LFrk. retain the older differentiated pl. endings in the verb paradigms. The 'Ingvaeonic' dialects, partly because of their extensive loss of nasal (see 1 (*a*) above), have only one pl. form ending in a dental, for the PGmc. third person pl. ending has lost the nasal: *nþ→-þ*; **beranþi→* Ingvaeonic **berað*. Cf.

OHG *berumes, beret, berant*, Neth. *baren, bar(e)t, baren* ≠ OE *berað*, OS *berað* 'we, you, they bear'.

3. *Syntactical.* OHG preserves the third person reflexive pronoun in the acc. case sg. and pl. *sih*, and in the gen. sg. *sīn*. Other WGmc. dialects use the oblique forms of the third person pronoun as a reciprocal and reflexive pronoun. NB. In OHG also the dat. forms of some pronouns can be used 'reflexively', namely the masc. and neut. sg. *imu* and the pl. *im/in*.

4. *Lexical.* The vocabulary of any language is prone to foreign influence and is an unreliable guide to linguistic relationships, especially between closely related dialects. Some isoglosses said to represent a LG ≠ HG opposition in modern dialects are so restricted regionally and stylistically that little weight can be placed on their absence from OHG: e.g. *padde* 'toad', 'frog', *kunte/kutte* 'female pudenda'.[24]

Since even the HG Consonant Shift has been claimed to affect other Gmc. dialects, we must conclude that this shift and the other features characteristic of HG are not exclusive to it, but by their frequency and by occurring together they can nevertheless serve to define it.

The term 'HG' applies here in a technical sense to 'language characterized by the HG Consonant Shift', and the dichotomy HG ≠ LG reflects an old geographical opposition between the 'Oberländer' of the mountainous regions in the south and the 'Niederländer' of the northern plains. The Roman provinces *Germania superior* and *inferior* and the modern names 'Netherlands', 'Niederlande' exemplify this. 'LG' is also ambiguous, for it can apply both broadly to any non-HG Germanic language—English, Dutch, or Danish, etc.—and narrowly to the present-day LG dialects within the borders of the Federal Republic and GDR. For the early period, we are dealing with an OLG comprising OS and OLFrk., both of which are mixed dialects; for instance, literary OS (*Hēliand* and *Genesis*) shows certain HG or Frk. features in its vowel system. These mixed 'literary dialects' are moreover, difficult to distinguish from one another, and we cannot plot the geographical distribution of the features that distinguish them ('isoglosses'), since our knowledge derives from texts written in some particular (not always indentifiable) scriptorium: we have no knowledge of the extent of dialect areas. Even today, with 'extensive' rather than 'punctual' information to work on, the dialects along the Dutch–German political border merge into each other almost imperceptibly. As a convenience, a morphological isogloss running roughly from the IJsselmeer to the Rhine is held to separate the Netherlandish (Flemish and Dutch) dialects in the west from the LG dialects in the east: whereas Netherlandish has a differentiated verb plural (e.g. *hebben* 'have', pl. *wij hebben, je hebt, zij hebben*), LG dialects show a single plural form for all three persons (west of the Elbe this is generally in -(*e*)*t*, e.g. *makt* 'we, you, they make', east of the Elbe forms in -(*e*)*n* predominate)[25]—see also feature 2 (*b*) above.

In the same way, the present-day isoglosses separating southern, HG dialects from these northern, unshifted LG dialects are impossible to map for earlier periods. The traditional boundary between HG and LG, the 'Benrath Line', is an isogloss separating medial /k/ in the north from medial /χ/ (a voiceless velar spirant), as represented by LG *maken* versus HG *machen*. At the end of the nineteenth century this demarcation crossed the Rhine at Benrath just south of Düsseldorf—see the map of German dialects *c.*1900 on p. 357—but its position and those of the other isoglosses subdividing

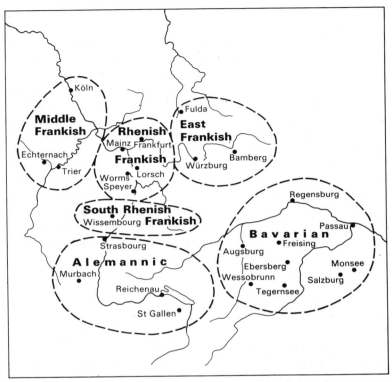

MAP 1. The Old High German monastery dialects and centres (after Sonderegger)

HG dialects as they have emerged from modern dialectological study cannot easily be projected back to the earliest periods:[26] no attempt will be made to indicate such boundaries in the map above, which sets out the main centres from which German evidence has been preserved, and gives a crude outline of dialect regions. It is customary to divide HG into 'Upper German' (UG), comprising Alem. and Bav. and 'Middle (or Central) German' (MG/CG) covering the (High) Frk. dialects, which may be subdivided into East, Rhenish, South Rhenish, Moselle, Middle, and Ripuarian Frk., although the differences are slight and not all dialects are well attested. During the later medieval period, from the twelfth century onwards, other dialects attain increasing literary and linguistic importance: Thuringian, Upper Saxon (US), and Silesian. The areas where such forms of German were spoken had been conquered and settled and these 'colonial dialects' are termed 'East Middle (or Central) German' (EMG/ECG), while the Frk. dialects of HG type which were dominant during the Early German period are similarly sometimes called 'West Middle (or Central) German' (WMG/WCG). For the moment, we are concerned with chronological and geographical factors affecting early forms of German, and we shall shortly turn to the questions of users and purposes. Meanwhile, we must bear in mind that the evidence for the earliest German dialects is written, and substantially different from the data of modern dialectological research. The 'dialect' map above therefore sets out in limited fashion regional distinctions in the attested forms of HG in the Early German period which we shall call 'monastery dialects' (see below, pp. 50–3). Texts attested from centres in these areas are, moreover, from different dates; nor can the picture they present reflect conditions in the immediate pre-textual period, say sixth-seventh centuries.

PEOPLES AND 'PARLERS'

Not surprisingly, the question is often asked: 'Who were the Franks, Alemanni, and Bavarians, Saxons and others?' There is in each case no simple answer; the names themselves are symbols,[27] attested relatively late and not denoting ethnically united and homogeneous groups. Apparently, the early Franks and others are loose agglomerations of speakers—'confederations' implies too formal a relationship—indeed, the name Alemanni (if correctly interpreted as 'all men') suggests just that. The name 'Frank' perhaps meant 'bold', 'free', cognate with mod. German *frech, frank* (Kluge (1967)), and it covers several, probably heterogeneous tribes, while scholars use it as a term of convenience. Still, Frankish attempts to create a pedigree also reveal an embarrassing ignorance of their origins.[28] The label 'Saxon' supposedly derives from a short curved sword— the *scramasax*—but these weapons are found widely in Frankish graves too, alongside the Frankish throwing-axe, the *francisca*. The Bavarians pose special problems: are they descendants of the Markomanni or of the Suebi (or Suevi)? A compromise solution regards the Bavarians as a 'macrotribe' comprising both Suebi and Markomanni which developed in the late fifth century, probably in part of the Roman province Pannonia. Moreover, the first element of Latinized forms of the name *bajuvarii* may reflect the early Illyrian (?) tribe, the *Boii*, preserved also in *Bohemia*.

All these 'federations' represent the linking of earlier smaller tribes in many different ways. The names of the minor tribes are often preserved for us in classical historians like Caesar (*c*.50 BC), Tacitus (AD 98), and Pliny the Elder (first century AD); in inscriptions; in place or regional names like Bardowick (< *Longobardi*), Hessen (< *Chatti*?), Betuwe (< *Batavii*), Schwaben (< *Suebi*); in later epic poetry (*Beowulf, Widsiþ*); and in the Merovingian historians Gregory of Tours and (pseudo-)Fredegar. A full discussion of the origins of the major tribes, or, 'Großstämme', then, involves a series of equations in which the earlier minor tribes migrating from their ultimate homelands in Scandinavia are combined to give plausible configurations as bases of our Franks, Bavarians, and others. Such issues lie outside the scope of the present book and are, in any case, peripheral to the linguistic history of German.

Nevertheless, the mixture of tribes we can discern through the mass of fragmentary detail gives us the keynote of the 'prehistoric' period of German and other Germanic languages. The Roman Empire was a barrier against which successive waves of Germanic invaders broke—literally, once extensive fortified defence-works known as *limites* had been erected to protect the Roman provinces on the Upper Rhine and in Rhaetia—only to fall back and regroup in new combinations. Thus, the empire in front and pressures behind, whether from climatic changes, lack of land, or fierce foes like the Huns and later the Avars, may have been the immediate agents of the chaotic population mixture. It is worth pointing up the discrepancy between the relatively homogeneous proto-forms PGmc, and WGmc. and this ethnic confusion. This either reinforces the ahistoric, 'metachronic', notional status of proto-languages, or else argues for relatively minor differentiation between Gmc. dialects in the prehistoric period, depending on one's viewpoint. (It should be noted, however, that non-Gmc. peoples, e.g. Celts, form some part of the mixtures.) Our three major 'tribes', then, are only in the process of evolving, they are not ethnically homogeneous, probably do not reflect clearly established cult groupings, are not distinguishable archaeologically, and are not uniform linguistically. Mixture and merger characterize the age and continue over centuries: a perpetual melting and merging only leading again to splitting and migration—a typically organic model. Indeed, the Frankish Empire can be seen as another such process on a larger scale: even as Charlemagne formed it into a more than usually coherent entity, it was already splitting up into precursors of the French and German states.

THE FRANKISH EMPIRE AND ITS LINGUISTIC IMPORTANCE

The Frankish Empire gradually extended its hegemony over Alemanni, Bavarians, Langobards, and others and used Christianity as an aid to political administration. In the process, missionaries preserved some details of Germanic customs and dialects much in the manner of their nineteenth-century colonial colleagues in Africa. The Frankish Empire, especially at its apogee under Charlemagne, thus provided the indirect stimulus for much of the early OHG religious material; it also needed administrators and so furthered literacy, which benefited the vernacular as well as Latin. Above all, the Empire gave a cultural continuity, however illusory, which contemporaries were still aware of in the ninth century and which linguistic historians gratefully exploit to give perspective to the first half of the Early German period.

We first hear of the Franks in the third century AD; two groups are distinguishable in the north and east. The northern Salians (*Salii*), whose name may derive from that of the river IJssel (*Isala* or *Sala*) or from the inland IJsselmeer, were settled in the regions of Betuwe and Toxandria in 358 as *dediticii*—allies accepting Roman rule but without fixed treaty. In the late fifth century they replaced the Roman administration under their leaders Childeric I (d. *c.*482) and Chlodowech (Fr. *Clovis*) (d. 511), and have given their name to an important codification of Germanic customary law, the *Lex Salica*.

The eastern Franks are known as Ribuarians, a late name, perhaps a hybrid formation from Lat. *ripa* 'river bank' (of the Rhine) + a Gmc. suffix *varii*, meaning 'men', 'people' (cf. 'Bavarian' = *Baiu* + *varii*). Sometimes we find eastern Franks inside the Roman Empire as allies (*foederati* or *dediticii*) or as farmers (*coloni*), and some Franks occupied important administrative positions, e.g. king Mallobaud, who was a *comes domesticorum* 'companion or count of the royal household', or Arbogast, count of Trier. The eastern Franks also defended the Roman Empire on occasion, as in 406–7.

From the evidence available it is not possible to distinguish northern from eastern Franks by language or place-names, or indeed by anything except the geographical context in which historical sources set them. But both groups maintained amicable relations with the Romans up to a point, for the *Lex Salica* reveals the Franks as farmers owning orchards, cornfields, bean- and lentil-fields, and vineyards,[29] while their place-names and grave-goods reflect centuries of contact with the Roman Empire and a taste for things Roman. The replacement of the Roman Empire by the incipient Frankish one was not, or not everywhere, a cataclysmic process: borrowings into the vocabulary of the German dialects support this view.

In 486 Chlodowech defeated the last Roman ruler Syagrius, so gaining virtual possession of northern Gaul. At some stage (503?) he became a Catholic Christian, and consequently both Frankish power and Catholicism were extended by him and his heirs over other Germanic tribes most of whom had become Arian Christians. For our purposes the defeat and subjugation of the Alemanni (496, 502–7, and 536) and of the Bavarians (536) are particularly significant. But the East Germanic Burgundians were also defeated, despite Chlodowech's marriage to a Burgundian princess, Chrodechildis, and their power was eventually broken by his sons Chlothar and Childebert in 534—events which together with the earlier Burgundian defeat by the Huns in 437 have passed in elaborated and altered form into the medieval *Nibelungenlied* (c.1200). In 555–6 the Saxons too were forced to render tribute, although they were subdued only by Charlemagne's campaigns against them in 772–804. In 774 Charlemagne also became *rex Langobardorum* through his successful intervention in Northern Italy. The Frisians and the Thuringians were gradually won over into Frankish dominion by a mixture of missionary activity and force. So, during the Merovingian and Carolingian periods, from the late fifth to the ninth century, Frankish power extended over all the so-called West Germanic tribes, except the Anglo-Saxons, and also over some Visigoths, whose hold over southern Gallia had been cut back to a mere coastal strip by the Frankish victory at Vouillé in 507.

Thus, the process of annexation and conquest begun perhaps unintentionally by the Merovingians was completed under their successors, the Carolingians. No integrated political unit resulted, and certainly nothing that could lead to linguistic integration or even the development of a standard language. Indeed, the Carolingian Frankish Empire burst asunder into the beginnings of France and Germany virtually at the very moment of its completion. But it did furnish an ideal, even after its collapse, and it had, by furthering the Church, extended widely the education and learning inherited from the Roman Empire. Under Charlemagne, the vernacular grew important for the dissemination of faith: the much-cited *Admonitio generalis* of 789 and other capitularies require the populace to know and understand the basic tenets of Christianity, and so prompted German translation of some catechetic writings. Among the populace at large the homiletic, preaching activities of monks and priests reinforced the meaning of the cult practices, encouraging through hagiography the regional cult of saints from Merovingian times on: the OHG *Georgslied* (text ninth century, manuscript tenth century) is an early vernacular example, significantly enough in a quite barbarous orthography. Frankish monasticism and its Christian 'politics' may have caused the creation and dissemination of much of the surviving OHG material, but, disappointingly, specific linguistic developments, like the spread of diphthongs (see below, p. 49), cannot be shown to have occurred as a result of the undoubted prestige of Frk.

Apart from important lexical influences to be examined later (pp. 57–8), four groups of interrelated linguistic problems are bound up with the Frankish Empire, some of them bearing upon OHG and certain OHG texts.

1. What was the density of the Frankish settlement on Gallo-Roman soil? Archaeology and historiography apart, the evidence is linguistic: personal and place-names and a few isolated Germanic words in Latin texts, including the corrupt glosses of the *Lex Salica*. The place-names testify to the symbiosis between Franks and Gallo-Romans, since hybrid types containing a Germanic personal name and a Latin or Celtic suffix are found, e.g.

Avricourt < *Eberhardi curtis*

Gmc. personal names are so abundant in inscriptions, on seventh-century Merovingian coins, and in documents that they probably reflect a vogue for Gmc. names among Romance populations, and strange elaborations of the principles of forming Gmc. names confirm this. The extent of the settlement has regularly been a political issue in times of Franco-German animosity, but few serious scholars now believe in a massive Frankish colonization. Instead, a fairly dense settlement near the present linguistic borders gradually thinned out towards the Loire boundary in the south: few Franks can have settled south of the Loire.

2. What are the origins of the present linguistic boundaries in the north and east between French and German dialects, and where did they run during the Frankish Empire? This problem still causes periodic friction in Belgium and has borne upon the Alsace and Lorraine question. Undoubtedly the linguistic border in the north did run slightly further south than it does today, and parts of the northern French *départements* Nord and Pas de Calais had pockets of Gmc.-speakers down to the end of the Middle Ages.

3. To what extent is modern French the product of mixture between a Gallo-Roman substratum and the Frankish settlers/conquerors? The differences between northern French and Provençal have been attributed to the different mixtures of Gallo-Roman with Frankish on the one hand and with Gothic on the other. However, the late imperial 'Latin' itself already had considerable dialectal differentiation. Major embarrassment accrues from our virtual ignorance of West Frankish and the EGmc. languages on Romance soil—Visigothic and Burgundian. Related questions concern the presence and age of Gmc. loan-words in French dialects,[30] and conversely the transmission of Romance loans into German dialects. Some scholars attribute the OHG diphthongs /ie/ and /uo/ to the influence of Gallo-Roman; compare the apparently parallel developments:

Lat. *pedem* > Fr. *pied*   Lat. *speculum* > OHG *spiagel*
                                     (NHG *Spiegel*)
Lat. *novem* > OFr. *nuef* (Fr. *neuf*)   Lat.   *domus* > OHG   *tuom*
                                     (NHG *Dom*)

However, attempts to prove causal connection are difficult to substantiate.[31]

4. What is the nature of *West Frankish*, the language of the Frankish settlers and conquerors of northern Gaul?[32] The almost entirely onomastic evidence (personal and place-names) is difficult to interpret, because of the notoriously unstable spelling in Latin texts of the Merovingian period. Moreover, since the replacement of the

Merovingian dynasty in 752 by the Carolingians probably increased eastern (Austrasian/'Rhenish') influence in the western colonial lands (Neustria), we should distinguish two periods of 'WFrk.': (1) up to 750; (2) after 750 until the language died out (perhaps as early as the eighth century, perhaps as late as 900).

The language from the western parts of the empire in period (1) does not appear to have been HG, for it lacks the HG Consonant Shift. WFrk. influence may be detected in certain orthographical features later current in OHG writings, notably the graphy ⟨gh⟩, occurring before the graphy ⟨i⟩ in 'WFrk.' personal names of period (1). e.g.

Ghiboino, AD 693; *Ghislemaro*, AD 688

(both from original Merovingian diplomas).[33] The glosses of the *Lex Salica* (manuscripts all post-750) are unfortunately too corrupt to differentiate WFrk. clearly from any other WGmc. dialect.

On the other hand, these texts from period (2) supposedly representing WFrk. all show the HG Consonant Shift in some degree, and even though they may have been produced on 'French' soil, we cannot discount 'Rh.Frk.' influence. The masterly *Isidor* translation (*c*.800), whose inspiration may have come from the highest intellectual circles of the Carolingian court, was perhaps written in the Lorraine area or by a scribe trained there.[34] The *Ludwigslied* (881/2) is also probably Rh.Frk., although it was transcribed on Neustrian soil and celebrates a victory over the Northmen at Saucourt in Normandy.[35] The tenth-century *Paris Conversations* ('Gespräche') are the work of Romance scribes attempting to transcribe a HG dialect, not simply WFrk.

Only when all the evidence, especially that for the Carolingian period,[36] has been fully analysed might we probe with greater confidence this particular hornets' nest.

MONASTERIES: OLD HIGH GERMAN MATERIAL
AND MONASTERY DIALECTS

Apart from epigraphic and onomastic evidence—inscriptions and names—the most important OHG material is found on parchment, preserved by scribes and archivists from an age when literacy was the monopoly of the Church, both for secular and ecclesiastical administration. So OHG 'literature' is a product of the cloister scriptorium, and much of it is catechetic, homiletic, and educational. Prolific glosses found throughout the period are the early dictionaries and cribs, bringing Latin texts and grammars, classical authors, and, above all, the Bible and exegetical writings within the reach of German monks. A recent catalogue of manuscripts containing OHG and OS glosses contains 1,023 entries,[37] and those already edited by Steinmeyer and Sievers run to four large volumes.[38]

Thus, the bulk of OHG evidence is far removed from the colloquial both in style and language. However, a few texts fall outside these categories: the *Hildebrandslied* (*HL*) and some magic charms, like the famous *Merseburg Charms*, preserved in a tenth-century manuscript but much older. Legal vocabulary has also survived, usually in Latin texts, and a skilful translation of the *Lex Salica* exists in a ninth-century EFrk. fragment. The great teacher, Notker III of St Gall, laid the basis of German philosophical vocabulary in his interpretations of Latin authors, which are written mainly in the curious *Mischprosa*, a mixture of German and Latin, inflexions being accommodated to the German syntax. This 'group language' may well have been actually spoken inside the monasteries, and later in the sixteenth-century grammar schools, and Luther himself used it in his *Tischreden*. Finally, Christian texts make stylistic concessions to vernacular poetic traditions, as shown by the *Wessobrunn Creation and Prayer* or the hell-fire sermon *Muspilli*. This holds true also of the 'biblical epics'—the diatessaron *Tatian* c.830, written in EFrk., perhaps at Fulda;[39] the *Evangelienbuch* of Otfrid of Weissenburg, c.865–70, in SRh.Frk., and the LG *Hēliand*, written in 'literary OS' in the first half of the ninth century, perhaps at Corvey.[40] All three works differ in style and form: prose, rhyming couplets, and alliterative verse respectively. The glosses, too, are no mere 'ink-horn words' but often give practical, technical terms for botany, anatomy, building, etc., particularly the so-called 'Sachgruppenglossare'. Moreover, the *Cassel Glosses* and the related *Paris Conversations* give us unique and tantalizing glimpses of 'German as she was spoke' in the tenth century. Finally, when characters speak to each other in Christian poetry and prose, we may find further evidence, albeit indirect, for early colloquial German.[41]

The monastic transmission of this material bears also on its linguistic analysis, since we are not dealing with dialects in the modern sense, but rather with local spelling traditions, 'Schreibdialekte', or 'monastery dialects'[42] as they are sometimes called. The written OHG evidence denies us direct information on the complex variations of speech—intonation, pitch, stress, changes in the colouring of individual sounds and words in differing phonetic environments, and so forth. At the same time, the orthographies of the scriptoria are based on the spelling traditions of Latin, are not internally consistent, and only partially 'phonetic'. The modern reader baulks at the apparently arbitrary spelling in many documents, and much variation is orthographical, not dialectal. Indeed, scribes make spelling and copying mistakes; scribes may collaborate who have completely different origins, or were trained in different scriptoria; a text produced at one scriptorium may be copied or partly transcribed in the conventions of another. The linguistic habits of a scriptorium sometimes alter considerably, reflecting changes in the composition of its staff,[43] while the language used inside the monastery need not simply be that of the surrounding region if its scribes were not locally recruited: the monastery of Fulda, for example, stood in RhFrk. territory, but in the eighth century Bav. and OE features occur in its scriptorium,[44] in the ninth century EFrk. characteristics (e.g. *pfund, apfel*) occur (in the *Tatian* translation—*if* it was written at Fulda), and eventually the monastery adopted the Rh.Frk. features (e.g. *pund, appel*) of the local area.[45] The coexistence of old and new spelling traditions within a scriptorium is shown in the *Tatian* translation, one of whose scribes, known as 'gamma', uses an 'outmoded Fuldese'.[46] However, gamma's language has also been considered to be Alem.-influenced, which illustrates how difficult it is to decide whether variations in spelling are due to orthographical development or dialectal factors. Before any phonological analysis can take place, a 'graphemic' study of the spelling is essential, but this is impeded by fluctuating forms and mixture of various kinds: most surviving texts are 'mixed', if only by virtue of having been copied.[47] Still, most early German orthographies show considerable regularity and refinement, especially when we compare them with the much more erratic *Paris Conversations* (see below, pp. 65-6) which are obviously closer to actual speech.[48]

We are therefore poorly informed regarding dialect in this early period: the spelling of texts is often ambiguous, the scriptorium staff not local, and the information restricted to distinct points on the map, not permitting us knowledge of the extent of dialect areas, some of which are sparsely represented in the early textual period. e.g. Alem. Moreover, the actual spoken dialects that to some extent underlie the written evidence are not linked to any vernacular supra-regional standard: Latin functioned as the diplomatic and administrative norm. For the practical purposes of comparison the EFrk. monastery dialect is chosen as a bearing, since this is represented by a major text (*Tatian*) and has a consonantal system similar to that of modern standard German. The names given to the monastery dialects are, moreover, hybrids of old 'tribal' names and modern geographical labels: we cannot say how much ethnic consciousness was linked to language in the eighth to eleventh centuries.

While we cannot say much about the users of German—whether pre-German *gentes* or monks preserving our texts—the language itself gives some clues in its vocabulary to the cultural contacts of speakers, and some texts give us glimpses of a surprisingly wide range of uses. So we turn first to the external stimuli of lexical borrowing, before assessing some of the stylistic forces shaping the language 'internally'

LEXICAL BORROWING AND EARLY GERMAN'S EXTERNAL HISTORY[49]

In several respects loan-words form an important, if tantalizing, piece of the early German puzzle. Historically, they can document and sometimes approximately date cultural contacts from periods poor in written records. From these linguistic 'zone fossils' in the chronological stratification of the vocabulary we assemble linguistic history: however, caution is called for, since the confused prehistoric (i.e. pre-textual) linguistic strata are often only randomly revealed. Socio-linguistically, we examine the place of loans within the borrowing language, as technical terms, or with stylistic overtones, or in the usage of particular groups of speakers. Linguistically, we are concerned with the formal and semantic adaptation of new elements into the borrowing language, which can give some indication about the structure of its phonology, morphology, and meaning—however, we may need to know about the sounds and structures of the donor languages as well.

A. PRE-GERMAN STRATA

Germanic tribes migrated southwards from Scandinavia and the Baltic littoral during the first millenium BC, coming into contact with a technologically superior Celtic civilization using iron (for example in the Hallstatt and La Tène cultures). During the lengthy Iron Age, Celts and Germans may have shared institutions, reflected in the surviving German words for political and military matters assumed to stem from this period:[50] *Amt, Bann, Eid, Erbe, frei, Fehde, Geisel, Reich*; *Brünne* 'breastplate', *Eisen, Beute, Ger* 'spear', *Heer*, and the ethnic terms *Germane* and *welsch*, are also Celtic (see above, pp. 31–2). OHG forms of probable Celtic origin which died out include *magu-* 'boy' (cf. *maguzogo* 'tutor'), *wini* 'husband', 'beloved', *wīg* 'battle', and the name element *hadu-* 'battle' (cf. 'Hadubrand'). Early bipartite personal names also show striking parallels; cf. Gallic *Catu-rīx* ≠ OHG *Hadu-rīh, Catu-volcus* ≠ OHG *Hadu-walh*, Gallic **Teuto-rīx* ≠ WFrk. *Theude-ricus*. Only *Reich* and *Amt* have phonological features clearly indicating their transmission via Celtic: OHG *rīhhi* shows long /ī/ instead of the long /ā/ we expect (cf. Lat. *rēx, rēgis*), while OHG *ambaht* (contracted to MHG *ambet, ammet*, mod. German *Amt*) shows an element *amb-* which probably represents the Celtic preposition *ambi*, whereas OHG has a form *umbi* (NHG (*her*)*um*).[51] Several of the words mentioned—and almost certainly others like *Tonne* 'ton'/'tun'[52]—may have gone into German through the Roman Empire or just after its end. Few place-names of indisputably Celtic origin are found on the right bank of the Rhine, which might support this view; examples are: place-names in the suffixes -(*i*)*acum* (mod. -*ach*, -*ich*), like Andernach (*Andernacum*), Jülich (*Iuliacum*), Zülpich (*Tolbiacum*); or in -*bona*, like Vienna (*Vindobona*) and Bonn (*Bonna*); or in -*dūnum* (cognate with English 'town', German *Zaun*), like (Kirch)zarten, near Freiburg im Breisgau (*Tarodūnum*), where a Celtic earthwork is still visible. A few river names may also be Celtic: the Glan (Celtic *glan* 'bright', 'clear'), the Tauber (Welsh *dubr* 'water'), perhaps also the Danube (*Dānuvius*).

In the next important phase of cultural contact, settlement of Germans within the Roman Empire and trade across its borders encouraged borrowings in the spheres of homes and (vegetable) gardens—*Mauer, Kalk, Keller, Küche, Fenster, Schindel, Stube, Söller, Ziegel*; *Pflanze, Pflaume, Minze, Pfeffer, Rettich*; weights and

measures—*Pfund, Unze, Meile*; trade and viticulture—*Kaufmann*
(OHG *koufo*, Lat. *caupo* 'wine-seller'), *Pferd, Zoll*; *Kelter, Most,
Wein*; and medicine—*Arzt, Büchse, Fieber, Pflaster*.[53] Most of this
vocabulary was preserved only long after it had been borrowed—
often in early monastic glossaries—but some words are obviously old
because they show the effects of the HG Consonant Shift; e.g. *Pferd*,
OHG *pferit* (< V.Lat. *paraverēdus*; cf. English *palfrey*), shows the
shift of *p* > *pf*; *Zoll* (< V.Lat. *tolōnēum* 'custom-house') shows that
of *t* > *ts* (spelt ⟨z⟩). Unshifted forms like *Kalk* (< Lat. *calx, calcis*)
suggest either that the word has entered the modern standard
language from those Frk. dialects where the sound shift was not fully
operative (contrast Old Alem. or Bav. *chalcha* with affricates ([kχ]),
and Old Frk. *kalka* with stops) or, alternatively, that the word was
borrowed after the shift was complete and hence remained unaffected
by it. Geographical distribution can obscure the chronological
stratification; for example, competing Latin names for 'winepress'[54]
give rise to German regional terms: (1) *Kelter* (fem.) (< Lat.
calcatura < *calcare* 'tread') may be a Gallo-Roman loan-word from
the fifth century, although it is attested only in ninth-century EFrk. as
calcaturun (*Tatian* 124. 1), which must have contracted to give the
much later form *kelter*, now found in Franconia along the Rhine
and Moselle, in parts of Baden and Swabia, and in Romania
(Siebenbürgen); (2) *Torkel* (fem.), a loan-word from V.Lat. *torcular*
(< Lat. *torculum* < *torqueo* 'twist'), is attested in Alem. *c.*1000
(Notker), was perhaps acquired from North Italy, and remains
current in Bavaria, Austria, eastern Switzerland, and southern
Swabia; (3) another Alem. term, *Trotte*, attested in the ninth century
as *trota* (cognate with *treten*, English *tread*), is a loan-translation
found in the south-west from Switzerland to Lorraine; (4) the
standard name (*Wein*)*presse* (from Lat. *pressa*) may have been
originally restricted to Franconian areas—ninth-century Lorsch
glosses have the form *pressiri* (from V.Lat. *pressorium*). (The
printing-press was later adapted from the winepress.)

B. GERMAN LOAN STRATA AND CHRISTIANITY

Christian influence on German intellectual and religious vocabulary
can also be—imperfectly—subdivided into phases. The earliest is
pre-German and linked probably with early Christian communities
in the Roman Empire, at Trier, say, or Cologne or Augsburg.

Borrowings from this time tend to be widely distributed in western European languages, are of 'Graeco-Latin' type, often attested early, and, where appropriate, have been affected by the HG Consonant Shift. For example, *Kirche*, OHG *kirihha* < Lat. kyrica < Gk. *kuri(a)kon* '(house) of the Lord'. Note the sound shift of pre-OHG *k* > *hh* medially, which suggests a date before the sixth century (see p. 40). The Gk. word, current briefly in about the fourth century, derives from a neut, adj.; Lat. forms are difficult to date but show a change of gender to fem. also shared by the Germanic languages. OHG *kirihha* appears in the place-name *Chircunwillare*, *Chiricunvillare* (Kirweiler in Alsace) AD 718. The origins and dissemination of this word remain puzzling in several respects.[55] *Bischof* (OHG *bisc(h)of* < V.Lat. *biscopu* < Lat. *episcopus* < Gk. *episkopos* 'overseer'), *Kelch* (< Lat. *calix/calicis*), *Mönch* (OHG *munih* < V.Lat. *monicus* < Lat. *monacus*), and *opfern* (OHG *opfarōn* < V.Lat. **opperare* < Lat. *operāri* 'give alms') all show the HG Consonant Shift.[56] Other loan-words with wide currency in the Gmc. languages include *Almosen* (OHG *alamuosa* < Graeco-Lat. *eleemosyna*), *Engel* (OHG *angil/engil* < Graeco-Lat. *angelus*), and *Teufel* (OHG *tiuval* < Gk. *diabolos*—phonology difficult). Some early Christian loans of Graeco-Latin type, and others which seem to be restricted to southern German religious terminology ('süddt. Kirchensprache'), have been attributed to Gothic missionaries, although no such mission is mentioned in historical sources. Words supposedly from Gothic include: *Engel* (Gothic *aggilus*; ⟨*gg*⟩ = [ng]); *Teufel* (Gothic *diabaulus*; ⟨*aú*⟩ = [ɔ]); *Heide* (Gothic *haiþns*); *Pfaffe* (Gothic *papan*);[57] *taufen* (Gothic *daupjan*); *barmherzig* (Gothic *armahairts*; ⟨*ai*⟩ = [ɛ]); *weih-* 'holy',[58] cf. *Weihnachten* (Gothic *weihs* (adj.); ⟨*ei*⟩ = [iː]; OHG *wīh*); *Pfingsten* (Gothic *paintekusten*). Other words, not necessarily religious, may have been introduced by Gothic or Langobard merchants, e.g. *Dult* 'market', 'fair' (Gothic *dulþs* (fem.)) and *Maut* 'custom-house' (Gothic *mōta* (f.); OHG *mūta*)—the place-name Mautern, on the Danube (*Nibelungenlied*, strophe 1329 *Mûtaren*), might mean 'bei den Zöllnern' (< Gothic dat. pl. *mōtarjam* < *mōtareis* (= NHG *Zöllner*)). Characteristic southern (Bav.) names for weekdays[59]— *Ertag* = *Dienstag*, *Pfinztag* = *Donnerstag*, and *Samstag* (rather than northern *Sonnabend* or provincial *Sater(s)dag*)—could derive from the same source, or even from settlers (the place-name Gossensaß = 'Sitz der Goten'?).

The growth of Frankish power during the Merovingian and Carolingian periods also spread Christian vocabulary. Words may be ascribed to this phase if they are attested in the fuller historical and ecclesiastical evidence remaining and also if they lack the HG Consonant Shift, making their adoption after its completion plausible—however, these cult words have sometimes resisted linguistic changes because of their sacred nature. Examples are:

> *Priester* (not **pfriestar*), OHG *priestar* < Lat. *presbyter* < Gk. *presbuteros* 'elder'.
>
> *Probst* (not **pfrobist*), OHG *probist* < V.Lat. *propos(i)tus* < Lat. *praepositus* 'superior'—lit. = 'Vorgesetzter'.
>
> *Zelle*, OHG *cella* < Lat. *cella*. Here the German pronunciation reflects the Romance palatalization of *c* before front vowels: the affricate [*ts*] < earlier *t* by the HG Consonant Shift was the closest approximation to this in German.

Surviving loans from this phase are possibly *Chor, Kapelle, Kerker, Kloster, Kreuz, Küster, Marter, Münster*,[60] *Nonne, Pilger, predigen, segnen*. Apart from the Frankish Church's contribution we know of two culturally most important waves of missionary activity—by Irish monks in the late sixth and early seventh centuries[61] and by Anglo-Saxon monks in the eighth—which must also have furthered the borrowing of Latin Christian terms, for very different reasons.

The Irish, since they spoke a language completely alien to their German converts, could either have promoted the spread of Latin loans or else invested native German words with special Christian significance ('loan-translation'): at any rate, only one loan-word is generally accepted as coming from Irish: *Glocke* < V.Lat. *clocca* < OIr. *clocc* 'bell'. Irish pronunciation has been held responsible for the form of some German loans from Latin: *Feier* (OHG *fīr(r)a* ≠ Lat. *fēria*), *Kreide* (OHG *krīda* ≠ Lat. *crēta*), *Pein* (OHG *pīn* ≠ V.Lat. *pēna* < Lat. *poena*), *Speise* (OHG *spīsa* ≠ V.Lat. *spēsa* < Lat. *expensa*), which all show a long /ī/ (and its NHG development /ei/) instead of (V.)Lat. long /ē/. Similarly, OHG *salm* (mod. *Psalm*) and *salteri* (from Lat. *psalterium*) show a loss of initial /p-/ found also in OIr. *salm, saltair*.[62] Irish influence in shaping a characteristic south German religious terminology remains only an attractive hypothesis.[63]

Few loan-words seem to have entered German as a result of the Anglo-Saxon mission either, but in this case OE and Old German, Frisian, and Saxon shared the same Germanic 'word-hoard'. The missionaries' role must have been catalytic:[64] native German words related to the OE ones could easily extend their meanings to cover the new religious concepts. At the same time, the similarity of the vocabulary makes picking out OE loans difficult. Surviving OE influence may be seen in *der heilige Geist* (OHG (EFrk.) *heilag geist* (*Tatian* 7. 4); cf. OE *se háliga gást*, contrast *wihes atumes* (gen. sg.) from the Alem. ninth-century *Murbach Hymns*),[65] also in *Heiland* ≠ 'Saviour' (*Tatian* has *heilant* throughout, translating 'Jesus'; cf. OE *haelend*), *Sonnabend* 'Saturday' (cf. OE *sunnanǣfen*), and possibly *Ostern* (perhaps from OE *eastron*).

Nevertheless, at the time, the Anglo-Saxon missions were of considerable cultural significance. Following Bishop Wilfrid of York's desultory attempts to convert the Frisians in 678–9, the Anglo-Saxon missionaries enjoyed Frankish protection. Because the English Church's close links with Rome (evident in the careers of Willibrord, renamed Clement (*c*.657–739), and Wynfrith, renamed Boniface (675–754)) suited Frankish political advantage, their missions in Frisia, Thuringia, Hesse, and Saxony were encouraged; and in Bavaria, too, Boniface reorganized the Church. But many monks and nuns participated in these missions, spreading literacy and the intellectual revival currently flourishing in Britain, particularly at Northumbria.[66] Alcuin of York (*c*.730–804) built on these foundations when he became Charlemagne's mentor in 789, bringing about a 'renaissance' of learning; and his pupil Hrabanus Maurus (784–856) made Fulda (founded by Boniface in 744) one of the important cultural centres in Germany with possibly as many as 600 monks[67]; Otfrid of Weissenburg was in turn Hrabanus' pupil.

Some OE must have been spoken and written in German monasteries, like Echternach (founded *c*.700 by Willibrord), and insular orthoepic and palaeographical features are found in OHG texts, e.g. the use of the rune wyn (ƿ) for /w/ or /hw/; or the Symbol Ð, *d* (modelled on OE eth, ð?), mostly for a voiced dental consonant (for example, in the *Hildebrandslied*, the OHG *Lex Salica* translation, and in the *Wessobrunn Creation and Prayer*), while a characteristic 'English' insular script was apparently retained in the scriptorium of Fulda until the mid-ninth century. Lasting lexical traditions which may stem from the Anglo-Saxon missions are, moreover, apparent in the EFrk. *Tatian* translation, which shares many forms with OE, OS, and Fris. which have failed to survive into modern German. Compare the words set out in Table 1.[68]

TABLE 1

Latin	(a) Common OHG	(b) Tatian	(c) OE
misereri	armēn (ir-bi-armen)	miltēn	miltsian
misericors	armherz (bi-armherzic)	miltherzi	mildheort
humilitas	deomuoti	ōdmuotī	éadméde
abrogans	deomuot (deomuot-ig)	ōtmuotig	éadmód
(= humilis)			
pati	dulten	tholēn	þolian
gaudere	freuuen	gifehan	ġeféon
gratia	ginάda	geba	ġiefu
evangelium	[various]	gotspel	godspel*
claritas	scōnī	fagarī	faeġer (adj)
consolatio	trōst	fluobara†	frófor
contristare	trūrēn	truobēn	[OS drobian]
dubitare	zwīfalōn	zuēhōn	twéoġan

* NB, godspel was originally gódspel ('good message'); Tatian shows the same association with got = deus; cf. other OHG forms like cuatchundida (Benedictine Rule) and diuri arunti (Otfrid).

† The form fluobara may show dissimilation of r > l; in dissimilation one of two similar (or same) sounds changes its manner of articulation, but not usually its place of articulation. See Paul (1968), 66.

Details apart, the words in column (a) become erbarmen, barmherzig, Demut, demütig, dulden, sich freuen, Gnade, Evangelium, Schöne/ Schönheit, Trost, trauern, zweifeln, whereas those in columns (b) and (c) generally die out: in English only 'fair', 'gospel', and 'mildhearted' remain. Moreover, competing terms occur in the text, e.g. anst (cf. NHG Gunst), geba, ginάda, and huldī all render Lat. gratia, so we have the choice of deciding whether these are regional forms, reflecting a north–south opposition, stylistic variants, or subtle interpretations of semantic nuances. The apparently OE elements in the Tatian vocabulary must thus be treated with caution; they may reflect nothing more than a particularly 'conservative variety of Middle German which has strong affinities with the north'.[69]

The Christian influences, by whatever agency, lay the basis for an abstract intellectual vocabulary in German which is most easily seen in the formidable range of Notker of St Gall (d. 1022), the third of that name, who was known as 'Notker Teutonicus' because of his great knowledge and love of German. A substantial part of the consolidation and elaboration of this vocabulary occurred in biblical scholarship, scholasticism, and learned mysticism down to the fourteenth century, eventually to enter the universities: but otherwise, and in the early period especially, it impinged only indirectly on the communities at large. Some impression of the sophistication already possible in the eighth century is gained from the *Isidor* translation, where theologically relevant distinctions regarding the 'essential' similarity or equality or identity of the persons of the godhead are rendered into German.[70]

STYLISTIC RESOURCES OF GERMAN IN THE EARLY PERIOD

Some impression of early German's versatility can be obtained from examining its native poetic, legal, and colloquial registers.

A. NATIVE POETIC TRADITIONS

The *Hildebrandslied* (*HL*) of unknown date and provenance is the unique example of a continental Germanic heroic lay. The events narrated are of the fifth/sixth century, much distorted in the generations of oral transmission behind the extant ninth-century manuscript, produced perhaps at Fulda, or Mainz.[71] The 'dialect' shows partial transcription of a poem in HG form into LG, with unshifted consonants—possibly an attempt to archaize and reproduce a pre-HG common poetic language.[72] Hence 'archaic' morphology and syntax, such as the use of the instrumental case without a governing preposition:[73] *cheisuringu gitan* 'made of imperial coin' (1. 34); *wili mih dinu speru werpan* 'you seek to hurl your spear at me' (1. 4); *scal mih swertu hauwan* 'shall hew me with (his) sword' (1. 53). The poetic and legal diction can blend, e.g. in *HL*'s use of the verb *gimahalen* 'to make (a formal) speech', as at the legal assembly or *mallum* (see below); moreover the form in *HL* is also old—later OHG texts have *malôn*; but compare mod. German *Gemahl*, *vermählen*. Several *hapax legomena* (words attested nowhere else in OHG) are found in other Germanic poetry. Unfortunately, since the OE and ON evidence post-dates our poem by a century or more, because of our ignorance of Germanic poetic traditions, and because there must have been differences of genre between lays and the longer epics that have not been preserved in OHG, stylistic assessment of the material is difficult. For example:

> *urhettun* 'warriors', 'challengers', cf. OS *urhetto*, OE *ōretta*.
>
> *hiltiu* dat. < **hiltia* 'battle', cf. OS *hild(i)*, OE *hild*, ON *hildr*.
>
> *gimahalta* 'spoke', cf. OS *gimahalda*, OE *madelode*.
>
> *giweit* < **giwītan* 'go', cf. OS *giwītan*, OE *gewītan*.
>
> *bure* < **būr* 'hall', 'bower', cf. OE *būr*.
>
> *gudhamun* 'battle-shirts', cf. the many compounds with *guþ*, peculiar to poetry in OE *gūþ-cearu, guþ-fana, guþ-freca, guþ-horn, guþ-lēoþ* etc., ON *gunnr, gudr*.
>
> *inwit* 'deceit', cf. OS, OE *inwid*.
>
> *wewurt* 'misfortune', 'terrible fate', cf. OS *wurd*, OE *wyrd* 'fate', ON *urdr*.
>
> *sceotantero* < **sceotant* 'shooter', 'warrior', cf. OE *scēotend*.

Some words are, indeed, only imperfectly understood.

Furthermore, the alliterative formulae and phrasing of *HL* also link it to other Germanic poetry, for example to OE, as in

> 8 *ferahes frotoro* 'more experienced in life', cf. *Battle of Maldon* 317 *Ic eom frōd feores* 'I am experienced in life'.
>
> 54 *ih imo ti banin werden* 'I (shall) become/cause his death', cf. *Beowulf* 587 *ðū þīnum brōðrum tō banan wurde* 'you were the bane of your brothers'.
>
> 43 *dat man wic furnam* 'that battle took men' (or *inan* 'him'), cf. *Wanderer* 80 *sume wīg fornōm* 'battle took some'.
>
> 68 *giwigan miti wabnum* 'fought with weapons', cf. *Battle of Maldon* where *wigan mid wǣpnum* 'warriors with weapons' shows a 'parallel' created by the alliteration.

Note also syntactic parallels, like the use of **lātan* + infinitive as a causative construction:

> 63 *do lettun se aerist asckim scritan* 'then they let fly with (ashen) spears', cf. *Battle of Maldon* 108 *Hī lēton þā of folman fēolhearde speru* | . . . *flēogan* 'Then they let fly from their hands file-hard spears', 149 *forlēt . . . flēogan*.

However, *HL* is restrained in its use of synonymy and lacks the expressive condensed compound metaphors known as kennings, which are common in *Beowulf* and especially in ON, where they contribute to the manneredness of this poetry—and to its virtual untranslatability. One exception is, perhaps, *HL* 65 *staimbort*

'shields', which may be a kenning ('stone(-studded) boards'?—the
Sutton Hoo ship burial yielded a shield with *cloisonné* work). We can,
however, presuppose some knowledge of kennings in OHG since
appellatives like *līhhamo* (NHG *Leichnam*) 'body', lit. 'life-shirt',
occur. Indeed, familiarity with this metaphorical tradition might
account for some loan-translations of Latin words which strike the
modern reader as inept or ridiculously transparent: *līhhamo* itself
has many derivatives and Notker even renders Latin *incarnatio*
by *līhham-wortani* (lit. 'the state of having become flesh'; NHG
geworden).

Not surprisingly, native poetic traditions influence OHG poetry
even where that poetry is Christian in intention and 'modern' in form,
like Otfrid's rhymed life of Christ with its sophisticated exegetical and
moral interpretations. Otfrid, too, uses alliteration and occasionally
the older type of vocabulary, e.g. *itis* 'woman', 'lady', and *ungisaro*
(= *ungerüstet*), cf. *HL saro* 'armour', and even near-kennings, e.g.
the synonyms for 'heaven': *sunnun pad* 'path of the sun', *sterrono
strāza* 'street(s) of the stars', *wega wolkono* 'ways of the clouds'
(*Evangelienbuch* 1. 5). Again, the *Murbach Hymns*, written at the
monastery of Reichenau on Lake Constance in the early ninth
century, while on the face of it a slavish word-by-word transposition
of the Latin *Ambrosian Hymns*, show alliterative embellishment and
older poetic vocabulary, e.g. *ortfrumo* 'Creator', *sedelcanc* 'sunset',
lit. 'throne-going'.[74]

So, despite all caveats and uncertainties, we can discern a diction
and vocabulary harking back to another poetic tradition, undoubtedly older and certainly in its own way as far removed from
colloquial language as the language of the Christian *Gebrauchs-
literatur*.

B. THE LANGUAGE OF LAW

Isolated Gmc. 'legal' words have been preserved in runic inscriptions,
tribal and personal names, and classical historians, but they are hard
to separate from general 'political' language reflecting social institutions. Legal vocabulary in a legal setting has come down in the
fascinating but hopelessly corrupt Frk. glosses in the Latin text of the
Lex Salica,[75] the *Malberg Glosses* (*MG*), so called because they are
often prefaced by *mal*(*bergo*) 'pertaining to the legal assembly',
(= *gerichtlich*). The glosses themselves are partly Latinized, e.g.

mallum 'court' < Gmc. **maþla-*,[76] *mannire* 'summon(s)', (= *vorladen*), *alodis* 'possessions', 'allodium', *fredum* = *Friedensgeld*, *mallare* 'hold court', *sunnis/sunnia* 'essoin', 'justifiable impediment to court appearance' (MHG *êhaftiu nôt*), *uuadium* 'pledge'. These terms become progressively incomprehensible to the Romance scribes, and in the revisions under Charlemagne (the *Emendata* and the *Lex Salica Carolina*) many are dropped. Indeed, even a ninth-century scribe of the original version omitted the Gmc. words as 'verba Grecorum' (MS A3)—all Greek to him!

If the *Malberg Glosses* do represent 'WFrk.' the relationship of this dialect to OHG is obscure: certainly the language was 'LG' ('pre-HG'?), since no shifted consonants appear. Other *leges barbarorum* contain Gmc. and 'German' words; some, like *morgingeba* 'morning-gift', 'dower', are common and the relationship of the individual legal codes to one another poses many difficulties. However, in the present context we note that several codes could be found in one monastery: an early library catalogue of 821-2 shows that Reichenau monastery possessed copies of the *Lex Salica* (*c.*507-11), *Lex Alemannica* (seventh century), *Lex Langobardorum* (seventh to ninth centuries), *Lex Ribvaria* (eighth/ninth century), and various capitularies of Charlemagne and Louis the Pious. Monks, then, were familiar with legal codes and could draw on their technical terms in biblical translation. The Old and New Testaments were themselves designated *ēa*, *ēwa* 'law'—the Bible is much concerned with legal matters; indeed, whole sections of Mosaic law were incorporated into thirteenth century vernacular codifications, the *Sachsenspiegel* and the *Schwabenspiegel*. In *Tatian* and *Hēliand* Germanic legal vocabulary is perhaps more striking to the modern reader than to a contemporary. Sonderegger[77] gives examples:

Latin	Tatian
praetorium	*thinghus* 'assembly-house'
	frīthof 'enclosed assembly-house'
rapīna	*nōtnumft* 'rape'
villicus	*sculdheizo* (NHG *Schultheiss*)
iudicium, iudex	*tuom, tuomo* 'judgment', 'judge'

Still, some legal terms take on specifically Christian meaning, often becoming abstract in the process, e.g. *trōst*, from meaning 'support', 'aid', has changed to 'comfort', 'hope'; *githingi* 'legal assembly', 'advice' becomes 'intercession', 'hope' (MHG *gedinge*); *suona* 'court' (cf. *suonatago* 'judgment') becomes 'atonement', 'peace' (NHG *Sühne); scult* 'debt' becomes 'guilt', 'transgression' (NHG *Schuld*). Finally, some terms acquire a wide currency, e.g. *thing* 'assembly', 'court' (cognate is the first element of the Isle of Man parliament, the Tynwald) gives NHG *Ding; sahha* 'case' becomes NHG *Sache:* both *Ding* and *Sache* now lack any clearly defined meaning.

But legal vocabulary is also appropriate to the Christian message because of its elevated level: the vocabulary of Germanic customary law was more adaptable for Christian purposes than was the older Germanic religious vocabulary, which consequently seldom survives.

Certain continuous OHG texts are specifically legal: the *Strasburg Oaths* of 842 preserve a piece of international treaty law; and a fragmentary translation of the emended *Lex Salica* in EFrk. dialect from the early ninth century (from Mainz?) copes skilfully with the original and generally paraphrases, for example Title lxi, *de chrenecruda* (about the transfer of 'wergild' to wealthier relatives),[78] is rendered simply *der, scazloos man, andran arslahit* 'he (who), (being) destitute, shall slay another'. Unfortunately, apart from summonsing practice, theft of various kinds of pig, and a few odd headings, we have no more of this text. Alliterative and archaic formulae reflect the age of German legal traditions and their solemnity—Jacob Grimm wrote of the 'Poesie im Recht'. The Frankish Empire had a hybrid administration, as the *Malberg Glosses* imply; later administrators dropped the Germanic tags. Whereas much OHG literature seems gradually to emancipate itself from Latin tutelage, with law increasing Latinization seems to be the rule. Not until the thirteenth century do we find written German legal codes: in keeping with the law's status it became the province of the highest administrators, whose language was Latin. The OHG *Lex Salica* shows that vernacular legists were adept, but by the tenth and eleventh centuries the educational standard of administrators and their lords must have been high enough to dispense with vernacular texts—another facet of the Ottonian cultivation.

C. COLLOQUIAL OLD HIGH GERMAN?

Curiously, it is in glosses that we find the traces of spoken German most clearly. Hitherto, scholars have edited and dated glosses, determined their provenance and textual traditions where possible, but seldom evaluated the material stylistically as a communicative process in which both Latin and German must be taken together.[79] However, two sets of glosses demanded stylistic analysis from the outset, and have, indeed, been labelled 'Gespräche', 'conversations'. The ninth-century *Cassel Glosses* (*CG*) and the late ninth-/tenth-century *Paris* or *Old High German Conversations* are complementary: the *Cassel Glosses* were written by a German, show regular Bav. features, and the odd error in glossing contemporary Romance (No. 54 *segradas* = *secreta* 'privy' is misunderstood as *sacrarium* 'sacristy'!); the OHG *Conversations* were written down by a Romance scribe in an orthography with characteristic Romance features,[80] with a disregard for morphology but a telling phonetic accuracy. The author of the CG allows himself a jibe at the expense of the Romance speakers, the Romance scribe of the OHG *Conversations* renders even German obscenities. Both texts are unusual in using Latin to understand German instead of vice versa.

The Cassel text deals with daily practicalities, the visit to the barber or contact with strangers: *Tundi meo capilli* = *skir min fahs*; *Radi me meo colli* = *skir minan hals*; *Radi meo barba* = *skir minan part*; *Unde es tu?* = *uuanna pist du?*; *Quis es tu?* = *uuer pist du?*; *Unde uenis?* = *uuanna quimis?*; *De quale patria pergis?* = *fona uueliheru lantskeffi sindos* [= *gehst*]? The *Paris/OHG Conversations* share some items with *CG*: *Guane cumet ger, brothro?* = *unde uenis, frater?*; *Gueliche lande cumen ger?* = *de qua patria?* But the phonology is unmistakably colloquial: the pronoun *ir* (or *ge*?) becomes the 'Cockney' *ger*; the *-o* on *brothro* has been interpreted as an intensifying suffix (= 'mate-y'?). The morphology is variable: *cumet* (second person pl.) alternates with *cumen*. In a string of commands we see the slurring of **gib mir* to *gimer*, as in *Gimer min ros, Gimer min schelt* ('shield'), *Gimer min spera* ('spear'), *Gimer min suarda* ('sword'). We find asseverations and expletives: *Semergot elfe* 'God 'elp me!', *Be gotta* 'by God', *en terue* 'in truth' (MHG *entriuwen*), and the coarse retort *Vndes ars in tine naso* = *canis culum in tuo naso*! We also have colloquially intensified negatives, e.g. *ne haben ne trophen* 'I haven't a drop',[81] and the pleonastic use of pronouns, e.g. *Narra er sarda gerre* = *stultus uoluntarie fottit*, '(Ein) Narr, *er* fickt(e) gerne'. The occurrence of the rare (taboo?) verb *serten/serden* (= *ficken*) is noteworthy: it is hardly attested again until the fifteenth-century *Fastnachtsspiele*. Here it is used literally, for practical purposes: *Gauathere, latz mer serte*, 'Lass mich bumsen, Püppchen'.

In some slightly later Terence glosses in the MFrk. dialect a frustrated and immature glossator reiterates the word in several heads: *faciam ut iusseris* = (*h*)*ich lazen thih serten*; *amatores mulierum* = *serdere* (agent noun pl.).

Earlier scholars saw in the *Paris Conversations* transcriptions of actual conversations, perhaps during a journey, and even identified speakers as 'nobles', 'priests', 'gemeine Knechte', 'innkeepers', or 'monastery porters' by their speech. This is unlikely: the glosses are entered with no discernible order along the top and in the upper margins of the ninth-century Abavus glossary into which they were copied, and they are supplemented by quotations in the same hand from a *Tatian* manuscript. These *Tatian* excerpts are clearly part of the *Paris Conversations*: the glossator compiled his phrasebook from several sources and the *Tatian* sentences illustrate points of grammar, and expand vocabulary and idiom. The order of elements in the Latin text of the *Tatian* has been changed to make the German syntax easier to master: for example, the phrase *gaudio magno* (*Tatian* 244 2) becomes *magno gaudio* to fit the German *mihilemo giuehen* 'with great rejoicing). The very triviality and repetitiveness of the vocabulary confirm the glossator's systematic intention; on occasion he inserts a phrase of his own. e.g. in a series dealing with 'sword', *Tatian* 185 *passim*: *mitte tuum gladium in uaginam* = *senti thin suert in sceidun*; *peribunt gladio* = *foruuerdent in suerte* ('perish'); *cum gladiis et cum fustibus* = *Ir mit suerton inti mit stangon*. His 'own' phrase, *nolo rogare meum fratrem suum gladium* = *Neguil bittan minan brother sin suert*, fits in well, whatever its origin. But the use of a literary source (*Tatian*) for conversational and idiomatic phrases confirms Sonderegger's opinion[82] that there may be colloquial OHG even in literature at this period.

SELECT BIBLIOGRAPHY

General presentations of Early German literature and language are listed here, with collections of texts and dictionaries. Grammars and phonological studies will be found at the end of Chapter II.

STUDIES OF EARLY GERMAN LITERATURE AND CULTURE

Baesecke (1921–52).
Bertau (1972).
Bostock (1976).
Brinkmann (1931).

de Boor (1949/1979).
Ehrismann (1932).
Schlosser (1977).
Sonderegger (1974).

TEXTS AND TRANSLATIONS

Barber (1951).
Braune and Ebbinghaus
  (1874–5/1979).

Müllenhoff and Scherer (1892).
Schlosser (1970).
Steinmeyer (1916).

For dialect specimens of Early German, see Appendix B.

FACSIMILES

Fischer (1966).

GENERAL STUDIES OF EARLY GERMAN LANGUAGE

Braune and Eggers (1886/1975).
Braune and Ebbinghaus
  (1891/1977)
Cordes (1980).

Naumann and Betz (1962).
Sonderegger (1973).
Sonderegger (1974).

DICTIONARIES

Graff (1834–46) [vol. vi of the original edn. contains an indispensable index by H. F. Massmann, *Gedrängtes althochdeutsches Wörterbuch oder vollständiger Index zu Graff's althochdeutschem Sprachschatze* (1846), which is vol. vii of the 1963 reprint].

Karg-Gasterstädt and Frings
(1952–) [in progress].
Köbler (1971).

Schützeichel (1969).
Starck and Wells (1972–)
[in progress].

LEXICAL STUDIES

Maurer and Rupp (1974) [with further bibliography].

CHAPTER II

THE PHONOLOGY OF EARLY GERMAN (OHG)

PROLEGOMENA

In the preceding chapter we have considered the background to the earliest German: periodization, the nature of the evidence available, the theoretical relation of German to other Gmc. languages, the main monastery dialects, and external and internal influences on the language. Now we turn to certain key features and developments in OHG phonology and to methods of examining and presenting them: the description and interpretation of the material depend both on the circumstances which produced it and on the analytical approach adopted to it. Unfortunately, our description of the material is hampered by its stemming from different areas and from its having been written in sometimes inadequate and inconsistent orthographies at different times and for different purposes: juggling these variables of time, place, and style, with spelling acting often as a blindfold, requires considerable faith and dexterity. To interpret OHG phonology chronologically we must, then, assume that the various forms of OHG might be placed into a chronological framework, with the texts representing different stages in the development of the 'same' language. But the texts also come from differing geograhical areas: their consonantism reflects the HG Consonant Shift in varying degrees,[1] and the vowel systems display differences in diphthongization or monophthongization, or in the unstressed syllables of weak noun and adj. declensions, as between, say, Frk. dialects and those of UG. The dilemma may be summed up as follows: can we view the language of the Frk. *Isidor* translation,[2] with its highly developed orthography, as an earlier form of the 'same' language which appears later in the no less sophisticated spelling of Notker's Alem. writings?

Stylistic features, conscious and 'unconscious', are notoriously complex and defy mono-causal explanation; and, so far as phonology is concerned, stylistic choice affects particularly the phonetic values of sounds, not necessarily their relationship to other sounds in the system. Whereas such variation occurs mainly in speech, and the OHG evidence is mostly far removed from everyday spoken language, the absence of any standard language at this period increases the possibility of spoken forms being adopted in spelling, and some of these might be stylistic, i.e. variants appropriate to certain speakers, contexts, and functions. The spread of some prestige pronunciation, or the errors and hyper-corrections which result when speakers vainly attempt to conform to some admired linguistic form, are well-known instances of style affecting a language's historical development. Prestige may have encouraged the spread of sound changes like the OHG diphthongization and monophthongization (see Chapter I, p. 49, and pp. 83-5 below), possibly even the HG Consonant Shift. The diphthongization in particular has been linked with parallel changes in Romance, and, even if linguistic borrowing is undemonstrable, catalytic reaction between German and Romance dialects must still have involved some degree of stylistic choice on the part of the speakers.[3]

Given the monastery scriptoria as the main sources of the written texts, we might also argue that the social effects of language-use are primarily reflected in the spread of, or inhibition of, spellings as well as sounds: again, it proves difficult to separate orthography and phonology. Some palaeographical and orthographical influence is attributable to the Anglo-Saxon missions, some graphies, like ⟨gh⟩ in the *Isidor*, are probably borrowed from Romance scribal traditions. Here we might see the prestige of a scriptorium favouring the spread of its spelling. Conversely, and more tentatively, developments occur in speech which may take many centuries to become recognized in orthography—spelling is often conservative, actually ignoring spoken forms.[4] Although political and cultural influences—the important court, social class, foreign languages—are often invoked as the vehicles for disseminating linguistic norms or even just individual words and sounds, prestige spellings within the closely knit cloistered world of monasteries may be more important for the kind of material that has survived, though this level of linguistic interaction, namely writing, was irrelevant to most of the speakers of German during the early period. This also accounts for the difficulty a linguistic historian has in trying to relate changes in the linguistic forms to changes in the speech-community. But at least we may say that the nature of the texts, their great variability, and the circumstances and manner of production relate to the monks, scriptorial traditions, and religious, political, and cultural functions they fulfil.

The problems of 'purifying the data' in order to construct phonological (or grammatical) systems, and the extreme tentativeness with which those systems can be placed into relation to each other and to the speakers, force historical linguistics to be an *interpretative* discipline. Plausibility is the highest achievable goal, though it often masquerades as 'explanation'. This is at once the crux and the charm of the subject!

METHODS OF ANALYSIS

As long as the status and interaction of the various levels of language—phonology, morphology, syntax, style, etc.—remain in dispute, particularly the relationship between syntax and semantics, it seems reasonable to exemplify internal features of OHG from phonology. Despite orthographical problems, the evidence at our disposal can be presented fairly coherently, and much work has already been done on phonology in early German: we shall, moreover, compare pre-structuralist, structuralist, and generative approaches to OHG phonology, assessing each method's basic assumptions, and their implications for the history of German sounds.[5] At the outset, Leonard Palmer's words should be borne in mind: 'A sound once uttered is gone and lost forever . . . Hence what is called a sound change is not a process in the external world independent of human action, but a change of habits by a group of speakers'.[6] This is valid equally for the drawing up of 'sound systems' from texts: we are representing in simple notation the relationships between complex articulatory processes.

A. PRE-STRUCTURALIST APPROACHES

A pre-structuralist theory may be defined as one concerned less with the functions and relations of sounds within a system than with the phonetic characteristics of individual sounds, their origins, and the changes they undergo. In pre-structuralist theory, the term 'sound' denotes both the phonetic quality of a sound and its function. This is so because pre-structuralists were aware of the systematic import- ance of certain sounds, but they were not, until Saussure, concerned to investigate this side of language. For example, although Jacob Grimm entitles the 'phonology' in the second edition of his *Deutsche Grammatik* (1822) 'Von den Buchstaben', he was aware of language as a system of oppositions—Grimm's *Buchstabe* corresponds partly to the use of *littera* by earlier Latin grammarians, and the concept is akin to that of the 'phoneme'; Hermann Paul[7] uses the term *Lautbild* in similar fashion. The emphasis on the origins of sounds reflects the nineteenth-century interest in the origin of language itself. Using the comparative method, scholars drew up 'genera' and 'species' of languages along Darwinian lines and we still resort to such 'genetic tables' or 'family trees' for taxonomic convenience (see Chapter I). Because nineteenth-century approaches are frequently 'atomistic' in their preoccupation with individual structural *elements* of lan- guage rather than with structural *relations*, they qualify as 'pre- structuralist'. For them, language change was virtually synonymous with sound change.

A younger group of Leipzig scholars, the 'Neogrammarians' (*Junggrammatiker*), established principles by which language, or sound change, operates and applied the 'sound-law' to any sound change taking place without exception and unnoticed by speakers.[8] However, a sound-law is not equivalent to a law of natural science:

Das Lautgesetz sagt nicht aus, was unter gewissen allgemeinen Bedingungen immer wieder eintreten muss, sondern konstatiert nur die Gleichmässigkeit innerhalb einer Gruppe bestimmter historischer Erscheinungen (Paul (1880/1963), 46).

Irregularities to the sound-law were explained by expedients like analogy (see below, p. 155) and 'interference'—borrowing from other languages. In attempting to assess why certain sound changes occurred at some period but not others, scholars turned increas- ingly to the phonetic analysis of language, and phonetics eventually

became a separate subject in its own right, linked with physics and physiology as well as language studies.
The two main types of Neogrammarian sound change are:

1. 'spontaneous' or unconditioned change, which takes place regardless of phonetic environment;
2. 'combinatory' or conditioned change, where some given phonetic or accentual environment produces a variation in the treatment of a sound from one stage of language's history to another.[9]

Conditioned change is recognized precisely by this variation of 'results' in grammatically or etymologically related forms and is sometimes called 'grammatical change', while structuralists use the more forbidding term 'morpho-phonemic alternation'; for the morphological effects in medieval German, see Chapter IV.

The classic examples of spontaneous and conditioned sound changes are the First or Germanic Consonant Shift, which distinguishes Gmc. languages from the other IE languages, and its corollary, Verner's Law. They take place before our era, perhaps even earlier than the first millenium BC, and so fall outside the scope of the present work, but their effects remain. All Gmc. languages show an initial voiceless spirant /h/ for a reconstructable PIE voiceless stop /k/; hence, in the word for 'hare':

> PIE *kaso- 'grey', 'grey-brown', 'pale'? (a taboo word for 'hare'?), cf.
> Lat. cānus < *casnos 'grey(-haired)', 'old'.
> PGmc. (1) *hasan-/ (2) *hazan-
> (1) OHG haso, OFris. hasa, MHG, MLG, MNeth. hase; mod.
> Neth. haas
> (2) OE hara, ON heri, mod. English, Danish, Swedish hare.[10]

While the change k > h is spontaneous and general, it was necessary to divide the attested forms into two groups with the PGmc. base-forms *hásan/*hazán having voiceless and voiced spirant respectively, depending on the position of the stress accent(´), which was movable in PIE and became fixed on the first syllable only in late PGmc. times. It will be seen that the occurrence of s or z (which subsequently deveops to r) is thus a conditioned sound change. Several spirants were affected by it in PGmc. and this accounts for variation in the consonantism of related words and, in the case of strong verbs, even in the morphology of one and the same word. Often this 'irregularity' is subsequently removed: the $s \sim r$ alternation occurring in the past tense of the verb 'to be' in OHG has been replaced in mod. German by levelling of the *r*: cf. OHG *ih was* ≠ *wir wārun*, mod. German *war* ≠ *waren*. In English, the alternation remains in the orthography: *was* ≠ *were*—although, of course, in standard British English pronunciation the *r* is not realized unless followed by a word beginning with a vowel. Karl Verner noticed the correlations between voiced fricatives in Gmc. and the positioning of word accent in Sanskrit and Greek. He recognized that the dynamic (or stress) accent must condition the consonants in the apparent exceptions to the First Consonant Shift: when the PIE stress accent, which was movable, immediately precedes a single voiceless stop in IE, that stop shows voiceless spirantal reflexes in Gmc.; if the accent does not immediately precede, voiced spirants occur which tend to become (voiced) stops in OHG.[11] For example,

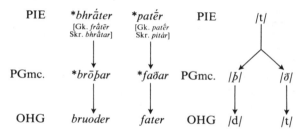

	PIE	**bhrā́ter*	**patér*	PIE	/t/
		[Gk. *frātēr* Skr. *bhrā́tar*]	[Gk. *patér* Skr. *pitár*]		
PGmc.		**brōþar*	**faðar*	PGmc.	/þ/ /ð/
OHG		*bruoder*	*fater*	OHG	/d/ /t/

When the movable stress accent became fixed on the first syllable in Germanic languages, the factors conditioning the alternation of voiceless and voiced spirants were obscured. The consonant changes described by Verner's Law have parallels elsewhere when voiceless and voiced spirants alternate according to stress pattern, e.g. English *execute* ['eksikju:t] and *executor* [eg'zekjutǫɹ].[12] Morphological complications arose from the alternating stress pattern as described by Verner's Law, especially in the strong verb (see pp. 162–3).

The Neogrammarians, then, fixed their gaze primarily upon the antecedents or successors of a sound; only if the phonetic context (i.e. the sound in its linear or 'syntagmatic' relations with other sounds) might account for some apparent irregularity did it attract their attention. They presented their findings in rigorous tabular form, often resorting to PIE. We take only the short vowels as examples. Wherever arrows diverge from an earlier 'sound' in the table,

conditioning factors have produced a more limited change—cf.
the developments of IE *e, i, u.*

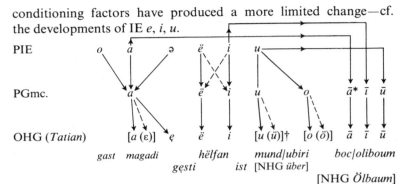

PIE   *o   a   ə   ë   i   u*

PGmc.   *a   ë   i   u   o   ā*   ī   ū*

OHG (*Tatian*)   [*a* (ε)]   *ę   ë   i*   [*u (ü)*]†   [*o (ö)*]   *ā   ī   ū*

gast   magadi   hëlfan   mund/ubiri   boc/oliboum
            gęsti   ist [NHG über]

[NHG Ölbaum]

* Some long vowels are listed here, since their number is increased in PGmc. by
lengthening of short vowels.

† The mutated vowels shown in parentheses are not indicated in the texts, and the
mutated *ö* is a late or analogical mutation occurring either in loan-words, e.g. *oli* (NHG
Öl), or in derivative forms, e.g. *böcklīn* (NHG *Böcklein*) from *boc* (NHG *Bock*) or the
new pl. *lohhir* (beside *luhhir*) from *loh* (NHG *Löcher*). See Braune and Eggers (1975),
§32. The problem is this: in PGmc. /u/ and /o/ were in complementary distribution,
/u/ occurring before high vowels, /o/ before non-high vowels; consequently /o/ ought
never to occur before high vowels and could thus not mutate to /ö/. That it does so is
explained by analogy, although this did not always operate, as pairs like OHG *gold*
'gold' and adj. *guldīn* 'golden' show: both derive from the PGmc. root **gulþ-*.

The greatly increased number of conditioned sound changes in OHG
should be noted: this is caused by mutation (umlaut), although its
effects are not generally indicated in the orthography of the texts
from this early period. If we compare *Tatian thū gibuti* and, later,
MHG *dū gebüte* (manuscript form *gebûte*) 'you (sg.) ordered', we see
no trace of the mutated [ü] in the *Tatian* orthography, but there are
grounds for holding that the sound was mutated none the less. The
long vowels *ā, ī, ū* also result from conditioned change:[13] when short
vowels preceded a nasal + velar spirant [χ] in PGmc., the vowel was
nasalized and lengthened while the nasal consonant itself disappeared; then the vowel lost its nasality:

short V + Nasal + [χ] > long Ṽ + [χ].

We can still see the effects of this in English *bring/brought, think/
thought*,[14] and in German, where the originally long preterite vowels
have been shortened: cf. *bringen/brachte* (OHG *brāhta*), *denken/
dachte* (OHG *dāhta*).

The great contribution of the Neogrammarians is their very
concentration upon regularity. Their grammars present the diachronic developments clearly, and also examine the phonetic

plausibility of the sound changes proposed. The standard OHG grammar—Braune and Eggers (1975)—still sets out its phonology under the individual PGmc. vowels and consonants. Moreover, placing the development of individual sounds in the forefront enables us to fit all the extant texts of the OHG period into a chronological framework according to their *progressive* features, i.e. sounds that are eventually to be adopted into later MHG literary dialects or into the modern standard language, or *conservative* features, sounds that are restricted to older texts or closer to reconstructed proto-languages. Pre-structuralists and Neogrammarians faced the perennial problems of philology—the collection of and arrangement of data—before they could theorize about language. It is a tribute to their punctiliousness that the pre-structuralist material is still regularly reinterpreted.

B. STRUCTURALIST APPROACHES

1. *The phonemic system*

Often the question is asked: 'How do we know what German sounded like at different historical stages?' The structuralist answers that we can never know exactly, although study of spellings and accents in the manuscripts (Notker employs a sophisticated accentual system), rhymes, isolated remarks by writers (Otfrid makes orthoepic observations in a letter to Archbishop Liutbert), and the later developments in modern dialects do provide clues; but in any case the question is not of prime importance. For the structuralist is concerned with the relational aspects of language, with the *langue*, while the phonetic problems of the realization of 'phonemes' (see below, pp. 76-7) in utterances are for him secondary. Saussure described the structural relations of language at a particular time as being like a state of play in a game of chess.[15] By another metaphor historical phonology is like a medieval tapestry. The colours of the threads (= phonetic values) may have faded beyond recall, but the stag-hunt or amorous encounter still emerges from the lie of the threads which make the structure of the picture (= the phonemic system). We can even rework the picture, inserting new threads in colours that seem to us appropriate, i.e. we may provide a 'modern' phonetic interpretation. (While this is not a requirement of the phonemic approach, for the generative school it assumes great importance.) Labouring the metaphor somewhat, we have lost certain details of the picture where these were conveyed by colour change alone, not by the direction of the threads: similarly, we have to deal with written evidence which does not always enable us to discern all oppositions we suspect must have operated in the spoken language.

The structuralist, then, examines the underlying regularities and relationships of the linguistic system—*langue* (above, pp. 8–9). These are discernible only via the substances—speech and writing. The historical linguist has thus to establish the relationship between speech and writing, and the relationship of each to the *langue*, since the two are seldom 'isomorphic',[16] i.e. they do not correspond exactly. Before establishing the phonemic system of any OHG text or dialect, we must decide which graphies (written symbols) are basic structural units (graphemes), and which merely orthographical variants (allographs). We expect graphemes and phonemes to correspond in large measure, although not absolutely: e.g. the dental spirant: [ß][17] and the dental affricate [ts] are not distinguished in many OHG texts, although we assume the underlying sounds differed: compare *Tatian gi-sezzan* (NHG *setzen*) and *gi-mezzan* (NHG *gemessen*) where the same graphy ⟨zz⟩ represents [ts] and [ß], and *Isidor dhiz* (MHG *ditze*, NHG *dieses*) and *dhazs* (NHG *das*), where ⟨z⟩ and ⟨zs⟩ are in opposition. The various definitions of the phoneme[18] are not equally relevant to the historian. For instance, the 'prosodic' or 'supra-segmental' phonemes like intonation and stress which serve to distinguish utterances or parts of them in speech are not adequately transmitted by writing. For early periods they are accessible only indirectly, particularly in their effects on the segmental phonemes: Verner's Law describes the effects of stress on consonantal phonemes; we see also alternations of vocalic phonemes in the 'ablaut'-series of the strong verb (see pp. 162–3) that were caused by 'tone', or pitch phonemes in PIE. But for the purposes of comparing sound systems we shall restrict ourselves in this chapter to the segmental phonemes.

Let us define a segmental phoneme as an abstract sound-unit belonging to the underlying system, *langue*, and represented in speech by sounds that may vary phonetically without, however, standing in opposition to each other so as to change the meaning of the utterance. In fact, these positional variants or 'allophones' of the phoneme are always distributed complementarily (or 'non-contrastively'): one allophone cannot replace another belonging to the same phoneme in a given environment.[19] Thus, the phoneme is a class of allo-phones, it has no 'total' physical realization, being represented in any given environment only by one of its allophones. In practice, the linguistic historian regards the phoneme as a 'physical'—or at least recognizable—unit for the purpose of constructing a phonemic system, and in this he is supported by the spelling, where this is phonemic. Understandably, the orthographical vagaries of OHG texts make identifying phonemes difficult, but in practice most orthographies are 'phonemic' rather than 'sub-phonemic'—i.e. allophones are not shown in the spelling. Notker is an exception, for his subtle spelling system clearly shows the varying phonetic realization of consonant phonemes: when $|b|$, $|d|$, and $|g|$ are preceded by voiced sounds, they remain voiced, but otherwise become voiceless—[p], [t], [k]; e.g.:

Alle gelúste hábent taz keméine . dáz sie die nîetegen gértendo iágônt ze dero tâte (Boethius, *De consolatione philosophiae* iii. 53).

All desires have this in common: that they drive their devotees with goads to practise them.

The superscripts [1] and [2] pick out allophones of the same phonemes.[20] Phonemes form linear, or 'syntagmatic', relationships with other phonemes that combine and contrast with them to give a word its phonetic shape; but each phoneme is potentially replaceable by others and with these it stands in 'paradigmatic' relationship. If we compare OHG *hant*, *lant*, *bant* (NHG *Hand*, etc.), then $|h| \neq |l|$, $|l| \neq |b|$: these phonemes are in opposition to each other, since they can occur in the same phonetic environment, and they each alter its meaning. Each of these three phonemes is in paradigmatic relationship to the other; they are in syntagmatic relationship to those following $|a| + |n| + |t|$, with which they combine and con-trast. But since not all phonemes can occur in every phonetic en-vironment,[21] some scholars have argued that any given word contains as many phonemic systems as it does segments: words of four segments give us four such sub-systems. While observations about the 'multi-systemic' nature of phonemes tell us much of the distribution of individual phonemes, in the interests of simplicity the historian works on the cruder principles of gathering together all phonemes, whatever their positional occurrence. These are presented according to their approximate manner of articulation, vowel phonemes being organized according to their main distinctive features: front vs. back of the mouth, tongue height, and degree of lip-rounding. Duration of articulation (length)[22] and simple or complex articulation dictate the setting up of short and long vowel systems and of diphthongal systems. The consonants are arranged in 'orders' according to the point of articulation: lips, teeth, hard palate, soft palate—hence labial, dental, palatal, etc.—and in 'series' according to the manner of articulation—stops, spirants, voiced, unvoiced, etc.

The sound systems that result are static, give no indication of the frequency or distribution of the phonemes, and they are 'monosystemic'. Phonemic analysis usually treats vowel and consonant phenomena and often even the short and long vowel systems separately. Finally, the phonetic values of the sounds are approximate, so that allophones are not shown, although several of the shifts from one stage to another in language are allophonic in their initial stages. It is, however, possible to incorporate allophones into the models, as we see from the vowel systems of the *Tatian*, which are set out in Table 2 according to co-ordinates in 'parallelograms': front $\neq$ back; high $\neq$ non-high; low $\neq$ non-low. Phonemes are usually placed between solidi, e.g. /i/, but in Table 2 these have been omitted to simplify the diagram. The allophones are bracketed together: their morphological importance emerges clearly from Moulton's examples, since they are found in plural, modal, and derivational relationships: by the MHG period, the allophones have become phonemicized and have grammatical, i.e. morphemic, function (see Chapter IV). The allophones of each phoneme share the same orthographical symbol, but note that the medial $\langle e \rangle$ of *geste* (NHG *Gäste*) (pl. of *gast*) links the root vowel to the /e/ phoneme orthographically, although later rhyme evidence shows that the two sounds belonged to separate phonemes.

2. *Types of phonemic change*

The structuralists William Moulton (1961), Paul Valentin (1969), and Herbert Penzl (1971), among others[23] have examined the changes in 'diasystems' by comparing phonemic systems constructed from the main OHG and later literary dialects. Several types of changes are seen: they cannot be fully discussed here, but it should be noted that they probably all begin as 'sub-phonemic', i.e. allophonic, changes. The main types are:

(i) *Phonemic replacement*, 'rephonologization'. Here there is no

TABLE 2. *The East Frankish vowel system of the* Tatian (*ninth century*)

Short Vowels

Front		Back
High:		
i	ü	u
snit	zugi	zug
(Schnitt)	(Züge)	
e·	ö	o
geste	holzir	holz
(Gäste)	(Hölzer)	
ë	weg	

Long Vowels

Front	Back	
ī	ǖ	ū
wīt	hūti	hūt
(weit)	(Häute)	(Haut)
ē	ȫ	ō
zēh	nōti	nōt
(zieh)	(Nöte)	

Diphthongs:

Front		Back	
iü	iu	üö	uo
liuti	liut	guoti	guot
(Leute)		(Güte)	(gut)
ie	io		
riet	nio		
	(nie)		
ei		öü	ou
ein		loufit	loufan
		(läuft)	

Low:

Front	Back	
æ	a	īā
mahti	maht	tāti
(Mächte)	(Macht)	(täte)
ǣ		(Tat)

* After Moulton (1961). Allophones have been placed in boxes: mutated allophones are mostly not shown in the spelling; not all the examples are actually attested in *Tatian*. Mod. German forms are placed in parentheses, but *zieh* shows analogical replacement from the past part. of the verb (NHG *zeihen* < MHG *zīhen* 'accuse', now archaic).

change in the structure of the sound system: all allophones of a phoneme in stage A remain in opposition to the allophones of other phonemes in stage B. It is the phonetic realization of the phonemes in the utterance that has altered, not their position in the system. For the moment, we may cite Penzl's ((1971), 24) example of the OHG reflexes of the PGmc. voiceless spirant /þ/ which gradually develops, via voiced spirant, to voiced stop in the monastery dialects without losing its opposition to other dental consonants: e.g., taking simply initial position, we find the different dialects of OHG preserve the following oppositions:

> þ ≠ d ≠ t: PGmc. *þingaz (NHG 'Ding'), *duhtēr (NHG Tochter), *tī-ði, (NHG 'Zeit')
>
> d ≠ t ≠ z (= [ts]): OHG (Alem.) ding, tochter, zît.

A schematic table of the OHG dialects showing only initial and medial position reveals how the phonemes are kept apart (Table 3). In the table note that the symbol /ß/ represents the dental spirant resulting from the Second Sound Shift, as opposed to the affricate [ts], written ⟨z⟩. In the tenth and eleventh centuries ⟨th⟩ appears as ⟨d⟩ in Rh.Frk. and MFrk. texts as well. If, as is often claimed, the sound shift and the change of /þ/ to /d/ both begin in the south and graduate northwards, the different dialectal systems also represent different chronological stages, the southern dialects showing a newer phonology, the more northerly being conservative. Such areal models of temporal processes are yet another instance of the close relation between the dimensions of time and space.

TABLE 3. *Initial and medial 'dental' phonemes in the late ninth century*[24]

	PGmc.	/þ/ initial	medial	/d/ initial	medial	/t/ initial	medial
North: LG	OS	th–	–th–	d–	–d–/–ð–	t–	–t–
MG	MFrk.	th–	–th–	d–	–d–/–t–	z–	–z–/[ß]
	RhFrk.	th–	–th–	d–	–d–/–t–	z–	–z–/[ß]
	SRhFrk.	th–	–d–	d–	–t–	z–	–z–/[ß]
UG	EFrk.	d–	–d–	t–	–t–	z–	–z–/[ß]
	Bav.	d–	–d–	t–	–t–	z–	–z–/[ß]
	Alem.	d–	–d–	t–	–t–	z–	–z–/[ß]
South:	Lgb.	t–	–t–	d–/t–	–d–	z–	–z–/ss

(ii) *Phonemic merger.* Allophones of one phoneme become indistinguishable from allophones of another and hence the two phonemes merge, either completely (in all environments) or partially: this appears to have happened in Alem. of the later part of the period, when we compare EFrk., e.g. *Tatian* (*c*.830) with Notker (*c*.1000):

$$\text{EFrk.}\langle ie\rangle \neq \langle io\rangle \qquad \text{Alem.}\ \langle \hat{ie}\rangle$$
$$\textit{hier} \neq \textit{tior} \qquad\qquad \textit{hîer, tîer}^{25}$$
$$\text{(NHG \textit{hier Tier}).}$$

(iii) *Phonemic split.* Some allophones of a phoneme become phonemes in their own right, and have thus split away from the phonemes to which they originally belonged. This 'phonemicization' of allophones is indicated when the phonetic environment conditioning them changes. The classic OHG case is the assimilatory change known variously as 'umlaut'[26] or 'mutation', 'modification'. Returning to the phonemic system of the *Tatian* (Table 2, p. 79), we see various mutated allophones in environments where an *i* follows, e.g. *zugi, holzir, nōti*. No change in the OHG orthography is found, but by the thirteenth century the mutated allophones are designated by separate symbols in most instances and, at the same time, the unstressed syllables containing the mutating factor, in this case the high vowel /*i*/, have become lax mid /ə/ (written ⟨e⟩—which is less likely to alter the root vowels:

$$\text{OHG \textit{nōt, nōti} > MHG \textit{nôt} \neq \textit{næte}}$$
$$\textit{zug, zugi} > \qquad \textit{zuc} \neq \textit{züge}$$

(iv) *Phonemic loss.* The total loss of a phoneme is rare, and the examples cited in grammars are nearly always interpretable as a merger with another phoneme, e.g. PIE /ā/ disappeared completely by merger with PIE /ō/ to give PGmc. /ō/. In OHG some allophones of /χ/ (voiceless velar spirant written ⟨h⟩) disappear, namely those initially before consonants; but others in pre-vocalic position remain: compare:

$$\text{OHG \textit{hlahhen} > \textit{lahhen} (NHG \textit{lachen})}$$
$$\textit{hwaz} > \textit{waz} \text{ (NHG \textit{was})}$$
$$\textit{hnīgen} > \textit{nīgan} \text{ (NHG \textit{neigen})}$$
$$\textit{but:}$$
$$\textit{hant} > \textit{hant} \text{ (NHG \textit{Hand})}$$

Turning from the change of individual items in the phonemic system to change in the system itself, we find striking advances over the

Neogrammarian phonology. Two presuppositions are important here: that sound systems have a limited number of phonemes and that these are distributed in a symmetrical or balanced fashion. Economy and equilibrium are the basis for a stable phoneme inventory, and the 'overloading' of any given phonemic opposition, or the existence of several phonemes that are too similar phonetically, could cause the system to change. We may disagree about what constitutes 'economy', 'overloading', and 'balance' in the system, but such labels can be used to interpret changes once they have occurred, although we might justifiably be wary of using them to predict change. Note also that this purely linguistic (*sprachintern*) approach need make no appeal to the circumstances of the speakers. Nor, it seems, is 'balance' sufficient to impede changes, for if we disregard the mutated allophones in OHG (of the EFrk. type) we find a 'balanced' vowel system containing five monophthongs, either short or long, and six diphthongs, four relatively high and two non-high:

$$
\begin{array}{llll}
(-) & (-) & & \\
/i/ & /u/ & /iu/ & /uo/ \\
& & /ie/\ /io/ & \\
(-) & (-) & & \\
/e/ & /o/ & /ei/ & /ou/ \\
\quad (-) & & & \\
\quad /a/ & & &
\end{array}
$$

The phonemicization of the mutated allophones caused disequilibrium in the OHG system, in particular by the creation of three *e* phonemes and by converting the binary system of contrasts front ≠ back in the monophthongal system into a system of 'triads', with two phonemes at the front of the mouth separated by lip-rounding, e.g.

	Front	Back		Front		Back
OHG long vowels:	/ī/ ≠	/ū/	> MHG	/ī/ ≠	/ǖ/	≠ /ū/
	OHG *sīgan* ≠ *sūgis, sūgan*		> MHG	*sīgen* ≠ *siuges(t)*		≠ *sūgen*
OHG short vowels:	/i/ ≠	/u/	> MHG	/i/ ≠	/ü/	≠ /u/
	OHG *kinde* ≠ *kundī, kunda*		> MHG	*kinde* ≠ *künde*		≠ *kunde*[27]

The apparent symmetry of the OHG system was jettisoned in favour of a 'lop-sided' MHG system.

While it is difficult for us to say exactly where the 'equilibrium' of a vowel or consonant system lies, we can sometimes see gaps in the pattern and observe the effects of any radical upset to the system, even without being able to predict them. André Martinet[28] suggested that gaps in a phonemic system can act as a vacuum, attracting allophones of some neighbouring phoneme so that a new phoneme arises. This he terms *chaîne de traction* or 'drag-chain' (German *Sog*), and it creates a chain reaction throughout the phonemic system. Conversely, where new elements are introduced into a stable system, they may make the system unstable and have a shunting effect on other phonemes causing them to change their realization: this in turn may affect other phonemes. Martinet terms this a *chaîne de propulsion* or 'push-chain' (German *Schub*). The 'shunting effects' are explained by (unconscious) avoidance of phonemic merger on the part of the speakers, since phonemic merger may entail a loss of important phonemic oppositions such that many words sound the same, i.e. become homonyms.[29] The actual triggering of the disequilibria in the system is usually impossible to identify. Moulton (1961) 19, draws up a pre-German (*urdeutsch*) long vowel system to show how monophthongizations created pressure on existing vowels:

Pre-OHG Long Vowels: 'Schub' or 'Sog'?

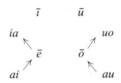

The monophthongization of /ai/ and /au/ creates new long vowels and the already existing long /ē/ and /ō/ diphthongize. The abstract shifts in the system may be related to external factors: their apparent spread can be charted and tentatively linked to foreign influence. Dialect geography and linguistic history are invoked in the OHG diphthongizations in this way, with the implication that they will 'explain' the changes. While such approaches are problematic, they do remind us that the history of a language reflects the behaviour of its speakers. Moulton holds that the monophthongization comes from the north and spreads southwards, since it affects the OHG dialects to a lesser degree than the more northern OE, OS: for in OHG both 'old' diphthongs have split, as the following formulae describe:

(1) *ai* $\swarrow$ $\bar{e}$ before *r*, *w*, PGmc. χ, and in final position;
$\searrow$ *ei* elsewhere.

PGmc. *maiz- > OHG *mēr*; PGmc. *hail- > OHG *heilant*. Cf. OS *mēr* 'more' *hēliand* 'saviour'.

(2) *au* $\swarrow$ $\bar{o}$ before dentals, PGmc. χ, and in final position;
$\searrow$ *ou* elsewhere.

PGmc. *brauða- > OHG *brōt*; PGmc. *baum- > OHG *boum*. Cf. OS *brōd* 'bread', *bōm* 'tree'.

But in the measure that the /ai/ and /au/ diphthongs monophthongize, the old long vowels diphthongize—so far as the texts show us. Historically speaking, both 'old' long /ē/ and long /ō/ have very different origins, but they undergo parallel developments—standard modern German has monophthongal reflexes of both, /[i:]/ and /[u:]/ e.g. *hieß*, *gut*. Interpretation in terms of the 'push-chain' (*Schub*) is only one side of the coin, however, for we have already seen (Chapter I) that there is little direct lexical OE influence on OHG, and there seems no clear OS influence: why should the monophthongization have 'moved southwards' from these other dialects? What 'natural vehicle' carries the spread? OE treats the PGmc. diphthongs /ai/ and /au/ differently in any case: they become respectively /ā/ and /ēa/. Moreover, in much literary OS (*Hēliand*)[30] we see a virtually complete merger of PGmc. /ai/ and /ē/ > /ē/, and of PGmc. /au/ and /ō/ > /ō/. Contrast

OS *mēr, hēliand, hēt* v. OHG *mēr* ≠ *heilant* ≠ *hiez* (NHG *hieß*)
  brōd, bōm, mōdar   *brōt* ≠ *boum* ≠ *muoter* (NHG *Mutter*)

We ought not to forget that scholars have in the past suggested a link between the 'OFr.' and the OHG diphthongizations (see p. 49). Although the evidence for the monophthongization appears first in the texts, it might yet be argued that, if there is some Gallo-Roman catalytic effect on and via Frk. dialects, we would have an example of *Sog.* The older monophthongs /ē/ and /ō/ would, by diphthongizing, have left a gap in the system which the diphthongs /ai/ and /au/ filled with some of their allophones. Furthermore, this interpretation avoids having to postulate an undemonstrable OS influence on all major OHG dialects, whereas Frk. influence *has* been detected on Alem. and Bav., and on OS also. Neither the *Schub* nor the *Sog* theory is entirely convincing: the problem seems incapable of solution.

But the structuralist view that rearrangements within a sound system arise from change to any part of it does at least permit a coherent presentation of the *effects* of sound changes, even if it does not identify their *causes*. Whatever the interrelationship of these pre-OHG diphthongizations and monophthongizations, we shall see that their parallel development has important effects on the morphology of the strong verbs (pp. 162–6). The structural 'push–pull chain' can also be applied to the OHG consonant system (Penzl (1975), 84–6). As the pre-OHG voiceless stops /p, t, k/ become spirants or affricates by the Second Consonant Shift (see Appendix A), gaps are created in the system. The voiced stops /b, d, g/ in the southern dialects Alem. and Bav., shift to voiceless in some environments[31]. This may, in the case of dentals, entail the further shift of PGmc. /þ/ to /d/. Looking again at the dental phoneme chart (Table 3, p. 80), we can represent the stages as:

(1) pre-OHG $t \nearrow^{ts}_{\searrow zz}$

(2) therefore pre-OHG $d \rightarrow t$
(3) then $þ \rightarrow d$.

However, such interdependence is at first sight lacking in the Frk. dialects, for both MFrk. and Rh.Frk. change $þ > d$ in late OHG, thus bringing about a merger with allophones of the already extant /d/ (from PGmc. /ð/). Nevertheless, Penzl (1975), 86, argues that in these two dialects and in SRh.Frk. there is pressure to remove the spirant written ⟨th⟩ because the dental–alveolar point of articulation is 'overloaded' with spirants and affricates from the Second Sound Shift as well as reflexes of the PGmc. spirant /s/, giving the following phonetically close phonemes: /th/, /ts/, /ß/, /s/. LG dialects, lacking the affricates and spirants, kept the spirantal *th* longer, since there was less pressure on this part of the system. Thus, both *Sog* for UG dialects and *Schub* for the MG ones could provide internal linguistic explanation of consonantal shifts: in both cases the Second Sound Shift developments of pre-OHG voiceless stops leads to rearrangements of the consonantal systems in the OHG monastery dialects.

C. GENERATIVE/TRANSFORMATIONAL APPROACHES

Generative grammarians examine the ways in which utterances are produced and interpreted according to underlying patterns or 'deep structures' and sets of rules applied to them. The historical generativist theorizes about change in the rules and in the deep structure, basing his hypotheses on the limited surface-structure material available. For OHG such material is limited in quantity, but, more important, in quality: for we have no access to the linguistic intuition of the native speaker. Moreover, the generativist copes poorly with variables in the data that result from geographical or social factors. In particular, the mixed features in many early texts form part of a more 'pragmatic' study of language, and they cannot be captured by generative rules without encumbering the analysis. Voyles (1976), 17 f., resorts to optional phonological rules to explain mixed texts and why the Second Sound Shift should have a differing distribution in different dialects; but this takes no cognizance of scribal factors, such as the deliberate use of 'compromise' orthographies that will have been understood over a wider area than local ones. Structuralist theory is more overtly descriptive and presents mixed features more clearly by not restricting itself to internal linguistic explanations.[32]

The types and refinements of generative theory cannot be treated here, nor can the mechanisms of language change it most frequently employs, namely the addition or loss of rules and the restructuring of the 'deep structure'. However, we must consider its basic approach to phonology. Whereas the structuralist, as we have seen (pp. 77–8), classifies his phonemes into systems according to the distinctive features which characterize them, the generativist views the oppositions of linguistic forms in terms of the distinctive features themselves. That the distinctive features may occur in bundles as the structuralist's phonemes is purely secondary: where the structuralist distinguishes Notker's *scado* (NHG *Schaden*) and *scato* (NHG *Schatten*) by the phonemic opposition between $/d/ \neq /t/$, the generativist sees the main opposition as one of + voice vs. − voice, the other distinctive features (+ consonant, + coronal, + anterior, etc.) being subordinate. The segments occurring in utterances, or the abstractions underlying them, can be set out in inventories of distinctive features, as shown by Voyles (1976), 30–1, but in practice only the features involved in the operation of any particular rule are described. That change in even one distinctive feature may affect segments in words and phrases is apparent in simple examples like *men* ≠ *bed* or *meine Beine* ≠ *beide*, *beide*: we need only delete nasality—by means of the common cold, perhaps—in order to change one into the other. More formally, the generative formulation is:

[+nasal] — — — — → [−nasal] in environment x, y, z,

Generative phonology provides, then, a superior model of the articulatory processes involved in communication, and in this respect it is less artificial than the structural sound systems. Also, the distinctions between vowel and consonant systems can be overcome by dealing with distinctive features, some of which, like voice, are common to both. Historically, too, sound changes can be convincingly explained by changes in individual distinctive features which affect several 'phonemes': Jean Fourquet's work on the First and Second Sound Shifts[33] is an early example of this type of approach. Pre-structuralists too, inasmuch as they considered difficult topics like intensity, intonation, and pitch, which might affect phrases, were also escaping from the view of phonology as an autonomous, closed system, independent of higher levels like morphology and syntax. In another sense as well, the generativists hark back to pre-structuralist linguistics, for their concentration on distinctive features involves them in phonetic values. They assume a set of 'canonical', i.e. universal, distinctive features holding for sound systems in different languages and also for those of one language at different times in its history. This inductive approach lays the historical generativists open to the charge that they are engaged in circular argument—arbitrarily attributing certain distinctive features to the elements on both sides of their equations in order to explain shifts in items whose true phonetic values they cannot know. For the historian, a more serious critique of generativism is that it underestimates the speakers' consciousness of units akin to, if not identical with, phonemes which form the basis for the orthographies which are the data of historical analysis. Even in modern speech it may be argued that the workings of language and the speaker's perception of it can differ. But, while the generativist presentation of phonological change is rigorous and has a quasi-mathematical clarity, its 'input' remains the old Neogrammarian philological data, and its explanations are often only descriptions. Such descriptions are more successfully given by the highly artificial structural models. However, the generative insights provide a welcome reminder that language is a process, and one in which phonology is the handmaid of higher levels, notably syntax and semantics.

So far, we have examined some problems of OHG phonology in the light of different approaches: it may be illuminating to contrast briefly the three views of an important set of changes: the OHG mutation, or 'umlaut'.

D. APPROACHES TO UMLAUT[34]

1. *Pre- or non-structuralist approaches*

Umlaut, the modification or mutation of a vowel, is in pre-structural parlance a combinatory sound change denoting the partial or total assimilation of a vowel to a sound in a following syllable. In OHG the change of *a* > *e* (a closed, fairly high sound) before the palatal sounds long and short *i/ī* and *j* in certain environments occurs in the earliest texts and in all HG dialects: it involves the raising and fronting of the *a*—'palatalization'[35] and can be interpreted as overcoming an articulatory 'hurdle' by anticipating the tongue movement from low *a* to following high *i*, e.g. pre-OHG **falljan* > OHG *fęllen* (NHG *fällen*); pre-OHG **tragit* > OHG *tręgit* (NHG *trägt*). Older scholarship termed this change 'primary umlaut'.[36] 'Secondary' umlaut is the apparently later change of vowel *a* to another more open (lower) *e*-sound in those environments where *i/j* followed (1) after another syllable, e.g. OHG *magadi, frafali* (NHG *Mägde, Frevel* (pl.)); or (2) after certain consonant combinations— notably velars that counteract the palatalizing effect of the high sounds, e.g. *-hs-, -ht-*: OHG *wahsit, mahti*. By 'MHG times' *a* in these environments had also become *e*, although of a much more open quality—[ɛ], which normalized grammars write ⟨ä⟩, e.g. *mägede* (NHG *Mägde*), *vrävel* 'bold' (NHG *Frevel*), *wähset* (NHG *wächst*), *mähte* (NHG *Mächte*), while the manuscripts often show simply a graphy ⟨e⟩, less usually ⟨æ⟩ or ⟨å⟩. The different quality of this secondary umlaut is deduced from examining rhymes, subsequent dialectal developments, and so forth. The other OHG vowels, namely *o, u*, long *ō, ū, ā*, and diphthongs *uo, ou*, also show mutation in late OHG and in MHG,[37] beginning with Notker's *hiuser* < *hūsir*, pl. of *hūs* (NHG *Haus*), where the graphy ⟨iu⟩ designates long mutated *ū* (phonetically [y:])—this diphthongal spelling arises because the old diphthong *iu* appears to have monophthongized in late OHG and merged with the new mutated *ū*.

Despite the testimony of the orthographies, attempts to establish two periods of mutation, one primary and one secondary, remain unconvincing for several reasons. First, by the thirteenth century the mutation factors /*i, ī, j* / in unstressed syllables had all merged in most dialects into a lax, short vowel often written with the graphy ⟨e⟩. This resultant unstressed central vowel is a priori less likely to have caused mutation than the high front phonemes it replaced, since its articulation was less extreme than before. Secondly, late loanwords from other languages provide very uncertain evidence for a continuing, or secondary, phase of mutation, since their foreign phonemes have usually been adapted to the nearest German ones; thus, *Grenze* borrowed from Slavonic in the thirteenth century does not show mutation any more than it shows the Second Sound Shift.[38] It is implausible to suppose that it was not until the later medieval period that scribes devised an adequate umlaut notation: there are sophisticated spelling systems, for example, in *Isidor* or Notker's writings. But this admission that mutation may have been present in the OHG period on a wide scale without appearing in the orthography was a promising lead: it was developed by structuralists.

2. *The structuralist view*

According to the phonemic approach to umlaut[39], all stressed vowels except the palatal /*i, ī*/ had raised or palatalized allophones, but these are shown in the texts only when they have become phonemicized, i.e. when they have become phonemes. For most vowels this means when the unstressed syllables containing the factors conditioning mutation have weakened to schwa ([ə]). Thus, at the very time when oppositions between phonemes in unstressed syllables—which were important since they contained information about case-forms or personal endings—were being neutralized as [ə], the stressed syllables still reflected some oppositions by the new umlaut phonemes. This provided the basis for morphological systems to develop in the MHG period and after (see Chapter IV).

However, short /*a*/ differs from other phonemes in having three sets of allophones:

(1) *ę* before /*i, ī, j*/: **gasti > gęsti* (MHG *geste*).

(2) *ä* before /hs/, /ht/, or intervening syllable + /i, ī, j/: *wahsit* > **wähsit* (MHG *wehset*); *magadi* > **mägädi* (MHG *megede*).

(3) *a* elsewhere: *magad* (NHG *Magd*) (MHG *maget*).

The closed ẹ allophones of phoneme /a/ were reattributed to the phoneme /e/, which had only open allophones (usually written ⟨ë⟩ in grammars).

PGmc. short /ë/ was either raised to /i/ before palatal sounds (*i, j*, nasal + consonant), or else it remained before mid and low vowels /a, o, e/. This means that the pre-OHG short /ë/ phoneme does not usually occur before the sounds that raised allophones of /a/ to /e/.

> PGmc.   **nëmandi* > OHG *nëmant* 'they take'.
>   **nëmisi* >   *nimis*   'you (sg.) take'.
> *But:*
> pre-OHG **lambir* >   *lẹmbir* 'lambs'.

Hence OHG /ë/ and the mutated allophone ẹ < /a/ are never in opposition and may be regarded as being in complementary distribution, i.e. belonging to the same phoneme.[40] At any event, it is clear that the early 'phonologization' (i.e. phonemicization) of /a/ > /e/ in OHG is based not so much on the disappearance of the mutation factors, since these are still visible in the final syllables, e.g. *tregit, lembir* (NHG *trägt, Lämmer*), but rather upon phonetic similarity with the allophones of the /ë/ phoneme. Moreover, symmetry may have played a role, since OHG /a/ would have been the only phoneme with three sets of allophones; all the rest have one mutated set and one unmutated set. Thus, phonetic similarity with the /ë/ phoneme, virtual complementary distribution with it, and imbalance in the sets of allophones may be the reasons why some allophones of OHG /a/ joined the /ë/ phoneme in the pre-literary period. To the extent that this is the earliest orthographically perceptible structural alteration caused by phonologization of the allophonic variants of OHG phonemes, it may indeed be called 'primary umlaut'.[41] However, since there is no reason why the allophonic values conditioned by palatal sounds could not have existed as early as PGmc., according to Antonsen,[42] primary umlaut is itself perhaps an example of late structural change resulting from mutation allophones. Umlaut is found in most Gmc. dialects (the Gothic evidence is difficult to interpret), but the phonologization of the mutation takes place in differing degrees and at different times. This is also true of the three main dialects that form the basis of German—Frk., Alem. and Bav. Secondary and other mutation is far less well represented in southern

German dialects even today—as attested by forms like *schlaft* (= *schläft*), *halt(et)* (= *hält*), *tragt* (= *trägt*), *drucken* (= *drücken, drucken*), place-names *Bruck, Innsbruck* (contrast the noun *Brücke* and the northern place-name *Brügge*). In parts of Switzerland (High Alem.) the final unstressed vowels still retain different qualities, and this might be one reason for the lesser degree of umlaut—it has not replaced inflexional endings to the same extent.[43]

The MHG vowel system differs from those of OHG mainly in the phonologization of the mutated allophones. This results in a vowel system that is clearly asymmetrical. The normalized MHG vowel system has nine short vowels, including three *e* phonemes, eight long vowels, and six diphthongs:

e phonemes $\begin{cases} & \\ & \\ & \end{cases}$

/i/	/ü/	/u/	/ī/	/ǖ/ (⟨iu⟩)	/ū/	/ie/	/üe/	/uo/
/ẹ/								
/ë/	/ö/	/o/	/ē/	/ȫ/ (⟨oe⟩)	/ō/	/ei/	/öu/	/ou/
/ä/			/ǣ/ (⟨ae⟩)					
	/a/			/ā/				

Note that /iu/ is problematic.[44]

3. Generative approaches to umlaut

The generativists interpret umlaut as *rule addition*.[45] Voyles (1974) treats it as part of the phonology of WGmc. languages, and elaborates the rule in his subsequent (1976) generative phonology of OHG based on *Isidor*, the OHG *Rule of St Benedict* (Alem., *c.*802), *Tatian*, and Otfrid's *Evangelienbuch*. In effect, the phonology is ninth century and the umlaut rules cover the so-called 'primary umlaut' only.

West Germanic Umlaut*

$$\begin{bmatrix} +\text{vocalic} \\ +\text{low} \\ -\text{long} \\ +\text{stress} \end{bmatrix} \longrightarrow \begin{bmatrix} ?-\text{low} \\ -\text{back} \end{bmatrix} \Big/ \underline{\quad} C_o \begin{bmatrix} -\text{consonantal} \\ +\text{high} \\ -\text{back} \end{bmatrix}$$

* Voyles (1976), 75–6, 141–3, 210–11, 307–10.

This means: /a/ → /e/ in positions before consonant (cluster) followed by high front vowel or /j/. Certain conditions must be specified:

(1) C ≠ /h/ or /l/ or /r/ [+consonantal]
    o ≠ consonantal + /w/

(Presumably the distinctive features for /h, l, r, w/ ought to be written in full, cumbersome though this is?) In other words: the

consonant cluster may not be /h/ or /l/ or /r/ followed by another consonant; nor may it be a single consonant followed by /w/.
(2) In some texts, e.g. *Isidor*, the stress must be defined as primary, i.e. main, stress, to account for exceptions like *bīnamin* (NHG *Beiname*) 'cognomen', without umlaut.
(3) The change operates across suffix (morpheme)[46] boundaries, but prefixes are not affected.

Various other remarks apply from text to text, but they do not affect the basic approach. We illustrate with the example in Voyles (1974), 25:

nom. sg. /lamb-/-∅-/-∅/   (NHG *Lamm*)
nom. pl. /lamb-/-ir-/-∅ ⟶ *lambir* or *lembir* (NHG *Lämmer*)

To non-generativists, this approach seems rebarbative and needlessly complicated, but it represents a *phonetic* interpretation which takes the orthography seriously. There seems no generative concept akin to the allophone to explain how a change takes place at one period but does not generally appear in spelling, which means a return to two periods of mutation, the early *a* > *ę*, and the later shifts. Generativists hold that the umlaut rule increased in frequency and range, affecting the other vowels. Voyles argues that morphological factors condition the increased use of mutation. This clearly emerges from his phonologies of the four texts mentioned, for we have deliberately simplified his analysis in one important respect: he gives morphological restrictions on the environments in which umlaut occurs. Thus, *Isidor* has weak verbs showing mutation, *Tatian* and Otfrid add strong verbs as well, and in Notker other vowels begin to be affected. So, arguing from morphology, we see good reasons why mutation should spread—it had become a convenient way of separating the different case- and verb forms. Moreover, an element of arbitrariness in the spread of mutation accords well both with the generative theory of rule addition and with the morphological function; for it has been pointed out that mutation is more common in inflexional morphology than in derivation: i.e., the forms with a syntactic role show umlaut more regularly than do those reflecting relations between word classes and individual words. However, there are problems, even in inflexional morphology: the preterite subjunctive of weak verbs, which was marked by *i*-endings in OHG, does *not* appear with mutation in MHG. Charles Russ,[47] in an examination of suffixes, points out that inflexional suffixation shows a more consistent use of mutation than derivational. Mutation has even been extended to words which could not have it 'phonetically' in OHG because they belonged to word classes that never had the mutation factors /i, j/ (the *i* may be long or short) in the following syllables; cf. mod. German *Bausch*, *Brauch*, *Gebrauch*, *Knall*, *Puff*, *Schluck*, etc. (Russ (1975), 60). The morphological importance of mutation has long been realized, but the generativists have fitted it into a different place in the language's inner development. Whereas for the structuralist, the development ran:

phonetic (i.e. allophonic) ⟶ phonemic ⟶ morphemic,

with the priority of the phonology, the generativists propound a phonetic change becoming harnessed to the morphology and *only then* becoming distinctive in language. In other words, any structuralist 'phonemic' status of the mutation depends upon and *succeeds* the morphemic stage.[48] Voyles quotes the apt statement of Dal (1967), 61, that in German the mutated vowels became phonemicized as the alternation between mutated and non-mutated vowels became morphemic.

Hence, even in the sketch given here, the generative approach deepens and supports interpretations of historical phenomena, not through phonology in isolation, but from higher grammatical levels: morphology and ultimately syntax and semantics.

SUMMARY

This chapter has concerned itself with facets of OHG phonology and with several main theoretical approaches to them. It is clear that our sympathies lie mainly with the functional structural approach, which deals in phonemic systems, largely because such systems, however divorced from communicative processes, are reconstructable from the data available. Moreover, we can also construct comparable systems for the modern language and for other periods and then gauge the differences between these models.

The generative school rightly emphasizes that language is a process, not a state, by rejecting the autonomy of the phonemic system and by denying a morphemic level in some types of the theory; some well-known phenomena like 'umlaut' are, moreover, well described by generative theory. Nevertheless, since we have no access to native speakers and little knowledge of styles, it seems wisest to restrict generative approaches to present-day languages, where problems posed by the data are not insuperable. Even at the risk of treating a highly complex motion picture as a random still life we shall at least be comparing like with like. Regarding the interaction of external history and language in respect to the phonology, we cannot do much more than suggest some factors that play a role: intermixture of speakers within an area or cultural contact over separate areas, as the possible causes of phonological change, spread of (fashionable?) features, etc. The phonological *effects* are perhaps describable as push- and pull-chains (*Schub* and *Sog*) in the vowel or consonant system, perhaps also in what appears to be geographical spread of certain features (like the diphthongizations or the HG Consonant Shift?) Those who regard polygenesis as accounting for the geographical distribution of sound changes are simultaneously divorcing them from external, social factors.

SELECT BIBLIOGRAPHY

GRAMMARS

Braune and Eggers (1975).   Schatz (1927).
Braune and Ebbinghaus (1977).   Sonderegger (1973).
Cordes (1980).   Sonderegger (1974).
Naumann and Betz (1962).

For dialects:

Franck (1909).   Schatz (1907).

PHONOLOGICAL STUDIES,   ESPECIALLY   STRUCTURALIST
AND GENERATIVE

Antonsen (1972).   Russ (1978).
Dal (1967).   Szulc (1974).
King (1969).   Valentin (1969).
Kiparsky (1968).   Vennemann (1972a).
Moulton (1961).   Vennemann (1972b).
Penzl (1971).   Voyles (1974).
Penzl (1975a).   Voyles (1976).
Russ (1975).

CHAPTER III

THE MEDIEVAL PERIOD
(1050-1500)

THREE important and interlocking issues will concern us in this chapter: the chronological extent and character of the period; the status of the literary language flourishing c.1170–1250, known as the *mittelhochdeutsche Dichtersprache;* and the origins—particularly the phonological basis—of the modern standard language.

PERIODIZATION[1]

Jacob Grimm saw no need for a linguistic period between the medieval one and the modern:

> ... da sich aber keine blühende poesie gründete, konnten niedersetzungen der sprache, wie sie zur aufstellung eigner perioden nöthig sind, auch nicht erfolgen. Die schriftsteller dieser zwischenzeit vergröbern stufenweise die frühere sprachregel und überlassen sich sorglos den einmischungen landschaftlicher gemeiner mundart ...[2]

The continuity of Grimm's 'MHG' period lies, then, in the progressive corruption of an earlier regularity due to insouciant authors, careless scribes, the 'decay' of inflexional morphology, and the resurgence of local, dialectal characteristics, especially in the later (fourteenth and fifteenth) centuries. His modern period begins afresh at 1500 with the literary and linguistic high point, Martin Luther. But Grimm's 'Mittelhochdeutsch' is ambiguous in several respects and too misleading to qualify the period as a whole: Grimm had an idealized view of the regularity of MHG based on important literary texts from around 1200, essentially southern/south-western in their language[3] with a common style and audience, and anyway often partially reconstructed in regularized orthography from manuscripts that were much later (see below, p. 116). Consequently, his label for the period, 'Mittelhochdeutsch', fails to do justice either to the important LG written language which flourished between about 1300 and 1500 as the koine of the Hanseatic League, or to a number of geographically and chronologically phased shifts in the German vowel system—monophthongization, dipthongization and vowel lengthening[4]—which were already under way in the twelfth and thirteenth centuries and some of which become characteristic of the modern German standard. In brief, there was no single supra-regional language at this time, any more than in the preceding Early German period, and the choice of the stylistically relatively homo-geneous literary language around 1200 provides only a reference point, but not continuity for the period as a whole: the needs of the historical grammarian who describes a narrow chronological 'slice' of language—a structuralist *coupe synchronique*—and those of the linguistic historian, interpreting several centuries of development and compassing stylistic and geographical variants, are here at odds. So, we shall keep Grimm's chronological period, but label it in historical terms 'Medieval', not 'Middle High German', and attempt to convey some impression of the social and linguistic diversity which marks it. The label MHG will be retained in citing linguistic examples, however, purely for convenience.

The end of any period is, of course, determined by the beginning of the next, and since Wilhelm Scherer (see p. 23) an intermediate period in German linguistic history known as Early New High German (ENHG) has been proposed, running from 1350 to 1650. The phonological basis of the modern standard language provides the focus here: the period begins with the presence around 1350 in documents from the imperial chancery of Charles IV at Prague of phonological features which recur in the modern standard, notably of the diphthongs /ei/, /eu/, and /au/ for MHG long monophthongs /î/, e.g. *mîn* (NHG *mein*), /iu/ (pronounced approximately [y:]), e.g. *liute* (NHG *Leute*), and /û/, e.g. *hûs* (NHG *Haus*). The end of the ENHG period in the mid-seventeenth century sees the spread of a book language of EMG type similar to the earlier Prague German which gains currency in the south-west, and in particular in the north, replacing LG almost entirely in printing-houses and chanceries.[5] We shall return to the vexed problem of the origins of standard German later, but a straightforward linear development from the imperial chancery at Prague in the fourteenth century can be discounted; on the other hand, the imperial chancery exemplifies processes of linguistic levelling and compromise evident in chancery documents of all areas from the thirteenth century onwards—compromise between dialect and local chancery usage, as well as compromise in the language of chanceries in different regions when they correspond with each other. The linguistic changes in the Prague chanceries do not mark any significant changes in the intellectual, political, cultural, or religious life of the community and are thus inappropriate for periodization in a socio-linguistic history of German. Instead, we shall favour the fifteenth century as a suitable turning-point, when the introduction of printing with movable type considerably facilitated inter-regional communication on a large scale, leading to the sloughing of local characteristics and

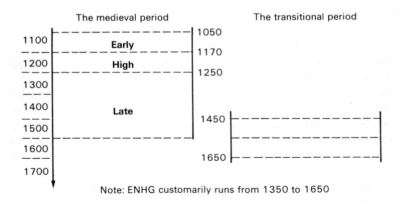

Note: ENHG customarily runs from 1350 to 1650

Fig. 4

eventually (by the seventeenth century) to a more or less identifiable HG book language. Moreover, in the late fifteenth century early German Humanism furthers the spread of ideas and intellectual vocabulary, while in the early sixteenth century the peasant unrest and the Reformation promote the use of printing for political and religious ends, in order to reach all members of the community.

So, a 'Transitional' period from about 1450 to 1650 will overlap the Medieval period from about 1050 to 1500, the latter being subdivided into an early section (1050–1170) leading up to the great literary epoch known as the *mittelhochdeutsche Blütezeit* with the poets Hartmann von Aue, Gottfried von Strassburg, Walther von der Vogelweide, Heinrich von Morungen, Reinmar von Hagenau, and Wolfram von Eschenbach, and the anonymous *Nibelungenlied*, and into a late medieval section from 1250 to 1500. This is represented schematically in Fig. 4. We are now free to examine some of the main characteristics of the Medieval period.

GENERAL CHARACTERISTICS OF THE PERIOD 1050–1500

Expansion and diversity characterize the period, especially the later (fourteenth and fifteenth) centuries: the population increases despite calamitous epidemics, new regions are colonized, towns established, and new social groups become literate, so that German is used increasingly as a written language beside Latin for political, legal, administrative, technical, and aesthetic purposes.

A. GEOGRAPHICAL EXPANSION

The movement eastwards that began with Charlemagne's campaigns against the Saxons in the eighth century, when Magdeburg and Erfurt marked the approximate borders of the empire, continued gradually, albeit with setbacks, until the twelfth century, when a new phase of colonization thrust deep into Slav territory. In the 1160s Henry the Lion overthrew Mecklenburg and Pomerania and extended German suzerainty to the Vistula, encouraging settlement and the building of towns. Henry's capitulation to the Emperor, Frederick Barbarossa, in 1179–80 meant a temporary halt to the expansion in the east, which was completed some fifty years later by the Order of Teutonic Knights, or 'Deutscher Orden' (founded at

Acre in 1190-1), under Hermann of Salza. Under the *Ordensritter* Prussia, Estonia, and other Baltic areas were subdued and their populations ruthlessly suppressed, often for ostensibly Christian motives, but in 1242 the Order was defeated near Novgorod and this marked the limit of the expansion. German colonists moved in from many different dialect areas, and Low Germans, including Dutch and Flemings, mingled with MG- and UG-speakers, creating the preconditions for a *koloniale Ausgleichssprache* which has since Adelung been regarded as the phonological basis of the modern German standard language (see below, p. 136, and n. 78). Relative stability under the protection of the Teutonic Knights until the fifteenth century, and the prosperity brought by the Hanseatic League, also produced flourishing towns and peasant farmers who were relatively free, unlike their Slav labourers.

In the south, too, there was some German colonization: the pockets of German-speakers in northern Italy known as the Cimbrian Enclaves arose from more sporadic settlement by Bavarian and Alemannic colonists from the eleventh and thirteenth centuries, while the sizeable German minorities in Romania—the *Siebenbürger Sachsen*[6]—came predominantly from Franconia at about the same period. Linguistic islands such as these are linguistically interesting since their isolation favours the preservation of features lost elsewhere: the language of the *Sette Comuni* in the north Italian province of Vicenza, for instance, still apparently has preterite verb forms and the genitive case in speech, while the reflexes of the MHG phonemes $/s/$ and $/z/$ (from pre-HG $*t$) are kept distinct. On the other hand, linguistic enclaves can also develop independently, reflecting in particular compromises and contaminations with the languages surrounding them.[7]

Among areas lost to German during the Middle Ages are the Netherlands, which split away politically and culturally, escaping from the expanding hegemony of the HG written language and establishing their own book language. In Bohemia the Hussite wars considerably weakened German's linguistic hold, although the language regained prestige during the Austro-Hungarian empire.

B. SOCIAL CHANGES

German society between 1050 and 1500 changes considerably: territorial principalities and centres of power begin to form, while many settlements and towns were established, reflecting population growth and contributing to greater social complexity. The courts in the twelfth and thirteenth centuries were the source of a rich vernacular literature, much of it imported from France, and the higher nobility provided its sophisticated audiences, the international connections, and the probable means of producing it, namely the court chancery—for it is likely that those who wrote and copied literary texts had a chancery education behind them. The courts at this time naturally differed in size and importance; some were situated in towns, which in their turn had chanceries and schools promoting literacy and sometimes literature, and the monastic and episcopal scriptoria continued their existence as in the earlier period—again, often close to or within the town walls. So we find the town not merely a commercial centre or a defensive bulwark, but a pot to mix the various ingredients of a literate intelligentsia.

Unfortunately, the individual social orders remain very shadowy, distorted by the idealized abstractions presented alike in legal codes and in literature; even the Latin or German terms used are ambiguous and subject to geographical and chronological shift of meaning.[8] For example, the labels *miles* or *ritter* do not designate a closed aristocratic 'class' until after the mid-thirteenth century: they imply first and foremost an equestrian fighting technique, regardless of social status. However, both words are progressively 'upgraded' in literature as the literary knight is stylized as a member of a group with its special code of honour and politeness based on service—to God, feudal lord, or liege lady. This paradoxical ideal of service in aristocratic circles drew attention to *dienestliute* or *ministeriales*, liegemen bound to their lords by service of several kinds who seem gradually to consolidate their position as a lower, 'unfree' nobility: such people might have projected an idealized image of self-abasement in order to enhance their own standing. But few poets of the Early and High Medieval periods are positively identified as *ministeriales*—Hartmann von Aue is an exception—and of some 140 *Minnesinger* in the fourteenth-century Manesse Codex only a handful probably belong to that category, including some important public figures.[9] For the term *dienestman* is as vague as *ritter* (the two are sometimes interchangeable, as are *miles* and *ministerialis*) and it covers both important imperial office and humbler functions like managing local estates: Eike von Repgow actually omits the *denstlude recht* from his vernacular legal treatise (*c.*1220) because of its diversity.[10] After the mid-thirteenth century, the *dienstman* often takes precedence over the *ritter*, which probably reflects the importance of administrators generally both in the new territorial courts and in towns; the word is adopted into Latin documents as a technical term, and by the fourteenth and fifteenth centuries the *ministeriales* have probably merged in town and country alike with hierarchy and squirearchy.

The townsmen or *burgenses*, too, represent new and economically important groups who eventually emerge as a widely differentiated middle class in the later Middle Ages. The wealthier merchant families and certain privileged craftsmen—goldsmiths, armourers and braziers, furriers, and so forth—blend with the aristocracy in a patrician stratum of *meliores*,[11] while humbler artisans might still be bondmen to a lord, or might live in the town but work as peasants on estates outside its walls. And even peasants, especially on the new estates in the east, might become relatively wealthy and rise socially, occasionally to knighthood, just as knights through impoverishment could sink to the status of peasant farmers: the existence of sumptuary laws regulating the dress of townsmen and peasants, and the satirical poetry of Neidhart von Reuental, *c*.1215, amply attest to peasant pretensions.[12]

The period shows, then, considerable social mobility, both 'horizontally'—the travels of merchants, the crusades, pilgrimages, and the more permanent drift to the towns or to colonial regions— and 'vertically', as new class structures emerge.

C. URBAN GROWTH

The word *stat* denotes firstly 'a place', then a 'larger settlement', and then a settlement with its own legal status and with considerable autonomy, perhaps subordinate directly to the Emperor, not to local magnates or bishops. Furthermore, town-dwellers could gain independence from their feudal lords on the principle *Stadtluft macht frei*—usually a year or so elapsed before civic rights were conferred, but then the burgher owed 'allegiance' to the municipal authority comprising men closer to him in status. The typical town, then, develops from a merchant trading-post via the privileged market town to a self-governing community with its own statutes and a council elected by local notables or *meliores*. During the thirteenth century towns might even combine against princes, as in the Rhine

Federation of 1254 (*Rheinischer Städtebund*). But the governance of towns also changes: the patriciate whose members predominate in the early surviving documents from towns increasingly drifted apart from the common artisans, who in turn formed themselves into guilds which then undermined the oligarchic patrician system, largely replacing it in the fourteenth and fifteenth centuries.

The growth of population and of towns can be assessed only very approximately[13] and the statistics in Tables 4 and 5 are tentative.

TABLE 4. *Towns in Germany*

Century	Number
9th	40
10th	90
11th	140
12th	250
13th	2,000
14th to 15th	3,000

TABLE 5. *Size of towns c.1500*

Population	Number
over 10,000	12-15
2,000-10,000	15-20
1,000-2,000	150
500-1,000	350
100-500	2,450

In 1500 Cologne had some 30,000 inhabitants, while the other important trading centres, Lübeck, Magdeburg, Erfurt, Augsburg, Nuremberg, Regensburg, and Strasburg had more than 20,000. Of a total population of some 12-13 million still only 10-15 per cent were town-dwellers.[14]

While many twelfth- and thirteenth-century towns were new foundations established by clearing forests—cf. place-names in -*rode*, -*reuth*, -*schwend*, -*schlag*, e.g. Bayreuth, Wernigerode—most develop from existing settlements; the word *stat/stadt* changes meaning from 'place' to 'town',[15] becoming virtually a place-name suffix, e.g. Wiener Neustadt (founded 1194, municipal charter 1380).

Most towns were tiny compared with their modern counterparts, but even so their citizens increasingly needed to be literate to cope with daily life—transferring property, making wills, taking legal action: as Luther observed in 1529, 'Ist doch kein dorff so klein, das eins schreibers emperen [=entbehren] kûnde'.[16] We shall see shortly the growth of the varieties of written German, but personal names also show the social and administrative developments, especially in the emergence of surnames. From the twelfth century second names or nicknames occur in some larger communities, often paternal or maternal names in Latin form in the gen. or even nom. case, e.g. *Ruprecht, Erenberti filius* (Mainz, 1104).[17] Some second names indicate a burgher's origins from another place or his abode in the town, e.g. *von der Mühlengasse, van den Boom*, more rarely in the earlier documents a trade, e.g. *Riemensnidere, Goldsleger, Duchmacher, Schilter, Hafener, Töpper*;[18] but with the artisan's increased importance this type becomes commoner—also 'indirectly' by tools of the trade, e.g. *hainrich hemmerli der smit, spitznagel, saltzfass,* etc., which lead over into a third type of name, the nickname proper, often pejorative, e.g. *peter snägg* (= *Schnecke*), *has* (= *Hase*), *lemli* (= *Lämmlein*), etc. The names are not constant; for example, in Villingen *c*.1380 the tradition of double names is established but the names themselves vary,[19] e.g. *ulrich der stark der smit den man ouch nembt fröstlin*. But some names last centuries and nicknames have then clearly become surnames (cf. English *surname* from Fr. *surnom*); humorous examples from Cologne are *Cobolt* (1140–80), *Gir* (= 'avarice') (1170–1417), *Hardevust* (= 'tight-fist'?) (1140–1435), *Vraz* (1149–78), *Unmaze* (1150–1200), *Overstolz* (1170–1435). The larger the town, the earlier double names occur: by 1150 only 18 per cent of Cologne citizens have an additional name, by 1250 the figure is 70 to 90 per cent, while in fourteenth-century Breslau persons are identifiable if they lack a surname: *Heinrich ane czunamen* (1361), *Nikolaus ane czunamen* (1369).[20]

D. NEW USES FOR GERMAN

Most striking is the extensive chivalric literature which flourishes from the mid-twelfth century at German courts influenced by French and indirectly by classical literature: the lyric poetry of Provençal troubadours and northern, French *trouvères* shapes German *Minnesang*, while classical material (the *matière d'antiquité*), the Celtic 'Arthurian' legends (*matière de Bretagne*), and quasi-historical *chansons de geste* are done into German verse, sometimes by great poets, Gottfried von Strassburg and Wolfram von Eschenbach. Native genres, too, are given courtly expression and written down. We shall return below to the status and nature of this literary language and to the French influence upon it, noting here that this literature has often been preserved in manuscripts from the fourteenth and fifteenth centuries, some of them produced for 'bourgeois', patrician circles.

German begins in the thirteenth century to be used for public and private documents of all kinds which would previously have been written in Latin. Many documents were produced in the chanceries[21] of local rulers and in town chanceries, they are in prose, they cover a wide range of matters often not treated in literature—disputes about planning permission, territorial claims, conferral of rights, bequests, even peace treaties—and the various types are repetitive in their formulae, facilitating comparison of documents from different chanceries; finally, their precise dating and localization make them an invaluable guide to regional written forms of German. But chanceries are of different size and complexity: from the fourteenth century larger chancery staffs with a chancellor and other grades of notary, sub-notary, and scribe[22] mean that several individuals combine in the production of a document and the rough drafts and archive copies which may be made of it. Hence, within the chancery, as in the scriptorium (see p. 52) and later in the printing-house, individuals may differ in their linguistic habits, especially if they come from different regions. The traditions within a chancery also need careful examination, since they will inevitably differ from those of the spoken dialect, and move progressively away from it. Finally, the spelling conventions are influenced by the conventions of the 'addressees' to whom a document is directed—indeed, the very choice of German or Latin may depend on whether the recipients are clerics or laymen. The earliest German documents occur sporadically about the mid-thirteenth century, and by its close run into thousands, as edited by Friedrich Wilhelm in his *Corpus der altdeutschen Originalurkunden.*[23] Vol. i–iv and supplements contain nearly 4,500 documents down to 1300. Geographically and chronologically they are unevenly distributed; the south-west predominates at first; the last decades preserve the bulk of the material (see Table 6). Some 500,000 Latin documents were produced in the same period. At a more local level registers of land-titles and revenues, the *Rodel/Rödeln* (Lat. *rotulus/ rotula* 'scroll') and *Urbare* (MHG *urbar* 'revenue'), are produced in chanceries and monasteries, and also show the shift from Latin to German: the earliest German *Urbar* comes from the Bavarian ducal chancery c.1229–37. From the fifteenth century the land registers from some regions are numerous—15,000 are preserved at Stuttgart alone.[24] Still, such humdrum material reveals the gradual sloughing off of local linguistic variants, especially in phonology and morphology, in favour of regional forms. Individual *Schreiblandschaften* are less important in this phase of German's development than the processes which shape them. But in the late thirteenth century

TABLE 6

Date	Documents
1240–50 ⎤	8 (3 genuine?)
1250–60 ⎪ (vol. i)	36 (4 Dutch)
1260–70 ⎪	197
1270–80 ⎦	383
1283–1300 (vols. ii–iv)	2,924

regional traditions are strong, even in imperial documents, as the following two decrees uttered by Rudolf von Habsburg in 1281 show: the one from Regensburg has Bav. features, while the other, from Mainz, is Frk. Rudolf is depicted in Ottokar von Steiermark's *Österreichische Reimchronik* (*c.*1300–10) demanding that imperial business should be negotiated in German for the sake of the temporal princes who had no Latin,[25] and several German documents survive from his chancery, the earliest from 1275. The first imperial edict with German versions (not necessarily 'official') is the Peace of Mainz (*Mainzer Landfrieden*) promulgated by Frederick II in 1235.

Beside these legal and administrative documents, the important legal treatise (in over 200 manuscripts), the *Sachsenspiegel*, a LG version compiled about 1220 by Eike von Repgow from the Latin, influenced other German codes like the *Schwabenspiegel*, *c.*1259. In general, legal language is well represented at this period—also in literature—and centuries of vernacular oral judicial practice account for its fluency in the earliest German documents; indeed, the punctuation system and the rhythmical structure of the clauses were aids to reading aloud.

But other kinds of German are increasingly written down which may be grouped beside the liberal arts as *artes mechanicae*: trades and crafts (including alchemy and mining); the military arts, like fencing; navigation, geography, and commerce; farming and husbandry; forestry and management of estates, including the courtly pursuit of hunting; medicine; and, finally, various courtly sports and pastimes, even horse-racing and tournaments. Most texts on these topics are found in manuscripts of the fifteenth century and later—an early exception is the veterinary manual known as *Meister Albrants Roßarzneibuch* from the thirteenth century, surviving in some 218 manuscripts and innumerable printings.[26] Another popular work is Gottfried von Franken's *Pelzbuch* (*pelzen* 'to graft'), a treatise on

Extracts from Documents of Rudolf von Habsburg (1218-1291)

[No. **475B**, *Corpus*, i. 408,
Regensburg, 6 July 1281]

WJR Rvdolf von goteſ gnaden
Rômiſcher chvnig vnd immer merær
des Ryches/ tv̂n allen den chvnt di
disen prief an sehent vnd hôrent/ daz
nah vnſerm gebot geſworn habent
vnser lieb fv̂rſten ·Lvdwich· vnd
hainrich · pfalzgrauen/ von Ryn vnd
herzogen ze baiern/ vnd Biſcholf
hainrich von Regenſpvrch/ vnd
welln vnd gebieten auch/ daz di
Biſchôlf di zv̂ dem lande ze baiern
gehôrnt/ daz iſt der Erzpiſcholf von
Salzburch ... der von Brichsen auch
ſweren diſen lantzfrid'/ biſ ze den
winahten di nv chompt von danne
vber driv iar/ vnď ſwer den vrid
vnder in niht ſweren welle/ der ſi auz
dem vrid'/ vnd ſol man im dahain
reht tv̂n/ vnd sol allen chlagærn von
im reht tv̂n/ Ez ſol auch diſer lande-
frid' nah ſinem zil den herren noh
dem lande an ir lantſreht niht
ſchaden. Wir ſezzen vnd welln daz di
piſchôlf vnd ellev pfafhait ir alt
vreihait vnd ir reht haben/ vnd daz
nieman div gotſhaus vnd ir levt
vnd ir gv̂t fv̂r den vogt/ oder im ze
laid/noh fv̂r niemen anders weder
pfenden noh rovben noh prennen
ſol/ ...

Bavarian features. New diphthongs (see
p. 112) in *vreihait, levt, ellev, gotshaus*
(MHG *vrîheit, liute, alliu, goteshûs*); old
diphthong /uo/ represented (*tv̂n*); /ei/
opened to /ai/ in *-hait, hainrich*; loss
of unstressed syllables by syncope (in
gnaden, gotshaus) and apocope (*vnd,
meraer*); inverse spelling suggests Middle
Bav. vocalization of /l/, as in *wald* to
['vɔit], has occurred (*bischolf*). Consonants show UG voiceless forms, e.g.
prennen, Regenspurch; graphy ⟨ch⟩ =
[k] (also voiceless /g/: *Regenspurch*) in
chvnig, chvnt and *Brichsen* (Brixen).
Morphology shows older third person pl.
verb forms in *-nt* (*sehent*).

[No. **493A**, *Corpus*, i. 434,
Mainz, 12 December 1281]

Wir Rudolf Von gotes genaden
Romes kunik . Vnde merere des
riches . dun kunt allen den di diſen
brif ſen oder horen leſen . daz Wir
allen den krik vnde di miſſehellunge
di zwiſſen Vnſeme lieben furſten
Wernhere deme erze biſſchofe Von
Menze Vnde ſime Stifte Vnde
Heinriche greuen Johannis brudere
Von Spanheim Vnde allen iren
helferen einhalp . Vnde greuen
Johannis Vnde greuen Heinriche
Von Spanheim Vnde iren Vrunden
Vnde iren helferen Was anderthalp .
han Virſlichtet Vnde Virrichtet Vnde
Virſunet genceliche Vnde luterliche
Vnde ewekliche Vmme alle di tat . di
in duseme kriche Vnde Vrlouge
zwiſſchen in geſchen iſt . alſo
hirnach geſchriben ſtat . § An deme
hus Von Beckelenheim Vnde an den
luten Vnde gute . daz der Vorgenante
erzebiſſchof da mite gekoufet hat.

Middle German features. No new diphthongs, but some monophthongization
occurs: *brif, krik, virsunet, dun, brudere*
(MHG *brief, kriec, versüenet, tuon,
bruodere*). Mutation is restricted, also in
spelling: *virsunet, horen, furſten*; MHG
/ae/ (= long open [ɛː]) appears as ⟨e⟩
(*merere*). Unstressed vowels are preserved (*merere, vnde, deme, missehellunge
(sg.)) and sometimes are written ⟨i⟩, as
in *virsunet, hirnach*. Medial ⟨ch⟩ may
represent a spirantal pronunciation in
kriche (MHG *kriege*). Morphologically,
the short formation *vnseme* without /r/ is
Frk.

WE, Rudolf, by God's grace King of Rome and perpetual enlarger of the Empire, do make known to all who see and hear this decree, that following our command there have given their oath our beloved Princes Ludwig and Heinrich, Counts Palatine of the Rhinelands and Dukes of Bavaria, and Bishop Heinrich of Regensburg. And (we) further desire and command, that the bishops which belong to the country of Bavaria, namely the Archbishop of Salzburg . . . and the (Bishop) of Brixen shall also swear (to uphold) this public peace from the coming Christmas, and thenceforth for three years. And whosoever amongst them shall not desire to swear, let him be outside the peace, and none shall grant him any justice, but shall grant justice to his accusers. Nor shall this public peace, after its appointment, impair the lords nor the land in their own legal code. We declare and decree that the bishops and all clergy shall retain their ancient freedom and jurisdiction and that none shall either impound or steal or burn the churches and their people and property, whether in the advantage of their feudal lord, or to injure him, or on behalf of any other Person . . .

WE, by God's grace King of Rome and augmentor of the Empire, do make known to all who may see this document or hear it read (out), that we have settled all that dispute and disagreement which was between our dear Prince Werner the Archbishop of Mainz and his foundation and Heinrich, Count Johannes of Spanheim's brother, and all those who assist them, on the one part, and Count Johannes and Count Heinrich of Spanheim and their relatives on the other part. (This we) have settled and composed and resolved utterly and impartially [*luterliche*] and in perpetuity, in respect of all those acts which have taken place in this dispute and quarrel between them, as is written hereinafter. *Item* [§]: In respect of that house of Beckelenheim and the Persons and property which the aforementioned archbishop acquired with it . . .

---

horticulture and viticulture compiled in Latin in the mid-fourteenth century whose German version was influential down to the eighteenth century. Naturally enough, some works derive from Latin sources, and Frederick II's famous book on falconry, the *De arte venandi cum avibus*, influences the first German treatises in the fourteenth century. Sometimes translations of the liberal arts were adapted for practical purposes: the *Geometria Culmensis* (c.1400) links geometry and surveying in the first vernacular agronomy. But many such works had little or no circulation—cookery books like the early *Bůch von gůter spise* (the manuscript dates from the 1340s) were probably from, and for, some well-appointed monastery kitchen, while the *Tegernseer Fisch- und Angelbüchlein* (*c*.1490), with early sections on wet-fly fishing, is again the isolated product of a monastery.[27]

Ephemeral, personal material survives even less often, for example, the account-books of merchants, like Vico von Geldersen of Hamburg, listing debts and rents in a mixture of Latin and LG, or private letters, like those of the sixteenth-century Nuremberg merchant Balthasar Paumgartner, diaries, traveller's accounts, and so forth all reveal a range of German styles. Curiously, few school-books appear to have been preserved from before 1500.

Towns also house asocial or *déclassé* elements—whores and tricksters, vagrants, and, with the growth of guilds and the foundation of universities, wandering students and apprentices. Glossaries were compiled of these idioms from the fourteenth century onwards. The important Jewish communities in many towns were also regarded as socially unacceptable, and many Yiddish forms have survived among the lower social strata as part of thieves' cant or 'Rotwelsch' (see Chapter IX).

The great popular preachers of the thirteenth century, Berthold von Regensburg (*c*.1210–72) and David von Augsburg (1200–72), found audiences among the masses in the towns, refining the art of the German prose sermon. More cerebral and innovatory were the mystics, notably Meister Eckhart (*c*.1260–1327) and his fellow Dominicans Heinrich Seuse (Suso) (1295–1366) and Johannes Tauler (1300–61), who sought to express the religious experience in the vernacular and in the process disseminated an abstract intellectual vocabulary drawn from theology and scholasticism but at once heightened and personalized (see below, pp. 130–3). German mystics were read in nunneries, since few nuns knew Latin: the Swiss nunnery at Wonnenstein (Canton Appenzell) had a library almost exclusively of German books, including Eckhart and Tauler.[28]

The later period also saw an increasing historical awareness and intellectual curiosity: chronicles, especially town chronicles, appeared, documenting the rights and privileges of the citizens and their struggles against secular or religious authorities. Early and much-travelled German Humanists, most of middle-class origins, began to renew Latinity for aesthetic and intellectual reasons. At the same time, the *Fastnachtsspiel* attests to cruder taste and language.

'MIDDLE HIGH GERMAN'—A CONVENIENT ABSTRACTION

The existence of some fairly uniform supra-regional language in the High Medieval period (*c.*1170–1250) to which poets strove to conform has been much debated. The issue is obscured by the small number of original or contemporary manuscripts surviving, by the preconceptions of editors and grammarians, who reconstruct texts and normalize spelling and language, and by the UG geographical bias of most of the literature, which was, moreover, largely composed before geographically and chronologically phased shifts in German vowel phonology had become established. It will thus prove expedient to examine first what is known of medieval German's regional differentiation as a foil against which to set the so-called *Dichtersprache*.

A. REGIONAL VARIATION

Literary texts in twelfth-century manuscripts and the administrative documents in German which begin in the second half of the thirteenth century clearly show regional, 'dialectal' features, and sometimes mixed, 'contaminated' forms, which may be variously explained by the influence of one 'dialect' on another, transcription by copyists from a different area, or even adaptation by the poet or author for the needs of the addressee or patron. Here lies continuity with the texts of the Early or OHG period, which are also diverse in spelling and language.

For example, two twelfth-century poems, the *Tobias* and the *Alexander*,[29] written by the same author—a cleric known as Pfaffe Lamprecht from the Trier area—show differing linguistic characteristics in their manuscripts. Whereas the Stargard fragments of the *Tobias* apparently show a fairly pure form of the Mosel Frk. literary dialect, the *Alexander* shows a mixture of MG and UG features. In the twelfth century the MG and UG literary dialects seem to have differed in several respects, including those illustrated in Table 7.[30] The Mosel Frk. *Tobias* does, however, show alternative forms, such as *dat ∼ daz*; *her ∼ er*; *van ∼ von*, and these have been interpreted (not very convincingly) as reflecting UG influence on MG at the dialect level, further evidence of a south-to-north movement which some scholars claim also for the isoglosses of the Second Consonant Shift.

TABLE 7

Middle German (Frk.)	Upper German (Alem./Bav.)
unshifted consonants:	shifted consonants:
paffe/porte/plegen	*pfaffe/pforte/pflegen*
draget	*traht(e)* (NHG *Tracht*)
gude	*guote*
node	*nôt*
daz ~ dat	*daz*
spirantal /*b*/:	stop /*b*/:
gescriven/geven	*geschriben/geben*
wîf, bleif (pret.)	*wîp, bleip*
pure rhymes:	'impure' rhymes:
sal/über al	*sol, über al*
deit/arebeit	*tuot, arebeit*
dienesthaft/maht	*dienesthaft, maht*
(shows [χt] for [ft]; see also NHG *Gerücht, Schacht*)	

The mixture of MG and UG features in the *Alexander*, on the other hand, probably reflects its manuscript tradition: the early MS V was a redaction for the monastery of Vorau in Styria, but MG forms still show through the Bav. transposition, especially in the rhymes. Both of Lamprecht's texts show mixture, then, but the interpretation differs in each case. An important literary text, *König Rother*,[31] is held to show LFrk., MFrk., and Bav. features and has variants like *penninc ~ pfennic* (NHG *Pfennig*), *weit ~ weiz* (NHG *weiß* 'know'), and *uoten ~ voze* (NHG *Füße(n)*). The comprehensibility of such texts is not seriously impaired by the mixture, however, and it is tempting to see the coexistence of variants as actually aiding comprehension by providing artificial compromises that were acceptable over a wide area.

UG literary dialects are distinguishable from most forms of Frk. at this time, but distinctions between Alem. and Bav. are less marked, suggesting a considerable degree of interaction; from the late thirteenth century, the 'Bavarian' diphthongization provides a criterion (evident in the Regensburg document of Rudolf von Habsburg, above, p. 106). Otherwise, representative 'isoglosses' are as illustrated in Table 8. Lexically, too, Alem. and Bav. are virtually

TABLE 8

Alemannic	Bavarian
kunne/krefte: graphy ⟨k⟩ presumably reflects the affricate [kχ]	*chunne/chrefte*: graphy ⟨ch⟩ seems to be Austro-Bavarian in the twelfth century
ir nement: second person pl. ends in *-nt*, like third person	*ir nemet*: second person pl. ends in *-et*
verbs 'go', 'stand' have regular contracted forms *gân/stân* (earlier **gangan, standan*)	verbs 'go', 'stand' usually contracted as *gên/stên*, but some ⟨â⟩ forms occur
mugen 'be able to' *kam* 'came' (pret.) *sîen* 'may be' (subj.)	*megen* *chom* *sîn*

indistinguishable in twelfth-century texts; stylistic factors are important, because some (presumably vulgar?) forms are not found until late: thus, the Bav. dual pronominal forms *ös, enk* (nom. and acc.), which must be old, are not attested until *c*.1280.[32]

So, the twelfth-century texts in no way reflect a supra-regional literary or standard language so far as spelling, sounds and forms are concerned, although they do not transmit a faithful image of local spoken dialect either, but follow instead the written traditions of the region where they were produced, traditions which were inevitably 'archaic', not homogeneous, and open to influences from other areas. We are better informed about regional written traditions in the thirteenth and fourteenth centuries because the chancery and private documents are usually of local interest, whereas literary texts pass along a network of social connections which was even international— French sources for German courtly poetry. The chancery scribes had no reason to adapt their language to any supra-regional norms (although we do perceive the influence of one chancery language on another)[33] and no constraints of rhyme or metre inhibited them from reflecting in varying degree the spoken forms of the localities in which they were produced. We cannot here consider the chancery languages for their own sake, but shall now briefly describe the main phonological developments of the twelfth to fifteenth centuries which readily appear in chancery and private documents, and which are constitutive of the modern standard language.

B. PHONOLOGICAL CHANGES WHICH INCREASE REGIONAL DIVERSITY

The main vowel changes are diphthongization, monophthongization, and lengthening of short stressed vowels in open syllables: their co-occurrence, together with the merger of certain old diphthongs with the new ones, in the EMG 'colonial' dialects has long been taken as evidence that the cradle of the modern standard language rocks in these regions.[34]

1. *Diphthongization*

		Phonetic interpretation
MHG *mîn*	NHG *mein*	[iː] > [ai]/[ae]
niuwez	*neues*	[yː] > [oi]/[ɔø]
hûs	*Haus*	[uː] > [au]/[ao]

Names in twelfth-century Latin documents from Carinthia first show this change, which is consequently sometimes called the 'Bavarian diphthongization'. By about 1215 the poet Heinrich von dem Türlîn rhymes *zît/geleit*. According to traditional monogenetic theory the change starts in the south and spreads northwards, leaving the south-west Alem. dialects (Swiss and Alsatian) and the northern Frk. dialects and LG unaffected.

The new diphthongs and three existing diphthongs, /ei/, /öu/ and /ou/, merge (though not in most dialects); e.g. MHG *mîn, ein;* MHG *liute, vröude;* MHG *hûs, troum* > NHG *mein, ein; Leute, Freude; Haus, Traum.* By 1350 the new diphthongs are used in documents of the imperial chancery at Prague.

2. *Monophthongization*

		Phonetic interpretation
MGH *liebe*	NHG *liebe*	[iə] > [iː]
guot	*gut*	[uo] > [uː]
güete	*Güte*	[yə] > [yː]

This MG development appears first in MFrk. and Hessian, *c.*1200, then in Thuringian and other EMG dialects; RhFrk. and, partially, EFrk. and North Bav. also show it. Otherwise, UG dialects remain largely unaffected: Bav. and Alem. show diphthongs in most positions. Unfortunately, conservative spelling often makes monophthongs difficult to detect, cf. mod. German *lieben* [li:bən]; but the extension of diphthongal graphies to forms with historical monophthongs provides a guide, e.g. MHG *geschriben* is written *geschrieben*, where the ⟨ie⟩ spelling indicates a long monophthong. Monophthongs occur in imperial documents from Prague in the fourteenth century.[35]

3. *Lengthening of short vowels in open syllables*

				Phonetic interpretation	
MHG	tages	NHG	Tages	[a]	> [a:]
	hoves		Hofs	[ɔ]	> [o:]
	über		über	[Y]	> [y:]
	gestigen		gestiegen	[I]	> [i:]
	leg(g)en		legen	[e]	
	nëmen		nehmen	[ɛ]	> [e:]
	vrävel		Frevel	[ae]	

Note that the three MHG *e* phonemes merge, and also that the MHG short vowels changed quality as well as quantity when they lengthened: short, relatively lax, open vowels have become long, tense, closed vowels in the modern standard pronunciation.

The lengthening may be attested as early as the late eleventh century in the Brixen area (spelling of place-names like *Gûrch* = Gurk, *Lisirahôvun*, with circumflex), and it occurs also in Carinthian documents of the twelfth and thirteenth centuries: hence a structural 'push-chain' (see p. 83) might have triggered the diphthongization, with new lengthened vowels 'shunting' the existing long vowels into diphthongs.[36] The lengthening occurs in the twelfth century in WMG—traces appear in Heinrich von Veldeke's rhymes—and by 1200 other MG texts show it; in the fourteenth century it is common in UG, but fails to reach Switzerland. Orthographical evidence for vowel length is unclear: graphies with doubled vowel (NHG *Haar*, *Moos*, etc.) or with the insertion of ⟨h⟩ or ⟨i⟩ or ⟨e⟩ (e.g. NHG *Ehre, gestiegen*, or medieval Rhenish spellings, e.g. *iair = Jahr*) are infrequent and/or regional. Certain consonants, especially dentals, seem to prevent lengthening, e.g. MHG *gesniten, genomen* > NHG *geschnitten, genommen*.

4. *Apocope and syncope (loss of final and other unstressed syllables)*

These changes may represent a further stage in the weakening of final syllables found in OHG times. Literary texts do not show them consistently, and indeed they have consequences for rhyme and metre as well as morphology: we discern here the conservative nature of the literary language and the gap between it and speech.

Apocope is attested in Bav. in the thirteenth century and in EFrk. and Swabian by the fourteenth century; in the second quarter of the fourteenth century other Alem. dialects are affected, and parts of Bohemia, although the EMG dialects generally resist it; RhFrk. is reached last, c.1450.[37]

Syncope is less well documented: MG dialects tend to preserve full forms, UG ones to syncopate, with Bav. doing so more than Alem. For example:

MHG		'post MHG'	
herze	>		*herz*
bote	>		*bot* (NHG *Bote*)
nime	>		*nim* (NHG *ich nehme*)
gelücke	>		*glück*
wonet	(third person pres.)		(NHG *wohnt*)
		wont	
won(e)te	(third person pret.)		(NHG *wohnte*)

5. *Consonantal Changes.* These include:

(i) *Merger of spirants /z/ (from pre-HG *t) and /s/.* In texts before the twelfth century the two spirants were kept apart medially and finally, but, starting with Alem. the merger developed throughout UG, becoming general in chancery documents about 1300.[38] For example, forms of the neuter pronoun merge:

MHG		NHG
nom./acc. *ez*		
	> →	*es*
gen. *es*		

(ii) *Development of shibilants from initial sibilants* ([s] > [ʃ]). A primarily phonetic change and consequently much obscured by conservative orthography (there was no structural need for a new symbol): in EFrk. and MG dialect areas, for example, the graphy ⟨sch⟩ before liquids and nasals (*l, r, m, n*) occurs only in the sixteenth century. For example:

MHG		NHG	
slange	>		*Schlange*
smecken	>		*schmecken*
snelle	>		*schnell*
swîgen	>		*schweigen*

But note the spelling before ⟨p⟩ and ⟨t⟩, as in ⟨spitz⟩, ⟨stein⟩, where the standard pronunciation is with shibilant, although several areas retain sibilants, e.g. Hamburg and Husum. Medial shibilants are found in some dialects, notably in Swabian, e.g. *ischt, hascht, Kaschperl* (= *ist, hast, Kasperl* 'Punch').

Changes with such varying geographical and chronological distribution increased dialectal diversity and made it seem that the German language had declined. Contemporaries, too, were conscious of the considerable regional variations in custom, dress, and language, as Hugo von Trimberg remarks in his didactic poem *Der Renner* (*c*.1300):[39]

> Ein jeglich lant hât sînen site,
> Der sînem lantvolke volget mite. 22260
> An sprâche, an mâze und an gewande
> Ist underscheiden lant von lande.
> Der werlde dinc stêt über al
> An sprâche, an mâze, an wâge, an zal.
> Swâben ir wörter spaltent, 22265
> Die Franken ein teil si valtent,
> Die Beier si zezerrent,
> Die Düringe si ûf sperrent,
> Die Sahsen si bezückent,
> Die Rînliute si verdrückent, 22270
> Die Wetereiber si würgent,
> Die Mîsener si vol schürgent,
> Egerlant si swenkent,
> Oesterrîche si schrenkent,
> Stîrlant si baz lenkent, 22275
> Kernde ein teil si senkent . . .

But this is a testimony to an underlying unity, as well as to diversity, for 'tiutsch' comprises all these dialects. Unfortunately, the terms used of the various dialectal pronunciations are vague, but Ehrismann[40] treats them in groups of four: the Swabians and Bavarians have a staccato articulation, separating their words strongly (*spalten* and *zezerren* 'tear to pieces'), while the Franks and Thuringians run their words together (*valten* 'fold') with a legato articulation (*ûf sperren*—opening the mouth to lengthen the sounds?). The Saxons and Rhenish speakers suppress syllables (*bezücken* and *verdrücken* 'cut off short' and 'suppress'—the verb *verzucken* means 'syncopate'), whereas the Wetterau speakers force their words out of a constricted throat (*würgen* 'choke') and the Misnians have an emphatic, strongly aspirated(?) pronunciation (*schürgen* = NHG *stoßen*). The last group of German dialects are characterized by differences of pitch (or musical) accent: the Carinthians seem to have a gravis accent with a falling tone (*senken*), and the Styrians perhaps have a rising tone or acute accent (*baz lenken* 'lead onwards'?), while Eger-speakers and Austrians have some kind of modulated pronunciation combining both acute and grave (*swenken* 'vibrate', *schrenken* 'interlock'). More important in the present context, the whole passage is inspired by classical authorities, notably Cicero's *De Oratore*, which reduces the value of Hugo's observations. But the kinds of pronunciation described are also treated by grammarians as faults (*vitia*), so by implication the dialects about 1300 may already have been regarded as regional and imperfect forms of some accepted norm—perhaps even a *Dichtersprache*?

C. THE MHG DICHTERSPRACHE

The language of medieval German chivalric literature around 1200 was supra-regional in style, vocabulary, and ethos (below, pp. 118f., but it was regional in spelling, sounds, and forms. The editors' texts and the grammars based upon them usually orientate themselves according to one regional type, namely UG of an essentially Alem. bias, following the practice of Karl Lachmann (1793-1851), who had taken as exemplary a limited number of literary texts. Lachmann was a classical scholar accustomed to editing texts in languages with a long literary tradition. He sought by detailed examination of the extant manuscripts to reconstruct the poet's original as closely as possible. Even though that original might itself be imperfect, Lachmann felt that the scribal errors and archaisms encrusting the evidence could be carefully chipped away, and the text made more accessible to modern readers by removing abbreviations and variant forms. Rhymes and metrical criteria were helpful here (but some doublet forms aided scansion); still, Lachmann respected the manuscript orthography, even if he and his successors were taken to task for having falsified it.[41] Dialectal differences interested him less—for he was no grammarian of medieval German—than uncovering the usage and pronunciation of individual poets, which he found remarkably consistent, noting that '. . . die Dichter des dreizehnten Jahrhunderts, bis auf wenig mundartliche Einzelheiten, ein bestimmtes unwandelbares Hochdeutsch redeten'.[42]

But we cannot dismiss the *Dichtersprache* as an editors' Esperanto, nor even treat it simply as a written idiom: when audiences were mostly illiterate poetry was 'social', and meant for reading aloud, and hence the language of literature had a phonetic reality. Within one dialect area, say Bav., the diphthongization (above, p. 112) must progressively have forced a wedge between the written (and declaimed) literary language and everyday speech. (Chancery documents probably mediate, being written in the same regional traditions as literature, yet not restricted by metre or rhyme from revealing the phonological changes like diphthongization). However, the poetic form did not assert itself, since late manuscripts update the spelling (albeit often inconsistently): Lachmann then blames the scribes for a linguistic corruption which may actually be scribal accuracy, both in reflecting spoken German and in working within the changed spelling traditions.

But there is also evidence that poets around 1200 were aware of regional differences and sought to compensate for them and reach a wider audience. Albrecht von Halberstadt in the prologue to his translation of Ovid's *Metamorphoses* (*c.*1190, or perhaps *c.*1210) expressly draws attention to the rhymes—he is no Swabian, Bavarian, Thuringian, or Frank, but a Saxon,

> des lât û sîn zû danke,
> ob ir vundet in den rîmen,
> die sich zeinander lîmen   50
> valsch oder unrecht . . .

Rhyming technique was particularly affected by transposition from one region to another, and so it has been argued that poets deliberately chose 'neutral' rhymes which were widespread. This is inordinately difficult to prove, given the lack of original manuscripts, the fact of copying and transcription of the manuscripts we do have, and the good intentions/prejudices of editors. Still, important poets like Walther von der Vogelweide, who was probably an Austrian, and Reinmar von Hagenau from Alsace (Low Alem.) both wrote for the court at Vienna, and neither they nor the Swabian Hartmann von Aue are narrowly localizable on the basis of their language. Particularly interesting is the case where a LG poet appears to be shaping his verse with an ear to its wider comprehensibility and, possibly, transposition into HG: Heinrich von Veldeke, a poet of the Limburg region which lies east of the Maas in the Ripuarian Frankish area, close to the Dutch linguistic border, has been much discussed. While he probably composed his songs and the *Servatius* in the LFrk. Limburg dialect, his *Eneide* is preserved exclusively in HG manuscripts, was eventually completed for a MG patron, Hermann of Thuringia, and has a rhyme distribution characteristic of HG rather than LG. Thus, HG /t/ and /z/ are kept strictly apart, although in LG their equivalents could rhyme. Moreover, rhyme words with medial /t/ and /k/ in a short open syllable in LG are consistently placed in lines with three stresses and not four, as though they had the long closed syllable we expect in the HG shifted forms, e.g. *gesezzen* (LG *geseten*); *sprechen* (LG *spreken*). The vocabulary of the *Eneide* also shows HG words which surely did not appear in Limburg dialect.[43] This makes reconstruction of a literary Limburg *Urtext* difficult, and despite the painstaking work of Theodor Frings and Gabriele Schieb, and the presence of LG dialectal rhymes which would be impure or impossible in a HG *Dichtersprache* (like *don* (NHG *tun*) ~ *son* (NHG *Sohn*), *vas* (MHG *vahs*, NHG *Haar*) ~ *was* (NHG *war*); *gelochte* (NHG *glaubte*) ~ *verkochte* (NHG *verkaufte*) etc.), the evidence for some HG forming of rhymes is inescapable. Moreover, Schieb's Limburg *Eneide* involved altering whole lines to 'restore the original', and it remains a construct of a literary dialect of which we have only an imperfect knowledge.[44]

As Hugo von Trimberg had observed, 'Swer tiutsche wil eben tihten, | Der muoz sîn herze rihten | Ûf manigerleie sprâche . . .' (*Renner*, 22253–5): conforming to UG consonantism and rhyming convention—the *Dichtersprache*—was only one solution. Another way of ensuring wide comprehensibility was to employ variant forms in the same text: Guchmann has also drawn attention to a group of mixed literary texts in the thirteenth century.[45] No standard language resulted in either case, for the 'Dichtersprache' became increasingly archaic as the diphthongizations and monophthongizations took place, and it had variant forms within the line (i.e. in non-rhyming position). We must not, then, see the medieval German literary language declining and becoming dialectal after about 1250. Instead, it failed to impose itself as the standard written norm.

CHIVALRIC AND OTHER STYLES IN MEDIEVAL GERMAN

Stylistically the language of chivalric literature is certainly supra-regional, expressing the values of an élite, aristocratic society. We shall consider briefly this aspect of the *Dichtersprache*, followed by an examination of other uses of German, chancery, commercial, and intellectual/mystical, to set it into perspective.

A. FRENCH INFLUENCE

French loan-words distinguish literary medieval German from religious, administrative, and most technical registers. Germans acknowledged French chivalry, manners, and dress as superior and increasingly emulated them: poets like Hartmann von Aue, Gottfried von Strassburg, and Wolfram von Eschenbach, and their heroes, especially Tristan, were familiar with French, and introducing French phrases was regarded as polite, indeed beneficial, since those unfamiliar with the language might learn 'der spaehen wörter harte vil'[46]—much excellent vocabulary. In the early lyric, loans are rare but some poets, for example Tannhäuser (flourished c.1250?), verge on mannerism:

> Ein riviere ich dâ gesach,
> durch den forês gieng ein bach
> zetal über ein plâniure.
> ich sleich ir nâch unz ich si vant die schoenen crêâtiure
> bî dem fontâne saz diu klâre süeze von faitiure . . .[47]

A rivulet I espied there, a rill ran through the forest and down a glade, and, following along its course, I found her, that fair creature, sitting by the stream, so radiant and sweet of feature!

Apart from the admiration for French culture in the literary context, trade, crusades, intermarriage with French and Provençal nobility, court festivals—several French and Provençal poets attended the famous *Hoffest* at Mainz in 1184—and tournaments all provided opportunities for cultural and linguistic borrowing, while along the lnguistic border in Alsace and Lorraine and parts of Switzerland bilingualism must anyway have existed: the lords (*Vögte*) of Hunoltstein (a Rhenish family) produced documents in Latin, German, and French.[48] Otherwise, the LG-speaking areas of Flanders and Brabant transmitted some Romance influence. The chivalry of these areas was itself much admired:

> Swelch ritter ze Henegouwe
> ze Brâbant vnd ze Haspengouwe
> ze orse ie aller beste gesaz,
> sô kan ichz mit gedanken baz[49]

In my thoughts I can outdo the best knights from Hainault, Brabant, and Hesbaye.

There seems to have been little French influence on German syntax, in keeping with the ornamental function of the borrowing—although loan-translation does occur, where the foreign expressions are not taken directly into German but are translated.[50] In the twelfth century some 300 French borrowings are attested, in the thirteenth century 700, and they reach their peak in the fourteenth century with some 2,000, of which approximately half are derived forms; the fifteenth century shows a decline, temporary as it turned out.[51]

Examples of twelfth- and thirteenth-century borrowing

(i) *Loan-words.* Words for armour and knightly exercise—most of which fail to survive—include *banier* 'pennant on lance' (OFr. *baniere*, NHG *Panier*); *harnas* (OFr. *harnais*, NHG *Harnisch*); *panzier* 'body-armour' (OFr. *pancier*, NHG *Panzer*); *lanze* (OFr. *lance*, NHG *Lanze*); *bûhurt* 'a game in which groups of knights attack each other with bated weapons' (OFr. *bohourt*); *tjoste, tjostieren* 'joust' (OFr. *joste, jost(i)er*); *puneiz* 'a charge at the opponent in a tournament' (OFr. *poigneiz*); *leisieren* 'let the horse run with free reins, (OFr. *esleissier*); *walopieren* 'gallop' (OFr. *waloper, galoper*). Hartmann von Aue's hero Gregorius baffles his mentor the abbot in a bravura eulogy of knightly technique (1593 ff.) These terms and others from courtly technical registers like venery and music were not restricted to literature. Gottfried von Strassburg[52] uses (for music) *folate, pasturele, refloit, rotruwange, rundate, schanzune, stampenîe*; (for hunting) *curîe* (OFr. *cuiriee* 'quarry'), *furkîe* (OFr. *forchie* 'choice morsels on a forked stick'), *quartier, panze* (OFr. *pance* 'paunch'), *gorge* 'throat', *zimer* (OFr. *cimier* 'haunch'). Some exotic materials come in via French, and trade, not literature alone, may have made them familiar: *samît*, (OFr. *samit*, MLat. *(e)xamitum*, Gk. *hexamiton* 'a cloth woven from six threads', NHG *Samt*); *baldekîn* (OFr. *baldekin*, MLat. *baldakinus* 'silk from Baldac (= Bagdad)'); *zendal* (OFr. *cendal* 'taffeta'); *scharlachen* (OFr. *escarlate* 'fine red or brown woollen material').

(ii) *Loan-translation and formation*

OFr.	MHG	MHG loan-words
court	*hof*	—
court-ois	*höv-esch* (NHG *hübsch*)[53]	*kurtois, kurteis*
court-ois-ie	*höv-esch-(h)eit*	*kurtoisîe*
douce amie	*süeze amîe*	

faire chevalerie	*ritterschaft tuon*
s'entresaluer	*sich undergrüezen* 'greet one another'
s'entrebaisier	*sich underküssen* 'kiss one another'
servir	*dienen* [a key word of the love lyric]
(des)mesure	*(un)mâze* '(lack of) moderation'
merci	*lôn, genâde*

Two suffixes may also have been borrowed from French and then extended to native words:

(1) OFr. *-ie* to MHG *-îe* (e.g. OFr. *prophecie, vilainie,* MHG *prophezîe* (NHG *Prophezeiung*), *vilanîe*); thence to native *jegerîe* 'hunting', *buoberîe* 'knavery', *zegerîe* (NHG *Zaghaftigkeit*). The suffix can be pejorative, as in *Lobhudelei* 'base flattery' or Schiller's *Empfindelei* 'false sentimentality' (vs. *Empfindsamkeit*), *Schweinerei,* etc., but also denotes a place where an activity occurs: *Bäckerei, Molkerei, Schlosserei, Ziegelei, Auskunftei, Kartei.*

(2) OFr. *-(i)er*, a verbal suffix, to MHG *-ieren* (e.g. OFr. *logier, parlier,* MHG *loschieren, parlieren*); thence to native *buchstabieren* 'spell out', *halbieren, hofieren.* The suffix becomes common from the fifteenth century onwards, doubtless reinforced by nouns in *-ier*, like *soldier, schevalier, zimier* 'crest'.

(iii) *Titles and forms of address.* The prestige of French is apparent in the use of *cunte, dame, damoisele, doschesse, markîs, seneschal,* while expressions in Wolfram von Eschenbach's *Parzival* are perhaps translations: *mîn her Gawan* < OFr. *messire Gauvains?*; *hêr iwer genâde* < OFr. *vostre merci (Parz. 362. 6)?* The polite use of the second person pronoun *ir* was also influenced by OFr. *vus.*

(iv) *Spoken influence.* We may safely assume that some French words were used in everyday speech—they are attested in sermons and even legal codes,[54] while hunting and jousting were popular spectacles, some of whose terminology must have spread beyond court circles. The forms of some words also suggest spoken transmission: MHG *lanze* and *panzer* show sound substitution with affricate, whereas *schumpfentiure* for OFr. *desconfiture* may show phonetic deformation linked with folk etymology, a wrong derivation from *schimpf* 'pleasure' and *tiure* 'rare', 'absent'; OFr. *osteiz!* (mod. Fr. *ôtez!*) becomes the expression of surprise *ohteiz!*; while

OFr. *sorcengle*, MLat. *supracingulum* (= *Obergurt*) appears as *schurzgel* (!) beside normal *surzengel*.

B. LOW GERMAN AND FLEMISH INFLUENCE

LG, Flemish, and Ripuarian Frk. dialects have many forms in common and are sometimes indistinguishable: but all three differ from HG in their consonantism: thus, LG *wâpen* (English *weapon*) contrasts with HG *wâfen*; it survives in courtly sense as *das Wappen* 'blazon', and in *wappnen* 'arm', *entwappnen* 'disarm(ing)'. Similarly, *dörpaere*[55] (LG *dorp* ≠ HG *dorf*), a loan-translation of OFr. *vilain* and the antithesis of courtliness; *dorperîe/dorperheit* render OFr. *vilainie*. Poetic *ors* 'charger' has metathesis for HG *ros* (PGmc. doublet forms **hursa* and **hrussa*)—the word is rare in compounds. The verbs *muoten* 'meet', 'encounter in combat', *tadeln* 'blame', and *trecken* (for HG *ziehen*) 'go', and the adjectives *blîde* 'blithe', 'joyful' and *kluoc* 'fine' (note HG *uo* for LG *ô*) are also LG/'Flemish'. So are the suffixes *-kîn*, as in *schapelekîn* 'chaplet of flowers (or laurel leaves)', *merlekîn*, 'blackbird', *negelkîn* (contracted to NHG *Nelke*) 'clove', also 'pink', 'carnation' (lit. 'little nail'), and *-ierse*, as in *soldierse*, *trippanierse*, both meaning 'camp-follower', 'whore'. The word *ritter* itself has been held to have been influenced by Flemish *ridder* because of the short vowel and double consonant (contrast HG *rîtaere* 'rider'); however, derivation from a PGmc. agent noun **ridjan* remains an attractive hypothesis.[56] Contemporaries were aware of the prestige of Flemish chivalry: Neidhart von Reuental (pre-1230) observes sarcastically of a pretentious peasant: 'mit sîner rede er vlaemet' (*Song* 82. 2), while in Wernher der Gartenære's *Meier Helmbreht* (c.1237-1300), a peasant farmer's prodigal son Helmbreht, addresses his father's labourers in bad LG and is taken for a foreigner from Brabant or Saxony—'vil liebe soete kindekîn, | got lâte iuch iemer saelic sîn!'—(line 717), he then insults his parents: 'Ey waz sakent ir gebûrekîn | und jenez gunêrte wîf? | mîn parit, mînen klâren lîf, | sol dehein gebûric man | zwâre nimmer grîpen an' (lines 764-8).[57] Indeed, some French loans enter German via the Flemish and Lower Rhine regions, are taken for LG, and then partially transposed into a HG form: OFr. *roc* 'rook' (a chess piece) and *eschec/eschac* 'chess' become LG *roc*, *schâc* and are then given 'hyper-correct' HG shifted forms *roch* and *schâch*. Similarly, OFr. *berser* to HG *birschen/pirschen* 'hunt with hounds' could come via LG **bersen* and show

HG */i/* for LG */e/* (cf. LG *kerke* ≠ HG *kirche*) and perhaps also HG */p/* for LG */b/*. MHG *fînlîche*, a hybrid form, may derive from a Dutch recasting of OFr. *finement* to *fijnlike*, thence transposed into HG, while the peculiar forms MHG *baneken/banekîe* 'amuse(ment)' may reflect LG modification of OFr. *esbanoier*.

C. ARCHAIC FEATURES?

Certain words found pre-eminently (though by no means exclusively) in the *Nibelungenlied*, in the minor verse epics treating Dietrich von Berne and related figures, and in the heterogeneous *spielmännische Epik*, have often been regarded as archaisms—although it might be better to treat this vocabulary as in some measure 'genre-specific': *degen, helt, recke, wîgant* 'knight', 'warrior', *balt, ellenthaft, ellensrîch, gemeit, snel, vermezzen, vrech* 'bold', 'brave', etc., *egeslîch/eislîch* 'terrifying', *ecke* 'sword', *gêr* 'spear', *rant* 'shield', *bouc* 'torque', 'ring', *brünne* 'breastplate', *îsengewant, sarwât, geserwe* 'armour', *wîc* 'battle', *wal* 'battlefield', *veige* 'doomed', *dürkel* 'riddled with holes', *verch* 'life', *wine* (masc.) 'friend', 'lover', 'husband', *wine* (fem.) 'wife', 'beloved', *vriedel* 'beloved'. The synonyms for 'warrior' and 'bold' probably reflect a different poetic technique employing a stereotyped variation closer to earlier oral alliterative poetry, so far as we can judge it. Some of this vocabulary became restricted to literature, or else changed in meaning, since it no longer represented the social conditions of the twelfth to thirteenth centuries. Thus, *recke* originally denoted an 'exiled warrior' (cf. English *wretch*) but it came to mean any fighting man; *geswâsliche* 'intimate', 'secret' once meant 'belonging to the household' (cf. *Hildebrandslied* 53: *suasat chind*)— later, the *swâshûs* or *swâskamer* meant a 'privy'! Words like *degen* are convenient for rhyme (*ritter* seldom appears in rhyme position), and *degen* occurs quite frequently in Hartmann von Aue (eleven times in *Erec*, four times in *Iwein*). The postpositioned adjective, e.g. *der degen balt*, was again probably literary rather than archaic phrasing— indeed, French influence might have encouraged this tendency, since French also has postpositioned adjectives; postpositioned adjectives remained common in popular poetry for a long time. The word *urliuge/urlouge* is rare in courtly literature, but it occurs elsewhere in religious and secular writing and in early vernacular legal documents; by contrast, chivalric literature was concerned rather with combat between individuals than with war, and here the terms *kampf* and *strît* were used. Most of the words in the list above are indeed *old*: they are attested early (some in alliterative poetry), they have cognates in other Germanic languages, and so forth—but this need not make them 'archaic' in medieval times. For example, the *Kaiserchronik*, (*c.*1140–50), a verse chronicle treating Roman and Church history, features most of these words, which were probably still in common use. True, late manuscripts of medieval poems do replace such vocabulary, which may have been becoming stylistically marked by the late thirteenth century, but we cannot easily assess whether contemporaries found it outmoded. By the fifteenth century most of it had died out, and it has not survived today, apart from *schnell* and *bald*, which are adverbs of time or motion, and *Held*—which can also be used colloquially: 'Du bist so 'n Held!'

D. COURTLY AND UNCOURTLY ELEMENTS

Feudal metaphor applies to the love relationship as part of polite usage—*dienen umbe lôn*; *iemen holt sîn*; *iemen undertân sîn*; *lônen*; *eigen sîn*; and politeness is expressed by understatement—*lützel iemen* 'no one', circumlocution *mîn lîp* (lit. 'my person') instead of *ich*, and the abasement of the self to a position which was obviously not one's true status. Keywords like *zuht* 'breeding', *êre* 'social status' *triuwe* 'loyalty', 'faithfulness', *tugent* 'excellence', *hôher muot* 'inspiration' 'exultation', *guot*, *edel*, *hovelîch*, *biderbe* (NHG *bieder*), *wünneclîch*, and other adjectives are difficult to translate out of their social and literary context: often they convey simultaneously degrees of social and moral worth. A writer's background and perspective also reflect his values and usage: naturally, some clerics disparaged courtliness, and the words *hovescen/gehofescen* could imply promiscuous behaviour even in the twelfth century, for example in the *Kaiserchronik* (lines 13041, 16555). Parodistic and satirical works can sometimes give an impression of how stereotyped such expressions had become even in the thirteenth century, while by the fourteenth and fifteenth several courtly terms had become generally debased: *minne* by then meant only coitus and had to be replaced by *liebe*; *hofieren* meant 'defecate', and the sixteenth-century *Zimmerische Chronik* (iii. 544. 14) bluntly observes of scandalous behaviour 'das si daselbst *curtisirt*, id est grosz huren gewesen (sind)'.

Conversely, obscenities (though not necessarily obscenity) are rare in the *Dichtersprache*—words like *fudenol* 'mons Veneris', *vut* 'vulva'

(NHG *Fotze*), both in Neidhart von Reuental, *visellîn* 'penis' in Wolfram von Eschenbach—and only become common later in the *Schwank* and especially the *Fastnachtsspiele*[58] and also in the Swiss poet Heinrich Wittenweiler's *Ring* (*c*.1400), an at times bawdy but entertaining and skilful parody of many courtly traits, written with a didactic purpose.

Descriptions of anti-courtly individuals are occasionally found as a literary device—the ugly damsel Cundrîe in Wolfram von Eschenbach's *Parzival* (313. 1 ff.) or the foul and infested rear of the allegorical Lady World in Konrad von Würzburg's *Der Welt Lohn* (217–38); while Heinrich von dem Türlîn, an Austrian, describes in revolting detail a broken-down nag with spavin and the glanders (*Diu Crône* 19804–900) (*c*.1220).

But some technical languages too—e.g. medicine—were not considered appropriate for courtly audiences: Gottfried baulks at a description of Tristan's wound and its cure:

> in edelen ôren lûtet baz   7942
> ein wort daz schône gezimt
> dan daz man ûz der bühsen nimt

CHANCERY STYLE

With chanceries, too, the language is local, but the style is supra-regional and the documents were meant for reading aloud, as a basic formula has it: *Wir NN tun kunt allen den die disen brief lesent vnd hærent* (or: *sehent oder hærent lesen*). Vernacular chancery practice evolved from classical traditions, which accounts for the similarity in form and style of documents from all areas—the universality of Latin is again evident. Chancery officials belong to the urban intelligentsia in the later Middle Ages, have close associations with universities and printing-houses, and were naturally aware of the different structures of Latin and vernacular grammar. Moreover, they collected, transcribed, translated, and themselves composed literary works: Meister Hesse, 'von Strasburg de(r) s(c)ribære' (perhaps scribe in the town chancery?), was a critical emendator of poetry in the thirteenth century;[59] a later minnesinger bears the name 'der Kanzler'; Johann von Neumarkt (*c*.1310–80), Imperial Chancellor under Charles IV at Prague, Johannes von Tepl (*c*.1350–1413/15), notary and author of the remarkable *Ackermann aus Böhmen* (*c*.1400), and Niclas von Wyle (below, pp. 201-2) all have well-attested literary interests. Occasional legal/administrative imagery in the chivalric poetry might reflect a chancery connection: the hero of Wolfram von Eschenbach's *Parzival* is described as *diss mæres sachewalte* 'this tale's advocate' (112.17); *urborn* 'provide income', is used of the May breezes which provide birds with their song (Wolfram's song 'Ursprinc bluomen'); and legal questions are important in some works, e.g. Gottfried's *Tristan*.

Conversely, chancery style itself was embellished, for it belongs to classical 'forensic' tradition, where rhetorical devices trick out an argument. The period, a complex sentence, with its double, sometimes triple and more, parallel clauses,[60] is a mainstay of German Humanist prose, but is characteristic of chancery style also, although in the chancery documents cumbersome deictic particles like *obgenannt*, *selbige*, *vorgenannt*, *egenannt* often limit the aesthetic effect by attaining precision at the expense of clarity. Abundant synonyms, too, can add variety and emphasis, as well as safeguarding contractual parties from ambiguity and overcoming regional lexical differences. The most impressive sustained example of artistic vernacular prose modelled on Latin chancery style is Johannes von Tepl's *Ackermann*, which, as we know from a letter of Tepl's, was an exercise in applying Latin rhetoric to German, and in this he anticipates the late fifteenth-century German Humanists. The work is a dialogue between Death and an author in the guise of ploughman of the rhetorical field; the ploughman, whose wife has died, puts up a spirited defence of humanity, individual and collective, against Death's scornful nihilism. The ploughman's opening accusation and curse, rearranged to show parallel clause structure, is shown opposite (italicized words are glossed below).[61]

Stylistically, the *Ackermann* is the keystone in Konrad Burdach's theory of the 'internal development' of the modern language: it both shows what was possible in German and documents the intellectual flowering at Prague, which in turn reinforced the linguistic importance of the EMG area in the century before Luther.[62] In particular, Burdach set out to prove the formative role of the Imperial Chancery under its gifted Chancellor, Johann von Neumarkt, whose links with the Italian humanists Cola di Rienzo and Petrarch had, Burdach claimed, introduced Renaissance ideas at Prague, including the new awareness of a national standard and literary language prompted by Dante's *De vulgari eloquentia* (pre-1305).

Grimmiger *tilger* aller leute,
schedlicher echter aller werlte,
freissamer morder aller menschen,→ir Tot,   euch sei verfluchet!
Got, ewr *tirmer*, hasse euch,
vnselden merunge wone euch bei,
vngeluck hause gewaltiglich zu euch: ⟶   zumale geschant seit immer!

Angst vnd not vnd jamer ⟶	verlassen euch nicht, ⟶	wo ir wandert;
leit, betrubnuß vnd kumer ⟶	*beleiten* euch ⟶	allenthalben
leidige anfechtunge, schentliche zuversicht vnd *schemliche verserung* →	die betwingen euch groblich	an aller state...

tilger = destroyer; *freissamer* = terrible; *tirmer* = creator; *vnselden merunge* = increase of misery; *beleiten* = *begleiten*; *leidige anfechtunge* = painful attack; *schentliche zuversicht* = expectation of dishonour; *schemliche verserung* = shameful affliction.

COMMERCIAL GERMAN IN THE MIDDLE AGES[63]

Latin, again, was the international trading language and influences German well before the twelfth century: surviving words with the Sound Shift (see p. 40) include *Kauf, kaufen, Münze, Pfund, Zoll*; other early forms are *Markt, Unze,* and *Zins.* In the later centuries, Latin loans often come in via French or Italian; they either acquire German morphology and form derivatives (*quitt: quittieren, quittanz, quittbrief; rente* (Lat. *rendita*)—*renten, verrenten*); or else they remain in Latin form as technical terms or 'tags' inserted into bills of sale, ledgers, and account books: e.g. *datum, pro, facit, dedit, summa, tenetur.* Such terms are even used in private correspondence, e.g. in the letters of the Kobergers, a family of printers and booksellers,[64] or in the letters of Nuremberg merchants like the Paumgartners in the sixteenth century[65]—but all this evidence is late, and in what follows we concentrate on vocabulary rather than style. However, native German expressions also form part of the merchant's language, and they are common in courtly literature too: *bürgen, borgen, bürgschaft, geleit(e), pfantbrief, pfenden, schult, schuldec, krâm, gelten, veile* (NHG *feil, wohlfeil), wert.* Indeed, merchants play a considerable role in literature: Gottfried's Tristan is abducted by them; Wolfram's Gâwân is mistaken for one; Rudolf von Ems describes a noble, idealized merchant in *Der gute Gerhart* (*c*.1225-30); in the lyric love can be debased to a transaction, etc.

Two main trading regions develop in the thirteenth and fourteenth centuries: a northern area with a trading union known as the Hanseatic League, and a southern one with important centres like Augsburg and Nuremberg, which traded across the Alps with Venice, Genoa, and the Levant.

A. THE HANSEATIC LEAGUE

The Gmc. word **hansō*, OHG *hansa*, once meant 'a group of warriors', but occurs in the twelfth century in mercantile contexts: *hanshûs* 'guild-house'. In 1358 the *düdesche hense* was a trading confederation which was to extend from Antwerp in Flanders to Königsberg (modern Kaliningrad) in Prussia. The language of the Hanse was LG with admixtures of Latin, English, Dutch, French, and Italian. The many LG words borrowed into Danish and Swedish attest to the League's importance, and it is surprising that the written LG language did not survive as a northern standard language. Indeed, the League still flourished in the sixteenth century, even after the power of the Teutonic Knights, who had controlled the colonial eastern regions, had been smashed, and after the discovery of new trading possibilities in the Americas. But probably the focus of trade had shifted: Lübeck, once the centre of the Hanse, declined in importance, overshadowed by the independent towns of Flanders and the Netherlands, which were centres of the continental wool trade and well placed to exploit the new American markets. Linguistically, the existence already of two emergent standard languages, Neth. and HG, must have 'sapped the strength' of LG—its lexical influence on mod. German is slight: see Kluge (1883/1967), s.vv. *bodmen* 'take credit on a ship and its contents' (*Bodmerei* 'bottomry'), *Kran, liefern, makeln, Schute, Stapel, Ware, Wimpel, Wispel* (a grain measure, 1,000 kilos). Non-LG words, like *Fracht* (< Fris.), *Kram* 'booth', 'tent' (< HG); *Prahm* 'barge' (< Russian *prám*?), and *Rolle* (< Lat. *rotula*), were disseminated by the Hanse, which may also have introduced a few English seafaring terms into German: *Boot*(?), *Dock*, and *Lotse* 'pilot' (earlier *Lootsmann* < English *loadsman*).

B. THE SOUTHERN TRADING REGION

Crusades and pilgrimages opened the way for trade with the Middle and even Far East, and Venetian merchants had contact with China even before Marco Polo and the Franciscan missionary Odorico de Pordenone travelled there in the thirteenth and fourteenth centuries.[66] German merchants established themselves in Italy—the 'Fondaco dei Tedeschi' on the Rialto is mentioned as early as 1228— and by the sixteenth century they were commuting regularly between the important German fairs, such as that at Frankfurt, and Italian towns like Lucca, Genoa, Florence, and, of course, Venice. These cities were important both as entrepôts and international centres of finance, so banking terminology as well as the names of spices, cloths, and other wares often come into German via Italian—and Italians themselves opened banks in Antwerp and London (cf. Lombardy Street). Medieval loans include *lumparte* 'money-changer' ('Lombard'), *gant* 'auction' (< It. *incanto* from Lat. *in quantum* 'how much?'), *karg, kargo* (< It. *karico* < Lat. *carrus* 'cart'), *bollette* 'customs note' (< It. *bolletta*), *tara* 'weight of goods' (from Arabic *tarḥah*). We may add the names of materials from courtly literature (*ziclât, scharlât, samît*), as well as from the Paumgartner letters (*rottcremasin, futtrattlas, daffat*)—some of which survive (*Scharlachtuch, Samt, Futteratlas* 'half-satin', *Taffet/Taft*). Words ultimately from Arabic and probably transmitted via Italian include *Bazar, Karawane, Magazin* 'store', *Tara* (English *tare weight*), and *Tarif*. Banking and commercial terms which still survive, often in Italian form, are *Bank, Baratt(o)* 'exchange deal' (English *barter*), *ditto, Konto, Konterbande, netto, per cento, Posten* (*Restposten* 'remnants'), *Sporko* (later replaced by *brutto*). Attested after 1500 are *Risiko, Saldo* 'balance', *saldieren, Valuta* 'monetary standard'; after 1600 *Diskonto, franko, frankieren, Giro* 'endorsement', *Kurs* (It. *corso*), *Tratte* 'bill of exchange', *Trassat* 'drawee', *trassieren*. Beside the loan-words are loan-translations or semantic loans: *Wechsel* for It. *cambio*; *Rechnung* for *conto*; *Soll* and *Haben* for *Debet* and *Kredit*. Subsequently, Italian terms are superseded by French ones, themselves sometimes originally Italian. Such technical terms either remain part of commercial language or become established in common usage; sometimes they are restricted to the south, to Swiss or Austrian with their closer associations with Italy. The Italian systems of book-keeping also reinforce their survival, and prompt

German technical treatises like that of the proverbial Adam Riese in the early sixteenth century.

INTELLECTUAL, PHILOSOPHICAL, AND MYSTICAL GERMAN

The OHG *Isidor* translation already shows German confronted with terminological distinctions regarding Christ's person in Trinitarian theological speculation, and copious glossaries from the Early German period amply attest to the value of German in teaching Latin and expounding the Bible and the Church Fathers; Notker of St Gall was its most vigorous champion. Later, vernacular religious verse and prose sermons of the twelfth and thirteenth centuries give glimpses of specialized vocabulary for Christian dogma, a terminology elaborated in vernacular prose translations of works by scholastics like Anselm of Canterbury (1033-1109), Hugh of St Victor (1096-1141), Albertus Magnus (*c*.1206-80), and Thomas Aquinas (1226-74). These translations, and original works in German in the same tradition,[67] are of paramount importance in the development of German Humanist prose and in laying the foundations for German intellectual and philosophical vocabulary: in this respect we cannot talk of a 'linguistic decline' in German after the mid-thirteenth century. Indeed, scholastic German prose was encouraged by the highest circles, and connections between court, chancery, and university are evident in the late fourteenth and early fifteenth centuries, notably at Prague and Vienna. At Prague the Imperial Chancellor Johann von Neumarkt (1310-80) himself translated a pseudo-Augustinian tract (his *Buch der Liebkosung*, *c*.1357-9) and a life of St. Jerome, and his example influenced others, including Johannes von Tepl. At Vienna the Habsburg court promoted German prose: the *Rationale divinorum officiorum* of Guillelmus Durandus (1230-96), a handbook on the rites, was translated for Duke Albrecht III in 1384, and Leopold Stainreuter, an Austin Friar, translated Cassiodorus' *Historia Ecclesiastica tripartita* for him in 1385, while the eminent theologian and university teacher Heinrich von Langenstein (1323-97) wrote his *Erchantnus der sund* (a free rendering of a Latin tract) for Albrecht's son, Albrecht IV.[68]

In the fourteenth century mystical writers of the new mendicant orders, especially Dominicans, use and develop the technical vocabulary of scholastic and theological writings and popularize it through their sermons. Older scholarship tended to emphasize the admittedly striking use of German by Meister Eckhart (*c*.1260–1327) and his pupils Johannes Tauler (*c*.1300–61) and Heinrich Seuse, or Suso (*c*.1295–1366), and credited them with fashioning a German intellectual vocabulary, by creating, *inter alia*, new abstract nouns in *-heit* (*-keit*) and *-ung*; subsequently, it was held, the eighteenth-century Pietists re-employed and passed these terms on to modern philosophers. However, German mysticism's linguistic debt to Latin via German scholastic and theological traditions has now been recognized.[69] Relatively few terms are loan-words, and these recur: *conscienzîe, difinieren, fantasîe, persôn, substanzîe, trinitât*, etc.; instead, loan-translation recasts the Latin formations into German equivalents—this probably also reflects the practice of using German to elucidate the structure of Latin technical terms. Certain suffixes show an almost mechanical correlation: for example, Latin verbal abstracts in *-io* are rendered by forms in *-ung(e)*, while Latin abstracts in *-tas* correspond to German formations in *-heit/-keit/-igkeit*.[70] For example:

ascensio	⟶ aufsteygung	aeternitas	⟶ ewigchait
dominatio	herschung	humilitas	diemuettigchait
inclinatio	naigung	humanitas	menschait
crucifixio	chrewzigung	sanitas	gesunthait
tentatio	vorsuchung	velocitas	snellychait

Prefixes, too, show equivalents in German, e.g. Lat. *com/con-*⟶*mit-* (*conformis = mitformig*; *concordans = mithellend*; *connaturalis = mitnatürlich*), Lat. *sub-/sup-*⟶*under-* (*subjectio = underwerfunge*; *subjectum = underwurf*; *subtractio = underziehunge*), Lat. *super-*⟶ *über-* (*supernaturalis = übernatürlich*; *superfluus = übervlüzzec*), etc., although competing forms are more evident here. At times the links with Latin are not obvious, perhaps because a German term no longer survives, as *widertragung* for Lat. *relatio*, perhaps because of Latin synonymy,[71] as when *înbildunge* translates Lat. *phantasia*, not *imaginatio* which is its close equivalent, or when *wesunge* glosses *substantia* (instead of *essentia*).

Both scholasticism and mysticism involve grammatical (or syntactic) abstraction and semantic abstraction: in syntactic abstraction, abstract nouns subsume the content of sentences or clauses, thus enabling them to be qualified and built into an argument; semantic abstraction is a form of semantic change, where originally concrete nouns acquire abstract meanings, for example *anstôz* 'boundary', *begrif* 'domain', 'area', and *eigenschaft* 'property' come also to mean 'objection', 'concept', and 'characteristic', respectively. However, scholastic, theological writing differs from mystical in intention, and may be described as didactic, expository, and analytical (within the limitations of a scholarship grounded in faith, Augustine's 'credo ut intelligam'), whereas mysticism not only describes religious dogma but seeks to convey the experience of the soul's union with the godhead, the *unio mystica*. Whereas scholastic style prefers *nomina actionis* in *-unge* for its syntactic abstraction, Eckhart increasingly uses the substantivized infinitive, which expresses action/activity more fully, e.g. *daz înstân* (NHG *Einstehen*), *daz însiczen* (NHG *Einsitzen*), *înbilden* (NHG *Einbilden*), *daz wâr haben* (NHG *Wahrhaben*), *ein wol wârnemen* (NHG *Wahrnehmen*), *ûfklimmen* (NHG *Aufklimmen*), and also *daz sîn*—more expressive than *daz wesen* (Lat. *esse*), whose association with the verb was no longer so strong.[72]

Mystical abstract terminology is also at times inconsistent and imprecise: scholastics keep *essentia* (*wesung*) and *esse* (*wesen*) apart in speculating on the unity of God, but mystics sometimes use *wesen* for both. Similarly, the various inner-Trinitarian processes or manifestations are differently treated: scholastics use a restrained, restricted terminology like *ûzgang*(*unge*) for *processio*, mystics prefer more dynamic, emotive words, such as *ûzfluz* (*emanatio*), *ûzbruch*, *ûzblüejen* (images of flowering), and *entgiezunge* (*effusio, diffusio*), etc.[73] German mysticism favours metaphor and its terminology therefore seems 'motivated' less by its Latin sources than by the network of associations found in the native language; for example, a technical term (ultimately from astrology) like *înfluz* (NHG *Einfluß*, Lat. *influentia*) has expressive links with *înfliezen, ûzfliezen, überfluz, überfliezen, zuofliezen*, etc. The literal meanings of the elements even of scholastic terms are 'reactivated' by setting them into a metaphorical context: thus, *erliuhtung* (Lat. *illustratio*) draws richness from the mystical images of light and darkness. (In the nineteenth and twentieth centuries, some philosophical terms are hyphenated for the same purpose, viz., to make us reinterpret them literally, e.g. Martin Heidegger's *Zu-fall* 'befalling', *Zu-kunft* 'the future as coming towards', etc.)

The mystics' attempt to express the inexpressible and perhaps also 'apophatic' (negative) mystical traditions falsely attributed to Dionysius the Areopagite (fifth-century mystical writings) explain the many negative formations in mystical German using affixes like *ent-, niht-, un-, ver-,* and *-lôs: entnemen, entsunkenheit, entwerden, entzücken; nihtheit, nihtsîn, nihtwesen, nihtwizzen; unbegriffenlich, unbekentheit, unwesen, unwizzen; vergân, vergangenheit, versinken; bildelôs, endelôs, grundelôs.* Other characteristics include intensified formations with prefixes *über* (Lat. *super*) (*übernâtûrlich,* Lat. *supernaturalis; überunbegreifenlich,* Lat. *superincomprehensibilis*), and *durch* (Lat. *trans*) (*durchformen; durchklæren* 'utterly elucidate'; *durchschînec,* Lat. *transparens*), and the substantivization of particles (*daz eine; daz al,* NHG *das All; daz wâ,* NHG *das Wo; daz nû,* cf. mod. German *im Nu* 'in a trice').

The transmission of philosophical, intellectual, abstract terminology into mod. German remains to be fully explained. Continuity between medieval mysticism and baroque mysticism provides a basis on which eighteenth-century pietism could build, as illustrated by the history of words like *Bildung, Eindruck, einleuchten, einsehen, rühren,* and *zerstreuen*—although French and English have also considerably influenced German philosophical terms. But with the founding of universities, and given the intellectual connections between university and court observable in fourteenth-century Vienna, it seems probable that some intellectual vocabulary was transmitted within the theology and philosophy faculties. At a more popular level, scholastic and mystical tracts for laymen in the towns—and we know that members of the patricians and artisan circles sometimes owned such works and even left them to monasteries—spread this vocabulary widely, especially after printing came in.

THEORIES OF THE ORIGIN OF MODERN STANDARD GERMAN

The chancery, commercial, scholastic, and mystical forms of German just discussed are deeply indebted to Latin, which was the universal language of European devotion, administration, trade, and intellectual enquiry. While lack of political unity in German-speaking lands and correspondingly strong local traditions impeded the development of a standard German language, the existence of a Latin standard effectively reduced the need for one: the splendid Latinity of the sixteenth century in Germany can indeed be seen as the vindication of Latin's importance as that nation's standard. Centuries elapsed before printing redressed the balance by establishing a HG-based book language (indeed, it was recognized enough by 1650 to inhibit radical innovations).

A. THE PRAGUE CHANCERY THEORY

Konrad Burdach saw the phonological basis for the modern standard language in the royal and imperial chancery at Prague under the Luxemburgs. Here a compromise, artificial *Kunstvokalismus* combined UG Austro-Bavarian diphthongs with MG monophthongs (see above, pp. 112–13); the consonantism had HG forms of the Frk. type (i.e. without velar affricates), and unstressed vowels were preserved or reintroduced (*Restitutionstrieb*) in chancery practice, so limiting apocope and syncope and regulating the language for artistic, rhythmically constructed prose.[74] According to Burdach, Prague's cultural importance during the reign of the Emperor Charles IV (1346–78), and particularly the literary prestige of the Imperial Chancery under Johann von Neumarkt, led other EMG chanceries to emulate it, not merely in style, but in external *habitus*—spellings and forms. Even after Prague's importance for German disappeared in the wake of the Hussite wars, the cultural impetus was still felt on the colonial German chanceries in Meissen, Thuringia, and Silesia, and this EMG language was used by Martin Luther in his translation of the Bible. A line of continuity thus runs from the Imperial Chancery, via the chanceries of the House of Wettin, the ruling dynasty of Saxony, to Martin Luther. The spread of linguistic features is made to depend upon the spread of cultural influence, according to the motto 'Sprachgeschichte ist Bildungsgeschichte', and the most important political and cultural centre, the imperial court, is credited with spreading the NHG type. Similar arguments had been advanced for the formative influence of the Hohenstaufen court on the 'MHG language', and for Charlemagne's court in OHG times: there had been a geographical shift also, first from Frk. to Swabian and thence to EMG/colonial regions.

Objections to Burdach's theory concern firstly the form and role of the Imperial Chancery language and secondly the source of the compromise phonology it supposedly disseminated:

1. According to L. E. Schmitt,[75] spelling in the chancery under Charles IV was not regular: diphthongal graphies ⟨ei⟩ and ⟨au⟩, ⟨eu⟩ alternate with apparently monophthongal ⟨i⟩ and ⟨u⟩.

Moreover, UG spellings tend to occur in documents with an UG connection, notably those written for Nuremberg, and after 1355 WMG features become quite prominent: the seventy-three (NB!) chancery officials came mostly from MG areas, some of them from the western chanceries at Mainz and Trier. Further, the chancery's composition probably remained as under Charles's father, for we have no proof that Charles or Johann von Neumarkt reformed it.

2. In 1437 the Imperial Chancery moved back to Vienna under the Habsburg Emperors Albrecht II (1438-9) and Friedrich III (1440-93) where the language assumed UG, Bav. features, as well as some apparently WMG Mainz characteristics reflecting the chancellorship of Adolph II of Mainz (1471-5).

3. The diphthongization and certain other features claimed as the contribution of the royal imperial Luxemburg Chancery at Prague occur already in the Prague municipal statutes (*Prager Stadtrecht*) (manuscript *c.*1310), and in other town documents as early as 1324.[76]

4. It is further apparent that other EMG chanceries show 'NHG features' from early in the fourteenth century, e.g. at Plauen, Gera, and Eger—indeed, from 1310 onwards the Eger chancery language closely resembles Luther's practice after 1522, i.e. Luther 'follows' orthographical traditions already established 200 years earlier. Similarly, the Saxon and Thuringian chanceries show diphthongs as early as 1325, long before the Imperial Chancery could exert any influence.[77]

So, the Prague Imperial Chancery's language must be set against a broader background of interaction between central and southern German-speaking areas, which the Chancery also reflects without significantly shaping it.

B. THE 'COLONIAL DIALECT' THEORY

Theodor Frings used linguistic geography to examine Rhenish dialects with signal success, viewing them not as static, ethnically conditioned, regionally discrete varieties of language, but as the products of social interaction. Even where no natural barriers (forests or mountains) separated speakers, dialect boundaries or clusters of isoglosses still occurred, revealing an interplay of cultural forces and habits of communication; according to Frings, dialect boundaries and the political and administrative boundaries of the various territories along the Rhine corresponded. Applying the same methods to the eastern dialects, Frings emphasized the spoken, dialectal basis of modern standard German and saw some of its characteristics as representing a mixture found only in central regions of Germany, the result of settlers and colonists from different parts of Germany (from UG, MG, and LG, and even Flemish and Dutch dialect areas) adjusting to each other's different linguistic habits in everyday speech.[78] Although these settlers came from different places and by several routes over a considerable period, they felt common ethnic and linguistic bonds separating them from the Slav native population, and this encouraged German linguistic levelling. The Meissen region mediates also between north and south, and the Wettin dynasty formed a powerful state much larger than the fragmented territorial states of the homelands, with Leipzig as an important trading centre. Intellectually, the *Studium generale* at Erfurt anticipated the founding of the first German universities. Thus, Frings does not merely argue for a *koloniale Mundart* or *Mischsprache* or *Ausgleichssprache*, but looks once more to the formative influence of a political and administrative unit, the territory.

The admixture of features produced according to Frings by linguistic interaction of different dialect speakers in the colonial east includes[79] (1) MG monophthongs with UG diphthongs; (2) the (southern) distinction between accusative and dative pronominal forms, e.g. *mich ≠ mir*, where the north has *me* or *mi* for both; (3) greater preservation of unstressed vowels, written ⟨e⟩ or ⟨i⟩, while UG shows apocope and syncope, e.g. EMG *Johannisbeere*; (4) diminutive suffix -*chen*, rather than LG -*kin* or UG -*lein*, -*li*, -*e(r)l*; (5) southern and eastern pronunciation of ⟨chs⟩ as [ks], e.g. *wachsen*, *sechs*, as against loss of the velar element in Rhenish dialects: *wassen*, *ses*; (6) fully shifted consonants except velar affricates [kχ]; (7) south-eastern forms of the contracted verbs *gên* and *stên*, not *gân*, *stân*. These mixed features provide the dialectal basis for chancery languages in the EMG regions, including the Imperial Chancery at Prague and the Saxon chanceries, and chancery influence on mod. German then comes in through the agency of Luther: Frings also cites a well-known passage from the *Tischreden* (cap. 70) to support the view that Luther followed and helped establish the Saxon chancery form of EMG as standard German. The colonial dialect theory still forms the background to research into chancery and administrative languages of the EMG area carried out by linguists in Russia and the GDR, but it must be modified in the light of several objections:

1. Frings provides little proof of the virtual identity of dialect and written chancery language which his theory implies.[80] Even if the *Ausgleichssprache* is regarded as a colloquial refinement of dialect, an *Umgangssprache* (see Chapter IX), its characteristics are still those of speech, not writing, and they remain inaccessible to direct observation.

2. Underlining this, some features of EMG, e.g. Meissen language of more recent times, are not found in standard modern German: e.g. *klēd* (NHG *Kleid*), *bōm* (NHG *Baum*), *schīn* (NHG *schön*), *tuchter* (NHG *Tochter*), *schlacht* (NHG *schlecht*); intervocalic /g/ is vocalized, palatalization is widespread, and unshifted forms like *appel* occur.[81]

3. The characteristics of NHG used by Frings as indices of the importance of the EMG/Meissen region occurred elsewhere in MG —in Silesia and in the HG areas of East Prussia (now part of Poland and Russia), and also in WMG in the western Rhineland Palatinate (especially at Mainz), and in important EFrk. centres—Nuremberg, Bamberg, and Würzburg.[82]

C. *SCHREIBDIALEKTGEOGRAPHIE*: THEORIES OF REGIONAL INTERACTION OF WRITTEN FORMS OF GERMAN[83]

Recent scholarship has been focusing attention on the regional distribution of linguistic features, orthographical, phonological, morphological, lexical, and syntactic, as they occur in chancery documents and other texts. Precisely because no standard language existed, written and early printed forms of German reflect local traditions—in the first instance local written traditions, then, less clearly, local dialectal features. By comparing texts of a similar kind from different places—ideally, by contrasting manuscripts of the same text which have been written in different areas—we can see where particular spellings and forms occur consistently, persistently, and systematically. Then, having so delineated *Schreiblandschaften* (areas with common written features), we can infer the influence of one area on another. In particular, HG has been encroaching upon the northern LG writing (and speaking) lands since the thirteenth

century—the preacher Berthold von Regensburg says as much—
and later we see a corresponding if less striking influence of UG
on MG, both in the east and in the west. But, as the example of
Magdeburg shows, the issue could be complicated.

Magdeburg in the Elbe/Eastphalian region was LG-speaking and
remained so until the nineteenth century. The town had trading links
and legal ties with the LG area to the north, but Magdeburg was a
Welf possession having administrative connections with Bavaria;
finally, it had diocesan attachments with the archbishopric at Mainz.
These circumstances account for the presence of two types of
documents produced at Magdeburg from the thirteenth century
onwards: (1) a predominantly LG group with a few HG elements,
used mainly for trading affairs; (2) a predominantly HG group with
occasional LG elements, used for mainly ecclesiastical matters. So,
HG was used for documents for particular addressees, the HG
influence predates the decline of the Hanseatic League, and it did not
reflect the town's spoken form.[84]

Taking a wider view, it appears that by the end of the fifteenth
century a number of areas ceased to be contenders for the basis of a
standard German language, whether in writing or speech. The north-
western region shows written characteristics which agree across
several dialect areas—Neth., LG, and LFrk./Ripuarian—but the
Netherlands had already gained political identity and a literary
Dutch was in the ascendant. The south-western region, Switzerland,
also became independent politically in the fifteenth century, and its
dialects remained peripheral to the development of German. The LG
north-east gradually declined in linguistic importance and many
towns went over to HG in chancery, printing-houses, and schools in
the course of the sixteenth and early seventeenth centuries. Effectively, the central German dialect areas EMG and WMG and the UG
dialects of Bav. together with Swabian represent the field of forces in
which the basis of NHG is eventually stabilized.

In his study of a popular devotional tract by Otto of Passau,[85]
Werner Besch suggests plausibly that the main interacting forces
which were to shape modern German lay in EMG and south-east
UG. Sometimes the irrelevance of western areas for this process
emerges clearly, as in the lexical division between *minne* in the west
and *liebe* in the east in the fifteenth century (Besch (1967), Map 54,
pp. 192 ff.): the split undoubtedly reflects the semantic deterioration
of *minne*, which came to mean exclusively 'coitus'. While *minne*

survived along the Rhine in all contexts in the fifteenth century, in the sixteenth the word is given up in favour of *liebe*. Similarly, a syntactic/morphological map (see Map 2) presenting the distribution of weak or strong adjective declension after the indefinite article *ein/ain* reveals the eastern and south-eastern written forms as progressive with the strong declension: *ain siecher, ain blinder* (NHG *ein Kranker, ein Blinder*); this is the construction which becomes established in the modern standard language, while the weak declension (*sieche, blinde*) was in any case vulnerable to the apocope and does not survive. We shall consider Luther's role in the development of mod. German later (Chapter V), but he remains for Besch an important reference point: Luther's (and/or his printers') usage can be set against the background of regional linguistic interaction at the close of the fifteenth century on the one hand, and against the established modern language on the other. Luther, then, seems to be caught up in processes of assimilation between EMG and UG which he can further but not oppose: his usage sometimes changes, and he adopts south-eastern UG forms, e.g. he gives up MG *brengen, quam, werlt,* and *dwingen/twingen* in favour of UG (often both south-western and south-eastern) *bringen, kam, welt, zwingen.*[86]

But in western areas, too, MG 'dialects' show southern influence, and Rhenish texts show the sloughing off of local forms like *dat, geven, ses, off, he, as* in favour of southern forms *das, geben, sechs, oder, er, als,*[87] and more work needs to be done on this and on the role of WMG at the turn of the sixteenth century.

Even in the twelfth century the UG literary dialects had shared many features, and Swabian and Bav. written forms remained close, although lack of the new diphthongization split off Alem. By 1500 southern regional orthographies are sufficiently close in the choice and distribution of graphies—and in vocabulary—to be regarded as sub-systems of potentially the 'same' graphemic and linguistic system, which was only in the process of emerging, 'Schriftdialekte einer (noch) nicht realisierten Schriftsprache'.[88] This is not to say that the southern dialects already constituted a regional standard language, for many variables persist; nor need the chanceries of Emperor Maximilian I or important printing centres like Augsburg be stressed as the focal points of any UG standard, since this involves making connections which remain to be confirmed by analysis.[89] Finally, the label *gemaine teutsch* attested sporadically from the late fourteenth century onwards cannot be convincingly interpreted as

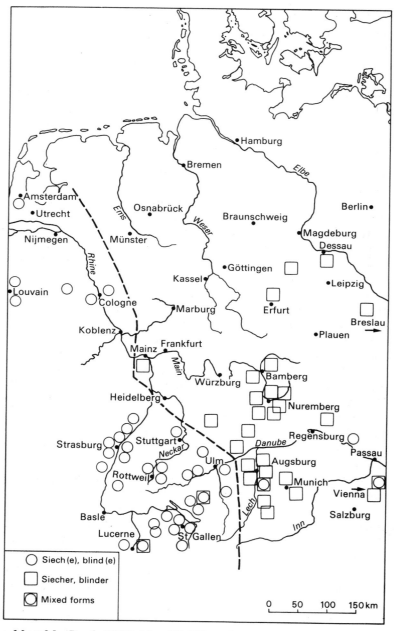

Sankt Gallen labels within figure:

Hamburg

Bremen

Amsterdam
•Utrecht
Nijmegen   Osnabrück
Münster   Braunschweig   Berlin•

Elbe

Weser

Ems

Rhine

•Göttingen   Magdeburg
Dessau

Louvain   Cologne   Kassel•   •Leipzig

Koblenz   Marburg   Erfurt   Breslau →

Mainz   Frankfurt
Plauen•

Main

Würzburg   Bamberg

Heidelberg•   Nuremberg

Strasburg   Stuttgart•   Regensburg   Passau
Neckar   Danube

Rottweil•   Ulm   Augsburg
Munich
Vienna →

Basle•   Salzburg
Lucerne   St Gallen   Lech   Inn

○ Siech (e), blind (e)

□ Siecher, blinder

◎ Mixed forms

0   50   100   150 km

MAP 2 [= Besch (1967), Map 87]. Fifteenth-century distribution of the
adjective declension after *ein/ain*

referring to a southern standard: in translations it is used to mean 'vernacular'; stylistically it denotes plain, everyday language as opposed to ornate Latinate prose or verse; otherwise, the phrase is not clearly used of any specific form of German, nor illustrated with examples.[90]

Nevertheless, the Imperial *Hofkanzlei* of Maximilian I does seem to have influenced the Electoral Saxon Chancery in the first quarter of the sixteenth century, as is shown by this chancery's adoption of the UG graphy ⟨ai⟩ for ⟨ei⟩, as in the suffix -*hait*; of UG suffix -*nus(s)* for MG -*nis(s)*; and negative particle *nit* for *nicht*.[91] But this does not prove even that the Imperial Chancery was the most influential form of written UG, let alone that an UG norm originated there: after all, the Elector Frederick of Saxony had been *Hof-marschall* in 1497–8 when the Imperial Chancery was reformed, and he was regent (*Reichsverweser*) after Maximilian's death in 1519— both of which might account for the presence of UG chancery features in Saxony. Moreover, in keeping with their importance and the scale of their business, both the Imperial and the Saxon Electoral Chanceries avoid local features occurring in lesser chanceries, and they are in this respect supra-regional. Indeed, Luther may even have been justified in maintaining that the Emperor Maximilian and the Elector Frederick the Wise had 'pulled German into a common form' (see below, p. 198), but this common form is not described, and need not have been identical with what we subsequently regard as NHG: rather, Luther recognizes the need for some standard vehicle of communication and seeks it in the interaction of the two most important chanceries of his time. In this he was out of date: the true standardizers of the external form of German were the printers, who perpetuated on much increased scale the assimilatory processes found in all chanceries.[92] For chanceries (and also the printing-houses themselves) reveal in microcosm the assimilation of linguistic variables which we encountered in the early monastic scriptoria; similar processes are discernible in documents and texts produced in towns and, wider still, across regions with differing written norms. While all spoken communication necessarily involves the control and adaptation of variables at all linguistic levels, comparable adjustments are also detectable in written data for periods un-trammelled by any fixed written standard.

So, by the end of the fifteenth century we find chancery norms comprising bands of variation,[93] the most extreme features of which are progressively reduced in frequency as chancery and other written/printed norms themselves function as the variables of a higher, 'standard', German in the process of crystallizing out. In the sixteenth century the explosion of printed material hastened this development, but on the other hand the lack of political (and then of religous) unity impeded it, as did the continued use of Latin for important political and administrative purposes. At first printers must have followed chancery traditions, but by the mid-sixteenth century the printers had overtaken chanceries and had developed house styles of their own. The authority of chanceries was still cited in discussion regarding linguistic norms, but their standardizing role was played out, and instead they were increasingly adduced as examples of poor style.

SELECT BIBLIOGRAPHY

STUDIES OF MEDIEVAL GERMAN LITERATURE

Bertau (1972–3).
Brandt (1971).
De Boor (1949/1979).
De Boor (1953/1979).
De Boor (1962/1973).
Ehrismann (1932).
Eis (1971).

Glier (forthcoming).
Michael (1971).
Salmon (1967).
Schottmann (1971).
Verfasserlexikon (1978–   ).
Walshe (1962).

GENERAL STUDIES OF MEDIEVAL GERMAN LANGUAGE

Besch (1973).
Burger (1980).
Eggers (1963–77) [esp. (1965), (1969)].

Härd (1973).
Lindgren (1973).
Objartel (1980).
Schieb (1970).

READERS AND ANTHOLOGIES

De Boor (1965).
Oksaar (1965).
Walshe (1974).

Wentzlaff-Eggebert and Wentzlaff-Eggebert (1971) [with useful bibliography to the many texts cited].

Both Oksaar (1965) and Walshe (1974) contain useful potted grammars and linguistic notes on selected passages.

ELEMENTARY GRAMMATICAL INTRODUCTIONS

(For the main grammars, see the Select Bibliography to Chapter IV.)

Asher (1967).

De Boor and Wisniewski (1969).

Gärtner and Steinhoff (1976).

Helm (1980).

Saran (1930/1975).

Weinhold (1881/1965) [rev. Ehrismann and Moser].

FACSIMILES/PALAEOGRAPHY

The series 'Litterae. Göppinger Beiträge zur Textgeschichte' (1971–) provides facsimiles for many important texts.

The series 'Deutsche Texte in Handschriften', vol. ii (1964–5), has a facsimile of MS B of Hartmann von Aue's *Iwein* (c.1200), which corresponds closely to 'classical MHG'.

Specimens of scripts are represented in Paul (1881/1969) [most recent edn. by Grosse (1982)].

Bischoff (1979a).   Petzet and Glauning (1910–30).

DICTIONARIES

Benecke, Müller, and Zarncke (1854–61) [= BMZ; difficult for the beginner, since it is set out according to etymological roots].

Lexer (1872–8) [acts as an index to BMZ and contains supplementary material].

Lexer (1879/1961) [a useful compact version of the above].

CHAPTER IV

THE MORPHOLOGY OF MEDIEVAL GERMAN (MHG)

Die Morphologie soll die Lehre von der Gestalt, der
Bildung und Umbildung der organischen Körper enthalten . . .

(Goethe, Nachlaß, 'Physiologie und ihre Hülfwissen-
schaften. Betrachtung über Morphologie überhaupt',
c.1795 [Stuttgart edn. (1959), xviii. 658])

In linguistics morphology is the study of the internal structure of
words viewed in isolation from their relationships in the sentence,
which is the province of syntax.[1] While *derivational morphology*
treats the formal links between etymologically related words, such as
Tag, täglich, vertagen, betagt, tagaus tagein, and the analogical
creation of new vocabulary[2] based on existing words or those
borrowed from other languages, *inflexional morphology* orders the
formal properties of words according to paradigms showing their
conjugation and declension. In what follows, we concentrate on
inflexional morphology, using examples drawn from the normalized
grammars of MHG, supplemented occasionally from contemporary
sources.

The nature and structure of the 'word' depends also upon the type
of language to which it belongs. A traditional linguistic typology
distinguishes languages according to whether their structure is predominantly isolating, agglutinating, or inflecting. Isolating languages, like Ancient Chinese, show invariant and unanalysable

words which do not combine with each other; agglutinating languages, like Turkish, use complex grammatical forms created by the addition of suffixes which remain identifiable and segmentable; inflecting languages—the class to which German belongs—resemble agglutinating languages in having complex, 'synthetic' forms, but individual inflexions are not readily segmentable and they may have several grammatical functions. German, like other IE languages (notably the Romance group), increasingly discards inflexions, and the medieval language already shows a considerable reduction of the endings found in OHG texts. This process was seen as 'decay' by earlier scholars, who regarded inflexional richness as both admirable and organic. We shall see how syntax played an important role in the structural changes in German morphology,[3] so that grammatical categories once conveyed by endings are now indicated periphrastically, by phrases and particles.

Traditionally, the formal properties of words in inflecting languages are presented in paradigms, or patterns for conjugation and declension. The earliest full grammars of German from the late sixteenth century do this, following the often inappropriate model of classical Latin grammars, and listing, for example, case-forms like the vocative or ablative which were not formally present in German at all—Gottsched in the eighteenth century still shows them. But although the paradigms of the grammar books are constructs of grammarians[4] not occurring naturally in language, they conveniently summarize the syntactic relationships contracted by the words belonging to them, and comparison of paradigms from different periods permits us to present models of syntactic change as well as changes in the morphology of individual words. Moreover, speakers must be aware of some paradigmatic patterns in German, since they have extended those patterns to loan-words, neologisms, and even to words long in the language which have then changed their inflexion; these analogical processes will be discussed later (see below, pp. 155 ff.).

MORPHEMES AND TYPES OF MORPH

In analysing German and other languages with many forms which are not segmentable into separate elements according to meaning and function, morpheme theory helps to distinguish between the problem structures that actually occur and the regularities which underlie them. Like all '-emic' units the morpheme is an abstraction, and it may be defined as the 'minimal unit of grammatical analysis'[5] and as 'the minimum meaningful unit of which the language is composed'.[6] Morphemes are of several kinds: lexical morphemes or lexemes, which in the case of verbs or nouns correspond to the recurrent meaning-bearing element customarily called the 'root'; and grammatical morphemes, such as inflexions, which are functional elements qualifying lexemes. Morphemes are represented in utterances by morphs, just as phonemes are represented by phones, and here a distinction is sometimes made between free morphs, which can occur on their own (these often correspond to lexemes), and bound morphs, such as suffixes, inflexions, prefixes, etc., which are normally never spoken alone.[7]

Morpheme Level (abstract)

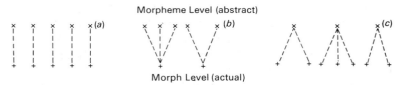

Morph Level (actual)

(a) Isomorphism, an exact correspondence between segmentable morphs and morphemes

(b) More morphemes than segmentable morphs, hence 'portmanteau morphs'

(c) More morphs than morphemes, hence 'discontinuous morphs'

FIG. 5

Three relationships between morphemes and morphs[9] are shown in Fig. 5, depending upon whether the same number, too few, or too many, morphs are discernible in the forms which occur in speech or writing. Past-tense forms from mod. German illustrate the possibilities: the preterites *liebte* and *flog* and the perfect form *ist geflogen* are analysable in terms of 'idea + completion', and have partially similar distribution, e.g. occurring in contexts with an adverb of past time, like *gestern, vor drei Wochen*. Using braces for the morphemes:

Morphemes	{LIEBEN} + {PAST}	{FLIEGEN} + {PAST}	{FLIEGEN} + {PAST}
Morphs	*lieb- te*	*flog*	*ist ge-flog-en*

Treating *flog* as a 'portmanteau morph' containing the reflexes of more than one morpheme is only one of several possible interpretations to account for the difference between this strong verb pret. form and that of the weak verb, *lieben*.[10] The perfect-tense form *ist geflogen* shows several morphs which signal {PAST}, namely the auxiliary verb morph *ist*, the prefix *ge-*, suffix *-en*, and the change of root vowel, *-flog-* (< *flieg-*).[11] These morphs are discontinuous, i.e. separated by other morphs, and even by whole phrases: 'Er *ist* am Freitag nach Hannover *geflogen*.' Discontinuous morphs bring us again to the boundaries between morphology and syntax. Moreover, the relations between morpheme and morph levels can be placed into chronological perspective to give three types of morphological change, again paralleling the phonological changes discussed earlier (Chapter II), namely (1) no change: isomorphism remains; (2) morphological merger: two or more morphemes cease to be distinguishable as morphs; (3) morphological split: morphemes are represented by several morphs in later stages of the language. The history of German morphology shows a reduction in the number and use of synthetic forms and an increase in the use of discontinuous morphs to show grammatical relationships: in other words, grammatical relationships are increasingly conveyed by syntax. A presentation of morphology in paradigmatic guise fails to do justice to the syntactic realization of morphemic relationships, but does convey successfully the reduction of marked forms available in any particular declensional or conjugational class. Indeed, the absence of marking can itself be functional within a paradigm, as often in mod. German number-marking, where the presence of a pl. ending contrasts with the absence of ending in the sg. The curious 'zero morph' (∅) is sometimes used to represent this, e.g. in contrasting the mod. German nom. sg. *die Frau*+∅ with the nom. pl. *die Frau*+*en*.[12]

Individual morphemes may be realized by several morphs, depending upon phonetic, lexical, and 'morphological' factors: such variant morphs are called 'allomorphs', for they have the same grammatical function and, like allophones (see Chapter II), they are not in opposition to one another. The weak verb pret. in both medieval and mod. German shows phonetically conditioned allomorphy. In MHG weak verbs with long roots ('root' here means the recurrent lexical morph), i.e. root syllables containing a long vowel, diphthong, or a short vowel followed by several consonants, formed their pret. in the suffix *-te*; the rest, i.e. weak verbs with short root syllable, added the longer form *-ete*, e.g.:

MHG (*a*) Long root syllable + *-te*	(*b*) Short root syllable + *-ete*[13]
kêren (NHG *kehren*) →*kêrte*	*denen* (NHG *dehnen*) →*denete*
teilen →*teilte*	*loben* →*lobete*
schicken →*schicte*	*nern* (NHG *nähren*) →*nerete*

In mod. German, the 'same' pret. allomorphs *-te* ~ *-ete* are distributed not according to the preceding root length but according to the consonant they follow: where the root ends in a dental stop (*-t/-d*) the longer allomorph occurs.

NHG (*a*) *schöpfen*→*schöpfte*	(*b*) *arbeiten*→*arbeitete*
löschen →*löschte*	*leuchten*→*leuchtete*
leben →*lebte*	*reden* →*redete*

Lexically conditioned allomorphy occurs in the varied pl. formation of nouns in MHG and mod. German: the allomorphs are phonetically dissimilar, as the following nom. pl. forms show:

MHG *bogen*	*buoch*	*geste*	*kleit*
NHG *Bogen/Bögen*	*Bücher*	*Gäste*	*Kleider*

MHG *tage*	*ûven*	*veter*
NHG *Tage*	*Uhus*	*Väter*

These plurals show segmentable morphs like *-e*, *-er*, *-en*, *-n*, *-s*, zero morphs as in *Bogen*, *buoch*, *kleit*, and non-segmentable morphs involving either mutation alone, as in *veter*, *Väter*, *Bögen*,[14] or mutation and a suffix *-e* or *-er*, as in *geste*, *Gäste*, and *Bücher*. The non-segmentable morphs could also be treated as segmentable in the case of mutation and suffix *-er*, since the lexical morpheme or 'root' always mutates if it has a mutatable vowel, *a*, *o*, *au*: e.g. *Mann/ Männer*, *Loch/Löcher*, *Haus/Häuser*. Difficulty arises with mutation and suffix *-e*—compare *Tag/Tage*, *Gast/Gäste*; *Land/Lande* (*die Niederlande*), *Hand/Hände*—for here the choice of unmutated or mutated root form is not predictable; nor is it with derivational suffixes: compare *täglich* ≠ *gastlich*; *ländlich* ≠ *handlich*. This perplexing plurality of pl. forms probably reflects the relatively late emergence of a German standard language, whereas other languages, like English and Dutch, have regularized one main pl. formation. The mod. German noun plurals must be learned by native speaker and foreigner alike, although some patterns are partially linked to gender:

thus, *umlaut* + *-er* does not mark fem. nouns, and *umlaut* + *-e* is not found with neuter nouns—except *Chöre* and *Flöße*[15] (both old masculines).

Morphologically conditioned allomorphy occurs in the ending of the third person sg. in strong verbs, where the present-tense form shows the person morph *-t* (*er sitzt, gibt, steigt*) vs. zero in the pret. tense-form (*er saß, gab, stieg*).[16]

Finally, just as homonyms are words that sound the same but have different meanings, *homonymous morphs* sound the same but have different functions: in mod. German the *-er* morphs appear in comparison of adjectives/adverbs, noun plurals, and in particle and adj. inflexion, e.g. *klein/kleiner als, Kind/Kinder, das Gejohle kleiner Kinder*. Homonymous morphs are especially interesting for the historian of German who traces their development in different periods and places (see below, pp. 150–2).

MEDIEVAL DECLENSION AND EARLIER MODELS

Disregarding prefixes, suffixes, and determinative infixes, the PIE nouns and adjectives are reconstructed with a tripartite structure consisting of (1) the *root*, the semantic core of the word, (2) the *stem-forming element*, usually a vowel or consonant which functions as a paradigmatic marker, (3) the *inflexional ending*, which conveys the word's syntactical relationship to other words in the sentence. In structural terminology, (1) is the lexeme, (2) the class morpheme and (3) the inflexional morpheme: since the PIE and PGmc. forms are reconstructions, they share certain 'ideal' features of deep structures and are readily segmentable. However, in some case-forms the thematic vowel and the inflexional vowel fuse; in other words, PIE and PGmc. forms are partly agglutinating (and hence segmentable into 'morphs') and partly inflecting. Compare:

PIE *$dhog^wh$-/-o-   /-s   →PGmc. *dag-/-a-   /-z   'day' (nom. sg.)

    root   /theme/ending   root /theme/ending

    $dhog^wh$-/-ōs (< *o* + *es*)   → *dag-/-ōs*   'days' (nom. pl.)

The various stem-forming elements (including lack of a theme, a zero morph) classify the nouns and also mark their gender, since not all classes comprised all three genders. The IE proto-languages's eight cases (nom., voc., acc., gen., dat., abl., loc., and instr.) and three numbers (sg., pl., and dual (referring to two objects)) imply a possible twenty-four distinct case-forms in the noun and adj. paradigms; however, even in IE the system displayed reduction and remodelling, hence difficulties are encountered in its reconstruction. The PIE declensions are classified according to their 'stems', where 'stem' = 'root + stem-forming vowel or consonant'. Some grammarians of PGmc. and OHG also adopted this practice, even though stem classes are difficult to identify from those stages, since the morphology had eroded considerably as a result of the removal of primary stress from inflexional syllables in PGmc. The principal stem classes for nouns (and adjectives) in PGmc. are held to be:

(1) *a* stems with 'diphthongal' subclasses in *-ja* and *-wa*: this class comprised masc. and neut. nouns;
(2) *ō* stems with 'diphthongal' subclasses in *-jō* and *-wō*: this class contained only feminines;
(3) *i* stems: originally comprising nouns of all genders, but neuters are not attested for German;[17]
(4) *u* stems: nouns of all three genders, but only residually neuters;
(5) *iz/az* stems: only neuters;
(6) *-n* stems, possibly with subclasses *-jan/-jōn/-īn*:[18] the class contained all three genders;
(7) minor consonantal classes.

These classes in Gmc. show some erosion: the dual number disappeared, apart from traces in pronominal forms, and only five cases (nom., acc., gen., dat., and in some dialects—including OHG— instr.) survive, and even these can derive from several different PIE morphemes: for example, PGmc. dat. sg. often reflects the form of the PIE locative case. Comparing the masc. *a*-stem declension for adj. and noun in PGmc. and OHG and MHG we find that eight different constructed forms of the adj. and nine of the noun are reduced in OHG to seven for the adj. and seven for the noun; by MHG the number of homonymous morphs has so increased that six distinct forms of the adj. and only four of the noun remain (Table 9).[19] While the nom. sg. PGmc. **dag-a-z* still shows tripartite structure with lexical, stem, and inflexional morphs, the OHG and MHG forms preserve only the reflexes of the PGmc. root, the other morphemes not being represented in the noun itself: OHG *tag* + $\emptyset$ + $\emptyset$, MHG *tac* + $\emptyset$ + $\emptyset$.

The primary stress accent had been 'free', or mobile, in PIE, shifting position in the paradigm of any given word, but in late PGmc. it became fixed on the initial syllable of words (usually the root), and unstressed syllables largely disappeared unless they were protected by following consonants or contained long vowels or diphthongs. Syntactic constraints on loss of inflexions may also have existed, since a convincing reconstruction of the vocalic system of inflexional syllables of late PGmc. actually shows more vowel oppositions than the stressed, or root, syllables, suggesting that the inflexions were more important syntactically.[20]

TABLE 9

	PGmc.		OHG		MHG	
Singular:						
nom.	*langaz	*dagaz	lang/langer	**tag**	lanc/**langer**	**tac**
acc.	*langanōm	*dagam	langan	**tag**	**langen**	**tac**
gen.	*langesa	*dagesa	langes	tages	langes	tages
dat.	*langezmō	*dagai	langemu	tage	langem	**tage**
instr.	—	*dagō	—	tagu	—	—
Plural:						
nom.	*langai	*dagōs	**lange**	taga	**lange**	**tage**
acc.	*langanz	*daganz	**lange**	taga	**lange**	**tage**
gen.	*langaizōm	*dagōm	langero	tago	**langer**(e)	**tage**
dat.	*langaimz	*dagamz	langēm	tagum	**langen**	tagen

Morphologically, the fixing of the stress accent meant a shift of the morpheme boundary, turning tripartite forms into bipartite ones, usually distinguishable as the recurrent lexical morph and an inflexional morph. Since the thematic or stem morphemes are no longer distinguishable as morphs, nouns change their declensional patterns, and minor paradigms, like that of the u stems, virtually disappear. Beside such 'inter-paradigmatic merger', the loss of case morphs within individual paradigms leads to 'intra-paradigmatic merger'; for example, nom. and acc. case-forms are distinct only in the sg. of masc. and fem. 'weak' nouns.[21] This loss of morphological distinctions can be linked to syntactic tendencies, like the growth of analytical constructions with particles, demonstrative pronouns, articles, prepositions, or marked forms of the adj. Since particles, pronouns and adjectives were not marked for nom. $\neq$ acc. opposition in the neut. sg. of any paradigm, nor in the pl., word order too must have been becoming increasingly 'grammatical', with the order Subject–Verb–Object (SVO) the norm, and OVS a stylistic variant possible with marked pronouns, weak nouns in the sg., or where intonation or context made the meaning clear. These discontinuous means of conveying syntactic relationships can only have reduced the importance of synthetic morphology still further, particularly where so many ambiguous forms existed.

THE WEAKENING OF INFLEXIONAL SYLLABLES IN LATE OHG

The noun classes in the texts of the Early German period are already unstable, with many words declining according to several different patterns.[22] A considerable weakening of inflexional and other unstressed syllables becomes apparent in texts of the eleventh century and becomes general, except in Alem., by the thirteenth. As the strong adj. and noun paradigms have already shown (Table 9), the full vocalic endings still found in OHG are reduced to a short mid vowel of indeterminate quality, approximately [ə], written ⟨e⟩, with a loss of marked case-forms, from seven to four; the weak noun was similarly reduced to only two forms, e.g. *boto* (masc.) 'messenger':

	OHG	MHG
Singular:		
nom.	*boto*	*bote*
acc.	**boton/-un**	**boten**
gen.	**boten/-in**	**boten**
dat.	**boten/-in**	**boten**
Plural:		
nom.	**boton/-un**	**boten**
acc.	**boton/-un**	**boten**
gen.	*botôno*	**boten**
dat.	*botôm*	**boten**

The weakening undoubtedly occurred in speech earlier than in writing; it is differently distributed in the early monastery dialects, and may also be linked to the spread of mutation, which itself becomes morphemic, separating in the root syllables pl. forms from sg. ones or subj. from ind. in the verbs. Nevertheless, the overall tendency is clear, viz. loss of oppositions in inflexional syllables.[23]

The reasons for the weakening remain obscure: the fixing of stress in PGmc. times is surely too remote in time, although it may have triggered imbalance in the morphology. The accentual differences between northern and southern German dialects are little understood for this period, while local spelling traditions may seem to preserve vowel qualities which had actually been weakened: Alem. texts continue to show a range of different vowel spellings in unstressed syllables as late as the fourteenth and fifteenth centuries.[24] An amusing (late thirteenth-century?) inscription from the wall of Oberzell church on the island of Reichenau shows an alternation of graphies ⟨e⟩ and ⟨v⟩ for unstressed vowels:

Ich wil hie shribvn | Von disen tvmben wibvn | Was hie wirt pla pla gvsprochvn | v̈ppiges in der wochvn | das wirt allvs wol gvdaht | so es wirt für den rihtvr braht.

THE MEDIEVAL GERMAN APOCOPE

A third phase of the reduction of inflexions is the medieval apocope, or loss of final syllables, which begins in Bav. in the thirteenth century (see pp. 113–14). In verse, elision and metre can favour reduced forms, but some inflexions were unstable anyway: the morph -e tended to drop after monosyllabic roots ending in -l and -r, and after polysyllabic roots ending in -el/-er/-em/-en.[25] The apocope reached Switzerland relatively late, as the following document from July 1251, relating to the rights of carters to hew wood, shows.

Wiſzen alle die diſen brief an geſehent · daz die wagenere von lintal · so ſi gedingent di dingen wellent · iergilich mit din probiſte von lutenbach · oldir mit ſinen bottinn · howen mŏgint ſweſ ſi bidorfint nv̈we wagene ze machinde · vnde nehein andir holz · ſcvzzent dir ſleiffin diz wartpuhilſ vndir michilun ſulzpach · vndi niman andire an diſ probiſtiſ vn diſ capitelſ vrlop. Wan die zi lutinbach geſezzin ſint die bi furint ſich mit dobime holze andimi wartpuhile. Di nuwe mulin du zi lintal gimachit waſ · wart mit rechte abe gebrochen · vñ ſol nieman da diheine machen an diſ probiſtiſ willen vn diſ capitelſ.[26]

Let all who see this document know that the waggoners of Lintal, if those who wish to do so negotiate individually with the provost of Lutenbach or his agents, can hew what they shall need to make new carts, and no other wood, between the track of the look-out hill and the great salt beck (place-names), and no one else without leave of the provost and chapter. For, those dwelling at Lutenbach take firing-wood from the aforementioned wood on the look-out hill. The new mill erected at Lintal was justly demolished, and none shall make another there without the will of the provost and chapter . . .

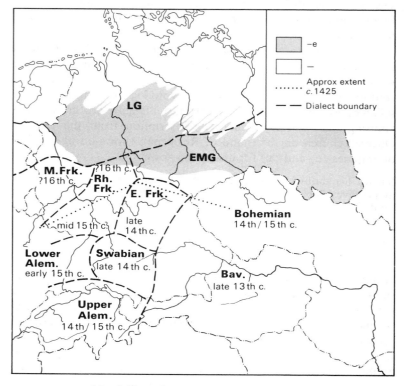

MAP 3. Upper German apocope (after Lindgren)

According to Lindgren,[27] by about 1425 the whole of the southern half of the German-speaking area had lost final unstressed -*e* in many forms (Map 3). Leaving aside details, the vulnerability of an inflexion apparently varies according to its function: as a number-marker the unstressed final vowel shows more resistance to loss than as a case-marker. Adjectives and pronouns tend to preserve it, since the nom. and acc. of all genders need it to mark the pl., while adverbs, by contrast, regularly lose the ending (OHG -*o*, MHG -*e*), so merging with the endingless forms of the adj. when used predicatively: formal distinctions between adj. and adv. have thus been replaced by distributional and functional ones.[28] Indeed, final -*e* becomes so unstable as to be added to forms that historically lacked it, which also

confuses the morphology. Certainly, early grammarians find unstressed final -e difficult to describe, and only after Martin Opitz
does poetic theory cope with it successfully.

The three phases of inflexional reduction (the PGmc. fixing of
stress on initial syllable, the late OHG weakening, and the medieval apocope) show the interconnection of morphology and syntax.
The phonological weakening and the emergence of an analytical
morphology by syntactic means like word order, periphrasis, and
particles are probably inseparable and simultaneous processes: no
priority need be assigned to either one. But in the nineteenth century phonological change was often blamed for the decay of morphology and for wreaking havoc with paradigms.[29] Limits were set
to the extent of the damage by the *Sprachgefühl* of the speakers, that
is, by their consciousness of the derivational and syntactic functions
of individual elements (i.e. morphemes) of the word: functionally
important elements escape loss. For Hermann Paul, the principle of
analogy repairs and restructures paradigms affected by sound
change, and is a fundamental factor in language.[30] His view of the
paradigm is a dynamic one—as an abstraction based on the syntactic
uses of the forms it contains. Speakers do not simply reproduce forms
from paradigms they have learned but instead create those forms by
reference to basic paradigms using their powers of combination.
Only the forms of a limited number of words need to be learned for
the speaker to be able to predict/'generate' the forms of other such
paradigms for any given word. It is immaterial if the new forms
contradict those usual hitherto, so long as the speakers themselves
remain unaware of any contradiction. Trouble naturally arises when
a word's 'ambiguous' shape qualifies it for membership of several
classes, so that its constituent forms may be constructed according to
different patterns. Which pattern predominates depends upon the
balance of power (*Machtverhältnis*) holding between the patterns
themselves, depending upon their frequency, number of members,
and so forth.[31] Analogy, then, may even further linguistic change,
although it can oppose the chaos threatened by sound change, acting
as a regulator to create a new equilibrium.

Combining a functional and analogical approach: syntactically
redundant elements, in this case certain inflexional morphs, are
allowed to weaken and disappear, others form the basis for the
development of new patterns, as illustrated in the MHG noun and
adj. paradigms.

THE DECLENSIONAL MORPHOLOGY (1050-1500)

The growth of homonymous morphs in noun and adj. classes and the medieval apocope greatly reduced the available differentiated inflexional syllables in many paradigms. Consequently, analytical syntax conveys linguistic relationships by particles qualifying the noun and by the use of stable, if homonymous, morphs which are bound to 'particles' (e.g. definite and indefinite article, pronoun, or strong adj.) in various combinations. Despite the radical recasting of its morphology, mod. German retains case, gender, and number, although (except for the pl.) these grammatical categories are signalled not in the noun itself but rather in the noun phrase.

In the nouns of medieval German number was subordinate to case, and many paradigms fail, for example, to distinguish sg. from pl. in their nom. and acc. case-forms.[32] But number is increasingly marked in the form of the noun itself, while its case and gender are shown discontinuously in particles. Two stages may be discerned: (1) the merging of originally separate paradigmatic classes; (2) the extension and redistribution of clearly marked pl. forms to create distinctions of number. At a time before grammarians were codifying German, morphological reshaping resulted from the naïve, though not entirely unconscious, analogical creation of new forms by the speakers. Two important factors are 'paradigmatic pull' (*Formzwang*) and 'paradigmatic push'.

Paradigmatic pull covers the merging of paradigms where the similarity of forms in one paradigm to those of another permits the analogical development of variant declensions, e.g. in strong and weak fem. nouns:

	MHG fem. ō stem	weak *n* stem
Singular:		
nom.	**gebe**	**zunge**
acc./gen./dat.	*gebe*	*zungen*
Plural:		
nom./acc.	*gebe*	*zungen*
gen./dat.	**geben**	**zungen**

Three overlapping forms, nom. sg. and gen. and dat. pl., probably sufficed for weak nouns to develop strong alternatives and vice versa; in this particular merger no change of gender has occurred. Eventually final -*n* disappeared from the sg. of these fem. nouns, giving a new pattern of historically 'strong' sg. as opposed to 'weak' pl.; NHG *Frau* ≠ *Frauen* belongs to this 'mixed declension'. Even strong singulars could be reformed: MHG *mülene* from Lat. *molina* 'mill' lost final *-e* after nasal (cf. *mulin* in the document on p. 153), and the new pattern *mül(e)* ≠ *mülen* appears: NHG *Mühle* ≠ *Mühlen*. Masc. nouns of the old *a*-stem and *i*-stem classes show a similar merger based on shared forms (indeed, complete identity in the case of *i* stems whose vowel could not mutate). The subset of masc. *i*-stem nouns showing mutation already had a marked sg. ≠ pl. opposition, and this was generalized especially in those southern regions where apocope prevented pl. marking, e.g. where *tage* became *tag*[l].

MHG	masc. *a* stems		masc. *i* stems	
Singular:				
nom./acc.	*tac*	*visch*	*tisch*	*balc*
gen.	*tages*	*visches*	*tisches*	*balges*
dat.	*tage*	*vische*	*tische*	*balge*
Plural:				
nom./acc./gen.	*tage*	*vische*	*tische*	*belge*
dat.	*tagen*	*vischen*	*tischen*	*belgen*

Curiously, although the UG south has a more restricted 'phonetic' mutation in the Early German period, it makes more extensive use of mutation as a morphological (i.e. morphemic) marker, and Alem. and Austro-Bavarian show many analogical pl. formations that have not been adopted into modern standard German, both in the colloquial (*Umgangssprachen*) e.g. *Ärme, Bsüech* (NHG *Besucher*), *Brünnen, Hünd, Pünkt(e), Täg, Wägen*,[33] and in dialects, e.g. *Stä* from *Stā*, for standard *Steine* ≠ *Stein*.[34]

Paradigmatic push is harder to illustrate, since it operates only in particular contexts, namely, where an ambiguous form from a particular paradigm is recast according to a different paradigm in order to clarify the syntax: the growth of marked noun plurals we have just discussed probably partly reflects this process of 'disambiguating' utterances. Early morphological reshaping in the strong adj. declension may be another instance. For the adj. declension, although parallel to the nominal, adopted certain endings from the pronominal declension in OHG (and Gothic), so preserving case distinctions lost in the noun itself, and distinguishing German from other dialects in the WGmc. group, like English, which did not introduce such forms and lost their case morphology.[35] In MHG the strong adj. forms are as follows in the nom. and acc. sg.:

	masculine	feminine	neuter
nom. (1)	*guot* (*man*)	*guot* (*frouwe*)	*guot* (*kint*)
nom. (2)	*guoter*	*guotiu*	*guotez*
acc. (1)	—	—	*guot*
acc. (2)	*guoten*	(*guote*)	*guotez*

The endingless forms are the old nominal ones based for masc. and neuter on the PGmc. *a* stems and for the fem. on the *ō* stems, the inflected forms (apart from fem. acc. *guote*) are pronominal. At first endingless and pronominal forms coexist, but the latter become obligatory in certain attributive uses, while in mod. German the nominal forms are choice, archaic, or proverbial: 'ein gut Teil der Leute', 'gut Ding will Weile haben'. In other usage, weak adj. forms based on the weak noun declension display homonymy, such that case-, number-, and gender-marking are possible only in combination with particles. The strong and weak adj. declensions distinguished by Jacob Grimm, although they differ in origin, could even be regarded as *one* adj. paradigm with variant forms which were largely in free variation in OHG and MHG, although they were tending to become distributed complementarily, i.e. attached to particular syntactic roles. Hence the interchangeability of strong and weak adj. forms in the early periods in many contexts. Paradigmatic push would dictate the use of strong, marked forms rather than unmarked, homonymous ('weak') forms where case-, gender-, or number-marking was necessary.[36]

However, analytical syntax, word order, and verbal concord help to clarify case and number, without recasting the nominal morphology, so paradigmatic pull and push are only ancillary developments. Context and the juxtaposition of marked and unmarked forms of the same noun also make consistent paradigmatic marking unnecessary. For example, a description of single combat from the *Prose Lancelot* shows some nouns unmarked:

Sie sprungen uff und zogen ir wolschnydende *swert* und schlugen sich off die *schild, helm* und *arm* also hart sie ummer [= immer] mochten. Sie zurbrachen ir *schild* oben und unden, sie entschlossen ir *helm* und zurbrachen ir *halßberg* ['hauberks'] . . .[37]

Here, number is marked in the first sentence by the adj. *wolschnydende* 'keen', then by the definite article *die*, which can only be pl. or it would otherwise conflict with the masc. gender of *schild*, *helm*, and *arm*. In the second sentence, context alone can distinguish the number, although we might argue that number is 'neutralized', since logically each adversary has only one sword, shield, hauberk, etc.: cf. mod. Fr. 'ils mettent leur chapeau' (not 'leurs chapeaux').

The apocope, then, which appears to devastate morphological paradigms, is easily compensated; it leads to uncertainty in the use of final -*e*, which nevertheless may be added to convey oppositions when required, and even appears in words whose paradigms originally lacked it (see below, pp. 171–2).

The morphology of the later medieval and ENHG period (say, the fourteenth to sixteenth centuries) appears chaotic, since, as in orthography and phonology, competing systems exist from region to region—sometimes even from text to text. The large dictionaries, Lexer (1872–8) and BMZ, simply record the variant forms without being able to dwell on their dialectal distribution: further studies are needed, and judicious interpretation of variant forms plotted on maps permits us to discern the outlines of late medieval *Schreiblandschaften*. Werner Besch, for example, illustrates clearly the fifteenth-century north–south split in gender in the word *luft* 'air', where northern manuscripts showed fem. gender, southern showed masc., and in between lay a zone of uncertainty where the word occurred only in ambiguous forms unmarked for gender.[38] Similarly, pl.-markers differ regionally (despite overlapping in some manuscripts and a degree of subservience to the forms of the original of which the manuscript is a copy), as in the pl. variants of MHG *buoch* (NHG *Buch*), a neut. *a*-stem noun originally without pl.-marking in nom. and acc. pl., where fifteenth-century competing pl. forms are *bůch* (= ∅), *bůcher*, *bůcher*, *buchere*, *boken/boeken*.[39] These and other pl. morphs derive from earlier paradigmatic patterns—the old stem classes—but they have been to some extent redistributed as geographical allomorphs, since most dialect areas adopt only one or two main ways of marking pl., but not all. The modern standard language clearly reveals its hybrid nature in the competing pl. patterns it retains, which again reflects the lack of any dominant area whose language became canonical. The standard is an overlying linguistic compromise drawing in differing degrees upon the regions, and in the noun classes its heterogeneous pl. formation shows it diverging from any particular dialect pattern. For the fifteenth century individual regions solve the problems of paradigmatic syncretism and ambiguity resulting from the weakening of inflexional syllables and the effects of apocope in their own ways: the UG south, where apocope was most evident, resorts to mutation with or without the -er ending;[40] in MG areas, especially in EMG, where unstressed vowels tended to remain, final -e functioned as a pl. morph, and mutation and the -er type are less common; in MFrk. and LFrk. the weak pl. morph -(e)n occurs; the -s pl. morph characteristic of Flemish and Neth. and some LG dialects appears relatively late in HG texts and remains sporadic, although it must have been reinforced orthographically by loans from Fr. in the thirteenth, sixteenth, and seventeenth centuries, and by loans from Neth. and English.[41]

The effects of this regionalism in pl. formation or gender are still observable in mod. German nouns with variant pl. formations or alternative genders. Such forms are not usually identical in meaning, or else they are stylistically distinct often to the point of becoming separate words, e.g. mod. German *Fahrt/Fahrten* 'journey' vs. the technical term *Fährte/Fährten* 'spoor', 'tracks' (hunting). Both originate from a fem. *i* stem, MHG *vart*, whose paradigm runs:

Singular:	Nom.	vart	Plural:	verte
	Acc.	vart		verte
	Gen.	verte/vart		verte
	Dat.	verte/vart		verten

Levelling had already occurred, as unmutated monosyllabic alternative forms in the gen. and dat. sg. show, and subsequently a split took place: the unmutated forms were levelled throughout the sg. and linked to a new weak pl. in -en (hence NHG *Fahrt*), while the mutated form was also levelled throughout the sg., again with a weak pl., but this time with a restricted, technical connotation (hence *Fährte*). In the same way, MHG *stat* 'place' gives rise to NHG *Stadt/Städte* 'town', *Stätte/Stätten* 'place', 'spot', and -*statt/-stätte* 'place', restricted to *Werkstatt/Werkstätte* 'works', 'work-place' and the archaic *Walstatt* 'place of battle' (also *Statthalter* '(Lord-) Lieutenant'). On occasion, grammarians suggest distinctions, e.g. between the pl. forms *Worte* 'words', 'discourse' and *Wörter* 'words', 'isolated words'.[42]

Variation in case-forms is less common in mod. German, although nom. forms with and without -en occur, which are sometimes more or less of equivalent frequency, as in the doublet *der Friede/Frieden*; or else one form is archaic/rare: *der Haufe* and *der Namen* are less common than *der Haufen* and *der Name*; sometimes semantic differentiation has occurred: *der Drache/des Drachen* 'dragon' ≠ *der Drachen/des Drachens* 'kite'.[43] In south-eastern UG the -*(e)n* of weak nouns was often levelled out into the nom. sg., creating forms like Viennese: *di Brukkn* (NHG *Brücke*), *Dekkn* (NHG *Decke*), *Fliagn* (NHG *Fliege*), *Nosn* (NHG *Nase*), *Schdrossn* (NHG *Straße*).[44] This doubtless accords well with the tendency not to use -*en* as a pl.-marker.

MEDIEVAL CONJUGATION AND EARLIER MODELS

The morphology of the verb also undergoes considerable recasting in the medieval period and later, again, analytical forms were increasingly used (see pp. 234 ff.). Basic morphemic oppositions of tense, mood, person, and number were altered by analogical levelling, although the weakening of unstressed syllables does not affect all of these categories to the same extent—further evidence that weakening and apocope are only concomitant changes and not first causes of the analogy.

Jacob Grimm[45] divides the Gmc. verb also into two main classes, the strong verb forming its pret. and past part. by changing the root vowel (a process known as apophony, or 'ablaut'), and the weak verb adding dental suffixes—an inferior, agglutinating formation. Compare:

> MHG   *singen* ≠ *sanc*   ≠   *sungen*   ≠   *gesungen*
> *machen*   *mach-(e)te mach-(e)ten gemach-et*

and note the differing past part. formation in *(ge)* + *en* for strong verbs and *ge* + *(e)t* for weak verbs. Weak verbs were usually secondary in meaning and form, being derived from roots found in strong verbs, nouns, adjectives, and adverbs: several contrasting doublets of strong and weak verbs existed in medieval German, where the weak verb had a causative force: compare *trinken* (strong) 'to drink' ≠ *trenken* (weak) 'to water' (horses etc.), i.e. 'to make them drink'. Similarly, *brinnen* (strong) 'be burning' (intrans.) ≠ *brennen* (weak) 'to burn something (down)' (trans.); *swîgen* (strong) 'be silent' ≠ *sweigen* (weak) 'to silence'. This distinction survives only occasionally in mod. German because phonological and morphological syncretism have obliterated it;[46] *trinken* and *tränken* remain; *brennen* is now contrasted with *abbrennen*, *verbrennen*, etc.; *schweigen* (actually the NHG equivalent of both MHG *swîgen* and MHG *sweigen*) now contrasts with the transitive *verschweigen*, the causative being conveyed by periphrasis—NHG *zum Schweigen bringen, schweigen lassen* (see Chapter VI).

Among the several anomalous verbs, the so-called 'preterite-presents' had a defective morphology and were, as the name implies, preterite in form but functioned as presents, developing new past-tense forms according to the weak conjugation. Most of these verbs became modal auxiliaries in the late medieval period,[47] i.e. they supplied modal marking where both strong and weak verbs lacked ind. ≠ subj. oppositions in their paradigms. Some 'athematic' verbs, e.g. *tuon* (NHG *tun*), *gân* (NHG *gehen*), *stân* (NHG *stehen*), and the old weak verbs of classes (2) and (3) (OHG *lobōn* and *sagēn*), derive from PIE forms which added personal endings directly to the root: these verbs, lacking any thematic (stem-forming) element, were always bipartite.

A. STRONG VERBS AND TENSE-FORMS

The regular alternation of root vowels in the strong verb formation ('ablaut') derives from the operation of PIE supra-segmental phonemes, i.e. from movable pitch and stress patterns. These qualitative (pitch) and quantitative (stress) accentual variations were possibly fundamental to PIE word-formation, but in the Gmc. languages their regularity can be only dimly discerned in the strong verb system and in a few sets of etymological cognates, like mod. German *Garten, Gerte, Gurt, Gürtel*; or English *and*, German *und*, OHG *inti, anti/enti, unti* (all meaning 'and'). The effects of pitch accent remain in the change of vowel between pres. ind. pl. and first and third person pret. ind. sg. in medieval German (technically this is called *Abtönung*):

	MHG			
	stîgen	≠	*steic*	(NHG *steigen*)
	binden	≠	*bant*	(NHG *binden*)
	nemen	≠	*nam*	(NHG *nehmen*)

The quantitative effects of the movable stress accent appear in the difference between the full vowels preserved in the pres. ind. and pret. sg., and the reduced vowels of the pret. pl. and past part.: cf. MHG *biegen* ≠ *bouc* vs. reduced grade *bugen* ≠ *gebogen* (*o* from *u*), where the *u/o* grades represent the remaining element of a PIE phonemic cluster *eu/ou*, reduced to *u* when unstressed. This may be presented schematically as follows:

PIE $C^1\acute{e}uC^2$ $C^1\acute{o}uC^2$ $C^1uC^{2/3}$ $C^1uC^{2/3}$

full grade   reduced grade
(*Abtönung*)   (*Abstufung*)

C = consonant(s); ′ = stress accent.

The fixing of the stress on initial syllable in PGmc., which is the phonologists' explanation for the decay of the PIE inflexional system in PGmc., also made irreversible the effects of pitch and stress accent. Stress affected certain consonants too—Verner's Law states that voiceless spirants become voiced between voiced sounds when strong stress does not immediately precede them. For this reason, C^2 in our model, when a voiceless spirant, becomes voiced in the pret. pl. and past part. of strong verbs and changes to C^3. By medieval German, the reflexes of the PGmc. alternating spirants are still recognizable as interchange between *h ~ g* (*slahen/geslagen*, NHG *schlagen/ geschlagen*), *s ~ r* (*was/wâren*, NHG *war/waren*), *d ~ t* (*snîden/gesniten*, NHG *schneiden, geschnitten*), and *f ~ b* (*dürfen/darben*).[48]

This variation is termed 'grammatical change', a Gmc. example of 'morphophonemic alternation': both designations indicate that the phonetic shape of the root changes in its different grammatical and derivational forms. Other such alternations have been introduced by sound changes like the WGmc. consonantal lengthening, the Second Sound Shift, the OHG diphthongizations and monopthongizations, umlaut, and medieval changes to stressed vowels, so that the regular patterns in the strong verb series have been considerably obscured, and the verbs are now felt to be irregular. Even in the medieval period, using normalized MHG, we can distinguish seven main ablaut classes, with ten or more basic patterns, allowing for variants (Table 10). The simplified MHG paradigms show partial number distinctions between sg. ≠ pl. in both pres. and pret. tense-forms, the result of mutation[49] and ablaut respectively. Consequently, some verbs show as many as six different vowels, e.g. Class II *biegen, ich biuge, bouc, du büge, bugen, gebogen*; others have only two, e.g. Class VII *heizen, hiez, du hieze, geheizen*. The second person sg. pret. ind.— originally a WGmc. formation (see p. 38)—contains the vowel found in the pret. subj. In medieval German it shows the consonantism and the root vowel of the pret. pl. ind., mutated where possible. By the

TABLE 10. *Ablaut series: MHG and NHG*

Class		Pres. Inf.	Pres. Sg.	Pret. Sg.	Pret. Pl.	Past Part.	2nd Pers. Pret.
I (*a*)		î	î	ei	i	i	i
	MHG	*strîten*	*strîtet*	*streit*	*striten*	*gestriten*	*du strite*
	NHG	*streiten*	*streitet*	*stritt*	*stritten*	*gestritten*	*du strittst*
I (*b*)				ê			
	MHG	*dîhen*	*dîhet*	*dêch*	*digen*	*gedigen*	*du dige*
	NHG	*gedeihen*	*gedeiht*	*gedieh*	*gediehen*	*gediehen*	*du gediehst*
II (*a*)		ie	iu	ou	u	o	ü
	MHG	*biegen*	*biuget*	*bouc*	*bugen*	*gebogen*	*du büge*
	NHG	*biegen*	*biegt*	*bog*	*bogen*	*gebogen*	*du bogst*
II (*b*)				ô			
	MHG	*bieten*	*biutet*	*bôt*	*buten*	*geboten*	*du büte*
	NHG	*bieten*	*bietet*	*bot*	*boten*	*geboten*	*du botst*
III (*a*)		i	i	a	u	u	ü
	MHG	*binden*	*bindet*	*bant*	*bunden*	*gebunden*	*du bünde*
	NHG	*binden*	*bindet*	*band*	*banden*	*gebunden*	*du bandst*
III (*b*)		ë	i			o	
	MHG	*hëlfen*	*hilfet*	*half*	*hulfen*	*geholfen*	*du hülfe*
	NHG	*helfen*	*hilft*	*half*	*halfen*	*geholfen*	*du halfst*
IV		ë	i	a	â	o	ae
	MHG	*stëln*	*stilt*	*stal*	*stâlen*	*gestoln*	*du stæle*
	NHG	*stehlen*	*stiehlt*	*stahl*	*stahlen*	*gestohlen*	*du stahlst*
V		ë	i	a	â	ë	ae
	MHG	*gëben*	*gibet*	*gap*	*gâben*	*gegëben*	*du gæbe*
	NHG	*geben*	*gibt*	*gab*	*gaben*	*gegeben*	*du gabst*
VI		a	e	uo	uo	a	üe
	MHG	*varn*	*vert*	*vuor*	*vuoren*	*gevarn*	*du vüere*
	NHG	*fahren*	*fährt*	*fuhr*	*fuhren*	*gefahren*	*du fuhrst*
VII*		â / a / ou	æ / e / ou	ie	ie	â / a / ou	ie
	MHG	*halten*	*heltest*	*hielt*	*hielten*	*gehalten*	*du hielte*
	NHG	*halten*	*hältst*	*hielt*	*hielten*	*gehalten*	*du hieltst*

* Class VII infinitives contain a variety of vowels: *ô, â, a, ou, uo*, and *ei*. The vowels recur in the past part.; in *hâhen* and *fâhen* (NHG *hangen* and *fangen*) the consonants in the pret. and past part. change by Verner's Law: *gehangen, gefangen*. In the pres. second and third person sg. the vowels mutate where possible, as do those of Classes II (*a*) and (*b*), III (*b*), IV, V, and VI. The vowels in the MHG examples are short unless marked long or digraphs; in NHG some have lengthened in an open syllable, but remain short in a closed one, e.g. Class IV, NHG *nehmen* (= [eː]) but *nimmt* (= [i]); contrast Class V *geben, gibt*, where standard pronouncing dictionaries (Siebs (1969) and *WDA*) prescribe ['giːpt]; NHG pret. *hing* and *fing* show shortening.

end of the fifteenth century it had virtually disappeared, but before that it must have weakened the resistance of the pret. sg. to analogical change, since in many ablaut classes the sg. contained two distinct root vowels. Where the vowel did not mutate, it was identical with that of the pret. pl., and this must have favoured the levelling out of that form: e.g. *stîgen*, pret. *ich/er steic, du stige, wir stigen, ir stiget, sie stigen*, where four out of six forms in the pret. paradigm show /i/. In mod. German the remaining strong verbs generally have a single form of the root in each tense, although mutation persists in the pres. ind. second and third person sg. of several classes, and some dialects have resisted the levelling of the pl. vowel into the first person sg. Compare:

MHG	NHG	Austrian
ich hilfe	*ich helfe*	*i hilf*
ich nime	*ich nehme*	*i nim*

But the disparity between pret. sg. and pl. has disappeared, and the vowel of the past part. can be identical, as in the modern reflexes of Classes I and II and some Class VII verbs (*scheiden/schied/geschieden*). Consonants have been generalized too, producing more consistent roots; sometimes the consonantism of the past part. and pret. pl. is levelled out into the present:

MHG	NHG
slahen/sluoc/sluogen/geslagen	*schlagen/schlug/*etc.
fâhen/fienc/fiengen/gefangen	*fangen/fing/*etc.
vriesen/vrôs/vruren/gevroren	*frieren/fror/*etc.[50]

Occasionally, levelling of consonants from the present is found, as in the example for Class I, *dîhen/gedigen*, NHG *gedeihen, gedieh* (the old past part. persists as mod. *gediegen* (adj.) 'solid', 'worthy'). Again, a few morphophonemic alternations remain, as in *schneiden/schnitten*, *leiden/litten*. The effects of Verner's Law remain dialectally, e.g. *hosd as net xeng? = hast es nit gesegen?* (i.e. *gesehen*), from the Viennese poet H. C. Artmann's spooky poem 'wos unguaz' (= 'Etwas Unheimliches') (Artmann (1958), 20, line 23).; similarly *geschegen = geschehen*. The levelling out of consonantal variations in the strong verb began early: by medieval German, the pret. and past part. of the verbs *fliehen* 'flee' and *fliegen* 'fly' are distinguished as *fluhen, geflohen* and *flugen, geflogen* respectively, whereas both should have fallen together with voiced consonants.

The overall developments are clear: the strong verb system has lost number opposition from root syllable and marks it by inflection or pronoun. The simplified ablaut forms retained instead a clear morphological function as tense-markers. This has created regularities within some verb classes, but only at the expense of older relationships between the classes themselves: their systematic nature is less evident than before, and many verbs have become weak or died out. The uncertainties felt by speakers can be seen from the plethora of variant forms even within one text, which provide a parallel to the phonological and orthographical diversity. The levelling processes between the various parts of the strong verb had begun in the thirteenth century,[51] although by the sixteenth century they were still not complete: Luther still has *fleucht* and *kreucht* (MHG Class II (*b*) *vliuhet, kriuchet*).[52] Only by the mid-seventeenth century, after some generations of printing and the grammatical codification that accompanied it, were variables increasingly discarded in favour of 'book spelling' and 'book norms'. The destruction of the strong verb system reached a climax in the medieval period as a result of morphological reorganization which entailed the strong verbs being drastically reduced in number between medieval German and the modern standard; for, of the 339 MHG strong verbs, 119 have not survived into the modern standard, 54 have become weak, only 3 weak verbs have become strong, and no new strong verbs are attested.[53] The system is clearly no longer productive; instead, the strong verbs are irregular and have been lexicalized. Although 169 such verbs still exist (fewer in some dialects), some of these recur with great frequency which preserves their idiosyncratic conjugation, while the influence of standard grammars retards changes to the rest, in writing at least. Again, the very lack of such canonical grammar-books must have furthered morphological uncertainty in the period from about 1350 to 1650 (late MHG and ENHG in the present book), which may have encouraged the growth of analytical, periphrastic verb forms like the perfect tense-form, and may thus have contributed to the loss of the pret. tense-form in speech, particularly in southern Germany (see below, p. 172).

B. WEAK VERBS AND TENSE-FORMS

The weak conjugation of the verb was an important Germanic development in verb morphology. In Gothic, the weak verbs fell into four classes, based partly on the suffix morphs and partly on meaning. Three classes are represented in OHG texts: (1) verbs in -(*i*)*en*, which often had a causative/factitive meaning;[54] (2) -*ôn* verbs, which were largely denominative formations, e.g. *salbôn* 'anoint' (*salba* 'unguent'); (3) *-ên* verbs, which were often durative, e.g. *wonên* 'dwell'. Classes (2) and (3) often interchanged their conjugation. The first class is morphologically interesting, since in PGmc. its suffix was *-jan*: the */j/* later caused consonantal doubling (i.e. lengthening?) and also mutation, but in the pret. of long-stem verbs (those containing a long vowel, diphthong, or short vowel plus consonant cluster) the *i* element was syncopated before it could cause mutation, triggering a morphophonemic alternation between forms in the present with mutation, and past forms without it, e.g. OHG *brennen/branta*, NHG *brennen/brannte*.[55] Jacob Grimm misnamed this phenomenon *Rückumlaut* because the mutation in the pret. seemed to have been undone, made *rückgängig*.

Curiously, the weakening of unstressed syllables and morphological recasting has affected the weak verbs differently from the strong verbs, for, by the processes of vowel weakening in inflexional syllable treated above (pp. 152–3), the various classes of weak verb fell together in medieval German and only the verbs with *Rückumlaut* stood out as a group because of their vocalic alternations:

	Class (1) -(*i*)*en* (< *-jan)		Class (2) -*ôn*	Class (3) -*ên*
	(*a*) short	(*b*) long		
OHG	*nerien/nerita*	*sterken/starcta*	*machôn/machôta*	*folgên/folgêta*
MHG	*ner(e)n/nerete*	*stercken/starcte*	*machen/machete*	*folgen/folgete*
NHG	*nähren/nährte*	*stärken/stärkte*	*machen/machte*	*folgen/folgte*

Not all Class (1) verbs with long-stem syllables contained vowels that could mutate, but these are still identifiable because they lack the *e* between root and pret. suffix in medieval German, ending simply in *-te*: cf. *teilen/teil-te*, *wîhen/wîhte* (NHG *weihen*), *schicken/schicte*. The syncope of unstressed syllables largely removed this distinction, making *-t(e)* the regular form of the suffix, although in mod. German the allophone *-ete* occurs after dentals, extended, oddly enough, even to long-stem verbs which lacked the syllable in MHG: *rihten/rihte* > NHG *richtete*, *leiten/leite* > NHG *leitete*. The two phases of inflexional reduction, weakening and syncope, thus regularized the weak verb system so that each tense-form showed internal cohesion between sg. and pl. while the root remained the same throughout the paradigm, with the exception of the *Rückumlaut* verbs. Of the many *Rückumlaut* verbs of MHG,[56] only six now survive: *kennen, brennen, nennen, rennen, senden,* and *wenden* (the last two with variant past forms *sandte/sendete, wandte/wendete*). The weak conjugation now accounts for 95 per cent of all basic verbs in German and has long been extended to foreign borrowings and neologisms.

SYNCRETISM WITHIN THE VERB PARADIGM

The 'OHG' personal endings of strong and weak verbs already mostly coincided, but they were characterized by differentiated vowels conveying oppositions of person, mood, and, to a lesser extent, tense. The weakening of inflexions reduces their morphemic oppositions, since many become homonymous morphs.

With the apocope, temporal and modal distinctions in the morphology of weak and strong verbs disappeared even more, though whether phonology or syntax was the overriding factor is again disputed.

In the Early German period, dialects show only four such homomorphs: the first and third person singular in the pres. subj., and pret. ind. and subj., and the first and third person plural pret. subj. Table 11 shows schematically the OHG verb-endings for both strong and weak Class (1) conjugations (weak Class (2) and (3) differ in the pres. forms).

TABLE 11

	Present		Preterite	
	Indicative	Subjunctive*	Indicative	Subjunctive
Singular:				
1st pers.	*-u*	**-e**†	**-∅, -ta**	**-i**
2nd pers.	*-is(t)*	*-ês(t)*	*-i, -tôs*	*-îs*
3rd pers.	*-it*	**-e**	**-∅, -ta**	**-i**
Plural:				
1st pers.	*-ames*	*-êm*	*-um*	**-în**
2nd pers.	*-et*	*-êt*	*-ut*	*-ît*
3rd pers.	*-ant*	*-ên*	*-un*	**-în**

* Longer forms of the pres. subj. are found in Alem. see Braune and Eggers (1975), § 310.

† Homomorphs are in bold type, and the distinctive pret. sg. formations have been separated: otherwise the endings should be added to the appropriate strong or weak verb root, the latter extended by dental suffix.

The growth and levelling out of homonymous morphs in the paradigm can be linked to the loss of modal oppositions and also to the change from synthetic to analytic verb morphology,[57] where particles and in particular auxiliaries convey mood (see Chapter VI). Although mutation preserves some modal distinction by transferring the grammatical information from the ending to the root—just as in the nouns umlaut was 'morphologized' as a number-marker in some classes—most weak verbs and many strong verbs retained little modal marking. The most extreme, but not uncommon, position is that of a strong verb with a non-mutable root vowel, e.g. *rîten* (NHG *reiten*), strong Class I (Table 12). With the levelling out of one form

TABLE 12

	Present		Preterite	
	Indicative	Subjunctive	Indicative	Subjunctive
Singular:				
1st pers.	*rîte*	*rîte*	*reit* ≠	*rite*
2nd pers.	*rîtes(t)*	*rîtest*	*rite* (←)	*rites(t)*
3rd pers.	*rîtet* ≠	*rîte*	*reit* ≠	*rite*
Plural:				
1st pers.	*rîten*	*rîten*	*riten*	*riten*
2nd pers.	*rîtet*	*rîtet*	*ritet*	*ritet*
3rd pers.	*rîtent* ≠	*rîten*	*riten*	*riten*

of the root in the pret. the syncretism increased: the second person sg. pret. ind., being anomalous, was progressively replaced, usually taking the ending *-st*, which was common to the pres. ind. and subj.[58] (Traces of old forms of the second person sg. pret. ind. persist in the sixteenth century.) The first and third person sg. pret. ind. also became *ich/er rit(t)*, distinguished from the subj. only by the notoriously unstable *-e* of the latter. However, by the apocope first person sg. pres. ind. and subj. and first person sg. pret. ind. and subj. were reduced in non-diphthongizing areas to two forms, *ich rît'* (pres.) ≠ *ich rit'* (pret.); and, while these were distinguished in speech, they were not always so in writing, although some (e.g. Alem.) texts tend to write ⟨ryt⟩ vs. ⟨rit⟩.[59] Where the diphthongization occurred, the distinction became *ich reit* phonetically [rait] vs. *ich rit'*, unless the pret. root had not been levelled, in which case *reit* [reit] could represent the old pret. sg. and there might even be a merger of present ind. and subj. and pret. ind. as against pret. subj.:

	PRESENT		PRETERITE	
	Indicative	Subjunctive	Indicative	Subjunctive
OHG	*ich rîtu*	*ich rîte*	*ich reit*	*ich riti*
MHG		*ich rîte*	*ich reit*	*ich rite*
diphthongization		*reite*		
apocope:		*reit'*	*reit*	*rit'*
merger:			*ich reit'**	*ich rit'*

* This potential merger may explain why strong Class I verbs tend to level out the pret. pl. form, while Class II (*b*) verbs occasionally level the pret. sg. root, e.g. MHG *bôt/buten* → NHG *bot/boten*. The past part. also influences the development.

The mergers and apparently arbitrary variations introduced by levelling out the strong pret. sg. and pl. contributed to the decay of the strong verb system.

Let us now briefly consider the personal endings as representing personal morphemes.

A. PERSONAL ENDINGS

Many personal endings contained consonants, and remained distinctive within a particular tense or mood paradigm. If the weakening of inflexions was triggered by the increased use of the personal pronoun with verbs, coupled with clearer number differentiation in the nouns, it is difficult to see why the endings did not erode even further, as happened in English. Indeed, such tendencies are found regionally: in Alem. and WMG (Middle Frankish) the first person sg. sometimes ends in *-en* in the medieval period, by analogy with the many weak verbs from classes (2) and (3) and with the common 'athematic' verbs, *tuon*, *gân/gên* and *stân/stên*, whose first person also ended in *-m/-n* in OHG. By this, the sg. ≠ pl. number opposition in the first person would have disappeared. Levelling also occurred in the pl.: in Alem. *-nt* from the third person pl. pres. ind. was early adopted into the second person pl., *ir nëmet* → *ir nëment*, and later extended even into the first person pl., giving the south-west a uniform pl. form (as had happened also much earlier in the northern OS and OLFrk. dialects). The new -*nt* form was extended throughout the pret. and subj. pl. in some regions, while in Alsace -*en* was levelled into all forms of the pres. ind. pl., reinforced probably by the first and third person pl. subj. endings. The third person pl. pres. ind. of the modern standard was reformed by analogy with the pres. subj., but the process of levelling stopped, giving the modern pattern for the pl. of all tenses and moods -*n*/-*t*/-*n*.

The standard has not adopted a uniform pl. (*Einheitsplural*) for historical, not 'grammatical', reasons, reflecting the prestige of the eastern and south-eastern German-speaking areas when grammarians and printers were working towards a standard. Even in the sixteenth century, printers continue to use single forms in the pl. in -*nt* and -*n* in all parts of the paradigm, although final -*n* was itself lost in several dialects, especially Swabian. Detailed geographical studies for the medieval period are lacking, but in the fifteenth century number distinctions were perhaps still important, since the levelling of -*en* into the first person sg. shows a complementary geographical distribution with the levelling of -*en* throughout the pl., it tends to occur rather in areas where the first person pl. ends in -*nt*.[60]

B. SYNCRETISM BETWEEN TENSE-FORMS

The strong verb is originally well-marked for tense oppositions, although the system becomes chaotic and decays. The weak verb morphology is poorly marked, since it is very sensitive to the effects of syncope and apocope, and syncretism of tense-forms occurs. In weak verbs with roots ending in a dental, this syncretism also affects the first person sg., for even in literary MHG we find verbs like *leiten*, *rihten*, *warten* with contracted pret. first-person forms: *ich leite, rihte, warte* for *leit-te, riht-te* (long-stem Class (1) weak verbs), and *wartete* (from OHG *wartēta*, Class (3) weak verbs); with apocope these become *ich leit, riht, wart*. But through apocope all weak verbs have ambiguous tense-forms in the third person sg. which can be pres. or pret. Compare *er folget, liebet, wonet* with *er folget(e), liebet(e), wonet(e)*. Indeed, final -*e* becomes so unstable that weak verbs in the first and third person sg. pret. ind. seem to have variant forms: *ich wart ~ ich warte; er liebet ~ er liebt ~ er liept ~ er liebte; er folgt ~ er folgte*. Such alternation may be one reason why -*e* was added to the first and third person sg. of strong verbs[61] also, creating forms like *ich gienge, er schwamme, er steige, er sahe,* the latter being especially frequent in Luther's writings. *Ich/er wurde* remains the sole survivor of these mixed preterites in mod. German, ousting *wart* (*ward*) and *warde* (*ward* remains in poetry and 'biblical' style).

However, the syncretism in tense-forms,

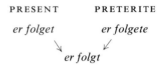

PRESENT   PRETERITE

er folget   *er folgete*

er folgt

is less serious syntactically than we might expect, since many contexts are quite comprehensible because of the interchange of the unmarked forms with forms marked for pret. —either strong verbs, mixed verbs, or *Rückumlaut* verbs. A random example from MS P of *Lancelot*[62] illustrates this:

Der schiltknecht stund ab, er ging zu syner frauwen und *sagt* ir die mere [= 'news'] von Parceval irem sone. Und als die frauw das verstund, da *weynt* sie zumal sere und begund solchen großen jamer zu triben das sie von rechter noth und we, das sie am herczen hett, *schickt* nach irem caplan.

The interchange of marked and unmarked forms is familiar in mod. German, where the 'pres.' subj. (Subjunctive 1) and 'pret.' subj. (Subjunctive 2) alternate with ind. in reported speech. Moreover, the fifteenth-century manuscripts of *Lancelot* preserve many *Rückumlaut* forms, e.g. *stalt < stel(le)n, dackt < decken, kußten < küssen, halßten < helsen* 'embrace'. Could such forms have persisted because they clearly mark the pret.?

The syntactic function of the tense-forms will be considered briefly in Chapter VI (pp. 241–5), but we note here that the syncretism of third person sg. in pres. and pret. is often adduced as a reason for the loss of the pret. in spoken German in the south,[63] where it has been replaced either by the perfect or by the pres. Indeed, the retention of the pret. in speech in northern areas might be seen as the result of LG-speakers having adopted HG as a literary language: the spoken use of the more literary pret. would thus reflect, like the purer pronunciation of the vowels of the HG book language, an artificially correct and choice transposition of written forms into spoken ones. At any event, the *Lancelot* seems to be written in pret. and other past verb forms, unlike the Fr. source, which frequently resorts to a historic, or narrative, present-tense form.[64]

C. MODAL SYNCRETISM

The imperative and pres. ind. had already merged in OHG, save for the second person sg., which in strong verbs was without inflexion, while the weak verbs ended in -i, -o, or -e depending on their class. In medieval German, by the weakening of inflexional syllables, all weak verbs ended in -e in the second person sg. imperative, and this was then extended into the strong conjugation. Again, the apocope contributed to the growth of variant forms—reformed *hære!* > *hær!*, *warte!* > *wart!*—so that the endless strong forms were also reformed with -e variants by a kind of 'hypercorrection': *heiz!* > *heize!*, *gib!* > *gibe!*

Syncretism between ind. and subj. moods in the paradigm of a strong verb of the non-mutating type can be seen from the example *rîten* above (p. 169). The verbs with mutation in the pres. sg. preserve the opposition with the subj., although the levelling of first person sg. reduces it. Compare:

MHG Indicative		Subjunctive	NHG Indicative		Subjunctive
ich nime	≠	*ich nëme*	*ich nehme*		*ich nehme*
du nimes(t)	≠	*du nëmes(t)*	*du nimmst*	≠	*du nehm(e)st*
er nimet	≠	*er nëme*	*er nimmt*	≠	*er nehme*
wir nëmen		*wir nëmen*	*wir nehmen*		*wir nehmen*
ir nëmet		*ir nëmet*	*ihr nehmt*		*ihr nehmt*
sie nëment	≠	*sie nëmen*	*sie nehmen*		*sie nehmen*

On the other hand, many strong verbs have completely distinct ind. and subj. paradigms in the pret., e.g. *binden* (*ich bant* ≠ *ich bünde*), *faren* (*ich fuor* ≠ *ich füere*). Unfortunately, here too the levelling out of a single form of the pret. root and the analogical extension of mutation has led to uncertainty, so that even in the modern standard some variants occur—*stände/stünde*,[65] *befähle/beföhle*, *gälte/gölte* (*gelten*)—although usually one variant is either regional or archaic: *hälfe* is rarer than *hülfe*, *begönne* rarer than *begänne*.[66] However, even in the strong paradigm, difficulties arise where the mutated vowel merges with the root vowel of the present. This is the case with *nëmen*, *gëben*, the reflexes of which show either long close or long open vowel in both pres. and pret. subj.: MHG *wir nëmen* (pres. ind. and subj.) ≠ *wir næmen* (pret. subj.). Mod. German preserves the orthographical distinction and the standard pronunciation prescribes a phonemic opposition between *wir nehmen* ['neːmən] and *wir nähmen* ['nɛːmən], but this is made only in careful, formal speech. Conversely, in the

middle period the distinction is not made in orthography, although it may have been in spoken language: so MHG *næme, gæbe* appear in the *Prose Lancelot* as ⟨nem⟩, ⟨geb⟩.[67]
The pret. of weak verbs, however, shows complete syncretism in medieval German, because for some reason the pret. subj. forms did not mutate, despite high vowels in the inflexions.[68] Let us take *salben* as an example, OHG Class (2) *salbôn*:

PRETERITE

	Indicative	Subjunctive
OHG	*salbōta*	*salbōti*
	salbōtōs(t)	*salbōtīs(t)*
	salbōta	*salbōti*
	salbōtum	*salbōtīm*
	salbōtut	*salbōtīt*
	salbōtun	*salbōtīn*

MHG	*salbete*
	salbetest
	salbete
	salbeten
	salbetet
	salbeten

The UG apocope also permits a merger between pres. ind., pret. ind., and pret. subj. in the third person sg.—which is after all an important form in any narrative:[69]

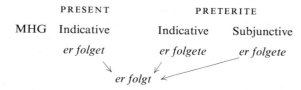

	PRESENT	PRETERITE	
MHG	Indicative	Indicative	Subjunctive
	er folget	*er folgete*	*er folgete*
	er folgt		

Again, word order, context, and other marked subj. forms alternating with these unmarked ones can usually make the utterance unambiguous. But doubtless this merger contributes to the loss of temporal oppositions found in MHG between the pres. subj. and pret. subj. verb forms, leaving them largely in complementary distribution in mod. German so far as tense is concerned,—although they do differ in some contexts as to their modality, degree of probability, etc. We should further note that in the medieval period the *Rückumlaut* verbs maintain modal oppositions to some extent by having mutated subjunctives, for example, in the *Prose Lancelot*:

> *kust* ≠ *kúst* (accent´ denotes umlaut)
> *saczt* ≠ *seczt.*

This however, scarcely survives now—NHG *küsste, setzte* are both ind. and subj. forms. Mutation can be extended to other verbs too, as in *fragt(e)* ≠ *fregt(e)*, a device not adopted into the standard. Periphrastic constructions using modal auxiliaries, especially *wolt(e)*, *solt(e)*, and *möcht(e)*, and the modally marked auxiliary verbs *haben* and *sein* will be treated later. They and modal or temporal adverbs ensure comprehension—and remind us that morphology, like phonology, is not autonomous but interacts with other levels of language.

CONCLUSION

Morphological developments are difficult to link with the external history of the speakers, although from the twelfth century to about 1500 the lack of a standard language and of standard grammars of German explains the continuing linguistic diversity and regionalism found in morphology as well as orthography and phonology. Stylistic factors in morphological change are hard to separate from geographical variants at this period—archaic forms are perhaps more obvious.[70] Inflexional morphology is also not much open to change by linguistic borrowing since social prestige attaching to the use of foreign tongues rarely affects grammatical endings, although later on, in the seventeenth and eighteenth centuries, preciosity and snobbery are sometimes suggested by keeping foreign words in foreign form even in German contexts; German inflexions are not involved.

Even internal, 'linguistic' explanations for the considerable morphological recasting are problematic, and mono-causal explanations are improbable.[71] Disregarding philological and text-critical considerations, like manuscript copying and dialectal transposition, or metre, the following four approaches interlock:

1. *Phonetic.* Unstressed syllables merge by weakening, syncope, and apocope; this involves loss of phonemic oppositions in inflexional syllables, and morphological recasting occurs. This traditional

phonological explanation sometimes looks outside the written evidence to the (at this period) virtually unknown supra-segmental quantities, like intonation. At any event, the primacy of phonological change is basic.

2. *Morphological.* Once morphological syncretism (the merging of inflexions) takes place, further changes to the paradigms occur in order to prevent ambiguity. However the original mergers were caused, subsequent change of declension or conjugation on the basis of morphological similarity or the need to distinguish between otherwise homonymous forms can be observed.

3. *Syntactic.* The existence of 'analytical' constructions makes the inflexions redundant in many contexts, hence vowel qualities and quantities are reduced and even disappear.

4. *Stylistic.* Some evidence suggests that weakening of unstressed syllables occurred earlier and more widely in speech than in writing.[72] This may hold also for the medieval weakening and apocope: in some areas, the changed morphology reflects a *rapprochement* between writing (the more conservative medium) and speech (the more progressive medium).

Emphasizing syntactic factors in weakening and apocope helps us to break out of the Neogrammarian dichotomy between sound change and consequent analogical readjustment. At the least, only the availability of analytical constructions using particles and word order permits the degree of syncretism in German morphology that has actually occurred; while, to state it more strongly, the increase in these analytical constructions makes the inflexional endings redundant, so furthering their erosion, perhaps even causing it. But so far as we can observe, analytical syntax and inflexional erosion are both aspects of the same linguistic phenomenon, occurring simultaneously in some degree: there is no need to attribute causal priority to either. (That analytical constructions are attested well before the medieval weakening and apocope need not discount their contribution, given the probable time-lag between the operation of sound changes and their becoming general in writing: after all, vowel reductions are also attested in OHG texts.)

The morphological developments we have considered occurred over several centuries and were anchored in regional, 'dialectal' traditions. The invention of printing and the upsurge in grammatical activity in German which seems to have accompanied it eventually established linguistic norms based on the printed or 'book' languages current in particular regions (see Chapter V), and gradually the zones of variation in phonology and morphology were reduced. School grammars later further filtered out local forms—a process not yet complete even by the end of the eighteenth century (see Chapter VIII). So, in the development of German, we should perhaps distinguish a 'pre-grammarian' phase, in which developments take place in the language itself, from a 'post-grammarian' phase, in which increasingly the focus moves to the traditions of analysis and codification adopted by generations of grammarians. Morphology illustrates the implications of this view clearly, since the pre-grammarian paradigms differ from the later ones, which are (with Humboldt, above, p. 145 n. 4) the creations of the grammarians. But early morphology is 'informal'; its paradigms are 'open' in that they contain variant forms, since for the speaker morphemic oppositions matter more than the cohesion of the 'paradigm': for example, in strong verbs the oppositions between tense forms are borne by vowel gradation ('ablaut'), but the phonemic oppositions between vowels are not of prime importance, since the paradigm can actually be inverted. Regardless of the origins of this 'mirror-image' ablaut,[73] the inversion itself commands interest. Compare the following NHG verbs listed in pairs with pres. ind. pl. followed by pret. pl.:

Present		Preterite	
liegen	≠	*lagen*	} Opposition between /ie/ ≠ /aː/.
raten	≠	*rieten*	
bieten	≠	*boten*	} Opposition between /ie/ ≠ /oː/.
stoßen	≠	*stießen*	
reiten	≠	*ritten*	} Shows /i/ in both pres. and pret. roots.
bitten	≠	*baten*	
halten	≠	*hielten*	} Shows /a/ in both pres. and pret. roots.
helfen	≠	*halfen*	

If the opposition between phonemes is more important than their distribution in the paradigm, speakers are relatively free to innovate by means of analogy. This happens in the volatile centuries before the grammarians impose restrictions to innovation by determining what they will allow as usage.

The important pre-grammarian phase in the history of the German language falls in the fourteenth and fifteenth centuries, when the writers, far from corrupting the rule ('die regel vergröbern'),[74] are gradually establishing regional norms from which influential grammarians, particularly in the seventeenth and eighteenth centuries, could select, and on which they could build.

SELECT BIBLIOGRAPHY

GENERAL PRESENTATIONS OF MEDIEVAL GERMAN, INCLUDING MORPHOLOGY

Bergmann and Pauly (1971). [discusses the origins of the modern noun and verb systems]. Bergmann and Pauly (1973). Ehrismann and Ramge (1976). Kern and Zutt (1977). Michels (1912). Paul (1881/1969) [contains a useful syntax by Ingeborg Schröbler; the most recent edn. is by Siegfried Grosse, 1982]. Paul (1916–20) [this grammar is based on historical principles and contains much information on the earlier forms]. Schmidt et al. (1969). Weinhold (1883).

ARTICLES

Hotzenköcherle (1962). Stopp (1974). Stopp and Moser (1967). Werner (1965).

Morphological material in relation to the historical and geographical background is also found in Besch (1967), Moser (1909).

For grammars and studies of the ENHG period, see the Select Bibliographies to Chapters V and VI.

CHAPTER V

THE TRANSITION TO
EARLY MODERN GERMAN
(1450-1650)

OUR Transitional period begins around 1450, with the earliest
German prints, and so overlaps with the end of the Medieval period
(see p. 98). At this time, no single regional form of German can claim
to be the standard, no literary genre or tradition holds the monopoly
of good taste and style, the inconsistent spelling in printed books
reinforces the impression of disorder, and the preoccupation of
educated men lies with languages other than their own. Throughout
the sixteenth century the early grammarians and orthoepists grope
blindly to regulate the language, basing themselves mostly on
grammars of Latin rather than observation of German—and citing
patterns of usage only in the vaguest terms. And yet, by the second
half of the seventeenth century a vigorous vernacular literature
flourished and was patronized in the courts of princes; aristocratic
and patrician language societies were fostering and purifying the
German language, which had been exhaustively codified by Christian Gueintz (1592-1650) and Justus Georg Schottelius (1612-76);
German's role in education, its prestige and appropriateness for a
wide range of technical purposes, had been acknowledged, and its
ancient heritage and supposedly unadulterated etymology were
invariably overstated. Most important of all, a generally recognizable, if not always recognized, HG 'book language' undoubtedly

existed throughout central Germany and the LG-speaking areas to the north—a norm, however fluid, which neither orthographical reforms nor regional, particularist interests could replace, even though they might still modify or influence its individual features. The present chapter speculates as to how this remarkable change came about.

The two main developments in German during this period are the emergence and spreading of supra-regional printed norms, and the elaboration of distinct styles in German for literary, everyday, and technical purposes. On both 'horizontal' and 'vertical' axes the newly perfected art of printing revolutionized communication, bringing people into contact with many different forms and styles of their native language. Contemporaries quickly grasped the significance of the invention, praising it as a divine gift to men so that the word of God might be spread among them; while for some the mystery of perfect multiple copies and the sheer output made printing seem rather a 'black art': one man produced in a day more than could be written in a year.[1] By the seventeenth century, when the costs of production had come down, Daniel Cramer, Superintendent at Stettin, observed that a whole book could be bought for the price charged by a scribe for copying half a page; moreover, books saved money, since one could carry around collections of sermons without having to buy the preacher supper.[2] Although printing did not immediately replace copying by hand in chanceries and monasteries, its advantages were so obvious that documents from both were soon printed; by the 1470s there were seven monastic presses, and even the conservative abbot of Sponheim, Johannes Trithemius (1452-1516), who defended the labour of scribes as keeping idle hands busy, encouraging diligence, devotion, knowledge of Scripture, still had his *De laude scriptorum manualium* printed. Less obviously, printing eventually influenced the external form of the language, partly because the very diversity of spelling and language it presented brought home the need for norms both within the individual printing-houses and outside them, partly because printed texts, in particular the Bible, provided a corpus of usage on which grammarians and their readers could readily draw.[3] At any rate, spelling guides and rudimentary grammars of several types become common in the sixteenth century—some thirty-seven prints of fifteen different works—since printing had taken spelling conventions out of the narrow confines of monastery and chancery and made them accessible to broader sections of the population. More people read, and people read more, since in all regions printing encouraged literacy and increased the potential audience, which ranged from churchmen, chancery officials, university and grammar-school teachers, and such, whose text- and hand-books were mainly in Latin, to the *gemeiner man* who turned to chap-books of all kinds (including grisly stories of Dracula the Impaler), to almanacs, folk-remedies, guides to husbandry, accounts of religious relics, simple catechisms and pious tracts, and so forth. The increased availability of old knowledge provoked new ideas, which the presses quickly spread, furthering intellectual and artistic developments, including German Humanism, social ferment, like the peasant movements, and religious unrest, culminating in the Reformation. Indeed, printing became a medium for agitation and propaganda, political and religious, taking over from the sermon as a means of communicating directly with the masses, and bringing stylistic alterations with it. Some of these refinements were characteristic of the shift from listening to reading as a whole, and, like punctuation, had implications for German syntax.

In the schools, too, printing revolutionized teaching by making grammars, phrase-books, dictionaries, and texts available to pupil and teacher alike. These works were designed to inculcate a knowledge of Latin and sometimes of Greek, but increasingly the informal classroom explanations which were often in German become incorporated into the textbooks themselves, giving us a fuller picture of centuries of teaching practice. Beside the 'Latin schools', German schools for the less gifted and the less well-off were set up to teach the rudiments of reading in German, and a few grammatical pamphlets were produced for these circles, and even for those no longer of school age who needed to teach themselves to read. Complete grammars of German, although desirable, were not strictly necessary for the humbler kind of school, and we see in the sixteenth century already a split between those catering for the poorer classes, and more ambitious grammarians conscious of the classical traditions of Latin grammar and anxious to apply them to German. The influential grammarians of the seventeenth and eighteenth centuries belong to the latter group and were preoccupied with the refinement of literary German and with grammatical philosophy and theory: they lead us away from changes taking place in the language itself and into the realm of theory about language variation. The choice of acceptable features of an educated norm is largely the work of these men who filter out many of the variants in forms, vocabulary, and syntax which were still more or less permissible usage in the sixteenth century.

PRINTING, ITS DEVELOPMENT AND LINGUISTIC EFFECTS

A. ORIGINS AND SPREAD

Printing with movable characters and the invention of paper are known first in the Far East[4] and travel westwards along the trade routes, before being perfected by the Mainz goldsmith Johannes Gensfleisch, called Gutenberg (c.1400-68), about the year 1439. In particular, the production of large amounts of movable type using an alloy of lead, tin, and antimony which was hard-wearing but easily cast revolutionized the primitive printing processes already in use— for the printers of block-books had already adapted the wine or domestic screw-press.[5] The new technology spread quickly, and by 1500 some 1,120 printing-houses were operating in between 260 and 270 European towns; in England William Caxton printed the first book at Westminster in 1477, and a year later printing began at Oxford. Estimates vary, but perhaps as many as 30,000 early prints, or incunables,[6] survive from before 1500.

Gutenberg's famous 42-line Latin Bible, printed in 1455, exactly resembles a manuscript, with coloured initials and rubrics added in later by hand, and some 290 separate symbols were used to print its various ligatures, diacritical marks, and abbreviations. The first psalter, printed at Mainz in 1457 by Gutenberg's colleagues Johannes Fust and Peter Schöffer, even describes itself in the colophon as 'spalmorum [sic] *codex*', and for a while the term *codex* also means 'printed book'. The first German books printed by Gutenberg were insignificant and popular in character: a fragment from a *Weltgericht* printed perhaps as early as 1445, a *Türkenkalendar* in 1454, and an *Aderlaß- und Laxierkalendar* for 1456.[7] The first complete German Bible was published by Johannes Mentelin at Strasburg in 1466.

Printing was both an art and a trade, and within the printing-house educated and skilled men worked beside semi-skilled and perhaps illiterate journeymen. Printers and correctors belonged largely to

urban educated circles, and might come from several backgrounds—
chancery officials, notaries, town clerks, scribes, physicians, university students, schoolteachers, even priests and abbots, lent a hand
when required; for example, Michael Greyff claims that his edition of
a work called *Dicta tintoris* (1486) had been corrected by 'peritos
magistros' of Tübingen University. At any event, knowledge of Latin
was desirable since Latin prints far outnumber German ones until the
late seventeenth century; indeed, of 288 works printed by the
Nuremberg family, the Kobergers, between the years 1470 and 1525,
only fifteen were in German, five of which were reprints of a tract
called the *Seelenwurzgärtlein*; in the same period the firm published
twenty-eight Latin Bibles, but only one in German.[8] Indeed, many
technical terms used in printing are of Lat. origin, the heritage of
scriptorium and chancery, e.g. *Alinea* 'paragraph' (§), *Exemplar*,
Folio, *Format*,[9] *Initiale*, *Kolophon*,[10] *Kolumne*, *Kopie*, *Korrektur*,
korrigieren, *Manuskript*, *Oktav*, *paginieren*, *punktieren*, *Quart*,
Rubrik, *rubrizieren*.[11] Most of these words relate to the book as a
finished product that had changed deceptively little in form, despite
the revolution in its production. For the actual processes of making
matrices, casting type, and printing new terms of art were required,
and these were often German, although sometimes loan-translations
from Latin: *drucken/trucken* itself is probably based on Lat.
(im)primere.[12] *Auflegen* 'print', 'publish' meant to put sheets of paper
on a pile ready for the press, hence *Auflagenhöhe* 'size (lit. "height")
of an edition'; *verlegen*, *Verlag* 'to make payment', 'financial outlay'
acquired the new meanings 'publish', 'publishing house'; *setzen* came
to be used also for setting up type—*Setzer* 'compositor'. The root
druck- spawned new forms and usages: *Druck* denoted the act of
printing and what was printed, 'print'; *Druckerei* meant the act of
printing and the place where books were printed; *Nachdruck* meant
'reprint' and 'pirated print' (later *Raubdruck*; Luther complains of
reubische Nachdrücker); *Schöndruck* and *Widerdruck* meant respectively 'first forme', or 'prototype' and 'second forme' or 'antitype'[13],
etc. Professional customs[14] and an informal printers' jargon developed: *Hochzeit* 'a word printed twice', *Leiche* 'word omitted',
Fliegenkopf 'letter round the wrong way'. In the early period no
consistent terminology could be expected, for printers moved about,
often running presses in several towns—Anton Koberger the Elder
had thirteen branches in central and southern Germany with twenty-
four presses and a hundred workers.[15]

B. LINGUISTIC EFFECTS

The scale of the printers' operations and their mobility meant that they seldom originated from the towns where they worked and did not always adopt local written traditions—of nineteen printers active at Vienna before 1582 only one was born there. Factors familiar to us from scriptorium and chancery still apply, for the form of the original (the *Druckvorlage*), the language and region of the addressees, and prominent features of dialect and written language of the printing centre itself may all blend in the finished printed book. Moreover, printing was a collective enterprise in which, since no single standard language as yet existed, the orthographical and grammatical habits of author, printer, compositor, and corrector played a part. Consequently, far from immediately favouring uniformity, printing actually introduced diversity into texts, and the individual elements in the mixture can be identified only through the study of particular printing-houses and their output, especially in relation to sources: unfortunately, printers and bookbinders tended to destroy original manuscripts from which they worked. Eventually, this variability itself favoured the growth of 'house styles' and brought home the need for normative spelling, but this development failed to make much ground in the sixteenth century, when as late as 1570 books in Latin still accounted for 70 per cent of all printed matter. The orthography of Latin was relatively stable, and the question of German orthography remained for most printers too difficult or of marginal interest. They undoubtedly do gravitate away from local speech, despite the persistence of individual features, but the evidence for any conscious striving for supra-regional norms is purely circumstantial; indeed, the extent to which printers felt commercial pressure to seek wider markets and hence, perhaps, to adopt more general linguistic forms, clearly varied considerably. Mostly the early vernacular prints show a tolerant attitude to variables, for alternative forms of the same word, even of personal or place-names, exist side by side, sometimes on the same page. For example, Johann Mentelin's German Bible was set by nine compositors whose work seems also to be characterized by changes in orthography.[16] Certainly, the first compositor fluctuates considerably, as a glance at Genesis 3, shows. Note especially (1) the coexistence of diphthongal and monophthongal spellings: ⟨au⟩ ~ ⟨û⟩ (*auff* ~ *uff*), ⟨ei⟩ ~ ⟨î⟩ (*sein* ~ *sin, dein* ~ *din, fygbaum*); (2) the alternations ⟨ou⟩ ~ ⟨au⟩

(*ougen* ~ *augen*, *hausfrouwe*, *-baum*) and ⟨p⟩ ~ ⟨b⟩ (*weip* ~ *weibs* ~ *weib*); and (3) several other variant forms: *nit* ~ *nicht*, *daz* ~ *das* ~ *dz*, *was* ~ *waz*, *het* ~ *hat*, *warumb*, *darumb* ~ *worumb*, *dorumb*, *getan* ~ *geton*, *wir essent* ~ *rŭrten*.[17]

So far as the reading public was concerned, printing confronted them with archaic, regional, and stylistically varied language, again increasing the diversity (this time of the 'inner form') but leading eventually to a stylistic enrichment. Chronology was at first 'suspended' to some extent, since the fifteenth-century printers scoured monastery archives for whatever manuscripts they could find. Johann Mentelin's 1466 German Bible was based on a translation dating perhaps from the fourteenth century, possibly from the Nuremberg area: neither dialectally nor stylistically does it reflect Strasburg usage of the late fifteenth century; in 1477 Mentelin printed Wolfram von Eschenbach's *Parzival* and Albrecht von Scharffenberg's *Jüngerer Titurel*, both works of the thirteenth century. Similarly, Ulrich Boner's aphoristic *Edelstein*, composed in 1350, appeared with illustrations in 1461, as did Johannes von Tepl's *Ackermann aus Böhmen*, some sixty years after it was written. Eventually, crass archaisms were removed from German Bibles. For example, Günther Zainer (Z) replaced some of the archaisms in his 1475 Bible (the fourth of the fourteen HG Bibles printed before Luther). In Genesis 1, Mentelin (M) has *anegang*, *geschieff* (pret.), *vinster* (pl.), *vestenkeit*, *michel* 'great', *merer* 'greater', while Z uses *anfang*, *beschüff*, *veinsternuss* (beside *veinster*), *firmament*, *groß*, and *grôsser*. M's *derschein* (subj.: 'let the dry land appear'), with the prefix *der-* which remains in some southern dialects today, is replaced by Z's *erscheyne*; and M's use of *rieff* ('vnd gott der rieff die durre die erde') is replaced in Z by *hieß* ('Vnd got hiess die dúrre das erdtreich'). Ambiguous forms of the pres. subj. are replaced by *sollen*: (M's 'Die wasser . . . die *werdent* gesamet an ein stat' becomes in Z 'Es sullen gesamlet werden die wasser . . .'. Word order and M's pleonastic articles *got der sprach*, *got der sach* are also changed; the old enclitic particle *en/ne-* disappears in favour of *nicht*; and Z and his successors replace the old forms *zeswe* and *winster* by *recht* and *link*. The perfect verb periphrasis tends to replace the pret.[18] Zainer's versions influenced successive printers, which may reflect the prestige of Augsburg as a printing centre in the fifteenth and early sixteenth centuries: nine pre-Lutheran Bibles appeared there, and Augsburg printing features have been detected in Swiss and Rhenish printing languages.

But Zainer and his colleagues, as well as updating the German version, probably also replaced expressions not current in their area, although the geographical distribution of morphology and vocabulary at this period is difficult to determine: the replacement of the prefix *der-* and of the Strasburg pl. verb ending in *-ent* are examples of the clash of regional forms. At any rate, printing makes simultaneously available to the readers regional as well as archaic varieties of German: unfortunately, the lack of any standard form of German meant that the value of these stylistic elements fluctuated from area to area—one man's archaism was another's provincialism or another's norm. In other words, printing overcame constraints of time and place and confronted individuals with a stylistic choice; and, indeed, the abundance of literary genres represents also the gradual evolution of recognized styles of German—Luther's Bible translation can be viewed in this light.

Printers also influence the style of the author; for example, the lively, if seemingly colloquial, diary of a semi-educated German *conquistador*, Ulrich Schmidl, differs from the formal language of the edition of 1567 produced by the Frankfurt printer Sigismund Feyerabend.[19] The print shows an economy of expression lacking in the manuscript: Feyerabend introduces synthetic constructions, like gen. and dat. case-forms without prepositions and subj. verb forms rather than modal verbs with dependent infinitives, and he uses the passive more frequently, prefers subordinate word order, and replaces pleonastic verbs, generally 'tightening up' the text; for example, Schmidl's 'da *khamen sÿ* . . . *vnd* paden vmb gennadt' becomes in the print 'in dem begerten sie gnad an uns'. Such editorial alterations imply that certain features were felt inappropriate to the traveller's tale printed for a wider market: Feyerabend has perhaps changed the genre of Schmidl's work, moving away from the diary's informal and personal character, which is closer to private correspondence and ultimately to speech. Private letters in turn differ from the formal missives produced in chanceries, which show the structure of Lat. documents, with increasingly elaborate forms of address and 'protocol' laid down in *Kanzlei-* or *Titelbüchlein.*[20]

Finally (a perennial problem), printers falsify the author's text by errors and omissions—as Luther complained (below, pp. 191–2), technical works were especially liable to vitiation, and Laurentius Fries issued a corrected version of his very early vernacular treatise on medicine, the *Spiegel der artzeney* (Colmar, 1518), in which he specifically castigates the 'vngelerten Setzer'.[21]

PRINTING LANGUAGES

Early prints down to the 1530s are characterized by fluctuating spelling and forms for the reasons just considered; indeed, since prints are directed to a wider and often less determinate readership than are chancery documents, they provide a less reliable guide to local written language. Broader, regional characteristics *are* usually noticeable, however: for example the shifted consonants of HG and the later diphthongs stand out, and their occurrence in the LG-speaking northern towns or in the Alem. south-west is distinctive, e.g. forms like *das* for LG *dat* or *mein* for Swiss *myn*, LG *mīn*. In Basle, for example, the diphthongal spellings are used as early as 1490 by the printer Lienhart Ysenhuot in his edition of Steinhöwel's *Aesop*, and texts with diphthongs become increasingly common beside the 'Swiss printing language', with monophthongs, which remains pre-eminent for centuries for local purposes.[22] Later, the imperial notary and grammarian Johann Rudolph Sattler was to observe in his *Teutsche Orthographey und Phraseologey* . . . (Basle, 1607), dedicated to the town council and mayor of Colmar, that not everyone 'in diesen Oberteutschlanden' knew that diphthongal spellings were required for writing 'rechte Teutsche Sprach', i.e. the non-local, supra-regional type of German.[23] The very variability of most prints makes the establishing of the boundaries of regional printing languages at this time difficult, and reinforces the impression of an increasing divergence, if not total divorce, between 'written' and spoken language in any one area,—one precondition for the spread and establishment of a standard language.

Similarly, the interaction between the printed languages of the different regions is hard to assess, and regional written traditions are eventually also eroded as they are influenced by the practice of other areas. Moreover, contemporaries failed to agree regarding the most acceptable norms to follow. The printed usage in individual printing-houses was not consistent, nor was it consistent between the printing-houses in any one town, despite the inevitable local features; consequently, regional printing languages are themselves nebulous entities. But printers do develop 'house styles' to differing degrees:

Hans Lufft's at Wittenberg used a highly regular orthography for the printing of Luther's works, and this could provide a point of comparison with other printing houses at Wittenberg, Erfurt, Jena, and Leipzig in order to establish the extent to which printers in the EMG area after Luther's death have common and characteristic features.[24] Looking at individual printing centres, Virgil Moser postulated shifts in the publishing and, by implication, linguistic importance of individual regions.[25] In the late fifteenth century the West UG region with the centres Augsburg, Basel, and Strasburg was pre-eminent (Cologne and Nuremberg were important too, but Mainz declined). In the second quarter of the sixteenth century the emphasis moves to EMG territory, and specifically Wittenberg, under the influence of Luther and the Reformation. But after 1560 the WMG printing centre Frankfurt becomes important, influencing the practice in the south-west; the LG-speaking areas increasingly adopt HG printed form, and in the south the UG printing languages tend to merge, in particular because the Alem. regions with monophthongal spelling traditions adopt diphthongal ones. According to Moser, after about 1620 the EMG area again assumes the lead, with Leipzig as the main centre, Wittenberg printing having declined; by this time the LG-speaking north had adopted HG printing habits of an EMG kind, and there was linguistic levelling in the central German regions between WMG and EMG printing languages. This meant in turn that parts of UG territory were influenced by essentially MG forms of printing language. This picture is, broadly, confirmed by a study of the number of printers producing German books at the printing centres during the sixteenth and seventeenth centuries,[26] although there are modifications: the WMG area was important in the first half of the sixteenth century and, indeed, produced more prints of Luther's Bible translation during his lifetime than the EMG area. At the end of the sixteenth century we have at least one detailed view of the regional printing languages which, interestingly enough, does not subdivide the central German zone. The discerning but uninfluential schoolmaster Sebastian Helber distinguished four kinds of printing in his *Teutsches Syllabierbüchlein, Nemlich Gedruckter Hochteütscher sprach Lesenskunst* ... (Freiburg in Vchtland, 1593),[27] the fourth of which, 'die Ober oder Hoch Teutsche', is printed in three fashions: 'die Mitter Teutsche', 'die Donawische', and 'die Höchst Reinische'. These varieties are identified geographically and by the way in which they treat diphthongal spellings (e.g. MHG *lîp* 'body', *bein* 'bone'):

(1) *Mitter Teütsche*: printed at Mainz, Speyer, Frankfurt, Würzburg, Heidelberg, Nuremberg, Strasburg, Leipzig, Erfurt, and Cologne (in HG prints). Characteristic: *bein, leib*. (NB. Wittenberg is *not* listed.)

(2) *Donawische*: printed in the old Bavarian and Swabian provinces, excluding the Rhine region, and in Austria. Characteristic: *bain, leib*.

(3) *Höchst Reinische*: the form used by the *Eidgenossen* or Swiss in the Wallis, and in the Constance, Chur, and Basle dioceses. Characteristic: *bein, lyb*.

Helber himself organizes his examples according to the 'Mitter Teutsch' model, with the spelling ⟨ei⟩ for reflexes of both MHG phonemes. Subsequently, in the seventeenth century, the linguistic importance of MG regions is reflected both in the number of printers working there and by contemporary statements about the best forms of German to follow: the praises of the Meissen and US language and of Luther, with whom it is often linked, outweigh all other patterns of linguistic excellence.

We cannot here review the various authorities and models of German usage, which include dialect areas, prominent individuals (notably Luther and Opitz), praise of good authors and books, institutions like the chanceries or courts, and 'internal' criteria based on analogy or etymology.[28] Generally, the references are vague—even contradictory—as when the grammarian Fabian Frangk invokes in 1531 Emperor Maximilian's Chancery, Luther's writings, and Johann Schönsperger of Augsburg's prints.[29] Curiously, printing languages are seldom cited, although all the good authors and many chancery documents were printed and so actually reflect *printers*' decisions on spelling. We shall shortly illustrate this using the example of Martin Luther, whose influence on the external shape of the nascent German book language has been exaggerated. For a book or printed language for literary and educated use was emerging, and in 1628 Martin Opitz (1597–1639) wrote to a friend, Venator, at Strasburg that there existed a form of German which, like the Attic among the Greeks, had to be followed unless one wished to fall into error. This Venator could call 'Lutheran' if he chose—the main point was that it transcended dialect.[30] Opitz, whose *Buch von der deutschen Poeterey* (Breslau, 1624) experimented with the adaptation of classical metres in German and so led to a poetic revival, had cause to pay close attention to the phonology and orthography for the sake of purity of rhyme, and his words must be taken seriously. For the aged Schottel, at any rate, the form of the book language was essentially fixed —presumably, in his opinion, through his own efforts—for he remarks in his *Brevis & fundamentalis Manuductio ad Orthographiam & Etymologiam in Lingua Germanica* . . . (Braunschweig, 1676):

Es ist aber numehr/ und vorlångst/ in gantz Teutschland durchgehends und offentlich bekant worden/ was die ausgeschmůkte/ regulirte/ reiche und herrliche Hoch Teutsche Sprache sey/ worin sie recht bestehe und bestehen můsse/ wie sie recht geschrieben wird/ und recht zuschreiben sey . . . (pp. A5f.)

In fact, even the book language continued to fluctuate and complete codification came only after the unification of Germany in 1870, as part of *Kulturpolitik* (see Chapter IX). However, probably by barely perceptible, almost organic, shifts in printed usage, a recognizable centrally based language with controlled zones of variation had come about which southern and northern speakers alike acknowledged. Despite the justifiable praise of Martin Luther's Bible translation, we can show that he was not responsible for the external shape of the German book language.

THE PRINTERS AND LUTHER

The skill and accuracy of Luther's Bible translation made it an institution in Protestant schools and some grammarians looked on it as an authority even in linguistic matters. In the sixteenth century Paul Rebhun and Johannes Clajus based grammars on Luther's Bible, in the seventeenth Johannes Bellin, Schottel, Johannes Bödiker, and others cited Luther, and in the eighteenth Elias Caspar Reichard's history of German grammar actually includes him among the grammarians.[31] Printing enabled Luther to reach vast audiences, making him the first German author to be read on a modern scale; at the same time, printing took control of the final form of Luther's works out of his hands (although he is credited with having supervised even the spelling of the Bibles printed by Hans Lufft at Wittenberg). In the matter of spelling, and to a lesser extent in vocabulary, the language of the Luther Bible was modified both regionally and with the passage of time.

A. CIRCULATION: THE POTENTIAL OF PRINTING

Luther's considerable and varied writings had a huge circulation, particularly his Bible translations (the New Testament in 1522, the complete Bible in 1534), not least because they were frequently pirated by printers, principally in southern Germany. Between 1518 and 1524 one in three German books published had been written by Luther (1,473 prints out of 4,205), and in 1520 of the 570 German works printed 234 were his.[32] The famous 'September Testament' appeared in 1522 and was revised in December of that year: by 1525 there had been fourteen authorized editions and translations into LG, Danish, and Neth., but sixty-six pirate editions had appeared. Adam Petri pirated the 'September Testament' at Basle in 1522, reprinting it with a glossary for the benefit of UG readers unfamiliar with Luther's language; Petri's edition was itself reprinted nearly forty times by printers in southern and western areas.[33] From the appearance of the complete Bible in 1534 until Luther's death in 1546 ten HG editions and some eighty partial editions were authorized at Wittenberg, but these compare with some 260, mostly pirated, editions from elsewhere in the same period. Luther had just cause to berate the 'reubische Nachdrücker' in a *Warnung* prefacing his Bible—they even added Luther's name or 'Wittenberg' to spurious works to boost sales. After Luther's death, another seventy-five HG Bibles were printed at Wittenberg,[34] and by 1626 the number of copies of complete Bibles produced there is believed to have exceeded 200,000—to say nothing of copies from the innumerable reprints. Hans Lufft himself may well have printed 100,000 copies of Luther's works in his fifty years as a printer, and these were mostly editions of the Bible, whole or in part.

Given this phenomenal success, Luther's opponents could not ignore his writings, and Duke Georg of Saxony commissioned Luther's former teacher Hieronymus Emser (1478-1527) to purge the New Testament of heretical errors.[35] When, after Emser's death, this adulterated version was published as Emser's own, without mention of the real author, Luther complained bitterly, but proudly:

Das merckt man aber wol/ das sie aus meinem dolmetschen vñ deudsch/ lernen deudsch reden vnd schreiben/ vnd stelen mir also meine sprache/ dauon sie zuvor wenig gewust ... es thut mir doch sanfft/ das ich auch meine vndanckbare iünger/ dazu meine feinde/ reden gelert habe.[36]

So, Luther's writings, especially his Bible, the catechism, and his translation of the Psalms, had a vast distribution throughout Germany in the sixteenth and seventeenth centuries, both directly and indirectly through the pirate printers and Luther's Catholic opponents. In 1710, Freiherr von Canstein's Bible society at Halle began to distribute copies of the Bible on a non-profit-making basis, bringing it within reach of the poor. Had the text itself remained unaltered, it might indeed have provided an orthographical and grammatical standard at a crucial time in the language's development. But the text was not immutable: Luther's own habits varied; his printers had their own, not always consistent, usage, often following regional or local traditions; and succeeding generations updated the language and revised the translation, while continuing to refer to it as Luther's own. In fact, as Opitz implies, Luther's name had become a watchword of good German, of symbolic significance, not related to a specific external linguistic form.

B. PRINTERS AND THE EXTERNAL FORM OF LUTHER'S LANGUAGE

Luther's own orthography remained inconsistent throughout his life, as variant spellings and even errors in his manuscripts show: in this he is typical of his age. He was no reformer of spelling, although he progressively regularizes his own practice, especially from the mid-1520s onwards.[37] Almost certainly Luther was influenced in this purification by his printers, although out of piety he has been held to influence them. Since discrepancies between Luther's manuscript and the spelling of the prints remain until the end of his life, he may have adapted his spelling for 'public' as opposed to 'private' purposes: for example, in the personal pronouns *ihr*, *ihm*, *ihn*, Luther continues to use the occasional forms *yhr* etc., while the 1545 Bible has the consistent forms *jr*, *jm*, *jn*; again, where the Wittenberg prints use capital letters for most nouns after about 1539, Luther restricts them to proper names and the like, or uses them for emphasis.[38] Luther's manuscript spellings are immaterial to the emergence of a modern German norm: not only are they inconsistent, but the potentially influential language is that which appears in printed form. For this reason Heinrich Bach bases his handbook of Lutheran language on Wittenberg prints, regardless of Luther's personal habits—*Luthersprache* as the sixteenth-century reader might understand it.[39]

The linguistic role of Wittenberg in the sixteenth century will emerge fully only after the practice of other centres has been adequately described. In particular, the connection between Wittenberg printed forms and the seventeenth-century book language needs further examination. In Luther's day the printers at other centres modified the external form of his writings, as regional reprints of his New Testament show.

Orthographical and Morphological Variables in Regional Prints of Luther's New Testament (Mark 1: 23-8)[40]

(1) *'Septembertestament'* (Melchior Lotther, Wittenberg, 1522)

Vnd es war ynn yhrer schulen eyn mensch besessen mit eynem vnsaubern geyst, der schrey vnd sprach, Hallt, was haben wyr mit dyr zu schaffen, Jhesu von Nazareth? du bist komen vns zu verderben, ich weys, das du der heylige gottis bist, vnd Jhesus bedrawete yhn vnd sprach, verstumme, vnnd fare aus von yhm, vnnd der vnsawber geyst reys yhn, vnd schrey laut, vnd fur aus von yhm, vnd sie ertzitterten alle, also, das sie vnternander sich befragten, vnd sprachen, was ist das? was ist das fur eyn newe lere? Er gepeutt mitt gewallt den vnsawberen geysten, vnnd sie gehorchen yhm, vnnd seyn gerucht erschall bald vmbher ynn die grentze Galilee.

(2) *Adam Petri's reprint* (Basle, 1522)

Vnd es war in iren schůlen ein mensch besessen mit einem vnsauberen geyst, der schrey vnd sprach, Halt, was haben wir mit dir zů schaffen, Jesu von Nazareth? du bist kommen vns zů verderben, ich weysz, das du der heilige gottes bist. vnd Jesus betrauwete jn vnd sprach, verstumme, vnd fare ausz von im, vnd der vnsauber geyst reysz jn, vnd schrey laut, vnd fůr ausz von im, vnd sy erzitterten alle, also, das sy vndernander sich befragten, vnnd sprachen, was ist das? was ist das für ein neuwe lere? Er gebeüt mit gewalt den vnsauberen geisten, vnd sy gehorchen im, vnd sein gerucht erschal bald vmbher in die grentze Galilee.

(3) *Hanns Schönsperger's reprint* (Augsburg, 1523)

Vnd es war inn jrer schůlen ein mensch besessen mit einem vnsaubern geyst, der schrey vnd sprach, Hallt, was haben wir mit dir zůschaffen, Jesu von Nazareth? du bist komen vns zůuerderben, ich weisz, das du der heylige gottes bist, vnd Jhesus bedrawete jn vnd sprach, verstumme, vnd fare ausz von jm, vnd der vnsauber geyst reysz jn, vnd schrey laut, vnd fůr ausz von jm, vnd sie erzitterten alle, also, das sie vntereinander sich befragten, vnd sprachen, was ist das? was ist das für ein newe lere? Er gebeüt mit gewallt den vnsauberen geysten, vnd sie gehorchen jm? vnd sein gerucht erschall bald vmbher inn die grentze Galilee.

(4) *Silvan Otmar's reprint* (Augsburg, 1524)

Vnd es was in irer schůlen ain mensch besessen mit ainem vnsaubern gaist, der schry vnd sprach. Halt, was haben wir mit dir zůschaffen Jesu von Nazareth? du bist kōmen vns zů verderben, ich waisz das du der hailig gotes bist. Vnd Jesus bedrôwet jn vnd sprach, verstum̃, vnd far ausz von jm, vnd der vnsauber gaist risse jn, vnd schry laut, vnd fůr ausz von jm, vnd sy erzitterten alle, also, das sy vnderainander sich befragten, vnd sprachen, was ist das? was ist das für ain neẅe leer? Er gebeüt mit gewalt den vnsaubern gaisten, vnnd sy gehorchen jm, vnd sein gerůcht erschal bald vmbher in die grenitz Galilee.

(5) *Melchior Ramminger's reprint* (Augsburg, 1526)

Und es was in jren schůlen ain mensch besessenn mitt ainem vnsauberen gaist, der schray vnd sprach: Halt, wz haben wir mit dir zeschaffen Jesu vonn Nazareth? du bist kom̃en vns zů verderben: ich waysz das du der haylig Gotes bist. Und Jesus beschalckt jn mit trōwen, vnd sprach: Uerstum̃, vnd far ausz von jm. Und der vnsauber gaist raysz jn, vnd schray laut, vnd fůr ausz von jm. Und sy erzittertend alle, also, das sie vnderainander sich erfragtend, vnd sprachend: Was ist das? Was ist das für ain neuwe leer? Er gebeüt mit gwalt den vnsauberen gaysten, vnd sye seind jm gehorsam. Unnd sein guter lümbd erschal bald vm̃her in die gegne vnd anstösz Galilee.

The most striking differences in the regional printings of Luther's NT are as follows:

Orthography

Petri's version (2) reduces the graphy ⟨y⟩ considerably; cf. (1) *ynn, yhrer, eyn, wyr, heylige, geysten* with (2) *in, iren, ein, wir, heilige, geisten*. The pronoun *sy* contrasts with (1)'s *sie*, the expected historical form.

Mutated ⟨ü⟩ in *für* contrasts with *fůr* (NHG *fuhr*) in texts (2)–(5), but not in (1). The mutated form *gebeüt* is probably not phonetically significant in (2), but might be in (3)–(5); see Moser (1929), § 82. 2; cf. Petri's *neuwe* and the form *newe* in 1, 3, 4 (MHG *niuwe; gebiutet*).

In the consonants, Petri employs ⟨sz⟩ (*weysz, ausz, reysz*) and reduces gemination before another consonant or in final position (*Halt, vnd, in, gebeut, gewalt, erschal*). The form *betrauwete* (NHG *bedrohte*) seems to show an UG ⟨t⟩ for MG ⟨d⟩, while *vndernander* shows an UG softening of *t → d* after a nasal. The medial ⟨b⟩ for ⟨p⟩ in *gebeüt* is unlikely to be of phonetic significance since most other reprints, including UG ones not considered here, show the form with ⟨b⟩.

This material shows sufficiently that Petri preserves Luther's text—

even to the error *vndernander* for **vnter eynander*—but not the Wittenberg orthography.

The other specimens, (3)–(5), from Augsburg, differ from (1) and also among themselves, illustrating the various 'house styles' current at the same printing centre. In particular, (4) and (5) are more 'southern' in separating the old and new diphthongs (MHG */ei/* as in *ein* and */î/* as in *sîn*), using the graphies ⟨ai/ay⟩ and ⟨ei⟩: cf. (1) *eyn, seyn* vs. (4) and (5) *ain, sein.* The Ramminger text, (5), is also less consistent in itself: *gaist/gaysten, mitt/mit, von/vonn, sy/sie/sye.*

Phonology

A phonological feature with morphological implications, if not causation, is the loss of unstressed */e/* (see Chapter IV). Again, our prints diverge: (1), (2), and (3) preserve the */e/*, while (4) and (5) drop it. Cf. (1) *heylige, bedrawete, verstumme, fare, lere, grentze* and (4) *heilig, bedröwet, verstum(m), far, leer, grenitz.* The verbal morphology in the imperative sg. and pret. sg. and the adj. and noun declension are affected.

One unstressed syllable appears in (1) in characteristic EMG form as ⟨i⟩, viz. *gottis*, replaced in the other texts; equally characteristic is the southern syncope in *gwalt* (Ramminger).

Morphology

Petri retains most morphology, but note that the original's weak sg. fem. noun (*ynn yhrer schulen*) is recast as pl. (*in iren schůlen*); cf. also (5) vs. (3), (4). In the verb forms, his Basle colleague Thomas Wolff in a 1523 reprint replaces the strong verb pret. *schrey* and *reys* (1) with *schry* and *risz*, showing analogical levelling of the vowel grade of the pret. pl. and past part. into the pret. sg.[41]. The Augsburg texts are again split: (3) and (5) preserve the old forms but with different orthography—(3) *schrey, reysz,* (5) *schray, raysz*—whereas (4) has analogical forms *schry* and *risse,* the latter showing further analogical development in having added final *-e,* as though it were a weak pret. The Ramminger, (5), shows pl. verb-endings in *-nd* for the third person pl. (*erzittertend, erfragtend, sprachend*), and shares this feature and some vocabulary with Christoffel Froschower's 1534 Bible (Zurich), which uses the expressions *beschalkt, erfragtend,* and which also replaces *gehorchen* by *gehorsam seind/sind, gerucht* by *lümbd* (cf. mod. German *Leumund, verleumden*), and *grentze* by *gegne vnd anstösz.*

These examples suffice to illustrate the regional variation in the orthography and morphology of reprints of Luther's New Testament, and we could add change of genders, increased use of perfect verb forms, and differing use of modal verbs. Luther's vocabulary remains relatively untouched, but even here glossing occurs, either in the text or the margin, or as an appendix. Similar deviation doubtless affects the external form of Luther's Bible and other writings when they were reprinted. Only exceptionally does a printer claim to retain even 'Luther's' spelling: Wendel Rihel in the preface to his 1535 Strasburg Bible states:

> . . . Vnd habe mich beflissen/ seine besunder wörter/ vnd orthographey so meer auff Sachsisch/ denn vnser hochteutsch gepraucht/ eygentlich pleiben zülassen. Die vbung wird solchs auch wol verstendig/ vnnd gepreuchlicher machen/ denen/ so zur H. geschrifft anmüt haben.

Rihel's claim needs checking—but even pirate printers might through their very haste retain a few Wittenberg features.

Wittenberg prints, like the Augsburg copies of the New Testament, differed among themselves. Melchior Lotther's version of the *Septembertestament* does not accord with the practice subsequently followed by Hans Lufft, and seems more 'local' in character.[42] The corrector Christoph Walther attacks pirate printers in 1563 for not keeping to the authentic spelling ('Ordnung und Orthographiam') devised by Luther and Caspar Cruciger,[43] and lists examples both to be followed and rejected. Interestingly, many forms advocated by Walther do not survive into the seventeenth-century book language, let alone into mod. German spelling, while forms from the pirate printers *do* correspond to later usage. Whereas Walther's separation of the homonyms *Rad* = Lat. *rota* from *Rat* = Lat. *consilium* survives, the plurals *Reder* vs. *Rete* lack the ⟨ä⟩ graphy; *Stad* = Lat. *civitas* vs. *Stat* = Lat. *locus* is now *Stadt* vs. *Stätte* or (*Werk-*)*Statt*. The Lufft orthography also makes scant use of ⟨h⟩ to indicate length, and consequently the personal pronouns are distinguished from the prepositions by the length of the symbol: '*jm . . . jn* mit einem langen j [NHG *ihm, ihn*] vnd *im . . . in* mit einem kurtzen i' (NHG *im, in*). The pirate printers have the 'modern' forms *Lehre, ohn(e), Sohn* (and also *Leuthen, Orth, Rath,* and *Theil*, which were 'normal' until the late nineteenth century), while Lufft prints *Lere, on, Son* (*Leuten, Ort, Rat, Teil*). Walther particularly attacks other printers for adding letters unnecessarily, although their use of double consonants seems both analogical and logical, since they extend them to final position, as in mod. German (*Komm, Mann, Brunn, Statt*), whereas Walther advocates *Kom, Man*, etc., reserving double consonants for distinguishing homonyms (*den* vs. *denn, wen* vs. *wenn, Veter* (NHG *Väter*) vs. *Vetter, ermanen* (NHG *ermahnen*) vs. *ermannen*). In short, Walther admonishes, 'Die Nachdrücker solten nicht allein wort auff wort (wie sie rhûmen) drucken sondern auch Buchstab auff Buchstab . . .', and in another tract directed against the Frankfurt printer Sigismund Feyerabend[44] he repeats that Luther had supervised the printing of his works and taught correctors and compositors even 'wie man recht Buchstabisch schreiben vnd drucken sol'.

With the passage of time even the Bibles published at Wittenberg distanced themselves more and more from the form of the 1545 Luther Bible. For example, the 1622 Wittenberg Bible printed by J. W. Fincelius and published by Zachariae Schürer shows considerable changes;[45] e.g. an increase in the use of capitals, of ⟨å⟩ in noun plurals (*båche, ståbe, ståmme, gåste*, etc.) and derivations (*gefåß, stårcke, waffentråger*), and in verb morphology: (*er gråbt, sie kåmen, sie bråchten*). Similarly, ⟨åw⟩/⟨åu⟩ is used for earlier ⟨eu⟩ (*såw(e), båwme, tråwme, glåubig*), although some forms in ⟨eu⟩ remain. The mutation sign ⟨å⟩, whether for the single vowel or for the diphthong, is extremely rare in Luther's works, and he invariably writes ⟨e⟩, ⟨eu⟩.[46] The conjunction *daß* occurs instead of earlier *das*, and is thus distinct from the article, and the 'Dehnungs-*h*' is much more frequent, e.g. in pronouns (*jhm, jhn, jhr, jhnen*), verbs (*führen, fahren, lehren*), and some nouns (*lehre, jahre*), but is still absent in the very frequent *son, sone*. In morphology, however (one striking example of continuity), the pret. sg. of Class I strong verbs still retains the /ei/ diphthong: *treib, erschein, schweig*, etc. These changes in the Bible's linguistic form represent the periodic updatings of printers and correctors, so that the concept of 'Luther's language' in respect of the external form—orthography and morphology—is probably a myth. But even if it were not, there is no compelling reason why the most widespread written or printed language need cause the readers to emulate its spelling and forms, reading and writing being different activities. Moreover, the sixteenth-century Bibles were made to last. An avid Bible-reader from Goslar, E. D. Pithan, lists his number of readings of the complete work on the flyleaf: around 1645 he had managed twenty-two readings, in 1655 the total reached a hundred and by November 1656 another four. But this Bible was printed by Rabe, Feyerabend, and Weigand Han's successors at Frankfurt in

1567, ninety years previously, and the orthographical influence must have been slight, since Pithan's entries show LG characteristics.[47]

Given the multiplicity of printed forms of Luther's text, his own famous pronouncement on the most common German seems scarcely relevant, although it remains intriguing. Luther's bilingual table talk collected by several friends in slightly differing versions contains an entry around 1532 expressing the need for a generally understood language:

Nullam certam linguam Germanice habeo, sed communem, ut me intelligere possint ex superiori et inferiori Germania. Ich rede nach der Sechsischen cantzley, quam imitantur omnes duces et reges Germaniae; alle reichstette, fürsten höfe schreiben nach der Sechsischen cantzeleien vnser churfürsten. Ideo est communissima lingua Germaniae. Maximilianus imperator et elector Fridericus imperium ita ad certam linguam definierunt, haben also alle sprachen in eine getzogen.[48]

Despite the juxtaposition of *rede* and *schreiben*, this quotation surely bears on the most widely current written form of German, not the style. Luther claims to avoid any one regional form of German (*certam linguam*), contrasting with this a koine or common form (*communem*) intelligible in south and north—this must mean HG, which was indeed being used in the LG-speaking north even before Luther. The most common form of HG is, as Luther has it, the language of the Saxon Chancery. We have already seen (p. 141) that the Imperial Chancery of Maximilian may indeed have influenced the Electoral Saxon Chancery, especially just after Maximilian's death. However, the Saxon Chancery's language was not uniform, and varied with the habits of individual scribes, although the Chancery does seem more progressive than the early Wittenberg printers, since it shows normative tendencies, is less local in character, and has forms not found in early prints of Luther's works and which have survived into the modern standard, e.g. *kaufen, Stroh, Turm, welch, zwanzig*, instead of the Wittenberg printers' forms *keufen, stro, thurn, wilch, zwenzig*. Luther, or his printers, may be following the Saxon Chancery practice when these forms are replaced.[49]

THE GROWING PRESTIGE OF HIGH GERMAN[50]

Increasingly in the sixteenth century the LG-speaking areas of northern Germany adopt HG as the formal written language in chanceries, lawcourts, printing-houses, and for Church and school administration, and finally even for religious services and in the classroom. This trend is attested well before the Reformation, in the fifteenth century, and has been linked with the decline of the Hanseatic League, as trading interests moved from the Baltic to more lucrative American and Venetian (Levantine) markets. For in the heyday of the Hanse LG had considerable status as a widely used administrative, commercial, and legal language which competed with Latin as a supra-regional koine for merchants and seamen. Moreover, LG dialects differed less radically than HG ones among themselves and the spelling was—relative to HG—less variegated; the links with other important trading languages—Dutch, Danish, and English—were closer: LG might well have become a German standard language. But the Hanse dwindled in importance, and the growth of absolutist states led to the loss of privileges of individual towns, which further weakened the cohesion of the north. New ideas—Humanism, Renaissance, and the Reformation—came from the south, often via HG intermediaries, and the prestige of the HG language gradually outstripped that of LG, starting in the aristocratic and educated circles. The Reformation, in particular, recast the organization of the Church and of education in most of north Germany.

The Brandenburg area has HG written language very early: the Berlin town chancery uses it from the first decade of the sixteenth century and Berlin schools are teaching in it by about 1550. The extreme north-western, Fris.-speaking region was the last to go over to HG as a teaching language in schools, by about 1680; the coexistence of Danish, LG, Fris., and HG in this area must have complicated matters. However, the shift to HG was no gradual geographical 'spread' northwards but a highly complicated and differentiated process affecting each court, town, chancery, church, and school at varying times and degrees.

Nevertheless, the spheres of influence and the sequence in which HG gains ground are, broadly discernible. First, it is recognized as an official administrative language in princely courts and chanceries, then in town chanceries and lawcourts; the origins and training of chancery personnel are significant here: Adam Thraciger, chancellor of Duke Adolf of Gottorp in Schleswig, was a HG-speaker, for example.[51] In the Church, the official administrative language of Church ordinances (*Kirchenordnungen*) is increasingly HG, for Church organization was influenced by the chancery. Parts of the actual religious service might also be HG, depending on the parson and the hymn-books and prayer-books used, but sermons generally remained in LG in order to reach the congregation; however, at Flensburg, for example, HG sermons were preached from about 1600. Where complaints against the use of HG are known, they reflect the problems of LG-speakers who could not follow it; for this reason Luther, who probably did not speak LG (though he understood it), relied on the LG preacher Johannes Bugenhagen (1485–1588) to deliver sermons in 'Plattdeutsch'; Bugenhagen probably also translated the Luther Bible into LG.[52] In the schools, the language of the statutes (*Schulordnungen*) is again official in character and appears as HG relatively early. The language of instruction usually remained LG for a few decades after, but a new HG rector and HG teachers led sometimes to an immediate change-over. Most HG teachers in the north came from Silesia, Saxony, and Thuringia, while most LG students—future teachers, preachers, lawyers, and chancery officials—attended university at Wittenberg, Leipzig, Frankfurt an der Oder, or Jena. Latin schools change to HG for teaching purposes before the German schools, and these before the humblest reading and writing schools (*Winkelschulen*). The change can be inferred from the introduction of textbooks with HG explanations, sometimes even from statutes: pupils at the Graues Kloster in Berlin are in 1574 expressly required to translate into HG, 'sich im teutschen des Meisnischen dialecti . . . zu befleißigen'.[53] School plays in HG become common, and Franciscus Omichius' *Damon und Pythia* 1578[54] and several plays by Duke Heinrich Julius of Brunswick (1564–1613) already have LG roles, as peasants, buffoons, and artisans, suggesting a social stratification in which LG ranked below HG.

Printing-houses reflect these developments and soon ceased printing LG altogether. Significantly, the only spelling guide printed in LG, the *Formulare vn duytsche Rethorica ader der schryfftspiegel ghenant des neuwen stylums* . . . (Cologne, 1527), written in Ripuarian Frk. spelling, had lost any relevance to printing by the end of the sixteenth century: while some 295 LG prints were produced at Cologne between 1500 and 1550, between 1576 and 1600 only 4 LG prints were published there.[55] At Magdeburg, by the end of the sixteenth century only 39 LG prints are found beside 138 HG ones. The last LG hymnal and Bible were printed at Goslar in 1618 and 1621.[56]

In a very general sense, Martin Luther could be credited through the Bible and the Reformation with having ensured that HG of an EMG type came to overlie the LG dialects as a standard book or written language, even if the *form* of that EMG was not his 'own'. An awareness of the gap between literary HG and spoken everyday, informal LG dialect is evident in many grammarians and writers from these northern areas:[57] whereas in the HG areas of the South stylistic differentiation is less crass. With central and northern Germany following a fairly recognizable book language in the late seventeenth century it was only a matter of time before grammarians and writers imposed this usage on the south, a process completed in the eighteenth century (see Chapter VIII).

MARTIN LUTHER AND THE 'INNER FORM' OF GERMAN

Martin Luther's Bible still strikes the reader by its freshness and vigour, its directness and expressiveness—this is a language for the ear, not for silent reading, even if time has removed it from modern spoken German and dignified it with an unintended patina of archaism. Luther's contemporaries, even his enemies, immediately perceived its worth and the dangers of its appeal to simple folk who would read it at home.[58] Yet Luther's biblical style was no naïve reproduction of colloquial speech, but rather a skilful simulation of it in a carefully considered form. The deliberate artistic shaping of his Bible is evident when we compare it with Luther's style in his less formal writings—polemical tracts, letters, sermons, and so forth— and also when we consider the constant revisions of the biblical text by Luther and his 'sanhedrin' of colleagues, including Philip Melanchthon (1497–1560), Professor of Greek at Wittenberg, Mattheus Goldhahn (Aurogallus) (c.1490–1543), Professor of Hebrew, Johannes Bugenhagen, the noted LG preacher and Latinist, and others. Luther also thought seriously about the translator's task, and it is illuminating to compare his views with those of the early German Humanists, who translated secular material for an entirely different audience and with a different purpose.

A. EARLY HUMANIST TRANSLATORS AND LUTHER

The best-known early German Humanists, the chancery official Niclas von Wyle (c.1410–78/9), the jurist Albrecht von Eyb (1420– 75), and the physician Heinrich Steinhöwel (1412–82), moved in aristocratic circles and often dedicated their German versions to patrons from southern German courts with literary interests and aspirations.[59] The sources are largely modern Italian authors of the Trecento and Quattrocento—Francesco Petrarch (1304–74), Giovanni Boccaccio (1313–75), Leonardo Bruni (1369–1444), Enea Silvio Piccolomini (1405–64), Giovanni Bracciolini Poggio (1380–1459), and others—whose refurbished neo-Latin elegance was much admired; classical authors and works are sparsely represented (Lucius Apuleius, Plautus, and Aesop) until the sixteenth century.

The translators responded to the perennial choice between literal translation and paraphrase in different ways. Niclas von Wyle was of the opinion that Latin rhetoric could be deployed equally well in German, and actually goes beyond his sources in using complicated periods, parallel clauses with participial constructions, present and past, and the un-German accusative and infinitive:[60]

ille feminam dicebat animal esse = 'er sprach ain frowen sin ain tiere vngezämpt, wild . . .' ('He said a woman was an untamed, wild animal . . .') (p. 53).

Sed invenies aliquos senes amantes, amatum nullum . . . = 'du findest alber [NHG *aber*] etlich alt liebhabend mane. aber liebgehapten kainen. Welche wort ich wol verstentlicher hett mugen [= *können*] setzen also. du findest aber etlich alt mane die frowen liebhabent. aber kainen alten findst du, der von frowen werd lieb gehept' (pp. 7–8).

Such apparent wilfulness demonstrates German's flexibility (and Wyle's own skill), but its aim is didactic: to reveal the beauty of Latin structures that have been literally transferred—Wyle's term is *transferieren*—to German. Popular appeal or even comprehensibility did not concern him:

. . . und nit geachtet, ob dem schlechten (NHG *schlichten*) gemainen vnd vnernieten (= *unerfahren*) man das vnverstentlich sin werd oder nit (p. 8).

Niclas von Wyle's *Translatzen* or *Translationen* can be seen as rhetorical exercises in writing Latinate German, recalling Johannes von Tepl's masterpiece, the *Ackermann aus Böhmen*. Both writers were chancery officials and also taught, and the *Ackermann* could have been known in these Humanist circles.[61]

Albrecht von Eyb's prose translations, particularly of two plays of Plautus, rely instead on paraphrase, setting the works firmly in the fifteenth century, Christianizing the classical pantheon, 'translating' the names of the characters and institutions, even replacing classical proverbs by German equivalents.[62] Steinhöwel, too, opts for prose rather than verse in his translation of Aesop (1476–80). While he renders the original closely, he is nevertheless guided by sense, not by the words themselves:

... uß latin ... schlecht (= *schlicht*) vnd verstentlich getütschet, nit wort uß wort/ sunder sin uß sin[63]

In 1530 while at Coburg Castle, Martin Luther set about refining and polishing Steinhöwel's *Esopus*,[64] and this may have prompted him to discuss his own principles of translation in the famous *Sendbrief vom Dolmetschen* published that year. The distinction between literal translation (*verbum e verbo*) and paraphrase (*sensum de sensu*) was in any case familiar to him from St Jerome, if not from Horace.

Luther is first and foremost a theological translator, for whom translating God's word is a religious act in which piety is as important as knowledge and zeal:

'Es gehöret dazu [*sc.* dolmetschen] ein recht/ frum/ trew/ vleissig/ furchtsam/ Christlich/ geleret/ erfaren/ geübet hertz ...'[65]

He was not interested in linguistic philosophy for its own sake, nor in theories of rhetoric,[66] but rather in its practical application. For language is the means by which the word of God is preserved for men and spread among them—and here Luther takes issue with *Schwermer*, 'enthusiasts' who claimed to communicate with God directly, without using language:

Vnd last vns das gesagt seyn/ Das wyr das Evangelion nicht wol werden erhallten/ on die sprachen. Die sprachen sind die scheyden/ darynn dis messer des geysts stickt. Sie sind der schreyn darynnen man dis kleinod tregt. Sie sind das gefess, darynnen man disen tranck fasset. Sie sind die kemnot, darynnen dise speyse ligt.[67]

Hebrew, Greek, or Latin are not intrinsically sacred, but are hallowed by the mere function of preserving God's message, which can be transmitted into other languages, including German, making them holy too. However, since each language has its own idiom and grammar, too much respect for the source language actually leads to misunderstanding. Exegetical interpretation of the Bible of a tropological-historical, allegorical, or anagogical kind—first found in German in Otfrid—also clearly took the scriptural message beyond the reach of the ordinary Christian layman. Luther wanted the text to speak for itself wherever possible, and to speak German. For this he was taken to task as a *Paraphrast* (Emser) who disregarded the letter of the Bible, where even punctuation was paramount. So in fact his critics claimed in one and the same breath that Luther stuck at the superficial, literal meaning of the text, and that he paraphrased it: their corrections of his heretical errors consisted in a return to older word-for-word renderings. But Luther too was prepared to compromise where important points of doctrine were at stake, even at the cost of writing bad German:

... wo etwa an einem wort gelegen ist/ hab ichs nach den buchstaben behalten/ vnd bin nicht so frey dauon gangen ... ich hab ehe wôllen der deutschen sprache abbrechen/ denn von dem wort weichen.[68]

Otherwise he ridicules the asinine *Buchstabilisten* for their barbarous German.[69]

Generally, the Catholic revisors and translators were conservative, but Johannes Dietenberger at least aims to be understood—perhaps an indication that Luther had forced his opponents to adopt his approach:

... Wo aber der bloß bûchstab/ an seiner dolmetschung/ dem rechten Christlichen verstand bey den leyen verhinderlich ist/ bedunckt mich besser/ daß man den rechten verstand dem lây dargebe/ ob gleich Grammatische dolmetschung nit so eigentlich erhalten werde. Dann die wort/ ... seynd vmb des verstands willē/ vñ sollen dem rechten verstand dienen/ vnd nit herwiderumb ...[70]

Significantly, Luther describes his translation as *dolmetschen*, implying perhaps then, as now, 'interpreting', both in the sense of oral, not written, translation—for Luther's style is declamatory—and also in the sense of explaining the message.

B. LUTHER'S STYLE AND VOCABULARY

... denn man mus nicht die buchstaben jnn der Lateinischen sprachen fragen/ wie man sol Deudsch reden/ ... Sondern man mus die mutter jhm hause/ die kinder auff der gassen/ den gemeinen man auff dem marckt drûmb fragen/ vnd den selbigen auff das maul sehen/ wie sie reden/ vnd darnach dolmetschen/ so verstehen sie es denn/ vnd mercken/ das man Deudsch mit jhn [NHG *ihnen*] redet.[71]

This is a call for idiomatic German, not Latin in German dress; for speech, not writing. Luther wanted the Bible to speak to everyone and he needed to choose the right level of diction, the most widely understood form: stylistic and geographical barriers had to be overcome.

Stylistically, Luther's Bible often imitates speech-rhythms and its syntax is less formal than mod. German's, with clauses linked loosely together, so that their relationship is clearest when they are spoken aloud. For instance, dem. and relative pronouns were not separated by differing word order at this time, and their degree of emphasis varies; in mod. spoken German the demonstrative can still 'replace' the relative, so avoiding complex subordinating clauses with verb clusters at the end. However, the Luther Bible is not always colloquial, but has the qualities of more serious and moving spoken language familiar from the sermon or from recitation. While chancery or legal documents can make the relationship between the parts of the period over-explicit by cumbersome particles, in the Bible grammatical and natural gender alternate, clauses are introduced by *und*, and pronouns or finite verbs are omitted:

Vnd da war ein Weib/ *das* hatte den Blutgang zwelff jar gehabt/ *vnd* hatte viel erlidden von vielen Ertzten/ *vnd* hatte alle jr Gut darob verzeret/ *vnd* halff *sie* nichts/ Da *die* von Jhesu hörte/ kam sie . . . (Mark 5: 25).

Double negation—not found in Latin—seems striking in the Bible— 'ein Füllen . . . auff welchem nie kein Mensch gesessen ist ~ Vulg. 'pullum . . . super quem nemo adhuc hominum sedit' (Mark 11: 2)— and is today dialectal and substandard.

The clausal frame (*Satzrahmen, Satzklammer*: see pp. 257-60) is also not found in the Greek or Latin sources, and reveals Luther's reshaping of the word order. Luther's alterations to his *September-Testament* create such clausal frames by separating finite verbs from their dependent infinitives, participles, or prefixes. Thus, Matt. 6: 14-15 in the *September-Testament*:

Denn so *yhr vergebt* den menschen yhre feyle/ so *wirtt* euch ewr hymelischer vatter auch *vergeben*/ wo *yhr* aber den menschen nit *vergebt* yhre feyle/ so *wirtt* euch ewr vatter auch nitt *vergeben* ewre feyle

becomes in the *Dezember-Testament*:

Denn so *yhr* den menschen yhre feyle *vergebt*/ so *wirt* euch ewr hymelischer vatter auch *vergeben*/ wo *yhr* aber den menschen yhre feyle nicht *vergebt*/ so *wirt* euch ewr vater ewre feyle auch nicht *vergeben*.

Similarly, comparing two examples from the *September-Testament* and the 1545 Bible, Mark 6: 56 'wo *er eyn gieng* ynn die merckte odder stett odder dorff' becomes 'wo *er* ynn die merckte odder stett odder dorff *eyn gieng*', and Mark 9: 22 'vnnd offt *hatt er* yhn *geworffen* ynn fewr vnd wasser . . .' becomes 'vnd offt *hat er* jn in fewr vnd wasser *geworffen* . . .'.[72] Whether or not the clausal frame is a feature of colloquial Wittenberg German in the sixteenth century, the translator's departure from the syntax of the original is clear. UG versions, like Zainer's (Augsburg, 1475) and Eck's Ingolstadt Bible (1537), are much more conservative than Luther in this respect.

Informal, *ad hoc* renderings of biblical passages abound in sermons and pericopes (liturgical readings in the vernacular), and Luther was not afraid to use them in his Bible, while his less daring rivals stick closely to the letter of the Latin. For example, whereas Luther translates Matt. 12: 34 (Vulg. 'Ex abundantia cordis os loquitur') as 'Wes das Hertz vol ist | des gehet der Mund vber', Emser—who had used precisely this wording in a polemic against Luther in 1521, perhaps even prompting him—reverts to a literal translation in his 1527 emended New Testament, 'aus fölle des hertzen redt der mund' and (Luke 6: 45) 'aus vberflus des hertzen redet der mund'.[73] But Luther had an ear for proverbial turns of phrase and even collected proverbs, like his contemporaries Johannes Agricola (1494–1566) and Sebastian Franck (1499–1542/3). The Bible itself contains many gnomic sayings, and Luther drew heavily on these in his pamphleteering: conversely, he imports everyday expressions into the Bible.

Luther constantly modified the vocabulary of his Bible translation, sometimes spending up to four weeks searching for the *mot juste*—even in vain—and sometimes barely managing to translate a line in a day.[74] The style of the Bible was to be simple and direct, and when Luther wrote to his friend Spalatin in March 1522 asking his advice about popular expressions he deliberately ruled out 'court or castle words' ('non castrensia nec aulica suppedites') as inappropriate. Later, in December, when he was already thinking about his translation of the Old Testament, he asked Spalatin for the names of several wild birds, animals, and reptiles.[75] Luther's biographer Johannes Mathesius, writing in 1567, reports that Luther once had a butcher cut up sheep and teach him the technical names for the cuts. Luther could also be critical of chancery word-formations in *be-* and *er-*, though history has not proved him right:

Ich hab auch noch bis her keyn buch noch brieff gelesen/ da rechte art deutscher sprach ynnen were/ Es achtet auch niemant recht deutsch zu reden/ sonderlich der herrn Canceleyen vnd die lumpen prediger/ vnd puppen schreyber/ die sich lassen duncken/ sie haben macht deutsche sprach zu endern vnd tichten vns teglich newe wortter/ Behertzigen/ behendigen/ ersprieslich/ erschieslich vnd dergleichen/ ia lieber man/ es ist wol bethoret vnd ernarret dazu.[76]

Replacement of vocabulary in subsequent editions of Luther's New Testament may be for stylistic or geographical reasons—the two are hard to separate. As early as December 1522 Luther replaced *spreysse* 'mote' (Matt. 7: 3) by *splitter* (hence *Splitterrichter*) and *spugnis* (Matt. 14: 26; cf. LG *spuk*, English *spook*) by *gespenst*. After 1527 he toned down colloquial expressions; thus, *anschnauben* 'reprimand' becomes *anfahren, schnurren* 'rush off' becomes *stürmen, die nase runzen* becomes *spotten, blastücker* becomes *teuscher* (NHG *Täuscher*), *kollern* becomes *sich wälzen, gruntzen* becomes *grollen, verstarrt* becomes *verwundert, schüttert er sich* becomes *entsetzt er sich, schrei* (NHG *schrie*) *Jesus* becomes *rief Jesus, Jesus . . . erwischt ihn* becomes *ergreif* (NHG *ergriff*) *ihn*, etc.[77] Luther's opponents also objected to some forms as too drastic: in 1529 Johannes Dietenberger revised Emser's version of Luther's New Testament in order to change 'vmb der Junckfrawen vnd vnschuldigen hertzen willen/ die frechen vnd ergerlichen wörter (der sich Luther in seynem Testament vil gebraucht) . . . in züchtigere wörter'.[78] Johannes Eck used Dietenberger in the New Testament of the 1537 Ingolstadt Bible: in these emended versions, *Lotterbube* (Acts 17: 18) was replaced by *schwetzer, plappern* by *geschwätz treiben, Hure* by *bübin/gemeines weib/gmaine, unzüchtige frau*, and *Hurerey* by *vnkeüschheit/vnzucht*. Eck also reintroduced some foreign words which Luther avoided; for example, Eck used *Ampel, Fundament, Glori, Kapitål, Orient, prophetisieren, Regent* instead of Luther's *Fackel, Grund, Herrlichkeit, Knauf, Morgen, weissagen, Herr*. Indeed, on occasion Luther even translated *Tetrarch* as *Vierfürst* and *Apostel* as *Zwelfbote*,[79] and in the *Sendbrief* he jokes that the papists do not begin to know how to translate the New Testament, whose opening words (Matt. 1: 1) are *Liber generationis*—rendered by Luther himself as *Geschlechtsregister*.

Geographically, barriers had also to be surmounted, and we have seen already that UG printers, starting with Adam Petri, added marginal glosses[80] and even glossaries to the Lutheran text. The next step is to incorporate the forms from glossaries into the text, either glossing the Lutheran word, or replacing it. Luther's Catholic opponents also changed some (E)MG forms to UG equivalents: *Lippe* they replaced by *Lefze*, *Hügel* by *Bühel* (Emser: *Hübel*), *Kahn* by *Nachen*, *fett* by *faist* (*feist*), *Hälfte* by *die Halbe*, *Ufer* by *Gestade*.[81] But the opponents were unsuccessful, while Luther's Bible has almost certainly established some forms in the modern Standard language which were originally geographical variants; for example, *Lippe* and *fett* are now standard, *Lefze* and *feist* are not.[82] However, *Lefze* persists for the 'lip of an animal', and in the technical sense of 'flange' on a machine, while *feist* and *Gestade* are from a higher, poetic style.

Inevitably, a gap opened between the language of the Luther Bible and speech: syntax, especially word order, morphology (*gebeut*, *kreucht* for *gebietet*, *kriecht*), and above all vocabulary, became archaic. Words no longer in common use include: *Aftersabbath* (NHG *Nachsabbat*), *äfern/efern* 'stir up', 'repeat', *altvettelische Fabeln* 'old wive's tales', *aufenthalten*, *arzneien* (but the nouns remain), *Barte* 'axe', *baß* (NHG *besser*), *dürstig* 'daring' (cf. also *thüren*, MHG *türren*, 'dare'), *Ehrenhold* 'herald', *gemach* 'gradually', *Krebs* 'breastplate' (NHG *Panzer*), *Mannsbild/Weibsbild* (NHG *männliches/weibliches Wesen*), *Narrentheiding* 'foolery', *Schweher* 'father-in-law', *Schwieger* 'mother-in-law', *Schnur* 'daughter-in-law', *Tartsche* 'shield', *wacker*, *weidlich* 'gallant', 'brave', *köcken* 'spew', *lecken* 'jump', 'kick' (*wider den Stachel lecken*). Other words have changed their meaning, becoming 'false friends': *arg* 'evil', *blöde* 'shy', *toll* 'mad' all remain in colloquial use: *arg beschäftigt, das ist zu blöd!* ('stupid'), *echt toll!* 'really great!' (but *Tollwut* 'rabies'); *aussetzen* no longer means 'provide with a dowery'; *beleidigen* now means 'insult', not 'damage'. The word *Dirne* once meant 'a young virgin', but now means 'prostitute'—apart from the surviving *Dirndlkleid*; similarly, *Magd*, once 'an unmarried girl', has come to mean 'servant'. *Schlecht* meant 'straightforward', 'simple'; *stillen* 'to silence' now means 'to breast-feed'; *strafen* denoted only a verbal rebuke, now it means 'punish'; *trunken* meant 'having enough to drink', not necessarily 'drunk' (*betrunken*) (Prov. 11: 26 'Wer trunken macht, der wird auch trunken werden'); *endelich* = NHG *eilig*, *emsig* (Luke 1: 39 'Maria gieng auf das Gebirge endelich'), *sorgfältig* 'full of care' comes to mean 'careful'.

Revisions of Luther's text were undertaken to overcome such barriers to comprehension: indeed, revisors were constantly at work, although they concentrated on changing the orthography, which anyway went unnoticed by those who heard rather than read the Bible. But those who publicly altered the Luther Bible inevitably faced criticism—among them Duke August of Wolfenbüttel (1579–1666).[83] In the eighteenth century biblical archaisms interested both grammarians and lexicographers for their stylistic value: in 1729 Johann Leonhard Frisch re-edited Johann Bödiker's *Grund-Sätze der Deutschen Sprache* . . . (1690) 'mit . . . einem völligern Register der Wörter, die in der Teutschen Übersetzung der Bibel einige Erläuterung erfodern'; Wilhelm Abraham Teller and Johann Christoph Adelung[84] examined all aspects of Luther's vocabulary. But in a curious sense, the language of the Luther Bible could not (until recent godless times) become obsolete so long as it was used in church. Instead, the passing centuries lent it a special and dignified flavour, made it a sacral language removed from speech and yet spoken, no longer of the people and yet familiar to them. Consequently, 'biblical language' especially appealed to poets, including Goethe and Brecht, since it provided an elevated and yet not arcane style.

In the sixteenth century, Luther's contribution to the external form of German may have been to provide some temporary and relative stability, enabling grammarians and others to codify some of his usage. 'Internally', he surely relativized the styles of his day, showing how German could be used even for the highest purposes, and for such religious, spiritual writing he was unequalled. But subsequently in other technical, scholarly, and cultural areas new and often borrowed vocabulary and other styles emerged for which Luther was not responsible.

THE POLITICAL USE OF GERMAN[85]

A considerable body of political writing has resulted from the social and religious unrest culminating in the Peasant War (1524–5) and the Reformation. Pamphlets and leaflets of various tendencies between 1519 and 1530 show German used for political propaganda and appealing for the first time, thanks to printing, to the masses, the *gemeiner man* or *gemein volck*. The language used was often colloquial in tone, sometimes even vulgar, but the authors were mainly educated men, capable of working in classical references as well as quoting the Bible. Lack of any single contemporary label reflects the heterogeneous origins of the polemical tracts[86] which are entitled *büchl(e)in, sendbrief, (v)ermanung, dialogus,* or *gesprech* (*büchlein*);

sometimes they baldly address their audience *An den Christlichen Adel* . . . The dialogue remains popular because it allows the adverse viewpoint to be pilloried: here the traditional rhetorical *jeu parti*, the *Fastnachtspiel*, and Humanist drama merge. The dialogue itself ranges from elegant Humanist Latin to occasionally drastic vernacular. For example, in the *Karsthans* (1521)[87] the mythological figure Mercurius, the peasant Karsthans, his student son, Thomas Murner, and Luther dispute together. At one point the student says to his (more intelligent) father, 'Was plaparst alweg dyn tand?' (NHG 'Was faselst du die ganze Zeit?'); Murner expands the hoary joke about Lat. *testes* into the grotesque imprecation 'das üch (NHG 'daß euch') bocks hoden plenden und schenden!', beside which Luther appears moderate in word and aims. While polemical writings take many different forms, they resemble each other in function and style; they have an ideological purpose and give a partisan bias to the concepts presented. This heightened, emotive use of language is typical of political writing of all periods, and also of the sermon, from which much sixteenth-century polemic naturally developed.[88]

We cannot here consider the complicated relationships between the various early pamphleteers. Broadly, the three main parties are the peasants, whose most interesting leader was Thomas Müntzer (1490?–1525), the Lutheran party, and the arch-Catholics, including some powerful writers—Hieronymus Emser (1478–1527), Thomas Murner (1475–1537), and Johannes Maier von Eck (1486–1543). After the peasants had been crushed, further disputes arose, especially within the Lutheran camp, and religion and politics continue inseparably mixed in a spate of publications, where the opponents are reduced to negative ciphers.[89]

We might expect the peasant writers—often anonymous—to be less articulate and more colloquial than their opponents, but they are not. An impressive pamphlet, *An die Versammlung gemayner Pawerschafft* (1525), bitterly parodies the feudal levies *handlon* and *haubtrecht* as *schandtlon* and *raubrecht*, and the peasants' grievances are advanced in formal, chancery style. For well before the sixteenth century peasants and townsmen (both nebulous terms!) had joined together in sporadic protests against feudal lords, the Church, and the patriciate. According to Marxist critics, the 'Peasant Revolt' represents the high point of a failed 'frühbürgerliche Revolution' and some of Müntzer's ideas anticipate Communism; at any event, the peasant movement had an educated, intellectual element.

So far as invective goes, the various parties rival each other, anticipating the comic style known to literary historians as *Grobianismus*.[90] Emser attacked Luther in 1524 as 'das wild Geyffernd Eberschwein Luthern/ so ynn dem weyngartten des Herren der krefften wûlet/ grabet . . . mit seynem besodelten Rûssel . . .'; Müntzer addressed Count Ernst von Mansfeld in 1525 as 'du elender dûrfftiger maden sack', and referred to Luther as 'Dr Lügner', 'Ertzbube', 'pott (NHG *Bote*) des teüffels', 'Eselisch fleisch', and 'das geistlose Sanftlebende fleysch zu Wittenberg'. Luther for his part puns on Emser's coat of arms, calling him 'Bock Emser', or, because of his revision of the New Testament translation, 'der Sudler ('botcher') zu Dresden'; Luther 'mistranslates' the name Cochlaeus (= 'Wendelstein') back into German as 'Rotzlöffel', with a complex pun on *Laffe* 'ninny', on Lat. *cochlearium* 'spoon' (also < *cochlea* '(snail(shell))'), and probably on *Kochlöffel*, and he rewrites Dr Eck as 'Dreck'.

Insults, proverbs, and humorous remarks, while not the sum of everyday communication, can sometimes reflect the freer syntax of speech. Political writing, diaries, private letters, and the sermon provide further indirect impressions of sixteenth-century spoken German and permit a tentative stylistic evaluation of some syntactic features. The satirical juxtaposition of learned Latin quotations or biblical passages and extreme coarseness also suggests what was still acceptable or tolerable, at least in polemical writing, before a stylistically and formally normative language had emerged.

HUMANISTS AND GERMAN

Humanism originated in Italy, where it constituted the intellectual background to the Renaissance in the form of a renewed interest in classical antiquity and especially language.[91] We have seen that the early German Humanists were influenced by Italian writers who had already assimilated and developed classical themes and styles; in the sixteenth century Latin and (more rarely) Greek texts were increasingly translated, and editions of the originals and of Greek, Latin, and even Hebrew grammars appeared.[92] The standard of Latinity rose, and Latin became a group language for intellectuals of all political and religious persuasions: they even 'translated' their names: Agricola (Huysman), Cochlaeus (Dobneck von *Wendelstein*), Dasypodius (Hasenfus), Desiderius Erasmus Roterdamus (Gerard

Gerard), Fabritius (Schmied), Melanchthon (Schwarzert), Oeco-lampadius (Husschin, NHG *Hausschein*). This is the counterpart of the crude deformation of names we have just met in polemical writing. Latin was admired as the international language of scholarship and civilization, with a well-regulated grammar and an impressive literature. German, by contrast, was not taught or officially used in schools and universities at this time: the odd early lectures in German, like those by Tilemann Heverlingh at Rostock in 1501 or by Paracelsus at Basle in 1526-7, are exceptions. The schoolmaster Valentin Ickelsamer remarked on the neglect of the native language:

Bey den Lateinischen wirdt die Orthographia/ das ist/ recht bůchståbisch schreiben/ so eben vnd fleyssig gehalten/ das ainer der gantzen lateinischen kunst unwissend würdt geachtet/ der nur ainen bůchstaben vnrecht/ oder ainen zůuil oder zů wenig setzet/ warumb soll es dann bey den Teütschen gleich gelten/ man schreib recht oder falsch? Kündt man doch dise sprach so wol regulieren als die Hebraisch/Ghriechisch oder Lateinisch sein . . .[93]

But at about the same time Valentin Boltz (d. 1560), who translated some plays of Terence for school use, considered that studying Latin might encourage the regulation and nurture of German:

Aber das ist das alt gifft vnd pestilentzisch übel/ das wir Teütschen nie vil acht auff vnser můtterspraach gehabt haben/ wie sie gepflantzt vnd auff bracht werd, Die ja gleich jr *facundiam* vnd zier wol hat/ als andere spraachen . . . Es ist der Lateinischen spraach ein treffelicher rům [NHG *Ruhm*] vnd hoher preiß/ das sie so hohe wunderparliche ding hinder jr verborgen hat gehan [NHG *gehabt*]/ vnd macht vns teütschen/ das mir [NHG *wir*] erst anfahen vnser eygen spraach regulieren vnd wolstellen.[94]

Translation and the school drama had their part to play in this; for in the Latin schools Humanists produced plays, annotated texts, edited grammars, and compiled vocabularies and dictionaries, and so indirectly worked with their native language. Moreover, regard for the vernacular had been one of the Italian Humanists' concerns, although in the German context this ideal was not much pursued in schools until the seventeenth century: Martin Opitz wrote his *Aristarchus sive de contemptu linguae Teutonicae* (1617) in Latin when he was at school. Whereas the younger boys inevitably acquired the rudiments of German grammar in the process of learning Latin, older pupils were at some schools expressly forbidden to speak German even at playtime, and a *lupus* or 'wolf' told on them if they did so.[95] Latin was to remain the foundation of all study until the

first quarter of the seventeenth century, when educational reformers
—in Germany notably Wolfgang Ratke (1571-1635)—argued for
a new method of instruction based on the native language. However,
the use of German for informal teaching purposes goes back to the
Early German monastery schools, although these subterranean
channels of communication come to the surface only in the age of
printing, when Latin grammars and word-lists appeared with printed
(i.e. teachers'), annotations and examples in German; moreover,
some native grammatical terminology used is consistent enough
to imply that it had a long tradition.

Typologically, grammars of German appear to develop out of
Latin grammars: isolated German glosses in commonly used Latin
texts, like the *Ars minor* of Aelius Donatus,[96] glossaries of technical
terms, then interlinear word-for-word translations, explanatory
paraphrases, and finally, in the 1570s, the earliest surviving grammars
of German, written in Latin and applying the structures of Latin to
German. The chronological sequence is inevitably blurred, and some
early grammars of German may have been lost, such as those
attributed to Johannes Krachenberger, a notary at the court of
Maximilian I, or to Ladislaus Suntheim, the court chaplain;[97] such
works were probably also inspired by Humanism. Interestingly, the
importance of LG is attested by several printed Latin grammars from
the late fifteenth century with LG glossing and examples, and such
grammars were even used to teach foreigners the vernacular—
presumably for trading purposes. However, merely doing Donatus
into German did not produce an adequate German grammar, as
Ickelsamer realized:

Darzu sag ich/ das der vns noch lang kain Teütsche Grammatic geben oder
beschriben hatt/ der ain Lateinische für sich nymbt/ vnd verteütscht sy/ . . .
dann so schon ainer der reden tayl mitt allen jren Accidentijs gantz wol vnd
recht teütschet/ vnnd aber jren rechten brauch in der rede nit klårlich anzaigt/
so ist sein Grammatic den teütschen wenig nütz . . .[98]

Nevertheless, many Humanist grammars with vernacular glossing
and translations were used in Latin schools, and if, as is the nature of
school-books, very few copies have survived, such modest works
were frequently reprinted: Jacob Henrichmann's *Institutiones* ran to
twenty editions between 1506 and 1520, printed at Hagenau (four),
Pforzheim (three), Leipzig (three), Tübingen (five), Strasburg,
Nuremburg, Basle, Augsburg, and Cologne, and some grammars
survived into the late eighteenth century, e.g. that by Johannes

Rhenius (1574-1639), which was based on Donatus. Humanists also produced their own Latin grammars, the most famous being Philipp Melanchthon's *Grammatica latina* (1525), which achieved a considerable circulation in later revisions, such as that by Joachim Camerarius (1500-74).

Latin proverbs and quotations from classical authors, such as those published by Erasmus in his *Adagia*, stimulated the gathering of German proverbs too. Similarly, collections of Latin synonyms and phrase-books or colloquies to promote the speaking of Latin soon appeared with bilingual and even polyglot glossing. Such simple vocabularies repay closer linguistic scrutiny, since the German glosses undergo regional shifts: an edition of Nicodemus Frischlin's *Nomenclator Trilinguis*, published at Nuremberg in 1614 but intended for use in Austrian schools, adds Austriacisms. These vocabulary books arranged according to subject-matter descend from the *vocabularius rerum* or *Sachglossar*; they often begin with words for God and the creation, and then work through the different parts of the human body, the animal and plant kingdom, and human institutions and activities. In the process they furnish useful lists of German technical terms: for example, Adam Siber's *Gemma Gemmarum* (itself based on the *Nomenclator* of the Dutch Humanist Hadrianus Junius (1567)) lists words under various *Berufssprachen*, as *Sutoria, Venatoria, Coquinaria* etc.; and an edition of 1603 from Leipzig translates the headings as *Schusterlatein, Jägerlatein, Küchenlatein*. Possibly, then, the designation *Latein* for German technical terms originated in the context of the Latin school word-list.

The larger dictionaries proper were also in the tutelage of Latin. The German-Latin dictionaries (as opposed to Latin-German ones) answer a need to write good Latin; they do not at first reflect any increased prestige for German, which also explains why the vernacular glosses are unsystematic and hence difficult to assess dialectally or stylistically. This is true of Petrus Dasypodius' important *Dictionarium Latino-germanicum/Germanico-latinum* (Strasburg, 1535-6) and of the dictionary produced by the Swiss Humanist Petrus Cholevius at Zurich in 1541, elaborated by Johannes Frisius.[99] Although Josua Maaler published his *Die Teutsche Spraach. Dictionarium Germanico-latinum novum* at Zurich in 1561—the first truly German dictionary, as Jacob Grimm called it, since it aimed to present the richness of the native language—this too was a reworking of Cholevius and Frisius; it was not reprinted and remained uninfluential. Georg Henisch in his unfinished dictionary, *Teütsche Sprach und Weißheit* . . . (Augsburg, 1616), gives a mixed bag of proverbs and etymological ballast, with a bias in favour of rare words: a learned tome, not a practical aid, and the same remains true for Kaspar Stieler's great dictionary of 1691, *Der Teutschen Sprache Stammbaum und Fortwachs oder Teutscher Sprachschatz*, which is aristocratic and learned in tone, the product of academic language-society circles (see Chapter VII).[100]

Given the Humanists' role in education and the dominance of Latin, it is not surprising that most terms for school and university[101] titles, classes, and practices should show their influence, notably as loan-words: *Akademie, Gymnasium, Kollegium, Klasse, Prima, Secunda, Tertia*, etc.; *Examen, Kandidat, Klausur, Kolloquium*; *Dekan, Dozent, Rektor, Professor* (originally a Latin teacher, by the late sixteenth century also a university teacher); *Fakultät, Seminar, studieren, disputieren, relegieren* 'rusticate', and so forth. And Humanists also helped shape the technical language of printing, since they published, edited, set up, and corrected texts: Fischart, for example, worked as a corrector at Strasburg.

But in many other areas intellectual curiosity and the questioning of old traditions made knowledge available to those who knew no Latin. The physician Laurentius Fries was prepared to risk the disapproval of his colleagues by translating medical advice into German, as we have seen (pp. 186–7). Some printers, like Christian Egenolff at Frankfurt-on-Main, seem to have specialized in the publishing of German legal and chancery texts. Humanism was not at first in conflict with Christianity and penetrated even to monastery schools: we gain some impression of the range of Humanist translation from the schoolmaster Ortholph Fuchsperger (*c.*1490– ?), who wrote a German introduction to logic, *Dialectica*, published at Augsburg in 1533 for the abbot of Mondsee. In the dedication, Fuchsperger draws attention to translations of the other liberal arts into German—rhetoric, music, arithmetic and mathematics, astronomy and astrology, as well as the Bible, law, and medicine; in his preface he pleads for the free availability of knowledge and asks: 'Warumb solt dann das vorhin von anderen erfunden und in frömbder spraach beschriben in die bekañt müterzung nit dörfen verkeert werden?'[102] In natural history, too, and comparative philology Humanists compiled data which included

German names and terms: the Swiss polyhistor and physician Conrad Gesner (1516-65) published his *Mithridates: De differentiis linguarum tum veterum tum quae hodie apud diversas nationes in toto orbe terrarum in usu sunt . . . observationes* in 1555, and produced great zoological studies on animals, birds, and fish which were soon translated into German (e.g. the *Vogelbuch*, in 1582).

While German Humanists have been taken to task for dissipating their energy on Latin instead of their native language,[103] the catalytic effect of Humanism on German intellectual development and the enrichment of the vocabulary by many loan-words and loan-formations drawn from classical languages can scarcely be denied. Luther too had used Humanist learning and method in his text-critical approach to biblical translation, and the knowledge of Hebrew which was indispensable for this owed much to the Hebrew grammar of Johannes Reuchlin (1455-1522). Above all, the Humanists gave German an abstract, internationally familiar store of 'ink-horn words' which owed nothing to Luther, yet which made possible the flowering of scholarship and literature in the later seventeenth century.

VERNACULAR GRAMMATICAL TRADITION IN THE SIXTEENTH AND SEVENTEENTH CENTURIES

Against this background of Latin school grammars may be set the first printed works treating German. These early vernacular 'grammatical' writings are practical rather than speculative and fall roughly into three types: brief spelling guides suitable for chancery, printing-house, and school; handbooks for teaching people to read; and the earliest more or less complete grammars of German, written in Latin or at best a hybrid of Latin and German.

A. CHANCERY SPELLING PRIMERS

This tradition may be best exemplified by Fabian Frangk, who published his *Cantzeley vnd Titel büchlin/ Darinnen gelernt wird/ wie man Sendebriefe förmlich schreiben/ vnd einem jdlichen seinen gebürlichen Titel geben sol* and his *Orthographia Deutsch/ Lernt recht buchstäbig schreiben* together at Wittenberg in 1531, because he saw both works as interrelated: they taught how to address people with the correct style and title in an accepted spelling. Frangk valued the German language highly, even desired a complete grammar for it, but his own emphasis is on *recht buchstâbig schreiben*, avoiding errors in writing German, whether they result from dialectal pronunciation— e.g. Silesian ('Neiderländisch') *treauter briuter* for *trauter bruder*, Meissen *die môyt sôyt* for *die Magd sagt* (p. J7a–b)—or from regional spelling habits. He gives no advice on the best pronunciation— indeed, his linguistic models are written or printed (Luther, Maximilian's chancery, and Johann Schönsperger; see above, p. 189). Pronunciation is important, in that words should be enunciated clearly and written accordingly so as to distinguish those which closely resemble each other. Indeed, separating near homonyms is a particular concern of chancery authors,[104] although Frangk allows latitude in the marking of vowel length, accepting the pronominal variants *jme, jne, jre* beside *jhm, jhn, jhr*, and mentioning doubled vowels in other words (p. J8 b). Several sections are devoted expressly to common vices in spelling, including the excessive use of doubled consonants, the omission of some letters, the transposition and replacement of others. The conclusion draws attention to the care lavished upon Latin and observes that errors in German letters lead to misunderstandings and also reflect poorly on a writer's abilities.

In the same tradition belongs the popular *Handbüchlin gruntlichs berichts/ recht vnd wolschrybens/ der Orthographie vnd Grammatic . . .* published by the Württemberg Hofgerichts-Sekretär Johann Elias Meichßner in 1538. After a few orthographical and grammatical rules there follow formulae for drawing up letters and documents for all occasions. The work had five editions at Tübingen and five at Frankfurt (changing its orthography in the process!), and the Frankfurt printer Sigismund Feyerabend claimed to have used it. In the south, the Imperial Notary and Clerk to the court at Basle, Johann Rudolph Sattler, wrote his *Teutsche Orthographey vnd Phraseology . . .* (1607), which, like Meichßner's work, was directed primarily towards young and inexperienced scribes and chancery officials. Sattler's models of correct usage are documents from the imperial and other princely chanceries, imperial edicts (*Reichstags-abschiede*), statutes of the *Cammergericht* at Speyer, formulary books, and other printed sources, especially historians; but he also consults printers and compositors, for instance on their aesthetically inspired preference for capital letters.[105] Sattler also compiled two guides for public speakers and a *Teutsche Rhetoric/ Titular- vnd Epistel-buechlein in sich haltend* . . . (1614).

While most chancery authors are keen to establish norms, they freely admit that usage varies and invite corrections. They also have close links with schools: Fabian Frangk used his orthography and formulary in an 'ordenliche deudsche schul' which he was asked to set up in Brandenburg (preface to 1538 edn.).

B. GUIDES FOR READING GERMAN—'LESEFIBELN'

In these increasingly numerous German schools the native language was not linked to learning Latin, Greek, or Hebrew, nor to correct spelling, but instead to reading, mainly the catechism and the Bible. Valentin Ickelsamer's *Die rechte weis auffs kürtzist lesen zu lernen* . . . (1527) includes such religious matter, as do ABC books down to the eighteenth century.[106] For Ickelsamer, reading is a divine gift:

ain herrliche gab Gottes . . ./ vnd das sy [= *die Gabe*] ain holtzhawer/ ain hyrdt auff dem velde/ vnd ain yeder in seiner arbeit one Schulmaister vnd Bucher lernen mag . . .[107]

and his phonetic description of the letters of the alphabet is linked to the sounds of God's natural universe:

Das /g/ so die zung das eüsserst des gůmens berůrt/ wie die Gens pfeysen wenns ainen anlauffen zůbeyssen . . . Das /m/ der Kue buchstab/ so man bede lebtzen auff ainander truckt[108]

Johannes Kolroß, a Basle schoolmaster, also wanted his *Enchiridion: das ist Handbuchlin tütscher Orthographi* . . . (1530) to make the Bible accessible even to parents who had to study in their free time:

ja, ettlich der elltern selbs/ ouch handtwercks gsellen/ vnnd jungkfrowen . . . tüdtsch schryben vnd låßen zelernen/ sich bemůyend/ die zyt vsserthalb jrer arbeit/ in erlustigung heyliger gschrifft nützlich zůuertryben (p. A2 a).

Since Kolroß is writing in Switzerland, however, some consideration of the regional use of monophthongal vs. diphthongal graphies is necessary. He appears already to regard the diphthongal forms as most generally used, although his text is printed with monophthongs, as the passage quoted shows. Nevertheless, discussion of the best form of German, spoken or written, is not strictly relevant to the authors of reading guides, although they do treat discrepancies between sounds and symbols, some of which are apparently regional.

Other authors of *Lesekünste* include Ortholph Fuchsperger, who writes specifically for younger children and their teachers, and in the seventeenth century Tilemann Olearius, who illustrates the letters of the alphabet by things which begin with them; hence A is depicted by an eel (*aal*) with its tongue in its mouth.[109]

C. COMPLETE GRAMMARS OF GERMAN[110]

In the 1570s three grammars of German appeared with little relevance for the common man, since they were in Latin and so meant for educated readers, whether German or foreign.

Laurentius Albertus (*c*.1535–83), called 'Ostrofrancus', published his *Teutsch Grammatick oder Sprachkunst*. *CERTISSIMA RATIO discendae, augendae, ornandae, propagandae, conservandaeque linguae Alemanorum sive Germanorum, GRAMMATICIS REGULIS ET exemplis comprehensa & conscripta* ('German Grammar. THE MOST SURE METHOD of teaching, enriching, embellishing, spreading and preserving the Language of the Alemanni or Germans, comprehensively collected and compiled WITH GRAMMATICAL RULES AND examples') at Würzburg in 1573, with the intention, *inter alia*, of enabling foreigners to learn the language for their various negotiations, commercial or diplomatic; and he wants also to raise the standard of German oratory and rhetoric by giving the language rules. Other interests, patriotic and scholarly, make Albertus the forerunner of baroque grammarians: the neglect of German contrasts ill with the care lavished upon other languages, particularly the bastardized modern Romance tongues, but also English. He criticizes the use of foreign words for elegance, and the emphasis placed upon Latin and Greek by those in high office: after all, 'cum Germanis enim germanicè agendum est' ('one has to deal with Germans in German') (p. a5 b). Albertus, who had studied at Wittenberg and then moved to the court at Würzburg, shows an interest in dialects, and provides a genealogical table[111] dividing them into 'Oberländisch' and 'Niderlendisch oder Sächsisch Teutsch'. *Oberländisch* is used in the sense of HG, and Albertus presents a language comprehensible to all *Germani Superiores* and found in the best prints from Mainz, Ingolstadt, Nuremberg, Augsburg, Basle, Frankfurt, and Wittenberg. There is some evidence that Albertus compromised, since MG features occur, especially as alternatives in the morphology— e.g. *ich werd* beside UG *ich wird*—but at this period no generally accepted printed norm current in MG and UG existed, as comparison with other grammars shows.

Albertus had converted to Catholicism, and even took orders at the end of his life, but he does not seem to have stressed the spiritual role of German: on the contrary, he regretted that the Bible was not exclusively read and expounded in Latin (p. a4 a). He gives a fuller prosody section than other grammars, has a section on accent, and shows a concern for style, in keeping with the rhetorical interest implicit in his elegant dedication to his patron and with the title of the work (*ornandae, propagandae*). The teaching purpose, while not absent, recedes, leaving a gentlemanly essay in grammatical presentation, elegant and restrained.

Albertus Ölinger drew more obviously on his experience teaching foreign noblemen's sons the German tongue, as his title implies: *Underricht der HochTeutschen Spraach: GRAMMATICA SEV INSTITUTIO VERAE Germanicae linguae . . . IN VSVM IVVENTUTIS maximè Gallicae* . . . ('Lessons in the High German Language: THE GRAMMAR OR FOUNDATION OF THE TRUE German Language FOR THE USE OF YOUNG PERSONS, particularly those who are French . . .') (Strasburg, 1573-4). The presentation and quality of the information reflect the practical intention, *Unterricht*, for example, the section on fluctuating gender of certain nouns (p. 48), or on the gender of loan-words from Latin and French (pp. 51 f.), on forms with alternative plurals, or with no plurals at all (pp. 72 ff.). Laurentius Albertus disregards these issues, except for one short paragraph on defective forms. While Ölinger certainly knew and used his predecessor's work, he has a different and much clearer aim; his pedagogical bent also shows through in his trilingual edition of twelve dialogues by the Spanish Humanist Juan Vives published in 1587, for in the German he gives alternative renderings. Moreover, his contrastive approach to German grammar using a modern (French) language, and his familiarity with French grammar books, may have led him to separate the noun and adj. declensions more clearly than other grammarians hitherto.

Johannes Clajus (1535-92) was undoubtedly the most influential early grammarian: his *Grammatica GERMANICAE LINGVAE . . . Ex BIBLIIS LVTHERI GERMANICIS ET ALIIS EIVS LIBRIS COLLECTA* ('Grammar of the GERMAN LANGUAGE . . . COMPILED FROM THE GERMAN BIBLES OF LUTHER AND FROM OTHERS OF HIS BOOKS') (Leipzig, 1578) ran to eleven editions by 1720, and was translated into Danish. Clajus was a 'theological grammarian', whose admiration for Luther's Bible translation and other writings made him feel that the Holy Spirit had spoken through 'electum suum organon Lutherum' ('his chosen instrument Luther') (p. 4). Hence, German enjoyed the same status as the original source languages of the Bible, Hebrew and Greek (and Clajus also wrote grammars for these languages). He is reticent about Latin, perhaps because of the emphasis placed on it by Catholics, including Laurentius Albertus, who had criticized vernacular Bible translation, claiming that German dialects were multiform and only confused and obscured the text. By contrast, Clajus stressed the clarity and richness of the Lutheran version, valuable for Germans and foreigners: 'perfecta et absoluta linguae Germanicae cognitio, tam indigenis quam exteris utilis et necessaria' ('perfect and entire knowledge of the German tongue, equally useful and requisite for natives and foreigners alike') (p. 4). Even if the reference to Luther in the title was removed from the second edition of the grammar, the preface praising him remained until the sixth, reinforcing the topos of the excellence of Luther's German.

Clajus' grammar naturally shows MG features, notably the retention of unstressed -e, and may be compared with the apocopating UG grammar of Laurentius Albertus,[112] who regards the use of -e as stylistic, marking 'orationis gravitas' ('gravity of diction') (p. H7 b). Thus, in the noun classes Clajus has classes of nouns with pl. in -e— der rock ≠ die röcke, die hand ≠ die hende, das schwein ≠ die schweine —whereas Albertus has only one type of noun with -e in nom. and acc. pl.—die farb (sg.) ≠ die farbe (nom. and acc. pl.) (but gen. and dat. pl. -en). Other nouns in Albertus are endingless (das schwein ≠ die schwein); many fem. nouns show -en in oblique sg. too. In the verbs, e.g. the first person sg. of haben, Clajus has ich habe (pres.), ich hatte (pret.), whereas Albertus has ich hab, ich hett.

All three grammars are weak on syntax and pass over mood, tense, word order, and sentence structure. Foreigners, merchants, and others were better served by the small polyglot phrase-books which become common in the later sixteenth century. Such works, like Der New Barlamont oder Gemeine Gespräche zu Teutsch vnd Frantzósisch beschrieben (Cologne, 1587), sometimes contain potted grammars, and they are important in examining contemporary colloquial language, but they lie outside the mainstream traditions of vernacular grammatical writing, and remained without influence on school or scholarly grammars.

SEVENTEENTH-CENTURY DEVELOPMENTS

In the seventeenth century the educational theories advocated by Wolfgang Ratke (Ratichius) (1571-1635) provided that in the elementary or German schools all children, boys and girls, should be taught to read and write German properly,[113] while in the Latin schools German was to be the foundation for all further study. Ratke felt the schools had a patriotic duty to cultivate the native language and teach a single agreed form of it, 'eine eindrächtige Sprache' convenient for Saxons, Franks, Swabians, Thuringians, and others;[114] he himself favoured Meissen language. At the same time, since he held that all languages reflected a single 'universal grammar', grammar books for individual languages—Latin, Greek, Hebrew, and others—could be written according to a set scheme. German grammar acquired a key role in this programme, since it introduced the basic linguistic structures, and· the translation of grammatical technical terms into German was the first step.

Ratke won over a powerful patron, Prince Ludwig von Anhalt-Köthen, a co-founder of the Fruchtbringende Gesellschaft (see Chapter VII), and soon German was being generally taught in the elementary schools of Weimar, Hesse, and Köthen. But Ratke also influenced other grammarians, most obviously in the matter of German grammatical terminology.[115] Some of his terms are borrowed from Dutch, e.g. *entlehnen* < *ontleenen*; the patriotic defence of the native language, the language societies, literature, and educational reforms all show influence from the Netherlands, and many Germans fled there during the Thirty Years War. Successful formations advanced by Ratke include *Ausrufungszeichen, Bedeutung, biegen, einsilbig, Nebensatz, Persohnendung, Sprachlehre, Wortbedeutung, Wortforschung, Wortfügung, Zusammensetzung.* Unsuccessful examples are: *Bug* 'case' (*Rufbug* 'vocative', *Kriegbug* 'dative'), *fräwlich* = NHG *weiblich*, by analogy with Neth. *vrowelijk*.

Pupils and sometime followers of Ratke included Christoph Helwig, Joachim Jungius, who was Schottel's teacher, Johannes Kromayer, who wrote the first wholly German grammar of German in 1618, and Christian Gueintz, who taught Philip von Zesen (see Chapter VII). Ratke's method is also mentioned in the title of certain grammatical works, including the universal grammar produced at Köthen in 1619, and through his connection with Prince Ludwig he contributed to the pedagogical activities within the Fruchtbringende Gesellschaft.

In 1641 two grammars were published which in their very different character and aims show something of the linguistic interests and tensions within these language-society circles, even if the authors, Christian Gueintz (1592–1650) and Justus Georg Schottelius (1612–76), became members of the Fruchtbringende Gesellschaft only after their works appeared.

Gueintz's essentially practical *Deutscher Sprachlehre Entwurf* is much the shorter (126 pages), but suffers from over-schematic presentation and inconsistent terminology. It opens tersely:

Die Deutsche Sprachlehre ist eine dienstfertigkeit der zusammensetzlichen Deutschen Wörter recht rein Deutsch zu reden.'[116]

Gueintz was no theoretician, but his pedestrian orderliness (he acquired the title 'Der Ordnende' when he entered the Fruchtbringende Gesellschaft) served him well in his not uninfluential *Die Deutsche Rechtschreibung . . .* (Halle, 1645), where he ostensibly organized and published the spellings advocated by Prince Ludwig ('Der Nährende') and other members of the Fruchtbringende Gesellschaft. The introduction to this second work stresses that contemporary usage should be the guide: 'Lutherus ist billich der Deutschen sprache in Kirchen Sachen Urheber/ die Reichs Abschiede in Weltlichen dingen die Haubtbücher'. While Gueintz acknowledges the value of antiquarian and philological studies in both his works, he denies their validity for German grammar: this is obviously a dig at Schottel, who had given his opinion of Gueintz's grammar before it was published, and had borrowed many German terms: cf. for example the nominal cases *Nenendung, Geschlechtsendung, Gebendung, Klagendung, Rufendung, Nehmendung.*[117]

Schottel was no plagiarizer. His flamboyant book is not just a grammar but a celebration of the antiquity, richness, purity, and excellence of German—of 655 pages the first 172 are taken up by ten eulogies on different aspects of the language. The title alone emphasizes the study of German as an art: *Teutsche Sprachkunst/ Darinn die Allerwortreichste/ Prächtigste/ reinlichste/ vollkommene/ Uhralte Hauptsprache der Teutschen auß jhren Gründen erhoben/ dero Eigenschafften und Kunststücke völliglich/ entdecket/ vnd also in eine richtige Form der Kunst zum ersten mahle gebracht worden.* As tutor and administrator at the court of the scholarly Duke August the

Younger of Brunswick-Lüneburg (1579-1666), Schottel profited from the linguistic, intellectual, and spiritual interests of his patron, and from the magnificent library from which he distilled the philological and poetic learning of his time, culminating in the great *Ausführliche Arbeit von der Teutschen HaubtSprache* . . . (1663). This is no classroom grammar, and Latin passages are included for the benefit of foreigners, that they may comprehend the status and purity of German. Schottel, sometimes called the second Varro, just as Luther was called the new Cicero, stands at the beginning of all the scholarly and 'literary' grammars which dominate the study of German until the nineteenth century—although he did, at the end of his life, produce a practical, orthographical excerpt for schools, the *Brevis & fundamentalis Manuductio* . . . *Kurtze und gründliche Anleitung Zu der RechtSchreibung Und zu der WortForschung In der Teutschen Sprache* . . . (1676). The purity, elegance, and origins of German and the number of ancient roots (*Stammwörter*) preserved in the language give it a new status. Grammar, linked again with rhetoric and philosophy (for Schottel had also published on poetics and ethics) in a vernacular *trivium*, had become 'emblematic', the civilized adornment of German culture. Martin Opitz and the rhetorician and poet August Buchner (1591-1661) helped shape a poetic German which the grammarians also aspire to: prosody and metre form part of grammar, as in the Latin tradition; important baroque writers consider themselves simultaneously poets and grammarians (notably Schottel, Georg Harsdörffer, and Philip von Zesen); and the search for the 'best', or standard, form of German is already conducted in literary, stylistic terms, despite obligatory references to Luther or the excellence of Meissen, and so forth. In short, *Sprachkunst* ('grammar'), as in classical times one of the seven liberal arts, is inextricably tied to *Kunstsprache*. Indeed, Schottel himself expressly set out to establish, codify, and actually to *create* this *Kunstsprache*, which was not to be left to the anarchic naïvety of usage as found in the *Pöbelsprache* or *Altagessprache*.[118] In keeping with this élitist, literary view of the ideal linguistic standard of his time, Schottel did not, as Gueintz had done, look to Luther even in religious language—and only in the second edition of the *Sprachkunst* (1651) does his fulsome praise of Luther appear.

After Schottel, normative discussion of the German language was to remain firmly linked to the literary or 'book' language for some two centuries. The printers had played an important part, first in bringing home the need for norms and secondly by themselves developing fairly consistent house styles, as Helber already saw, but they and the chancery officials and schoolmasters lacked the authority to promote the forms of language they themselves were using. Nor could the early grammarians of German provide an adequate basis for the normalization of the language, for we have seen the fairly primitive and derivative character of their grammars, uneasily modelled on Latin and with little or no detailed and consistent dialectal or stylistic interpretation of their grammatical 'rules'. But with Schottel and his colleagues grammar assumed a symbolic, patriotic function and it became an expression of intellectual, philosophical, and literary interests. In particular, the 'neo-classical' preoccupation with German literary style narrowed down and identified those printed works on which grammatical analysis might properly be based: defined the data base, as it were. We shall see how aesthetic and philosophical considerations lay behind grammatical description in the eighteenth century (Chapter VIII), but already in the seventeenth century the basic issue was one of style: whose norms should prevail? Without political unity, such a question (a 'questione della lingua') could not be definitively answered, and it is indeed striking that the ultimate imposition of a standard form of German occurred only through the political unification at the end of the nineteenth century, specifically via the agency of educational ministries (see Chapter IX). Curiously, although the developing literary language is beginning to be understood as a standard language, the discussion of the best German at this period continues to be conducted in geographical, dialectal terms—say, Meissen vs. the rest. However, Schottel himself well realized that a 'national' literary language could not be bound to any one area but must be supra-regional.[119]

SELECT BIBLIOGRAPHY

BIBLIOGRAPHICAL AIDS

Moser and Stopp (1970–8).   Piirainen (1980).

Moser and Stopp (1970–8), i/2 (1973), 254–356, esp. 339 ff., contains a bibliography of sources and secondary literature compiled by Helmut Graser and others; see also ibid. i/3 (1978), 293–9.

GENERAL STUDIES ON THE ENHG PERIOD

Besch (1973).
Brooke (1955).
Eggers (1963–77), vol. iii.

Erben (1970).
Philipp (1980).
Schirokauer (1952).

LITERARY HISTORY

Newald (1967).
Rupprich (1970).

Rupprich (1973).

ANTHOLOGIES AND READERS

Coupe (1972).
Erben (1961).
Götze and Volz (1976).

Gravier (1948).
Kettmann (1971).

LANGUAGE

Bahder (1890).
Moser (1909).
Moser (1929–51).

Moser and Stopp (1970–8).
Penzl (1984).
Stopp (1976).

For syntactic studies see the Select Bibliography to Chapter VI.

VOCABULARY/GLOSSARIES

Bahder (1925).
Claes (1977) [a list of contemporary glossaries].

Götze (1912).
Ising (1968).

PRINTING

Eisenstein (1979).

Hirsch (1967).

MARTIN LUTHER AND GERMAN

Arndt (1962).
Arndt and Brandt (1983).
Bach (1934).
Bach (1974).
Berger (1943).
Bluhm (1965).
Bödiker (1690, 1746).

Erben (1974).
Franke (1913–22).
Reinitzer (1983a).
Reinitzer (1983b).
Schwarz (1955).
Teller (1794–5).
Wolf (1980).

HUMANISM

Bernstein (1978).

Rosenfeld (1974).

SCHOOL GRAMMAR

Ising (1959).
Ising (1966).

Ising (1970).
Müller (1882).

For early grammars, see the Select Bibliography to Chapter VI.

CHAPTER VI

SYNTAX IN THE TRANSITIONAL PERIOD (ENHG)

As yet, comprehensive syntactic studies of the early stages of German, in particular of the Early German (OHG) period and of the fourteenth and fifteenth centuries, do not exist, despite detailed work on individual texts and authors.[1] Nor do the sixteenth- and seventeenth-century German grammars provide much characteristically German syntax, since they start from the premiss that Latin syntax can serve as an adequate descriptive model: as Ölinger (1573-4), 172, put it, 'Germanica lingua ferè omnibus in locis (paucis exceptis) Latinorum Syntaxin sequitur' ('The German tongue follows Latin Syntax in almost all places (with a few exceptions)').

Consequently, without being able to draw on any coherent syntactic study of the ENHG period as a whole, the present chapter can only sketch a few developments between about 1450 and 1650, at the risk of missing some of the more subtle changes and of overemphasizing striking differences which set ENHG apart from the modern standard language. In particular, shifts in the distribution of central or core features of German (the areas where continuity is often most obvious) are very hard to perceive, especially since we are ill-informed regarding regional and stylistic variants in the 'pre-grammarian' ages. Furthermore, the boundaries between speech and writing are less determinate for early stages of German, and little is known of the spoken language; but some changes in the written language may be inferred to be the influence of speech—the increasingly used perfect tense and other periphrastic verb forms, for instance. Some kinds of material—private letters, diaries or travellers' accounts, phrase-books, and scenes in plays—present language seemingly close to speech,[2] but even here considerable refinement and stylization prevent us from taking these as speech pure and simple. At the other extreme an ornate, Latinizing German favoured by certain Humanists employs constructions which belong in a written, educated tradition from chancery and university. Yet in polemical pamphlets both styles coexist and even blend: the absence of a standard literary language permits stylistic variability as well as geographical diversity.

Finally, syntax is not easily separated from other levels of language, having close links with morphology in particular. We have already (Chapter IV) linked certain morphological and indeed phonological changes (inflexional weakening) to syntactic developments. The growth of analytical structures, the noun phrase and the complex verb morphology, is already well advanced by the sixteenth century, replacing inflexion as the dominant means of relating the elements of the sentence to each other.

SYNTAX

As the German term *Satzlehre* implies, syntax traditionally describes and interprets the relationships and functions of elements within the sentence, which constitutes its basic unit. But sentences vary considerably in complexity and in completeness, so some syntactic rules inevitably extend beyond the confines of one sentence: choice of tense or pronominal forms depends much on the context, while the situation of the speakers, gestures, or some prior knowledge of the participants may even make it unnecessary to complete every sentence. Consequently, syntax involves semantic, psychological, and 'situational' factors and is in some degree context-bound. Strictly, this applies to the syntax of utterances produced in speech, but written material is more limited in ways of conveying information, lacking gesture, intonation, and situation; consequently, its syntax is more easily described. So the written data of linguistic history represent language in simplified form, and the sentences are closer to the idealized sentences which are usually presumed to underlie the often incomplete or ill-formed utterances of speech. However, we have just noted that speech and writing are less distinct in the ENHG period, so the constructions of its texts will show much greater variability than in later times with a more or less established standard language taught in the schools. Nevertheless, part of the history of German syntax examines the shedding of some variants and the generalizing of others, the growth of 'new' constructions—difficult to date since they usually arise in speech and so escape observation—and the falling into desuetude of others. We shall regard these constructions as belonging to sentences, not utterances.[3]

Relations between parts of the sentence can be expressed in several ways in spoken and written language, principally by:

(1) *word order*, whether mere juxtaposition or some sequential rule, like the position of the finite verb form at the end of subordinate clauses in mod. German;

(2) *stress*, that is, by using more energy to articulate the main or important parts of the utterance;

(3) *pitch*, namely by musical accent or intonation;

(4) the *speed of delivery* of parts of the utterance: in the sixteenth century, the virgule (/) was used to divide the utterance into 'breath' or sense groups;

(5) the use of connecting or relational *particles* like prepositions, conjunctions, and auxiliary verbs;

(6) *inflexion*, which either separates forms belonging to different parts of the utterance, or else, by congruence or agreement, links them together.[4]

No direct and few indirect historical data are available for (2) stress, (3) pitch, and (4) tempo,[5] but punctuation, emphatic particles (like *ja*, *halt*, *doch*), and the use of periphrasis with auxiliary verbs (like *tun* and *stehen*) do provide clues. Therefore, in what follows we concentrate on changes to 'particles', inflexion, and word order between ENHG and modern standard German.

INFLEXION AND THE USE OF PARTICLES

A. CHANGE FROM SYNTHETIC TO ANALYTIC STRUCTURE

We have already discussed under morphology the erosion of inflexions and the emergence of analytical structures in which particles ('accessory words')[6] convey syntactic relationships. One such important structure is the noun phrase, which consists of the noun itself accompanied by other elements, whether demonstrative pronouns, articles, adjectives, or pronominal words. PIE and PGmc. both lacked articles, and only traces appear in Gothic, but German, like English, has developed a definite article from what was originally a demonstrative pronoun[7] and an indefinite article from the numeral 'one'. In OHG texts nouns often appear without any qualifying particles, e.g. *Ludwigslied* 48 *Sang was gisungan, wîg was bigunnan* '(the) song was sung, (the) battle joined'; but by ENHG articles were regularly used syntactic markers, as a comparison of extracts from the *Magnificat* shows:

OHG Tatian *translation* c.830	Martin Luther's New Testament (1522)[8]
Teta maht in sînemo arme, zispreitta ubarhuhtîge muote sînes herzen,	Er hat gewalt vbet [NHG *geübt*] mit seynem arm, vnd zurstrewet die da hoffertig sind ynn yhrs hertzen synn,
nidargisatzta mahtîge fon sedale	Er hat *die* gewalltigen von *dem* stuel gestoßen,
inti arhuob ôdmuotîge,	vnd *die* nydrigen erhaben,
hungerente gifulta guoto	*Die* hungerigen hatt er mit guttern erfullet,
inti ôtage forliez îtale	vnd *die* reychen leer gelassen.

Articles (and pronouns and auxiliary verbs)[9] were often left out in certain kinds of writing in the fifteenth and sixteenth centuries, for example in chancery style. Even today *Kläger, Beklagter, Unterzeichneter* can appear without articles in legal German;[10] similarly with certain tags like *gemelt/obgemelt* (= *obgemeldet* 'aforementioned'), *besagt*; *obgenannt, gedacht*. This occurs also in diaries and travellers' accounts by merchants, who were influenced by chancery usage, e.g. in Samuel Kiechel's description of the Lord Mayor's show: 'Denn 29 *gemeltes* monats octobrüs sahe ich zu Londen in Engelandt einen maior oder burgemeister erküsen [NHG *erkiesen*] . . . Wann nun *vorgemelter* herr maior . . .'.[11] Conversely, the definite article is used pleonastically, as in modern spoken German, which probably reflects its continued emphatic or demonstrative force in some contexts.[12]

The distinction between definite and indefinite article was primarily semantic: the definite article referred to objects or entities already familiar to the hearer, while the indefinite article was used mainly for introducing unfamiliar objects or entities. As case-, gender-, and (to a lesser extent) number-markers the articles have acquired additional syntactic functions as part of the noun phrase.[13] They further interact with the adj. declension, which, as we have seen (pp. 157-8), had strong and weak variant forms. The newer, weak adj. (it developed only in PGmc., based on the *n*-stem noun declension) qualified a familiar or definite concept or object, and so it tended to occur attributively (i.e. before the noun it qualified) with the definite article, as this became established in the language. Strong adjectives, while probably not associated with marking indefiniteness, tended to be used with the indefinite article, and were used where no article was present, for example in the pl.[14] Despite exceptions and a measure of interchangeability depending, perhaps, on whether syntactic marking of grammatical relationships or semantic marking for degree of definiteness or individualization was uppermost, the two adj. patterns seem, then, to have become complementarily distributed. In the fifteenth and sixteenth centuries, however, the picture is blurred by the endingless forms of adjectives which derive from the old endingless strong nom. forms, or arise from apocope, especially in UG. The endingless forms occur after both definite and indefinite article and for all genders, and this is one of the striking differences between ENHG adjectival usage and that of mod. German. Eventually, in the course of the seventeenth and eighteenth centuries, the uninflected adj. forms were increasingly restricted to neut. gender, whereas the masc. and fem. nouns show weak adj. endings after the definite article.[15] The weak adj. ending in the nom. sg. of all three genders and in the acc. sg. neut. and fem. was -*e*, a pattern which the UG apocope was bound to disturb, and one whose survival has consequently been attributed also to the important EMG area.[16]

After the indefinite article (and possessive pronouns *mein, dein, sein*) the strong adj. became established in the nom. and acc. sg., but a mixed declension with -*en* weak endings in the other oblique cases evolved, giving the mod. German model:

(1) definite article + weak adj. + noun.
(2) strong adj. + noun (no particle).
(3) *ein/kein/*possessive adj. + mixed adj. + noun.

This somewhat artificial system seems to have been promoted by grammarians and was adopted in nineteenth-century school grammars under the influence of Adelung in particular.[17] Still, the distribution of strong and weak adj. forms was probably important in conveying syntactic relationships before the grammarians formalized it, as we have mentioned in connection with paradigmatic push (pp. 157-8). Like the definite and indefinite articles, the weak and strong adjectives may have provided (partial) solutions to the problem of how to distinguish general and familiar elements in discourse from particular and unfamiliar ones being introduced into it. Subsequently, these primarily semantic functions recede behind syntactic ones, as both articles and adjectives become number-, case-, and even gender-markers, conveying information analytically that had once been marked in the noun morphology by inflexions. Although not systematized as at present, the analytical noun phrase was already a developed syntactic unit during the ENHG period: its regional variants need further examination.

B. CASE AND THE PREPOSITIONAL PHRASE

The oblique case-forms of the nouns have also in time ceded to more analytic structures with prepositions. Prepositions, like demonstrative and anaphoric pronouns, originate as markers inserted into the utterance to clarify the relations between the verb and other parts of the predicate, between the subject and its qualifiers, and adjuncts of both—qualifying the time and place of the action, for example. Consequently, prepositions have affinities with adverbs, and mod. German has homonymous prepositional/adverbial morphs: *an, auf, aus*, etc.[18]

The instrumental case-form has been entirely replaced in the recorded history of German: it was dying out in OHG texts, and the archaic *Hildebrandslied* shows it already linked with prepositions (*mit sinu billiu* 'with his axe'); in MHG texts it survives virtually only in the particle *diu*[19] in combinations like *bîdiu, von diu* (NHG *deshalb*), or with the comparative, *diu baz* 'the better' (also *deste baz* < *des diu baz*, NHG *desto besser*). More recently, the gen. case-form has considerably decreased in frequency, and has disappeared in dialects and colloquial German, and even in the written, standard language many originally genitival constructions have been replaced or have become stylistically marked as poetic, archaic, stilted, and so forth.[20] But in ENHG the gen. case-form is common, both in the Luther Bible and in more informal writing, like the private letters of the Nuremberg merchant Balthasar Paumgartner and his wife.

Double gen. constructions occur too: 'Des Scheürl Muhmleins begehrten samt und damast auch eingedenk sein will' = 'Ich werde an das Samt denken, das die Muhme von Scheürl [proper name] begehrt'.[21] Admittedly, Balthasar as a merchant was presumably influenced by chancery style, but the gen. was probably still common in everyday language in the sixteenth century. The decline in the frequency of the gen. post-dates the weakening of inflexions and cannot obviously be attributed to any change in noun morphology: after all, the weak noun class (unlike the weak adj.) has been much reduced, and only the fem. nouns lack a distinctive strong gen. form. Consequently, we may surmise that stylistic factors account for the increasing circumscription of the originally gen. constructions. Morphological syncretism in the anaphoric pronoun is frequently cited to explain the change from MHG *er vergizzet es* (gen.) to NHG *er vergißt es* (acc.):

$$
\begin{matrix}
\text{MHG} & \text{nom.} \\
 & \text{acc.} \\
 & \text{gen.}
\end{matrix}
\left.
\begin{matrix}
ez \\
\\
es
\end{matrix}
\right\}
\longrightarrow \text{NHG } es \text{ (nom./acc./gen.)}
$$

Yet this is improbable.[22] At any event, the gen., so common in MHG and ENHG, is replaced in mod. German—often by prepositional phrases.

   The growth of such prepositional phrases, as in *sich erinnern an* + acc. instead of earlier *sich erinnern* + gen., or *frei von* for earlier *frei* + gen., *reich an*, *voll mit* etc., raises the question of the very nature of case relations. If such changing constructions do not apparently alter underlying semantic relationships—and variant structures are often available—then it might be possible to identify certain basic 'semantic' case relations, which resemble the generative phonologists' canonical distinctive features (p. 87). These various case relations might be conveyed by several devices, including noun morphology, prepositions plus marked or unmarked case-forms, word order, and so forth, and the linguistic historian would trace the change in the distribution of the various devices to render a particular underlying case relation.[23] In practice such distributional shifts are probably stylistic in origin; certainly the analytic constructions replacing the genitive case-form are colloquial, and some dialectal patterns, such as a possessive dat. construction of the type *meinem Vater sein Haus* for literary *meines Vaters Haus*, fail to gain acceptance as standard.

   An important implication of this approach is the destruction of the noun paradigm's autonomy, since individual case-forms represent only one way of marking case relations. Those early grammarians who drew up paradigms based on Latin with an 'abl.' case governed by the preposition *von* may possibly have sensed this.[24] And the more frequent use of prepositional cases which is attested in the ENHG period also shows German changing from a semantic-based syntax, where context and meaning suggested the obvious grammatical relationships, to a much more regulated and explicit syntax, in which relations between elements of the sentence are shown formally (see below, pp. 260–1).

see p. 37

ANALYTIC STRUCTURES IN THE VERB PHRASE

The verb in early periods of German was marked morphologically for the features of person and number, aspect, tense, mood, and voice, but here too the language has developed analytical structures with pronouns and auxiliary or modal verbs functioning as grammatical particles in recurrent patterns.

A. PERSON

The passage of the Magnificat quoted above in OHG EFrk. form (p. 230) shows several third-person verbs *teta, zispreitta, nidargisatzta, arhuob, gifulta, forliez*) without personal pronouns, whereas Luther's version uses them consistently. By ENHG, pronouns were usual with verbs, but this has not resulted in the erosion of the morphology in the modern standard (although some dialects, notably in the north and in the south-west (Alem.) have uniform pl. forms).[25] Doubtless, the personal pronouns in OHG texts were emphatic, but by ENHG they have become the rule, although in some contexts and styles—e.g. in the letters of the Paumgartners—they can be omitted:

> ... Hieige [NHG *hiesige*] doctores vermaindtten mir wol zu helffen, [ich] mag mich aber nitt einlassen, gleichwol [ich] an der zeitt auch nitt hab, [ich] wills den lieben Gott alls dem besten artztt wallten lassenn, der, da [er] will, wol helffen khann. [Ich] Verhoff auch, wann [er] mir nun widerumb zu dir verhelffe, [es] schon widerumb besser umb mich stehen soltt.[26]

This might be the influence of chancery style, perhaps politeness or modesty, possibly even businesslike brevity.[27] At any rate, omission of the pronoun—or its pleonastic use—must have a stylistic effect in mod. German; the verb form alone does not sufficiently convey person.

B. ASPECT

Verbs may be grouped according to the nature of the 'action' they describe—for instance, whether that action is repetitive (iterative), completed (perfective), beginning (ingressive or inchoative), momentary (punctual), or extensive in time (durative). This feature is known as 'aspect', and, while it does involve time, that time is not at the disposal of the speaker, but is trapped within the verb itself as the 'temporal distribution or contour' of the verb's action, event, or state:[28] in other words, an iterative verb action, e.g. *wobble, wiggle*, remains iterative whatever tense-form of the verb is employed—*will wobble, wobbled*, etc. Some languages, like Russian (from which the term 'aspect' is derived), have a fully developed morphologically marked system of aspect, but in German no thoroughgoing marking with prefixes or suffixes exists;[29] compare *schneiden/schnitzen, reißen/ritzen, neigen/nicken*; or *kommen/ankommen/aufkommen/ auskommen/verkommen, blühen/anblühen/aufblühen/ausblühen/verblühen*. Not all verbs can combine with any prefix or suffix; some are aspectual without being marked as such—e.g. *wohnen* and *schweigen* are duratives. The occurrence of prefixes with a verb root is unpredictable: *erblühen* exists, but **erkommen* (OHG (*sih*) *arqueman* 'be terrified') died out. Intensifying suffixes are even more word-specific, since few pairs like *schneiden/schnitzen* exist. Thus, there are no unmarked forms of *flattern* 'flap', *kichern* 'titter'—although nonce-creations for humorous purposes can occur, as when Johannes Fischart (*c.*1550–89) extends the iterative suffix *-eln/-(e)len* to verbs which normally lack it: *schertzlen, stertzelen, mertzelen*, etc.[30] Aspect may also be conveyed by periphrastic constructions using auxiliary verbs and participles or infinitives, and by suppletion, i.e. the use of another verb. Sixteenth-century grammarians were familiar with aspect in Latin, and with the means of translating it into German, e.g. Albertus Ölinger (1573–4), 148 f.

Quædam sunt inchoativa, quæ apud Latinos in -sco plærunque desinunt, apud Germanos in -le exeunt: vt, nigresco, ich schwertzle; rubesco, ich rôdtle, vel circumscribuntur: vt, Ich fahe an schwartz zů werden/ oder würd schwartz/ etc.

Some are inchoatives which mostly end in *-sco* among the Latins, among the Germans they end in *-le*: as *nigresco* 'ich schwertzle' ['I darken'], *rubesco*, 'ich rôdtle' ['I redden'], or they are circumscribed: as, I begin to grow black, or, I become black, etc.

Ölinger also knows 'meditativa seu desiderativa' ('meditatives or desideratives') in *-ren*, e.g. 'Es lauffert/ weinert/ dantze(r)t/ reittert jhn/ id est, er hat ein lust zǔ lauffen/ weinen/ dantzen/ reitten etc.', and also 'diminutiva, frequentativa, imitativa' (*ich Ciceronisier*) (p. 149). No single consistent system of marking aspect has emerged in the history of German; instead, some of the older devices have become isolated, others incorporated into the tense morphology of the verb, whilst others again have become stylistic.

1. *Prefixes as aspectual markers*

The origins of separable and inseparable prefixes in German cannot concern us in detail. One theory holds that in PIE particles were inserted into the sentence to convey the relationship of the verb to the other elements in it. Such particles were increasingly attracted either to noun phrases or to the verb itself and were correspondingly positioned in the sentence. Particles associated with noun phrases developed into prepositions and in all stages of German are felt actually to govern cases, rather than merely mediating the case relations of the verb. But if a particle was attracted to the verb it could develop into a verb prefix (or 'preverb'), either separable or inseparable. Thus, the PIE particles—'adverbs' in that they expressed the verb relation—split into three separate but related functions: prepositional, 'prefixal', and adverbial.[31]

Since the medieval language, the ordering of particles has changed and several adverbs and prepositions have become separable prefixes (e.g. *empor, fort, los, zusammen*), although earlier texts often permit us only to observe that they are increasingly used as preverbs. Today, inseparable prefixes are weakly stressed and thus differ from cognate, corresponding prepositions or adverbs (where these still exist): consequently, *be-, emp-/ent-, er-, ge-, ver-, zer-*, and (irregularly) *miß-* have a purely aspectual 'meaning' largely unrelated to parts of the sentence other than the verb itself. We shall restrict ourselves to these inseparables. However, separable prefixes are clearly also aspectual, e.g. *ausgeblüht, ausgehurt* (Luther), *ausgeredet, aufgegessen*, etc. Probably the complex and ill-defined relations between preverbs, prepositions, and adverbs actually impeded the development of a single aspectual system using prefixes.

Moreover, the inseparable prefixes in particular can alter the verb's meaning in several, sometimes conflicting, ways. The preverb *er-*, probably cognate with *aus*, can express inchoative (ingressive) aspect, as in *erblühen, erröten, erwarmen, erschrecken* intrans. 'to give a start'; or it can perfectivize, as in *erdrosseln, erschlagen, ertrinken, ertränken, erhören*. One of the most striking developments since medieval times has been the restriction of the once common perfectivizing prefix *ge-*. This prefix could distinguish perfective verbs from imperfective ones, as in the following list:

> *sitzen* 'be sitting' ≠ *gesitzen* 'sit down' (result), NHG *sich setzen*
> *stên* 'be standing' ≠ *gestên* 'to fare', NHG *ergehen*
> *swîgen* 'be silent' ≠ *geswîgen* 'fall silent', NHG *verstummen*

It could be added to the pres. ind. verb form on occasion, to render the future tense, and to the pret. verb form to render the pluperfect.[32] Infinitives dependent upon 'modal' verbs (*kan, mac, wil, sol*)[33] often showed it, and it regularly marked the past participles of non-perfective verbs. Perhaps this pluralism, plus the fact that there was no preposition related to the preverb, encouraged its eventual decline.[34] Paradoxically, the many past participles in fifteenth- and sixteenth-century texts which lack the *ge-* prefix may show that it had not yet degenerated into a mere past part.-marker. Once that happened, and even the past participles of originally perfective verbs—e.g. *kommen, funden, bracht*—took the prefix (as *gekommen, gefunden, gebracht*), the opposition between verbs with *ge-* and those without it was neutralized. Consequently, when infinitives or pret. forms were constructed from past participles marked with *ge-*, these 'back-formations' invariably lacked *ge-*: thus, the form *geschlagen* yielded the infinitive *schlagen*, not *geschlagen. With other verbs *ge-* became firmly linked, which again removed the possibility of an opposition with unprefixed forms—e.g. *glauben* (MHG *gelouben*), *gebären, gebühren, gedeihen*. But other devices could replace the loss of *ge-*, and regional forces operate here. In the south, for instance, *zusammen* (like *ge-* originally a spatial, local particle) is used aspectually, and may be compared with the noun formations in the standard language using *Ge-*, e.g. *Gerede, Gesinge* vs. *etwas zusammenreden, zusammensingen* 'to talk a lot', 'sing a lot (of rubbish)'.[35]

2. *Suffixes and aspect*

Germanic marked aspectual distinctions in the weak verbs by various suffixes, as in Gothic, where the suffixes *-jan*, *-an*, and *-nan* conveyed causative, durative, and inchoative aspect respectively—e.g. Gothic *fulljan* 'fill', 'make full', *liban* 'be living', *fullnan* 'become full'. Early German texts show three classes of weak verb in suffixes *-(i)en* (< *-jan*), *-ōn*, and *-ēn*, but these are much augmented by new formations from several sources: for example, beside *-ōn* verbs we find forms in *-alōn/-ilōn* (NHG *-eln*), *-arōn/-irōn* (NHG *-ern*), and *-isōn* (NHG *-sen*). The elaborated forms with consonants resisted the weakening of final syllables and apocope, remaining recognizable even in mod. German, where they retain aspectual function, often as intensifying or iterative suffixes.[36] Some phonetic erosion has occurred, however, for example in the suffix MHG *-etzen* (from OHG *-etzen/-azzen* < PGmc. *-atjan*), which survives in several forms, e.g. *blitzen* (MHG *bliczen* < OHG *blechazzen*), *schluchzen* (MHG *sluckzen*), *rutschen* (< MHG *ruckezen?*), *mucksen* 'protest' (OHG *irmuckazzen*). However, the durative verbs (in OHG *-ēn*) could no longer be marked by suffix once that had weakened, and many of the verbs with intensifying suffixes in *-ern/-eln* or *-sen* which were recognizable were isolated, i.e. not obviously aspectually related to other unmarked verbs, so the suffixal system of aspect has also been reduced in scope in mod. German. The intensifying suffixes do nevertheless represent the continuing use of synthesis in mod. German, and their success lies partly in their being segmentable morphs, potentially productive in new formations.

3. *Suppletion and aspect*

In suppletion words with independent meanings and functions are used in certain constructions as auxiliaries. These suppletive elements are reduced in meaning and usually unstressed and subordinated to the construction of which they form part; they may eventually develop into prefixes or suffixes, dissociated from any independent use they may otherwise have.

Periphrastic ways of conveying inchoative/ingressive aspect include *beginnen*, *anfangen*, or *anheben* and a dependent infinitive, while constructions with *pflegen* are durative, and *lassen* and *tun*, *heißen* and *gebieten* can be used as causative auxiliaries.[37] Possibly these structures belong to speech rather than writing, and sometimes they merely intensify an action, e.g. the southern German *ich tu's schon machen* for *ich mache es*. Luther seldom uses these constructions.

Mod. German has periphrastic structures with verbs like *bringen, geben, gelangen, geraten, kommen, nehmen, setzen, stehen, stellen, ziehen* and a dependent verbal noun or noun with clearly verbal force (e.g. a noun in -*ung*), e.g. *ins Reden kommen, ins Stocken geraten, zur Erörterung kommen*. Such periphrasis may avoid the passive, provide stylistic variation, and so forth, but often its function is aspectual:[38] inchoative (*in Wut geraten*), causative (*zum Ausdruck bringen, in Gang setzen*), durative (*zur Diskussion stehen*). Grammarians over the centuries have railed against such nominal style, labelling it chancery or 'paper' style, but examples of it before the eighteenth century are sporadic, and vary from one suppletive verb (*Funktionsverb*) to another: *bringen* + verbal noun is late, but examples with *geraten* occur in MHG and ENHG: 'so minne an tumben kinden | ir spil *gerâtet vinden* . . . (Gottfried von Straßburg, *Tristan* 12436); 'bei nacht, so es *gerot* [NHG *gerät*] vinster *werden*', 'die sonn *geriet undergon*' (Johann Geiler von Kaisersberg (1445–1510), a popular preacher).[39] As an aspectual device suppletion is convenient, and English too uses it (*keep laughing, get talking, give a start, go on crying*), but in English the construction is mostly informal, colloquial, or slang,[40] whereas in German it seems 'bureaucratic' and ponderous, which can add nuance: *in Frage stellen* is more cautious than *bezweifeln*; *zur Kenntnis nehmen* and *in Betracht/Erwägung ziehen* imply greater deliberation than *erkennen, betrachten, erwägen*.

4. *Periphrastic verb forms conveying aspect*

Pres. and past participles can be combined with various auxiliary verbs to mark the uncompleted or completed nature of the verb 'action'. The resulting structures are ambiguous, in that the auxiliaries convey time relations between an action and the time of reporting it, whereas the participles are aspectual. Considerable overlap between the categories of aspect and tense thus occurs, aggravated by the lack of one coherent aspectual system.

The pres. part. could combine with the auxiliary verbs *sein* and *werden*, and was aspectually durative or progressive. It failed to survive for two main reasons: firstly, the pres. part. which ended in -*ende* frequently lost its final dental and merged with the infinitive;[41] secondly, and more important, the marking of perfective aspect by prefixes or past participles made the retention of the progressive marking unnecessary. Certainly, in sixteenth-century ENHG participles and infinitives are interchangeable, e.g. in the Luther Bible (1545) 'Es *waren* . . . Jüden zu Jerusalem *wonend* . . .' (Acts 2: 5), '. . . funden sie jn im Tempel *sitzen* . . .' (Luke 2: 46), '. . . vunden sie den Menschen . . . *sitzend* . . .' (Luke 8: 35); or in the Paumgartner letters (1592) 'Und *bin* zu vernehmen *wartten* [NHG *wartend*], was du . . . weytters [NHG *Weiteres*] bedürfftig (bist) . . .'.[42] The use of the pres. part. has subsequently been much restricted and was pilloried by grammarians (e.g. Gottsched) as foreign. Nevertheless, the part. has survived, supported perhaps by the influence of Lat., although it has not established itself within the tense morphology of the verb as has the past participle. In the formation of the future tense, it was ousted by the infinitive form, in combination with *werden* (see below, p. 242). Possibly the pres. part. was once quite common in speech, where its adjectival nature related the action more directly to the subject of the sentence and so intensified it. In the Paumgartner letters the part. acts sometimes as a conjunction, linking clauses, e.g. '. . . *besorgend*, ja schier gewies [NHG *gewiß*] dafür *halltennd*, er es nitt in gutten von mir aufnemenn würde' ('concerned, indeed, thinking it virtually certain, he would not take it well from me . . .');[43] and Niclas von Wyle sometimes uses participial, progressive forms not found in the Lat. original, as when he translates 'non credulus fui nec praebui' as 'was [NHG *war*] ich nit . . . gelöbig noch . . . für war [NHG *wahr*] *ufnemend*'.[44] However, both Paumgartner and Wyle may be influenced by Latinate, chancery style.

If we argue that perfective aspect was increasingly marked in German by the use of prefixes and preverbs (including *ge-*, which was eventually demoted to a past part.-marker), no additional marking of imperfective/non-perfective aspect was required, hence the loss of the pres. part. constructions. Even in MHG these seem to have been often stylistic variants, particularly the humorous use of the 'progressive infinitive': 'er und sîn pfärdelîn | muosen [NHG *mussten*] *vallende* ûf die bluomen sîn' (*Parzival* 154. 30). The lack of progressive forms distinguishes the mod. German verb system from that of English, which retains an equivalent construction with verbal nouns in *-ing* (the suffix is cognate with German *-ung*).[45]

Past participles, particularly those of the auxiliary verbs (*gehabt*, *gewesen*, (*ge*)*worden*) participate in several periphrastic constructions, are well integrated in verb morphology, and will be treated under the category of tense.

C. TENSE

Tense is deictic: it relates the time of the action, event, or state in the sentence to the time at which the sentence is being uttered. It also relativizes several actions, events, or states being talked about. The earliest German texts show a simple tense division into pret. and pres. tense-forms, but the use of adverbs or similar particles enabled more complex time relations to be conveyed. Hence German, like the other Germanic languages, showed at first a morphological but not necessarily a semantic impoverishment of the PIE verb system. Even in mod. German the pres. tense-form can be used for a range of functions: the 'historic pres.' in written and colloquial narration, the future, a durative/progressive with linking to the past ('ich schreibe dieses Buch seit geraumer Zeit' = 'have been writing'), and a timeless, proverbial use; the pres. tense verb form is not temporally defined, but neutral.[46] Increasingly, new analytical structures have elaborated the verb morphology since medieval German. These are very evident in fifteenth- and sixteenth-century texts, disturbing the simplified system which can be drawn up for MHG in both ind. and subj., where four distinct verb forms participate in a two-way contrast, e.g. *tuon* (NHG *tun*):

		Indicative →		← Subjunctive
Present	↓	*er tuot*		*er tuo*
Preterite	↑	*er tëte*	≠	*er tæte*[47]

Tense distinctions are poorly preserved in the morphology of the subj. (see pp. 173–4), and tense has been 'neutralized' in the mod. use of subj. (see below, p. 247).

1. *Future periphrasis*

Early translators used the pres. ind., or more rarely the pres. subj., to render Lat. future tenses into German. Presumably the subj. marked the uncertainty and unpredictability inherent in the concept of futurity. Periphrastic future tense-forms using *sollen* and *wollen* with a dependent perfective infinitive (usually marked by *ge-*) also involve modality: *sollen* implies external pressures on the subject, perhaps the will of others, or simply force of circumstance, while *wollen* (MHG *wellen*) relates the coming events to the subject's own volition or intention. Whereas LG dialects retain *sollen* and equivalents as their future auxiliary, and in English *shall* and *will* are often in free variation, in HG this modal periphrasis is already dying out in the sixteenth century: Luther seldom uses it in his Bible translation, and few contemporary grammarians mention it.[48] There seems to be a geographical split here: the LG north uses a *sollen*-type future, the central and southern areas show the *wollen*-type losing out to a relatively new periphrasis with *werden* plus infinitive.[49] Gottsched in the eighteenth century still draws a distinction between an 'uncertain' future tense (*ungewiß zukünftige Zeit, tempus futurum incertum*) formed with *wollen* and a 'certain' one (*gewiß zukünftige Zeit, tempus futurum certum*) with *werden*, but failed to establish this compromise.[50]

The *werden* periphrasis originally combined with the pres. part., as we have seen (above, pp. 239f.), and was doubly aspectual, both progressive (marked by the part.) and inchoative/ingressive (marked by *werden*). From the twelfth century onwards *werden* + infinitive occurs, which survives as the mod. written future, although in present-day speech it is regarded as stilted, the present tense and adv. of future time being preferred. The inchoative aspect is most apparent in past tense-forms, e.g. in the Luther Bible (1545) 'Moses aber *ward* zittern' (Acts 7: 32) (no longer possible in mod. German, which marks this aspect either by suppletion with *anfangen/beginnen* or by word-formation, e.g. *erschauern* 'shudder', 'give a shudder'). Even today, the *werden* auxiliary implies that an action is not completed and has not yet begun, although in many contexts it is simply a stylistic variant for the future.

But *werden* has modal overtones, implying supposition, which leads to ambiguity in constructions with a dependent perfect infinitive (past part. + *haben/sein*) that may be understood (*a*) temporally as future perfects, or (*b*) suppositionally (possibly even both simultaneously). The Paumgartner letters show that such forms were not exclusively literary:

1 '. . . da [es] mich . . . zu vernehmen verlangt, wann und wie du noch endlich . . . hinaus gen Altdorf *wirst gezogen sein*' (= temporal; future perfect?).

2 '. . . [ich] will mich aber jedoch versehen [= 'hope'], [daß du] dich nach meinem verreisen nit lang mehr in Nürnberg *gesaumt* [= 'delayed'] . . . *wirst haben* . . .' (= suppositional past).[51]

The suppositional force of *werden* may have been strengthened by MHG constructions like 'er solte ez gemachet hân', which NHG has replaced by 'er hätte es machen sollen'.[52]

2. The Preterite and its periphrastic competitors

In older periods of German the pret. was the unmarked form for the past, just as the present was the unmarked for the 'non-past'. Gradually, however, the perfect and pluperfect periphrases, using auxiliary verbs *haben* and *sein* plus the past part., have taken over several functions once fulfilled only by the pret., and so compete with it.

(i) *Perfect*. In written mod. German the perfect and preterite verb forms can often occur with roughly equal frequency (depending on the kind of text or style), but in non-dialogue, i.e. narrative or discursive contexts, the pret. predominates. In the spoken language, however, whether dialect or colloquial, the perfect is more common, and has indeed replaced the pret. entirely in southern Germany, a development which may have occurred about 1500.[53] Whereas past narrative shows only some 1 per cent of perfect periphrasis around 1300, and it remains below 10 per cent *c*.1450, the proportion rises dramatically and after 1530 may even exceed 50 per cent. But the pret. never entirely disappears from written German, and even regains some of its former importance in the seventeenth and eighteenth centuries—further influence, no doubt, of the codified literary norms. (The persistence of the pret. even in speech in northern Germany may reflect the influence of the HG book language on LG speakers.) In the fifteenth- and sixteenth-century texts, moreover, the perfect and pret. forms are manifestly in free variation, not in stylistically complementary distribution, say for dialogue and narration respectively;[54] this implies that the tense-system too was a relatively open one, allowing the speakers some freedom. Still, the upsurge of perfect forms in sixteenth-century texts and the present-day lack of pret. in the south make it reasonable to assume that the pret. was already becoming stylistically marked in spoken German.[55] Moreover, the increased use of the perfect in writing may represent the influence of the spoken language on the written at this period: the 'historic pres.' also seems to become common in literature from the sixteenth century onwards, and it too is characteristic of speech.[56] Comparable influence of speech on writing in the period has been seen in vocabulary and idiom in sermons, polemical tracts, and *Grobianismus*—an anti-polite style used in parodies of courtly literature in Lat. and German; Luther, too, uses everyday and sometimes drastic expressions in his pamphlets and sermons.

In the perfect periphrasis, the auxiliary verb relates the action to the circumstances of utterance, while the past part. has become an invariant aspectual particle marking completed action. In German, as in the Romance languages, the part. was originally adjectival, agreeing with the object in the case of a trans. verb and with the subject if the verb was intrans. However, the inflections were soon lost, and the past part. had become part of the verb morphology.[57] Nevertheless, the composite, indeed ambiguous nature of the tense-form persists in mod. German, encouraged perhaps by word-order patterns. The *haben* periphrasis with trans. verbs implies 'having at one's disposal a completed state or activity relating to the object of the sentence',[58] but in mod. German the primary interpretation is actional (*er hat seinen Bogen gespannt* means 'he has drawn his bow'), not stative ('he has his bow drawn'), which would be *er hat (s)einen gespannten Bogen*. Word order in English is distinctive here, but in mod. German the juxtaposition of finite verb and part. is stylistic in main clauses: in the sixteenth century the verbal frames characteristic of modern written German are not yet fully established, and partial or 'broken' frames are common.[59] The separation of the past part. from the finite auxiliary verb only strengthens the independence of both parts of the construction. Consequently, the perfect verb periphrasis can replace the future perfect: *Nächstes Jahr hat das Kind die Grundschule absolviert = wird . . . absolviert haben.* Here, the auxiliary in pres. tense-form (*hat*) is replacing the future (*wird haben*), the past part. describes the action as completed. Constructions with *sein* (usually intrans. verbs, which often have perfective force) are also ambiguous and can be interpreted adjectivally, with the part. qualifying the subject: compare *das Haus hat gebrannt* with *das Haus ist abgebrannt*, which is ambiguous, meaning (1) 'it burned down' or (2) 'it is a burned-out shell'. Similarly, adjectival constructions can resemble the perfect tense formally: *ein Unglück ist bald geschehen* 'accidents happen easily' and *ein Unglück ist letzten Freitag geschehen* 'an accident happened last Friday'.[60]

(ii) *Pluperfect.* The pluperfect employs the auxiliaries *sein* and *haben* in the pret.-tense-form: *war geblieben, hatte gekauft.* Again, the simple pret. could fulfil the pluperfect function of marking an action as anterior to other past events,[61] e.g. *Hildebrandslied* 33–4 *wuntane bauga . . . so imu se der chuning gap* 'torques the king *had given* him'. The preverb *ge-* added to the pret. verb form also expressed completed aspect in medieval German: 'Da die messe [= 'mass'] gesungen wart, die spise was bereit, und man ging eßsen. Da man *gaße* [= NHG *nachdem man gegessen hatte*], da ging der konig . . . zu mym herren Gawan . . .'[62] However, where the pret. verb form had fallen out of use (notably in spoken southern German) the auxiliary verbs *war* and *hatte* were themselves replaced by perfect tense-forms, creating new periphrastic forms:

> *ich hatte gegessen* → *ich habe gegessen gehabt*
> *er war weggegangen* → *er ist wegegangen gewesen.*

The pluperfect periphrasis remains literary and relatively rare, since the pret. in combination with adverbs still competes with it, even if the temporal relations are less precise. A hypercorrect use of the pluperfect is occasionally met with in regions which lack the pret. form in speech, e.g. 'Ich bin heute im Dorf gewesen' becomes 'Ich war heute im Dorf gewesen', the pret. being equated with polite, literary usage.[63]

(iii) *Supercomposed or past anterior forms.* The supercomposed forms of the type *ich habe gegessen gehabt* are well attested in the sixteenth century, and employ the past participles *gehabt* and *gewesen* (and dialectal forms of these—*gesy, gewest, gehott*, etc.) as aspectual particles marking a stronger degree of perfectiveness.[64] This proves particularly useful in texts like the Paumgartner correspondence, where auxiliary verbs are frequently omitted altogether, so that the past part. *gehabt* emphasizes the completed nature of the activity and, as it were, replaces the auxiliary verb: 'Demnach ich aber wol gewüest unnd ausgerechnett gehabtt . . .', '. . . den futterattlas vor diesem [tag] schon bestellt gehabtt . . .'.[65] Relative degrees of past time can, as usual, be conveyed by temporal particles (*schon, bereits*, etc.), so strictly obviating the need for any past anterior forms. Nevertheless, they serve useful stylistic purposes, creating variation, but also retaining the colloquial flavour of a conversation even in reported speech: 'Er sagte, er habe sein Frühstück schon um sieben Uhr gegessen gehabt', where *habe gegessen* alone would be choice. The stylistic value of supercomposed forms in the sixteenth century is unclear, and their use in speech is probably geographical (southern?).[66] Gottsched condemns them and they have never counted as standard. Moreover, writers from Austria (or its Empire) occasionally use an even more markedly aspectual form of the type *hatte gegessen gehabt* which cannot be explained by avoidance of the pret.[67]

D. MODALITY

Modality may be defined as the expression of some attitude to what is being said, and this modal colouring is conveyed in several ways, of which verb morphology or 'mood'[68] is one. Such a wide definition of modality means that most utterances will be modally marked. Depending on one's approach, as many as eight kinds of modal marking occur in modern spoken and written German, sometimes in combination: (1) intonation, e.g. to express doubt, sarcasm, irony, etc.; (2) modal particles interpretable only from context, e.g. *schon, doch, halt, ja, auch, eh*, etc.; (3) modal 'adverbs' with independent lexical meaning, e.g. *möglicherweise* 'possibly', *veilleicht* 'perhaps', *wahrscheinlich* 'probably', etc.; (4) verbs whose meaning is necessarily modal, e.g. *bezweifeln, glauben, hoffen*, etc.; (5) modal auxiliary verbs, *dürfen, können, mögen, müssen, nicht brauchen, sollen, wollen*; (6) modal infinitives, e.g. 'das Haus ist *zu verkaufen*' = 'kann/muß verkauft werden'; (7) auxiliary verbs with a clearly marked subj. form which act as modal particles, e.g. *sei, wäre, habe, hätte, täte, würde*; (8) mood (i.e. subj. forms of verbs), e.g. *er komme/er käme* vs. ind. *er kommt/er kam*. To these might be added (9) word order, since first position of the verb is a feature of questions, commands, and conditional constructions (*Hätte ich nur Zeit gehabt, so . . .*), and could be taken as expressing uncertainty or volition. Here we can discuss only mood, notably the subj. verb forms, and the modal auxiliaries.

1. *Replacement of synthetic modal forms by periphrasis*

Having treated morphological syncretism in the subj. forms of the verb already (see pp. 173-4), we can appreciate here too the change from synthetic ('morphological') structure to analytic ('syntactic') structure: modality is marked not by any single verb form or modal morph, but rather within a verb phrase, or else by one of the other modal devices just listed. Moreover, the loss of distinctive subj. forms goes hand in hand with changes in the frequency and use of those marked forms which survive: in brief, subj. verb forms occur more frequently in medieval and early mod. German and show a different distribution.[69]

Both modality and tense distance a speaker—the spatial metaphor is significant—from what he is saying, since events outside the speaker's experience and immediate situation, whether they occur earlier or later or even simultaneously with the act of speaking but in some other place, are open to question regarding their factual status. In the modern language, residual subj. forms represent one way in which the speaker, or more usually the writer, dissociates himself from his report. The nature of this dissociation varies: a speaker may be reporting someone else's opinion which he does not share, uttering a wish, issuing a command which may or may not be followed, or setting out hypothetical conditions. In such instances the two subj. moods, 'pres.' and 'pret.', mark differing degrees of dissociation and contrast with the ind., which is unmarked concerning the speaker's commitment to his statements. The precise kind of distancing or dissociation depends on the particular context in which the subj. is used, since levels of volition, potentiality, or unreality are context-bound and dependent on the speaker's viewpoint, and perhaps even character. Tense has been neutralized in the subj. mood in mod. German, and the old labels 'pres. subj.' and 'pret. subj.' have usually been replaced by 'Subj. I' and 'Subj. II' (SI, SII).[70] But in medieval German a 'sequence of tenses' appears to govern the use of subjunctive forms in many dependent clauses: a pres. subj. (SI) occurs in a clause dependent on a main clause with pres. (or occasionally perfect) ind. or subj.; a pret. subj. (SII) is found where the governing clause contains a pret. ind. or subj. Translation problems bring home the change in the use of the subj., in particular the loss of temporal force of the 'pret.' subjunctive. Thus, *Nibelungenlied* 963 'dô sprâchen die daz sâhen, er *wære* ein kreftic man' must be rendered into NHG using SI: 'diejenigen, die das sahen/gesehen hatten, sagten, er *sei* ein kräftiger Mann' (to use *wäre* would imply that Sîvrit was not in fact as strong as the bystanders maintained). Similarly, the synthetic SII can in MHG convey a range of past meanings no longer possible. Thus, *Nibelungenlied* 927 'het er sîn swert enhende sô *wær* ez Hagenen tôt' can only be rendered into mod. German by periphrastic forms: '*Hätte* er sein Schwert in der Hand *gehabt*, so *wäre* es Hagens Tod *gewesen*.' By ENHG SII occurs in clauses dependent on main clauses with the verb in the pres. tense, as in Luther's version of the Aesop fable of the dog and the bone: 'als er den schemen vom fleisch ym wasser sihet, wehnet er, es *were* auch fleisch'.[71]

The medieval language, then, has dependent subjunctives distributed complementarily according to their temporal setting,[72] but this system decays, as is evident both from morphological syncretism and the fact that modern dialects have retained only one set of subj.

forms: Alem. and the neighbouring Austrian and Bav. dialects preserve only the pres. subj. (SI), while all the rest—LG, the MG and Frk. dialects, and the remaining Austro-Bav. dialects—have kept the pret. subj. (SII).[73] Only the standard German language (in this respect, as in its phonology, a curious amalgam) has both SI and SII, which are often used indiscriminately in opposition to the ind., depending upon the availability of identifiable subj. forms, which varies from verb to verb. Whether the regional loss of one or other subj. mood had already occurred in the sixteenth-century dialects, as Behaghel maintained, is a moot point, since the early grammarians discuss only the written language, and their indebtedness to Lat. and perhaps Fr. grammatical traditions blinded them to some features of contemporary German usage.[74]

For instance, following Donatus, they distinguish *five* moods—ind., imperative, optative, conjunctive, and infinitive.[75] The optative and conjunctive moods depend primarily on the use of particular conjunctions which are taken over into the paradigms, and the verb forms given are neither temporally nor modally marked in some instances; some are actually ind. forms. Thus, the optative pres. *and* pret. is formed from the conjunctional expressions *wolt Gott/ach/oh das* (NHG *daß*) (which render Lat. *utinam*) plus pret. ind. or pret. subj., as in Ölinger (1573–4), 109 'Ach oder wolte Gott das ich hette/ du hettest etc.', 123 'Oh oder wolt Gott das ich schrieb etc.';[76] whereas the conjunctive pres. is formed by *so/wie/wenn/als* plus pres. ind. forms; as in Ölinger (1573–4), 110 'wie ich hab/ wie du hast etc.', Clajus (1578), 119 'Cum amem, So ich liebe . . . so er liebet etc.' As for the actual subj. verb forms, the pres. subj. is poorly represented in the grammarians: Albertus (1573) mentions it only as part of the imperative mood, i.e. third person sg. *Der hab/hab der* (p. I 6b); Clajus (1578) includes it in a few conjunctive constructions (after *auff das/das*, e.g. *auff das er sterbe* (p. 138)), and does give a rudimentary 'sequence of tenses' rule for dependent clauses (p. 250):

Ich gebiete dir/ das du anfarest	*Impero tibi ut exeas*
Ich gebot dir/ du soltest das thun	*Mandabam tibi ut hoc faceres.*

Ölinger (1573–4) establishes a whole 'modus dubitativus' (pp. 152f.) based on the pres. subj., but the dubitative use of the pret. subj. is not discussed,[77] past tense-forms being rendered, as in mod. German, by periphrasis with the past part., e.g. *Er sagt er schreibe/Er sagt er hab geschrieben.* Ölinger uses this mood where Lat. has acc. plus perfect infinitive. Thus, *Dicunt eum occidisse Petrum* 'They say he has killed P.' becomes *Man sagt er habe den Petrum umbgebracht/ . . . man sagt das er den Peter zů todt geschlagen habe.* So, apart from Clajus' sketchy statement, SI and SII are not treated as tense-forms of the subj. by the grammarians, nor is their relationship to each other discussed. Ölinger's dubitative mood also shows past participles marking completed aspect pressed into service to indicate time relations. Clearly, the subj. morphology in the sixteenth and seventeenth centuries was already too depleted to allow thoroughgoing tense oppositions. The more fully differentiated modal auxiliaries increasingly fill in the gaps in the verb morphology, a form of periphrasis involving suppletion.

2. *Modal auxiliaries*

The modal auxiliary verbs of modern standard German mostly derive from a small class of defective verbs known as 'preterite-presents', since in their pres. tense they show what are actually old past tense-forms. In early texts these verbs are already used modally and they increasingly supplement the subj. morphology. Notker, for example, already translates Lat. subjunctives with *darf, mag,* or *sol* plus infinitive, e.g. *Boethius* iii. 51. 10 *loquar = Uuaz mag ih chôsôn,* iii. 71. 5 *possis . . . petere = hólôn súlîst . . . bíten súlîst.* Similarly, the early grammarians incorporate the modal auxiliaries *sollen* and *müssen* into their paradigms for the imperative mood, especially the pl. Albertus (1573), p. I 6b, has *wir sollen haben/ihr sollent/Die sollen haben*; while for a future tense imperative he prescribes *Ich wird/Du wirst/Der wirdt sollen oder müssen haben,* etc. Ölinger's imperative future takes the form *Du solt haben/er soll haben/wier sollen haben* etc. (Ölinger (1573–4), 108 f.), whereas his future ind. is formed with *wollen* or with *werden/würden.*

Geographical (i.e. dialectal), stylistic, and contextual (semantic) factors will have contributed to the regulating influence of grammarians to account for the system of modal auxiliaries found in mod. German. The present system can be divided into several opposing but overlapping subsets according to function, showing how modal verbs qualify parts of the sentence.[78] First, necessity and obligation (NHG *muß* and *soll*) are opposed to possibility and permission (*kann* and *darf*); a second dimension, according to whether the modal factor lies within the subject or whether it depends on an outside agent or frame of reference, may be termed 'intra-subjective' (*will*) vs.

'extra-subjective' (*soll* and *darf*). Finally, 'objective causality', where the subject's situation is determined by forces akin to natural laws (*muß*, *kann*), is opposed to 'autonomy', where the subject's volition participates (*will*, *mag*, *soll*, *darf*). If we project this system (here only the first dimension) back into the past, we can describe the changing distribution of the verbs within it, thus:

NECESSITY/OBLIGATION VS. POSSIBILITY/PERMISSION

(1) MHG	*darf*	*scal* (*sol*)	≠ *mac*	*muoz*
(2) NHG	*muß*	*soll*	≠ *kann*	*darf*

This shows that the modern equivalents of medieval *muoz* and *darf* have changed places: MHG *muoz* implied permission but now conveys necessity, whereas *darf* once implied necessity (cognate with *Bedürfnis*) but now involves permission. Medieval *mac* (NHG *mag*) expressed possibility (cf. *vermögen*, *Möglichkeit*) but has been replaced by *kann*, which relates to mental ability.[79] A full interpretation of shifts occurring within this first dimension must naturally consider the other dimensions too, and also special uses of particular forms, like the SI: in MHG wishes and greetings can be formed with *müeze*, e.g. *Nibelungenlied* 480. 2 'got müez iuwer êre die zît wol bewarn', but in NHG *mögen* would be used ('Gott möge Eure Ehre erhalten'). Regional forms also differ: southern speakers often use *möchte* for standard *könnte*, for example, as in 'Das möchte wahr sein'. Moreover, there are contexts in which the modal oppositions are neutralized and the modal auxiliaries are virtually interchangeable.[80] Above all, modal verbs must be seen as part of the whole system of modality in which individual modal verbs participate in different and changing degrees. The verb *wollen*, for instance, seems to have ceded many functions to other constructions. Firstly, *wollen* (and *sollen* and *müssen*) were used in future tense forms, but growth of the *werden* construction has replaced the competitors. The parallel development *würde* plus infinitive in the conditional construction has again largely ousted *wollen*. Furthermore, the semantic shift of *mögen* away from 'possibility' towards 'like', 'wish' has restricted the occurrence of *wollen* here too: it can now sound abrupt or curt. The Paumgartner letters give an impression of the earlier frequency of *wollen* in sixteenth-century Nuremberg:

(1) . . . der selbige [= Gott] *wölle* uns in seinen gnaden . . . erhalten (NHG 'möge uns erhalten') (Letter No. 2).

(2) Bitte dich freundlich, *wöllest* mit gelegenheit also fortfahren . . . (NHG 'du *möchtest/würdest*') (ibid.).

(3) [Ich] *Wollt* uns solche Muhm auch gern . . . zu freundin erhalten (NHG 'ich *würde* uns gern/*möchte* gern') (ibid.).

(4) *Wöllen* . . . den zorn . . . [dar] aufgehen lassen (NHG '*Laßt uns*'; less usually '*Wollen wir*') (ibid.).

(5) . . . wann ich nun west [NHG *wüßte*], du sonst wohlauf, frisch und gesund wärest, so *wolt* ich schon zufrieden sein (NHG '*würde* ich') (Letter No. 3).

The letters also show two modal verbs overlapping in some contexts but not in others, as *mögen* is being replaced by *können* and is in turn replacing *wollen*:

> '[ich hab] dich . . . weiter nicht betrüben *mügen* (past part., where *mügen* clearly means 'wish', 'desire'; NHG 'ich habe dich nicht betrüben *wollen/mögen*') (Letter No. 2).

BUT

> [wird] nit regnen *mögen* oder *können* (here ability and 'intention' are difficult to separate: does *mögen* mean 'can' or 'will'? Cf. NHG 'Es *will* regnen' 'It's trying to rain') (Letter No. 3).

Finally, some modal verbs have died out, e.g. MHG (*ge*)*tar*, cognate with English 'dare', has sometimes been replaced by *dürfen*, partly because the meaning 'dare' and the new meaning of *dürfen* ('be allowed to') are close in some contexts, partly because of similarity of form (e.g. subj. *thürste* and *dürfte*) at a time when *getar* was no longer understood.[81]

WORD ORDER

Ordering grammatical elements is one of the main ways of indicating their relationship to each other, and a central concern of syntax. Medieval German word order was not so rigidly fixed as in the modern language, for the earlier syntax was closer to that of speech— most medieval texts, poetic, legal, or religious, were intended for reading aloud, so that intonation, context, and situation (gesture etc.) played an important part in understanding them. The more complex morphology, with its greater number of inflexional morphs, also permitted more flexible word order, while grammarians had not as yet begun to codify the German language: in the sixteenth and seventeenth centuries they have little to say about word order either[82] beyond trivial statements that adjectives when inflected precede the nouns they qualify, and so forth. This earlier 'syntax for the ear' contrasts, then, with the modern 'syntax for the eye',[83] where, in the case of word order, sets of conjunctions tie the main and dependent clauses together in fixed patterns.

Comparison of medieval and modern syntax must also take into account the fact that much medieval literature is in verse and correspondingly idiosyncratic. For example, the positioning of inflected adjectives before the possessive pronoun was unusual and 'formulaic' even in medieval literature: *Nibelungenlied* 2038-9 'Dô schuzzen sie die gêre mit krefte von der hant | durch die vesten schilde ûf *liehtez ir* gewant' (*lieht* 'bright', 'shining'). Even so, often not so much the actual word order as the frequency and functions of certain constructions shifted: the position of the finite verb, rightly considered the basis of mod. German word order, still shows four variants, but their 'functional loading' and stylistic values have changed. In what follows we consider only the positioning of the finite, or inflected, verb, dependent and subordinate clauses and their marking, and the development of the verbal frame characteristic of modern written German.

A. FINITE VERB POSITION

In German, past and present, four basic positions for finite verb occur: (1) non-initial/non-final with preceding subject; (2) non-initial/non-final with following subject; (3) initial; (4) final. Assuming for simplicity that either an object or an adjunct (e.g. an adverbial phrase) is potentially present in all environments, these patterns may be listed according to two types using the symbols S (subject), V (verb), O (object), A (adjunct):

	(a)		(b)
(1)	SVO	or	SVA
(2)	OVS		AVS
(3)	VSO		VSA
(4)	SOV		SAV

The frequency, stylistic value, and environments of these patterns change as the complex morphology of periphrastic verb forms, the use of dependent infinitives, and the use of separable prefixes introduce further variables. In modern standard German, in independent or main clauses the word orders (1) and (2) are normal, although variant 2 (*a*) is less frequent and thus more emphatic than

2 (*b*). Compare 2 (*a*) 'Den Sohn tröstete der Vater' (emphatic, poetic, etc.) and 2 (*b*) 'Gestern weinte er ganz toll' (colloquial). Pattern (3) is normal in questions, commands, and conditional constructions, but elsewhere poetic, particularly in folk-song: cf. Goethe's 'Sah ein Knab' ein Röslein stehn'. Word order (4) is nowadays unusual outside dependent clauses, and where it does occur in main clauses it is poetic.

Syntactic and stylistic constraints on verb position did not apply to sixteenth-century German to the same extent: word order (4) competed with other main clause word orders and had not yet become linked with subordinating conjunctions and particles to mark dependent clauses. Instead, medieval German dependent clauses were sometimes distinguished from main clauses not by word order but by using the subj.; so the decay of subj. morphology is linked also to the growth of word-order rules governing the verb position in dependent clauses.

If we consider the relationship of the noun phrase to verb position, we find that morphological factors do not contribute to significant changes in word order, since subject (nom.) and object (acc. or dat.) marking has changed little since medieval times. The only loss of morphemic opposition is between nom. and acc. fem. sg.: MHG *diu* ≠ *die* have coalesced as NHG *die*.[84] Indeed, word order was already grammatical in distinguishing subject from acc. object even in OHG texts, if the absence of nom. ≠ acc. oppositions in most noun and adj. paradigms is any guide. However, the word order of German noun phrase and verb phrase remains freer than in English, when we compare patterns (1), (2), and (4) in both languages:[85]

(1) 'Der Vater tröstete den Sohn' = 'The father comforted the son'.
(2) 'Den Sohn tröstete der Vater' ≠ 'The son comforted the father'.
(4) 'Der Vater den Sohn tröstete' ≠ 'The father the son comforted'.

The German examples show no change of grammatical relationship, whereas the English ones do, (4) being a relative construction, 'the father whom the son comforted'; similarly, a fifth possibility, OSV, highly unusual in normal German, would be relative in English:

(5) 'Den Sohn der Vater tröstete' ≠ 'The son the father comforted'.

B. DEPENDENT CLAUSES

In older stages of German main or independent clauses are often hard to distinguish from dependent ones:[86] the grammatical structures are not consistently marked formally and their relationships emerge from the meaning, rather than conveying it. Thus, dependent clauses are not necessarily introduced by a conjunction, their word order varies, with finite verb placed in positions other than final, and their finite verbs are not necessarily in subj. mood. Parataxis (the parallel juxtaposition of clauses) is common in medieval German poetry, and the 'logical operators' which show how parts of the sentence fit together are not yet established: conjunctions do not form a separate class, and instead 'conjunctional adverbs' have variously adverbial or conjunctional function depending on meaning. For example, MHG *dô* may mean 'then' (adv.) or 'when' (conjunction), and translators into mod. English or German may face awkward choices. Moreover, some particles can be prepositional as well, or may relate so closely to the verb as to be virtually verbal prefixes, separable or inseparable. Similarly, the relative pronoun is not distinguishable from the demonstrative pronoun or definite article in every context, although the compounded relative pronoun *der dar*, found already in OHG texts, marks a stage in the formal separation of different grammatical functions. The medieval use of subj. mood to mark dependent clauses—perhaps by distancing the speaker from the matter contained in them—was once common, but has virtually died out, and subj. morphology has become inadequate for the task. For example, the MHG 'negative exception clause' (= 'unless' clause) was a dependent clause marked by negation and subjunctive: 'mînes herzen tiefiu wunde diu muoz iemer offen stên *si enküsse mich* [= 'if she do not kiss me'] mit friundes munde' (Walther von der Vogelweide, 74. 14 f.).[87] In mod. German the word order would change from SVO or a conjunction would be supplied (NHG 'küßt/küßte sie mich nicht' or '*wenn* sie mich nicht küßt/küßte'), or else a 'conjunctional phrase' based on the medieval construction we are discussing would be used, namely *es sei denn (daß)* + SVO (or, after *daß*, SOV).

By the sixteenth century, despite a considerable growth of hypotaxis (i.e. encapsulated clauses) and the formal devices for marking it, especially in chancery and administrative texts, the modern system of marking dependent clauses by conjunctions and/or final position of the finite verb is still not fully established.

1. *Conjunctions*

The functionally and formally ambiguous particles of OHG which were probably distinguished by emphasis and intonation begin to separate out into more clearly marked conjunctional and adverbial sets some time in the late medieval period. Here one example must suffice: the MHG homonymous morph *daz* can act as conjunction, article, demonstrative, and relative pronoun. Of these, the article function is recognizably part of the developing noun phrase, but the other less easily distinguishable functions become differentiated by spelling and word order, though at varying rates. Certain fourteenth-century manuscripts already mark the conjunctional use by spelling, and Steinhöwel in his Boccaccio translation (1473) distinguishes 'ain kurcz daz' (conjunction) from 'ain lang das', and about the same time the Court Chancery of Maximilian I also separates conjunctional *daz* from the article *das*. In the sixteenth century, the printers at Frankfurt also make consistent orthographical distinction, but the modern spelling *daß* for conjunction is not yet established even in the seventeenth century.[88]

The demonstrative and relative uses remain close throughout the sixteenth century, but diverge as the relative pronoun becomes linked to the final position of finite verb in relative clauses. In Luther's Bible translation, for example, 'demonstrative'/'relative' constructions abound, e.g. Mark 5: 25 (1545 version) 'Vnd da war ein Weib | das hatte den Blutgang zwelff jar gehabt . . .', but to the modern ear they sound perhaps more colloquial than Luther intended, even though he wrote for the common people. In fact, before the finite verb has become fixed in final position in dependent clauses introduced by a relative pronoun we cannot be certain whether examples like the one just given are to be taken as relative or demonstrative. The meaning differs little, and the sixteenth-century stylistic values are elusive.

Whether orthographically distinct or not, *das* (*daß*) was added during the thirteenth to fifteenth centuries to a whole series of pre-positional or conjunctional particles as a neutral but clearly marked conjunctional morph. Surviving examples (modern spelling) include *als daß, auf daß, bis daß, damit daß, ehe daß, nachdem daß, seit daß,* and these all acquired the fixed subordinating word order with the finite verb used finally.[89] The many complex conjunctions with *daß* and hypotaxis have been considerably pruned back, and even those which survive are felt to be clumsy or stilted, the products of chancery 'paper style'—although evidence is now pointing to the successful influence of the chancery in other aspects of word order, notably the final position of the finite verb in subordinate clauses and the growth of the verbal frame (see below).

Co-ordinating conjunctions with parataxis seem to have been fewer in number than the subordinating conjunctions ('subjunctions'), and to have survived more frequently into mod. German.

2. Verb-final position in subordinate clauses

In modern written German subordinate clauses are characterized by showing the finite verb in final position unless it governs two infinitives, in which case it immediately precedes them: compare 'daß er kommen konnte' and 'daß er hat kommen können'.[90] While elements of the sentence may sometimes follow the finite verb in a subordinate clause, these are always felt as a breach of normal word order, a *Nachtrag* or afterthought outside a now obligatory frame or parenthesis, formed usually by the separation of the subject at the beginning of a subordinate clause from the finite verb at or close to the end of it. In the sixteenth century, however, as has been noted, final position of the finite verb in subordinate clauses was not yet the established word order:[91] Albertus (1573), in a rare comment on word order (p. I 7a), accepts for the optative paradigm the alternative word orders

(1) 'Wolt Gott das ich gehabt hett' ($= daß \ldots + V + AUX$).
(2) 'Wolt Gott das ich hette gehabt' ($= daß \ldots + AUX + V$).

At Nuremberg the order $V + AUX$ becomes the rule in subordinate clauses by the end of the sixteenth century, the result perhaps of the influence of the administrative style of the town chancery on local writers, who seek to emulate it in informal letters, diaries, chronicles, and so forth.[92] But not until the eighteenth century do school grammarians prescribe it: Karl Friedrich Aichinger (1717–82) requires verb-final position in subordinate clauses in his *Versuch einer teutschen Sprachlehre* (1754), while in 1759 the educational theorist Johann Bernhard Basedow (1723–90) actually distinguishes main and subordinate (dependent) clauses by this positional criterion.[93] The final position is by then virtually established in classical literary German. This positioning leads to the development of a clause frame embracing the elements of subordinate dependent clauses.

The position of the finite verb in dependent clauses has been viewed in terms of the theory of 'relief',[94] according to which topics are relegated to the foreground or background of a speaker's consideration and, as it were, 'thrown into relief'. Among the devices of the background, those of interest here include the subj. of the verb in dependent clauses, and the position of the verb at the end of subordinate clauses.[95]

While the relief theory is illuminating, it is unfortunately 'subjective'. Before the subordinate word order became obligatory (i.e. 'grammaticalized') some time in the seventeenth and eighteenth centuries, the use of second or final position for the verb must presumably have depended on the speaker's perception as to the main topic of his discourse. Consequently, the speaker's word order is coloured by personal considerations, whereas the historian of syntax is anxious to extrapolate from the individual context in the interests of constructing a model of syntactic change.

C. THE VERBAL FRAME (*SATZRAHMEN*)

One of the most striking word-order patterns of modern written German is the 'verbal frame', or *Satzrahmen, Satzklammer*, where a finite verb and other elements of an analytical verb phrase (participles, dependent infinitives, separable prefixes, pronominal subjects) are separated in a main or dependent clause, spanning the other elements of the clause, and organizing and identifying its components. This pattern—called the *Distanzstellung*[96]—is sporadic in OHG and MHG texts and becomes frequent only in ENHG, facilitated both by analytic verb morphology and by word order, with the finite verb increasingly occupying the final position in subordinate clauses. The load-bearing structures of main or independent clauses are of four main types:

1. Compound past tenses using the auxiliary *haben/sein* + past part.
2. Future and modal periphrasis with auxiliary *werden*/modal verb + dependent infinitive(s).
3. Often aspectually marked finite verb + separable prefix.[97]
4. Passive constructions with the auxiliary *werden* + past part.

In dependent clauses with the finite verb in final position the framework is created by the spatial (and temporal) gap between the subject and the finite verb: bridging or frame structures of the main clause 'collapse' into new dispositions in which the subject or a reflexive becomes prominent. Where the frame occurs in speech—and it is not uncommon in short segments—intonation and stress are superimposed on it.

The verbal frame occurs even in OHG, for example in Notker,[98] but is far from being the rule, and in medieval German poetry the demands of rhyme and metre bear also on its use. Compare *Nibelungenlied* 1762–3 'Alsam tier diu wilden *wurden gekapfet an* | die übermüeten helde von den Hiunen man', where the contact position of the passive would be recast into the frame in a modern prose translation: 'Wie wilde Tiere *wurden* die stolzen Helden von den Mannen der Hunnen *angestarrt*.' But even in the sixteenth century the frame is not yet obligatory, and main and dependent clauses alike show frameless word order beside complete frames and broken frames—i.e. frames enclosing some elements but not others.[99] For the moment, the geographical distribution of the frame construction is unclear. In early biblical translation from the fourteenth to the sixteenth centuries EMG versions have been claimed as progressive, showing frames from the mid-fourteenth century,[100] while UG Bibles from the late fifteenth century still lack it—even Zainer's Augsburg Bible (1475), which shows a marked increase in analytical verb morphology, e.g. in periphrastic perfect tense-forms, such as should have favoured the frame. In the LG-speaking area, the Cologne Bible of 1478 shows frame structures, albeit of the broken kind. Eck's UG Ingolstadt Bible (1537) does make some use of the frame, though not as much as Luther, who has often introduced it in revisions of his translation, notably in revising the *September-Testament* of 1522.

However, Bible translations represent too limited a material to show how common the frame construction was in the sixteenth and seventeenth centuries, or indeed if it originated in colloquial language. Certainly, the incidence of the frame in Luther's Bible does show his independence of the Hebrew, Greek, and Latin source languages, which do not have the construction; but can this be used as evidence that Luther turned to the constructions and rhythms of speech to make his translation more widely accessible? Surely not, for outside the Bible (for instance, in the lively and polemical *Sendbrief vom Dolmetschen*) Luther does not use the frame exclusively: broken frames and frameless clauses are common, in contrast to Wenzeslaus Linck's introduction to the same work, which (barring the position of the modal auxiliaries etc.) uses the frame as in mod. German. Conversely, Luther's 1545 Bible shows many instances of demonstrative clauses with contact-position word order.

A recent computer-run statistical survey of the use of the sentence frame in forty-one Nuremberg writers between 1300 and 1600 emphasizes the important role played by the town chancery.[101] In dependent clauses the chancery at first uses slightly fewer frame constructions than do individuals, but in the fifteenth century the chancery outstrips them, and by the late sixteenth century the chancery material regularly shows the full frame, with the finite verb in final position in dependent clauses. In main clauses, too, full frames increase in the sixteenth century, with the town chancery markedly to the fore. Direct Lat.' influence can probably be ruled out, since Lat. lacks the frame construction and has no tradition of placing finite verbs last in dependent clauses.[102] Ebert (1980) groups the Nuremberg individuals according to variables of time, style, education, and profession, and makes a plausible case for the administrative usage of the town council having influenced them in differing degrees. For instance, the frame is more frequent in informal letters than in formal ones or in diaries and chronicle-type material:[103] the Paumgartner letters show a high proportion of clauses with the complete frame (although the firmness of the load-bearing structures is weakened by the omission of auxiliary verbs). Balthasar Paumgartner, as a merchant, was presumably familiar with the city administration and must have corresponded regularly with the town council.

The less educated writers—secular women (as opposed to nuns)—tend to use the frame less frequently: where Balthasar Paumgartner uses the frame 98.1 per cent of the time in main clauses, his wife Magdalena uses it 85.7 per cent; in dependent clauses, Balthasar uses the frame regularly (100 per cent) and Magdalena 86 per cent of the time.[104] Ebert's study provides no evidence that the frame originated in speech: its origins remain uncertain. Possibly it became popular in the chancery because it provided a range of clause structures suitable for rendering into German the rhythmical *cursus* used as an embellishment in Lat. chancery documents: Lat. influence would be indirect and catalytic in this case.[105] The part played by printing in the spread of the sentence and clause frames also needs examining: in the WMG area, the stylistic refinements made to Ulrich Schmidl's travel account by the Frankfurt printer Sigismund Feyerabend in his 1567 edition show, *inter alia*, the introduction of clause frames into the text.[106]

Modern spoken German tends to limit hypotaxis, avoiding long encapsulations by using the demonstrative pronoun instead of the relative, or by using the present tense for narrative in place of periphrastic verb forms, both future and perfect. Short frame structures, especially partial or broken frames, are common in speech, but the contact position which was already becoming archaic in the sixteenth century has now been given up. It occurs frequently in the Bible, which probably accounts for its associations of pathos and poetry, e.g. in Revelation 3: 10 (Luther, 1545):

Die weil du *hast behalten* das Wort meiner Gedult | wil ich auch dich behalten fur der Stunde der Versuchung | die *komen wird* vber der gantzen Weltkreis | zu versuchen, die da wonen auff Erden.

CONCLUSION

This chapter has given a brief account of the change from synthetic to analytical structure, as revealed by the 'grammatical machinery' of the German language. A truly 'historical' interpretation must inevitably await further detailed study of the social, and above all educational, influences on sixteenth- and seventeenth-century German from all geographical areas and stylistic levels, but we can nevertheless see quite clearly the emergence of competing structures in the written and printed evidence.

In particular, the morphology of the noun and verb are increasingly replaced by more discrete and discontinuous means of marking their grammatical role, namely by the noun phrase and by periphrastic verb forms respectively, and also (for the verb) by the use of suppletion to convey the categories of mood, tense, and aspect. By the sixteenth century German syntax was well on the way to its established mod. German form, although considerable stylistic latitude remained, particularly in word order, which has nowadays become much more restricted in standard written form. Despite the erosion of morphological endings, the syntax of written German in the Transitional and Early Modern periods shows developments which tended to express more clearly the formal relations between the elements of the sentence than in many medieval texts: the fixing of word order, the growth of prepositional phrases and of conjunctions, mark a shift away from a syntax based on, and vaguely discernible from, the *meaning*, towards a formal, elaborated, and explicit system with logical clause connections.[107] However, the complexities of earlier aspectual marking should warn us against underestimating the subtlety of the medieval language—as should the great works of medieval literature. Instead, the medieval syntax was, perhaps, still 'less abstract', in other words, more closely tied to context and situation—in this respect, again, closer to speech. But whether word order or particular modal verb forms reflect the speakers' perception of a topic as being in the background or foreground of their focus of attention remains open to debate.

Attempts to link syntactic developments with social ones include theories of foreign, notably Lat. influence, either directly via the Humanists or indirectly via chanceries and schools. Unfortunately, the observable effects of school grammars fall mainly after the sixteenth century, although their influence prior to that must have been considerable. Nevertheless, the theories of Lat. influence are now out of favour, and at least two important features of German word order cannot derive from Lat.: the final position of the finite verb in dependent clauses, and the characteristic clausal frame (*Satzrahmen*). Both *might*, however, be attributable to what contemporaries *thought* was Lat. style, and both seem redolent of the chancery, or, to be more cautious, they seem less probable in the speech of the mass of the population outside the educated patriciate. And again, some Lat. influence may be smuggled back indirectly where there is an obvious discrepancy between the standard written norms and everyday speech. For example, double negation remains common in present-day dialect and vulgar colloquial, and it was once found in medieval administrative and chancery texts: its loss in the modern standard language might reflect the influence of Lat. school grammars on the German grammars.[108]

In general, the picture of sixteenth-century syntax in the 'pre-grammarian era' accords well with the other levels, phonology and morphology: norms are developing but have not yet become canonical. Geographical, stylistic, and semantic differences complicate and blur impressions, while the earliest grammarians of German, even in the seventeenth century, were primarily concerned with other issues, notably with word-formation. They treated syntax very much as *Wort-fügung*, not as *Satz-fügung*.

SELECT BIBLIOGRAPHY

GENERAL:

Behaghel (1923–32).
Dal (1966).
Ebert (1978).
Erdmann (1886–98).
Grimm (1819/22–37) [esp. *Syntax* (1837)].

Lockwood (1968).
Naumann (1915).
Paul (1916–20) [esp. vols. iii–iv, *Syntax* (1919–20)]
Schröbler, in Paul (1881/1969).
Wunderlich (1892).

EARLY NEW HIGH GERMAN SYNTAX

Kehrein (1854–6) [esp. vol. iii, which is still useful as a source of material].

BRIEF SUMMARIES

Brooke (1955).
Philipp (1980).

Schmidt *et al.* (1969) [esp. pp. 281–358, notably 352 ff.].

MARTIN LUTHER'S SYNTAX

Franke (1913–22).

Erben (1974).

SPECIAL STUDIES (mostly not available before completion of this chapter).

Admoni (1979).
Guchmann and Semenjuk (1981).

Kettmann and Schildt (1976).
Scaglione (1981).

EARLY GRAMMARS USED

Albertus (1573), ed. Müller-Fraureuth.
Clajus (1578), ed. Weidling.

Ölinger (1573–4), ed. Scheel.

For other early grammars, see Müller (1882), Jellinek (1913–14, and especially the systematic account of German grammar in vol. ii (1914).

CHAPTER VII

THE EARLY MODERN PERIOD (I): THE DEFENCE OF THE LANGUAGE (1600–1700)

CHANGES in vocabulary, in particular lexical growth, caused by foreign influences of various kinds, are the stuff of traditional linguistic history, for here internal and external factors themselves interact more directly and obviously than in phonology, morphology, or syntax. The present chapter discusses linguistic and social aspects of borrowing from other languages during the seventeenth century, especially from Fr. Contemporaries reacted to the influence from abroad in several ways, including purism, which was fostered in language societies newly established to cultivate and improve the native language. This 'feedback' from the speech-community on the use of foreign forms in German contexts gives insights into the stylistic role played by borrowing in the language's vocabulary. The puristic attacks on loans are not proof that German was being overrun or adulterated, however, for in many circles and contexts the new vocabulary was an enrichment, both for technical and stylistic purposes. Instead, the often superficial and subjective attacks on Fr. can be seen as a vindication of the native language, marking the growth of the conviction that German was an important language worth nurturing. So the 'defence' of the German language is actually a stage in its development, regardless of the amount of influence from outside—indeed, most loans at this time had come from Lat., for centuries the language of learning, yet attacks on Lat. influence are relatively rare. The structure of the German language was hardly altered by the foreign influence at this time, and most of the words borrowed eventually disappeared along with the cultural settings which produced or required them. Moreover, the aristocracy sought to learn Fr., read Fr. novels, and corresponded in French. They had little real desire to eradicate a group language which was a badge of breeding, though they might enjoy laughing at it now and again. The purists, on the other hand, who generally profited from some aristocratic patronage, were mainly bourgeois writers who parodied the excessive use of foreign words in poetry or satirized the inappropriateness of certain kinds of speakers aspiring to foreign tongues. At the same time these writers marked themselves out as gentlemen who knew enough Fr., Italian, and Spanish to criticize those who did not. Finally, the satirists were especially preoccupied with form and style in literature, for in style, too, writers were increasingly aware of standards of acceptability, just as the grammarians looked for spelling and grammatical norms. In spelling and morphology, perhaps in syntax too, regular, if regional, bands of variation in the printed or book language already existed whose limits could not be exceeded. So that, for example, individual attempts to reshape and reform the orthography on rational grounds failed because of widely accepted traditional spelling based on usage.[1] But whereas the forces of inertia in orthography and morphology were acting on relatively circumscribed levels of language, the vocabulary, especially in the sphere of meaning, was less limited. Seventeenth-century satirists and purists sometimes sought vainly to purify German from all foreign influence, regardless of where and why foreign words were being used—not surprisingly with limited success, since those who used German for everyday, non-literary purposes had a less self-conscious attitude to loans and followed their own convenience. At any event, it would be unwise to rely on the antagonistic view of foreign borrowing often expressed in satirical literature of the period or in grammatical, rhetorical, or poetic handbooks. The chanceries, schools, various 'technologies'—notably architecture and warfare—dictionaries, and more popular texts like newspapers seem not to have been avowedly purist: they give a better guide to the actual level of borrowing which occurred and, by implication, to the tolerant attitudes to it.

FOREIGN BORROWING AND THE GERMAN VOCABULARY

Foreign influences on a language may be considered in three main ways: (1) the *historical* and *'etymological'* approach looks for the reasons for the influence and asks why, from what sources, and by what routes the borrowing has occurred; (2) the *linguistic* approach establishes a typology of influence, examines the extent of changes that have taken place at all levels of language—in phonology, morphology, syntax, and in the semantic systems; (3) the *sociolinguistic* approach combines elements of the other two in examining the main areas of cultural and political life affected by the borrowing, and discussing reactions to it.

A. POSSIBLE CAUSES OF LINGUISTIC BORROWING IN THE SEVENTEENTH CENTURY

The 'reasons' underlying linguistic borrowing are not easily determined for any period, whether the seventeenth century or the present day. Certain types of semantic influence are so subtle that speakers are hardly aware of them, while the individual speaker's ability to recognize foreign words from their form varies, for example, with the degree of education and with the similarity of structure between the foreign words and native ones.[2] Some borrowings lack native equivalents and remain restricted to technical usage, while others become fashionable and are deliberately, even provocatively, flaunted in the speech-community at large. Class, the speaker's status, genre, context, situation of use and purpose all bear upon the unconscious and conscious use of foreign or foreign-influenced forms. The 'situational', psychological factors in linguistic borrowing ought not to be entirely forgotten in a history of German vocabulary, although in a general survey the emphasis must fall on historical, cultural, and economic forces favouring the receptiveness to influences from abroad.

War, in particular the Thirty Years War (1618–48), has since the seventeenth century been given as one of the main reasons for the apparent cultural and linguistic susceptibility of the German vocabulary to outside, especially Romance, influences. A considerable influx of foreign military vocabulary did indeed occur: some 30 per cent of French borrowings between 1575 and 1648 were military, the bulk of them (75 per cent or 342 out of 453 terms) attested before

1625.[3] Moreover, the war meant that many army expressions—names of weapons, ranks, and units—must have become familiar to the civilian population, while early newspapers which appeared in the opening decades of the seventeenth century spread them through their war reports. In literature the braggart soldier, familiar since Plautus' Pyrgopolynices (*Miles Gloriosus*), reappears as a *Sprachmischer* who naturally includes soldiers' slang. Andreas Gryphius (1616–64), in his *Horribilicribrifax Teutsch* (Breslau, 1663), introduces 'twin' captains, the Italian-speaking Horribilicribrifax, and the French-speaking Daradiridatumtarides, both of whom mangle their foreign tongues. Despite the literary sources—Horribilicribrifax is modelled closely on a captain from the *commedia dell'arte*—the German audience were presumably credited by Gryphius with understanding the linguistic jokes.[4] More debatable is the view that the Thirty Years War had so sapped the resources of Germany as to weaken the native language and inhibit the emergence of a national literature. For the devastation of the war was selective, some regions surviving relatively untouched, although epidemics and emigration considerably reduced the population overall.[5] Perhaps the most far-reaching social effect of the war was the weakening of the urban bourgeoisie which had begun to dominate intellectual life in the sixteenth century, and the strengthening of the position of the aristocracy through the debris of absolutist states (some 343) left behind after the Treaty of Westphalia. The individual states lacked the economic and intellectual cohesion to produce any outstanding 'national' literature, which a single cosmopolitan capital might have achieved. Nevertheless, the princes provided opportunities for the bourgeois officials who carried out the state duties, although membership of the court was often limited to the nobility, who acted as advisors and companions of the prince. The aristocracy was indirectly responsible for the adoption into German of many foreign words because of the princes' concern for spectacle and pomp. Architects from abroad were commissioned to build castles and palaces and to lay out gardens; musicians, singers, stage and theatrical engineers worked in the theatres and later opera houses, and in all these spheres the technical vocabulary was foreign. In Vienna Spanish court ceremonial was imitated rather than French, and operatic, musical, and dramatic influences from Italy were prominent.[6]

Dynastic links with Spain explain the Spanish influence on the

Viennese court, but many lesser German princes had intermarried with French aristocracy and had developed a taste for things French. The ties between German and French princely families in border areas, like the Palatinate, were particularly close—Liselotte von der Pfalz (1652–1722), daughter of the Elector Karl Ludwig, married the duke of Orléans, brother of the 'Sun King', and her letters give a vivid glimpse of court life in France at this period. Moreover, in the age of Louis XIV (1638–1715), of the *salons* and of French classical theatre, French culture was at its height, and by an almost physical law its influence flowed to lower levels all over Europe, mainly through aristocratic and literary channels. In the eighteenth century German princes still had residences built in imitation of Versailles, giving them French names: *Favorite, Monrepos, Sanssouci,* and *Solitude.* But even in the early seventeenth century French language teachers, not all of them reliable, are known to have come to Germany to teach the nobility, while young nobles sometimes went on a *Kavalierstour* to France, especially to Paris (for example, the poet Hofmannswaldau). So the interest of the upper classes in French is amply attested. Indeed, just after the most prestigious and aristocratic German language society had been established in 1617, a rival society for the furtherance of foreign languages was set up by a group of noble ladies under the leadership of Anna, the wife of Christian I of Bernburg. This body, 'La noble Academie des Loyales' or 'L'Ordre de la Palme d'Or', had its statutes written in French.[7] About the same time Caspar Laudismann, a court official and teacher of French, emphatically denied that German was inferior to French, as some Frenchmen were claiming:

Sed quod Galli linguae suae nimium attribuant et dicant: Qu'il faille parler par la langue Francoise seulement aux grands Seigneurs, mais par la langue Alemande aux mechaniques & aux Rustiques . . . In hoc turpiter errare Gallos dicit hujus Consilij Author & Publicator. Transferant se Galli hoc dicentes Wiennam Austriae, Lipsiam, Augustam Vindelicorum, & Ulmam, & audiant ibi loqui selectiores Viros et Domicellas, & admirabuntur & leporem, & gratiam, & jucunditatem linguae Germanicae.[8]

But as to what the French immoderately claim for their Language, saying that 'one should speak French only with the great Lords, but keep the German tongue for talking to labourers and peasants . . .' The Author and Publisher of the present Guide holds the French to err basely in this. Let the Frenchmen who assert this go to Vienna in Austria, to Leipzig, to Augsburg, and Ulm, and let them there listen to noble men and ladies talking and they will admire the elegance, grace, and suavity of the German language.

Over a century later, another itinerant Frenchman was still making
the same observation on a visit to Potsdam:

> Je me trouve ici en France. On ne parle que notre langue. L'allemand est pour
> les soldats et pour les chevaux; il n'est nécessaire que pour la route.[9]

I might as well be in France. Only our language is spoken. German is for
soldiers and horses; you do not need it, save when travelling.

In the second half of the seventeenth century economic factors
tipped the trading balance in France's favour,[10] and leading German
and Austrian mercantilists argued for the banning of foreign imports,
including clothes and other fashionable luxuries. Imperial edicts
forbidding French wares and manufactured goods were promulgated in 1676 and again in 1702 and 1703, but remained ineffective.
Precisely at this period the foreign fashions and conspicuous display
on the part of some princes were most evident.

Large-scale francophone immigration in parts of Germany from
the late sixteenth to the early nineteenth centuries must not be
discounted as a factor in borrowing. The Huguenots fled religious
persecution after 1572, the Massacre of St Bartholomew, and again
in 1685, following the revocation of the Edict of Nantes, when as
many as 20,000 refugees may have settled in Brandenburg alone
at the invitation of the Calvinist Elector Friedrich Wilhelm ('Der
Große Kurfürst'). By 1703 about 5,690 French Protestants had
settled in Berlin, constituting perhaps a third of the population of
that town, and possibly explaining some of the considerable 'French'
element in recent Berlin slang. Possibly this also accounts for the
impression gained by Voltaire a generation later that French was
the genteel lingua franca.[11] Subsequently other waves of French
aristocrats escaped the excesses of the Terror following the French
Revolution.

B. QUANTITY AND QUALITY

The quantification of borrowing in the seventeenth century is a
difficult undertaking. The bulk of loans continues to derive from
Latin, reflecting an increasing use of German for purposes hitherto
virtually closed to it. For, until the seventeenth century German
culture had been effectively bilingual, with Latin the scholarly and
(international) administrative language, and only in the last quarter
of the seventeenth century did the number of German books printed

annually in Germany outstrip the number of Latin ones. There is correspondingly little criticism of Latin, although in some contexts, such as education, the German case was forcefully advanced: Wolfgang Ratke's followers Christoph Helwig (1581–1617) and Joachim Junge (1587–1657) attacked a 'Tyranney der Lateinischen Sprach', seeing it as a linguistic barrier to all other learning.[12] Similar views about translating Latin medical or legal language in order to make the subject-matter comprehensible are known from the sixteenth century, but Latin itself remained the respected biblical and learned tongue; only its abuse by the wrong people or for the wrong purposes attracted criticism—for instance in the (ultimately classical) stock figures of the charlatan stage lawyer and medico. German satirical writing in the seventeenth century often pilloried not Latin as such, but the curious 'macaronic' mixture of German and other languages,[13] although behind the conventional literary caricature speakers may actually have interlarded their conversation with technical terms on occasion: Georg Philip Harsdörffer (1607–58) commented on the use of Latin in church services and the desire of scholars to impress the ill-educated by filling their speech with Latin tags.[14]

French influence increased markedly from the late sixteenth century on, and intensified at the end of the seventeenth. As we have seen, the presence of Frenchmen in Germany, whether as soldiers or refugees, played a small part in the adoption of French loans; only in border areas can much bilingualism have occurred, and even then largely at dialectal level. The relatively minor traces of spoken influence in the kinds of borrowing which occurred confirm this (see below). Instead, a 'literary bilingualism'[15] affects foreign modes of address and foreign pastimes and pursuits with all their attendant vocabulary. In literature, art, music, manners, and dress an often uncritical mimicry is found: for instance, the ideals expressed by French classical writers were taken in Germany at face value, not contrasted with the reality of French society. The very fashionableness of much of this borrowing is significant, for the outcry against French, especially in the early seventeenth century, far exceeded its quantitative effects. Even the less influential languages like Spanish and Italian were roundly condemned on occasion. Again, the fashionable setting is important. While Latin gradually declined as the language of law, learning, and religion, German painlessly replaced it, filling a vacuum, so to speak. But Latin was never the language of fashion and politeness, and for these newer demands German competed in an unequal struggle with French, which prompted polemical and satirical writing. Still, the relationship between German and French was not inevitably one of conflict, and depended on the purpose involved. For example, the famous jurist and philosopher Christian Thomasius (1655-1728)[16] lectured in German at Leipzig University (on Balthasar Gracian's maxims), and also developed German legal and philosophical terminology by adapting foreign words to German morphology. But at the same time Thomasius admired the gallant and polite French influence and advocated imitating it within reason:

. . . man ahme denen Frantzosen nach, denn sie sind doch heut zu tage die geschicktesten Leute, und wissen allen Sachen ein recht Leben zu geben.

Thomasius specifically mentions the French intellectual achievements, beside which the old reactionary Latin-based scholarship in Germany was quaint, unworldly, out of date, and unappealing to men of the world. French scholars had already translated many classical authors, such learning was encouraged by the king, and was, above all, alive and developing. Germans, on the other hand, showed scant regard for their own language since they either mangled Greek and Latin technical terms by obscure and ludicrous attempts to translate them, or else gave up altogether and denied that German could be used for scholarly discourse at all. Thomasius argues that French is so widely known in Germany that, instead of attempting the impossible task of eradicating it, it should be used, along with German, to educate those who are to play a part in everyday life, or who have learned only German and French and have no stomach for Latin.[17] Moreover, the undoubted refinement of French culture will civilize German society too. In short, Thomasius was arguing for a reform of the German universities to make them more relevant to the needs of his time: this extended even to using the German language in lectures, and also to dress, for he was censured for lecturing 'im bunten Modekleid mit Degen und zierlichem goldenem Gehänge'.[18] So, respect for German was combined with admiration for things foreign. Gottfried Wilhelm Leibniz (1646-1714) is another who had a very warm respect for his native language, and yet his published works are invariably in Latin or French. Leibniz opposed extreme purism—his own (?) ironical term for the purist is *Rein-Dünkler*[19]—but he did note that related languages like Dutch could provide German with technical and philosophical vocabulary, and judicious borrowing from this source or from dialect could enrich the language.

The more informal language used in letters, newspapers, diaries, and 'conversational pieces' confirms the picture that Latin loans are far ahead of the rest (73 per cent), with French quite prominent (25 per cent) and other languages insignificant.[20] Moreover, there is *more* borrowing at this level than in didactic writing—although popular works translated from French and Italian abound in loan-words for local colour and so forth. In these contexts the social rather than technical or aesthetic aspect of borrowing is to the fore. The reactions against foreign influence, and indeed the contemptuous catch-words given by contemporaries to the fashion-conscious, *Alamode* or *allomodo*,[21] express the opposition to Romance in-fluence, *not* to Latin. French borrowings were much less common than Latin, but were clearly felt to be much more objectionable because they were borrowed for social, not 'functional', reasons, and from a living European rival, not a dead classical model.

To sum up, the main European languages contributed technical terms in those spheres either where German lacked vocabulary, or where the ideas and cultural innovations were borrowed with the terms themselves. From Italian came the language of commerce and book-keeping, of Humanism, of the *commedia dell'arte*, of music and opera, and of architecture. Spanish had a geographically limited influence on court ceremonial, namely at the Viennese court, and in literature the translations and adaptions of the picaresque novel were popular, but little linguistic effect is discernible. Dutch acted as an intermediary for other languages (particularly French), and was related to German in form, so that loans were recast in German shape; its influence affects commerce, horticulture, seamanship, textiles, and probably siege-craft and modern military techniques.[22] The transmission of loans into German can be complex: in par-ticular, the contributions of the individual Romance languages to international military terminology cannot always be clearly dis-tinguished because of their similar structures. English influence is discernible in literature; however, only in the eighteenth century does significant linguistic borrowing occur. Other languages provide isolated words, for example *Flinte* 'musket', perhaps from Swedish *flinta*, *Pallasch* 'sabre', from Turkish via Hungarian *palloš*, *Tornister* 'knapsack' from Czech (seventeenth-century form: EMG *Tanister*).

At any event the social critics primarily attack borrowing from Romance (*Welsch*), as *Die Alamodische Hobelbank* (a satirical tract of 1630) has it:

> ... der eine geht französisch alamodisch, wie ein rechter Pantalon, der andere italienisch, der dritte spanisch, der vierte halb und halb, wie man die Hund schiert.

One follows French fashions, like a right clown, another the Italian style, a third Spanish, and the fourth goes half-and-half, just like a trimmed poodle.

The order of priority of Romance languages given here is supported by the evidence, but the virulence of the attack on them is out of all proportion to the quantity of the loans and to their usefulness; after all, some 20 per cent of French loans before 1648 have survived into mod. German.[23]

TYPES OF LINGUISTIC AND LEXICAL BORROWING

All linguistic borrowing can be seen as the 'interference' of one language system on another, and ultimately such borrowing reflects the conscious or unconscious linguistic behaviour of individuals who are to some extent 'bilingual'.[24] While all levels of language— phonology, morphology, syntax, and semantics—are affected by this interference, the extent of influence varies from level to level, and our ability to observe it depends on the kind of data available. The seventeenth-century evidence is written, which obscures the phonetic structures of German and the donor languages alike; moreover, 'dialectal' forms may be involved on both sides. Lack of a completely consistent German orthography complicates matters. In any case, depending upon the fluency and intentions of the user, the phonetic rendering of foreign words varies from relative conformity to the pronunciations of the language of origin to complete recasting according to the phonetic patterns of German, the recipient language. Despite concentrating on lexical borrowing, some consideration of the other linguistic levels is necessary and desirable since they bear upon the processes of assimilation of foreign forms into German. Also, we should note the relatively slight influence on German phonology, morphology, and syntax, belying the fears of patriotic contemporaries and their nineteenth- and early twentieth-century successors.

At the level of phonology we have scant information regarding intonation and stress ('supra-segmentals') or the pronunciation of individual phonemes. Some loans remain in mod. German with a 'non-native' stress pattern, presumably reflecting their foreign pronunciation (*Brigáde, Cavallerie. Fortifikatión*), while others retain a foreign stress even when modified by the addition of a new suffix (*avancíeren*, from Fr. *avancer*); others change their syllabic structure while retaining the foreign stressed syllable (*Pistóle* [pis'tolə], trisyllabic, from disyllabic); while some monosyllabic forms become disyllabic (*Truppe*, from *troupe*): morphology affects this change, since a new pl. **troupe+n* would be disyllabic and a new sg. was formed by analogy. Borrowing from Romance languages has introduced many words with stress elsewhere than on the first, or root, syllable, but this has not caused any recasting of the German patterning. Moreover, suffixes like *-tíon* and particularly *-íeren* are always strongly stressed and may have impeded the full assimilation of words whose grammatical adoption they facilitate. Similarly, the phoneme inventory has remained relatively unaffected by borrowing. The rendering of /r/ as a post-dorsal uvular trill [R] is sometimes attributed to the influence of Fr. pronunciation. However, there is good evidence for a uvular [R] even in OHG, beside an apical one, since pre-OHG /ai/ monophthongizes before velar sounds, namely /h/ (= [χ], /w/ [= u̯], and /r/ (e.g. PGmc. **air-* > OHG *êr* 'formerly'). Still, Fr. influence might have encouraged the frequency of uvular rather than apical /r/, as a 'catalytic' effect.[25] Similarly, a sparsely attested palatal nasal (ñ), as in *Pinie, Linie*, might be supported by Fr. *ligne, seigneur*. The occurrence of nasalized vowels, e.g. in the suffix *-ment* [-mã(ŋ)], is stylistic rather than phonemic and, like a 'variphone', changes from speaker to speaker according to situation: minimum pairs are hard to find. Nor does the colloquial pronunciation of mod. German (*gemäßigte Hochlautung*) distinguish between open and closed quality in the unstressed syllables of foreign loanwords; and they have been arbitrarily prescribed.[26]

In the morphology catalytic Fr. influence has again been detected in the increase in *-s* as a pl.-marker, although LG dialects, Neth., and English influence may also have promoted it. Some Fr. words are treated as invariable, since the pl. *-s* is pronounced only before a following vowel or mute /h/,[27] but they soon adopt German inflexions, for the transfer of bound morphs such as inflexional endings is extremely rare. The influx of foreign words from different sources does, however, reinforce certain suffixes, like -*ade*, -*anz*, -*at*, -*erei*, -*esse*, -*ie*, -*eur*, *ität*, -*teur*, -*tor*, -*tion*, also adjectival ones -*abel*, -*ant*, -*ös* (from Fr. fem. forms in -*euse*). In verb morphology, the suffix -*ieren* and weak conjugation are the means of assimilation, although in the formation of the past part. the *ge*- prefix is often omitted. The orthography sometimes tells us when a suffix is felt as part of German, since the foreign word (or 'root') regularly appears in roman type, while the inflexional morphs appear in the *Fraktur* or 'German' type; this even happens in contemporary manuscripts (where foreign words are written in Humanistic cursive), e.g. letters, as well as in printed books and newspapers. Less 'bound' morphs, like the Fr. comparative particle *plus*, may have encouraged the German comparative circumscription with *mehr* + adj./adverb.

Syntactic influence is slight: the tendency to adopt isolated foreign words hardly affected the native sentence structure. Since German case and number relations are partly dependent on gender and are conveyed syntactically, the attribution of gender to loan-words is syntactic rather than purely morphological. Among the factors involved are the influence of natural gender in animate nouns, the phonetic similarity of the borrowed word to gender-related classes in German, and the gender of semantically close equivalent words in German, e.g. *le malheur* > *das Malheur* (~ *das Unglück*).[28] Again, whereas grammatical resources of German are extended to cover new forms, the resources themselves remain largely unaltered. In specific areas word order seems to change, as when the hypotactic chancery style of official and private letters gradually gives way, at least in the epistolographic handbooks, to a more simple and direct phrase structure.[29]

The use of third person sg. pronouns (*Er* and *Sie*, hence *Erzen*, *Siezen*) as a polite style of address may have arisen in imitation of Spanish *Usted* (< *vuestra merced* 'Your Grace'). Medieval texts show the pl. pronoun *ir* for polite or formal address and the singular *du* elsewhere, a usage still surviving among the lower orders in seventeenth-century Silesia, as Andreas Gryphius shows in his remarkable comedy *Verlibtes Gespenste*/*Die gelibte Dornrose* (1660). The main HG-speaking characters of the *Verlibtes Gespenste* address each other in the third person sg., reserving *Du* for servants or informality. But servants among themselves and the peasants in the Silesian dialect play *Die gelibte Dornrose* use *Ihr* for politeness and *Du* otherwise; only the self-opinionated local magistrate Wilhelm von hohen Sinnen addresses everyone as *Du*. So Gryphius's cleverly constructed double play shows polite pronouns of address in complementary social distribution—*Er* and *Sie* sg. in the bourgeois setting vs. *Ihr* in the peasant world.[30] By the end of the seventeenth century the third person pl. (*Sie*) was itself increasingly used for politeness and has now taken over from both *Ihr* and the third person sg. Indeed, in eighteenth- and nineteenth-century plays the sg. form is applied to social inferiors and servants (Schiller's *Kabale und Liebe*, Georg Büchner's *Woyzeck*) and it soon died out. The pl. form *Ihr* (apart from functioning as an informal pl.) remains the formal style in aristocratic circles in eighteenth-century classical drama, so the once fashionable third person sg. usage, whatever its origin, did not become established at the German courts.

Undoubtedly, however, the linguistic interference in the seventeenth century was mainly lexical. Sometimes the foreign word is adopted totally (within the limitations of a given context), i.e. both the expression (*signifiant*) and its content (*signifié*) are taken into German; sometimes native, i.e. German, resources render a foreign 'meaning'. Less commonly, foreign and German elements are combined into hybrid forms, while a few spurious 'foreign' forms are actually created, either on purpose or in ignorance.

A. LOAN-WORDS (*LEHNWÖRTER*)[31]

Discussion revolves round definitions of the *Fremdwort* and *Lehnwort*, although the distinction is to some extent subjective; most loan-words can be said to undergo a phase in which they are accepted and yet exotic. Here, the term 'foreign loan(-word)' distinguishes those foreign words which are used in German contexts from foreign words which 'import' their own foreign context (e.g. quotation from a foreign source). Seventeenth-century purists were little concerned with the phonological, morphological, and orthographical ways in which foreign 'phonemic sequences' (Weinreich (1953), 47) might be assimilated into German.[32] Only the more discerning theorists, like Georg Harsdörffer, distinguish the foreign loan from the established and non-exotic assimilated loan-word. Harsdörffer accepts foreign words in specialist use, provided (1) that German lacks the concept or can express it only by circumlocution; (2) that the loans are widely known and understood by those who speak only German; (3) that 'selbe [viz., the words] sich Burgerlich halten | ich will sagen | Teutsch

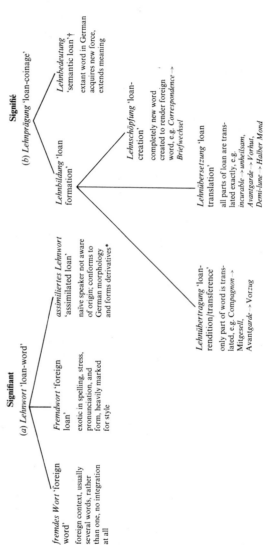

Signifiant
(a) *Lehnwort* 'loan-word'

fremdes Wort 'foreign word'
foreign context, usually several words, rather than one, no integration at all

Fremdwort 'foreign loan'
exotic in spelling, stress, pronunciation, and form, heavily marked for style

assimiliertes Lehnwort 'assimilated loan'
naive speaker not aware of origin; conforms to German morphology and forms derivatives *

Signifié
(b) *Lehnprägung* 'loan-coinage'

Lehnbildung 'loan formation'

Lehnbedeutung 'semantic loan'†
extant word in German acquires new force, extends meaning

Lehnschöpfung 'loan-creation'
completely new word created to render foreign word, e.g. *Correspondence → Briefwechsel*

Lehnübersetzung 'loan translation'
all parts of loan are translated exactly, e.g. *incurable → unheilsam, Avantgarde → Vorhut, Demi-lune → Halber Mond*

Lehnübertragung 'loan-rendition/transference'
only part of word is translated, e.g. *Compagnon →* Mitgesell, *Avantgarde → Vorzug*

(c) *'Bastardwort'* (Schottel) 'hybrid loan'
partial 'loan transfer/-translation':
one foreign element remains as in donor language, e.g. *contremine → Gegen-Mine*

Note. Einar Haugen has the following English terminology: *Lehnprägung* 'loanshift', *Lehnbildung* 'creation', *Lehnübersetzung* 'literal creation', *Lehnübertragung* 'approximate creation', *Lehnbedeutung* 'extension', *Lehnschöpfung* 'creation'. See Betz (1974), 139.

* Assimilation may involve 'folk-etymology'.

† It is difficult to prove that a new meaning results from a foreign word: it may be a native development, or it may be a coinage based on the borrowing of an institution or innovation, invention, regardless of how it is labelled in other languages. Compare mod. German *Flaschenhals* (1) 'neck of a bottle' (old metaphor), (2) 'bottle-neck', 'obstruction', 'traffic congestion' (new metaphor). In English, the compound form 'bottle(-)neck' can occur in both meanings albeit with different stress, whereas 'neck of a bottle' cannot be used in sense (2); *Flaschenhals* means both.

Fig. 6. Types of lexical interference (after W. Betz)

geschrieben | und Teutsch geendet werden'.[32] The paleographical/ typographical distinctions in writing and printing foreign words as opposed to native ones give a rough guide to the consciousness of the writers and printers that words were of foreign origin: yet the roman type or Humanist cursive might imply respect rather than distaste.

B. LOAN-COINAGE (*LEHNPRÄGUNG*)

The more subtle influence of type (*b*) (Fig. 6) involves complex theoretical issues like the identification of semantic loans. Moreover, individual examples can often be considered under several heads: *Flaschenhals* might be a semantic loan or a loan-translation. The seventeenth-century purists tend either to translate the foreign word more or less literally or else create a completely new word ('loan-creation'), usually by juxtaposing words already in the language: German's facility for forming compounds helps here.

C. HYBRID LOANS

Hybrid formations are common in satirical contexts. Especially striking are blends of foreign and dialect or colloquial, as in Schottel's masque, the *Neu erfundenes Freudenspiel genandt Friedens Sieg* (1648),[34] where the pretentiousness of the Fr. clashes comically with the homely vulgarity of the LG context: . . . den *Contribuzie-Kerl*, . . . den *Servis-Kerl*, den *Gasi-Kerl* (= *Gage-Kerl*), den *Furasi-Kerl* (= *Fourage-Kerl*)/ un wo dei Kerls alle hetet . . .' (= 'und wie die Kerle alle heissen'). Where a loan is reinterpreted consciously or unconsciously in terms of native words, the assimilation involves 'folk-etymology', although satirists produce mock-naïve formations with deliberate distortion for humorous effect, e.g. *Hexekution* (~ *Exekution*), *Jungfraumation* (~ *Information*), *Könneralität* (~ *Generalität*), *Rantzwinkel* (~ *Rendez-vous*). Some of these have resulted in hybrid formations, generally by extension of a familiar foreign suffix to the recast, unfamiliar foreign root: *Jungfrau* + (*m*) + -*ation*. Confusion also results from 'scholars' etymology', where expressions are interpreted incorrectly in terms of foreign words, whether for humour, as *Dame* from Lat. *dāma* 'chamois', 'antelope', see below, p. 283), or apparently seriously, as when 'ein Baselman

machen/ das ist/ eine Königliche/ verdrehete vnd zierliche Hander-
bietung thun . . .' is explained as from Gk. *basileōs* 'king' and Lat.
manus 'hand'.[35] Even more curious is *Schiffbrod*, said to be from
Pißboten (It. *biscotta*, Fr. *biscuit*, from Lat. *bis coctus*, lit. 'cooked
twice'), where the spelling may have suggested associations with
German *schiffen* 'to piss'.[36]

D. PSEUDO-LOANS (*SCHEINENTLEHNUNG*)

The interesting 'pseudo-loan' is defined by Jones (1978), 26, as 'not
itself a borrowed word, but a formation composed of foreign
morphemes, for which no parallel exists in the donor language', e.g.
Bloquade 'blockade', *canaillös* 'vulgar', 'coarse' and *Piquanterie*
'grudge', 'disappointment', apparently not attested in Fr.

The bulk of the words borrowed from Fr., some 63 per cent, and
presumably also those taken from other foreign languages, were
nouns, and most of these were concrete rather than abstract; verbs
and adjectives account for about 15–16 per cent each of the
borrowing, adverbs for under 5 per cent.[37]

Lexical interference, whether by borrowing or creating new forms,
inevitably alters semantic relations between the words in the recipient
language. The addition of items to a given 'semantic field' changes
nuances among its members, usually involving homonymy,
synonymy, and antonymy. Moreover, foreign words are a stylistic
enrichment as well as convenient—the foreign word as a 'cultural
token' carries with it exotic associations, of elegance perhaps, or
refinement. On the other hand, the foreign word is also vaguer and
may cover a range of precise native terms. Hence, the introduction of
Mademoiselle and *Dame*[38] as a polite address overlays the social
distinction between *Fräulein*, the aristocratic girl, and *Jungfer*, the
bourgeoise, which then begin to be applied to unmarried females of
both classes. Even where foreign words appear to be synonyms for
already existing native words, true synonymy seldom persists for long
before stylistic or semantic differentiation occurs: *Jungfer* became
archaic (cf. the characteristic expression *eine alte Jungfer* 'an old
spinster'), while *Fräulein* became the general form of address, though
it has itself recently been replaced by *Frau* for all adult women,
whether married or 'liaised', or single in some circles—for example,
at university or among feminists.

THE SOCIAL EFFECTS OF BORROWING

A. AREAS OF INFLUENCE

The social settings and technical registers in which loan-words and other borrowings appear are not always easily defined or exclusive, since metaphor and other kinds of polysemy break through the boundaries of any categories that have been drawn up. Nevertheless, the vocabulary of certain spheres of activity has been recognizably influenced by foreign borrowing; some words are felt to be foreign and are used by speakers for stylistic effect or for some technical purpose, or both.

From the sixteenth century onwards the terminology of warfare and military language became internationally dominated by loans from Fr.: German examples include *Attacke, attackieren, avancieren, Bataillon, Batterie, Charge, chargieren, Kapitän, Leutnant, General, Regiment, Truppe, marschieren, Pistole*; the following may come from or via Italian: *Alarm* (from *all'arme!*), *Kavallerie, Front, Grenate, Kanone, Soldateska*; and others, like *Armada, Brigade*, are from Spanish.[39] Despite Gottsched's recommendation that German equivalents be found for designations of ranks and military units,[40] the reforms were not successful until the late nineteenth century, with the eclipse of French power (see Chapter IX). Terms for fortification and siege-craft at this period are *Bastion, Fortifikation, Glacis, Kasematte, Kurtine, minieren, rasieren* 'raze', *Ravelin, Redoute, sapieren*, with the odd loan-translation (*Halbmond*, from *demi-lune* 'defensive outworks') or hybrid (*Halbbastion*, from *demi-bastion*). Foreign oaths used by the soldiery were sometimes distorted because of taboo,[41] and swearing in other languages was more exotic, emphatic, and at the same time perhaps less obviously obscene or blasphemous: *bougre, diable, par ma foy, mort de ma vie, ventre (dieu), parbleu (= pardieu), sambleu (= sang de dieu), safferment/sapperment (= sacrament)*. In complete contrast are the polite forms of address and titles: *Monsieur, Madame, Baron, Baronesse, Cousin, Cousine, Dame, Kavalier, Mama, Papa, Onkel, Tante*; while foreign phrases and words are common also in letters, together with set formulae like *à votre service, votre trèshumble serviteur*. Common catch-words and slogans include *brav, Compliment, Discours, Estime, excellent, Gala, galant, Galanterie* (these last from Spanish), *Manier, nett, rar, Reverenz*, and, naturally, *Alamode*—roughly translatable as 'abreast of the fashion', 'fashionable'—with thirty-two compounds attested before the mid-seventeenth century, including *Alamodo-Bauchpurgation*, *alamode-bekleidet*, *alamode-Flüche*, *Allmode-Latein*, *Allemodo-Monsieur*, *Alamode-Tracht*, and also derivatives, such as *alamodisch*, *allemodische Venus-Knaben*, *unalamodisieren*, *Alamodist*.[42] Even names were given Romance form, especially in literature. Fashions in dress, too, reflected foreign influence in materials and styles: *Brokat*, *Gaze*, *Kattun*, *Kostüm*, *Mouche* 'beauty spot', *Muff*, *Robe*, *Taille*, *parfümieren*, *Perrücke*, *Plüsch*, *Pomade*, *rasieren*, *Toupet*; whilst older, exotic words became more common: *Samt*, *Satin*, *Seide*. Young gallants with trimmed beards were known as *Stutzer* and their beribboned dress and large hats are satirized.[43] Eating habits, too, change, and German cuisine reflected the new taste for once exotic vegetables like tomatoes and potatoes, and new ways of preparing familiar food: *Bouillon*, *delikat*, *Delikatesse*, *Gelee*, *Kaffee*, *Kakao*, *Karbonade*, *Kompott*, *Kuvert*, *Limonade*, *Makrone*, *Marinade*, *marinieren*, *Marmelade*, *Ragout*, *Sauce*, *Schokolade*, *Service*, *servieren*, *tranchieren*. Homes and gardens were laid out formally on the foreign model, especially late seventeenth-century castles; hence the names for architectural features (*Altan*, *Balkon*, *Fresko*, *Galerie*, *Korridor*, *Loge*, *Parkett*, *Palais*) and for the formal garden (*Allee*, *Bassin*, *Boskett*, *Fontäne*, *Grotte*, *Parterre* 'flower bed', *Rabatte*, *Spalier*) with its exotic fruits (*Aprikose*, *Ananas*, *Marille*, *Pistazie*, *Zitrone*) and vegetables (*Artischoke*, *Kohlrabi*, *Kartoffel*, *Tomate*)—some of which are now merely homely. Almost the watchword of the later 'rococo' society, *Plaisir*, translated as *Lust*, gave rise to a whole range of fashionable compounds: *Lustschloss*, *Lustschiff*, *Lustgarten*, *Lustgang*.[44] Sports and pastimes included card-games, like *Hasard*, *Lomber*, *Pikett*, and *Solo* (with their terminology *Atout* (= *à tout*), *Trumpf*, *kaputt*), and dancing, e.g. *Ball*, *Menuett*, *Pavane*, *Promenade*, *Quadrille*, as well as billiards, fencing, equestrianism, and the theatre: *bravo*, *Dacapo*, *Maskerade*, *Posse*, *Soffitte* 'scenery drop', *Spass*. Musical entertainments and church music of the period flourished, with Italian providing technical terms for pieces, instruments, and, of course, the opera: *allegro*, *andante*, *Arie*, *Bass*, *Bratsche*, *Fagott*, *Kantate*, *Kanzone*, *(H)oboe*, *Oper*, *Tempo*, *Violine*, etc. The practice of paying calls (*Visite geben*), probably in a *Karrosse* accompanied by an *Equipage*, completed the social whirl.

War in the first half of the century and conspicuous consumption in the second had lasting effects on German vocabulary, but not until the eighteenth century did many words listed here filter down into bourgeois and lower circles. The seventeenth-century culture was an absolutist, aristocratic one, and relatively small groups followed or set the trends that so enriched the vocabulary. A strong backlash, partly aristocratically inspired, enriched German vocabulary by forming new words ('neologisms') from native elements to replace the loan-words. There is a geographical bias here: the Catholic south was more open to baroque architecture and music—especially Venetian opera—from Italy, and transmitted these to central and northern Germany, while the grammarians of the century were nearly all central and northern Germans, receiving the foreign influence at second hand and reacting with hostility to the technical vocabulary that came with it.

B. REACTIONS TO THE INFLUENCE

The first *Fremdwörterbuch* of Simon Rot (1571)[45] lists some 2,800 foreign words—almost all Latin—with the aim of helping Germans to understand them; in the seventeenth century, theorists attacked and replaced them. The purists and satirists were mostly bourgeois men of letters who followed a literary convention, repeated each other's censure, and had little observable linguistic effect. They are unreliable witnesses to the frequency and importance of the borrowings they decried, and may even have helped to spread them. Indeed, the purists' xenophobia, the attempts to determine and codify a standard German norm, the increased awareness of older forms of the language, the exaggerated claims regarding its antiquity, and the experiments of rhetoricians and poets following Martin Opitz[46] can be interpreted as signs of the language's enhanced status. Opitz had attacked foreign borrowing from modern tongues as inelegant in his *ARISTARCHUS, sive DE CONTEMPTU Linguae Teutonicae* (Beuthen, 1617): 'Jam a Latinis, jam Gallis, Hispanis etiam ac Italis mutuamur, quod domi nascitur elegantius' ('We borrow, now from the Latins, now from the French, from the Spaniards, and even from the Italians that which grows more elegantly at home') (p. B4 a). He averred that all the verse forms of those foreign peoples could be imitated in German, which had been handed down as a fair, noble, decorous, most worthy and unadulterated language—'venusta', 'decens', 'gravis', 'dignissima', 'integra & incommista' (pp. D 1a– D 1b). The satirists' concern at the adulteration of the language represents a clearly recognizable phase in the rise of German, based on the crude theoretical position that language and life are in a direct and reciprocal relationship. As Johann Michael Moscherosch (1601–69) put it:

Wie die Zeiten sind, so sind die Wort; und hinwiderumb, wie die Wort sind, so sind auch die Zeiten. *Verba ut Nummi* ['That holds true for words and money both'].[47]

The passage continues with an elaborate and punning comparison of the debasement of language and coinage, both common currency:

Es ist unsere Sprach dißmahlen in ein recht Kipper-Jahr gerathen [*Kipper* = 'coin-clipper', 'debaser']; Jeder beschneidet, bestimmelt ['bestümmelt'] dieselbe, wie er will, gibt ihr einen Halt [*Feingehalt*, 'value'] und Zusatz, wie er will. Vnd wie solche leichte Müntzen, wie weiß sie auch gesotten sind, dannach anderst nichts in sich haben als Kupffer am Halt, also alle solche heutige Auffschneidereyen ['showing off': pun on clipping coins], wie schön sie äußerlichem Thon nach lauten ['however fine they may ring/sound'], sind im Hertzen doch nicht eins drecks werth . . . (p. 184).

Still, one of the earliest attacks on foreign habits of speech seems popular in tone, as is the melody to which it was set; *Der Teutsche Michel Das ist/ Ein newes Klaglid/ vnd Allamodisch A.B.C. Wider alle Sprach-Verderber* . . . (Innsbruck, 1638).[48] Some fifty-five strophes catalogue foreign words from several languages, and the song opens and closes with the words:

Ich teutscher Michel, versteh schier nichel [= Lat. *nihil*, 'nothing'] In meinem Vaterland, es ist ein schand.

Despite its shaky verse, the text shows a suspiciously impressive command of the multitude of foreign words pilloried, and may be more sophisticated than it seems; Michel himself survived into the nineteenth century to become a national stereotype, albeit of a good-natured simpleton: in this context he is the plain-speaking embodiment of common sense. In somewhat similar vein, a tract of 1629, *Der Kleyder Teuffel*, attacks foreign dress and foreign speech: the Germans are denying their birthright: '. . . Da gibts Teutsche Spanier, Teutsche Franzosen, Teutsche Italiener, Teutsche Engelländer, Summa: der Teutsche Mann ein Allemodisch Mann.' And in 1643 another satire, *Der Vnartig Teutscher Sprach-Verderber. Beschrieben Durch Einen Liebhaber der redlichen alten Teutschen Sprach*,[49] also equates linguistic and moral purity. These works share the view that

mixing foreign elements with German defiles the language and
weakens the moral fibre of the speakers, e.g. Moscherosch: 'Bastart-
Hertzen, Bastart-Sprachen.'[50] Individual borrowings are unmasked:
Complimenteur was interpreted as 'boaster', 'deceiver', 'liar', with a
pun on *menteur*; *Dame* (ultimately from Lat. *domina* via Fr.
dame) was derived from Lat. *dāma* = 'eine Gåmbs oder stinckende Berg-
Zieg' (*Der Vnartig Teutscher Sprachverderber*),[51] foreign words, like
foreign people, being unreliable. Such anonymous works appeared
during the Thirty Years War, and can be interpreted as a reaction
to the endangered state of some German lands; the excessive and uncritical attacks even on well-established words reflect the writers'
distress and anger. Subsequently, the themes and targets became
literary topoi and the fop, or *Stutzer* (so called because of the
trimmed beard), remains a butt for a long time. Moreover, writers
often attack not foreign words as such, but the language mixture,
or the inappropriateness of the users—peasants with pretensions—
(e.g. ploughboys, chimney-sweeps, knife-grinders, ratcatchers, pork-
butchers, ne'er-do-wells (*Bärenhäuter*), and ostlers)—speaking
snippets of Latin and French, for example.[52] Joachim Rachel
(1618–69) in his eighth satire, *Der Poet*, parodies the inappropriate
use of mixed language in the pulpit (!), by putting the speech of the
captain of Capernaum (Luke 7: 1–10) into 'Alamode':

> *Monsieur*, ich bin nicht werth, daß ihr zu meiner Thûren,
> Und in mein schlecht *Logis* solt mit mir hin *marschiren*.
> *Un mot*, sprecht nur ein Wort, ich weiß zu dieser Stund,
> *Et tout incontinent*[a] so wird mein Knecht gesund.
> Zwar ich bin nur ein Mensch, und daß ichs gern gestehe,
> Ein schlechter *Cavallier*, noch wann ich einen sehe,
> Von meiner *Compagnie*, und ruff ihn zu mir her:
> *Ça garçon?* Er ist *prompt*, verrichtet sein *devoir*![53]
>
>   [a] = 'directly'.

The military connection and third person pronoun in commands(?)
are noteworthy; a few lines earlier the *Mengelmueß* ('pot-pourri') of
soldiers has been criticized (276 ff.). Schottel, in his masque, the
Friedens Sieg, even has a peasant using a LG mixture with foreign
elements, again mainly military:

Ai, man werd jo tho grandig *vexeret*, ek *spintesere*, work wil ene *Suplicazie*
maken an den *Major*, de syn *Quarteer* un *Losomente* hier harre bi het. Denn
man *palert* davon et schôllen *Soldaten* im *marseren* syn, un den wolle si bi
ösek *inquarteren* . . .[54]

Other places where loans were so evident as to excite parodists to exaggerate them include letters and newspapers, in particular the gallant love letter and the 'war report'. The *Alamodebrief*, liberally sprinkled with *Fremdwörter*, becomes a literary topos in satirical writing, but the satirists themselves do not shrink from mixing language in their own polite correspondence. Seventeenth-century epistolary style still owed much to the chanceries, whose documents and letters favoured the use of synonymy: the 'mixed' letters often continued the same tradition by different means, since they tended to gloss a foreign expression by a native one, ensuring comprehensibility but also adding gravity and, supposedly, elegance. Real as opposed to fictive letters of the period can show a considerable number of loans—Wallenstein's letters use French, Latin, and Italian words and phrases, partly as technical military vocabulary, partly as the hallmark of an educated gentleman. For example, his much-quoted report of an attack on Nuremberg in a letter to the Emperor of 1632:

Das *combat* hat von frühe angefangen und den ganzen Tag *caldissimamente* gewährt. Alle *Soldaten* Ew. kaiserli. *Armee* haben sich so tapfer gehalten, als ichs in einiger *occasion* mein Leben lang gesehen, und niemand hat einen *fallo* in *valor* gezeigt. Der König hat sein Volk über die Maßen *discoragirt*, daß er sie *hazardosamente* angeführt, daß sie in vorfallenden *occasionen* ihm desto weniger trauen werden. Ew. *Majestät Armee* aber, indem sie gesehen, wie der König *repussirt* wurde, ist mehr denn je *assekurirt* worden.[55]

Newspapers, too, often reported military matters and were open to ephemeral social and linguistic influences. The earliest had foreign names—the *Relation* at Strasburg and the Wolfenbüttel *Aviso* (both *c*.1609). Indeed, the *Vnartig Teutscher Sprachverderber* (1643) complains:

. . . Es were von nöthen bey dieser jetzigen zeit/ daß/ wann einer die Zeittungen lesen will/ er zween [NHG *zwei*] Männer bey sich stehen habe/ auff der rechten seiten einen Frantzosen/ auff der lincken einen Lateiner/ welche die frembde Wörter jhme außlegten.[56]

This is one of the clearer statements that foreign words prevented comprehension and created linguistic barriers. Christian Weise, in a pamphlet on the functions of the newspaper, actually omits any discussion of military and naval terms because of their obscurity:

Nihil dicerem de MILITIBUS ET NAUTIS, nisi terminorum militarium & nauticorum ignorantia plerisque narrationibus induceret obscuritatem.[57]

I should say nothing of SOLDIERS AND SAILORS, lest ignorance of military and naval terms should introduce obscurity to the majority of accounts.

But most contemporary satirists were little concerned with the effects of linguistic borrowing on ill-educated classes. The better-known writers were in the service of princes or dedicated their works to them, aspiring to the very circles where the foreign, especially French, influence was most evident. Complaints that other, lower classes were using language inappropriate to their station are known, of course, from medieval times,[58] but a new note is struck by the claims that German is an ancient and pure language, to be preserved and nurtured on patriotic grounds. Here too the rejection and replacement of foreign words was linked to aristocratic interests in some areas—particularly northern Germany, home of the most famous language society, the Fruchtbringende Gesellschaft.

C. PURISM AND LANGUAGE SOCIETIES[59]

In the seventeenth century several learned societies were founded in Germany which were forerunners of the academies. They strike the modern reader as a curious blend of guild, gentlemen's club, and masonic lodge, and the extreme linguistic purism of some members and their personal squabbles, especially in the Fruchtbringende Gesellschaft, seem ridiculous and disproportionate nowadays.[60] However, linguistic purism was only one of the activities of these patriotic organizations established to nurture all aspects of German culture—manners, dress, literature, and especially poetry. Their members were interested in educational theory, discussed philosophical topics like the origins of language, produced treatises on grammar and spelling, translations, and even works on epistolary and chancery practice. The Humanist studies of the history of German and of the origins of the German dialects and their speakers were continued, old texts were cited, sometimes even quoted—e.g. Otfrid's Gospel harmony, the medieval German didactic poems *Winsbeke* and *Winsbekin* (thirteenth century), and the Marner (a thirteenth-century didactic poet). Opitz edited the early MHG *Annolied* just before his death (1639). The Gothic Bible was claimed to enhance German's status (since the term *Teutsch* was generously interpreted) and Charlemagne's lost grammar of the vernacular and Rudolf I's use of German in his political deliberations recurred as scholarly ballast in contemporary linguistic historical writing, an encouragement and courtly legitimation for continued efforts. Indeed, in literary works ancient heroes were summoned to sit in judgement on the moral and cultural decay of their effete successors: Moscherosch confronts his Philander with (among other more obscure figures) Ariovistus, Arminius, Witukind, and Saro,[61] while Schottel, in his masque the *Friedens Sieg*, sets Arminius and Henricus Auceps (Henry the Fowler) against the fop Bolderian. Bolderian claims:

Die heutige *manier* zu *parliren*, wie sie die *Damen* und *Cavalieri sauhaitiren* und belieben ist *a la modo* und die *delicateste*, darin ich mich auch mit *contentement* kan *delectiren*.

To which Henricus observes that 'Auf die Enderung der Sprache folget eine Enderung der Sitten . . .'.[62] This is significant, for the ultimate interest of the societies lay in social morality and behaviour, and purism was only one means to attain it. The societies were not solely bulwarks against incursion by foreign borrowings; ironically, they were themselves modelled on institutions from abroad.[63] Finally, in a Germany carved up into petty and parochial absolutist states the societies provided forums for exchanging ideas.

The first and most famous of the German *Sprachgesellschaften*, the Fruchtbringende Gesellschaft, later known as the *Palmenorden*, was founded by Hofmarschall Kaspar von Teutleben at Weimar in August 1617, together with its first president, Prince Ludwig von Anhalt-Köthen, who had become a member of its Italian prototype, the Academia della Crusca, in 1600. The Fruchtbringende Gesellschaft was aristocratic and exclusive, although bourgeois members were eventually elected, including important grammarians and writers—Gryphius, Gueintz, Harsdörffer, Logau, Moscherosch, Opitz, Rist, Schottel, and Zesen. By 1680 when it was already moribund, its membership had reached 890,[64] and in the horticultural metaphor copied from the Italian society each had a plant emblem and a motto: Opitz was 'Der Gekrönte', Schottel 'Der Suchende', Zesen 'Der Wolsetzende', Moscherosch 'Der Träumende', Stieler 'Der Spate' (NHG *Späte*). Other societies soon appeared, initiated by members of the Fruchtbringende Gesellschaft:

1633   *Aufrichtige Gesellschaft von der Tannen*, founded by Jesaias Rompler von Löwenhalt at Strasburg. A mainly bourgeois circle, whose pine-tree emblem was less exotic than the Fruchtbringende Gesellschaft's palm.

1642   *Die Teutschgesinnte Genossenschafft,* founded by Philipp von Zesen at Hamburg. Its various 'guilds' included one for women.

1644   *Hirten- und Blumenorden an der Pegnitz* (*Pegnitzschäfer*) founded by Georg Philipp Harsdörffer at Nuremberg.

1656/8   *Elbschwanenorden,* founded by Johann Rist at Hamburg or Lübeck.

1697   *Deutschübende Poetische Gesellschaft,* founded at Leipzig and remodelled by Gottsched in 1726 as the *Deutsche Gesellschaft.* Most of the many eighteenth-century societies were influenced by this one.

All these societies had varying composition and aims, and their wider influence, in particular on the German language of the time, is difficult to assess. After the death of Prince Ludwig in 1651 the Fruchtbringende Gesellschaft declined; mostly its members were obscure establishment figures who made no striking grammatical or literary contributions. Nevertheless, individual rulers, like Prince Ludwig himself or Duke August of Wolfenbüttel, were passionately interested in such matters and extended their patronage to bourgeois men of letters: Gueintz's grammar and orthographical recommenda-tions were dedicated to Ludwig and enshrined his views,[65] while August had Schottel as his protégé. To some extent the differences between Gueintz's and Schottel's approach to German grammar reflect the conflicting interests of Ludwig and August (who had joined the Fruchtbringende Gesellschaft in 1634 as 'Der Befreyende'). Whereas Gueintz undertook a rigorous and pedantic codification of a usage which was essentially Misnian, Schottel ('Der Suchende') had a more philosophical approach, arguing for a supra-regional, non-dialectal norm, purer and more venerable than any language in daily use. We shall return to these problems later (Chapter VIII). But in the present context, Schottel's great *Ausführliche Arbeit von der Teutschen Haubt-Sprache* (1663) would be unthinkable without the intellectual background of Wolfenbüttel and the Fruchtbringende Gesellschaft, whose emblematic, patriotic, and literary inspiration it shares. The grammar has been called the 'barocke *summa philologica*',[66] but this label applies primarily to the magnificent library of Duke August which Schottel used extensively, assimilating most of the earlier grammarians and theorists of eloquence and rhetoric. Schottel's purism is of a special kind, since he wanted to preserve the dwindling stock of 'primeval' roots—*Stammwörter* (*radices; voces primitivae*)—which had survived in German from the time of the earliest language spoken by Adam, the *lingua adamica*. The old roots were supposedly recognizable *inter alia* by their onomatopoeic rendering of the sounds of Nature (they too are 'emblematic'), and consequently German's rich store of expressive words seemed to qualify it as *the* natural language. As Georg Harsdörffer put it:

Sie redet mit der Zungen der Natur, in dem sie alles Getön und was nur einen Laut, Hall und Schall von sich giebet, wol vernemlich ausdrücket; Sie donnert mit dem Himmel, sie blitzet mit den schnellen Wolken, stralet mit dem Hagel, sausset mit den Winden, brauset mit den Wellen, rasselt mit den Schlossen [= 'hailstones'], schallet mit dem Luft, knallet mit dem Geschütze, brüllet wie der Löwe, plerret wie der Ochs, brummt wie der Beer, beeket wie der Hirsch, blecket wie das Schaaf, grunzet wie das Schwein, muffet wie der Hund, rintschet wie das Pferd, zischet wie die Schlange, mauet wie die Katze, schnattert wie die Gans, quacket wie die Ente, summet wie der Hummel, kacket wie das Huhn, klappert wie der Storch, kracket wie der Rab, schwieret wie die Schwalbe, silket wie der Sperling . . .[67]

German's status was enhanced by its highly motivated vocabulary: words reflected the sounds of nature, while compounding and derivation enabled new words to be formed which were recognizably related to the old ones. This too was purism—a continuing use of native German word-formation, rather than importing foreign words. In comparison, the less transparently motivated vocabulary of French appeared cerebral and abstract, while English was a hopeless pot-pourri. The leading French grammarians of the time in any case regarded language as a system of *arbitrary* signs and were not concerned with defending their language on diachronic, etymological grounds.[68]

But we must not think of the language societies as obsessively purist, even if purist aims were listed among their statutes; they were concerned primarily with establishing norms of literary language, both in form and style. Many of the attacks on foreign borrowing by writers associated with the societies must be seen in the context of their theoretical statements outlining criteria according to which foreign words were acceptable. Schottel, for instance, says that words which had acquired a 'Teutsches Statrecht' should be kept, i.e. those with a 'Teutsches Kleid, Ausspruch und Endung'.[69] Other writers pillory particular kinds of inappropriate borrowing. Georg Wilhelm von Sacer (1635–99), for example, parodies the excessive use of foreign words in poetry in an amusing tract dedicated to Hans Wurst;[70] Hans is advised:

(Es) Stehet sehr *decor*, wenn man *frequenter* die Deutschen Worte *changiret* und die heutige *Mannier requiret* es *totaliter*. Ob du gleich nichts mehr als deine *langue maternelle* verstehest/ so bist du doch *obligat*, wo du ein frembdes *raisonables* Wörtchen *observirt* hast/ dasselbe bey allen *occasionen* deinen Versen zu *inseriren* und *ala mode* sehr *nettement* [= *artiglich*] (jedoch *pro posse* [= *nach Möglichkeit*]) zu *lardiren*/ wenn du bey den Neulingen dich nicht als einen *miserablen* Gesellen wilst *exagitiren* [< Lat. *exagito* 'pursue with criticism'] lassen . . .[71]

But note that Sacer had other targets too, such as the excesses of orthographical reform and bombastic style, and he also condemns the unnecessary replacement of words which had long since gained citizenship, 'Bûrgerrecht' (Sacer (1673), 82). Such attacks on extreme purism were levelled less against the societies than against individuals, and Sacer is clearly mocking Philipp von Zesen (see below). Those who pilloried over-zealous purism were indeed more often than not themselves members of a language society, while writers who joined might endeavour to purify their style. It is hardly coincidence that Andreas Gryphius was moved, after being admitted to the Fruchtbringende Gesellschaft as 'Der Unsterbliche' in 1662, to replace some foreign expressions in his last revision of his works.

Translation formed an important part of the literary activity of the Fruchtbringende Gesellschaft, so the problems of grappling with foreign vocabulary were familiar. Borrowing foreign words in technical translations aroused less opposition than using them in literature, where they appeared unnecessary; nor did technical usage play much part in moralizing or satire, apart from the stock comic jargons of doctors and lawyers. Some technical terms were translated into German for patriotic reasons, e.g. the grammatical terms (see Chapter V), and the language societies must have encouraged their use, while individuals proposed replacements which have sometimes remained current today, e.g. Harsdörffer's *Aufzug* for *Akt*, *beobachten* for *observieren*, *Briefwechsel* for *Correspondence*, *Fernglas* for *Teleskop*, *Irrgarten* for *Labyrinth*, *Rechtschreibung* for *Orthographie*, and *Zeitschrift* for *Chronik*.[72] More important, but less easily discernible, the societies must have contributed to the stylistic differentiation of seventeenth-century loan-words and loan-translations where competing forms existed, thus enriching the language even though the 'aliens' were not completely banished. Whereas the societies were clearly of great importance in their own day, their direct contribution to the modern standard language remains slight: in this way they are no different from other formative influences in the past history of German.

The organized reaction to foreign influence began in the seventeenth century and revived in the nineteenth, but with different emphasis. The patriotic, moralizing approach of the early aristocratic and select societies stems partly from inferiority and demoralization; these are factors mentioned by contemporaries. In the nineteenth century, the xenophobia was fuelled partly by the Napoleonic occupation, partly by the growing conviction that Germany was militarily and culturally superior to France (and to England). By the First World War, a broadly based nationalism encouraged warmongering against foreign words of all kinds (see Chapter X). The rhetoric remains the same, as does the conflation of language, life, and morals, so that nineteenth-century nationalists would have had no difficulty in agreeing with the following sentiments of Sigmund von Birken of 1663:

> Pfuy/ Teutscher! schäm dich doch! Und wilst du dich nicht schämen:
> So wird Gott dir die Ehr und deine Freyheit nehmen:
> Machst du die Sprach zur Magd: So wirst du werden Knecht
> Der Fremden/ weil dir ist dein Vaterland zu schlecht.[73]

Even the seventeenth-century slogans 'treu-teutsch', 'frey-teutsch', and 'ur-teutsch' remained usable.

Probably less to the taste of the nineteenth century, but more in the emblematic spirit of the seventeenth, is the frontispiece to Christoph Ernst Steinbach's *Vollständiges Deutsches Wörterbuch* (1734), with its implicit equation of foreign modes of dress and speech (Fig. 7: reproduced from the copy in the Niedersächsische Staats- und Universitätsbibliothek, Göttingen, shelfmark 8° Ling. VII, 5036). Here we see the simpering German Language in all her splendour, literally denuded of fashions from abroad, the centre of the somewhat dubious attention of entirely male representatives from other nations, including one (an Englishman, perhaps?) with a spyglass . . .[74]

To bring into clearer focus the equally ambivalent and often uneasy relationship between purism and baroque literature, we now turn to Philipp von Zesen—certainly a minor figure by modern

Nuda Splendet.

Strahowsky Sc: Wrat

FIG. 7

account and a far lesser poet than Martin Opitz, but more controversial in his own day and by his very limitations linguistically more representative of it.

PHILIPP VON ZESEN (1619-1689)[75]

Zesen attended the grammar school at Halle where Christian Gueintz was rector, and studied at Wittenberg and Leiden. During his long stay in the Netherlands he became a prolific and varied translator of everything from manuals on siege-craft to works of piety, medical treatises, and novels; his own *roman-à-clef*, the *Adriatische Rosemund*, published at Amsterdam under the pseudonym Ritterhold von Blauen (= Philipp, Caesius/Zesen) in 1645, remains readable despite its mannered style and radical purism. In 1642 Zesen founded a language society and in 1648 he was admitted to the Fruchtbringende Gesellschaft, despite reservations regarding his translation of everyday loan-words long in the language, and even stronger objections to his orthographical reforms. In a letter of 1652 Harsdörffer even described him as 'ein Ketzer in unserer Sprache'.

But some successful loan-translations and transfers have been suggested or supported by Zesen: *Freistatt* (*Asyl*), *lustwandeln* (*spazieren*), *Sinngedicht* (*Epigramm*), *Gesichtskreis* (*Horizont*), *Verfasser* (*Autor*), *Vertrag* (*Kontrakt*), *Urschrift* (*Original*), *Zeughaus* (*Arsenal*), *Zweikampf* (*duellum*). He may also have helped to establish older words, e.g. *Augenblick* for *Moment* (he also used *Zeitblick*). Technical terms like *Mundart* for *Dialekt* and *Wörterbuch* for *Lexikon*, first published by Zesen, probably derive from Ratke via Gueintz, and they recur in the grammars of Gueintz and Schottel (see Chapter V, pp. 222-3). Zesen has been criticized for failing to distinguish between *Fremdwörter* and *Lehnwörter*, since he sought to replace well-established words and in consequence made himself look foolish. However, most of Zesen's neologisms accord with German word-formation patterns, even if more than one-third are based on foreign models, like the following element-for-element loan-translations from Dutch:[76] *Schauburg*, Neth. *schouwburgh* (later ousted by (*Schau*)*bühne*); *Lebensmittel*, Neth. *levens middelen*; *Abbildung* Neth. *afbeeldinge*; *Abschneidung*, Neth. *afsnydingen*; *Sternschauerey*, Neth. *starrekijkerij* 'astronomy'; *Augenartzt*, Neth. *oogharts*; *Baukunst*, Neth. *bouwkonst*; *Schimpfdichter*, Neth.

schimpdichter 'satirist'. Many of Zesen's neologisms are loan-translations or transfers, which had its disadvantages, since the educated circles who read his works knew the foreign originals and found their German clothing quaint or unbecoming. At the end of his *Adriatische Rosemund* Zesen unfortunately included a glossary of his purist translations, and his renderings of classical divinities in particular made it easy for opponents to attack them, although other poets used similar circumscriptions. For instance Zesen replaced the following: *Kloster > Jungfernzwinger*; *Fenster > Tageleuchter*; *Grotte > Lusthöhle*; *Natur > Zeugemutter*; *Urne > Leichentopf*; *Pistole > Reitpuffer*; *Venus > Liebinne, Lustinne, Schauminne* (Venus = Aphrodite, Gk. *aphros* 'foam'); *Juno > Himmeline*; *Cupid > Liebreiz*. Zesen's imagination sometimes led him astray, he has been criticized for being 'als Dichter zu sehr Philolog . . ., und als Philolog zu sehr Poet' (Cholevius), and mis-translations like *Herzenschlüssel* for *Clavichordium* made him look foolish.[77] On the other hand, in his prose works and translations many of Zesen's neologisms appeared in practical, everyday con-texts, and he experimented, suggested alternatives, and admitted his mistakes: when *Tageleuchter* was ridiculed, he reverted to *Fenster*—although now claiming it as an original German word, not a loan from Latin! Joachim Rachel satirized him as a 'Hirsenpfriemer' or 'millet-piercer', considering Zesen's purified German as wretched as the Alamode mixture:

> Der *Ertz-Gott*[a] Jupiter, der hatte, sich zu letzen,
> Ein Gastmahl angestellt. Die *Weidinn*[b] gab das Wild,
> Der *Glutfang*[c] den Thobak, der Sahl ward angefüllt,
> Die *Obstinn*[d] trug zu Tisch in einer vollen Schüssel,
> Die Freye saß und spielt mit einem *Liebes-Schlüssel*[e].
> Der kleine *Liebr(e)itz*[f] sang ein *Tichtling*[g] auf den Schmauß,
> Der trunkne *Heldreich*[h] schlug die *Tageleuchter*[i] aus,
> Die *Feurinn*[j] kam dazu aus ihrem *Jungfer Zwinger*[k]
> Mit *schählblau*[l] angethan, Apollo ließ die Finger
> Frisch durch die Seiten gehn, des *Heldreichs*[m] *Wald-Hauptmann*[n]
> Fing lustig einen Tanz mit den *Huldinnen*[o] an.[78]

[a] ruler of the gods   [b] Diana   [c] Vulcan   [d] Pomona?   [e] lyre?
[f] Cupid   [g] verse   [h] Mars   [i] *Fenster*   [j] Vesta   [k] *Nonnen-kloster*   [l] *bleu-mourant*   [m] Mars   [n] Lieutenant (probably Silvanus is intended)   [o] Graces.

Schottel bridled at *Zeugemutter*: 'Schendlich ist es, der alten Haubt-Sprache dieses Wort Natur entziehen wollen, und eine grosse

Zeugemutter mit Zitzen daraus machen . . .'[79] Other apparently
grotesque expressions attributed to Zesen were not his, or were used
humorously: he did not himself coin *Löschhorn* for *Nase* and he used
it comically, while *Gesichtserker* for 'nose' is not found in the seventeenth century, and *Windfang* for *Mantel* comes from thieves'
jargon.[80]

   Zesen's orthographical reforms discredited him hugely. His two
main criteria were, alas, incompatible: first, a phonetic/phonemic
approach reflecting, somewhat inaccurately, the priority of Meissen
language; secondly, an etymological approach designed to make
the origins and morphological relationships of words transparent
in the spelling.[81] Both criteria neglected already existing conventions
(*Gebrauch*). Zesen used ⟨h⟩ extensively to indicate long vowels in
closed syllables (as in Dutch), while he simplified consonant clusters
after short vowels. Zesen's inconsistent orthography changes as time
goes on: e.g. he wrote *hohch, sprahch* in *Rosemund* (1645), but his
Deutscher Helicon (1643) often shows forms *Hooch* and *Spraach* with
geminated vowels. He toyed with introducing accents: acute for short
stressed vowels, circumflex for long stressed, and unmarked for unstressed, a system which obviated double consonants altogether:
fál/fálen/nâm for *Fall/fallen/nahm*. Whereas Schottel prescribed
double consonants in final position where they occurred medially in
related forms of the same word, e.g. pret. *schwamm < schwimmen*,
Zesen argued phonetically. But the spoken language of the EMG
area did not distinguish rounded from unrounded vowels, so that the
signs ⟨ä⟩/⟨e⟩/⟨ö⟩ and ⟨ü⟩/⟨i⟩ were variants.[82] Hence, where the
pret. of strong verbs showed an ⟨a⟩ or ⟨u⟩ in sg. or pl., Zesen chose
the symbols ⟨ä⟩ or ⟨ü⟩ for the infinitive and pres. ind. forms also,
producing spellings like *läsen, hälfen, nähmen, gäben, bärgen* for
lesen, helfen, etc. because of preterites *las, half*, etc., and also *bünden,
fünden* for *binden, finden* because of pret. pl. *bunden, funden*. Similarly, *fechten* appears as *föchten* because of the pret. *focht*; and even
more curious *ich weus* instead of *weis* by analogy with *wuste* (NHG
wußte). The length-sign ⟨h⟩, the 'etymological' choice between
rounded/derounded vowel graphies, and the use of doubled consonants in the case of *ff, ss* to distinguish them from voiced single
ones, lead to some bizarre spelling: *tühffen* = NHG *tiefen*. Moreover,
the etymology involved other Germanic languages: Zesen advocated
Lücht for *Licht* by analogy with Neth. *lucht*. Zesen rejected the letter
⟨c⟩ except in the graphies ⟨ch⟩ and ⟨sch⟩; he replaced ⟨qu⟩ by

⟨kw⟩, also ⟨ph⟩ by ⟨f⟩ and ⟨th⟩ by ⟨t⟩: hence spellings like *blikte*, *kwär, Saffo*.

Undoubtedly Zesen's orthography most upset his contemporaries, provoking several parodies, for example, by Christian Weise (*Erznarren*, XI): Weise attacked the spelling, purism, and the circumlocutory baroque poetic style, as the passage below shows. Clearly, orthographical innovation in the seventeenth century had limits, and a disregard for traditional spellings did not go uncriticized. However, Zesen's mystical and sometimes muddled approach to language (he claimed that the four vowels *a, e, o, u* were 'uhr-selbst-laute' or 'uhrklånge' representing the elements water, earth, air, and fire respectively) does not suffice to damn him.[83] He was an experienced translator, and a lively and humorous writer; while his orthography lacked rigour, it had system. Zesen strove in his renderings of technical works to accommodate the foreign terminology to German, and he experiments to find the best translation. The more exceptionable attempts to translate even accepted, established loan-words into German can be viewed as part of an emblematic baroque style where condensed circumlocution acts as poetic decoration.

There follows an example of Zesen's writing and a parody by Weise:

Philipp von Zesen, *Adriatische Rosemund* (1645), ed. Jellinek (1899), 189.

A Walk in the Garden[84]

Der tahg wahr sehr schôhn, der himmel klahr, und das wetter über=aus- lihblich [*exceedingly pleasant*]: di sonne blikte mit ihren anmuhtigen strahlen, welche râcht laulicht [*most mild*] waren, den frohen wålt=kråus [*orb, world*] so fråundlich an, daß man fast nicht mehr lust hatte in den håusern zu bleiben. Di Rosemund mahnete den Markhold zu einem lust=wandel an, und di Stil=muht [*Rosemund's sister, Serena?*] selbst baht ihn dahr=ûm, daß er sich mit ihnen in das grûne begåben môchte. Si gingen hihr=auf in den garten, da sich di lihblichen rosen von der wårme der sonnen schohn auf=getahn hatten, und såzten sich ehrstlich zum brunnen, hår=nahch unter di lust=hôhle, da sich Markhold an den zihrlich=gesåzten und über=kôstlichen [*most precious, Fr.* très-/sur-cher] muscheln sonderlich erlustigte. Es waren ihrer daselbsten wohl hunderterlei ahrten, immer einer schôner als di ander, zu såhen, dahrinnen man di wunder der grohssen zeuge=mutter nicht gnugsam betrachten konte. . . . Di schau=glåser, so auf allen seiten und in allen winkeln hårfûhr blikten, gahben einen sehr lustigen wider=schein. In dåm einen stein= wårke [*rockery*] wahr ein kleiner teich, dahrinnen der Se=got mit seinem drei=zank=stabe hår=ûm-fuhr. Er sahs in einer långlicht=rundten ofnen muschel als auf seinem kôniglichen stuhle; ûm ihn hårum schwummen allerlei kleine Se=wunder [*sea-monsters*], Mehr=ammen [*mermaids*], und wasser=kålber [*seals*]. Auf der andern seiten wahr noch eine kleine Se, welche fast halb fol gisch [*foam, yest, NHG* Gischt *masc.*] wahr, und di Lustinne, in einer ahrtigen [*pretty, exquisite*] muschel, aus=warf, welches in dåm nåhsten schau=glase ein solch ahrtiges aus=såhen [*spectacle*] gahb, daß auch Markhold sagte: wan einer nicht begreiffen kan, wi di kunst und selbheit [*Nature, as opposed to Art*] mit einander streiten kônnen, so darf er nichts mehr als dises wunder=wårk anschauen.

Christian Weise, *Die drei ärgsten Erznarren* (1672), ed. Braune (1878), 65.

A New-fangled Letter

Hoochgeneugter und Follkommen
liebender Freund.

Daß seine sich=so plôtzlich fergnûgenwollende Jugend, in das lûstrende und augenreizzende Lachchen der holdreuchesten Fenus angefåsselt worden, haabe ich wohl fernommen, lasse auch den Preißwûrdigsten Einladungs= Brieff deswegen in dem Tageleuchter liegen, dahmit ich das Ahndånkken der fohrstehenden Lustbarkeit nicht auß den Lichtern meines Haubtes ferlihren môhge. Di Fakkel des Himmels wird nicht fihlmahl umm den Tihrkreuß lustwandeln fahren, so wird die gånzzlich=herfor gekwollen seynde Sûssigkeit der freundlichsten Libinne, sein gantzes Låben erkwikkend beseligen. Und da mûste Zizero sålbst ferstummen, ja dem Firgilius und Horazius ingleichen dem Ofidius wûrde es an gleichmåssigen Glûckwûnschungs=Wohrten fermangelbahren. Bei so angelaassenen Sachchen, solte ich schweugen, umb meine in der Helden sprachmåssiger Wohlsåzzenheit gahr wånig außge= kûnstelt habende, und nicht allzu woortsålig erscheunende Schreibrichtig- keit, oder daß ich båsser vernûnfftele, umb meine sich unwissend erkånnende Gemûths=Gebråchchen nicht zu ferblôssen. Entzwischen ist die Ohngedult meiner begirig auffsteugenden Hårzzens=Neugungen so groß, daß ich den Mangel der an den Himmel der Ewigkeit zu schreiben wûrdig seinden Worte, mit gegenwårtiger Geringfûgigkeit zu er såzzen beschlossen habende, mein Ohnvermôgen entschuldigt zu haben bittend, und in forliebnåhmender Gunst=gesinnenschafft aufgenommen zu werden hoffend, mich in ståter und unwandelbahr blûhender Dienstfårtigkeit wûnsche zu nånnen

Gegåben mit flûchtiger   Meines Hårzzengebieters dienstsamen und
Fåder den 10.   auffwarts=bahren Knåchts
deß Rosenmonds
im 1656. H. Jahre.   N.N.

Approximate translation:

Highly Esteemed and Wholly Affectionate Friend,

I have indeed heard that His Youth, so suddenly bent on Diversion, hath been captivated by the provocative and enchanting Smiles of the gracious Lady Venus, wherefore [I] leave the most inestimable Letter of Invitation lying in the Daylighter [Casement], that I may not lose out of the Lights of mine Head the Remembrance of the forthcoming Festivity. The Torch of Heaven will not travel oft around the Zodiac but that, all the Sweetness of that most amiable Goddess of Love being utterly effused, [it] will bless His entire Being with Refreshment. And Cicero himself must needs fall dumb, Yes, Virgil, Horace, and Ovid to boot would be sensible of Want of suitable Expression of Felicitation. In such occasioned Business I should properly be silent, on Account of mine own Accomplishment in Letters in the rhetorical Style befitting our noble and heroic Tongue having contrived but little of Worth, and it appearing none too eloquent, or if I should cavil yet further, in order not to expose the Frailties of mine Humour that openly own themselves ignorant. Meantime, the Impatience of mine eagerly climbing sincerest Affections hath so increased, that I, having resolved to make good the Deficiency of Words worthy to have been writ in the Heaven of Eternity with this poor present Trifle, requesting to have mine Inadequacies excused, and in Expectation of being received in a Spirit of forgiving Favour, wish to declare myself in constant and immutable flourishing Obligation,

Indited, with hasty Quill, this	the most willing and humble
10th Day of the Rose-Month	Servant of the Lord of mine
[= June] in the Year of Our	Heart,
Lord 1656	N.N.

BAROQUE STYLE AND PURISM

The similarities between purism and the elaborate baroque[85] style sometimes known as *Schwulst* did not escape contemporaries, for they both involved circumscription, and both could be involuntarily comic. The purists attempted to eradicate words of foreign origin whose morphology and derivation were unknown to the speakers, often replacing them by compound nouns which were so transparently motivated in their formation as to be disproportionately expressive and consequently out of context in everyday use. For example, as a formation *Tageleuchter* is no more preposterous than English 'window', from ON *vindauga* 'wind-eye' (compare also Goethe's *Tageloch* 'sky-light'), but beside the long-established, 'neutral' *Fenster* the neologism is too striking outside poetry. However, for poetic effect the emphatic, unusual form or juxtaposition of words was desirable, and the manneristic metaphor deliberate, part of the emblematic conception of language. Indeed, the high baroque style aims to be understood on several levels simultaneously, and consequently sometimes defies consistent or logical interpretation, since individual words and phrases have independent associative meanings which dominate the contextual meaning. Such 'uneigent-liches Sprechen'[86] implies not merely a figurative, metaphorical use of language, but a 'non-literal speech', where the priorities of normal communication have been altered so that associative, oblique messages are conveyed. Syntax can be sacrificed to the discrete, isolated compound noun or adj. where the tension between the overall meaning of the compound and the meanings of the elements juxtaposed to create it arrests the audience's attention.[87] For example, Catharina Regina von Greiffenberg (1633–94) in a poem to autumn strings together a series of compound nouns whose condensed images are independent yet loosely associated with the season;[88] *Freud'-Erfüller, Früchte-bringer, vielbeglückter Jahres-Koch, Grünung-Blüh, Zeitung-Ziel, Werkbeseeltes Lustverlangen, Zeiten-Schatz, süsser Mund-Ergetzer*, etc. Christian Hoffmann von Hofmannswaldau (1617–79) wrote sensual love poetry, indulging in a long paean in praise of his lady's breasts, including:

Die brüste sind mein zweck/ die schönen marmel-ballen . . .
Zwey schnee-balln/ welche doch unmöglich schmeltzen können/
Womit das jungfern-volck der männer seelen schmeist.
Zwey aufgestelte garn/ und schlingen freyer sinnen/
Aus denen gar kein mensch/ wie klug er ist entreist.
Zwey kräme [*booths, stalls*]/ wo man huld und freundlichkeit ausleget/
Und wo ein rother mund nur kan der kauffmann seyn.
Zwey körb'/ in welchen man bloß marcipan feil träget/
Nach dessen süßigkeit die lippen lechsend schreyn . . .[89]

And in another of his poems, the sonnet 'Vergänglichkeit der schönheit', antithesis goes as far as 'Der schultern warmer schnee wird werden kalter sand . . .' (ed. Windfuhr (1969), 95, line 4). A writer on epistolary style, Johann Kaspar Suter, gives a lover's elucidation of a kiss in the following terms:

Der Kuß ist . . . Ein Abtruk brünstiger Zuneigung auff einer Corallinen Presse: Ein Paar gegen einander schlagende Feuersteine: Ein Carmesin-rothes/ Wundenpflaster der Liebe: Ein süsser Lippen-Biß: Ein holdseliger Mund-Truk: Eine Speise/ die man mit rothen Löffeln zu sich nimmt: Ein Zukkerbrod das nicht sättiget: Ein Obst/ so man zu gleich pflanzet und abbricht[90]

The mannered style was easily parodied by taking it to extremes, as when Sacer writes of a dog and cat 'Das Mur- und Belle-Thier mit viergebeinten Füssen | lief uns unmenschlich an . . . Des Kürschners Ebenbild/ lebendige Mäusefalle | Mit Peltze überdecket/ die mauete mit Schalle';[91] or when Weise in the satirical letter above replaces *Augen* by 'aus den Lichtern meines Haubtes'.

Nevertheless, this style encouraged lexical experimentation, and it had respected analogues in other European countries—euphuism in England, Gongorism in Spain, Marinism in Italy. Set against this background, Philipp von Zesen's style appears unexceptionable. His puristic neologisms even interpreted the foreign words they replaced; indeed, purism provided an inexhaustible source of inspiration for new compounds. Only when the neologisms in the *Adriatische Rosemund* are confronted with the replaced foreign term do they stand out, otherwise they blend into the diction of the novel: in the passage quoted above, *schau-gläser*, *wider-schein*, *drei-zank-stab*, *segot*, *länglich-rundt*, *königlicher stuhl* are probably not all immediately apparent as renderings of the foreign words *miroir*, *reflection*, *trident*, *Neptunus*, *ovale*, *thron*, while *lust-höhle* (~ *grotte*) and *Lustinne* (~ *Venus*) fit into the whole range of compounds with *lust-* which run through the work. Nor is *Natur* always rendered *Zeuge-Mutter* (= 'Mother Nature'), but occasionally *Selbheit* (see the passage quoted above, pp. 295–6).

Quoting Zesen's neologisms out of context and confronting them with the already current foreign loans makes him look ridiculous. But Zesen himself was partly to blame for claiming general validity for what were really poetic devices, and for drawing attention to the original loan-words in his glossary. Finally, Zesen's linguistic views were, with variations, not untypical, and even some opponents shared them, without, however, attempting to put them into practice.

SELECT BIBLIOGRAPHY

LITERARY HISTORY

Goedeke (1887).   Szyrocki (1968).
Newald (1967).

STUDIES ON LANGUAGE

Blume (1973).   Hankamer (1927).
Blume (1978*b*).   Langen (1957).
Eggers (1963–77).   Sperber (1929).
Fleming and Stadler (1974).

FOREIGN INFLUENCES ON THE VOCABULARY (including other periods)

Brunt (1978).
Brunt (1983).
Ganz (1955).
Ganz (1957).

Jones (1976).
Palmer (1950, 1960).
Stiven (1936).

LANGUAGE SOCIETIES

Blume (1978a).
Engels (1983).
Otto (1972a).

Schultz (1888).
Stoll (1973).

BIBLIOGRAPHIES OF BAROQUE LITERATURE

Dünnhaupt (1980–1).

Pyritz and Pyritz (1979–   ).

PHILIPP VON ZESEN

Otto (1972b).

Van Ingen (1970).

CHAPTER VIII

THE EARLY
MODERN PERIOD (II):
GRAMMARIANS,
LITTÉRATEURS, AND
CULTURAL POLITICS
IN THE
EIGHTEENTH CENTURY

THIS chapter treats the changing role of the grammarians in the eighteenth century and particularly their contributions to the evolution of a standard German language, a question much debated at the time, so that contemporary theorizing about the best German enables us to add a 'metalinguistic' level to our history of the language. However, the selection by grammarians of those linguistic features they saw as the basis for a standard language can itself be seen as a very special form of linguistic levelling drawing on less conscious processes of regional and social interaction which had been given new impetus by the spread of printing.

So, eighteenth-century grammarians seek to describe and regulate the norms of their day, often starting from different theoretical positions to justify linguistic descriptions which are very similar. Much of the controversy concerned style, since three main factors influencing language change—time, place, and social level[1]—were discussed indirectly in grammatical and lexicographical writings under the guise of archaisms, provincialisms, and 'vulgarisms' in literary style. In attempting to fix grammatical and stylistic norms, the grammarians inevitably rejected features they considered archaic or provincial, and these then often came to be regarded as vulgar: taste, ever a difficult criterion to apply, dictated the choice of the best German and the best authors. Dialect and spoken usage were poorly distinguished and both were branded 'incorrect'; and this very preoccupation with what was 'correct', 'good', or in Enlightenment terminology *vernünftig, aufgeklärt, klar*, represents a characteristic phase in the establishment of a linguistic norm. Only when the standard is relatively established, at the end of the century and in the course of the nineteenth century, do we find the dialects regaining general popular appeal, both for romantic reasons, as exotic and quaint, and for patriotic and even nationalistic motives, as part of the cultural heritage of the unique assemblage of peoples in the 'Reich'.

Nevertheless, despite the great importance of literary considerations, especially style, we shall not deal in detail with the great writers of the century,[2] nor does space permit mention even of all the important grammarians,[3] while the influence on schools and printing-houses remains largely unexplored. Instead, we must restrict ourselves to considering three figures—Gottsched, Klopstock, and Adelung—in whose work all the major grammatical controversies of the time are reflected, in particular, the identity and character of the written standard (*Hochdeutsche Schriftsprache*), the status of dialect and speech, and the contribution of 'literature' (of authors and printed writings) to establishing written norms. Conflicting criteria, often subjective, ambiguous terminology, and false premises concerning the grammarian's task and historical change in language frequently obscure the grammarians' theoretical pronouncements. First, they stand in a grammatical tradition which prevents them from viewing clearly the very language they wish to describe, and secondly, their exclusively literary viewpoint and philosophical approach limit the value of their grammatical descriptions in the schools, where they had most success in stabilizing the relatively 'closed' systems of language—phonology, morphology, and orthography. In fact, some grammarians had too grandiose a view of their own role, and actually neglected the very sectors of the populace most in need of their advice.

THE BASIC APPROACHES TO THE QUESTION OF THE STANDARD LANGUAGE

The eighteenth-century debate about the nature and situation of the best or standard language employs old arguments of the seventeenth century with more rigour and intensity. Three main positions may be discerned, supported by highly varied aesthetic, historical, political, and social arguments:[4]

1. The *analogical* model favoured by Schottel claims that correct German is supra-regional, not identifiable with any particular dialect. The structures of this ideal language are to be revealed by deduction using the principle of analogy. The rationalism may aim at identifying the regularity lying behind actual linguistic performance, and is hence 'structuralist', but it can seek the reflexes of old 'roots' (*Stammwörter*) and so has comparativist, etymological aspects. Both LG and UG grammarians alike found the approach attractive, since it did not exalt any one dialect to canonical status. The *written* form of language is the prime concern of such theory.

2. The *anomalist* position (anomaly is here equivalent to 'usage': *consuetudo, usus*) identifies and describes the usage of a particular group of speakers. In the seventeenth century the US or Meissen usage is considered exemplary, albeit in purified form, and is held to be the German equivalent of the Attic dialect of ancient Greece. Philipp von Zesen's orthographical reform is anomalist to the extent that it is partly inspired by Meissen pronunciation. Theoretically (though seldom in practice) the *speech* of a particular region is paramount.

In their extreme form, these two approaches to language are incompatible,[5] but in practice theoreticians of all periods attempt compromises: the analogist must after all base his speculations on material which in turn must come from some source, while the grammarian's need to impose rules leads to the tempering of usage by insight gained from analogy. But a third approach, which is in fact such a compromise, is important here:

3. Essentially this is the description of the supra-regional form when it has been adopted by a particular region. The idea probably emanated from Italian grammarians who maintained that the best Italian resulted from the Roman pronunciation of the Florentine,

Tuscan form of the language, summed up by the slogan *lingua toscana in bocca romana*. Applied to German, it was argued that LG-speakers who had to acquire HG from books learned it as a foreign tongue with care and respect. Adelung later used the curious term *Nieder-Hochdeutsch* by which he understood the standard ('Hochdeutsch') when spoken by LG-speakers;[6] Klopstock adopted a position not unlike this in his attempts to devise a phonetic orthography for the declamation of poetry. It involves the blending of *written* and *spoken* forms of language.

Despite the existence of compromise solutions like the above, much eighteenth-century grammatical theory involved attempts to mediate between the analogist and anomalist positions. In the process there is little doubt that the written traditions of the EMG area became increasingly accepted, although it became apparent that they did not reflect the spoken language of the region, whether dialect or 'town colloquial'. The labels *Obersächsisch* and *Meißnisch* become disembodied slogans and are used synonymously: given the patchwork of absolutist states this is not surprising; in fact, on a rough dialect map of the EMG area in the eighteenth century, Misnian is at the core of the US region (see Map 4). Thuringian, Lusatian, and parts of Silesian, at least as represented by authors, are often reckoned as belonging to this 'US', though, unlike its pendant Low Saxon, US covers a relatively small area. Low Saxon, by contrast, is used to mean LG generally and has many dialects: doubtless this led some grammarians to view US as fairly homogeneous. At any event, when we attempt to see clearly just what contemporaries understood by US and Meissen language, we see the limits of their method and observations. Precisely this inadequate empirical basis for the US claims became apparent in the course of the century and led to attacks on both Gottsched and Adelung, who took up the slogan in their different ways.

GRAMMATICAL TRADITION IN THE EIGHTEENTH CENTURY

Many important baroque grammarians had regarded themselves as poets—Harsdörffer, Schottel, and Zesen—so that grammar was inseparable from prosody, metre, and aesthetics: the question of the best German was debated in litarary, stylistic terms.[7] The same approach, *Kunstsprache* as the basis for *Sprachkunst* (grammar),

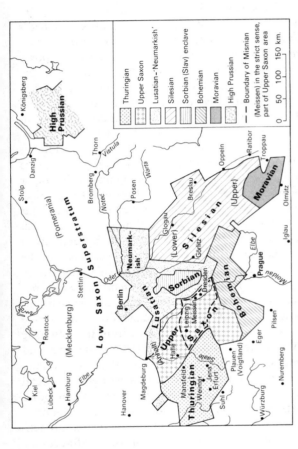

Note. This map presents approximate dialect areas which play a role in the eighteenth century linguistic controversy regarding the standard or 'book' language, HG. While towns and regions are given, neither eighteenth century nor modern political circumstances are considered, and terms like 'Bohemian', 'Moravian' imply only a regional form of German overlying the indigenous Slavonic. The map, based on that given by Putschke (1973), 346, reflects conditions about 1900.

Gottsched's broad definition of US/Meissen includes the written language of Thuringia, Mansfeld, Anhalt, the Voigtland, Lusatia, and Lower Silesia. See Gottsched (1748, 1762), 67–9, including note (*f*). The passage is unclear: Gottsched is arguing for the primacy of the written language in the most cultivated area, but he refers also to educated speech in these other regions—'ein recht gutes Hochdeutsch gesprochen [NB!]: welches man a potiori, nach dem Sitze des vornehmsten Hofes, das Obersächsische zu nennen pflegt'. See the edition by Penzl (1978), i. 105–7.

MAP. 4. The East Middle German dialect area in the eighteenth century.

remains current in the eighteenth century too, and awareness of it helps us to understand how grammarians fail to distinguish clearly between the formal closed systems of grammar (phonology, morphology, and orthography) and the open stylistic and lexical ones. In effect a *literary* language is being imposed as a *standard* language, which leads to problems when the differing needs of everyday communication are considered. We shall see that Gottsched's grammatical writings were subordinate to his literary, aesthetic, and philosophical interests, and their inadequacy for practical purposes is partly explained by this. Moreover, his preoccupation with the Enlightenment philosophy of Leibniz and Wolff made him view language inflexibly, as though it were a philosophical, logical system. The same rigidity limits his canons of good taste and blinds him to certain styles of writing: with the rejection of his aesthetic standpoint, his grammatical writings were also discredited. But even Adelung in the last quarter of the eighteenth century is forced to take cognizance of the writers, although he makes the spoken language of the upper classes in the US area the basis for his prescription. Despite this, Adelung's pattern is as unrealistic as Gottsched's, and no clear definition of the 'oberen Classen' is offered, although naturally such circles are the model for bourgeois aspirations too. Still, Adelung did have practical experience in writing textbooks for schools, and he does move away from the refined literary use of language as a pattern; moreover, he presents vocabulary in his *Grammatisch-kritisches Wörterbuch* (1774–86) in a practical manner, for he uses *style* not to discuss abstract questions as to the best language, but to determine the value of individual words and expressions within the linguistic norms. Literary style is merely one level, not the basic one, and Adelung acknowledges, as Gottsched had not, that poetry may require the use of archaic and even provincial words for special purposes: this, like the borrowing of technical terms from other languages, represents a permissible broadening of the standard language. Adelung's theory claims to embody a practical approach, although it is still exclusive in tone, unlike the sixteenth-century religiously inspired popular grammatical traditions. But his work looked beyond high literary considerations, while its thoroughness made it indispensable to later grammarians as a basis for further discussion.

We must also consider the degree of literacy of the eighteenth-century society, if we are to understand the grammarians' role within it. This also involves discussing such issues as the relationship of spoken and written language and the position of dialects. Not surprisingly, since such entities are themselves subject to variation and are imperfectly preserved in texts, we shall probably never attain ultimate clarity. Still, it is salutary to see just how little these early grammarians agreed, even on fundamental issues, and how vague and ambiguous much of their terminology turns out to be.

SOCIETY, DIALECT, AND LITERACY IN THE EIGHTEENTH CENTURY

The copious printed and written material from the eighteenth century does not enable us to see the relationship between spoken and written language clearly, although we can observe 'interference' in the written forms which must reflect spoken language. Nor can we distinguish between 'dialect' and everyday spoken language, which is regional in character (*regionale Umgangsprache*). Contemporary studies of dialect were in their infancy and were antiquarian in character and not based on direct phonetic observation; worse still, dialect was regarded as the medium of lower social classes whose idiom could not appeal to writers of the day for serious purposes. In southern German areas where the use of dialect extended higher up the social scale, and where social distinctions between the different dialectal strata were (and are) difficult for the foreigner to assess, little was produced in the way of grammatical writing in the early part of the century, while in the north the very noticeable gap betwen the HG-based norms and the LG dialects forced a deep social wedge between those who spoke dialect and those who aspired to higher status. At any rate, a suitable phonetic orthography which would have rendered subtle phonetic distinctions accurately, did not exist.[8] Even in the drama, where dialect was used for comic, often satirical, effect or for characterization, or at least for local colour, no phonetic accuracy was necessary or even possible, since the stabilizing standard written language itself lacked a consistent orthography. Indeed, such dialect transcription as occurred was carried out by educated men using the fluctuating orthographical traditions of the written language and in no way provides a faithful rendering of the sounds themselves. Even in the great upsurge of serious dialect poetry prompted by Herder and practised first by Voss, an idealized 'literary dialect' was intended. Naturally, regional pronunciation had considerable bearing upon the poets' use of rhyme, but this depended also upon the orthographical traditions of the regions where they were writing and the extent to which they wrote for audiences beyond the immediate vicinity. Nevertheless, interest in dialect was primarily stylistic, not phonetic, and concerned the use of dialect words and expressions rather than sounds and spellings. Since the stylistic standards have yet to be generally established, such apparently neat categories as 'provincialisms', 'archaisms', 'vulgarisms', and 'poetic forms' are subjective, depending directly upon the origins and outlook of the observer. The various regional dictionaries or *idiotica* which appear during the century are coloured by the same subjectivity and are of little practical value. For the most part they are inspired indirectly by Leibniz, who saw that dialects might usefully supplement the limited vocabulary of the standard language by giving technical terms for various special arts and crafts and expressions to replace foreign words.[9] But most dialect lexicographers produced books based on poor theory and imperfect observation, where the collector's joy overwhelmed any analytical urge, and where rare specimens borrowed from earlier writers were uncritically set beside current dialectal usage. Here the antiquarian, patriotic motives of the previous century remained prominent. Sometimes, the desire to overcome barriers to comprehension is apparent, but the barriers are viewed primarily in geographical rather than social terms; dialectal differences are registered, but forms considered vulgar because restricted to certain social classes are avoided. Instead of the lexicographers enriching German by their collections, we have to look to the writers, who are then roundly criticized by grammarians for going beyond the canons of acceptable taste, and for obscurity.[10] So, eighteenth-century dialect dictionaries give an imperfect picture partly because the sophistication of the lexicographers isolated them from the lower strata of society, partly because of their naïvety in approach, and partly because they were primarily concerned with lexis rather than phonology.

A further problem concerns the relationship between dialect and the spoken language of towns and other cultural centres, which differed from dialect and the regional written traditions alike. The term *Umgangssprache* ('colloquial language'; see Chapter IX) is applied to such usage, which remains today recognizably regional in sounds and expressions. Gottsched and other grammarians were aware that the forms they codified in their grammars were idealized inasmuch as they were based on written language. In practice, for example, unstressed *e* might be dropped in speech, e.g. *redete* reduced to *redte*, *ich habe* reduced to *ich hab*; but the spoken language of the lower social classes was not an appropriate object for grammatical description. Even in the nineteenth century dialect poetry is purified by the Romantic imagination, so that attempts to present an idiom close to the language actually spoken are criticized.[11] In the eighteenth century the poorer classes in town and country were largely illiterate and ill-provided with either reading material or school-books.[12] Old-fashioned biblical tracts, peasant calendars, almanacs, and chap-books, the Bible itself—widely distributed by the Bible Societies[13]—formed the staple reading diet of these circles. Although some states had introduced compulsory schooling nearly a century before (e.g. Saxe-Coburg-Gotha in 1642, Württemberg in 1649, and Brandenburg in 1662), parents remained unconvinced of the benefits of reading, unable or unwilling to send their children to schools. In towns primitive abecedary schools—*Winkelschulen* or *Klippschulen*—gave rudimentary education to the children of artisans, but schoolmasters and children alike lacked books and training. The authorities sometimes opposed education for the bulk of their subjects as the political implications of literacy became plain, especially after the French Revolution, and reading by servants, artisans, and peasants was frowned upon and branded an unhealthy *Lesesucht*. In respect of education too, the lower classes were of little concern to eighteenth century writers and grammarians, and where the schoolmasters themselves were not conversant with the forms of the HG book language, as was frequently the case in rural areas, further barriers to overcoming illiteracy existed. To some extent the proponents of orthographies and grammars based on local varieties of German draw attention to this problem, but they too are concerned mainly with the education of 'middle-class' children.

Consequently, although book production increases tremendously in the latter half of the eighteenth century—some 66 per cent of a total of approximately 175,000 German titles were published after 1750— the circles catered for remain bourgeois or aristocratic. These classes also read newspapers and the new 'moral weeklies',[14] but even at important cultural centres like Leipzig and Hamburg probably well under 10 per cent of the population were reading at all, while among Frankfurt merchants only 28 per cent of wills mention legacies of books. Still, the spread of literacy among the middle classes in particular is well attested and borne out by the decline of Latin books: of titles published at Leipzig in 1700, 38 per cent were Latin, in 1740 this dropped to 28 per cent, and in 1800 only 4 per cent of Leipzig books were in Latin.[15]

Women were generally less well educated than men, and among the peasantry and even middle classes reading was not felt necessary at all by some.[16] It comes as no surprise to discover phonetic spellings like *Efijenige* (~ *Iphigenie*), *Grüdick* (~ *Kritik*), *Eeckibbasche* (~ *Equipage*), *dies Kaste* (~ *Tischkasten*), *dehedansag* (~ *Thé dansant*), *Biebeldäck* (~ *Bibliothek*), *Liedratdur* (~ *Literatur*) in the letters of Christiane Vulpius-Goethe, but Goethe nowhere criticizes her for bad spelling, although he admits to having to read her letters several times; indeed, for his own works he prudently leaves orthographical matters to his printers.[17] But such phonetic spellings abound in the letters of rulers, too: Kåre Kaiser compares the autograph versions of letters written by King Friedrich Wilhelm I (1713–40), the father of Frederick the Great, with the official correspondence produced by his Chancery:[18]

Potsdam den 23. Nove(mber) 1725.

Euer Lieben schreiben mit die beide *obersten* habe wohll erhalten auch den gestrigen (Brief) es tuet mir vo(n) hertzen leidt das alles was ich getahn nits fruchten wierdt ich überschiecke *itzo kaht(sch)* und den *gen(erall) Ma(jor) Bechewer* mit Euer Lieben recht zu sprechen den(n) ich kan nit glauben das die herren *obersten* aus *respect* vor Ihrn feldt *Mar(s)chall* alles gesaget haben werden was sie hatten deswegen sagen wollen den(n) wen(n) ich die sache nit ausmache ich das blutt das dar möchte vergossen werden ich gewiss auf mir haben werde da bewahr mir Gott vor kein rein gewissen zu haben den(n) biss *itzo* habe guht gewissen gehabt aber wen(n) die sache nit ausgemachet ist und *Blut* vergossen worden ich mein dage es mir *Reprochiren* muhs also Euer Lieben sehen in was vor *chagrin* bin da es auch *itzo* in der weldt*constellacion* nach eingrossen *krig* aussiehet und Euer Lieben solten wegen der *affere chagrin* haben würde mir sehr leidt tun aber wer ist s(ch)uldt das sein Euer Lieben den(n) sie die sache ümmer schlimmer machen und fast nit zu *redressir*en Gott bekehre Ihre Sache der ich stehs Euer Lieben frundt sein werde . . .

Compare a letter written by the 'Kabinett', his Chancery (note also the syntactical and stylistic differences):

Potsdam 28. November 1725.

Es haben Mir der p. von Katsch und Generalmajor v. Beschefer so mündlichen als schriftlichen allerunterthänigsten Rapport von demjenigen abgestattet, was sie nach Meiner Instruction mit Euer Lieben gesprochen, und wohin Dero Erklärung gegangen. Euer Lieben werden wohl versichert sein und aus allen Meinen Umbgang genugsam spüren können, dass Ich Sie liebe und an Conservation Dero Person Mir gelegen. Ich werde auch vor Euer Liebden alles gerne weiter thun, was nur nach meinem Gewissen gegen Gott und nach der Gerechtigkeit vor der raisonnabelen Welt zu verantworten. . . .

Typical variants in Friedrich Wilhelm's letters include the alternation of ⟨j⟩ and ⟨g⟩: *jejaget* ~ *gegaget* ~ *iegaget* (NHG *gejagt*), *sehr guhng* ~ *die jünjen Herren*; also in foreign loans: *Kannalge, alljirten, artilgerie, Campange, Battalge*. Some unshifted consonants occur: *Perde, Plaster, Paffen, Plicht, 3-Pünderkanonen, Kop, Schnupen, tapper, appell*; also 'hypercorrections': *pfeldt, pfahren, pfertig, anpfandt, hundespfott*. There are also ⟨s⟩ spellings instead of ⟨sch⟩: *sreiben, gesrieben, surcken, söhne* (NHG *schöne*), *hübs, fals*. In morphology, *-s* plurals are common: *angers, apostels, arbeitters, Barons, Bataillons, Bürgers, deuffels, docktors, jägers, junckers*; and there are several in *-er*: *gelegenheiter, Rebeller, hander, Kamisöhler, brücher*.

We should note that the informal, handwritten material was not designed for publication and shows less attention to external form: it is relatively unselfconscious. At the same time, the deviation between the written form of Friedrich Wilhelm and of his Chancellor allows us to recognize that there was already a fairly homogeneous educated usage, a 'Mundart der Gelehrten, oder auch wohl der Hôfe', as Gottsched puts it, not identical with any one dialect, but to some extent general: 'eine gewisse, eklektische, oder ausgesuchte und auserlesene Art zu reden, die in keiner Provinz vôllig im Schwange geht'.[19] This language must be reformed and purified. Corroboration comes also from an anonymous tract (listed in Kaiser (1930), p. ix), *Wohlgemeinte Vorschläge Zu einer Allgemeinen und Regelmäßigen Einrichtung und Verbesserung Der Teutschen Sprache In dem Ober-Sächsischen und Nieder-Sächsischen Kreise* (Halberstadt, 1732), where the recommendations made are expressly for educated people only: 'Es kommt hier allein auf die Gelehrten an. Die Ungelehrten bleiben in allen Ländern bey ihrer Schreib-Art . . .' (pp. 28 f.: quoted in Henne (1975), 88 n. 44). The problem is further complicated by the existence of local written (more importantly, printing) conventions, which are themselves influenced by local dialect and by the urban 'intermediate' forms of colloquial language that have moved away from dialect and yet are not simply the spoken rendering of the local written or printed language (*Schreibe*).[20] The main factors in the debate about the emergent standard form can be illustrated diagrammatically (Fig. 8). All four types of language interact and influence each other, but the degree of influence is not shown by the model, since it varies according to region and circumstances. Clearly, the dialectal and local spoken forms inevitably affect regional written

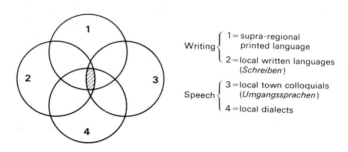

Writing { 1 = supra-regional printed language
2 = local written languages (*Schreiben*)

Speech { 3 = local town colloquials (*Umgangssprachen*)
4 = local dialects

FIG. 8 (after Schenda (1977), 29)

forms, which in turn may influence the supra-regional written form. But dialectal features may be taken directly into the 'standard' for poetic/stylistic reasons, while the standard language may influence some dialects, actually accounting for some of the non-dialectal features of local *Umgangssprache*.

The supra-regional 'written' language was not uniform in itself, and made concessions to local printed languages. Nevertheless, in such basic features as shifted consonants and diphthongizations, this language occurs, with due modification, both in the LG north and in Switzerland in literary works and editions of the Bible since the seventeenth century, and it was recognized as an educated form of language.

This spread of a recognizable but imperfect written (and printed) language had begun in the sixteenth century, as we have seen (Chapter V). Taking three important areas—the north, south-west, and south-east—scholars have documented the spread of a central form of HG, usually claimed by modern scholars as EMG, by eighteenth-century writers as 'obersächsisch' or 'meißnisch'.[21]

HG as an administrative and church language in north Germany stands out, because its consonant system differs from those of LG dialects. Whatever the reasons for the HG takeover, it must have been complete by the early seventeenth century, as the cessation of the printing of LG Bibles and the declining number of other LG prints suggest. This is corroborated by the relatively early use of LG dialect for literary purposes in satires, plays, and comic interludes in operas: from the late sixteenth century LG roles in plays indicate rustic, local, and uneducated speakers. Stylistically, LG was the most common 'non-standard' form of language, implying already a considerable degree of consolidation in the position of HG as 'standard'.

The extreme south-west area also increasingly adopted a HG *habitus* in orthography and morphology, particularly in works printed with an eye to wider markets. A well-known example is the 1665-7 Zurich edition of the Bible, which adopted diphthongal spellings, although preachers at the end of the seventeenth century are still exhorted to avoid pronouncing diphthongal forms during the service for their congregations' sake. In the eighteenth century, Swiss efforts to emulate specifically EMG habits are well documented in the literary feud between Gottsched and the Swiss writers Bodmer, Breitinger, and Haller (see below, pp. 321 ff.).

In the south-east, the Austro-Bavarian area seems apathetic towards the linguistic issue, although even before Gottsched's grammar there is evidence of the influence exercised by (Upper) Saxon language: in one of the rare linguistic contributions to the Bavarian moral weekly *Parnassus Boicus*, Agnellus Kandler notes:

Denen Herrn Lutheranern hingegen, und fürnemlich denen Ober-Sachsen solle der durchgängige richtige Gebrauch zum Grund liegen und deß D. Luthers Übersetzung der Bibel soll in zweiffelhafftigen Fällen den Ausschlag geben. Dises können und sollen sich jene Catholische Schreiber und Buchdrucker wohl zur Gedächtnuß nemmen welche blindhin alles nachmahlen und nachaffen, was sie in einem Sächsischen Buch lesen und aufklauben da doch solche Schreib-Art mehrmahlen kein andere Brunn-Quell als die Lutherische Bibel und keinen tiefferen Grund hat als des Luthers Willkuhr.[22]

The eighteenth-century scholars viewed the ideal standard in literary, aesthetic terms which made such language difficult to attribute to any group of speakers. This stylistic issue was nevertheless reinterpreted as a geographical one, and a fruitless search for *the* home of the

Schriftsprache began. Confusion is apparent in the use of the term *Mundart* itself, for it could apply to all *four* types of language in Fig. 8, as well as meaning spoken language in general[23] and German as a whole—one *Mundart* of the Germanic family of languages. It was necessary to introduce social and stylistic distinctions into the concept of spoken German, and this is increasingly apparent in the grammarians' pronouncements as the century progresses, culminating in the attempts by Adelung to produce a description based on the everyday discourse of the upper classes in the US area. This view, apparently reflected in the *Encyclopaedia Britannica* at the end of the eighteenth century (1797 edn., vol. viii, p. 506)—'*HIGH Dutch* is the German tongue in its greatest purity and c. as spoken in Misnia & c.' —is actually much older, and pre-dates the major pronouncements of both Gottsched and Adelung, for it is lifted verbatim from Ephraim Chambers's *Cyclopaedia* of 1728 (vol. i, p. 250). Both these German grammarians, then, can be seen as embodying already existing popular opinion on where the best German was to be found.

JOHANN CHRISTOPH GOTTSCHED (1700–1766) AND THE TYRANNY OF TASTE

Gottsched was born and educated at Königsberg in the LG-speaking part of East Prussia and subsequently moved to Leipzig, where he lectured on philosophy, rhetoric, and poetry. From the outset he was interested in language, in particular the diction of poetry, although his influential grammar, *Grundlegung einer deutschen Sprachkunst, nach den Mustern der besten Schriftsteller des vorigen und jetzigen Jahrhunderts* did not appear until 1748. In his moral weeklies, too, *Die Vernünftigen Tadlerinnen* (1725–7), based on *The Tatler*, and *Der Biedermann* 1727–9), some sociolinguistic contributions appear— satire against linguistic mixture or Gallicisms, much in the tradition of the seventeenth-century *Sprachgesellschaften*. Indeed, in 1727 Gottsched became the 'Senior' of the Deutschübende Gesellschaft at Leipzig, changing its name to the Deutsche Gesellschaft, revising the statutes, and placing in the forefront of its activities the study, improvement, and purification of the German language; under Gottsched the society flourished and similar bodies in many other towns were set up to emulate it, e.g. Jena (1728), Weimar (1730),

Berne (1739), Königsberg (1741). In addition to his university lectures, Gottsched published treatises on rhetoric—*Grundriß zu einer vernunfftmäßigen Redekunst* (1729, expanded in 1736); and on poetry—*Critische Dichtkunst* (1730), which also discusses vocabulary in terms of archaisms, provincialisms, neologisms, and vulgarisms, anticipating his later work on synonymy, *Beobachtungen über den Gebrauch und Misbrauch vieler deutscher Wörter und Redensarten* (1758). From 1732-44 Gottsched edited and contributed to the learned journal *Beyträge zur Critischen Historie der deutschen Sprache, Poesie und Beredsamkeit*, many of whose articles represent the groundwork for the *Sprachkunst*. He also conducted a voluminous scholarly correspondence and undertook many translations, helped by his gifted wife Louise,[24] including plays which formed part of the *Deutsche Schaubühne* (1741-5) and were intended to shape the taste of the theatre-going public, replacing the vulgar, ill-constructed, and unedifying harlequinades—(*Hanswurstiaden*)—borrowed from Italian comic opera, and the *Haupt- und Staatsaktionen*[25] of strolling players. His dramatic theory drew particularly upon the French classical theatre and its theorists whose conventions Gottsched sought to introduce on to the German stage with the aid of the well-known actress Caroline Neuber and her troupe.

By any standards this output displays an impressive energy, and the strength of his personality and the bitter controversies about poetry and style which marked the waning of his career nevertheless helped to spread his writings. As Bodmer remarks in his anecdotes: 'Gottsched hatte in dieser Zwischenzeit ganz Deutschland vergottschedet.'[26] The *Sprachkunst* itself ran to five editions during Gottsched's lifetime and one after (1776); it was pirated at Vienna (by Trattner) and translated into Latin, French,[27] Dutch, Russian, and Hungarian, while even as late as 1819 the German preacher F. A. Wendeborn's *Elements of German Grammar* defers to Gottsched's authority.[28] An extract designed for schools, the *Kern der deutschen Sprachkunst* (1753), reached its eighth edition in 1777 despite being roundly criticized as inadequate for school use; Lessing, too, in his *Literaturbriefe* (No. 65, 1759) accused Gottsched of blind vanity, while the Lüneburg Rektor Johann Michael Heinze, whose observations Lessing quotes, reproached him for superficiality, inaccuracy, arrogance, tediousness, and prolixity. In particular, Gottsched had failed to improve on the grammar of Bödiker and Frisch,[29] from which he can frequently be corrected, while the converse is not true, and he displays 'unbedächtige Urteile und schnöde Verachtung gegen angesehene Schriftsteller oder gar gegen unschuldige Städte und Provinzen'. This last point was taken up by many opponents of Gottsched's grammatical views who disagreed less with his grammatical regulations than with his theoretical justification for them. Gottsched's theory was confused and subjective, but even so severe a critic as Jellinek emphasizes his catalytic effect on German grammatical writing, which experienced a sudden upsurge during the years 1748–81, particularly in southern Germany (Jellinek (1913–14), i. 244–5). Whether writers were opposed to Gottsched or not, most used arguments put forward by him: the appeal to such authorities as 'Gelehrte' or 'gute Skribenten'; internal linguistic reasons, like 'Sprachrichtigkeit' or analogy; historical and etymological arguments; the championing of individual dialect areas, particularly in respect of orthography and pronunciation. Such arguments had been used subjectively by Gottsched and his predecessors, and were easily applied to assumptions other than Gottschedian ones.[30] Above all, Gottsched's emphasis on the relationship between correct grammar and reason (*Vernunft*) made the linguistic issue fashionable in Enlightenment circles.

GOTTSCHED'S 'HOCHDEUTSCH' AND LEIPZIG USAGE

In its title the *Sprachkunst* upholds as linguistic models the best authors of the seventeenth and eighteenth centuries, which represents a stylistic departure from the archaic, if admirable, Luther Bible, from outmoded chancery prolixity, and also from baroque rhetoric, *Schwulst*; moreover, in practical terms, *written* language had recognizable orthographical and grammatical traditions and was more stable and hence more easily codified than speech, whose irregularities were, it seemed, caused by ignorance, carelessness, or haste. Still, the criteria for selecting the 'best authors' are not discussed, nor is Gottsched's grammatical codification systematically related to the authors on which it is ostensibly based.[31] Indeed, Gottsched deliberately (?) conflates written and spoken language,[32] since his aim is prescriptive rather than descriptive: he seeks to establish norms for pronunciation as well as grammar and style. But his attempts to identify the 'best speakers' geographically and socially are at odds with the claim to describe supra-regional literary German, and they were bitterly opposed by those who knew that no such spoken norm existed. Gottsched maintains that 'das wahre Hochdeutsch' is the language of educated people and of courts:

> Doch ist noch zu merken, da man auch eine gewisse eklektische, oder ausgesuchte und auserlesene Art zu reden, die in keiner Provinz völlig im Schwange geht, die Mundart der Gelehrten, oder auch wohl der Höfe zu nennen pflegt . . .[33]

But it becomes increasingly apparent that both are identified with a purified (and undoubtedly non-existent) form of US, for the 'best authors' are chosen from those following EMG written traditions,[34] and the model court is the Saxon Electoral Court at Dresden. With further simplification and characteristic overestimation of the grammarian's (i.e. his own) role, Gottsched arrives at the formula 'rules from Leipzig plus polite pronunciation from Dresden':

> So werden wir in Deutschland ohne Zweifel der chursächsischen Residenzstadt Dresden, zumal des Hofes angenehme Mundart [NB], mit den Sprachregeln und kritischen Beobachtungen verbinden müssen, die seit vielen Jahren in Leipzig gemachet, und im Schreiben eingeführet worden . . .[35]

The 'Leipzig rules' were sometimes established by the internal linguistic criterion of analogy: yet again, Gottsched generally restricts his handling of analogy to the EMG area and seldom considers other provinces except to blame them. For example, the forms *du kömmst, er kömmt*, rather than the widespread *kommst, kommt* are held to be 'correct' because irregular verbs (*unrichtige Zeitwörter*) should have vowel change in the present, and because they occur in Meissen and Silesian usage, Opitz rhyming *kömmt* with *nimmt*.[36] But the language of the courts was almost certainly neither homogeneous nor 'pure'; and, as Gottsched was aware, French still held sway as the language of polite conversation. Here Gottsched's literary theory is of interest, for in equally vague and over-simplified terms he prescribes as the language of tragedy the spoken rendering of the elevated written standard language, 'Hochdeutsch', since this is appropriate to the pathos of the action and to the 'vornehme Leute' who are the protagonists. By contrast, the language of comedy is 'eine ganz natürliche Schreibart' appropriate to 'Bürger, oder . . . Leute von mäßigem Stande' or to 'Bürger und geringe Personen, Knechte und Mägde',[37] and if necessary minor aristocrats; coarseness was to be avoided, and the result was a classical 'mediocre style' suspended between the poles of *Prachtsprache* and *Pöbelsprache*. Once more, language is rigidly tied to social class or education, and in drama, at

least, characters are not allowed more than one style. Nor was the
language of comedy to be provincial, but here Gottsched asks the
impossible of the dramatist: to produce a realistic, informal language
uncoloured by local characteristics. Such language did not exist in
Gottsched's day, and it is doubtful if it does even now. The Viennese
dramatic critic Sonnenfels claims (Sonnenfels (1768), 97–103; No. 17,
1 April 1768) that German lacks a language of comedy precisely
because there is no general *Umgangssprache*—the circles which might
have produced a refined language suitable for refined comedy speak
French![38] The ideal nature of Gottsched's approach to language
is evident, and his opponents could easily point to discrepancies
between the grammatical prescriptions and Leipzig usage. Whilst
Leipzig speech is naturally lost to us, we can gain some impression
of certain salient features indirectly, partly from Gottsched's
own work.

For example, in his moral weekly *Die Vernünftigen Tadlerinnen*
Gottsched published a presumably fictive letter from a young lady of
quality from Leipzig:

Werdeste Frau muMe,

Mir han lange uf en Schraiben aus den lieben Halle kewart, mit kraußen
schmerzen. Maine Mama Môchte kârne wissen Ab se och Noch fain kesunt
sain se kummen Jo keen Eenzich mohl hâr, un Mir han Ihn doch nischt ûbels
getaan. Mir sind hieben noch Alle wolloff nur Der kleene Pruter ist en
pißgen Mallate, sonst wirter schon Lange trûbben kewesen sain. Mir
laipzsche jumfern sind in kraußer kefahr, Weil der daud vaur etliche wochen
so stharck unter se kummen, das ihr flucks zwee uff emahl gestorben eens is
auch Braut Worden, und ich soll zur hochzich geyen . . . Ich ha disse nacht
Nich waul keruht drimme tût mir der kop wey, und ich kan nischt mer
schraiben. Atge dausentmahl atge [= *adieu*]

Meiner hauchgeerdesten Frau muMe

kehaurschamste tienerin N.N.

P.S. Es kummen klech pay ihn trûbben solch Schriften raus die von waibsen
Gemacht werden [i.e. *Die Vernünftigen Tadlerinnen*], Ich ha eens Gelesen
aber es doocht mit alldem heele nischt. Die Menscher mûssen keenen
Spinn Rocken oder Stricke Nateln han . . .[39]

Gottsched criticizes the language of this letter as 'pôbelhaft' and
indicative of a 'verderbte Aussprache'; typical features are the monophthongized forms in *keen*, *Eenzich* ($\bar{e} < ei$) and *doocht* (NHG *taugt*)
($\bar{o} < au$); the paucity of rounded vowels, as in *hieben* (NHG *hüben*),
wirter (NHG *würd' er*); and the lack of distinction between voiced

and voiceless consonants in initial and medial position (contrast *trübben* and *dausent*, *werdest* and *Pruter*, and compare *Gemacht* and *doocht*, where the spirantal value of non-initial /g/ is evident, as in *Eenzich, laipzsche* and (inversely) *atge*). In *kop* (NHG *Kopf*) an unshifted consonant occurs, and the affricate /pf/ was also rare, having become /f/ initially (this isogloss still separates EMG from WMG dialects); as a mnemonic note the Leipzig form *Feifengopp* (NHG *Pfeifenkopf*). In some 'hypercorrect' spellings, the diphthongal symbols ⟨au⟩ and ⟨ey⟩ are used for long monophthongs: *krauß* (NHG *groß*), *daud* (NHG *Tod*), *hauchgeerdest* (NHG *hochgeehrt*), and *kehaurschamst* (NHG *gehorsamst*); *geyen* (NHG *gehen*) and *wey* (NHG *weh*). Probably this reflects simply the fact that for semiliterate speakers the symbols ⟨ei⟩ and ⟨e⟩, ⟨au⟩ and ⟨o⟩ are in free variation and represent monophthongs, but such forms may also have a basis in speech when speakers seek to upgrade their language, which results in a Leipzig town colloquial between the extremes of dialect and written language.[40]

While Gottsched avoids monophthongal forms like *Kleeder* and *Boom* (NHG *Kleider* and *Baum*), and provides lists of words like *Leder* ≠ *Leiter*; *klauben* ≠ *kloben*, which are to be kept apart (Gottsched (1748, 1762), 126-8, ed. Penzl (1978), i. 166-8), he may himself have used unrounded forms in everyday discourse, since his list of 'zweifelhafte Wörter' in the *Sprachkunst* includes examples like *Beil/Beule, geil* (= *unzüchtig*)/*Gåule/geel* (= *gelb*), *Geleit/Gelåut*.[41] Gottsched, as a native of East Prussia, seems to have apocopated unstressed *-e* more readily than US-speakers, but he retains it as a marker for fem. nouns, objecting to forms like *Gnad', Gût'*. In consonants he is concerned to separate voiced from voiceless forms, including sibilants: at Leipzig *reisen* and *reißen* were homonyms. Final nasals, *-m* and *-n*, were also confused in Meissen, with morphological consequences: acc. and dat. cases were often not distinguished. Hence we can glean information about Leipzig and US speech, by scrutinizing precisely those features Gottsched wished to eradicate, supplemented by statements from other grammarians from the region.[42]

In his *Sprachkunst* Gottsched draws on his wife's play *Der Witzling*, which appeared in 1745, i.e. three years before the grammar.[43] This little satire defends Gottsched's aesthetic and linguistic ideas and is a typical rationalist comedy with *Vernunft* characters opposing foolish characters whose behaviour is tasteless and language incorrect. The linguistic errors are printed in heavy type in the editions of the *Schaubühne*, presumably for emphasis; the play would have sounded highly artificial on the stage, and was probably never performed. Nevertheless, useful insights into the Leipzig *Umgangssprache* are provided in the (ab)usage of the three foolish characters—the anti-hero Vielwitz, a young student who has come to Leipzig from Lower Saxony; Sinnreich, a pedant; and Jambus, a poetaster, who are natives of the town. The 'unrichtige Ausdrückungen' and 'Provinzial-Redensarten' are divided artificially into Low Saxon errors and US ones (Gottsched (1748, 1762), 455, note (*a*)).

Vielwitz's 'Niedersaxonismen' involve confusion of *für* and *vor*, the splitting (tmesis) of particles (e.g. '*Da* habe ich nicht schuld *an*' for *daran*), and, most importantly, confusion of *mich* and *mir* (e.g. 'bey *mich*', '*mir* dünkt', 'ich mache *mir* . . . drüber'), which represents general confusion of acc. and dat., especially after prepositions. These errors are not, however, simply dialect but rather the 'interference'[44] of the dialect system in Vielwitz's handling of the standard as the Gottscheds see it: the playlet's language is Leipzig *Umgangssprache* viewed as an incorrect version of the standard, indicative of lack of intelligence, education, morality, reason, and taste! The US characters Sinnreich and Jambus are the mouthpieces for aesthetic and linguistic ideas unacceptable to Gottsched, and parody the break-away group of Gottschedian supporters, including Christian Fürchtegott Gellert (1715–69), Gottlieb Wilhelm Rabener (1714–71), Johann Elias Schlegel (1719–49), Abraham Gotthelf Kästner (1719–1800), Friedrich Wilhelm Zachariä (1726–77), and Friedrich von Hagedorn (1708–54).[45] Sinnreich and Jambus persistently confuse *Sie* and *Ihnen* (e.g. 'ich bin erfreut, *Ihnen* zu sehen'), while Jambus's construction 'in Willens haben' infringes the Gottschedian prescription 'des Willens sein' by analogy with 'der Meynung sein' (but 'in Willens haben' is common in Leipzig books—e.g. Zedler's *Universal-Lexicon* (1732–54)).

This material demands caution—*Der Witzling* also attacks chancery style, the use of participles, and other features unlikely to be colloquial. Nevertheless, some impression of the relationship between the Gottschedian canons and actual spoken usage in Leipzig can be gained. We must next turn to the question of how other regional written and spoken forms differed from that prescription, which brings us to consider Gottsched's literary feud with the Swiss writers.

GOTTSCHED, THE SWISS, AND REGIONAL PRINTED NORMS

In 1738-9 Gottsched resigned from the *Deutsche Gesellschaft* in a dispute over the rhymes of Silesian poets; at about the same time he broke with the Swiss poet Albrecht von Haller (1708-77),[46] and in the 1740s and 1750s he was deserted by some of his own disciples (the *Bremer Beiträge* supporters) and involved in acrimonious feuds with the Swiss scholars Johann Jakob Bodmer (1698-1783) and Johann Jakob Breitinger (1701-76).[47] These essentially literary controversies concern us only peripherally here, but Bodmer and Haller had both been influenced by Gottsched in the external forms of their writings, since, like many countrymen before them, they had sought to adopt written traditions of Germany, and Leipzig in particular, in order to overcome the linguistic barriers imposed by their own Swiss German. For, in eighteenth-century Switzerland, dialect remained—as still today—the means of everyday communication, with French the language of polite conversation and literature among the middle classes, certainly at Zurich. Consequently, Swiss German was barely *literaturfähig*, and books were printed in a curious medley of dialect words and 'German' forms, riddled with French or Latin words that were often immediately glossed into German, so creating a kind of polyglot synonymy that smacked of the chancery. This language appeared quaint and old-fashioned. Haller actually called his poetry 'Swiss' because he was aware of the local character of the language: 'Aber ich bin ein Schweizer, die deutsche Sprache ist mir fremd ...'[48] In some parts of Switzerland, notably at Basle, Gottsched enjoyed considerable support, while the opposition to his literary ideas is based at Zurich. In 1740, even Bodmer acknowledges the superiority of Meissen pronunciation (but not of the vocabulary),[49] and in 1742 he revises his translation of Milton's *Paradise Lost* to give it a more German form.

Bodmer and Breitinger's moral weekly *Discourse der Mahlern* (1721-3) and Albrecht von Haller's *Versuch schweizerischer Gedichten* (1732) reveal some characteristics of this Swiss German language. The titles already show that we are dealing with a regional written norm (*regionale Schreibe*): the gen. plurals in *-n/-en* cannot be pure dialect, since the gen. case-form had long ago ceased to exist in the spoken language. Haller's poetry was immensely popular, and he continued to modify its forms towards the EMG patterns even after

his quarrel with Gottsched. The 1734 edition has some 200 alterations, of which about one-third involve noun morphology; the use of
für/vor was also adjusted along Gottschedian lines. Taking examples
both from Haller and the *Discourse*, some of the salient morphological features of this Swiss German are:

1. *Nouns.* (*a*) Pl. forms in *-en/-n*, e.g. *Äpfeln, Bäumen, Böcken,
Hunden, Lusten, Gedichten, Malern.* (*b*) Different gender, e.g. *die
Bach, der Last, das Quell.* (*c*) Forms with an additional, perhaps
hypercorrect, *-e*,[50] e.g. *der Moraliste, Prophete, Geschmacke, Schlaffe*
(NHG *der Schlaf*), *das Weibe.*

2. *Verbs.* Regional 'ablaut' grades in the strong class (again a mark
of printed language, since the pret. was rare in speech), e.g. *fund,
zwung*, later changed by Haller to *fand, zwang, ward* changed to
wurd, schwall changed to *schwoll*. But (the pres. tense-forms of)
strong verbs of the second ablaut class pose problems in Swiss.
Gottsched, in rare preference for an archaic, Lutheran form,
advocates the rounded diphthong */eu/*, e.g. *er fleug(e)t* (MHG
fliuget).[51] But Swiss dialect lacked the diphthongization of the
phoneme */[y:]/* (= MHG *iu*) and when speakers attempt to write/
speak HG they create hyper-literary forms like *beuten* ('bieten'),
schleussen ('schließen'), *zeuhen* ('ziehen') etc. The modern standard
forms have levelled out the vowel of the plural into the singular, while
the Swiss have transposed the singular root phoneme into its HG
equivalent and then levelled that into the plural and infinitive.

But most striking of all, and the subject of considerable literary
controversy, were the lexical differences between Swiss and German.
While the Swiss compromised with Leipzig over the external form of
language, they would not relinquish regional expressions and words
which heightened poetic effect and appealed to the emotions.
Gottsched, despite protestations to the contrary ((1748, 1762), 13, ed.
Penzl (1978), i. 49), treats language as a closed system which ought
ideally to approach the clarity of a philosophical language: the
grammarian's task is to establish the different linguistic forms and
their meanings. Indeed, 'Man muß aber auch nur alle Wörter seiner
Sprache kennen, und in seiner Gewalt haben, um sich deutlich
auszudrücken . . .'[52] (!), which implies an identifiable and finite
corpus of concepts which are mutually defining and within the
competence of at least some speakers. Synonymy is impossible, and
any synonyms ('gleichgültige Wörter') reflect abusage rather than

enrichment. For, as well as in the copiousness and clarity of its vocabulary, the true richness of any language lies in its brevity and expressiveness, i.e. in the number of *meanings* which can be distinguished, not in the superabundance of words: Gottsched sums this up in the phrase 'mit wenigen Worten, viele Gedanken entdecken' (Gottsched (1748, 1762), 15, ed. Penzl (1978), i. 51). Again, in his *Beobachtungen*, Gottsched observes:

Verwandte Bedeutungen sind . . . noch lange nicht einerley. Das eine Wort sagt mehr, das andre weniger, das eine ist edler, das andre verächtlicher, oder doch gemeiner; das eine bedeutet ganze Geschlechter oder Gattungen der Dinge, dahingegen das andre nur gewissen Arten derselben eigen ist. Eben so kann das eine wegen der Nebenbegriffe, die man damit zu verbinden gewohnt ist, eine höflichere, oder gefälligere Art des Ausdruckes abgeben: dagegen das andre etwas ungesitteter, bäuerischer und gröber herauskömmt.[53]

And in practice this amounts to a rigorous application of semantic-field theory: the precise determination of connotations and core meanings is possible only within a clearly defined corpus, and this is another reason (besides the traditional, patriotic reasons) why Gottsched penalizes foreign, regional, and archaic usage.[54] However, because he treats context superficially, ignores the possibility of partial semantic overlapping, and neglects the historical development of language and its potential for change, Gottsched once more fails to satisfy his contemporaries. In particular, his rejection of provincial and archaic forms led him into conflict with Bodmer and Breitinger. The ensuing *Literaturstreit* centred on the expressiveness of poetic vocabulary and aesthetic criteria; its linguistic implications were less obvious.

Bodmer, too, was a rationalist who recognized language as a system of conventions and opposed any diminution of its efficacy by homonyms or synonyms. But Bodmer sees the limitations of rationalism in the poetic sphere and argues for the primacy of the feelings and imagination: naïve and untutored individuals, unconversant with the rules of rhetoric, will often intuitively find appropriate expression for their emotions. Indeed, foreign, provincial, or archaic words could contribute to poetry precisely because they were richer in associations than the '*nervenlose* Sprache der sächsischen Magister'.[55] Both Bodmer and Haller were familiar with foreign words and phrases—especially from French—in everyday conversation in Switzerland, while the literary traditions of the area were naturally coloured by local forms. Moreover, the dialectal elements in Haller's poetry were necessary for local colour and dictated by the subject-matter; even for Saxon audiences the context generally made their meaning plain, while the very presence of these 'provincialisms' had an appeal akin to the picturesque in landscape painting. Finally, Bodmer's love of older German literature—the *Nibelungenlied* (edited as 'Chriemhild's Rache'), Wolfram's *Parzival* and *Willehalm*, and especially the Minnesinger in the Manesse manuscript, with its Swiss connection—made him aware that archaic expression might be revived to contribute to the forceful expression of emotion. In addition, the cultivation of the 'altschwäbische Sprache' was a patriotic act to the enhancement of the Swiss and south-western areas, as well as demonstrating Swiss superiority over the Saxon lands which, being of younger foundation, lacked any comparable cultural pedigree.

A vigorous, independent, and somewhat bizarre attack from the Swabian region was launched against Gottsched in 1755 by the dominican monk Pater Augustin Dornblüth (d. *c.*1760) from Gengenbach. The full title of his *Observationes* (1755) is in its length as 'baroque' as the outmoded linguistic models he proposes— essentially chancery usage of the seventeenth century[56]—and a subsequent edition seems to have been linguistically updated. The work could serve as no adequate basis for a grammar of the written 'book language', even if most of its features are found in other printed works from the same area. Perhaps the best one might say in defence of Dornblüth is that he was theorizing about how best to translate primarily religious writings into German. In the process, the style which he found suitably dignified and clear—by its preference for conjunctions and particles, encapsulations, and qualifying adjuncts —was chancery style. In this respect, too, he turned away from the Protestant traditions of the Lutheran Bible and its often almost conversational directness. At any event Dornblüth is unwilling and unable to adduce any strong regional literary traditions to support his claims for a more Swabian form of language. The same is true of the other Swabians, Friedrich Karl Fulda (1724–88) and Johann Nast (1722–1807),[57] who view the standard language as supra-dialectal and best codified by using older forms of language as criteria for correctness. This could not appeal to the generality of those eager to learn what was correct German without the need to study linguistic history, and attempts to modify the orthography on etymological lines were similarly doomed to failure: tinkering with spelling remained fatal for linguistic reformers, even after centralized bodies and legislation existed to promote their decisions. Still, these writers were in agreement in claiming that some cognizance should be taken of southern German.

In the south-east, Vienna was an important intellectual centre where a linguistic model might have developed. But here, too, Gottsched's grammar gained in popularity, and even those opposed to him seem to have accepted the superiority of the HG book language he was essentially defending. Johann Balthasar von Antesperg published a grammar entitled *Die Kayserliche Deutsche Grammatick* (Vienna, 1747), the year before Gottsched's *Sprachkunst* appeared. Antesperg's motives were patriotic and practical: to raise the quality of German letters, poetry, and eloquence in Austria, to combat undue foreign influence, and to allow the arts and sciences to be practised more rationally 'in dem eigenen Vernunftlicht (ich meyne in der eigenen Sprache)' (Antesperg (1747), preface, § 28). Antesperg corresponded with Gottsched and was a member of the Leipzig Deutsche Gesellschaft, and his work favoured the use of a printed, literary, and administrative standard language with few local features: he had little interest in dialect and makes no systematic reference to Austrian habits.[58] Even usage seemed acceptable to Antesperg only where it could be supported by etymological or morphological relationships: clearly he took his cue from Leipzig. By contrast, Johann Siegmund Valentin Popowitsch (1705-74), an irascible Slovene and an autodidact, was a vigorous opponent of Gottsched and was all the more disappointed by the *Sprachkunst* when it appeared in 1748 because Gottsched had discouraged him from producing a guide of his own to help Austrians avoid provincial errors ('stiriacismos und austriacismos') when they write HG.[59] Popowitsch never doubts that HG is the book language which must be cultivated and purified; spoken Austrian is provincial and care must be taken to avoid barbarisms and solecisms when writing HG. Moreover, Popowitsch sees that the schools provide the best way of inculcating the correct HG, which needs to be thoroughly learned, and he regrets that time spent on this endeavour is not taken seriously. But he also respects the antiquity of UG dialects in general compared with US, and sees analogies between them and English or Scandinavian; sometimes Austrian forms have better claim than Saxon ones to a place in HG. Popowitsch is also convinced that language is not separate from reality: 'Sachforschung' and

'Sprachforschung' go together. This promotes empiricism, and here too he differs from Gottsched, the abstract rationalist. Indeed, the *Untersuchungen vom Meere* (1750) contains observations of what Popowitsch has actually heard, details of spoken Austrian unavailable elsewhere. He notes, for example, that the pronunciations *kômmst*, *kômmt* (prescribed by Gottsched) are considered vulgar ('bâuerisch') in Austria, while in the towns *kommst, kommt* are normal (p. 416); similarly, the old declined forms of the numeral *zwo* and *zwen* (favoured by Gottsched) occur only in peasant speech (p. 420); the word *Arzt* is used in Austria only with negative associations ('mountebank', 'quack'), *Medicus* or even *Docter der Arzneykunst* being the normal terms (pp. 426-7). But Popowitsch strives to follow the HG form, even where he believes it to be wrong on etymological or observational grounds: hence he continues to write *Geschlecht*, although convinced that *Geschlâcht* is correct because of the connection with *schlagen*:

Man wûrde es als eine Vermessenheit ausgedeutet haben, wenn ein Steyermârker sich unterstûnde, Neuerungen in die Teutsche Sprache einzufûhren oder dieselben zu bestâtigen. Ich lief dem grôssern Haufen nach.[60]

Popowitsch's preoccupation with etymology and comparative grammar in the *Untersuchungen* leads to his misunderstanding the limited objectives of Gottsched's *Sprachkunst*, which is no universal grammar. But Popowitsch is surely correct in claiming that only an Austrian could fully appreciate the difficulties experienced by his countrymen when they attempt 'standard HG' (pp. 404–5). A Saxon had less scope for error since his language was closer to HG: 'Des Sachsen angebohrne Sprache, welche dem Hochteutschen sich mehr nahert . . .' (ibid.).

Looking back, Goethe recalls the paralysing and bewildering process of 'having the linguistic edges knocked off him' when he went to study at Leipzig in 1765; he generalizes from his own experience, talking of provinces that have suffered the linguistic tyranny of Meissen:

Jede Provinz liebt ihren Dialekt: denn er ist doch eigentlich das Element, in welchem die Seele ihren Atem schöpft. Mit welchem Eigensinn aber die Meißnische Mundart die übrigen zu beherrschen, ja eine Zeitlang auszuschließen gewußt hat, ist jedermann bekannt. Wir haben viele Jahre unter diesem pedantischen Regimente gelitten, und nur durch vielfachen Widerstreit haben sich die sämtlichen Provinzen in ihre alten Rechte wieder eingesetzt.[61]

This ought to remind us that the problem of a standard language was not, for the creative writer at least, so abstract as the arguments in which it was discussed.

KLOPSTOCK'S POETIC DICTION AND RATIONAL ORTHOGRAPHY: THE BANISHMENT OF BANALITY

Friedrich Gottlieb Klopstock (1724–1803) is commonly acknowledged to have revitalized German poetic language by emancipating writers from Gottschedian constraints of normative grammar and rationalist style. His verse epic *Der Messias* (1748–73), prompted by classical literature (especially Homer) and by Bodmer's translation of Milton's *Paradise Lost*, was written in hexameters, and figured prominently in contemporary linguistic and stylistic controversies. Klopstock's poetic achievement outweighs the theoretical and often polemical literature that surrounds it, and despite his indebtedness to other writers, notably Bodmer and Breitinger and the poets Haller and Pyra,[62] he had a decisive influence on the development of German poetic diction.[63] Klopstock writes from the heart and for the heart, while the grandeur of the subject-matter required an idiom far removed from everyday language. In other words, poetry was distinct from prose,[64] and its aesthetic value depended on its power to move the audience: the task now was to forge an evocative, expressive instrument, and in the process Klopstock aroused the ire of Gottsched and his supporters. In vocabulary, he uses archaic words drawn often from the Lutheran Bible, e.g. *Hain, Halle, hehr, Kü(h)r, Schöne* [NHG *Schönheit*], *Waller* 'pilgrim', and *Wonne*, while his religious terminology shows pietist influences, and leads to accusations that he is a free thinker or religious fanatic.[65]

Neologisms in particular proved offensive, and Klopstock creates them in two main ways: first, by forming new compounds; and secondly, by modifying already existing words, e.g. by changing or omitting prefixes and suffixes. New compounds were naturally striking, but also expressive in their compressed syntax, since they obviated the need for prepositional phrases or clauses: *Todesstille, Flammenwort, grabverlangend, das Grabheulen (Messias* (1780); earlier versions had *der Gräber Heulen).* Klopstock held that such compounding actually led to swifter thought, but his opponents found it obscure because of the often ambiguous syntactic relationships between the compounded elements. Klopstock was aware of the comic value of neologisms and employs them satirically, e.g. *Heiligerömischereichdeutschernazionsperioden, die Wasistdaswasdasistwashaftigkeit,* and *Clubbermunicipalguillotinoligokrat-Tierepublik.* To modify existing words, unstressed vowels might be omitted, e.g. 'er weißagt' und trank' (a practice reminiscent of the apocopated 'preterites' of the fourteenth century), or added, e.g. 'spiel*e*ten Knaben', 'glaub*e*test', 'führ*e*ten' (the last two are 'unhistorical' forms; MHG *gloubtest, fuorten*). Metrical requirements are important here, although Klopstock shows that the hexameter with its juxtaposition of two long or two short syllables (in German terms stressed/unstressed) was more versatile than the iambic measure, which forbade certain kinds of word order because of the alternation of stressed and unstressed syllables it required. Prefixes are also dropped, e.g. '*fernt* mich von dir' instead of *entfernt, Frischung* instead of *Erfrischung, heitert* instead of *erheitert, mürbt* instead of *zermürbt.* The Gottschedians, especially Gottsched's protégé Christoph Otto von Schönaich,[66] condemned this as 'Enthauptung', 'Worthenkerei', or 'Silbenschluckerei'. This 'Verfremdungsprinzip' (Schneider) removed words from their usual everyday form and increased their impact—in meaning and expressiveness but also by conciseness. The participles and formations in *-ung* also add dynamic force to the adjectival and nominal phrases, sometimes at the price of syntactic ambiguity. These and other devices, like the omission of the articles, asyndeton, and polysyndeton, and particularly word order, illustrate the ways in which poetic syntax too differs from that of everyday prose. Its special sentence structures are emphatic, raise expectation or surprise, or they may be simply decorative:

Unvermuthetes, scheinbare Unordnung, schnelles Abbrechen des Gedankens erregte Erwartung. Alles dieß setzt die Seele in eine Bewegung, die sie für die Eindrücke empfänglicher macht.[67]

Understandably, Gottsched, for whom the language of poetry and prose was essentially the same and, moreover, guided by reason rather than emotive force, could not countenance the poetry of Klopstock with its 'associative syntax', where the grammatical relations emerge often from context rather than from particles, conjunctions, or word order.

This recalls the 'looser', semantic-based syntax of medieval German poetry (see Chapter VI), just as the heightened significance of the individual *Machtwort* can be seen as a survival of the seventeenth-century emblematic use of vocabulary and imagery (see Chapter VII). Indeed, Klopstock was sometimes compared with the baroque poet Lohenstein, who stood for the bombastic literary style to which Gottsched was utterly opposed; *Klopstockianismus*, like *miltonisches* or *hallerisches Dunkel* (a key insult in the age of Enlightenment), was regarded as positively anti-grammatical, a negation of normative and prescriptive approaches to language and literature alike. We shall not here consider further the ramifications of that particular stylistic dispute, although it had implications for grammar too. Instead, we turn to Klopstock's views on orthography, which take up the issue of the best form of German and result in a phonetic orthography of great skill and elegance, well suited to the declamation of the author's poetry but much maligned, despite its rational basis. Here we see Klopstock the Enlightenment thinker unafraid to break with the spelling conventions of his day—more or less those of Gottsched—in the interest of relating letters to sounds.

In some respects, Klopstock's orthographical interest was unfortunate. It stimulated other less able and consistent reformers, so that by 1783 Wieland speaks of 'eine Art von Orthographischer Influenza' that has reached epidemic proportions;[68] and it discredited him by recalling Zesen, another link with the baroque seventeenth century.

Klopstock's total absorption with poetry[69] leads him to devise a perfectly phonetic orthography for the purpose of declamation. Other theorists had paid lip-service to the criterion *Schreib wie du sprichst!*, but they promptly introduced extraneous elements, like etymology, analogy, or tradition (*Gebrauch*, *Gewohnheit*), which proved incompatible with this principle, while Klopstock maintained rigorously that spelling was 'ein Ding fürs Ohr und nicht fürs Auge'.[70] This stance enabled him to distinguish, where others had not, between *Sprachgebrauch*, in which pronunciation is paramount, even tyrannical, and *Schreibgebrauch*, which is a heterogeneous collection of conventions subject to historical and arbitrary developments in a way that the pronunciation is not. Even allowing for the weaknesses in this extreme formulation, it freed Klopstock from the trammels of traditional spelling and allowed him to innovate where phonetic accuracy demanded. In modern terms, linguistic form is represented in the primary substance which is sound, and this phonic substantiation can be rendered in spelling: 'Di Aussprache ist

geredete Sprąche, und das Schreiben geschrịbne Aussprąche' (Klopstock (1779–80), 389). Evidently, some canonical pronunciation must
be presumed, viz. 'di richtige Aussprąche', which Klopstock first
seeks in the US/Meissen area, partly modified by his own, albeit
'purified', pronunciation. Finally, by a subtle blend of traditional
orthographical and phonetic interpretation he reaches an original
and interesting compromise:

1. In certain areas pronunciations are heard which are not reflected
in the most generally accepted written forms of German, e.g. the UG
diphthongs /oa/, /ie/, /ua/, or the medial /[ʃ]/ in *bischt* or *ischt* (NHG
bist, ist).

2. Conversely, some very general spellings, like those of the
rounded vowels /eu/, /ö/, /ü/, or of the consonant /g/, are not
pronounced in certain areas, notably in EMG dialects, including US
and Silesian. Distinctions between voiced and voiceless consonants
initially are not upheld in either UG or EMG dialects: /d/ ~ /t/ and
/b/ ~ /p/, etc.

3. However, in certain other areas one hears the second set of
sounds but not the first and it is here that the basis for standard
pronunciation must be sought. These areas are in fact the LG regions
where the HG book language had in any case been acquired as a
'second' or 'elaborated code', hence the preservation of distinctions
founded in spelling.

In brief, Klopstock's phonetic orthography describes 'Hochdeutsch
in niederdeutschem Munde' although he avoids the vexed question
of the extent to which a supra-regional HG book language (in the
sense of spelling) actually existed. Certainly, correct pronunciation
('di richtige Aussprąche') is distinct from regional accents ('Aus-
sprecherei'), and by this token US speech is provincial. Taking the
basic features required for the canonical pronunciation as broadly
recognizable in the contemporary printed usage, Klopstock next
regularizes that pronunciation's symbols and their distribution,
aiming at economy and generality. Among the fundamental rules to
be applied as exclusively as possible, regardless of the consequences
for traditional spelling, we find:

(1) 'man schreibe nicht was man nicht spricht';
(2) 'kein laut sol durch merere buchstaben ausgedrüket werden';
(3) 'ein jeder buchstab sol nicht mer als einen laut anzeigen'.

Consequently, some symbols that are inconsistent or of foreign origin can be replaced: ⟨ei⟩ replaces ⟨ai⟩ because it is more common; ⟨f⟩ replaces ⟨v⟩ where voiceless spirant is intended; ⟨qu⟩ is simplified to ⟨q⟩; the symbols ⟨ph⟩ and ⟨th⟩ are replaced (e.g. *Orthographie → ortografi*), as are ⟨y⟩ and ⟨c⟩. But ⟨sch⟩ and ⟨ch⟩ are retained. Vowel quantity is indicated (alas inconsistently) by giving long vowels in closed syllables a subscript loop (e.g. ⟨gewǫnlich⟩, ⟨wir̨⟩), and by marking short vowels in open syllables[71] by doubling the following consonant, so that the oppositions in the words *Kahn ≠ Kahne ≠ kann ≠ Kanne* (closed long; open long; closed short; open short) are conveyed as: ⟨kan̨⟩, ⟨kane⟩, ⟨kan⟩, ⟨kanne⟩. The 'stenographic' forms proposed to cope with morphophonemic alteration, with metrical requirements, and with the informality of speech were highly controversial. Where simplifying *sitzen → ⟨sizen⟩* was acceptable, the change of *flieht's* into ⟨fliz̨⟩ or of *Glücks* into ⟨glüx⟩ was not. As the aphorist Georg Christoph Lichtenberg (1742–99) remarked somewhat scurrilously:

Was die Engländer in der Füsik, die Franzosen in der Metafüsik sind, sind die Deutschen unstreitig in der *Ortokrafi*. Das Süstem, das uns H(err) K(lopstock) hierüber gegeben hat, ist vortreflich. Fürz gleich nicht überall Überzeugung bei sich, so fürz doch auf Einigkeit, und hilfz nichz, so schatz doch auch nichz.[72]

Klopstock's orthography was employed in several of his works, notably the essay on 'Rechtschreibung' and the 1780 Altona edition of the *Messias*,[73] but it was much attacked, and he eventually dropped it even from his correspondence. Nevertheless, it constitutes a considerable intellectual achievement in the best Enlightenment tradition. Alas, the time was not ripe for Klopstock's 'phonetic alphabet', partly because the study of phonetics was still based on antique tradition rather than observation—Klopstock mocks Adelung for his unsuccessful German designations for labial nasals (*Mampflaut*) and velars (*Gacklaut*)—partly because Klopstock was isolated, contradicted by other more extreme and certainly less discerning orthographical reformers. As a result, Klopstock appeared as wayward as Zesen, and his readers turned in relief to the hardening orthographical norms proposed by Gottsched and largely adopted by a prosaic, unimaginative, but thorough and observant grammarian, Adelung.

JOHANN CHRISTOPH ADELUNG (1732–1806): THE GRAMMARIAN VS. THE LITTÉRATEURS[74]

Adelung exemplifies the split between littérateur and linguist which marks the end of grammatical continuity from the seventeenth-century language societies; indeed, he ventures to deny writers any serious contribution to the establishment and refining of a standard language.[75] Language is for him a social phenomenon, a vehicle for the clearest possible communication: 'Die wahre und einige Absicht der Sprache ist die möglichst leichte Verständlichkeit in dem gesellschaftlichen Leben . . .'[76]

Dispassionate prose ('kaltblütige Prosa') constitutes the norm, while poetry is irrational and obscure, certainly not the most essential purpose ('Absicht') either of language or social existence, but a mere attendant embellishment ('eine Nebenzierde'), properly inferior to higher qualities.[77]

Not unnaturally, therefore, Adelung attempts to codify actual usage, seeking the basis for standard German in the everyday social intercourse of the upper classes in southern Saxony. This constituted, in his view, the highest form of German from the most cultivated and flourishing province in Germany; it was the product of historical development and, purified still further from the imperfections of speech, the language followed by the best literary writers:

. . . unser gegenwärtiges Hochdeutsch, d.i. diejenige deutsche Mundart, deren sich alle Deutsche Schriftsteller von Geschmack in ihren Schriften bedienen, ist nichts anders, als die gewöhnliche Gesellschaftssprache Obersachsens in den obern Classen, welche von hier zu den Schriftstellern ausgegangen ist, und sich von der Schriftsprache in nichts unterscheidet, als daß diese mehrere Sorgfalt, Aufmerksamkeit und Auswahl nicht allein verstattet, sonder auch erfordert, als der schnell vorüber gehende mündliche Ausdruck.[78]

The polemics unleashed by this standpoint (the most important by Wieland in his *Teutscher Merkur* of 1782) cannot concern us in detail, but three aspects are important: (1) the relation of HG to a particular province; (2) the role of authors in establishing and improving the standard; (3) the nature of the spoken *Gesellschaftssprache* of the upper classes in Upper Saxony.

From the outset terminological ambiguity vitiates Adelung's statements about the kind of language he is describing in his grammatical and lexicographical work. In a broad sense *Hochdeutsch* covers all southern dialects as opposed to the northern ones, *hoch* here referring in the first instance to the geographically higher terrain, with the added associations of greater sophistication and refinement. But, more specifically and most usually, HG is identified with Meissen or US dialect:

> Allein im engern und gewôhnlichsten Verstande bezeichnet dieses Wort [*sc.* Hochdeutsch] die meißnische oder obersächsische Mundart, so fern sie seit der Reformation die Hofsprache der Gelehrsamkeit geworden ist, und durch die Schriftsteller aller Mundarten theils viele Erweiterungen, theils manche Einschränkungen erfahren hat. In diesem Verstande ist gegenwârtiges Wôrterbuch ein Wôrterbuch der hochdeutschen Mundart.[79]

These views were unexceptionable in seeming to grant authors the ability to modify the form of the current educated koine, which is also held to contain features from southern and northern areas and therefore to be less easy to regulate than a more homogeneously based idiom. But in time Adelung rejects the role of authors as a mechanism for changing and refining language and increasingly equates the standard educated usage with the speech of the upper classes in southern Saxony. He seems here to be guided by two main principles: his awareness of the historical importance of US, which made him loth to see it adulterated; and his fundamental view of language as living speech, not to be divorced from the group of speakers whose usage shaped it.

For Adelung social and linguistic history reflect the progress of civilization (*Culturgeschichte*), and he adopts an almost medieval view that culture and taste move from one province to another in the course of time—a *translatio gustus*. With the ascendancy of Charlemagne, the earliest linguistic pattern had been the old Frk. dialect, then the cultural centre moved to the Swabian area during the Hohenstaufen period, but this 'altschwâbische Sprache' was in turn superseded from the sixteenth century, when the southern parts of Saxony began to flourish in technology, trade, book production, and even population growth, providing the foundations for prosperity and linguistic cultivation with a resultant literary flowering. The mechanism for the transfer of 'culture' remains vague, however, and Adelung avoids the question of what, if any, continuity existed between the different cultural regions.[80] In any event, neither the authors nor any individual could resist the historical forces purifying taste and shaping language, and in the same spirit Adelung sees the grammarian's role as primarily descriptive:

Er [sc. der Sprachlehrer] ist nicht Gesetzgeber der Nation, sondern nur der Sammler und Herausgeber der von ihr gemachten Gesetze . . . Er stellt die Sprache so dar, wie sie wirklich ist, nicht wie sie seyn kônnte, oder seiner Einbildung nach seyn sollte.[81]

But Adelung's description of a particular form of language actually, of course, constitutes a prescription which was unacceptable to fellow grammarians on theoretical grounds and attacked by authors who did not share his aesthetic preferences.

Adelung insists that the authors should follow the usage of the most cultivated province, but was a good enough observer to see that the literary experiments of his own day often did not accord with what he regarded as correct. His dictionary had begun to appear in the same year as Goethe's *Werther* (1774), while the 'Storm and Stress' writers and their imitators were producing literature in many styles which seemed detrimental to linguistic unity. Adelung recognizes that languages may decay and declares the most uniformly refined literature to have been written during the period 1740–60 by writers from the US area: he selects Gellert in particular, but also Weisse, Johann Elias Schlegel, Rabener, Cramer, Giseke, and Ebert, in fact largely the members of the anti-Gottsched *Bremer Beiträge* group.[82]

If authors are left to do with language as they will, Adelung feels that they introduce arbitrary innovations which will eventually lead to barbarism; even in 1774 literary fashions are held responsible for the rapid change of language in towns as opposed to the conservatism of rural dialects: 'Die so genannte hôhere und poetische Schreibart arbeitet unaufhôrlich an dem Untergange der Mundart des tâglichen Umganges.'[83] So a HG dialect that is merely a 'book language' will inevitably be subservient to fashion, a 'Sklavin der Mode'. Language as a social phenomenon develops according to the spread of constructions by analogy, but such analogy must, for Adelung, relate to a language system, not to the individual's own whim. The authors' freedom to innovate must be limited to experiments against the background of the higher authority of the spoken language in its most cultivated form. However, the examples of objectionable features stemming from the authors' interference in language are predominantly from orthography or morphology,[84] not style—

e.g. variables like *Gebet* for *Gebeth, er weist* for *er weiß*, preterites like *schnid, sod, schrit, sof* for *schnitt, sott, schritt, soff,* etc.— (such variables persist even till the end of the nineteenth century). Wieland particularly disputed Adelung's claim that authors ever necessarily followed the speech of the upper classes of the most flourishing province, asserting that important French authors were more conversant with the classics than the court, while, even after 1760, German could still be refined and developed by authors; and, furthermore, not all the best authors of the seventeenth and eighteenth centuries had resided in southern Saxony—some had even moved away from it. Adelung gave no adequate reply to the first point, but in any case, literature was of secondary importance for him and was, like language itself, subordinated to the authority of taste; he was not legislating for artistic writing or attempting to restrict genius.

Adelung regards real, 'living' language as spoken, and the products of authors are dead language if they are not rooted in speech. The authors cannot have access to the proper systematic 'analogies' through which language changes unless they work within a social framework, i.e. follow a particular spoken form of German. In this respect, Adelung is a socio-linguist born before his time, but the modernity of his view that 'Die Sprache ist ganz das Werk des engern gesellschaftlichen Lebens'[85] is counterbalanced by his implicit assumptions that it is a closed, well-defined system which is relatively static. This very 'staticity' is corroboration of Adelung's having actually codified written/printed usage, the *Büchersprache* rather than speech; so he is closer to the authors than he admits, and this is doubtless one reason for the enduring success of his dictionary.

On the issue of the upper-class language of southern Saxony Adelung was again criticized: the class boundaries were difficult to determine, while the actual pronunciation even of the most refined speakers had certain US characteristics which were not those of the standard Adelung was prescribing (see pp. 318–20 above for Leipzig colloquial). J. C. C. Rüdiger,[86] for example, listed a series of US solecisms which Adelung either flatly denied that the best speakers at Leipzig used, or else dismissed as momentary distortions of speech which did not detract from US's inherent closeness to the structure of standard HG. Rüdiger's US 'idiotikon' (Rüdiger (1783), 61–134) is difficult to evaluate at this remove of time, but some forms can hardly have been used in polite circles (e.g. calls to attract cows: *Motsch!*

Motsch!, p. 102). Words like *Aschkuchen* [NHG *Topfkuchen*], *die Demse* [= *schwüle Hitze*], *die Glander* 'a slide', *glandern* 'to slide', *Holdersprossen* 'freckles', *kalmen/galmen* 'doze', and the child's term *Pusekatze* 'pussy' strike one as regional; others, like *eete peteete* 'fussy', 'fastidious', *grunzen* used in the sense of *klagen, weinen*, and *Maul* for 'mouth' seem colloquial; a few words, e.g. *kuttentoll* 'boisterous', seem to have obscene connotations;[87] yet other words seem unexceptionably standard nowadays: *Behagen, bimmeln, grell*. In brief, eighteenth-century vocabulary is difficult to assess stylistically, and Adelung's attempts to clarify the position are welcome, despite their inadequacy.

Still, Rüdiger's phonetic observations reinforce what has already been noted about Leipzig colloquial—an inability to distinguish voiced from voiceless initial stops, or between rounded and unrounded vowels, and a preference for medial spirants etc.,[88] e.g. *Bôwel = Pöbel, Kinste = Künste, ein Amt begleiten = ein Amt bekleiden* (p. 135). Rüdiger notes further some difference in quantities: *an, nach, gern, kucken, Tobak* have long vowels (*Tobāk*), while *Boden, Feder, Stube, gestohlen, Distel*, and *dir* are short (p. 136). Stress patterns also differ: *Mittágsbrod, Brantwéinschank* (p. 136). Even more noteworthy, Rüdiger questions the monolithic status of US and declares that the language spoken at Halle differs from that of Leipzig; other scholars criticized Adelung for tending to Dresden pronunciation in his treatment of some *e* sounds as open, e.g. in *bêben, dêhnen, gêben*, where ⟨ê⟩ indicates long open [ɛ:] (*ä*).[89]

At this remove of time, it is difficult to decide on which side truth lies, but mostly Adelung is held to be wrong: for example, when he declares that the best US-speakers separate initial voiced and voiceless consonants. Here his own Pomeranian background may have led him astray, but conceivably, several decades after Gottsched, printed/written language was impinging on spoken to the extent that some individuals were making conscious efforts to make their pronunciation accord with written usage.[90] At any event, Adelung's attention to spoken, not written, language and the emphasis on upper social classes must have appealed to schools and schoolteachers in providing a codification of plain language without philosophical or literary pretensions.

The importance of Adelung's grammatical writings and their practical value emerges from the many editions they reached during his lifetime, to say nothing of reprints after his death, translations, and influence on grammars and dictionaries produced by and for foreigners.[91] His school grammar (1781) reached its fifth edition in 1806; an extract ran to three editions by 1800, and an enlarged version (1782) provided a scholarly commentary. Other works, also reprinted, were devoted to orthography (1788) and style (1785). But most important of all was the dictionary itself (1774-86), which Adelung had been commissioned to write by the printer Breitkopf after Gottsched's death.[92] Adelung proved well-equipped for the task both by disposition and circumstances, for after losing his job as a teacher he was for a long time a free-lance writer, translator, popularizer, and compiler of school textbooks. His precarious existence furthered a talent for assimilating vast amounts of material and reducing it to fluent generalizations, while the range of his writing—from current affairs to diplomatics, from metallurgy to histories of navigation and of the Jesuits, brief surveys of the principal arts and sciences, potted biographies of famous men of letters, and even a chronicle of human folly[93]—sharpened his awareness of German's different registers, especially the non-artistic ones. He also pursued interests in the history of the German language, its dialects and its earlier literature, and in the English language (1783-96), while his last work, *Mithridates* (1806), compares versions of the Lord's Prayer in as many languages as possible.

The dictionary is practical and 'synchronic': ostensibly based on the upper-class speech in southern Saxony it provides information for the 'ordinary user' in an accessible manner. Thus, the words are arranged alphabetically, not according to abstruse etymological principles involving *Stammwörter*, or roots. In accordance with its title it gives grammatical details of pronunciation, stress, morphology, gender, word-formation, and even constructions, and the second edition (1793-1801) uses an asterisk ('ein vorschimmernder Unglücksstern', according to Voss!—see below, p. 340) to indicate archaic or unusual words, and a dagger for low or vulgar ones. Moreover, the dictionary was 'critical', and in particular its stylistic and semantic pronouncements are of great interest. Adelung classifies expressions according to their rank (*Würde*) into five groups:

1. die höhere oder erhabene Schreibart; 2. die edle; 3. die Sprechart des gemeinen Lebens und vertraulichen Umganges; 4. die niedrige, und 5. die ganz pöbelhafte.[94]

The first level is that of poets, who often elaborate and embellish by importing archaic or provincial words, phrases, and constructions, principally from UG (probably a reference to Bodmer and the Swiss): Adelung is not much concerned with it. The fifth level is beneath the grammarian's consideration except in special circumstances, and the fourth is considered only because it commonly occurs on the stage and in comic writing. Proverbs too are entirely rejected as vulgar, along with other 'schmutzige Blümchen des großen Haufens'. Level 2, a 'Schreibart' for formal purposes, and level 3, a 'Sprechart' for daily communication, remain—although Adelung includes examples also from the Luther Bible or from older authors where they are current ('gangbar'). However, his stylistic entries in the dictionary do not consistently relate words to these five levels, whose characteristics are nowhere fully discussed; he soon abandoned this over-simple yet inflexible scheme.[95]

Adelung did not exclude expressions of which he disapproved: instead, he qualified them as not part of HG; among words belonging to the coarsest level are *brunzen* 'to urinate' and *scheißen*.[96] Typical of the more prudish entries, the sg. *die Brust* is said to be acceptable, whereas the pl. *die Brüste* is best avoided; on the other hand, in the 'anständige Schreibart' even animals are equipped with *Brüste*, rather than the usual *Euter*; by contrast, the 'basest dialects' apply the words *Dutten*, *Titten*, *Zitzen*, and *Bietze* to human breasts.

Among archaic words he lists *Abenteuer*, *Buhle*, *Degen* 'warrior',[97] *Fehde*, *Gau*, *hehr*, *Minne*, *Recke*, and *Wonne*, objecting particularly to attempts to revive the last (also in compounds like *Wonnetag* and *Wonnetod*). Sometimes archaic forms survive in poetic use, e.g. *Harm*, *wallen*, and *Woge*, while *Mahl* 'meal' is archaic, pl. *Mähler*, with an alternative poetic and UG pl. form *Mahle*. The provincial or dialectal expressions, again, sometimes overlap with poetic or archaic categories; frequently Adelung equates UG words with poetic style and was understandably criticized for so doing. However, he did not have suitable dialect dictionaries for the southern areas at his disposal, and consequently the ultimate objective of a truly complete German dictionary presenting material from all regions and periods was not yet attainable.[98] Among LG words are *Ärger* (for *Ärgernis*), *binnen*, *Bucht*, *dicht* 'close', *düster*, *ebben/Ebbe*, *flott*, *hapern*, *Koje*, *Mischmasch*, *schmuck*, *Wirrwarr*; while the following are UG: *Ahn*, *behend*, *deuten*, *dumpf*, *förderlich*, *gemeinsam*, *gestalten*, *Hader*, *kosten*, *kostspielig*, *lugen*, *unbefangen*.[99]

Adelung treated foreign borrowing with tolerance; since literary

German concerned him less than speech, his sensibilities were not offended by foreign words which formed part of polite conversation and of technical and scholarly writing.

Words under 'F' ((1774–86), ii, cols. 243 ff.) include derivations from *Form* relating to bookbinding (*Format, formiren, Formrahmen*), metallurgy, goldsmithing, and mining (*Formbank, Formbrot, Formerz, Formflasche, Formpresse, Formsand, Formspath*); military usage (*sich formiren*), wig-making (*Formkugel*), and so forth. For this he was taken to task by Joachim Heinrich Campe (1746–1818), who published a supplement to Adelung's dictionary listing foreign words and attempting to replace them by German ones from dialects, older periods of the language, or even by neologisms of his own devising.[100] Adelung was himself no enemy of neologisms, provided always that they conform to the regular patterns of German word-formation: in fact, he omits many compounds from his dictionary, arguing that German had an infinite capacity to create them, and that most were in any case perfectly comprehensible. Indeed, his dictionary contains entries for various suffixes which seem to him particularly productive; this again squares with his approach to language as a functioning system governed by analogy (*Sprachgebrauch*).

The presentation of meanings in the dictionary is also functional: Adelung attempts a definition of the word, shows by examples how it is used, assesses its stylistic level, and gives a brief etymology. Sometimes he differentiates it from near 'synonyms', and this desire to draw distinctions leads to errors, as when he claims that the suffix -*ig* denotes a property belonging to a concept, while -*icht* (-*lich*) denotes similarity:[101] actually, both are in most instances phonetic variants. Hardly surprisingly, Adelung's definitions of the meanings of words are least effective when he deals with abstract or poetic vocabulary, and this only enhanced his reputation as a pedant; but he does give valuable definitions of the many technical terms which occur, and they do at least reflect contemporary usage as Adelung understood it, not some hazy etymological 'original' meaning.

More work needs to be done on the influence of Adelung's dictionary on individual authors. Klopstock, Goethe, Schiller, Voss, Wieland, Campe, E. T. A. Hoffmann, and Heine all know and use it, and some give it grudging praise: Schiller refers to it as 'dieses Orakel'[102] and Wieland supposedly nailed it to his desk to keep it handy.[103]

But the poets and authors are not the best authorities to follow when assessing Adelung's importance for German grammar and lexicography, since they could hardly approve wholeheartedly of an approach to language which worked within practical limitations and did not include the whole range of German, the older authors, the dialects, and the most recent literary giants: consequently, most refuse to assess Adelung in terms of his own aims. So he was criticized persistently for his special use of the term *Hochdeutsch* and for neglecting the best authors. Johann Heinrich Voss (1751–1826), in a vitriolic review (written, as it happened, using Schiller's copy of the dictionary, which had been lent to him by Goethe!), attacks Adelung's 'Idiotikon des galanten Obersachsens' as '. . . ein maaßgebendes Gemisch von neumodischer Kathedersprache, und ceremonienhafter, halb höfischer, halb kleinstädtischer Galanterie'[104] But Voss and the others, for all their brilliance and good taste, were facing the wrong way on the threshold of an era in which literature and the circles that produced it were to be considerably reduced in importance, so far as their influence on literacy was concerned. The growth of 'democracy' and emergence of urban proletariats, the industrial revolution and national unification all furthered linguistic standardization by making literacy essential for strata of society hitherto denied a voice. The fairly homogeneous literary standard of the Enlightenment was not, stylistically speaking, adequate for the masses, and those who cultivated it in the nineteenth century were often producing escapist or sentimental pap. Instead, the writers had to discover the lower classes and their lives and language: the *Pöbel* which had remained neglected and beyond consideration in the late eighteenth century, where the term *Volk* denoted an idealized and comfortingly abstract collective body, now constituted a group whose language and way of life increasingly attracted notice (see Chapter IX). Adelung admittedly claimed to draw on the speech of the upper classes, and was in other respects conservative, pedantic, and simplistic: but he had grasped that the literature of his age did not represent linguistic reality as manifested in most everyday social communication. Moreover, Adelung had actually assimilated the scholarship and insight of his predecessors, embodying it in sober and sensible form in his grammars and dictionaries. That his theory was occasionally weak or inconsistent is a minor blemish beside the intelligent, practical presentation.

Even Adelung's contemporaries recognized that his practice and theory diverged: 'Ueberhaupt ist er in der Ausûbung richtig und fehlt nur ein wenig in der feinen Theorie, die auf jene nur selten Einfluß hat.'[105] His grammars and dictionary were practical guides to a fairly neutral German which could pass as a 'non-literary' standard, a starting-point for many nineteenth-century grammarians and teachers who were more concerned with education and literacy than with art.

The relationship between Adelung's grammatical pronouncements and the codification of non-literary German in the nineteenth century, especially in schools, needs further examination, for it is here that his main contribution to the development of the German language must be sought. In brief, Adelung had become the 'Duden' of the late eighteenth century, an institution who had—paradoxically in view of his own theories—achieved the status of oracle and legislator on a whole range of linguistic issues. The individual could after all shape language, even a humble grammarian who claimed only to describe, not prescribe.

SELECT BIBLIOGRAPHY

On the development of German literary style, but with useful chapters on Gottsched's grammatical contribution, see the excellent study in Blackall (1959/1978).

THE GRAMMARIANS

Jellinek (1913–14).
Kaiser (1930).
Nerius (1967).

Socin (1888) [has a good section on language in the eighteenth century, pp. 360 ff.].

GOTTSCHED'S THEORETICAL WRITINGS

See the reprints in the series 'Ausgaben Deutscher Literatur des XV. bis XVIII. Jahrhunderts', edd. Hans-Gert Roloff and Käthe Kahlenberg, specifically:

Birke and Birke (1973) [edition of the *Dichtkunst*].
Mitchell (1978) [commentary on the *Dichtkunst*].
Penzl (1978) [edition of the *Sprachkunst*].
Penzl (1980) [commentary on the *Sprachkunst*].

See also:

Penzl (1975*b*).
Penzl (1977).

Rieck (1972).

FRAU GOTTSCHED

Richel (1973).

ADELUNG

Henne (1968*a*).
Henne (1968*b*).
Jellinek (1913–14), i. 184–385.
Müller (1903).

Raumer (1870), esp. 204–42 [Adelung's contribution to syntax is especially praised on pp. 227–9].
Scherer (1875).
Spiridonova (1963) [not used here].

ADELUNG, CAMPE, AND LEXICOGRAPHY OF THE PERIOD

Henne (1975).

EMG AND US DIALECT IN THE EIGHTEENTH CENTURY

Eichler and Bergmann (1967).
Grosse (1955).

Henne (1968*a*).
Putschke (1973).

For Haller see Siegrist (1967), and for Bodmer and Breitinger see Bender (1973).

CHAPTER IX

THE MODERN PERIOD (1800–1945) (I): UNITY AND VARIETY

THE last two chapters of this book examine the German language in the Modern Period (1800–1945). Chapter IX discusses the various forms and styles of German and also their changing interrelationships which are conditioned by historical and social factors. Chapter X treats the internal, semantic structure of German, neglected up to now, combining accounts of purism, political language, and German under the National Socialist regime, with the underlying issues of the links between language and life and between language and thought which are key problems in linguistic history.

The present chapter outlines the limits and subdivisions of the period 1800–1945 in more detail against the background of important historical, political, and cultural changes which affect the German language. Next, the establishing of standards of spelling and pronunciation provides a basis for comparison with the other main varieties of German, including 'dialects'—rural, urban, and regional—and technical and group languages. Such linguistic varieties can in theory be taken to constitute the state of a language at any given time:

Die Einheitlichkeit der Sprachsituation einer Gesellschaft läßt sich aber auch als ein stabiles Gleichgewicht, bestehend aus einer Vielzahl von unterschiedlichen Sprachvarietäten, beschreiben.[1]

However, the relationships between varieties are not stable or static, either objectively or subjectively, for the varieties themselves change, while the individual's contact with, and perception of, the various styles of language differs throughout his life. Taking such styles in the absolute, the history of modern German shows how the mobility of labour and improved communications have made inroads into the use of dialect. Indeed, dialects and technical languages are now largely separate, although in the early nineteenth century they were still closely linked (e.g. LG and the language of littoral fishermen or peasant farmers).

THE PERIOD 1800–1945

In default of any obvious and widespread phonological or other linguistic changes like the Second Sound Shift or 'NHG' diphthongization, the Modern Period must be established on extra-linguistic grounds. The debate about the nature of the best or standard German language (*Hochdeutsch*) continued to bear upon the distribution of variables within already established literary and written traditions: consequently, regional phonological and morphological developments in the spoken language were effectively debarred from consideration. The syntax of this literary standard remained also fairly stable, and authors from the beginning of the nineteenth century remained the models for grammarians of the beginning of the twentieth[2]—although some constructions became less common and were felt as archaic, choice, or stilted outside special contexts. While the sounds, forms, and structures of German were linked to the relatively closed literary variant, the vocabulary, being an open system, changed rapidly. However, even groups of words are seldom sufficiently important or general to periodize a language except from periods where the surviving linguistic evidence is sparse and more or less homogeneous.[3] So, to periodize, we fall back on historical factors which impinge on language—wars, revolutions, population growth, and movements, technological change, the emergence of new classes, improved communications, and so forth—developments often commented upon in literature and art, long before linguists discussed them.

By about 1800 the egalitarian ideas and vocabulary of the French Revolution had become familiar in Germany through reports in the

German journals and press. A few years later Napoleon introduced democratic administrative reforms in the territories gained by his successful campaigns, and he considerably reduced the number of absolutist states, so weakening further the power of the aristocracy.[4] This external French influence persisted through a growing Francophobia and nationalism and through the gradual increase in political awareness among almost all sectors of the population, which was intermittently fuelled by revolutionary protest of several different kinds. Indeed, the period might be subdivided according to revolutions and their linguistic repercussions in the growth of political vocabularies, party names, and slogans (see Chapter X), for in 1830 and again in 1848 and in 1918 Germany experienced revolutionary upheaval with considerable political and social effects, particularly regarding the polarization of public opinion. At other times, wars encouraged political and cultural nationalism and xenophobia, accelerated communication between speakers of different dialects, and added new terms to military language and soldiers' slang which, because of large-scale conscription, reached into general everyday usage. In such ways the Napoleonic wars of 1805-15, the wars against Denmark and Austria in the 1860s and against France in 1870-1, the First World War (1914-18), and the Second World War (1939-45) have all left traces in the German language.[5]

Less dramatically, but no less radically, the improvements in communications broke down the geographical barriers by bringing people from all areas into contact. In the nineteenth century the railway, and in the twentieth the motor car, aeroplane, wireless, telephone, and film newsreels destroyed the insularity of life in the provinces—as had the reduction in the number of absolutist states, the removal of customs and tariff barriers by the Customs Union (*Zollverein*) of 1834, and political unification in 1871. The establishing of the Second Empire also created the political basis for economic growth and industrialization, whose social effects included new styles of work and living, and increases in the size of towns. Here too linguistic levelling favoured the use of non- or substandard colloquial languages between speakers from differing dialect backgrounds. The standard language itself gained in prestige as a vehicle for educated and polite communication, and consequently as a means for social betterment. At the same time, in the north at least, social linguistic barriers were strengthened, and new ones created by technical and specialist jargons used at the industrial work-place.

The population increased by almost as much again in the last quarter of the nineteenth century as in the first three-quarters:[6]

Year:	1816	1846	1870	1880	1890	1900	(1915)
Population:	25m.	34m.	41m.	45m.	49m.	56m.	(68m.)

Increase 1816–70: 16 million; increase 1870–1900: 15 million.

Moreover, the Imperial Constitution of 1871 guaranteed individuals of all classes the right to change their domicile (*Freizügigkeit*: Articles 3 and 4), which must have significantly swelled town populations, again with social and linguistic effects. The mobility of the masses can be seen from the records: in one year in Berlin there were 235,611 new registrations, and 178,654 deregistrations.[7]

The growth of urban population occurred at different rates, although a marked acceleration—a doubling, in fact—is evident in the last quarter of the century, as a comparison of five towns shows (Table 13).[8] Berlin dominated all other towns, and in 1895 already had a population of 1,680,000 (2,120,000 including the suburbs), while the densely populated towns on the Ruhr by 1910 accounted for over 1.5 million people. Still, even in 1895 some 69 per cent of the population remained rural, despite the continuing flight from the land.[9] These developments favoured the emergence of a fourth class, the urban proletariat, which needed to be literate to cope with industrial life and state bureaucracy. The spread of (limited) education among these sections of the population brought with it an increased political awareness. The decrease in illiteracy shows in the quality of recruits to the Imperial army and navy between 1876, when 212 men per 10,000 were illiterate, and 1896, when this number had dwindled to 15.[10]

TABLE 13

	1500	1800–10	1848–50	1872–5	1900
Hamburg	16,000	132,000	220,968	340,000	768,349
Munich	13,500	45,000	118,000	210,000	422,368
Frankfurt-on-Main	12,000	40,000	59,000	103,000	288,989
Hanover	5,000	23,400	41,000	106,677	235,649
Basle	9,500	16,600	29,000	55,000	112,227

Literacy and reading do not go hand in hand: the reading public in the nineteenth century consisted mostly of the middle class and upwards, few even of the petty bourgeois (*Kleinbürger*) will have read much, the workers only exceptionally.[11] The ephemeral literature designed for mass (middle-class) consumption thus remained firmly tied to the standard book language, not the colloquial speech of towns, and so ought to have reinforced the standard and further contributed to the decline of dialects. Schools were also hostile to non-standard language, regarding it as incorrect, while after unification the new centralized bureaucratic machinery of the empire promoted spelling reform and linguistic purism with unparalleled effectiveness. Only towards the end of the century, under the influence of Zola and the French naturalist writers, did German authors discover the substandard norms of the industrial masses which they used for social themes on the poverty and deprivation of the underprivileged strata of society.

The collapse of Germany in 1945 marks the end of an epoch, although there is continuity within change, since the basic phonological, morphological, and syntactic structures remained virtually unaltered, and some German-speaking areas (Switzerland) were comparatively unaffected anyway. But for the rest of Germany and Austria dialectal, stylistic, semantic, and lexical changes resulted, even if they did not become fully apparent until the early 1950s. Geographically, large areas that had had German-speaking superstrata for centuries were lost, and these sections of the population driven out or resettled. Thus, the East Prussian dialect area became part of the Soviet Union and of Poland, Silesia became Polish, and the German minority in the Sudeten region of Czechoslovakia was largely driven out. In all, some 13.5 million German-speakers left the eastern territories, about 9 million settling in the Federal Republic, and 4.5 in the German Democratic Republic.[12] The linguistic consequences were twofold: first, some dialects, like East Prussian, have become 'disembodied', living on in speakers without any geographically localized speech-community; secondly, the settlers and refugees adulterate the dialects of the Federal Republic and German Democratic Republic and disturb the linguistic homogeneity of those regions.

Socially, the collapse of Germany led to the emergence of a new class structure in East Germany but not in West Germany or Austria —although the power of the aristocracy has virtually disappeared.

Politically, the split into two German states with very different ideologies is reflected in their official political vocabulary, particularly the positive and negative polarization of key concepts. Despite differences in vocabulary and idiom, it is not yet clear that the standard language used in the two states will diverge significantly in sounds, forms, and syntactic structure. The difference may be no greater than that between the 'standard' German of the Federal Republic and that of Austria or Switzerland.

Culturally, German literature and art regressed for a while to the pre-National Socialist period before a new beginning could be made. Authors sought to avoid a language 'tainted by Nazism', and whether this problem was a real one or not, for a time no new literature was produced.

THE STANDARDIZATION OF SPELLING AND PRONUNCIATION

Spelling and pronunciation were not finally codified until the early years of the twentieth century, by conferences in 1901 and 1908, and even then inconsistencies and alternatives persisted, as they did in morphology and syntax.[13] University professors participated in the standardization, but it did not spring from the study of German at universities, which was of a philosophical or historical rather than practical kind. In 1818 Jacob Grimm had openly set himself against the tradition of rationalist normative grammar which he felt did not belong in school: school grammars of the mother tongue stunted the children's linguistic development, were sterile, contributing nothing to the true, historical study of German, and could safely be left unread.[14] At about the same time the comparative philological study of the Indo-European languages began to attract attention.[15] A rift developed between practical school grammars and the philological, comparative, and historical study of German, although school grammars sometimes became excessively preoccupied with abstract grammatical speculation or with the earlier history of German.[16] Unfortunately, neither the scholars nor the schoolmasters concerned themselves with the developments taking place in the German language of their own day: Grimm concentrated his considerable energies on earlier, more synthetic, and 'richer' stages of German, not on the contemporary language;[17]

the school grammarians were obsessed with correctness and regarded dialects as barriers to learning or as quaint survivals of the national heritage which they were busily fabricating, while the actual speech of the urban industrial masses they considered vulgar and valueless.[18]

A. SCHOOLS, PRINTERS, POLITICIANS, AND GERMAN SPELLING

The spelling problem was particularly acute in the schools, since children had to be taught to read and write at a time when no standard pronunciation existed as a guide and when the orthographical conventions of the printed or 'book' language were not fixed either. The complacent view that printed usage was already well established and could be accepted as a standard for school spelling is rebutted by comparing the divergent practice of different publishers, who are not even themselves consistent. Gustav Freytag's *Die Geschwister* (*Ahnen*), published by S. Hirzel at Leipzig in 1878, printed by Breitkopf and Härtel, contains variant spellings like *Schooß ~ Schoße*; *Der Tod ~ der Tot ~ Todfeind ~ tot ~ todschlagen ~ töten ~ tödten ~ getötet ~ tödtlich*; *hantiren, hofiren, studiren ~ regieren, hausieren, stolzieren*. Joseph Viktor von Scheffel's *Trompeter von Säkkingen*, published and printed by Metzler at Stuttgart in 1859, has variants like *Blüthe, Gluth ~ Blut, Geblüt*; *Gehülfe ~ hilfreich*; *Concert ~ Conzert*. Capitalization and word division cause headaches to all printers, accounting for variants like *dies Mal ~ diesmal ~ dießmal* or *zum ersten mal ~ zum erstenmal ~ zum ersten Mal ~ zum Erstenmal*.[19] Some words could be spelled in five or six different ways: *Ernte ~ Ernde ~ Erndte ~ Ärnte ~ Ärnde ~ Ärndte*; and, adding the many words in *-ieren* and uncertainties in spelling loan-words, as many as 900–1,000 quite common words fluctuated.[20] Mostly, such trivial variation does not hinder comprehension, and it is reducible to a number of typical cases ($\langle d \rangle \sim \langle t \rangle \sim \langle dt \rangle$, $\langle e \rangle \sim \langle ä \rangle$, $\langle i \rangle \sim \langle ie \rangle$, etc.), which are easily mastered. Inevitably, foreign words are spelled in different ways—often according to the degree to which they have been adopted into German—and, usually this is not particularly serious, provided they are recognizable and comprehensible. Nevertheless, a printed language which is not entirely normalized—especially in ephemeral publications like newspapers or pulp novelettes—is inadequate as a spelling guide for schools, and the degree of confusion in the classroom is evident from a Prussian edict of 1862 laying down that each school shall follow only one orthography.[21] Sporadic reforms were initiated in various states and schools—at Hanover in 1855, Leipzig in 1857, and Württemberg in 1861—but were neither consistent nor co-ordinated, and not until after the unification of Germany in 1871 were serious attempts to impose uniformity undertaken. At this time, too, the headmaster Konrad Duden (1829–1911) published a highly successful pamphlet of spelling conventions for his grammar school at Schleiz[22] and was in consequence invited to the first German orthographical conference held in Berlin in 1876 at the request of the Prussian Minister of Education, Dr Falk. The participants at the conference included university professors, teachers, publishers, and printers under the guidance of Rudolf von Raumer, who maintained that the orthographic reform had two main aims: to achieve unity by establishing one spelling practice throughout German-speaking areas, and to achieve consistency within the system used. The first aim was more important than the second.[23] Unfortunately, the heady atmosphere of the conference table and the avid attention of the nation's press tempted the delegates to consider more radical purification of the spelling system, and von Raumer tabled issues which had not been agreed beforehand, in particular the regularization of the means of indicating vowel length, one of the thorniest problems of all.[24] The nature and purpose of orthographical systems in general cannot concern us here,[25] but the three main approaches are phonetic, historical, and traditional. The extreme 'phonetic school', dubbed by Scherer the *fi-partei* (*fi* = *Vieh!*), were not invited to attend the conference at all: lack of a canonical pronunciation and the havoc wrought on established spelling by this approach made it unacceptable. The historical approach had the weight of Jacob Grimm's authority: he had, for example, rejected the use of capitalization for nouns, favoured a reduction in consonantal clusters, and had even privately advocated a return to medieval spelling.[26] Grimm's ideas were elaborated by the medievalist Karl Weinhold (1823–1901), who suggested spelling *Helle, Leffel, schepfen, schweren, zwelf* instead of *Hölle, Löffel*, etc., and it was to counter such absurd proposals that Rudolf von Raumer produced his own reforms which were eventually discussed at the conference.[27] In the very first sitting Duden demanded that the historical principle be dropped if incompatible with modern pronunciation, while phonetic considerations were to be limited by etymological ones. But the voting was sometimes arbitrary. The etymologically unjustified distinction *wider* 'against' ≠ *wieder* 'again' was rejected with eight votes, and held to be pedantic and detrimental to pronunciation. The form *wider* was accepted for both with nine votes. However, the historically justified distinction between *Lied* and *(Augen)lid* was retained with eight votes in favour. Distinctions between originally foreign words like *Fiber* 'fibre' and *Fieber* 'fever', or *Mine* 'mine' and *Miene* 'mien', 'expression', were rejected in favour of one form—*Fiber*, *Mine* for both—again with eight votes.[28] The traditional approach to spelling sought merely to establish the status quo in so far as it existed, ironing out inconsistencies. Not surprisingly, the printing representatives, notably Daniel Sanders, favoured a conservative approach, backed by the press and the general public—who very soon lost interest in the whole business. The members of the conference disagreed amongst themselves and its recommendations were not accepted.

Nevertheless, Duden published a modified form of his pamphlet with the somewhat unfortunate title *Die Zukunftsorthographie nach den Vorschlägen der zur Herstellung größerer Einigung in der deutschen Rechtschreibung berufenen Konferenz* . . . (Leipzig, 1876), where *Zukunftsorthographie* implies a radical recasting of the whole system, rather than the moderate and cautious compromise actually proposed. In 1879 Austria and Bavaria published orthographical reforms for their own schools along the lines of Rudolf von Raumer's original proposals, but adopting some of the less controversial solutions of the conference. Meanwhile, Daniel Sanders, who was working for the Leipzig publishing firm Breitkopf and Härtel, had introduced a system of his own for use by printers, but the Prussian authorities refused to license it for schools and hastily commissioned Professor Franz Wilhelm Wilmanns (1842–1911) to produce a guide for schools that would not differ too much from the Bavarian one— *Regeln und Wörterverzeichnis für die deutsche Rechtschreibung zum Gebrauch in den preußischen Schulen* (Berlin, 1880). Bismarck spoke against it in Parliament, and an edict of the Imperial Chancellery forbade its use in Imperial or Prussian ministries. The Prussian Government's attempt to nullify its own reforms was only partially successful, however, for Oldenburg, Weimar, and other states followed them, while Saxony, Baden, Württemberg, and Switzerland produced guidelines differing only slightly from the Prussian ones.[29]

Also in 1880, Konrad Duden published his own *Vollständiges ortho-graphisches Wörterbuch für die Schule. Nach den amtlichen Regeln der neuen Orthographie,* which is very much larger than the Prussian pamphlet (about 27,000 words to approximately 3,300 in the latter) and contains a full list of foreign words, with footnotes outlining the main points of dissension. Duden had consulted Wilmanns and followed the Prussian rules where deviations occurred, e.g. Prussian *Litteratur, Moritz, Möwe, Wiederhall* vs. Bavarian *Literatur, Moriz, Möve, Widerhall.* In compounds where three consonants of the same type occurred, Duden and the Prussians generally leave them, while the Bavarians drop one: Prussian *Betttuch, Schwimmmeister* (but there were exceptions, e.g. *Schiffahrt, Dritteil, Brennessel*), as against Bavarian *Bettuch, Kammacher* (but *Rückkehr, Schutzzoll*).

At this period, then, the chaotic state of German orthography looked like being aggravated by the confused state of orthographical theory, with different systems operating in Bavarian, Austrian, and Prussian schools, in Prussian and Imperial Government departments and offices, and in some printing-houses.[30] Still, appearances were deceptive, for the Bavarians and Prussians had liaised informally regarding the reforms, while Duden and Wilmanns had also collaborated. The regional orthographies in Saxony, Baden, Württemberg, and Switzerland were themselves based on the Prussian school rules. Indeed, in 1892 Switzerland accepted Duden's *Orthographisches Wörterbuch* before it had become the official code in Germany itself, testifying to his success. In 1901 a second Orthographical Conference was held at Berlin (17–19 June), of which no minutes survive; but no radical alterations to the spelling were suggested. Thus, ⟨th⟩ was removed from the initial position of some eight native roots (*Tal, Taler, Tat,* etc.),[31] while ⟨k⟩ and ⟨z⟩ replaced ⟨c⟩ and double ⟨cc⟩ in foreign words which had become assimilated into the language: *Kanzler, Akzent, Publikum,* etc. The basis for discussion was the Prussian rule-book of 1880, and both Wilmanns and Duden participated. The revised edition appeared in 1902 and was accepted by Austria, and also in effect by Switzerland, since Duden incorporated the reforms into a new edition of his own pamphlet, *Die deutsche Rechtschreibung nebst Interpunktionslehre und ausführlichem Wörterverzeichnis nach den für Deutschland, Österreich und die Schweiz gültigen Regeln zum Gebrauch für Schulen und zur Selbstbelehrung neu bearbeitet,* 7th edn. (Munich, 1902). The orthography itself was not 'new' and it was not 'radical': the use of capital letters, the indication of vowel length, and the use of spelling to separate homonyms remained inconsistent. But at last an orthography existed which was regulated, universally taught in schools, and used officially; unity and uniformity, if not total consistency, had been achieved.[32]

B. PRONUNCIATION AND THE STAGE

An idealized standard German pronunciation, ostensibly based on the established practice of the stage, was eventually laid down about the turn of the nineteenth century. As early as 1803, Goethe observes that provincial pronunciation could offend the audience's sensibilities by destroying the effects of a tragic speech: 'Kein Provinzialismus taugt auf die Bühne! Dort herrsche nur die reine deutsche Mundart, wie sie durch Geschmack, Kunst und Wissenschaft ausgebildet und verfeinert worden.'[33] But his actors are given only the vaguest directions as to how to avoid dialectal habits: they should 'adhere to the general rules of the German language', enunciate clearly, and pronounce all the sounds (*Buchstaben*) occurring in their words. Such a model pronunciation is implicitly linked to the spelling, just as in contemporary grammars, so that a vicious circle is drawn: the spelling is to give visible shape to the sounds of language, but the proper pronunciation depends partly on the rules of the HG book-language (*Schriftsprache*).[34] In fact, a phonetic alphabet was needed so that the grammarians could discuss phonetic values without becoming lost in the orthographical maze; this problem affected dialect writers too, although they were aiming not at absolute phonetic fidelity but only at a rough approximation of dialectal sounds, so as to suggest dialect without impeding comprehension.

Hermann Paul distinguished clearly between spoken and written norms, and already looked to the stage pronunciation as the ideal,[35] but on the other hand, the grammarian Friedrich Blatz, while noting the 'ziemlich übereinstimmende Aussprache des Theaters', denied the existence of a recognized pronunciation: 'Eine mustergiltige, allgemein anerkannte und von den Gebildeten angenommene Aussprache besteht nicht.'[36]

In 1896 the Germanist Theodor Siebs (1862–1941) approached several theatre managers on the question of a standard pronunciation for the stage, and in 1898 a conference at the Royal Theatre in

Berlin[37] produced a series of recommendations under the title *Deutsche Bühnenaussprache*, which were also welcomed by school-masters at the 'Philologenversammlung' held in Bremen the following year. No actors were represented at the conference, but Siebs's guidelines claimed to have taken careful note of the way they spoke on stage. No detailed account of the deliberations of this conference has survived, and the quality of the data is in doubt. Moreover, the actors being studied were probably (like Goethe's company) following the written scripts. In fact, the stage pronunciation was ultimately a 'spelling pronunciation' and had been so since the eighteenth century and perhaps even earlier.[38] Since all areas of Germany have some pronunciations which are 'substandard', only the written forms of the HG book or standard language are truly supra-dialectal, the result of interaction and compromise. Schools and the stage came up against the dislocation of sounds and signs in the crassest fashion, and both these institutions had, for different reasons, a vested interest in keeping pronunciation and spelling closely linked.[39]

After a second conference at Berlin in 1908, prompted in part by the Genossenschaft deutscher Bühnenangehöriger, 200 questionnaires were sent to theatres to elicit views on difficult points. This time actors and singers had also participated, and they influenced—but only marginally—the eighth and ninth editions of Siebs's *Deutsche Bühnenaussprache*. These editions, which appeared in 1910, even asserted, somewhat polemically, that spelling could never be a criterion for pronunciation: 'die Schreibung kann niemals Maßstab für die Aussprache sein' (p. 10).

To those who feared the tyranny of the new standard pronunciation outside the theatre as well as in it, Siebs replied[40] that the language of the stage cannot mirror everyday speech because of two special characteristics: (1) *Fernwirkung*, the need to project the speech into a wide auditorium; (2) *Gesamtwirkung*, the need to be more consistent than in daily speech, so as to avoid unfortunate dissonances created by actors with variant pronunciations. To apply these in everyday conversation would sound hopelessly artificial, so stage pronunciation can only be a guide, not so much by 'Gebot des Bühnenmäßigen' as by 'Verbot des allzustark mundartlich Gefärbten'. Inside the theatre, the rules claimed to be descriptive, not innovatory, and applied only to the classical German verse drama of the most refined type, not to the so-called 'Konversationsstück, dessen Ausdrucksweise sich der Umgangssprache des täglichen Lebens nähert', where even dialect had its place at times. We should remember that, just as this ideal stage pronunciation was being established, Gerhart Hauptmann, Arno Holz, and others were using dialect and colloquial language for political and social criticism. The 1910 editions of the *Bühnenaussprache* sought to extend its norms even to the *Konversationsstück* as well, in the interests of protecting the standard of pronunciation in the serious drama. Regional pronunciations could easily be adapted in the direction of the norm without actually attaining it. Siebs, for instance,[41] made the following stipulations: in Silesian, long vowels were to be pronounced (e.g. in *Trug, Sieg*), and unrounded vowels avoided (e.g. in *trübe, Größe*); in Saxon, the consonants *p/b* and *t/d* were to be distinguished; in Swabian, nasalized vowels should be avoided (e.g. not *uagnehm* for *unangenehm*) and *-schp* and *-scht* were inadmissible medially and finally (e.g. not *Haschpel, Geischt* for *Haspel, Geist*).

The pronunciation of the stage was not, then, established expressly to be a general norm, although it could serve several purposes: in school, university, and pulpit it was a vehicle for formal speeches and lectures (akin to declamation on stage); it gave an educated spoken norm for the whole of Germany; foreigners could base themselves on it; eventually it might assist orthographical reform and overcome the 'dialectal' distinctions between north and south. Gradually, the *Bühnenaussprache* gained ground as a norm: in 1904 the American grammarian George Curme regarded Berlin pronunciation as 'the most representative form of the spoken language', but in the revised edition of 1922[42] he changed his mind in favour of the 'standard of the stage'. Also in 1922, the title of Siebs's manual changed to incorporate the term *Hochsprache*, and under the National Socialists attempts were made to apply it more generally, in radio broadcasting, for example. Only in 1961 was the label *Bühnenaussprache* relegated to the subheading; in 1969 (the nineteenth edition) it was removed altogether and the existence of a less formal but still purified level of pronunciation accepted, the 'gemäßigte Hochlautung',[43] which also takes account of the Austrian and Swiss variations in rendering the standard.

DIALECTS: DECLINE AND CULTIVATION[44]

The approximate geographical lie of German dialects *c*.1900 is shown on Map 5. The following points should be borne in mind:

1. The modern political and linguistic boundaries do not coincide. In the north, LG dialects are influenced by Danish and Fris. and vice versa; some polyglot speakers speak, however imperfectly, Danish, Fris., HG, Danish dialect, and LG. In the north-west, the LG dialects shade barely perceptibly into the LFrk. dialects of Holland. Some areas, notably Alsace and Lorraine in the west and parts of the Tyrol in the south, have been much disputed politically, sometimes on linguistic grounds. In the east, a German superstratum (sometimes thinly spread) has overlain Slav populations since the twelfth century; Map 5 shows only the geographical spread of German dialects, not the density of German settlement.

2. Some dialects are difficult to separate from one another because of broad transitional zones: South Bav. and Middle Bav. merge into each other, and in the west into Alem. North Bav. and EFrk. have common features, while the status of SFrk. as a distinct dialect is disputed. Northern parts of Rh.Frk. are often regarded as Hessian dialects in their own right, whereas Ripuarian and Moselle Frk. are commonly bracketed together as MFrk.

3. We have divided the LG dialects into West Low German and East Low German, since this terminology is more modern. However, 'Saxon' was the common term in nineteenth-century parlance, and Gottsched in the eighteenth century contrasts 'Niedersächsisch' with the 'Obersächsich' of EMG areas, so effectively comparing a large LG-speaking area with its own dialects with a smaller and more homogeneous territory.

The very factors which favoured the normalization of spelling, pronunciation, and grammar hastened the erosion of the everyday use of dialects; the number of contexts in which dialect was felt appropriate decreased. Dialect eventually became restricted to familiar, domestic, informal situations and to rural life and work, like farming, or to certain regional but traditional occupations, like mining or fishing. In the south, in country areas, dialect class and occupation probably remained fairly identifiably linked, but in the industrialized conurbations of the centre and north dialect

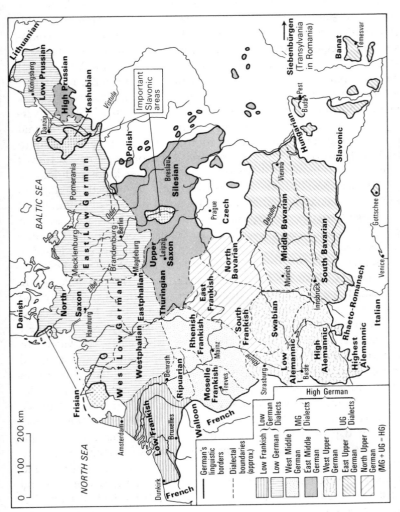

MAP 5. Linguistic map of German dialects c.1900

increasingly ceased to be the language of work and daily life, and was replaced by urban or regional colloquial languages (*Umgangssprachen*), which are group languages used by speakers of various social and dialectal origins in their everyday conversation.[45] An old, essentially geographical, 'horizontal' differentiation of the German-speaking regions was thus superseded by a social or 'vertical' stratification in the towns, where language played a more important role in separating the various groups in the community; in smaller, less complex, and less shifting communities the linguistic differences were subordinate to other distinctions. Colloquial languages overcame barriers to comprehension, principally by providing less formal and less regulated alternatives to the standard language and to dialect. However, new social and political groupings, new forms of work, and technological advances created other kinds of linguistic barrier as specialist and group languages developed, so that in industrialized communities dialect became only one of a number of language varieties or 'registers'[46] with which people were at least partially familiar. As dialect became socially more and more limited and consequently stylistically marked, since using it reflected a conscious or half-conscious choice on the part of the speakers, the possibilities for successive generations to learn and use dialect were restricted, making it rarer still. The process differed regionally and according to social class, education, and so forth. Paradoxically, where the dialect was most quickly and drastically eroded, namely in the LG-speaking north, dialect was also early cultivated for literary purposes.[47] Of course, before the emergence of the standard 'book language' all writing could be regarded as 'dialectal', but in eighteenth- and nineteenth-century literature dialect was used deliberately and almost invariably self-consciously in contrast to the educated standard. Indeed, after Johann Gottfried Herder (1744–1803) had promoted an idealized folk-poetry,[48] dialects and their speakers were regarded as the repository of certain basic and inalienable national values, such as common sense, tradition, and loyalty, coupled with heightened awareness of the seasonal round of nature. 'Literary dialect' was an acceptable vehicle for bucolic, idyllic writing, just as in classical antiquity (Theocritus, for example), and its practitioners were educated men with a sentimental and philosophical distance from their chosen means of expression. Unfortunately, most such writers were untalented, even if they had any mastery of the dialect they were writing in—and some had not. They treated dialect with puristic rigour, cleansing it of contamination with the standard language, other dialects, and foreign languages, so making the language as artificial as the verse medium itself. Naturalistic topics were also avoided as vulgar, and much of this poetry was escapist, ignoring or at best simplifying social, economic, and political problems, safely distanced from writer and reader alike. Although dialect represented a serious barrier to general comprehension, in the nineteenth century the dialect lyric and story were suitably refined and edited for, and largely by, the middle classes, complete with glossaries and footnotes: this literature raised new barriers between genuine dialect-speakers and the educated consumers of artificial dialect writing.[49] Such sentimental *Heimatdichtung* reflected further stages in the process of dialectal decay, rather than any new vigour: writers were preoccupied with the dialect form but not with the social reality that lay behind it in the country life, just as they neglected the predicament of the masses in towns and factories.[50] Political unification also spread a patronizing interest in dialects as part of the national heritage which ought to be preserved, and greatly stimulated the historical and geographical study of dialect in the latter part of the nineteenth century—though there had been some, including Jacob Grimm, who held that LG dialects had no significant part to play in the history of the nation, or that they might actually impede unity. The 'herbarium approach' prevailed in dialectology even after sophisticated techniques had been developed for the description and analysis of actual speech, techniques themselves indirectly related to technological advances in reproducing images by photography and sounds by the phonograph. Nor did linguists ask the fundamental questions about the feasibility of describing utterances faithfully, and they also usually left to philosophers and literary writers the thorny issues of the relationships between language and thought and between language and social reality (see Chapter X).

Written dialect—often felt to be a contradiction in terms, since the many and varied phonetic characteristics of speech are inevitably simplified in writing—falls into two basic types: the (often only apparently) naïve and unpretentious, and the consciously artistic.[51] The first has a long tradition in most areas, and still survives in regional jokes, 'Fastnacht' revels along the Rhine, occasional poetry for weddings, family, or local celebrations, the dialect column in local newspapers, and so on. The serious literary use of dialect has a more chequered history, differing according to genre as well as region. In the drama, dialect had often served humorous or satirical purposes,[52] but the Gottschedian stage reforms of the eighteenth century had banished it from the stage for German classical theatre, although it survived in Vienna—for example in the *Possen* of Johann Nepomuk Nestroy (1801–62).[53]

At the turn of the eighteenth century lyric poetry in dialect appeared which was to enjoy a tremendous vogue and which led to theoretical and polemical argument, as well as stimulating a multitude of epigones. Johann Heinrich Voss (1751–1826) wrote a series of idylls, two of which, *De Winterawend* (1776) and *De Geldhapers* (1777), gave an idealized form of LG, refined still further in the 1801 edition in accordance with Voss's complicated theory of the classical hexameter.[54] While Voss's 'Platt-Deutsch' dialect writing was very much a learned experiment in purified form, he nevertheless believed that LG could be more expressive than the HG book language. The Alemannic poet Johann Peter Hebel (1760–1826)[55] reports that Voss translated Homer into Platt-Deutsch first before transposing its phonology—but not, he claimed, its thought patterns—into HG.[56] Hebel himself certainly knew the first versions of Voss's LG idylls; he had met Voss and discussed with him basic problems and principles of presenting lyric poetry in purified and elevated dialectal form and classical metre. Moreover, Hebel too was an educated man, who studied theology and taught at a grammar school; his own *Alemannische Gedichte* (1803) are no narrow transcription of a local dialect but a purified, literary Alem. general enough to render the main characteristics of language used over a wide southwestern area:

Der Dialekt, in welchem diese Gedichte verfaßt sind . . . herrscht in dem Winkel des Rheins zwischen dem Fricktal und ehemaligen Sundgau und weiter hin in mancherlei Abwandlungen bis an die Vogesen und Alpen und über den Schwarzwald hin in einem großen Teil von Schwaben.[57]

However, Hebel's essentially HG spelling conventions are often ambiguous and inconsistent when applied to dialect: e.g. the graphy ⟨ie⟩ has diphthongal value in *lieb, Dieb, vier, verdiene*, but in *Wiese, Frieden, sieht* it represents a long monophthong; moreover, he wrote both *Bub* and *Bueb*, and failed to separate the open and closed *e* sounds characteristic of spoken Alem. His dialect form was clearly a *Manier* (his term), a vehicle for moral, philosophical, and allegorical ideas. Nor did Hebel theorize about his language, leaving later editors to decide whether to print what Hebel wrote (with all text-critical variants), or whether to provide an accurate phonetic transcription allowing readers from non-Alem. areas to gain a better impression of how the poetry sounded. The purity and homogeneity of the dialect seem to have been taken for granted by Hebel, but transcription problems, and the naturalistic fidelity and the genuineness of dialectal thought and expression were to become important issues later in the century; there was even a misguided attempt to rewrite Hebel's famous poem *Die Wiese* in a more phonetic orthography.[58] In Alem.-speaking regions no serious linguistic controversies existed at this time,[59] and educated and uneducated alike accepted the superiority of the HG book language beside whatever local gradations of dialectal speech—and sometimes writing—they employed in everyday usage. Hebel's poetry enjoyed tremendous success: it ran to six editions by 1821, and a HG translation by R. Reinick in 1850 to at least four, and there sprang up a vogue for 'Alemannic poetry', of which Goethe's *Schweizerlied* (1811) and the North German Hoffmann von Fallersleben's *Allemannische Lieder* (1826) are the most notorious specimens.[60] More important in the present context, Hebel's example inspired the LG writer Klaus Groth (1819–99) to try out a new lyric in Platt-Deutsch which, thanks largely to the phenomenal success of Groth's collection of poetry *Quickborn* (1852), established dialect poetry as a respectable and even patriotic form of literature, besides appealing to his readers' romantic and escapist feelings. While Groth was arguably a lesser poet than Hebel, he gave much thought to the role of dialect poetry, particularly in LG, which, unlike Alem., enjoyed little prestige and had been under attack for centuries;[61] indeed, the writer Ludolf Wienbarg argued that Platt-Deutsch should be utterly eradicated, since it hindered the spread of arts and sciences and, above all, was a barrier to the full appreciation and mastery of HG.[62] In some respects, Klaus Groth was a belated Enlightenment grammarian bent on purifying, ennobling, and disseminating a canonical, 'pure' dialect for literary purposes. He had studied the grammatical writings of Gottsched, Adelung, Grimm, Karl Ferdinand Becker (1775–1849), and Simon Heinrich Adolf Herling (1780–1849), among others, and so set himself above other LG poets, like Sophie Dethlefs (1809–64) and Fritz Reuter (1810–74). Moreover, Groth and the Germanic scholar Karl Müllenhoff (1818–84) worked together on a suitable orthography for Platt-Deutsch, and this scholarly endeavour formed part of Groth's intention to raise the status of LG, although it also entailed a move away from everyday speech. After Fritz Reuter's collection of light and humorous verse, *Läuschen un Rimels* (1853), had been favourably compared with his *Quickborn*,[63] Groth became embroiled in an acrimonious dispute with Reuter which clearly reveals the difference between a naturalistic, insouciant treatment of speech for humour, local colour, social satire, and anecdote (*Läuschen* = 'anecdote', *Rimels* = *Reimereien* in Mecklenburg Platt) and the pretentious artistic lyric. Like Voss, whom he despised as artificial,[64] Groth saw LG as an ideal, venerable, and archaic language. Despite his spirited defence of LG and the claim that some nine million people still spoke it in his day, Groth tried to create a written literary standard for Platt-Deutsch, in whose 'correct' pronunciation educated speakers played an important part— 'bei einer gereinigten Aussprache im gebildeten Munde';[65] he expressly rejected the claims of the 'Naturalists' to emulate speech.[66] Groth, indeed, set himself up as an authority on the 'true' way of life of LG-speakers and on 'genuine' dialect, and he reproached Reuter for defaming and caricaturing peasants and others as ludicrous, vulgar, stupid, and sly, and for presenting their speech as impure, a 'Judenplattdeutsch' and certainly not a 'Christenhochdeutsch'![67] But such adulterated 'Gräuelhochdeutsch' ((1858), 40) and 'ohrzerreißendes Kauderwelsch' ((1855), preface, p. vi) was undoubtedly spoken, particularly as the curious LG–HG mixture 'Missingsch', itself a regional colloquial language.[68] Reuter had accurately observed the speech of his area, and several of his characters, notably Onkel Bräsig, speak Missingsch. Groth could not approve because he treated dialect as a closed system to be protected from contamination. Even though he accepted that dialect changed with time, Groth did not suggest any mechanism for the change: he deplored the HG admixture to Platt-Deutsch, just as he rejected foreign influence on patriotic, chauvinist grounds. The topics appropriate for LG dialect poetry therefore remained limited, since Groth repudiated borrowing, which might have provided an intellectual, technical, and philosophical vocabulary. The speakers belong instead to an idealized rural or littoral community with a technology based on agriculture or fishing and with a mainly biblical abstract vocabulary.

In the last quarter of the nineteenth century there was a great upsurge of dialect poetry, much of it apparently in the mould of Groth.[69] Gerhart Hauptmann in his autobiography claimed to have been reacting against the sentimental *Heimatkunst* and *Heimatdichtung* with its salon dialect when he used Silesian in the social dramas *Vor Sonnenaufgang* (1889) and *De Waber* (1891-2): he saw dialect as a vehicle for serious drama and even tragedy: 'Ich wollte dem Dialekt seine Würde zurückgeben.'[70] However, the German Naturalists did not distinguish clearly between dialect and urban colloquial language, nor was accurate or consistent phonetic transcription essential to the social points they were making: the controversies surrounding Hauptmann's plays were not linguistic. Nevertheless, it is writers, rather than scholars, who take credit for discovering the speech of the masses.

Groth and Reuter were both patriots, who saw LG dialects as nationally important: both served as rallying points for LG emigrants. German ethnic minorities in America erected statues in their honour and founded societies to promote 'Platt'. The first major 'plattdütsch Volksfest' at New York in 1875 was attended by forty-five such clubs, and Groth made a telephone greeting to another at Chicago in 1880. Both writers had become symbols of nostalgic idealism, monuments to a language that could no longer seriously contend with the HG standard.

THE STUDY OF DIALECT AND THE DISCOVERY OF COLLOQUIAL

Nineteenth-century dialect studies reflected, as did English dialectology of the same period, a desire to preserve threatened local forms of language as part of the national heritage. Idealism, possibly escapism, made rural speech appear the expression of static and idyllic communities; moreover, some dialects had archaic features which made them suitable objects for historical study. Dialect also seemed a relatively closed and identifiable form of language where social variations were less important than the geographical ones. Historical continuity was taken for granted and made it seem possible to trace some contemporary dialects back to those spoken by tribes of the early Middle Ages, perhaps even to the Migration Period: this soon proved to be an illusion. Notwithstanding, the nationalistic motivation for dialectology persisted—popular literary histories subscribed to the 'tribal fallacy' and sought to demonstrate the continuity of Germanic and German ethnic and ethical consciousness in the old tribal regions. Empirical studies, especially on phonetics, were soon applied to dialect, both for the study of particular dialects and in the newly developed 'dialect geography' which set out from the premiss that geographically conditioned linguistic variables could be precisely localized and cartographically presented using 'isoglosses'. In 1876 Georg Wenker (1852–1911) consulted local schoolmasters about the lie of dialectal boundaries in their Düsseldorf area, especially that separating LG from HG; his questionnaires resulted in *Das Rheinische Platt* (1877). With the support of the Government through the Berlin Academy, Wenker extended his survey of phonological isoglosses over the whole Empire.[71] However, it soon became apparent that morphological and lexical differences supervened[72] and that dialect fluctuated, and was far from homogeneous or static. Similar insights into the fluid nature of language in all its manifestations were being made in phonetics. Since German dialectology neglected sociological factors, such dialectal variation was interpreted in terms of chronological change, dialectal mixture, transitional dialect zones, population movement, and the like.

As dialectology was being put on a serious, scholarly footing, another, even less determinate kind of language began to attract the attention of writers interested in social milieu—the *Umgangssprache* used by Theodor Fontane (1819–98) in his novels and by Gerhart Hauptmann in the social drama. The professional linguists mostly ignored it (Hermann Wunderlich is the exception), and in 1888, the year before Hauptmann's *Vor Sonnenaufgang*, the respected linguistic historian Adolf Socin dismissed the language of the urban proletariat as a corrupt jargon. This view is typical:

Die Verhunzung der guten Sprache in den großen Städten ist kein Volksdialekt, sondern ein Jargon, und kann höchstens zu komischen Zwecken nachgeahmt oder parodiert werden.[73]

Town language had progressively deviated from dialect for a long time, certainly since the Middle Ages, and the changes brought by industrialization, urbanization, and improved communications created conditions in which a sub- or semi-standard spoken language could emerge and spread into the areas surrounding towns. Probably around 1800 most Germans were still primarily dialect-speakers;[74]

already by 1900 most of them were speaking some form of regional colloquial language, and for them, too, dialect had become stylistic. Today, *Umgangssprache* in some form or other is spoken by nearly all German-speakers in most circumstances (although modified dialect remains the local everyday norm in Switzerland, Luxemburg, and the South Tyrol),[75] while few if any Germans speak the standard language at all outside the formal circumstances of the lecture hall, pulpit, classroom, radio or television interview, or official ceremony. Perhaps fewer than one-third know dialect[76]—and then only passively rather than actively. Since modern German-speakers regard *Umgangssprache* as their main form of language, it might more properly be relabelled 'Normal-' or 'Alltagssprache'; on the other hand, dialect and the standard language are systems in which the average Germans have an imperfect competence and for which they have only a limited need.

But grammarians and lexicographers remained unimpressed— they were too preoccupied with giving the final touches to the codification of the standard language to treat any deviation from it sympathetically. Popular works of *Sprachkritik*, like Gustav Wustmann's *Allerhand Sprachdummheiten. Kleine Grammatik des Zweifelhaften, des Falschen und des Häßlichen* (Leipzig, 1890), or Theodor Matthias's *Sprachleben und Sprachschäden. Ein Führer durch die Schwankungen und Schwierigkeiten des deutschen Sprachgebrauchs* (Leipzig, 1892), typify the usual attitude to colloquial German: one of censure if it is used in writing. The Muret-Sanders *Encyklopädisches Wörterbuch* (1891–1901), which uses letters and symbols to convey the stylistic value of vocabulary, treats *Umgangssprache* as spoken standard.[77] Even Ludwig Sütterlin's ostensibly contemporary grammar, *Die deutsche Sprache der Gegenwart* (Leipzig, 1897–9), accords the *Umgangssprache* scant mention, although he at least recognizes that it differs in all respects from the standard: in sounds (*habm* for *haben*), in morphology (*hauen/haute* instead of *hauen/hieb*), in word-formation (*Lauferei* for *Gelaufe*), in syntax (preference for Subj. II rather than Subj. I, which has virtually disappeared), and in vocabulary (LG *Stulle* 'bread roll' is 'gewöhnlich', i.e. 'common', 'vulgar' if used in HG).[78] This neglect of the town colloquial is explicable partly because the language itself is extremely variable, having different strata and also regional variations; moreover, the term *Umgangssprache* is ambiguous.

UMGANGSSPRACHE AND COLLOQUIAL[79]

Like the English term 'colloquial', the German *Umgangssprache* can be regarded as a spoken approximation of the standard or literary language as used by educated speakers in their everyday communication where situation and context permit a degree of syntactic flexibility, ambiguity, and looseness of construction; in this sense *Umgangssprache* remains stylistically linked to the form of the standard. The special characteristics of speech, as opposed to writing, as a medium for language cannot here be considered in detail. 'Broken' constructions (*apo koinou*), ellipsis, aposiopesis, avoidance of encapsulation and complex clause structures, the preference for demonstrative pronouns rather than relative clauses, repetition (especially of pronouns), and, above all, the use of emotive particles and interjections for opening conversation and qualifying what has been said, both in order to express the speaker's view and to win over the interlocutor, are common in spoken German, whether dialect or not.[80]

But, unlike colloquial English, German has markedly regional features in vocabulary, intonation, and phonology, and to a lesser extent in syntax and morphology: in fact, German has several regional colloquial languages[81]—(*Umgangssprachen*) associated especially with important towns—in the nineteenth century notably with Berlin and Vienna, the two main German-speaking cultural centres.

The informality of *Umgangssprache* and its provincial manifestations explains why the term also implies 'slang' in the sense of 'unacceptable', 'vulgar', 'incorrect' usage. Moreover, the special and technical vocabulary of certain groups of speakers may be taken over into the colloquial language for metaphorical purposes, depending on the importance of the groups that use it; conversely, technical jargons borrow from the colloquial. In short, the parameters of *Umgangssprache* are hard to define, since it mediates between standard and dialects, between different social classes, and between different scientific, technical, and 'professional' groups, overlapping and changing in the process.[82]

As a stylistic level, *Umgangssprache* lies between the standard and dialect, sharing features of both in varying degree, depending upon geographical and social factors, as illustrated in Fig. 9.[83] This tells us

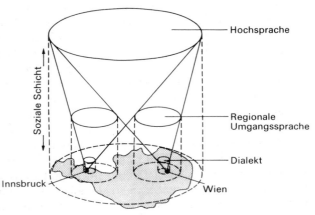

FIG. 9. The communicative range of standard, colloquial, and dialect in Austria (= König (1978), 132)

nothing specific about the form, for this language is characterized by variation, even within the speech of one individual. The standard language and dialect are not closed systems either, though they are relatively more stable than *Umgangssprache* for different reasons: the standard has been codified, while the dialect is closely associated with a particular group of people which it identifies, whereas *Umgangssprache* is more 'anonymous' because of its variability. The colloquial language of a particular town can consequently only be represented by the most commonly occurring variants.

Umgangssprache's Janus-like nature may be illustrated by its phonology, which may have the same phonemic system as the standard language, but with a dialectal intonation and phonetic realization of the phonemes. For example, the phonemic opposition represented in the MHG numerals *ein, zwei ≠ drî* has disappeared in standard German, where an open diphthong [ai] occurs in all forms. In Berlin dialect the older opposition remains as *eens, zwee,* with the monophthong [e:], vs. *drei,* with a diphthong. However, Berlin colloquial sometimes generalizes one phoneme, usually the monophthong; thus *meene Beene,* 'incorrect' for dialectal '*meine Beene*'. At Vienna, too, the dialectal forms *āns, zwā* vs. *drei* become *eins, zwei, drei* in the speech of younger or educated speakers, but the diphthong has a more closed quality than that of the standard, more like [ɛi]: ['ɛins], ['tsvɛi], ['drɛi].

The in-between status of colloquial language led to its being attacked on the grounds that it was 'incorrect' or 'vulgar standard', and not pure dialect either, which again reflects a conception of standard and dialect as ideal systems having rules, or at least norms. The 'openness' or relative freedom of *Umgangssprache* may also explain why it does not arouse strong feelings of identity in the speakers, and may account for its greater comprehensibility over wide geographical areas. Hence, *Umgangssprache* is an intermediate level, with a wider communicative range than dialect, although not so wide as the standard language which overlies both. Moreover, in most areas *Umgangssprache* is used by speakers higher up the social scale than those who speak dialect. On the other hand, in contrast to English, German *Umgangssprache* is regionally differentiated in vocabulary, and in this respect is closer to dialect: this is shown by regional equivalents, like *Fleischer ~ Fleischhauer ~ Fleischhacker ~ Metzger ~ Schlachter ~ Schlächter* or *sich erkälten ~ sich verkälten ~ sich verkühlen*, which are not stylistically differentiated.[84]

The regional differences do not all derive directly from older dialectal forms, however, since new words resulting from technological advances or cultural contact with foreign speech-communities also vary according to geographical area in stress, pronunciation, and gender.[85] For example, in Berlin we find *Tábak, Káffee* (= the beverage, as opposed to *Café* 'coffee-house'), and *der Túnnel*, whereas in Vienna we find *Tabák, Kaffée* and both *das Túnnel* and *das Tunnél*. Influence of Fr. stress patterns may be seen in three of the Viennese cases, but in *Kópie* (= ['ko:pje]), *Úniform*, and *Mathemátik* the Viennese forms show greater assimilation, whereas Berlin keeps the Fr. pattern: *Kopie, Unifórm, Mathematík*. The pronunciation of *Chemie* and *China* shows a palatal spirant at Berlin [çemí:] etc.) but a voiceless stop at Vienna (['ki:na] etc.); in *Offizier, Bürokratie* Berlin prefers assimilated forms with [ts] ([ɔfi'tsi:r]) and [t] (['ti:]), whereas Vienna has 'French' forms [ɔfi'si:r] and [byrokra'si:]. Such differences reflect varying degrees of phonological assimilation of foreign borrowings; the regional distribution reflects the cultural importance of urban centres. Sometimes competing designations for new inventions arise showing a mixture of foreign and German terms: the horsedrawn tram was at first called *Pferdebahn* at Berlin, but *Tramway* at Vienna and *Trambahn* in other parts of southern Germany; with the change to electric power it became *die Elektrische* or *Straßenbahn*.[86]

All the above variation can be regarded as resulting from the lack of centralization in German-speaking lands—though we shall see (below, p. 398) that with unification a single, official term has usually become current beside the local ones with which it competes, at least in Germany (Austria and Switzerland have generally retained their own bureaucratic and regional forms).

In southern areas *Umgangssprache* is closer to dialect and thus more restricted in range, whereas further north *Umgangssprache* moves closer towards the standard language in sounds and forms— though not in vocabulary—with a consequent increase in communicative range. Historically, this reflects the imposition of the HG language on LG-speakers whose colloquial language then strove to conform to the overlying standard language, adopting its shifted consonantism, for example. Northerners, therefore, lacking the dialectal basis of the standard language, tend to be particularly critical of *Umgangssprache* and to view it as substandard or nonstandard. However, in the south the regional colloquial languages were rooted in dialect and never lost touch with it; late sixteenth-century printers' norms in the South are probably largely the written reflection of such regional *Umgangssprachen*. Again, it should be borne in mind that any sounds or forms or words that are not either standard or dialect are relegated to *Umgangssprache*, which has many levels, even in the South.

In its function as informal spoken language, *Umgangssprache* is also a half-way house between the esoteric technical and scientific languages ('jargons') used at work, for example, and the standard language. There is interchange here too, since some everyday expressions are borrowed over into jargons and given special, technical senses. Below *Umgangssprache* lies the language known as *Rotwelsch* —perhaps better called *Ganovensprache* or *Gaunersprache*—with a long history and a variety of forms composed of many different elements, including soldiers' and students' slang and elements of Hebrew/Yiddish. *Gaunersprache* (= English 'thieves' cant') also applies best to a function of language rather than to any particular form: it is used by the anti- or asocial criminal fraternity as a secret language and changes rapidly to preserve its cryptic nature. In this respect it is like certain types of children's language.[87]

THE HISTORICAL CONTRIBUTION OF *UMGANGSSPRACHE*—
ESPECIALLY THAT OF BERLIN

The emergence of urban colloquial as an identifiable and increasingly important variety of German beside dialect and the standard was clearly brought about by cultural, economic, social, and political changes, and it illustrates, even if only in vague fashion, the links between the history of a speech-community and its language. Curiously, the grammarians virtually ignored developments in the spoken language except to criticize them; it was the writers who began to experiment with actual speech to heighten the veracity of their controlled experiments in social drama. The distinction between dialect and urban colloquial was not in itself important, except in so far as authentically conveying the wretchedness of the milieu was concerned, but it had implications for general comprehensibility. Hauptmann, for instance, obviously felt that the Silesian dialect in *De Waber* was restrictive, for in 1892 he wrote a second, modified version, *Die Weber*, which was closer to HG; in fact he had put the play into a regional *Umgangssprache* close enough to that of Berlin to be readily comprehensible there. While this colloquial was still relatively unfamiliar in printed form, it was much easier for audiences to understand than dialect, and this in turn is indirect evidence of the widespread acceptance of, and familiarity with, such a colloquial language as the everyday idiom of the urban masses. Fontane in his *Irrungen Wirrungen* (*Vossische Zeitung*, 1887) and Hauptmann in *Der Biberpelz* (1894) and *Die Ratten* (1911) show us writers drawing directly on Berlin colloquial, which remained influential throughout Germany until the end of the Second World War.

While other large towns will inevitably have affected the speech of the surrounding areas, the task of tracing their wider influence is difficult. At the period under discussion only Vienna, as the other major European German-speaking cultural and imperial capital, could rival Berlin—Munich, Hamburg, and Cologne were in a different league. Moreover, the colloquial of Berlin, as we have seen, had become well known through the literary experiments of Naturalism: the prestige of the city as a centre of popular culture and its avant-garde literature must have helped to spread many catchwords and phrases, including a few expressions from criminal and asocial groups. Furthermore, Berlin's colloquial usage had long differed from the surrounding LG dialects, for its HG colouring reaches back to the sixteenth century.[88]

The originally LG language spoken there had been declining since the sixteenth century—in 1504 the town chancery adopted HG—and in speech too the cultural ascendancy of the EMG region asserted itself, although in intonation, phonology, syntax, and vocabulary LG remains an important element in the HG 'Neuberlinisch' of later centuries. In fact, Berlin adopts 'Missingsch' *sensu stricto*: it borrows the generally acclaimed, though only vaguely described, Meissen form of HG ('mîsnisch') spoken in the contiguous MG areas, and characteristic 'errors' of HG usage criticized by eighteenth-century grammarians in the speech of Leipzig (above, pp. 318 f.) are also current at Berlin.[89] Subsequently, Berlin language has deviated from Saxon in many respects, particularly because of the continuing influence of the surrounding LG dialect and of lower, LG-speaking strata of society amid the growing urban population. At the end of the eighteenth century Karl Philip Moritz (1756–93) produced popular grammatical guides for Berliners listing common 'errors': among the forms expressly marked 'pöbelhaft' are the relatively new LG *ik/ikke* for *ich*, *wat* for *was*, and *det* for *das*, now felt to be hallmarks of the Berlin language.[90]

The Berlin *Umgangssprache* became highly influential at the close of the nineteenth century, thanks to the city's size and importance as metropolis and cultural centre. Even—and perhaps especially—outside literary circles Berlin had gained prestige and self-awareness: music-halls and variety theatres, humorous almanacs and magazines, like those of the popular author Adolf Glassbrenner (1810–76), published from 1832 onwards—particularly his *Berlin wie es ist und — trinkt*—helped to spread catch-phrases, and in 1878 Hans Meyer published *Der richtige Berliner in Wörtern und Redensarten*, a phrase-book which ran to several editions. For the Berliners, especially the new arrivals, of whom there were many, were looking for a sense of identity and were growing in self-importance. Indeed, trivial writers like Glassbrenner and Meyer anticipate the Naturalists in their interest in milieu, if not in their treatment of it: and, because they lacked literary pretensions and appealed to a local audience, they could use ephemeral catchwords and allusions uninhibitedly.

Characteristic features of Berlin colloquial language[91]—not necessarily restricted to the city but associated with it—include:

1. *Phonology*. (i) The assimilation or loss of final consonants, especially dentals: *und, nicht, ist, sind* > *un, nich, is, sin*; the reduction of articles and pronouns: *t* can represent *et, det* (NHG *es, das*), *n* represents *ihn, den, een, eenen*, (NHG *ein, einen*), and *eine* is reduced to *ne*. (ii) Medial consonants also drop: *Mädchen* > *Meechen, ordentlich* > *orntlich, kriegst* > *krist, werden* > *wer(n)*, etc.; and sometimes particles can be run together: *donnich, nonnich, zeidomma* = *doch nicht, noch nicht, zeig doch mal*. (iii) Some more local features include the well-known *j* for HG initial /g-/: *Jott, jut, Jurke, jenau, jekonnt* for *Gott, gut, Gurke, genau, gekonnt*; also sometimes medially: *Jejend, jejen* = *Gegend, gegen*. There are unshifted consonants in some words: *ik, det, wat, Schafskop* (= *Dummkopf*).

2. *Morphology*. (i) The pl. forms differ in their distribution of the endings *-er, -s*, and *-en* from the modern standard language: *Dinger, Rester, Stöcker, Steener* (NHG *Steine*); *Bengels, Fräuleins, Gärtners, Jungs, Meechens, Kerls, Kinderkens* (= *Kinderlein*); *Fenstern, Messern, Stiebeln* (NHG *Stiefel*). (ii) The nouns *Vater* and *Mutter* show *-n* in the oblique cases with possessive forms *Vatern sein Hund, Muttern ihr Kind*, and are treated like proper names. (iii) The adj. shows an *-et* ending in the neut. sg., although this cannot be LG, since LG adjectives are endingless in this case: *nischt Neuet, 'n kaputtet Fenster*.

3. *Syntax*. (i) Confusion of acc. and dat. forms, especially of *mich/mir*: in a verse of the court actor Johann Ferdinand Rüthling (1793–1849) 'Ich liebe dir, ich liebe dich | Wie's richtig ist, das weeß ich nich | Un's is mich ooch Pomade [= 'es ist mir egal'] . . .'.[92] (ii) Replacement of the gen. case by circumscription with *von* or the possessive construction, e.g. *Bollmann sein Hund*. (iii) The modal verb structures are also noteworthy: *Det konnste dir jedacht haben* instead of standard 'hättest . . . denken können'; and even *Det hätt' ick mechten sehen, det hättste ja jleich konnten sagen*. (iv) The use of the future—and even future perfect—for narrative: 'Kaum werde ick nu meinen Freund die Maulschelle jeimpft haben . . . so entsteht eine Keilerei . . .' = 'I've just give me mate a slap round the kisser . . . then this punch-up starts'.

4. *Particles*. (i) Especially common are *I* to introduce an utterance: *I nu . . ., I, Gott bewahre!* (also *Na* or *Nanu*). (ii) The form *man* is used in the same manner as HG *nur*: 'Na, binde man alles gut zusammen!'

But it is undoubtedly in vocabulary that Berlin has contributed most to everyday spoken German, making fashionable and disseminating expressions of disparate and even dubious origin. Some such forms are relatively new: *Kladderadatsch* (masc.) 'crash', 'scandal', early nineteenth century, then, since 1848, the name of a satirical journal; *Klamauk(e)* (masc. and fem.) 'noise', 'din'; *Radau* (masc.) 'uproar', 'riot' (*c.*1870), *Radaubruder*, -*macher*; *Tingeltangel* 'music-hall', 'variety theatre' (1870s), *Tingeltangelmädchen*; *manoli* 'messed up' (= *verdreht*), from an illuminated neon sign in Berlin which revolved with the name of the cigar firm Manoli (1890s); *knorke* 'splendid', 'super', perhaps also from a name (also *vollknorke*, *edelknorke*); *etepetete* 'fussy', 'prudish'; *Quatsch* 'nonsense'; *forsch* (from Fr. *force*) 'flash', 'stylish' may also have become common via Berlin. Not all these terms still survive.

A conspicuous number of expressions originating in soldiers' slang, thieves' cant, Yiddish, and student jargon have become socially acceptable and fashionable in Berlin, perhaps in the brothels, beer- and dance-halls (*Tabagien*), the (variety) theatre, or the cheap novelette, or through journalism. Semantic change can occur: e.g. *keß* 'pert', 'smart', 'attractive' once meant 'experienced in thieving', from Hebrew *ḥākām* 'wise', but abbreviated to the initial letter, Hebrew *ḥēθ*, which in Ashkenazic pronunciation had become Yiddish *xes*. Similarly, *Klamotte(n)* 'togs', 'clothes' originally meant 'broken tiles', 'rubble'. Expressions still current include: *Kaschemme* 'boozer', 'thieves' den'; *Ganeff/Ganove* 'gangster', 'criminal'; *Kassiber* 'a stiff', 'secret message smuggled out of prison'; *Kies, Moos, Pinke, Pinkepinke, Zaster* 'money'; *Kluft* (fem.) 'clothes', 'uniform'; *ausbaldowern* 'to spy out', 'find out'; *Schmiere stehen* 'keep look-out'; *mies* 'bad'; *schofel* 'mean', 'shabby'; *meschugge* 'crazy'; *mogeln* 'cheat'; *pleite* 'bankrupt', 'stony-broke'; *pumpen* 'lend'; *pennen* 'sleep'; *Penne* 'dosshouse'; *Pennbruder* 'tramp', 'dosser'; *Rotwelsch* 'thieves' cant'; *schmusen* 'flirt', 'talk'; *schnorren* 'cadge'; *schnuppe* 'worthless' (= *egal*); *Tinnef* 'trash', 'rubbish'; *Stuß* 'nonsense' (*rede keinen Stuß!*); *dufte* 'smashing', 'ace'.

Berlin colloquial occurs in the unusual context of an advertisement for French corsetry, probably from about 1900, shown in Fig. 10 (Schultze and Müller are two well-known Berlin 'characters' from the mid-nineteenth century).

Mangled French loan-words (*Foxterieur* for *Exterieur*) are also typical of the half-humorous but semi-serious aspirations of Berliners

CORSETS
DE PARIS
C.P. À LA
SIRENE
DIE ERSTE MARKE
DER WELT!

Müller: Schulße, pump   Schulße: Aber Müller,
mir dein Tafchentuch.   deshalb brauchfte doch
lck muß weenen.   nich weenen. Koof'
Schulße: Nanu, wat is?   deine   Olle   een
Müller: Ach, wenn ick   C. P. - Korfett, da
een Ooge uff det nette   follfte mal fehn, wat
Mächen werfe, wie   die nen anderes Fox-
fchick die jebaut is,   terieur kriegt.
un wenn ick denn be-   Müller: Det is ne jroß-
denke, wat for ne   artige Idee, un deiner
doofe Fijur meine   Ollen koofe ick jleich
Olle hat.   eens mit.

An Plätzen, an denen C. P. - Korfetts nicht zu
haben, weifen nächfte Bezugsquelle nach, von
wo ein C. P.-Luxuskatalog gratis zugefandt wird:
ETABLISSEMENTS FARCY & OPPENHEIM
PARIS / 15 RUE DES PETITS HÔTELS
'Société anonyme au capital de 2 625 000 frs.)

FIG. 10 (from Waas (1967), 42–3).

to stylishness and *savoir-faire*: compare such catch-phrases as 'Mit 'n
jewissen Awek', 'Jeder nach seinen Chacun', 'dusemang' (Fr. *douce-
ment*), 'Pläsirverjnüjen', 'partuh nich', 'Verstandez-vous?', 'vis-à-
schräj' (= *vis-à-vis*), etc. (For the French influence of Huguenots in
Berlin, see Chapter VII.)[93]

SPECIALIST AND GROUP LANGUAGES

Centralizing and standardizing tendencies in the recent history of the
German language were offset by the growing diversity of forms and
uses of the language which confronted individuals of all classes in
their daily lives. Scientific and technological advances created new
kinds of work demanding special training which sometimes brought
with it elaborate technical jargon. The new goods and inventions
profoundly affected the language as well as the life of the man in the
street; the railway, for example, introduced a whole new vocabulary
composed of heterogeneous elements, including loans from English

and French. In the mushrooming cities, bureaucracy delimited the individual's freedom and defined his responsibilities in language barely understood by most of the populace. Indirectly, such varieties of German were spread through politics, the press, and advertising, while the individual's own language varied according to the social groupings in which he participated—at home, at work, in working men's clubs, at political gatherings, in places of entertainment, and during military service. Despite the often enthusiastic reception of modern developments, technical and professional languages represented new barriers to general comprehension, especially to the poor and ill-educated masses,[94] not least because some terminology was borrowed from other languages, or artificially created, or, worse still, translated into stilted German 'officialese'. But even for the educated and semi-educated middle and lower middle classes (*Bürger- und Kleinbürgertum*) the awareness of other linguistic forms could be disturbing and seemed to threaten the cohesion of the literary standard language.

Since the nineteenth century technical and specialist languages have been influencing and enriching the German regional colloquial languages and the standard language. They represent major sources of linguistic innovation affecting all levels of language, but especially morphology, vocabulary, and semantics. Because technology is usually international, these specialist languages are open to influence from abroad and pass it into general usage: here too they encourage language change.

We shall subdivide specialist languages into two main but not always easily distinguished groups: technical and scientific languages or 'technolects' (*Fachsprachen*), and group languages (*Sondersprachen*[95] or *Gruppensprachen*). Technical, scientific languages are functional registers related to certain kinds of work; they aim at objectivity, precision, consistency, and economy, and are in their purest form written rather than spoken, supra-regional and perhaps international. Group languages, on the other hand, are social and often emotive; they are spoken as well as written, and are close enough in purpose to everyday spoken language to influence it or even to borrow everyday expressions from it; group languages tend to be less fixed and formal, ephemeral, and not infrequently regional. Any technical language is potentially a group language, but the users do not necessarily intend to set themselves apart from other members of the speech-community; on the other hand, speakers of group languages have a strong sense of group identity and may wish to create language barriers. However, within technolects different gradations of formalism blur the distinctions yet further: whereas the formal theoretical language may have a mathematical notation and a precise nomenclature based on Greek or Latin, and an 'objectivizing' syntax with impersonal and passive constructions, informal but still technical discussions between scientists display many more features of everyday colloquial language, especially a tendency to use metaphor. Finally, some form of popularization brings the technical development—and a limited amount of technical vocabulary—to the wider public. The extent to which the three levels of technical language can be distinguished depends upon the technology or science involved. In the history of modern German the links between the technical registers and the colloquial and standard languages are important: journalism, political debate, school textbooks, popular manuals (*Sachbücher*), and especially advertising, are some of the main routes by which technical jargon became familiar in Germany before 1945.

Certain professional languages of long standing have changed in character considerably: even the languages of farmers and fishermen have become modernized and technical as a result of scientific advances in animal physiology, biology, and farming methods. Thus, farmers and fishermen now draw upon the theoretical and experimental insights of agricultural and fisheries research, and the old *Berufs-* or *Standessprachen* have become intermediate levels between the scientifically trained experts and the layman. But in the nineteenth century (and until quite recently) these professional languages were informal and firmly based in local dialect. By contrast, in the Middle Ages the language of huntsmen already had a markedly group function (cf. Gottfried von Straßburg's *Tristran*), and for most of those who hunt it has become a prestige group language for leisure. The language of soldiers is another occupational language with a chequered history: warfare has increasingly become a science rather than an art, and the soldier a technician; at the same time civilians have been conscripted for limited periods into modern armies, which has shaped their language as a group and helped to familiarize the rest of the speech-community with many of its expressions.

We shall now compare an important technical language, military language, with its related group language, soldiers' slang.

A. MILITARY LANGUAGE (*MILITÄR*- OR *HEERESSPRACHE*)
AS TECHNICAL JARGON

Military language is the technical level of language in the armed forces. Many of its basic terms are international and derive from the sixteenth and seventeenth centuries when the structure of modern armies was established under French, Spanish, and Italian influence: e.g. *Armee, Arsenal, Artillerie, Bagage, Bataillon, Batterie, bombardieren, Bombe, Bresche, Brigade, Defensive, defilieren, Deserteur, desertieren, Division, Dragoner, Epaulette, Eskadron, exerzieren, Flanke, Fort, Furage, furagieren, General, Kaliber, Kamerad, Kommando/Kommandant/kommandieren, Kommiß, Kompanie, Korporal, Korps, Leutnant, Major, Parade, Parole, Patrone, Patrouille, Sergeant, Spion, Train, Truppe*, etc. Some of these are replaced by German equivalents as the result of linguistic purism (see Chapter X). But technological development opens up new areas in warfare—aeroplanes, tanks, submarines, field communications, to mention only the most obvious—and eventually new terms enter the military manuals, as can be seen in the changes to small arms and, on a larger scale, in the emergence of new 'arms' of the forces.

1. *Changes in small arms: the rifle and the automatics*

Only a few salient developments can be picked out:

Firstly, *Gewehr* (from *wehren*) replaces *Flinte, Büchse*, and *Feuerrohr* as the designation of the 'rifle'. The old muzzle-loader (*Vorderlader*) was replaced by the breech-loader (*Hinterlader*), thanks to the invention of the percussion system (*Perkussionssystem*) using a percussion cap (*Zündhütchen*). This increased the rate of fire considerably, and in the Prussian wars of 1864 and 1866, the needle-gun (*Zündnadelgewehr*) invented by J. N. von Dreyse in 1836 achieved a rate of five or six shots per minute. The accuracy was improved by the adoption of rifling (*gezogener Lauf*). Next, a magazine (*Magazin*) was added, taking up to five bullets. The jacketed bullet (*Stahlmantelgeschoß*) enabled high-velocity rifles to be developed. The basis for the German rifle of the First World War was the Mauser-Gewehr 98, a multiple rifle (*Mehrladegewehr*) with a bolt action (*Schlagbolzenzündung*) using the metal cartridge (*Metallpatrone*) invented in 1860, filled with smokeless powder (*rauchschwaches Pulver*) invented in 1884.

Automatic weapons (*Maschinenwaffen*) also appeared in the

second half of the nineteenth century and eventually replaced the rifle. At first some foreign forms occur, e.g. *Mitrailleuse* (this is replaced by *Maschinengewehr*). The Maxim Gun, named after the American inventor Hiram Maxim, was introduced into the Austro-Hungarian army in 1888 as the *Maxim-Maschinengewehr* or MG; the German army acquired it in 1899. Various types of MG were used, with both ammunition belts (*Gurtzuführung*) and magazines (*Magazinzuführung*). There were also in the First World War *Maschinenpistolen* using pistol ammunition and *Maschinenkanonen* using shells; their automatic movements were either by recoil (*Rückstoßlader*) or gas (*Gasdrucklader*). The MGs were further subdivided into l.MG (= *leichtes Maschinengewehr*) and s.MG (= *schweres Maschinengewehr*). The German MG 42 introduced in 1939 managed between twenty-five and thirty shots per second.

2. New arms of the forces

Tanks replaced cavalry towards the end of the First World War, and the old word *Panzer* ('armour'), already used for fortifications, battleships, and trains in the mid-nineteenth century (cf. *Panzerschiff* 'iron-clad', *Panzerzug*, etc.), was transferred also to *Panzer(wagen)* 'tank'. New compounds were formed with the determinative element *Panzer-*, translated into English variously by 'tank-' (*Panzerführer* 'tank-commander') or by 'armour(ed)' (*Panzerdivisionen* 'armoured divisions'). Other terms include *Panzerangriff*, *Panzerschlacht*, *Panzerabwehrkanone* (abbreviated to *Pak* (fem.)) 'anti-tank gun', *Panzerfalle* 'tank-trap', etc.

The air force (*Luftwaffe*, cf. English 'air-arm') required a whole new terminology, involving at first distinctions between craft that were lighter than air (balloons and dirigibles, 'Zeppelins') and those that were heavier than air (kites and aeroplanes). In particular, the elements *Flieger-* and *Flugzeug-* were productive in the new compounds;[96] *Fliegeralarm* 'air raid warning'; *Fliegerangriff*, *Fliegerbombe* 'aerial bomb'; *Flugzeuggeschwader* 'air(craft) squadron'; *Flugzeugstaffel* 'flight'; *Flugzeugträger* 'aircraft carrier'; *Fliegerabwehrkanone* (abbreviated to *Flak*) 'anti-aircraft (AA) gun'; etc.

Similarly, with the deployment of submarines (*Unterseeboote*), a new set of terms, this time prefixed by *U-boot-* or *Unterwasser-*, evolved, based partly on the already existing naval language.

Those technical terms from military language adopted into civilian life are usually general in nature: *Front, Kampf, Attacke, Gefecht, Feldzug,* for example, are common in political contexts (cf. *Klassenkampf, Kulturkampf*). Some show change of meaning: *Barracke* 'barracks' means a 'hovel', 'hut'; *Kaserne* is attested at Berlin in 1872 in *Mietskaserne* 'tenement house'; *Platzpatrone* 'blank cartridge' meant 'someone easily roused to anger'; *abblitzen* 'to misfire' (the powder flashes in the pan without any explosive force) is used of unsuccessful admirers (*ich habe ihn abblitzen lassen*); *die Werbetrommel rühren* 'to beat up (for) recruits' came to mean 'to advertise', as *Werbung* itself changed in meaning. Such semantic change can result from technical terms having been taken over first into the servicemen's slang, so that they are only in origin technical, no longer in function.[97] The relationships between military and soldiers' language, and between each and the general colloquial language (*Umgangssprache*), are complex and shifting.

B. SOLDIERS' SLANG (*SOLDATENSPRACHE*) AS A GROUP LANGUAGE[98]

Like the technical military language, soldiers' slang changes with time, although much more rapidly. Since many expressions are ephemeral and peculiar to individual arms of the forces and to regiments (dialect also contributes here), the slang is difficult to describe chronologically. We may broadly distinguish an old *Feldsprache*, with elements of *Rotwelsch*, which predates the nineteenth century (see above, p. 373); next, a second layer, essentially regional in character, which extends to the First World War;[99]—then, First World War slang (labelled I below) and finally Second World War slang (labelled II). The slang of the two World Wars is clearly distinct from earlier equivalents,[100] more ironical and coarser, reflecting the grimmer and more devastating features of modern warfare and its effects on civilian populations. Several social and functional variants of the slang occur: the language of officers remained a 'caste' language down to the First World War, for they had traditionally come from aristocratic backgrounds, and even in 1913 some 30 per cent of all officers were noblemen;[101] the language of parade-ground instructions differed from that of the field, and so forth. Contact with the enemy was also sometimes linguistic: parallel formations include 'hedge-hopping' ~ *Heckenhüpfen* and 'shit-house rumour' ~ *Latrinengerücht, Latrinenparole,* also in the RAF 'elsan gen'

(='phoney/unreliable information'). English loans from German show semantic change: *blitz* 'air raid' (from *Blitzkrieg*); *flak* 'anti-aircraft fire' (from *Fliegerabwehrkanone*, abbreviated to *Flak*); *strafe* 'make a low-flying attack firing indiscriminately' (from *strafen*).[102]

Soldiers' slang has had a wide influence, perhaps because of the social levelling which occurred in the German army, especially in the Second World War. In any case, it was rooted in the everyday colloquial language, and contributed to the decline of dialect and the spread of new or hitherto socially restricted expressions. Moreover, in almost every generation since the early nineteenth century conscription and war have brought the experience of soldiering to the man in the street for limited, if intense, periods, familiarizing the civilian population with soldiers' language on an unprecedented scale, since the soldier passed on its often colourful expressions when he resumed his old life in Civvy Street.[103] Conversely, the conscript attempted to demilitarize his existence and trivialized the institutions of war by using civilian expressions: a machine-gun became a *Gießkanne* (I and II);[104] a bomb was an *Ei* (I and II) (*Eier legen* 'to bomb'); in the navy a torpedo was an *Aal* (*veraalen* 'to torpedo'). Euphemism and circumlocution replaced expressions for death, destruction, wounding, and killing; but the very triviality of the replacements could seem sinister or brutal, an impression enhanced by their vulgarity: *absaufen*, *abrotzen* 'drown' (intr.); *er ist fertig gemacht, er ist zur Sau/zur Minna/zur Schnecke gemacht, er ist im Eimer, er hat einen kalten Arsch, der Arsch ist weg* 'he's dead'; *einen vor den Latz geknallt bekommen* 'be wounded'; *er bekam eins von mir über gebraten* 'I did for him'; *sich die Radieschen von unten ansehen, sich von der Verpflegung abmelden, abkratzen, verschütt gehen* 'to die'; *abgeschrieben* 'posted missing'; *umlegen* 'kill'. A crash landing became *abschmieren, hinrotzen*, even *Klavier aus dem 5. Stock*; to sink a ship was *einen Dampfer wegstecken/ abtakeln/ fischen/ knacken*; exploding shells were referred to as *Masern* 'measles' (I and II); a grenade explosion was a *Wattebausch* (II); bursts of anti-aircraft fire were *Feuerwerk* (I) or *Feuerzauber* (II); fighter planes were reduced to *Püppchen* (I and II); and spitfires were *alte Damen*. Other colloquial expressions for aircraft included *Drachen* (I), *Kiste* (I and II) (cf. English *crate*, (*box-*)*kite*), *Eierkiste* (I), *Molle* (I), *Mühle* (I and II), *Furzmolle* (I), *Wolkenkutsche* (I), *Schaukel* (I and II), *Schlitten* (I and II), *Kahn* (I), *Dampfer* (II), *Badewanne* (I and II), *Möbelwagen* (I), (*olle*) *Klamotte* (I),[105] and *Krähe* (II), but some of these (especially *Dampfer*, *Kiste*, *Schlitten*, and *Kahn*) were applied also to tanks, lorries, and other vehicles. Inevitably, the disparity between the thing described and the label applied to it was incongruous, and black humour figures prominently in soldiers' slang. Abbreviations also served to diminish and familiarize, as well as lending an air of military curtness: *Flak* (= *Fliegerabwehrkanone*), *Pak* (= *Panzerabwehrkanone*), *Stuka* (masc.)[106] (= *Sturzkampfflugzeug*), *MG* (= *Maschinengewehr*), *Wabo* (fem.) (= *Wasserbombe*), *Kaleu* (= *Kapitän-Leutnant*), *Sani* (= *Sanitäter*), *kv* (['ka:'fau]) (*kampfverwendungsfähig*); some of these short forms originated as slang but then became technical terms. Eventually, in the reverse of the process we have been considering, technical military terms were applied to everyday concerns: *Schanzzeug* 'eating irons' (lit. 'sappers' tools'); *am Boden zerstört* 'dead drunk'; *auf Tauchstation gehen* 'to sleep'; *Feuer frei!* 'smoking allowed'; ESAK/KASAK = *evangelische/ katholische Sündenabwehrkanone* 'padre' (!); *Frühzünder/Spätzünder* 'person who is quick/slow on the uptake'; *Blindgänger* 'dud', 'failure'.

Either way, by demilitarizing the military existence linguistically and by reapplying military terminology in civilian life, a considerable degree of polysemy is created.

The more extreme features of soldiers' slang result from the tensions of mainly young men subjected to the pressures and compulsions of strict military discipline, frustrated by long periods of boredom, and exposed to the experience and risk of death and injury. To relieve boredom, even banal activities of regular type were expressed in many different ways: in the First World War sleeping was termed *pennen*, *bofen* (*pofen*), *dachsen*, *koksen*, *kuscheln*, *sich lang machen*, *sich hinhauen*, while eating was *picken*, *acheln*, *prumßen*, *flapsen*, *spachteln*, *wampen*, *schlabbern*, *müffeln*—even within the same regiment.[107] Released from responsibility, away from the civilizing influences of home, women, and children, and required to disregard a basic taboo—not to kill—the soldier relieves his feelings in obscene or vulgar language drawn from other taboo areas, notably sexuality and excretion: *Scheiße* and derivatives abound, e.g. *anscheißen* 'reprimand', *Anschiß*, etc., even *ausgeschissen haben* 'be dead'. Some bizarre terms were undoubtedly isolated or nonce formations: e.g. *Tripperspritze* 'machine-gun' (*Tripper* = 'gonorrhea'); or *die Pinkulative ergreifen* 'urinate', a blend of military phrasing (*Initiative ergreifen*) and vulgar *pinkeln*.[108]

TECHNOLOGICAL DEVELOPMENTS AND THE
SPEECH-COMMUNITY[109]

Specialist and technical registers are in themselves systematic varieties of German, with their own functions and history, but individual
elements from them influence the standard language and everyday
spoken German, perhaps via advertising or newspapers. Such words
and expressions are cultural tokens—*Kulturwörter*—introduced with
the new concepts or inventions, and often borrowed from abroad.
In other cases a whole bureaucracy swathes inventions which affect
the daily lives of citizens. For example, as householders were provided with mains services, water and sewage, gas, electricity, and
the telephone, they had to master a new vocabulary, e.g. *Wasser-
versorgung, Wasserwerk, Wasserzuflußrohr, Wasserleitung, Leitungs-
wasser; Gasversorgung, Gasleitungsröhre, Gasleitungen legen, Gasherd;
Elektrizitätswerk, elektrisches Licht, elektrische Klingel, Elektroherd;
Strommesser, Stromsperre, Stromschwankungen, Anschluß* 'service
connection' (for all services), *Anschlußgebühr, Telephonanschluß*, etc.
Parallel formations were common, but at first technical vocabulary
existed in several variants, e.g. *Gasanstalt, Gasbeleuchtungsanstalt,
Gasfabrik, Gasbeleuchtungsgesellschaft, Gasgesellschaft*, although
time, convenience, or centralized bodies[110] eventually favoured one
term. Similarly, *Gasometer* for a time competed with *Gasbehälter*
'gasometer' and with *Gasmesser* in the sense 'gas meter'. German's
facility for compounding and derivation produced readily understood neologisms, such as those for domestic lighting, often based on
existing words from the time when candles were the main source of
light: *Gas + -armleuchter, -wandleuchter* = 'gas bracket'; *Gas + -krone,
-kandelaber* (masc.), or *-armleuchter* = 'gas chandelier', 'gaselier',
'gas (lighting) fixture'. Metaphor added other terms, e.g. *Glüh(licht)
strumpf* 'gas mantle' (lit. 'stocking') or *(Glüh)birne* 'light bulb' (lit.
'pear'). Such forms look like informal creations of the 'workshop or
laboratory language' rather than accepted technical terms, but they
are listed in Muret–Sanders in 1899,[111] and must have gone into
popular parlance relatively early. Such metaphors were readily accessible to the man in the street, and at this time nationalistically inspired
purists (see Chapter X) sought to replace foreign terminology where
possible, so encouraging further the metaphorical use of the native
language. The scientific and technical theoretical language, on the

other hand, will have entered the standard dictionaries via technical journals, manuals, and glossaries and did not come via the colloquial language.

Moreover, the metaphors of one technology or science are very often borrowed into another. For example, the word *Netz* comes to mean 'network' and is applied in turn to railways (*Eisenbahnnetz*), roads (*Straßennetz*), electricity (*Stromnetz*), telephone (*Telefonnetz/ Fernsprechnetz*), radio (*Funknetz*); similarly, the word *Anschluß* (lit. 'connection', 'annexation') comes to mean 'train connection', 'electrical contact', 'subscriber number' (telephone), 'house connection' (for mains services), etc., so that polysemy increases. As Mark Twain notes in his appendix on 'The Awful German Language', some words, e.g. *Schlag* and *Zug*, both on their own and combined with other words, can convey a formidable array of meanings.[112]

Some inventions can be dated and placed in chronological sequence (e.g. the *Druckknopf(verschluß)* 'press-stud', invented in 1885 by Heribert Bauer, or the *Reißverschluß* 'zip-fastener', invented by A. B. Drautz in 1889), but since the items themselves became household names only somewhat later, the enrichment of standard and colloquial language by this technical vocabulary is less easily datable. Moreover, the informal levels of technical language were more important than the formal, theoretical ones—partly because they used metaphor to supply terms of art, partly because they resembled group languages, with the added attraction of seeming modern and progressive to the layman. The resulting polysemy was a reciprocal process: technical jargons borrowed everyday words in metaphors, and then returned some of them enriched with a technical meaning as new metaphors in everyday language. Because technical jargons interact, terms can be difficult to attribute to particular fields; furthermore, existing metaphors may be 'revivified' by being applied to a new content or context—a process akin to semantic borrowing:[113]

1. *Transport*. From steamships/trains: *abdampfen* 'go off (in a huff)'; *tu' das gleich und mach' Dampf dahinter* 'get a move on'. From railways: *Pufferstaat* 'buffer state'; *Türpuffer* 'door-stop'; *Dampf ablassen* 'let off steam'; *entgleisen* 'come unstuck'; *Schmalspurakademiker* 'second-rate academic', 'hack teacher'; *auf dem toten Gleis* 'at a dead end'; *du verstehst Bahnhof davon* 'you haven't a clue'; *es ist höchste Eisenbahn* 'high time'. From railways or transport

generally: *in ein Geschäft einsteigen/aussteigen* 'join/leave a business'; *den Anschluß verpassen* 'fail to get married' (of spinsters, cf. English 'to miss the boat').

2. *Technology*. From electricity: *wie elektrisiert* 'electrified'; *die Polizei wurde eingeschaltet* 'the police were brought in'; *die Konkurrenz wurde ausgeschaltet* 'the opposition was foiled'; *er schaltet langsam, hat eine lange Leitung* 'slow on the uptake'; *Deutschland wurde gleichgeschaltet/Gleichschaltung* (lit. 'parallel electrical circuitry')— these terms refer to the creation of a Nazi infrastructure from 1933 controlling all aspects of life; *Kontakt aufnehmen mit jemand* 'get into contact with someone'. From engineering and other industrial processes: *Reibungspunkt* 'source of friction'; *reibungslos* 'smoothly'; *zusammenschweißen* 'weld together'; *Belastungsprobe* 'endurance test'; *völlig ausgelastet* 'busy'; *steuern* 'steer', 'direct'; *(ab)drosseln* 'cut back'; *am laufenden Band* (lit. 'conveyor belt') 'continually'; *auf Touren laufen* 'at full output'; *die Panne* 'breakdown'; *Sicherheitsventil* 'safety valve'; *er dreht durch, ist überdreht* 'he's crazy'; *Steuerschraube* (lit. 'tax screw'), as in *die Steuerschraube anziehen* 'to raise taxes' (cf. mod. *Preis-Lohnspirale*). From photography and film: *unterbelichtet* 'stupid' (lit. 'underexposed'); *Rückblende/rückblenden* 'flashback'; *auslösen* 'start, set off'.[114]

At a different level, technical terms from psychoanalysis and philosophy enriched the abstract language of literary criticism and intellectual debate and have become current—partly via literary feuilletons in newspapers—without becoming 'popular'. Examples from Psychoanalysis are: *das Unter-/Unbewußte* 'the sub-/unconscious', *Lust-/Unlustgefühl, der Komplex, das Ich, das Überich, das Es, Verdrängung, Minderwertigkeitskomplex, Hemmung* 'inhibition', *Neurose, Geltungsdrang, Narzißmus, abreagieren*.

Finally, specialist terms from various sports and pastimes have become familiar as sport itself became increasingly popular, albeit vicariously, initially among the middle classes and then, with regulated working hours, increased leisure, and wages, among the masses. In consequence, the role of sport was naturally reinforced by politicians who drew metaphors from it and saw in it a means of communicating with the masses; callisthenics (*Turnen*) had been established by Friedrich Ludwig Jahn (1778-1852) with a partly nationalistic aim. The word *Sport* was itself borrowed from English sometime before the mid-nineteenth century, and in the last quarter successive sports emerged—horse-racing and tennis, and, at a more popular level, football, boxing, and others. Sporting terms with a metaphorical meaning include: *Außenseiter, Favorit, Schrittmacher* 'pace-maker', *Endspurt, ein guter Tip, gehandikappt, in (guter) Form sein, Konkurrenz, trainieren, Rekord, eine Hürde nehmen, sich durchboxen* 'to fight through', *gerade noch über die Runde kommen* 'just manage to do something', *ich bin ganz k.o.* 'I'm worn out'. Considerable foreign, especially English, influence is found in the language of sport, including written reports of matches in newspapers. Because of its popular appeal, sporting jargon quickly attracted the attention of purists (see Chapter X), although in this area, which was not susceptible to bureaucratic diktat, they seem to have been unsuccessful.

CONCLUSION

The codification of spelling and pronunciation more or less completed by the early twentieth century represents centralizing forces linked to the political unification of Germany and its long cultural hegemony over Austria and parts of Switzerland. While barriers to comprehension had been overcome, since the dialects were reduced in importance to stylistic or cultural variants, social barriers were to some extent reinforced by the codifications. The colloquial urban languages remained strongly regional in character, but were heterogeneous, vehicles for social and linguistic mobility, yet flexible enough to represent the basis for most daily communication. However, the new technical and scientific languages and the less formal jargons dependent on them create new linguistic barriers and set apart groups of speakers. Innovations in daily living, in the press, advertising, housing, consumer goods, and so forth, transmit many originally technical expressions to the community at large. The technical and scientific varieties of German clearly represent powerful forces for linguistic change, able to reshape the standard language even in its codified state. Much work remains to be done in describing the huge growth of German scientific and technical vocabulary at the end of the nineteenth century. Such 'industrial etymology', as we may call it, has the added attraction that the exact dates of innovations and new inventions lie tucked away in the many technical journals or in the archives of the larger firms, while the names and terms for the inventions may themselves be discussed or laid down in Government directives, local council regulations, and so forth. The major technical dictionaries give guidance to the capturing of these new labels, while museum collections permit the study of *Wörter und Sachen* in close conjunction.

SELECT BIBLIOGRAPHY

A comprehensive history of German in the nineteenth and twentieth centuries remains to be written. The standard linguistic histories have sections on it: see especially Bach (1965, 1970), Eggers (1963–77), iv (1977), Keller (1978), Polenz (1978), and Tschirch (1966–9, 1971–5). A very readable account of vocabulary and style from the late nineteenth century to the most recent past is given by Mackensen (1971). The older work by Socin (1888) treats some nineteenth-century aspects from a contemporary viewpoint. Some work on present-day German has historical perspectives, e.g. Bausinger (1972), Braun (1979), while dialectology is largely based to this day on material collected before 1945.

GENERAL INTRODUCTORY ARTICLES ON STANDARD AND LITERARY LANGUAGE

LGL contains several useful articles:

Eggers (1973*b*).	Frühwald (1973).
Eibl (1973).	Leibfried (1973).

HISTORICAL AND CULTURAL BACKGROUND

Ramm (1967).	Sagarra (1980).
Sagarra (1977).	Taylor (1954).

Still useful as a source of information is the *Deutscher Kulturatlas*, edd. Lüdtke and Mackensen (1928–38).

SCHOOL GRAMMARS AND EDUCATION

Cherubim (1980).	Schieb (1981).
Chorley (1984).	Vesper (1980).
Glinz (1967).	

See also the work on literacy by Engelsing (1973) and Schenda (1977).

SPELLING AND PRONUNCIATION

Althaus (1980).   Schlaefer (1980).
Lotzmann (forthcoming).   Ungeheuer (1969).
Mentrup (1980).

DIALECTOLOGY

Bach (1950).   Mitzka (1957).
Keller (1961).   Schirmunski (1962).
Martin (1939).   Schwarz (1950).
Mitzka (1943).   Weifert (1964-5).
See also Goossens (1977).

DIALECT ATLASES

Deutscher Sprachatlas (1926-56) [the *DSA* evaluates material collected by
Georg Wenker in the late nineteenth century].

See also *Deutscher Wortatlas* (1951-80), and Mitzka (1952).

For other atlases and dialect dictionaries for Luxemburg, the Tirol,
German-speaking Switzerland, and Pennsylvania, see Goossens (1977),
128 ff. For specimens of modern German dialects, see *PHONAI* (1969) (with
tape) and Weifert (1964-5) (with records).

INDIVIDUAL DIALECT WRITERS

Braak and Mehlem (1961) [on   Kully (1969 [on Hebel].
    Groth].   Töteberg (1978) [on Reuter].
Christiansen (1975) [on Reuter].

COLLOQUIAL LANGUAGE (*Umgangssprachen*)

Bichel (1973).   Küpper (1955-70).
Eichhoff (1977-8).   Wunderlich (1894).
Kretschmer (1918).

VARIETIES OF GERMAN (Technical and Social)

See the introductory articles by Möhn (1980) and Hahn (1980) in *LGL*, and
especially:

Fluck (1980).   Olt (1981).
Mackensen (1954).   Wolf (1956).

CHAPTER X

THE MODERN PERIOD (1800–1945) (II): SEMANTICS, PURISM, AND POLITICS

THE philosophical question of the relationship between language and life bears also upon the history of the German language in the Modern Period to 1945, for it has often been assumed by purists, linguistic historians, writers, and politicians that the German language and the social and physical reality of Germans stood in direct, perhaps even reciprocal, relationship. By '*the* German language' was usually meant the educated standard or literary language, since this prestigious variant of German had come to furnish a symbol of the cultural cohesion of Germans in the period before political unification in 1871. In this respect it resembled the nebulous concept *tiutschiu zunge* in the Middle Ages (see pp. 31–2). The modern written and printed literary standard had been considerably codified, and so was relatively stable in spellings, forms, and syntax. However, the very processes of unification and centralization which highlighted the need for linguistic standardization also broke down the older, absolutist states, leading eventually to larger and more complex social structures at national level, and this social diversity conflicted with the apparently relatively homogeneous standard language. From being a symbol of unity, *Hoch-* or *Schrift-*

deutsch was increasingly felt to be a barrier to social mobility by those who did not use it. Moreover, dialect no longer provided an adequate means of communication for the changed society, as we have just seen (Chapter IX): for only a sentimental escapist view of dialect still regarded it as the traditional and unchanging expression of a sheltered and structured community, again linking language and life directly.

Paradoxically, despite the apparent dislocation between the increasingly unified standard German and the diversifying and complex social reality, the growing importance of other varieties of the language—colloquial, technical, and group registers—did reflect new social circumstances. The changing relationships between these varieties of German in the nineteenth and twentieth centuries has become a central part of the recent history of the German language, since the varieties themselves are distributed in society according to the functions and intentions of those who use them—no longer, as in the eighteenth century, primarily according to class and region.[1] In particular, political emancipation and awareness gave a voice to hitherto barely represented groups among the poorer artisans and workers who made up the urban proletariat at the close of the nineteenth century: their interests and their language alike differed from those of German literary circles in absolutist days. Indeed, some major literary movements from the 1850s onwards can be seen as reactions to the new circumstances, as a search for more adequate, or at least novel, expression for them. Individual authors felt their alienation and inability to communicate as a weakness of the language they were using, especially in its semantics—words and things seemed separated by a widening gulf. Several factors contributed to this sense of ill ease with the German language: first, the multiplicity of varieties of German entailed shifts of meaning according to degree of formality, technicality, and intention; secondly, the literary language of the classical writers Goethe and Schiller had addressed an identifiable and close-knit audience of upper and upper middle classes, but attempts to perpetuate this language in the later nineteenth century resulted only in cliché; finally, the authors were inhibited by a sense of linguistic crisis (*Sprachverwirrung*),[2] partly of their own making, based on an oversimplified approach to meaning.

This chapter will show some linguistic effects of purism, of the politicization of German society, and of National Socialism, which also tended to assume a one-to-one relationship between language and reality (*Wort* and *Sache*) and a corresponding one-to-one relationship between expression and 'thought' (*Worte* and *Gesinnung*). The purists were often nationally inspired, and claimed that foreign words did not merely obscure the content, but somehow weakened the moral fibre of those who used them. Purism, particularly institutionalized purism, represents a form of linguistic manipulation and therefore has some affinity with the political use of language to place value-judgements on the interpretation of social reality.[3] The National Socialists attempted to impose their ideological view by means of propaganda, and their totalitarian regime gave National Socialist usage an unrivalled importance, allowing us to scrutinize its effects on the speech-community in some detail, and especially to perceive the positive or negative associations words had acquired. In the immediate post-war period, attempts were made to 'denazify' the German language, but paradoxically these efforts often shared the underlying assumptions regarding the close relationship between language and life which had been those of the National Socialist propagandists.

SEMANTICS AND SEMANTIC CHANGE

Wilhelm von Humboldt clearly stated that words were not simply representations of objects even in the case of concrete nouns:

In die Bildung und in den Gebrauch der Sprache geht aber nothwendig die ganze Art der s u b j e k t i v e n W a h r n e h m u n g der Gegenstände über. Denn das Wort entsteht eben aus dieser Wahrnehmung, ist nicht ein Abdruck des Gegenstandes an sich, sondern des von diesem in der Seele erzeugten Bildes.[4]

While constrained by the regularities of the language, each individual was, according to Humboldt, free to understand something slightly different behind the words, so that each act of comprehension also included an element of misunderstanding—this is one of the mechanisms of language change. For Humboldt, the crisis of the gulf between words and things perceived by some writers was part of the actual functioning of language. Despite certain weaknesses, the 'semiotic triangle' provides a similar analytical model of the possible relationships holding between thought, reality, and the linguistic symbol, and it can perhaps clarify the kind of semantic assumptions behind purist and political manipulation of German, while also identifying the limited type of semantic change produced by ideological factors.

Fig. 11 shows a traditional model of this triangle.[5] The symbol relates to its referent—the action, event, or thing in the 'real world'—only via thought; hence the broken line implying that the relationship between symbol and referent is indirect. Moreover, both symbol and thought are abstractions, and they combine inseparably to give the

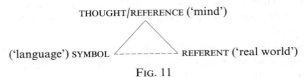

THOUGHT/REFERENCE ('mind')

('language') SYMBOL ← - - - - - - - - → REFERENT ('real world')

FIG. 11

linguistic 'sign', which can only be a sign if it signifies something. Indeed, Ferdinand de Saussure described the symbol as an acoustic *image*, to distinguish it from the actually occurring sounds (or written characters): in other words (from the listener's point of view), acoustic images enable us to pick out familiar blocks of sound and link them to meanings which relate to reality. Saussure's linguistic sign is abstract and bipartite, comprising an acoustic image, the 'signifier' (*signifiant*) and some concept or meaning, the 'thing signified' (*signifié*), which is itself abstracted from reality. Hence, we cannot simply see the sign as a label applied to the real world; instead, it is a complex entity of form and meaning, so that the linguistic form or symbol or acoustic image—however we prefer to term it—refers to some object or event in reality only indirectly, via thought. This relationship is called 'referential' or 'denotational': words denote features of reality.

Signs relate to other signs both conceptually and formally, and such primarily intra-linguistic relationships (disregarding the external world of experience) are termed 'sense relations' and are of several kinds. For instance, the different symbols *small, minute, teeny, tiny, titchy*, etc. convey very similar meanings, so that these signs are in a sense-relationship of (partial) synonymy.[6] Conversely, two identical acoustic images (symbols) can express different meanings, e.g. *die Bank* 'bench' (pl. *die Bänke*) and *die Bank* 'financial institution' (pl. *die Banken*), where the relationship is one of homonymy; the different plurals reinforce the view that we are dealing with two distinct words. At times homonymy is difficult to distinguish from polysemy where one acoustic image has more than one meaning, e.g. *die Tasche* (pl. *Taschen*) (1) 'pocket', (2) 'attaché case'. The dictionary-compiler must decide whether to give one entry or two.[7] Other types of sense-relation include oppositeness (antonymy) and conceptual hierarchies (hyponymy). Turning to the formal links between signs, we find associations of several kinds based on the similarities of their acoustic images: some are morphological and paradigmatic, reflecting the functions of word-formation and grammar, others are phonetic and are most evident in assonance, rhyme, punning, and so forth, although such 'acoustic echoes' are present in all communication in some degree.

Concentrating on sense-relationships rather than referential ones avoids the problem of incorporating the referent (i.e. the experiential world of reality) into semantic study. But the linguistic historian must consider at least the social reality, if linguistic shifts are to be related to changed circumstances of the speakers. Moreover, sense and reference are sometimes closely connected, as in the often-cited 'lexical field' for 'female human', where MHG *wîp, frouwe, frowelîn juncfrouwe, dame, dierne, maget, magedîn* differ from their formal modern German equivalents *Weib, Frau, Fräulein, Jungfrau/Jungfer, Dame, Dirne, Magd/Maid,* and *Mädchen.* Rank and status blend with generic and functional factors to account for the shifts in distribution, some of which have undoubtedly been triggered off by borrowing from French, as in the case of *dame/Dame* (and also *Mademoiselle/Mamsell* and *Madame* in the seventeenth and eighteenth centuries).

While sense and reference affect the German language as a system, the context and situation of use also bear upon meaning: just as statements can be used as commands or made ironical given the appropriate intonation or qualified by the right gestures, so the meaning of words and expressions depends also on their use. Furthermore, language changes through use, and it is surely context and situation which permit shifts of meaning to occur—which is not to deny that such shifts may be supported by 'structural' factors present in the language system. Contextually, some words and expressions may be more likely to occur than others, and in idioms their 'collocation' is actually determined, even down to tense-forms, e.g. *er hat etwas ausgefressen* 'He's been up to mischief', not **er fraß etwas aus.* Sometimes the simple contextual collocation of one word with another makes it become pejorative. Yet another kind of meaning is the 'connotation' or emotive value or 'overtone' which words and expressions acquire when used by certain social groups in particular situations: religious and political ideologies impose such connotations. Collocational and connotational meaning relate mainly to the use of language to convey attitudes, not just information.

Many nineteenth-century writers failed to distinguish these different types of meaning sufficiently clearly, and either contented themselves with linking language directly to reality as a form of 'naming', or else held that language actually shaped thought and thereby imposed a view of reality rather than reflecting it. Either way, they overemphasized only part of the semiotic triangle. Purists and politicians did likewise. In particular, the modern purists concentrated on the formal rather than semantic issues and wished to remove un-German words: but meaning was important because the introduction of new ideas or things inevitably changed sense-relationships. If foreign words are accepted, if they are replaced by neologisms, or if existing words are extended in meaning to accommodate the new concept, the result is *always* a shift in the sense-relationships holding within the language, either by partial synonymy, or by homonymy or polysemy. Those who seek to manipulate others politically often insinuate that some change in referential semantics is involved in interpreting reality 'correctly', whereas political opponents have misunderstood it. They claim to be using language 'correctly' or 'truthfully', giving an adequate interpretation of 'the way things really are', while opponents are peddling inadequate or 'false' concepts. But the imposition of a view of reality by politicians is mostly restricted to collocational and connotational use of language, and involves little more than an emotive colouring of expressions in certain contexts and situations for ideological purposes. While this can be pernicious—as National Socialism shows—it hardly amounts to altering referential relationships, still less to reshaping reality.

THE LATER PURISM[8]

Nineteenth-century linguistic purists might often see themselves as descendants of the seventeenth-century language societies (Chapter VII), but most drew on the theory and practical example of the influential educationalist Joachim Heinrich Campe (1746–1818).

Campe had submitted a prize essay on purism to the Preußische Akademie at Berlin in 1792, and his lifelong interest in the subject culminated in his *Wörterbuch zur Erklärung und Verdeutschung der unserer Sprache aufgedrungenen fremden Ausdrücke* (1801) and in his and Theodor Bernd's five-volume dictionary, *Wörterbuch der deutschen Sprache*, (1807–11). Campe was set on gradually eradicating all foreign words, including technical terms, because he felt that science and learning would be more generally accessible if presented in German. The stylistic and literary value of loan-words did not impress him, although he obviously recognized them as emotively marked, since his dictionary often suggests alternative replacements for foreign words according to whether they are being used positively or negatively: thus, for *Aristokrat* he proposed either *Adelherrscher* or, more critically, *Herrscherling*, *Adeling*; *Patriotismus* could be rendered favourably as *Vaterlandsliebe*, or criticized as *Vaterländerei*.[9] Replacement ('*Ver*deutschung'), rather than adaptation of foreign words to suit German phonology and morphology ('*Ein*deutschung'), was Campe's intention,[10] and his late-Enlightenment rationalism even led him to purify Kant's philosophical vocabulary by 'translating' the Graeco-Latin terminology, although those interested in such matters were likely to be from the educated middle classes with a grounding in the classics. Campe also replaced the traditional foreign terminology of grammar, going far beyond Gueintz and Schottel. Goethe and Schiller ridiculed his pedantry in their *Xenien* (1795–7) (see especially Nos. 79, 124, 125),[11] while Wieland rejected his 'Sprach-Jakobinismus',[12] his penchant for 'guillotining' words which, while not necessarily citizens, had nevertheless acquired some customary right to exist. As well as suggestions from puristic predecessors and rivals, Campe's dictionaries contain about 3,500 neologisms of his own, of which some 250 (a large number) gained a measure of acceptance, in some cases despite—possibly even because of—the hearty criticism they provoked. Words like *Zerrbild* (for *Karikatur*), *Kerbtier* (for *Insekt*), *folgerichtig* (for *konsequent*), and *Stelldichein* (for *Rendez-vous*) have survived, though without ousting their foreign rivals; however, other formations along similar lines failed: *Schmollwinkel*[13] (for *Boudoir*; from *schmollen* 'pout', 'sulk', Fr. *bouder*), or *Wandelbahn* (for *Promenade*). While Campe did accept some loans as having become naturalized German 'Staatsbürger', neither he nor his immediate successors saw fit to distinguish between the *Fremdwort* and the

Lehnwort, and in this respect they had not advanced beyond the insights of the abler seventeenth-century purists like Harsdörffer (see Chapter VII).

Because of the conviction that language and thought are so interrelated that language shapes thought as well as expressing it, nineteenth-century purists wished to eradicate foreign words in order to promote clearer and more nationally conscious thinking. When we consider some of the more extreme rationalist purists, we may question the wisdom of this approach. C. H. Wolke (1741–1825) and K. F. C. Krause (1781–1832) were co-founders of the Berliner Gesellschaft für deutsche Sprache (1815–25), and were both extreme rationalists. Wolke reformed the orthography and rejected common usage and the leading authors as models for reform; he also believed that individuals can change language. His grammatical terminology includes forms like *die Nunzeit/das Nun* 'present tense', *di Fortzeit/das Fort* 'perfect tense', *di Komnunzeit/das Komnun* 'future'. Krause even wished to replace the language of religion, philosophy, and chemistry, but became hopelessly abstruse: he 'translates' 'Dieser Mensch ist Gottes Sohn' as 'Dieses orendliche Geistleibinvereinwesen ist durch Wesen als gleichwesentliches Nebenausserwesen miteigenlebverursacht.' Whereas, to reform chemical terms, he resorts to the 'old' root *mell-* (not authenticated!): *mellen = chemisch behandeln, mellig = chemisch, Mellner = Chemiker, Mellung/Mellnis/Mellebnis = chemischer Prozeß*.[14] Such rationalist purists were insensitive to the historical development of the German language, convinced that it could and should be made utterly systematic, blind to its poetic qualities, and naïvely out of touch with the forces of usage and inertia ranged against change of any kind.

A second contention of linguistic reformers—already commonly held in the seventeenth century—was that foreign borrowing undermined German culture and was a sign of decadence. To purify the language was an act of national loyalty: indeed, the words *Volk* and *völkisch* replaced *Nation* and *national* in certain contexts. The old organic metaphor of the baroque language societies recurred, presenting the German language as a living plant to be nurtured or as a healthy organism to be protected from alien diseases; for foreign words were products of the forcing-house, exotic and ill-suited to robust German soil, where they must inevitably degenerate[15] (*degenerieren, entarten, verkrüppeln*). Such imagery and language abounded in the nationalist movement known as the 'Deutsche

Bewegung', whose members included prominent writers, political journalists, and educationalists—notably Johann Gottlieb Fichte (1762–1814), Ernst Moritz Arndt (1769–1860), and Friedrich Ludwig Jahn (1778–1852), 'Turnvater-Jahn', whose callisthenic vocabulary remains current today.[16] These writers naturally regarded the German language as *the* cultural bond, shaping its speakers, and identifying them as belonging to a specific group, the *Volk*, whose *Volksheit, Deutschheit, Volkstümlichkeit* are 'natural' and 'sacrosanct'. For example, Arndt observes, 'Will also ein Volk nicht verlieren, wodurch es Volk ist, will es seine Art mit allen seinen Eigentümlichkeiten bewahren, so hat es auf nichts so sehr zu wachen, als daß ihm seine Sprache nicht verdorben und zerstört werde';[17] and again, '. . . was sind die Naturgrenzen eines Volks? Ich sage: die einzige giltige Naturgrenze macht die Sprache.'[18] Later, much of the language and all of the pathos recurred in National Socialist style, but racial rather than linguistic purity was stressed, and the political purpose was totally different. It is noteworthy that waves of purism break at times of political upheaval—at the time of the Napoleonic Wars, around 1848, after unification in 1871, and in the First World War period. At first, the accompanying xenophobia is directed against French loans (*Französelei*), then, towards 1900, with the growth of competitiveness with England, against borrowing from English. The English influence, for example, occurred particularly in social and cultural contexts—the names of children, racehorses, dogs, types of carriages, clothes, material, and food and drink; in fact, the language was used for its snob appeal. Equally objectionable were the mixed or incorrect forms which ranged from *Hemetex* 'ham and eggs' to *Mehlkutsche* 'mail coach' and *Lehmanns Quatsch* 'lemon squash'.[19] In general, as befitted the political potential of the movement, criticism was directed primarily against loans in everyday social life—entertainments, sport, and literature—but in technology and science also new inventions increasingly favoured the use of German, reflecting a new awareness of German industrial and commercial prestige. However, as late as 1911 a particularly extreme purist, Eduard Engel, observed in a mixture of horticultural, medical, and religious imagery:

Ein Gebiet unsers geistigen Lebens jedoch ist von der Veredelung unsrer Sprache so gut wie unberührt geblieben, die . . . Wissenschaft; ja sie verschmutzt die sprachlichen Blutbahnen, die sich säubern möchten, immer von neuem mit dem fremden Blutgift. Bei der hohen sachlichen Geltung der

Wissenschaft in Deutschland ist diese Versündigung an einem der vornehmsten Volksgüter unverzeihlich . . .[20]

The unification of Germany in 1871 marks a turning-point in the history of recent purism, as Kirkness shows, since centralized bureaucracies for post and telecommunications, railways, law, education, and administration all needed corresponding linguistic standards. The choice of new German designations was sensible, because it aided clarity and overcame the multiplicity of regional usages, and to these practical advantages we may add national pride. This was particularly so in the military sphere, where the superiority of German armies seemed to some incompatible with the continued use of a French-based *Heeressprache*. In 1871 the *Militärliteraturblatt* and the *Militär-Wochenblatt* came out in favour of Germanizing the military language, and this was reinforced by re-editions of the Field Service Regulations and Firing Regulations (*Felddienstordnung* and *Schießvorschriften*) in 1886 and by edicts of Emperor Wilhelm II:[21] in 1887 he prescribed *Gelände* (instead of *Terrain*) and *Abteilungen* (instead of *Detachements*), and in 1899 he replaced several ranks by German ones: *Second-Lieutenant* became *Leutnant*, *Premier-Lieutenant* became *Oberleutnant*, *Charge* became *Dienstgrad*, *Avancement* became *Beförderung*, and *Anciennetät* became *Dienstalter*, etc.; the Emperor refers explicitly to the 'Reinheit der Sprache in Meinem Heere'. Gradually successive army regulations went over to German terminology (*bajonettieren* becomes *gewehrfechten* in 1909, for example) and the technological advances in weaponry and tactics also encouraged breaking away from historical tradition.[22]

Official linguistic norms ('amtliche Sprachregelungen'), like school grammars, permit individuals to influence German in considerable degree, although their names may remain virtually unknown to the community at large. One of the best remembered is the first imperial Postmaster-General, Heinrich von Stephan (1831–97), who was made an honorary member of the newly founded Allgemeiner Deutscher Sprachverein in 1887 for his contribution to purism in removing some 765 foreign terms from Post Office usage. His directives of 1874 and 1875 imposed the forms *Postanweisung* (instead of *Mandat*), *eingeschrieben* (for *recommandiert*), *Fahrschein* (for *Billett*), *postlagernd* (for *poste restante*), *Rückschein* (for *Retour-Recipisse/-Billet*), *Merkbuch* (for *Notizbuch*), *Dienstalter* (for *Anciennetät*), *Briefumschlag* (for *Couvert*), and so forth; *Postkarte* (now replacing *Correspondenzkarte*) occurs already in the eighteenth century in several senses, including 'map' and 'ticket'; *Anschrift* (for *Adresse*) is another revival, probably from Zesen, while Wolke's neologism *Fernsprecher* (for *Telephon*) was introduced in 1877.[23] Although there was opposition to Stephan's purism, largely on the grounds that it replaced expressions that were international, the purification of official and administrative languages was no aggravation to the man in the street, who scarcely needed such language himself and complained only if he could not understand it. On the contrary, purism in official language symbolized a proper national pride. Anyhow, foreign designations have remained common in everyday speech—*Billet, Kuvert, Etui*, etc.—whereas German 'officialese' prefers German,[24] often relying on compound nouns that appear quaint or cumbersome to the foreigner, like *Fahrzeug, Kraftwagen, Personenkraftwagen, Last(kraft)wagen, Straßenverkehrsordnung.*[25] These official or administrative languages were laid down in Germany after 1871, but they were not fully adopted in other German-speaking countries, and Austria and Switzerland frequently retain their own foreign-based official jargons, much to the consternation of well-meaning 'pan-German' purists.

THE ALLGEMEINER DEUTSCHER SPRACHVEREIN

Within Germany itself the official purism probably encouraged creation of the most successful German language society in the language's history, the Allgemeiner Deutscher Sprachverein, founded in 1885 by the Brunswick art-historian Herman Riegel (1834–1900). Riegel himself was moderate in his purism and sought to eradicate only unnecessary foreign words from the language, a policy summed up in the slogan 'Kein Fremdwort für das, was deutsch gut ausgedrückt werden kann' (admittedly a subjective issue). Given a choice between no foreign words in German or all, Riegel claimed to prefer all. Purism was in any case only one of the Society's aims, besides the nurture of the mother tongue and, characteristically, the strengthening of national consciousness in the German people. In an early appeal for new members of the Society, Riegel observes that a German is a German by language as much as by birth, nationality, rights, duties, and so forth: 'Gedenke auch, wenn du die deutsche Sprache sprichst, daß du ein Deutscher bist!'—a phrase which became a slogan in the Society's publications.[26] The Society's journal, the *Zeitschrift des Allgemeinen Deutschen Sprachvereins* (*ZADS*), was, moreover, written in plain language devoid of learned jargon and accessible to the interested layman: unlike its baroque forebears, the Society was not to be the arcane citadel of academic learning, nor the playground of aristocratic amateurs. The *Zeitschrift* also ran competitions for the Germanization of foreign words. The suggestions which won the prizes were not always successful; thus, *Rauchrolle* for *Zigarre* (1889), and *das Aut* for *Auto*, with the useful derivatives *auteln*, *Autler* (1901), sank without trace.[27] Reviews of books, discussion of newspaper articles, reports of meetings and lectures held at the Society's branches, and a section for reader's letters and queries make the journal informative and up to date. Monographs were devoted to individual purist endeavours, and a series of *Verdeutschungswörterbücher* were issued for several purposes; specimen German menus were available to members of the Sprachverein, for example, to be passed on to unenlightened waiters. Probably this general appeal of the Society and its journal accounts for its tremendous success, for it had caught the mood of the time. Many branches sprang up throughout Germany and overseas: by 1887 it had some 6,000 members, by 1902 there were 20,180 members and 231 branches, by the twenty-five-year jubilee in 1910 there were 30,090 members and 324 branches, and by 1917 there were 37,210 members. A London branch founded in 1899 under the chairmanship of Professor Aloys Weiß had 402 members by 1902, rising to 600 in 1910—and falling to 376 in 1914. In comparison, the Sprachverein was less popular in Vienna, where the local branch had only 67 members in 1902, rising to 303 in 1910,[28] while in the same period Switzerland seems to have had no branches but only individual members, preferring instead to found its own Deutschschweizerischer Sprachverein in 1904, centred on Zurich. This was mainly stimulated by the existence of francophone/francophile societies, not out of any pan-German conviction.

In its early years the Allgemeiner Deutscher Sprachverein had to come to terms with extremists—'Sprachpeiniger', as Karl Kraus later calls them—whose radicalism threatened to split the Society from within and who aroused opposition from without: the *Preußische Jahrbücher*, 28 February 1899, published a statement attacking the Sprachverein as obsessive and tyrannical, signed by writers including Theodor Fontane, Gustav Freytag, Klaus Groth, and the historian

Heinrich von Treitschke. Gradually, however, the Society began to influence those who drew up official and administrative usage; it gained a large following among schoolteachers and lobbied politicians. For example, the president between 1900 and 1921 was Otto Sarrazin, a civil engineer and editor of the official gazette of the Prussian Ministry of Works, and he replaced foreign words in railway terminology: *Abtéil*, with stress on the second element (for *Coupé*), *Bahnsteig*, by analogy with *Bürgersteig* (for *Perron*), *Fahrgast* (for *Passagier*), and *Fahrrad* (for *Velo*) are credited to him among some 1,300 replacements between 1886 and 1893. Sarrazin exemplifies the committed nationalist bureaucrat working within the Sprachverein—he wrote many reviews and articles, and some monographs—whereas Heinrich von Stephan had already completed his purist work before the Society existed. Moreover, Sarrazin must have maintained strong links with engineering and other colleagues: in 1901 at the Society's annual general meeting there were present representatives of the military, the imperial railways, and the Post Office, and nearly all the presidents of the railway boards were members. Again, neither Switzerland nor Austria-Hungary followed the purist line taken by the German imperial institutions, and they kept foreign expressions.[29] In the schools, too, the Sprachverein gained in popularity, and school and university teachers are prominent in its ranks: leading professors of German studies associated with it include Otto Behaghel, Friedrich Kluge, Paul Pietsch, Theodor Siebs, Wilhelm Wilmanns, and Hermann Wunderlich. The influence of the Sprachverein could reach even the highest political level: in 1902 Sarrazin writes to the Imperial Chancellor von Bülow regarding the corrupt German being spoken in German South-West Africa, and receives a warm reply. A newly founded branch of the Society at Windhoek (1900–1) had 101 members in 1903, while Vienna had only 92.[30]

The Society survived the First World War intact, and in 1925 the name of its journal was changed to *Muttersprache*.[31] In the 1930s, under Alfred Götze, the Society became enthusiastically National Socialist, and the cruder currents of *völkisch* nationalism present from its inception came again to the surface, accompanied by anti-Semitic and racialist articles; the membership dropped from 35,000 in 1932 to 29,310 in 1934. But, contrary to expectation, neither Hitler nor Goebbels had time for radical purists and the Society's activities were eventually suppressed.[32] With hindsight, the Society's political heyday extended to the outbreak of the First World War, when the purism it had encouraged was furthered by the anti-French and anti-British feeling, when firms and restaurants even changed their names. With the codification of the administrative official languages already completed, the Sprachverein had little positive contribution left to make, and lapsed into a largely critical, unfashionable, and outdated nationalism of elegiac character. Its linguistic theory remained old-fashioned also; little attention was paid to the semantic influences from foreign tongues, or to their positive stylistic contribution.

The Allgemeiner Deutscher Sprachverein shows how politics and purism were linked at the turn of the century; its reactionary and nationalistic attitudes are unfashionable nowadays, but the Society's aims were not pernicious. While it made no obviously striking contribution to the German vocabulary, its strong position in the schools made it influential, and its journal is an excellent repository of material on German usage painstakingly culled from local newspapers and regional branches of the Society, from official notices, and from book reviews.

LANGUAGE AND POLITICS IN THE NINETEENTH CENTURY

Throughout the nineteenth century the German population increasingly participated in political processes, a 'democratization' stimulated by the French Revolution of 1789 and intensified by the revolutions of 1830 and 1848. The end of the absolute power of princes and their cabinets necessitated techniques of negotiating, persuasion, and political control which were relatively new to Germany. The working classes too began to organize, and their language is correspondingly influenced by political jargon: conversely, the political importance of the masses favours the increasing importance of *Umgangssprache*, as politicians address all sections of the population.

Any human activity is potentially a political issue, and the language associated with it can be given a political function. But in a more technical sense we may distinguish three main manifestations of political language: (1) as part of the old, forensic tradition of rhetoric, where opponents are to be persuaded and positions defended or attacked; (2) as the language of political procedures and institutions for governing, i.e. a technical register; (3) as the ideological language of a political group, with its positively and negatively coloured slogans and expressions. We shall not here consider the first of these aspects of political language, although it might be said to combine both technical and ideological elements and also to be the true definition of political language, as Walther Dieckmann observes:

Die Funktion der Sprache in der Politik ist zu einem guten Teil Verhaltenssteuerung. Was und wie etwas gesagt wird, richtet sich, am deutlichsten in der Propaganda, nach den Absichten des Sprechers und den erwünschten Reaktionen beim Hörer. Isoliert man die sprachliche Aussage von den Kommunikationspartnern, so verliert man den Gegenstand, der in der Sprache der Politik von besonderem Interesse ist.[33]

Clearly, coping adequately with the political use of language involves a stylistic analysis of the debates of individual parliaments or parties, which lies outside the scope of this chapter.[34] But even procedural and ideological terms cannot strictly be treated in isolation as part of an atomistic historical presentation of the vocabulary (*Wortgeschichte*), since they refer to complex institutions or to political points of view which equally require a whole range of terms to be discussed together. Political activity takes many forms, including debates, legislation, administration, diplomacy, and the shaping of public opinion, and consequently impinges on society at many points, prescribing ideological postures for the man in the street and filling his mouth with the catchwords of the day. In this chapter we can consider only the technical, procedural vocabulary and some ideological usage: the former reflects the evolution of parliamentary structures and procedure, including party configurations, the latter reflects the growth of political consciousness.[35]

TECHNICAL TERMS AND POLITICAL INSTITUTIONS

The basic technical terms for political procedures and institutions have usually entered the German language from England or France, whether as loan-words or loan-translations. This vocabulary has precise meanings within its particular institutional framework and, like other *Fachsprachen*, is subject-orientated, non-emotive, and consistently used—although we shall see that some terms can be used ideologically and carry positive or negative associations, as when the particular structures and procedures of an opponent are attacked. (But other technical registers, too, can acquire ideological overtones: the National Socialists used biological terms for political purposes in highly emotive fashion; see below, pp. 416–17). Undoubtedly, the French Revolution spread democratic ideas and its own political vocabulary throughout Europe.

Many terms are ultimately classical, French political philosophers having culled them directly from classical sources or via eighteenth-century English parliamentary traditions and writers; revolutionary intellectuals then simplified the terms for the benefit of the masses, whose slogans and catchwords they became. As Dieckmann says, existing words were given a new lease of life, increasingly heard and widely disseminated, and technical political language was brought into public debate.[36] Reporting the Revolution in the foreign press was a major means of spreading the new expressions; in Germany Wieland's *Neuer Teutscher Merkur* was especially influential: in 1789 he introduced *Staatsbürger* as a translation for *citoyen*, and in 1790 *öffentliche Meinung* for *opinion publique*, but many more words are simply left untranslated. Some loans retain their association with the Revolution (*Revolutionär, Terrorismus, Jakobiner* etc.), but others have become so general that speakers are no longer aware of their origins: *administrativ, Demokrat, demoralisieren, Diplomat, Expropriation, fanatisieren, Initiative, Ministerielle, Monarchist, Propagandist, Reorganisation, Taktiker, Zentralisation, Zivilisation.*[37] Not all 'revolutionary' vocabulary enters German at the same time; some forms, like *Anarchist, Bürgerkönig, Konservatorium, liberal, Nationalhymne, Proletarier, Reaktionäre, Trikolore*, seem to come in only after 1830. Loan-translations include *Belagerungszustand* (= *état de siège*), *Königtum* (= *royauté*), *gemäßigt* (= *modéré*), *auf der Höhe sein* (= *être à la hauteur de*), *Tagesordnung* (= *ordre du jour*). *Sansculottes*—which actually refers to those who have given up knee-breeches in favour of long trousers—is variously mistranslated as *Hosenlose, Ohnehosen, Ohnbehosigte*, and *Unbehoste*.

Some political terms relate closely to the French Revolution and its aftermath, while others again applied—together with loans and translations from English (*Budget, Parlamentarier, Defizit, Legislatur, Linke, Rechte, Jungfernrede, Ober-/Unterhaus, Stimmvieh* 'voting cattle', *Selbstverwaltung*)—to German institutions and circumstances. All these terms become familiar in the daily press, and so too do nineteenth-century party constellations, many of which label themselves with the elements *Bund*, *Verein*, and *Partei*:[38]

1. *Bund*. The element *Bund-* continues to form part of several technical terms in modern German (*Bundestag*, *Bundesregierung*, *Bundesstaat* 'federation' and 'member state', *Staatenbund* 'confederation', etc.), some of which, like *Bundesrat*, have slightly different functions in the different countries Austria, Switzerland, and West Germany. Indeed, some terms are retained with changed meaning as the constitution changes; hence, *Bundesrat* meant originally the representative body of the *Bundesfürsten*, but in the 1871 constitution the *Bundesrath* consisted simply of representatives of members of the federation (Article 6). After 1945 *Bund(es)-* became identified with institutions of the Bundesrepublik, replacing earlier compounds with *Reich(s)-*, e.g. *Reichstag* > *Bundestag*, *Reichsbahn* (retained in the GDR) > *Bundesbahn*, *Reichpost* > *Bundespost*, *Reichswehr* > *Bundeswehr*, contrast the element *Volk(s)-* in the GDR (*Reichsheer* > *Volksarmee* etc.). We can trace the growing popularity of *Bund* in the names of various nineteenth-century political groupings: the 'Rheinbund' (1806), 'Der Deutsche Bund' (1815–66), the 'Bund der Kommunisten' in the 1830s, 'Der Norddeutsche Bund' (1867), 'Der Deutsch-Israelitische Gemeindebund' (1869), and the politically, motivated 'Bund der Landwirte' (1893).

2. *Verein*. The word *Verein* remains a general term for associations of all kinds, for sport ('Turn- und Sportverein', TSV) and cultural pursuits ('Gesangverein'), and for official, legal purposes ('eingetragener Verein', e.V.). As a party-political label the element appears in the 'Zollverein' (1834), and some ostensibly religious or cultural groups had a political aim, e.g. the 'Deutscher Arbeiterbildungsverein', founded in London in 1840, later called the 'Kommunistischer Arbeiterbildungsverein'. The 1848 unrest led to a number of 'Vereine': the 'Piusverein für religiöse Freiheit' in Mainz, the Trier 'Christlich-Demokratischer Verein', and radical democratic groupings known as the 'Märzvereine'. Conservative groups included 'Vaterlandsvereine', 'Preußenvereine', 'Vereine für König und Vaterland', and the 'Verein zur Wahrung der Interessen des Großgrundbesitzes und der Förderung des Wohlstandes aller Volksklassen'. In 1859 the liberals founded the 'Deutscher Nationalverein', while in 1861 the conservatives founded the 'Preußischer Volksverein', but

the designation was not popular afterwards, and gradually declines in favour of *Partei*.

3. *Partei.* This denotes 'a group of people with the same interests', but comes to mean a political party with a particular ideology. Tracing this process in German is difficult, since English and French influence may be involved; briefly, however, the *Manifest der Kommunistischen Partei*, written by Marx and Engels in 1847–8, is the first manifesto of a German political party in the modern sense. After the founding of the liberal 'Deutsche Fortschrittspartei' in 1861, many other parties appeared, the 'Sächsische Volkspartei' (1866), 'Nationalliberale Partei' (1867), 'Sozialdemokratische Arbeiterpartei' (1869), 'Monarchisch-Nationale Reichspartei' (1872), 'Deutsch-Konservative Partei' (1876), 'Christlich-Soziale Arbeiterpartei' (1878), 'Deutsche Freisinnige Partei' (1884), 'Freisinnige Volkspartei' (1894), 'National-Soziale Partei' (1896). (The latter did not survive the first decade of the twentieth century, but its name was taken over by the 'National-Sozialistische Deutsche Arbeiterpartei'.)

More general political designations appearing in the nineteenth century are: *Liberal(er)*, found in German *c.*1820 and later translated as *Freisinniger; Reaktion/Reaktionär*, from the opening decades of the century; *Sozialist/Sozialismus*, in the 1830s and 1840s; *Konservati(vi)smus*, after 1830; *Kommunist*, in the 1840s (used by Heine in 1841 and taken up by the *Junges Deutschland* writers); *Sozialdemokrat*, in the 1850s; and so forth. These terms also figure increasingly in the party labels we have just discussed, they are open to wide interpretation, and are used as slogans or symbols which change according to the standpoint of the speaker. *Sozialdemokrat* means both 'social democrat' and 'revolutionary socialist', and can be a precise party label or a crude term of abuse.[39]

POLITICAL IDEOLOGY AND ITS LINGUISTIC EFFECTS

The technical language of politics also distinguishes politicians as a group, regardless of party affiliation, and a parliamentary group language with metaphors like *Jungfernrede, Stimmvieh*, and *Hammelsprung* naturally attracts the attention of the community at large. More important, each political interest represented has its own ideology with a characteristic connotational[40] usage which extends outside parliament and party to the 'grass roots' in the country. Ideological language shares characteristics of group languages, since it expresses group loyalties and attitudes and deliberately marks political opponents as outsiders. On the other hand, ideological usage tends to be more coherent in its affective, emotive language because it reflects an unnaturally consistent system of concepts and values; moreover, proponents of political ideologies seek converts to their group, they employ propaganda to persuade and convince, and they usually aim to impose their system exclusively. In this respect, political and religious faith are similar; as we have seen at the Reformation (Chapter V), words from the religious sphere (*heilig*, *ewig*, *Glaube*, *Bekenntnis*, and *Apostel*) and quotations from the Bible form part of political rhetoric.

Where words and expessions are used as slogans or catchwords (*Schlagwörter*, *Schlagworte*, *Fahnenworte*, *Losungen*), their referential or denotative meaning is subordinated to their political function as a rallying cry or focus of abuse. Conceptual meaning becomes secondary and may result in some keywords becoming ambiguous,[41] e.g. *democracy*, which needs defining particles to refer to any specific system of government (*constitutional*, *parliamentary*, *liberal*, *political*, *formal*, *western*(*-style*), *presidential*, *plebiscitary*, *social*, *people's democracy*, etc.); while 'democracy' unqualified is used 'connotatively' as a positive slogan in many systems. The slogan value of words like *national*, *liberal*, *christlich*, *sozial*, *deutsch*, *Arbeiter*, *Volk* is evident in their recurrence in party names, as we have just seen, and the National Socialists, by their very party label ('National-Sozialistische Deutsche Arbeiterpartei'), combine several—from some standpoints antithetical—elements so as to appeal to a wide ideological spectrum, or at least to both disaffected extremes. Similarly, opponents were attacked in 'meaningless slogans', and the *Communist Manifesto* (1847-8) was written partly to counter such misuse by providing a clear statement of what the term *kommunistisch* stood for.[42]

While language itself is not intrinsically good or evil, despite the assumptions of purists and others, it may be used for contemptible, inhuman, and deceitful purposes.[43] Although words are essentially neutral in value, they can be charged up emotively and used as slogans. An article in the *Neuer Teutscher Merkur* (October 1792), pp. 216, 218, 223, employs the expressions 'das Volk elektrisieren', 'Volkselektrisierer', 'Elektrisiermittel', 'sich elektrisieren lassen' to describe the effects of the revolutionary demagogues on the masses,[44] aptly enough, considering the polarization of political reality into positive and negative values. One polarizing technique is to deny the political opponents any claim to a correct view, partly by qualifying the desired view in some way as *echt, wahr, gesund, artgemäß*, etc., partly by demoting the opponents' view as *falsch, unecht*, or by ironizing it through the use of *sogenannt* or inverted commas. Otherwise, word-formation sometimes provides alternative formations with pejorative force: suffixes like *-ismus/-ist, -ler, -ling, -ei/ -erei/ -lerei*, or prefixes like *ultra-* 'extreme', 'extremist' (originally from *ultramontan* 'beyond the Alps', applying to extreme Catholic politics), *hyper-* (e.g. Bismarck's *Hyperkonservative*), etc. Campe's proposed translations of foreign loans are of interest here, since a pejorative equivalent is often given beside a positive (or, perhaps, neutral) one:[45]

	(+ or neutral)		(−)
Aristokrat ⟶	*Adelherrscher*	∼	*Adeling, Herrscherling*
Aristokratie	*Adelherrschaft*		*Herrschelei*
Machiavellismus	*Machiavelslehre*		*Machiavelei*
Patriotismus	*Vaterlandsliebe*		*Vaterländerei*
Republicanismus	*Freibürgersinn*		*Freibürgerei*

This 'symbol splitting' or polarized synonymy possibly indicates the extent to which the Revolution had promoted political consciousness in Germany. By yet another familiar technique, words were heightened in their positive value or defamed by association with other words, and under the National Socialists certain collocations were expressly forbidden for this reason, as we shall see.

NATIONAL SOCIALISM AND THE GERMAN LANGUAGE

The first post-war linguistic studies of the National Socialist regime identified a language of National Socialism which they felt must be eradicated because it corrupted those who spoke it. German itself must be 'denazified':

Soviel und welche Sprache einer spricht, soviel und solche Sache, Welt oder Natur ist ihm erschlossen. Und jedes Wort, das er redet, wandelt die Welt, worin er sich bewegt, wandelt ihn selbst und seinen Ort in dieser Welt . . . Der Verderb der Sprache ist der Verderb des Menschen . . . So hat der Mensch auch als Unmensch seinen Wortschatz, seine eigentümliche Grammatik und seinen eigentümlichen Satzbau . . . dieses Wörterbuch hat eine Aufgabe, die derjenigen der übrigen und gewöhnlichen Wörterbücher genau entgegengesetzt ist: es soll uns diese Sprache fremd machen . . .[46]

And again:

. . . zu verschwinden hat ja nicht nur das nazistische Tun, sondern auch die nazistische Gesinnung, die nazistische Denkgewöhnung und ihr Nährboden: die Sprache des Nazismus. Wie viele Begriffe und Gefühle hat sie geschändet und vergiftet![47]

Of course, there are undeniably certain National Socialist institutions whose mention now always recalls the Nazi period, for example, the political and administrative structures and their labels: starting with the *Führer* (copied from Italian *Duce*), which was restricted to Hitler and even now is seldom used; then the twenty *Reichsleiter*, the regional *Gauleiter*, communal *Kreisleiter*, the local *Ortsgruppenleiter*, down to the *Blockwart*, the lowest party official of a *Block*, which comprised some forty to sixty households. Terms with *Reichs-* and *Volks-* are also common: *Reichsleitung* (the Imperial Directorate of the Nazi Party), *Reichsministerium für Volksaufklärung und Propaganda*, *Reichskulturkammer*, *Reichs-Pressekammer*, *Reichs-Rundfunkkammer*, etc.; *Volksgerichtshof* 'People's Court', *Volksgemeinschaft* 'racial community', *Volksgenosse* 'fellow countryman' (this word derives from Herder), *Volksliste* 'Racial Register' (list of ethnic Germans), *Volkssoldat*, etc. Abbreviation is common, but not exclusive to National Socialist German:[48] SA (*Sturmabteilung*), SS (*Schutz-Staffel*), HJ ('Hajot', *Hitler-Jugend*), BDM ('Bede Em', *Bund Deutscher Mädel*), SD (*Sicherheitsdienst*), Pg (*Parteigenosse*), DAF (*Deutsche Arbeitsfront*), WHW (*WinterHilfswerk*), KZ ('Kazet', a doubly abbreviated form from *Konzentrationslager*), *Gestapo* (*Geheime-Staats-Polizei*), *Oflag/Stalag* (*Offiziers-/Stamm-Lager*), *Osaf* (*Oberster-SA-Führer*), *Promi* (*Propagandaministerium*). Moreover, some National Socialist technical terms were meant to be suggestive and affective (thus, *Reich* and *Volk* are rich in associations, *Gau* is an archaic territorial division); while, yet more striking, the reorganization of factory management along neo-feudal lines as a *Betriebsgemeinschaft* with a *Betriebsführer* and *Gefolgschaft* (for older *Gefolge* 'retinue'), composed of the *Arbeitsmann* and the *Arbeitsmaid*—idealized new terms for workers (*Maid* is a poetic word from Romanticism)—implies a sentimental, paternalistic attitude to labour.

Nevertheless, the names for specifically Nazi terms are relatively few, have become historical, and are in themselves unimportant for present-day German. The earlier critics of National Socialist language are really concerned with more fundamental stylistic issues governing the ideological use of German—which they mistake for that regime's lasting influence.

But Klemperer, Sternberger, and others are actually attacking the Nazi regime under the pretence of criticizing its language, and are thus tacitly in agreement with the National Socialists in directly equating language with thought or with reality. Paradoxically, even the style of the post-war critics mirrors that of Nazi polemic: Klemperer writes of National Socialist language as an insidious *Gift*, describes anti-semitism as *Krankheit, Infektion, Seuche*, and fascism as 'spezifische deutsche Krankheit, eine wuchernde Entartung des Fleisches' and 'eine Entartung des deutschen Wesens'; Sternberger and colleagues deal with the abstract *Unmensch*, as empty and aggressive a *chiffre* as the National Socialist *Jude*.[49] Such pathological style is not specifically National Socialist; it occurs in nineteenth-century political writings, and even in the linguistic purists (see poor Engel—himself, alas, Jewish—pp. 396-7 above). Indeed, since the National Socialists lacked any coherent political philosophy they failed to develop a consistent ideological language either, and borrowed from a hodgepodge of sources. Their political style is, like other political styles, geared to gaining and retaining power, and shows the features of political language discussed earlier in this chapter (pp. 401-2 above). But by masterly propaganda, total control of the news and cultural media, and political supervision of all important spheres of activity, the National Socialists imposed their disparate ideological language with unparalleled intensity. In the process many common expressions were charged with special, political significance, some becoming euphemisms for repression and genocide. As Zeitblom observes in Thomas Mann's *Dr Faustus*:

Einzelnen Vokabeln können Leben und Erfahrung einen Akzent verleihen, der sie ihrem alltäglichen Sinn völlig entfremdet und ihnen einen Schreckensnimbus verleiht, den niemand versteht, der sie nicht in ihrer fürchterlichsten Bedeutung kennengelernt hat.[50]

Whether coined by National Socialists or not, some expressions remain so tainted as to be unusable now, and in this respect we can indeed talk of 'the language of National Socialism'; but the issue is primarily semantic, concerning the ideological distortion of existing expressions.

The ideological polarization of German propaganda is an extreme attempt to impose a view of reality, even to shape reality through language. As we have seen earlier in this chapter, the relation between reality and language is complex (above, pp. 390–3), but language can be used to instil feelings of solidarity with one particular group or hatred against another if the masses can be sufficiently 'fanaticized' or whipped up. While it is inadvisable to identify a particular 'totalitarian style', Dieckmann observes that in a totalitarian state loyalty to the regime and criticism of its opponents are promoted in a particularly intense fashion: tension between rulers and ruled is a constituent of the political system and actually calls for an emotive style.[51] If necessary, a mood of crisis must be artificially created to unite the mass of the people: in pre-war Nazi Germany anti-Semitism partly served this purpose with its claims of a Jewish plot to dominate the world and to debase the purity of the 'master race'. National Socialist style *is* highly emotive, as the stark polarization of connotations shows, and hence also the choice of vocabulary and imagery provoking strong emotional response.

Against this background let us now consider three questions: the linguistic effectiveness of Nazi propaganda, the characteristics of National Socialist political style as exemplified by Hitler, and the main sources of that style.

THE PROPAGANDA MACHINE AND LANGUAGE

In the sixth and eleventh chapters of *Mein Kampf*, Hitler discusses the theory of propaganda: it must appeal always to the emotions of the masses, adapt its intellectual level to the lowest common denominator, present only a limited number of points, and hammer them home by slogans and repetitiousness. The inculcation of belief in a susceptible audience was the aim, not the reasoned presentation of an intellectual argument. Joseph Goebbels, who became Hitler's *Propagandaminister* in 1933 when the National Socialists took power, removed freedom of the press by promulgating various press laws as part of the general *Gleichschaltung* or reorganization of Germany on National Socialist lines. Many newspapers were temporarily or permanently suppressed, and party harassment led those editors who remained to impose self-censorship.[52] Simultaneously, Goebbels curbed the press by controlling the German news agency, the DNB ('Deutsches Nachrichten-Büro'), which supplied most of the news in the first place. We must not disregard the skilfully stage-managed political rallies, often arranged at night to heighten the effect, the cleverly designed banners and symbols, and, above all, the speech-making as part of Nazi propaganda, but control of press and radio provided the basis for manipulation of language on a massive scale: total *Sprachlenkung*. Unlike linguistic regulations (*Sprachregelung*) proposed by the purists, which sought to establish acceptable German norms for administration or technology, *Sprachlenkung* seeks to impose a view of reality on speakers in order to influence them, so that manipulating people (*Menschenlenkung*) lies behind it. Some of the ministerial directives, which were issued often daily to the media, have survived;[53] they determined which news was to be reported or omitted, whether irony was called for, and even the expressions to be used. Hence, the phrase *gelbe Gefahr* was to be avoided in deference to the Japanese, while *antisemitisch* was subsequently replaced by *antijüdisch* to avoid offending the Arabs. Although for a while the claim to establish a 'großdeutsches Reich' was tactfully played down, in 1936 the designation *Brudervolk* for Austrians was to be replaced by *das deutsche Volk in Österreich*, in preparation for the annexation of 1938. After the break with Russia, Soviet politicians were to be identified as Jews where possible, e.g. 'der Sowjet-Jude Litwinow-Finkelstein, Volkskommissar des Äußeren'. When war started, any mention of *Krieg* was to be studiously avoided (directive of 1 September 1939); instead, 'Deutschland schlägt einen polnischen Angriff zurück'. Naturally, war intensified the propaganda, especially the practice of symbol-splitting (see above, p. 407): *Propaganda*—itself a positive term—was to be restricted to National Socialist propaganda, while enemy propaganda was branded as *Greuelhetze, Greuelagitation, Hetzreden, Greuelkampagne*, and so forth; the English Ministry of Information was referred to only as *Lüge- and Reklameministerium*. Other terms were used solely of the party, e.g. *Parteitag* and *Kongreß*, while *Führer* was restricted to Hitler, *Leiter* being the equivalent for other party members. The allies were not to be termed *Allierte*, their troops not described as *tapfer*, and their attacks, especially aerial bombardments, were called *Terrorangriffe* or, somewhat incongruously, *Gangsterangriffe*.[54] Similarly, partisans were not to be called *Partisanen*, since the word had positive, patriotic associations, but were instead to be labelled *Mordbrenner, Räuber, Stalin-Banditen,*

Heckenschützen, Banden, Räuberhorden. In later stages of the war the propaganda usually attempted to gloss over uncomfortable news: *Katastrophe* was replaced by *Großnotstände, Katastropheneinsatz* by *Luftkriegseinsatz.* Finally, a few pseudo-mythical Germanic words like *Thing, Kult, kultisch,* or Germanicized names of months, like *Lenzing,* were outlawed.

The effectiveness of National Socialist propaganda is hard to assess: but linguistically it failed to do more than make the prescribed designations reasonably common. For example, although the word *Propaganda* itself was restricted to political contexts and ceased to mean advertising of a commercial kind (*Werbung, Reklame*), it increasingly acquired negative associations, and as late as 1943 directives had to remind the press to restrict the word to positive German contexts; nevertheless, compounds *Greuelpropaganda* and *Lügenpropaganda* still occur, and even Goebbels in 1942 and 1943 was inconsistent in speaking of 'Zersetzungspropaganda gegen das deutsche Volk' and 'die englische und bolschewistische Propaganda'.[55]

NATIONAL SOCIALIST STYLE AND RHETORIC

Speeches at mass rallies and broadcast over the radio are the characteristic form of National Socialist political language: it is a language of oratory. Hitler in *Mein Kampf* and in political speeches represents this style which Goebbels emulated, churning it out through the propaganda ministry. Indeed, Hitler consistently regarded himself as an orator (*Redner*), not an author:

Ich weiß, daß man Menschen weniger durch das geschriebene Wort als vielmehr durch das gesprochene zu gewinnen vermag, daß jede große Bewegung auf dieser Erde ihr Wachsen den großen Rednern und nicht den großen Schreibern verdankt.[56]

Mein Kampf was compiled from speeches, which accounts for its often poor grammar and style and probably also for its unreadability (for it seems to have been little read); but Hitler considered that the manner of delivery, not the content, was the orator's principal concern, and success could be measured by his grip on the audience's hearts. Hence, Lloyd George's speeches seemed 'psychologische Meisterstücke seelischer Massenbeeinflussung' despite, indeed because of, their banal content, primitive homeliness, and simplistic examples.[57] Hitler and Goebbels set out to woo the masses (and at times resorted to vulgar slang to establish a rapport with them), but their main intention was to rouse the crowd to such an emotional pitch that all critical faculties would be suspended.

Hitler composed his speeches as he was dictating them, indeed actually delivering them to his secretary, working himself into a fanatical frenzy, his voice at times reaching breaking point—and yet his prosody is curiously independent of the sense, as sound-recordings show: misplaced pathos picks out unimportant parts of speech, trivial points are hammered home with increased volume and rising pitch, exaggerated ungrammatical pauses, falling intonation, and oddly placed stress tear the syntax apart, confusing the audience and creating a monotonous, hypnotic intensity.[58]

There is a similar dislocation of rhetorical devices and content as Hitler needlessly intensifies his style by synonyms (*groß und genial, bereit und entschlossen, Energie und Tatkraft*), hyperbole (including superlatives and intensifiers like *gigantisch, ungeheuer, unerhört, total, monumental, graniten*, e.g. *granitene Dummheit*), and repetition: the rhetoric is 'empty'[59] but contributes, like the prosody, to a hymnic language of 'conjuration'.[60] But, on the other hand, sentence structures lacking logical relation to the content are also used to simulate dialectic; in particular, conditional, modal, and adversative constructions using pairs of conjunctions like *wenn . . . dann, je . . . desto, nicht . . . sondern* suggest a logical, rational argument, but behind them lie baseless assertions, or arbitrary ideological comparisons:

Wenn ein Volk aber in seiner Masse aus körperlichen Degeneraten besteht, *so wird* sich aus diesem Sumpf nur höchst selten ein wirklich großer Geist erheben.[61]

Denn *wenn* das Perikleische Zeitalter durch den Parthenon verkörpert erscheint, *dann* die bolschewistische Gegenwart durch eine kubistische Fratze.[62]

Je niederträchtiger und *elender* die Erzeugnisse einer Zeit und ihrer Menschen sind, *um so mehr* haßt man die Zeugen einer einstigen größeren Höhe und Würde.[63]

Die Größe des Christentums lag *nicht* in versuchten Vergleichshandlungen mit etwa ähnlich gearteten philosophischen Meinungen der Antike, *sondern* in der unerbittlichen fanatischen Verkündung und Vertretung der eigenen Lehre.[64]

The combination of bombast and hyperbole with rigid 'operational syntax' makes the language turgid and monumental as well as enervating, strident, and yet reminiscent of bureaucratic, chancery style. The same blend of emotional content and vocabulary and antithetical, dialectical syntactic structure contributes to ideological polarization and creates slogans in which connotations are important: Goebbels speaking to students at the burning of the books in the Opernplatz in Berlin (10 May 1933) expressly contrasts the values of the National Socialist state with what he sees as the false values of the Weimar Republic, the *Unwerte* of the *Unstaat*. Certain terms with positive values within the National Socialist system have, not surprisingly, subsequently become negatively charged: *Antisemitismus, Brutalität, Fanatismus, Propaganda*, and especially the adjectives/adverbs *barbarisch, blind/blindlings, brutal, fanatisch, hart, rücksichtslos*. Together with militaristic imagery (see below) these words conveyed an impression of dynamism and power, whereas *Pazifismus, Humanität*, and similar concepts were sneered at or devalued by the addition of *sogenannt*. Contrasting pairs of words include *Propaganda* (+) vs. *Agitation* (−), *national* (+) vs. *international* (−), *Gemeinschaft* (+) vs. *Gesellschaft* (−),[65] *geistig* (+) vs. *intellektuell* (−), *Organisation* (+) vs. *System* (−), *gesunder Instinkt* (+) vs. *(zersetzender) Intellekt* (−). Purely denunciatory terms include *Bolschewismus, liberal, Marxismus, Materialismus, Objektivität, Plutokratie*, and above all *Juden-/jüdisch*, which can be combined with other words. Indeed, negative stereotypes like *demoplutokratisch* (a blend of *demokratisch* and *plutokratisch* coined by Goebbels), *jüdisch-amerikanisch, kapitalistisch-bolschewistisch, amerikanisch-bolschewistisch, jüdisch-freimaurerisch* are often interchangeable.

SEPARATE STRANDS AND SOURCES OF NATIONAL SOCIALIST LANGUAGE

The separate strands of National Socialist style contributing to its emotive force include (1) dynamic, martial, and heroicizing terms; (2) religious terms; (3) pseudo-mystical, mythological, and archaizing language; (4) biological and medical expressions; (5) sporting imagery; (6) technological vocabulary and metaphors; (7) foreign expressions; (8) euphemism. Not all of these can be dealt with in detail here.[66] The dynamic, militaristic language (1) emphasizes the primacy of action over thought, appeals to the popular admiration for the heroic and monumental, and, most important, stresses the existence of a crisis which is to be overcome by struggle—hence the frequency of *Kampf*, *kämpferisch*, *Feind*, etc. At the same time, the nation is organized in institutions with paramilitary ranks, and co-ordinated into uniformity: normal peacetime activities of production, food supply, work and even birth are stylized into the *Erzeugungsschlacht*, *Ernährungsschlacht*, *Arbeitsschlacht*, and *Geburtenschlacht*, and the workers are dragooned into the *Deutsche Arbeitsfront*. Technological imagery (6), together with depersonalizing constructions using infinitives, the passive voice, accusative case, and so forth has also been held to reduce the individual to a cog in the state machine. However, caution is necessary, for the National Socialists have no monopoly of bureaucratic impersonal style,[67] and technical metaphor is natural in industrial Germany (see Chapter IX). *Gleichschaltung/gleichschalten* is probably the most notorious technical image; Goebbels especially used electro-technical imagery, and said of Hitler, 'Er hat das ganze Volk wie einen Akkumulator aufgeladen'.[68] *Leistungsgemeinschaft* is also a significant combination of technical *Leistung* 'output of a generator or machine') and the nebulous, emotive *Gemeinschaft* ('community', 'union').

Religious vocabulary was used politically in the French Revolution for its highly emotive value, and Hitler also used it in *Mein Kampf*, both pejoratively, to discredit opponents (*marxistische Kirchenväter*, *marxistisches Glaubensbekenntnis*, *Hetzaposteln*, *bolschewistische Kunstaposteln*), and positively, to sanctify *die Mission der national-sozialistischen Bewegung*, described in terms like *heilig*, *ewig*, and *Glaube*; early casualties became 'martyrs', *Blutzeugen der Bewegung*. Goebbels especially in his speeches speaks of National Socialism as 'eine Lehre des ewigen Lebens', or of 'das heilige Tuch der Blutfahne', or praises Hitler as Germany's saviour. At other times religious concepts are trivialized ('Der Krieg ist ein Glaubensbekenntnis der Waffen'), while technical terms were given a National Socialist, racialist sense: *Erbsünde* 'original sin' becomes a crime against the genetic origins ('Die Sünde wider Blut und Rasse ist die Erbsünde dieser Welt'); *Mischehe*, once used for inter-confessional marriages, applies to those between members of different races.

Hardly surprisingly, Catholics and Protestants alike objected to this profanation of religious language.[69] Pope Pius XI, in an encyclical (14 March 1939) requested, and partly drafted, by German cardinals and bishops, asserted that God could not be bound to one nation or race, and complained expressly of the misapplication of *Offenbarung, Glaube, Unsterblichkeit,* and *Erbsünde* to National Socialist doctrine. Protestants also deplored the state's supplanting the Christian faith by a secular one, extolling concepts like *Blut, Rasse, Volkstum,* and *Ehre* as eternal values; moreover, both anti-Semitism and the deification of Hitler broke the Commandments. In defiance, some Catholic priests actually reinterpreted National Socialist symbols as Christian ones: Göring complained that 'HJ' was being interpreted as 'Herz-Jesu-Jugend', BDM as 'Bund der Marienmädchen', and the Nazi salute applied to God: 'Unser himmlischer Führer Jesus Christus, Treu Heil!'[70]

More emotive still are metaphors drawn from biology and medicine (4), for these had been used increasingly since the late nineteenth century in anti-Semitic circles. At about this time anti-Semitism becomes based on biology rather than religion.[71] A new slogan *Rassenkampf*—the word goes back at least to 1848—came to rival *Klassenkampf;* the latter must partly have prompted it, but the *Rassenkampf* reflected a static, deterministic view of race which held Jews to be different and inferior. Here no compromise was possible: the genetic structures of German and Jew were irreconcilable, and the Germanic race must be kept pure. (Paradoxically, the racial stereotype of 'the Jew' should by this theory have been 'purer' than that of the 'master race'.) At any event, most of the vocabulary and much of the virulence of National Socialist anti-Semitism are already well established in the Bismarck era and just after in writers like Wilhelm Marr, Paul Lagarde, Eugen Dühring, and Houston Stewart Chamberlain.[72] Genetic technical terms like *Rasse, Art* 'species', *Erbe* 'heredity', and others from stock-breeding, such as *Abstammung, Kreuzung, Mischung, Ziehung, Zucht, züchten, weg- herauszüchten,* now acquired political, ideological value: *Rassenbewußtsein* (cf. *Klassenbewußtsein*), *Rassenhaß* (cf. *Klassenhaß*), *Rassenfrage, Rassenmoral, Rassenpolitik; Aufartung, artbestimmt, artblütig, artecht, artfremd, Entartung, entartet; Erbmasse, Erbgesundheitspflege, Erbsünde, Erbwertigkeit, erbgesund, erbtüchtig,* etc.[73] The National Socialists took over this terminology, some of it from pseudo-mystical contexts (see below), especially the notion of purity of blood. *Blut* as a highly emotive word entered into many compounds: *Blutbewußtsein, blutecht, blutgebunden, blutlich, Blutopfer,*

Blutschande (this last changed its meaning from 'incest' to 'miscegenation'). The mystical overtones of *Blut* are evident in the slogan *Blut und Boden*, which associates racial purity with territorial claims (sometimes abbreviated to *Blubo*).

Biological language shades off into medical, pathological imagery. Hitler attacks 'the Jew' as a *Schmarotzer, Parasit, ewiger Spaltpilz der Menschheit, Schädling, schädlicher Bazillus*, implying an insidious, clandestine physiological threat to the *Volkskörper* and playing on the fear of the masses. So synonymous with disease is 'the Jew' that words like *judenfrei* or *Entjudung* are used analogously to *keimfrei* and *Entseuchung*.

Archaizing and pseudo-mystical elements of National Socialist style (3) are drawn partly from Hitler's acquaintance with certain obscure anti-Semitic and anti-Christian 'Germanic' cranks, including the 'Thule Gesellschaft' at Munich. Early twentieth-century writings like the 'Ariogermanic' novels of Guido von List (1848–1929) or the periodical *Ostara* of Jörg Lanz von Liebenfels (= Adolf Josef Lanz) (1874–1954) already mix biological, religious, and archaic language in ill-informed fashion, and National Socialism adopts and spreads in particular the racialist terms. Words probably from such sources include *Rassenblut, Rassenchaos, Männermaterial, Erbsünde, Mischehe, Mischlingsblut, Sippe, Schädling, Dünger des Blutes, Volkskörper, Völkerbrei*.[74] There were some archaisms, like *Rechtswahrer* 'Jurist', *Maiden, germanische Lehrburgen* (cf. National Socialist *Ordensburgen*, where the party élite were schooled), but Hitler mocked 'völkische Propheten';[75] some archaisms, like *Thing*, were suppressed (see above, p. 412), and the revived word *Odal* 'hereditary farm', from a common Germanic root, did not become widely used.[76] Only in racial terminology did the older-sounding vocabulary thrive, and then the various labels *arisch, indogermanisch, deutsch, germanisch, nordisch* are used virtually interchangeably, certainly without proper scientific foundation: *Arier, Ariertum, arische Abkunft, arisch-christlich, christlich-arisch, arischer Geist, arische Völker, Indogermane, indogermanische Rasse, deutscher Geist, Deutschtum, undeutsch, Entdeutschung, Germane, germanischer Volksgeist, nordische Männer, die nordischen Germanen, aufnorden, aufgenordet, nordrassisch, germanische Uranlagen*. But many of these words occurred in the work of serious scholars in the later nineteenth century, although *Arier* was discredited quite early. Chamberlain and Hitler take its diachronic validity for granted and use the concept as a synchronic, positive stereotype to set beside the negative *Jude*; they use it vaguely, like the label 'Caucasian'.[77]

As for foreign words (7), we have seen (above, p. 400) that the National Socialists were not in sympathy with linguistic purism. The Allgemeiner Deutscher Sprachverein was at first tolerated, but in 1938 a *Presseanweisung* forbade any mention of *Sprachreinigung* in the press, and in 1940 Hitler himself put an end to any further attacks on loan-words.[78] For Hitler and Goebbels understood the opacity and exotic appeal of foreign words, which were strongly affective and consequently easily polarized.

Finally, certain National Socialist expressions were euphemisms (8): Polenz (1967), 120, argues that *Sterilisation* in the eugenic law of 14 July 1934 sounded more scientific than *Entmannung* or *Unfruchtbarmachung* and camouflaged a morally reprehensible law euphemistically; similarly, *arisieren* 'to drive out Jews from their shops and homes and give them to Gentiles' (e.g. *ein arisiertes Geschäft*) covered up the real action, whereas *Konzentrationslager* was vaguer than *Straf-* or *Zwangslager*. Indeed, euphemism is most prevalent in the context of the *Konzentrationslager* and Gestapo: notoriously, *Endlösung* (*der Judenfrage*), i.e. 'genocide', but also other words for killing,[79] especially compounds with *Sonder-* (*Sonderbehandlung* 'special treatment', *Sonderaufgabe*, *Sonderaktion*, *sonderbehandeln*, *sonderbehandelt*, *Sonderbehandlungsangelegenheit*, *Sonderbehandlungsfälle*, *Sondereinsatz*, *Sonderkommando*, *Sonder-zubehandelnde*, *Sonderwagen/S-Wagen* 'mobile gas-chambers'); also, *betreuen*, 'take care of', *Betreuung*, *überstellen* 'take to another camp for execution'. In civilian contexts, euphemism appears in the course of the war when economic shortages occur: *Engpaß* instead of (*Versorgungs-*)*Krise*, *Austauschstoff* instead of *Ersatz*, and so forth. In popular usage, even party words like *organisieren* acquire the meaning 'steal', an example of unofficial euphemism.

Central to euphemism is the disparity between what is said and what is meant, and Cornelia Berning links it with the National Socialist desire to mislead the population by nebulous, emotive language—the whole Nazi style is one of *Verschleierung*. Para-doxically, however, euphemism for death and destruction fails in this, since the euphemistic expression comes itself to be identified with the very content it is intended to conceal, and so appears all the more sinister and even absurd to the speakers: the harmless expression and the appalling meaning actually intensify the emotive force of the word (soldiers' slang is similar in this respect). The National Socialists undoubtedly intended to mislead, but their use of language, though reflecting this intention, did not of itself create the lies. For speakers are familiar with metaphorical or transferred expression: metaphor is a prominent source of variation and rhetorical emphasis, but can also act as a mechanism for readjusting the relationship between the linguistic 'symbolic code' and the real world. When speakers become aware of a discrepancy between what is said and what is meant, they take what is said as a metaphorical (or ironical or euphemistic) mode of expression. Perhaps for this reason the National Socialists were unsuccessful in introducing lasting changes into the conceptual system of meaning in German; instead, they imposed particular collocations and connotations, altering the associations of many words—but again, mainly in official contexts. Consequently, most varieties of German (other than the official, political kinds) between 1933 and 1945 did not differ radically from their equivalents before and after that period.[80] Nevertheless, even the (semantically speaking) much more limited objective of propagating ideological values throughout the nation contributed to the maintenance of a regime which murdered millions of innocent people.

CONCLUSION

One further issue needs mention before this chapter is closed, for the topics just discussed bring us back to the fundamental question of linguistic history—the relationships between language and the speech-community. Much of the linguistic historiography of the nineteenth century and down to 1945 shared the tacit assumptions of purists and politicians that the relationship between language and the social reality of the speakers is direct and stable and, above all, reciprocal. Indeed, it seemed that gaps in the historic and 'prehistoric' record might be filled by studying language, which could supply information about societies for which texts were lacking: the scanter the evidence the more compelling (less refutable) such suggestions appeared to be. Some of the motivation for the study of the German language and its dialects was nationalistic—and in moderate, idealistic form, not necessarily pernicious for being so—but it was nevertheless misguided in working uncritically with over-simplified conceptions of language and society, both of which were treated as homogeneous and determinate (see for example, the approaches to dialect discussed in Chapter IX). The last two chapters of this book have tried to stress that language and society are complex and the relationships between them far removed from any crude congruence, or 'isomorphism'.

Language change through time and the variability of language according to place and purpose do make plain the differing communicative needs of speakers, and the speakers are themselves aware of the reasons for these stylistic shifts. Variability and change themselves interact, as particular linguistic varieties—geographical, social, or technical—become prominent at different periods. The task of the linguistic historian is to attempt some interpretation of these processes looking at as many varieties of a given language and at as many linguistic levels as possible. The history of the speakers is perhaps most obviously reflected in vocabulary, but the other levels of language also lend themselves to interpretation against the social background, however imperfectly and with whatever difficulty. The diversity of the Early German evidence can indeed be explained by the circumstances of the speech-community, as seen through the phonology in the multifarious phonological systems and their spellings. Regional forces everywhere apparent in the morphology of the fourteenth to sixteenth centuries, the increasing awareness of style and changes in syntax in the era of printing, notably in the sixteenth century, and the role of the purists in the seventeenth century or of grammarians in the eighteenth can all be linked with socio-economic and cultural developments. Different levels from those which we have considered might have been chosen to illustrate the various periods, but it seemed possible following the scheme here adopted to present a history of German which would remain close enough to already existing schemes not to appear wilful, while perhaps being new enough to provoke discussion. Finally, I am convinced that German in the nineteenth and twentieth centuries is the best testing ground for hypotheses regarding linguistic history, because of the vast sources of material which survive, some of it, indeed, in spoken form (old recordings, newsreels, and so forth). But, for whatever period, I see the task of evaluating historical changes in German (or any language) as an interpretative one, as rich and as challenging as the language itself with its ever-altering continuity.

> Ach, und in demselben Flusse
> Schwimmst du nicht zum zweitenmal.

SELECT BIBLIOGRAPHY

SEMANTICS
Lyons (1977).

PURISM AND BORROWING

Bernsmeier (1977).
Bernsmeier (1980).
Bernsmeier (1983).
Engel (1916).
Henne (1965).
Sanders (1871)

Sarrazin (1889).
Schulz–Basler (1913–83).
Steuernagel (1926).
ZADS [each volume contains a useful index of topics and words].

POLITICS

Bartholmes (1970).
Cobet (1973).
Dieckmann (1969).

Dieckmann (1981).
Schildt (1977).
Schildt (1978).

See also Moser (1974), Wagner (1974).

Slogans and keywords
Ladendorf (1906).

Meyer (1900).

NATIONAL SOCIALISM AND LANGUAGE

1. *Material*
Goebbels (1932–45).
Goebbels (1942–3).
Goebbels (1943).

Hitler (1925–7) [10,643,000 copies by the 1943 reprint].
Inter Nationes (1979).
Kinne (1981) [not used here].

2. *Studies*
Berning (1960, 1961, 1962, 1963).
Berning (1964).
Bork (1970).
Glunk (1966–71).
Klemperer (1946).
Pechau (1935).

Polenz (1967).
Seidel and Seidel-Slotty (1961).
Sternberger, Storz, and Süskind (1945).
Winckler (1970).
Wulf (1963).

[See also the useful documentations in Wulf (1963–6), (1964–6).]

APPENDIX A

THE HIGH GERMAN CONSONANT SHIFT[1]

THE HG or Second Consonant Shift is a series of changes to the consonant systems of certain dialects in the WGmc. group which differentiates them from the other members of the group.[2] Not all the resultant HG dialects are affected in the same degree, and the shift appears in most complete form in the southern dialects, Bav. and Alem. The Frk. dialects show gradations of the shift varying from complete lack of it (LFrk.) to the dialect of the *Tatian* (EFrk.), which lacks only the velar affricate and does not shift WGmc. -*bb*-, -*gg*- to -*pp*-, -*kk*-, as happens in UG. WFrk. before AD 750 seems not to show the shift. Langobardic reveals a few clear instances beside unshifted forms: /t/ shifts but /p/ does not, cf. Langobardic *sculdhais* but *plovum*, EFrk. *sculdheizo*, *phluog*, NHG *Schultheiß*, *Pflug*.

THE SHIFT

In its complete form, as represented by UG dialects, the shift affects the pre-OHG (strictly speaking 'pre-Old UG') voiceless stops ('tenues') */p/, */t/, and */k/, which developed from PIE voiced stops ('mediae') */b/, */d/, and */g/. These phonemes split into three sets of allophones according to their phonetic environment, position, and length; two of the sets of allophones were new, and subsequently became phonemicized as affricate and spirant phonemes.[3] The loss of pre-OHG voiceless stops—or possibly the accentual causes underlying it—also affected pre-OHG voiced stops, which tend to become voiceless, filling the gap in the phonemic system.[4] The three main aspects of the sound shift, viz. (1) voiceless stops to affricates, (2) voiceless stops to spirants and (3) voiced stops to voiceless stops, are difficult, on the

evidence available, to separate into chronological sequences. It is impo
to distinguish theoretically between the occurrence of the shift an
subsequent geographical distribution in German dialects, as will be ͙
Those who hold that the changes began in southern dialects and spread into
Frk. often distinguish phases of the shift in terms of the degree of its spread;
hence the shift of the voiceless dental stop pre-OHG */t/ is assumed to be
earliest because it extends over most HG dialects; next comes the voiceless
labial stop */p/, and finally the voiceless velar stop */k/, where the resultant
affricates are restricted to UG.

The phonetic processes involved in the shift remain obscure: it has been
attributed alternatively to strengthened or to weakened articulation of the
consonants concerned. A period of aspiration may have split the pre-OHG
voiceless stops into aspirated reflexes vs. a small number of unaspirated
reflexes in certain consonant clusters which impeded aspiration, viz. /sp, st,
sk/, /ft/, /χt/, and /tr/.[5] Next, the aspirated sounds developed into affricates,
and then a further split into spirantal vs. affricate allophones[6] occurred,
resulting in three sets of allophones all told. Fig. 12 exemplifies this with
regard to the dental. Following this interpretation of the phonetic developments[7] we examine in turn the shifts to affricate and spirant, then the possibly
related shift of other pre-OHG consonant phonemes.

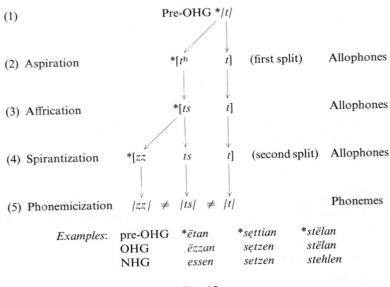

(1)		Pre-OHG */t/			
(2) Aspiration		*[tʰ	t]	(first split)	Allophones
(3) Affrication		*[ts	t]		Allophones
(4) Spirantization	*[zz	ts	t]	(second split)	Allophones
(5) Phonemicization	/zz/ ≠	/ts/ ≠	/t/		Phonemes

Examples:	pre-OHG	*ëtan	*settian	*stëlan
	OHG	ëzzan	setzen	stëlan
	NHG	essen	setzen	stehlen

FIG. 12

A. AFFRICATES

Initially, medially and finally after consonants, and when long (i.e. doubled), the pre-OHG voiceless stops *|p|, |t|, |k| becomes voiceless affricates |pf|, |ts|, |kχ|. The velar affricates are found only in UG. Compare:

OS	*plëgan*	≠ OHG	*pflëgan*
	hëlpan	≠	*hëlpfan**
	skeppian	≠	*skepfen*
	tiohan	≠	*ziohan*
	swart	≠	*swarz*
	settian	≠	*setzen*
	korn	≠	*chorn†*
	wërk	≠	*wërch*
	wekkian	≠	*wecchen*

* Rh.Frk.; others shift further > hëlfan.
† Alem. and Bav. only.

B. SPIRANTS ('FRICATIVES')

In all other positions, i.e. medially and finally after vowels, voiceless double spirants result, and these long consonants are generally, though not consistently, shortened to single spirants when following a long vowel or diphthong, or when in final position. Compare:

OS	*opan*	≠ OHG	*offan*
	slāpan	≠	*slāfan*
	ëtan	≠	*ëzzan*
	that	≠	*daz**
	makōn	≠	*mahhōn*
	ik	≠	*ih*

* EFrk. *thaz.*

To see the complementary distribution, compare the following two paradigms of the verb 'to sit':

OS	*sittian*	*sat*	*sātun*	*gi-sëtan*
OHG	*sitzen*	*saz*	*sāzun*	*gi-sëzzan*

Note that both of these phases result in a shift of the syllable boundary, since the affricates and the medial double spirants, where not simplified, would presumably be divided by that boundary: compare OS *o=pan* and OHG *of=fan.*

C. VOICELESS STOPS

PGmc. had a series of voiced spirants *|b|, |ð|, |g|, which developed stop allophones in differing degree. These pre-OHG voiced stops become devoiced in Alem. and Bav. in early texts. While the devoiced dental $/t/$ remained, voiced stops $/b/$ and $/g/$ are apparently reintroduced, at least in the spelling, this has been viewed as Frk. influence. Compare:

OHG EFrk. *geban* ≠ UG *kepan/keban* (NHG *geben*)
  gotes   *cotes* (NHG *Gott*)

The dental stop $/t/$ remained in EFrk., Bav. and Alem. and has sometimes entered the modern standard, as in *Tochter, Vater* (cf. OHG Rh.Frk. *dohter, fader*). Linked with this is the change of another PGmc. phoneme, $/þ/$, to voiced stop $/d/$ via a voiced spirant stage $/ð/$. At no point do these two dental phonemes merge, and perhaps for this reason the shift of pre-OHG media $/d/$ to $/t/$ was not reversed. Compare:

PGmc. *þingaz- ⟶ OHG *ding* ⟶ NHG *Ding*
  *dagaz   *tag*   *Tag*

The affricate and spirant phases can also be described in terms of generative rules[8] as follows:

(A)
$$\begin{bmatrix} p \\ t \\ k \end{bmatrix} \longrightarrow \begin{bmatrix} pf \\ ts \\ k\chi \end{bmatrix} \Bigg/ \begin{Bmatrix} C_1 + \underline{\quad} \\ \# \underline{\quad} \begin{Bmatrix} V \\ C_2 \end{Bmatrix} \\ \begin{bmatrix} p \\ t \\ k \end{bmatrix} + \underline{\quad} \end{Bmatrix}$$

C_1 = any consonant except /s, f, χ/; C_2 = any consonant

(B)
$$\begin{bmatrix} p \\ t \\ k \end{bmatrix} \longrightarrow \begin{bmatrix} ff \\ zz \\ hh \end{bmatrix} \Bigg/ V + \underline{\quad}$$

V = any vowel

$$C_2C_2\# \dashrightarrow C_2\#$$
$$C_2C_2 \dashrightarrow C_2 \Big/ \acute{V}\underline{\quad}$$

C_2 = any consonant; $\#$ = word boundary; V = any vowel; $\acute{V}$ = any long vowel or vowel cluster; ′ = stress

DATING

The sound shift occurred before the eighth century, from which we have the earliest HG manuscript material (apart from isolated names). The duration of the shift and the relative chronology of its affricate, spirant, and voiceless stop phases are disputed, probably impenetrable, issues. Still, the WGmc. doubling of consonants must precede the affricate phase, and since that doubling also affects OE and probably took place before the migrations of Angles and others to the British Isles in the fifth century, we may assume that the affricate phase was not at that time complete. Otherwise, random onomastic and epigraphic material has often been used to date and perhaps localize some features of the shift, although seldom without rebuttal. Thus, *Etzel* in the *Nibelungenlied* (*c.*1200) seems to show the dental affricate (*Attila* > *Etzel*, with mutation of *a* > *e*), and since Attila died in 453 the affricate shift cannot have been completed by that date. But *Etzel* might involve sound substitution as a hypocoristic, or familiar, name (? from Gothic **attila* 'little father'; *atta* 'father') with intensified consonants.[9] Similarly, the name *Idorih* on a spearhead dated *c.*600–50 from a grave at Wurmlingen in southern Württemberg is supposed to show the velar spirant shift in early Alem.: but the date of the inscription is uncertain, the spearhead—a highly portable object—tells nothing of the owner's ethnic origin, the name itself may be Celtic, and the element *-rih*, even if it is Germanic, is unstressed and unstable in other parallel name types. With place-names in particular we must sometimes reckon with a tradition of unshifted Latin forms: whereas a number of early place names in Alem. areas show the shift (Zabern, from Lat. *ad tavernas*; *Ascapha*, Aschaffenburg; *Ziurichi*, Zurich), Gregory of Tours has *Strateburgum* for Strasburg, while Bishop Arno of Salzburg still has unshifted Latinized or traditional forms as late as *c.*790: *ad Lauppiom* beside *ad Laufom* (Laufen near Salzburg); *ad Diupstadun* and *iuxta Tiufstadun* (Tiefstadt); *Hulthusir* (Holzhausen).

DIALECTAL DISTRIBUTION

The Second Sound Shift is not fully represented in all HG dialects, as shown by Table 14 illustrating the shift of tenues (voiceless stops).[10] The striking discrepancies among the orders of consonants (the dentals shift more generally than the velars) and between the series (the spirants are more widespread

TABLE 14. *Shift of Voiceless Stops*

	t					p						k			
Position	t-	-tt(-)	-Cons. -t-	+t	-t	p-	-pp(-)	mp	lp	rp	-p(-)	k-	kk	-Cons. +k	-k(-)
Pre-OHG	t	tt	t	t	t	p	pp	mp	lp	rp	p	k	kk	k	k
OS	t	tt	t	t	t	p	pp	mp	lp	rp	p	k	kk	k	k
MFrk.	z	z	z	zz	z./t	p	pp	mp	lp	rp	p	k	kk	k	k
Rh.Frk.	z	z	z	zz	z	p	pp	mp	lp/	rp/	f(f)	k	kk	k	ch
SRh.Frk.	z	z	z	zz	z	p	pf	mpf	lpf	rpf	f(f)	k	kk	k	ch
EFrk.	z	z	z	zz	z	pf	pf	mpf	lpf	rpf	f(f)	k	kk	k	ch
Bav.	z	z	z	zz	z	pf	pf	mf	lf	rf	f(f)	kχ	kχ	kχ	ch
Alem.	z	z	z	zz	z	pf/f	pf/ff	mf	lf	rf	f(f)	ch	kχ	ch	ch
Lgb.	z	z	z	s(s)	s	p	p(p)	mpf	lpf	rpf	p/f(f)	k	kk	k/kχ	ch

than the affricates) are puzzling. It has been argued that the dental order shifts earliest because of its greater geographical extent, while the velars shift last: loan-words like OHG *tunihha* < Lat. *tunica* are claimed to show that the word was borrowed after completion of the shift /t/ > /ts/, but before completion of /k/ > /xx/. But this approach of separating orders of consonants runs counter to the structuralist's wish to look at the changes in series, which may be interrelated. Moreover, the absence of labial and velar affricates from some of all Frk. dialects is problematic if affricates are regarded as an intermediate stage in the shifting to spirants: indeed, the spirants are more common in Frk. than the affricates.

The isoglosses of the Second Sound Shift seemed to Theodor Frings to have spread gradually northwards, fanning out as they did so to produce the characteristic divisions of Frk. dialects known as *der rheinische Fächer*. The individual isoglosses are sometimes named according to the place where they cross the Rhine, hence the Frk. dialects are strung out between the Ürdingen (*ik/ich*) line in the north, and the Germersheim (*appel/apfel*) line in the south, which separates them from Alem. This is represented schematically in Fig. 13. The stability and age of the isoglosses have been much debated, in particular the Benrath line. Frings argued that the sound shift drifted northwards, reaching Cologne by about 1000, and was subsequently moulded by the territorial and ecclesiastical (diocesan) boundaries in the later Middle Ages—a linking of linguistic with political/cultural history.

The stimulus for a south → north spread of the sound shift and the political and social vehicles which carried it remain unclear: for until the ninth century cultural superiority lies with the Franks and might rather have favoured a north → south spread. Applying 'vertical' interpretations to this 'horizontal', geographical picture, we may identify groups of speakers—say nobles or ecclesiastical/political administrators—who would be likely to borrow from the language of other regions, or we may invoke the undoubtedly potentially supra-regional spelling conventions of writing vs. the local spoken language; but still the reasons for a movement northwards are unclear.[11] Alternatively, 'spread' might be rejected altogether: recently it has been claimed that in MFrk. areas, notably in Ripuarian, an autochthonous shifting occurred which is consistent and attested early.[12] The intricate and often acrimonious debate about this theory of polygenesis of the Second Sound Shift cannot be discussed here,[13] but some of the evidence seems to suggest the existence of shifted forms in MFrk. at least as early as the Merovingian period (pre-750). However, undoubtedly unshifted forms and place-names in present-day dialects and in earlier texts and documents cannot readily be explained away (as imports from the north, or for other reasons), and so the consistency and homogeneity of the shift are impaired, making polygenesis unlikely. The issue is complicated by the survival of pockets of Romance speakers in the Moselle Frk. and probably also the Ripuarian areas, accounting perhaps for unshifted place-names which were used in Romance contexts and consequently unaffected by the shifting. We have, in fact, a counterpart to the 'West Frankish problem'—which involves assessing the linguistic influence of groups of Germanic (Frk.) speakers on Gallo-Roman soil—only here we have Romance settlements in Franconia.

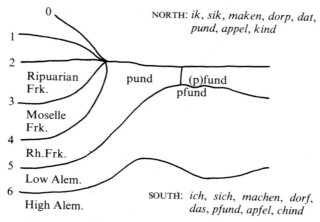

0 = the *sik/sich* line: one of several minor isoglosses north of Ürdingen.
1 = Ürdingen line, *ik/ich*.
2 = Benrath line, *maken/machen*: often taken as the 'baseline' for the LG/HG dialect division, since the other isoglosses merge into it.
3 = Bacharach line *dorp/dorf* separating Ripuarian from Moselle Frk.
4 = *dat/das* line separating MFrk. dialects (Ripuarian + Moselle Frk.) from Rh.Frk.
5 = Germersheim line, *appel/apfel*, separating Frk. from Alem.
6 = *kind/chind* line (not strictly part of the Rhenish Fan), separating Low Alem. from High Alem.

Note. All these isoglosses are complex zones of features reflecting the dialectal position at the end of the nineteenth century. The isogloss *(p)fund* is not part of the fan: in the early period it separates Rh.Frk. *(pund)* from EFrk. *(pfund)*, later it separates WMG *(pund)* from EMG *(fund)*. Otfrid's SRh.Frk. has *pad* (NHG *Pfad*) and *aphul* (NHG *Apfel*), again demonstrating that the isoglosses of the Rhenish Fan must be used with caution when evaluating OHG monastery dialects.

F IG. 13. The Rhenish Fan

The shifted forms of MFrk., albeit probably of early date, still look 'secondary'—i.e., they have been adopted subsequently and represent sound substitution rather than sound change—partly because they are less systematic than the UG shifting (for example no corresponding shift of voiced stops to voiceless), partly because of the unshifted 'relic' forms. Hence, the old view of geographical spread of the sound shift remains attractive. However, the polygenesis theory might still have some relevance, in much weaker form, since speakers will most readily adopt new features which are compatible with their own language: so spread could trigger certain already existing predispositions to the shift in a catalytic manner.

APPENDIX B

EARLY GERMAN MONASTERY DIALECTS WITH SPECIMEN TEXTS

UPPER GERMAN: ALEMANNIC, BAVARIAN (LANGOBARDIC)

A. GENERAL

Jacob Grimm postulated a common consonant system for Alem. and Bav. in the eighth and ninth centuries, and this *Strengalthochdeutsch* provides a useful frame of reference of an ideal, 'metachronic' type (for it is not attested 'in time'). Here the HG Consonant Shift is fully represented (see Appendix A), with the resulting affricates and spirants in complementary distribution; the spirants appear as long (doubled) medially following a short vowel; single spirants appear after a long vowel or diphthong and in final position. Pre-HG voiced stops appear devoiced, and are usually interpreted as voiceless lenes.[1] Thus, pre-HG *b > p* (*ḅ*), *d > t* (*ḍ*), *g > k* (*g̣*); and the PGmc. voiceless dental spirant *þ* (as in English *thin*) appears as *d*, perhaps the result of a chain reaction of the push-pull type (*Schub* and *Sog*; see Chapter II), with the following possible stages: (1) Pre-OHG *t > ts/z* (affricate) or *zz* (spirant), creating a gap which was filled by (2) pre-HG *d > t*, resulting perhaps in (3) pre-HG *þ > d*; essentially, then, a 'pull-chain'. The system was even more 'unbalanced' in the labial and velar orders, which lacked oppositions between voiceless and voiced stops during the earlier centuries. However, in the dental order, note the imbalance in the spirantal series, where *zz/z* and *ss/s* are in opposition: no comparable complication exists in the labials and velars. The subsequent merger of *ss/s* and *zz/z* in medieval texts (MHG) lightened the system in the spirantal series; similarly, lenition (*Lenisierung*)

TABLE 15. *Oppositions in the dental order of* Strengalthochdeutsch*

	Initial	Medial	Final
STOPS	t- tac [Tag]	-t- cotes [Gottes] -tt- mitti [Mitte]	-t cot [Gott]
	d- (< þ) daz [das]	-d- (< þ) snîdan [schneiden] -dd- (< þþ) kleddo [Klette]	-d (< þ) smid [Schmied]
AFFRICATES	ts- zît [Zeit]	-ts- sizzen [sitzen]	-ts scaz [Schatz]
SPIRANTS		-ʒʒ-, -ʒ- wizzan, âzun [wissen, aßen]	-ʒ waz [was]
	s- sela [Seele]	-ss- rosses [Rosses] -z- (voiced s) lesan [lesen]	-s des [des]

* Modern German equivalents are given in square brackets.

increased the representation of voiced stops by causing initial and medial voiceless stops to become voiced, e.g. *tac* > *dac* (NHG *Tag*), *weter* > *weder* (NHG *Wetter*).[2]

In UG vocalism /iu/ appears as the regular reflex of PGmc. /eu/, whereas Frk. texts have /io/, e.g. PGmc. *leuba-* > UG *liup* (NHG *lieb*), but Frk. *liob*. But in UG /io/ appears where the following consonant reflects a PGmc. velar spirant /χ/ or a dental, thus: UG *lioht, biotan* (NHG *Licht, bieten*).

In UG morphology, the weak noun and adj. endings are usually -*in* in gen. and dat. sg. masc. and neut. (but in Frk. they are usually -*en*); the acc. sg. masc. and the nom. and acc. pl. masc. and neut. appear as -*un* (Frk. -*on*). Contrast *des êuuigin lîbes* from Otloh's Prayer (Bav., post-1060) with *in themo iungisten tage* from *Tatian* 82. 7. 11 (EFrk., ninth century). The strong adj. shows the ending -*iu* in the nom. sg. fem. and nom. and acc. pl. neut., in contrast to Frk. -*u*. Furthermore, UG shows weak verbs in -*ên* which they appear in -*ôn*: contrast *hazzon, sparôn, zilôn* (NHG *hassen, sparen, zielen*) in the Vienna manuscript of Otfrid's Gospel harmony (SRh.Frk.) with *hazzên, sparên, zilên* in the Bav.-coloured Freising manuscript.

There are lexical differences: UG religious terminology differs from Frk., and has generally survived (see Chapter I): contrast UG *diemuoti* (NHG *Demut*) with Frk. *ôdmuoti*.

B. INDIVIDUAL DIALECTS

1. Alemannic

Centres. St Gall (613–14); Reichenau (724); Murbach (727). *Main Features.* Affricates are shifted further to spirants in late Alem. (Notker): $k\chi > \chi$, *pf > f*. But certain graphies ($\langle$ch$\rangle$ and $\langle$ph$\rangle$) are ambiguous; cf. Frk. *starck* ~ Alem. *starh*; Frk. *p(f)legan* ~ Alem. *flegan*. Devoicing of mediae is less radical than Bav.: Alem. *keban, sibun* ~ Bav. *kepan, sipun* (NHG *geben, sieben*). There is alternation of voiceless/voiced initial consonants following a pause or voiceless environment and a voiced environment respectively (Notker's *Anlautgesetz*); e.g. *ter bruoder unde des pruoder sun* 'the brother and the brother's son'.[3] Semivowels i̯ and u̯ are lost in some environments: *j > ∅* (Frk. *jener* ~ Alem. *ener*); *kw > k* (Frk. *quidit* ~ Alem. *chît* 'says'; Frk. *quedan* ~ Alem. *chedan* 'say' [cf. English *bequeathe*]). Pre-OHG *ô* diphthongizes, appearing first as $\langle$oa$\rangle$, then as $\langle$ua$\rangle$, which remains characteristic till Notker when $\langle$ûo$\rangle$ is found. Pre-OHG *ê²* diphthongizes, appearing as $\langle$ia$\rangle$ (Notker $\langle$îa$\rangle$). Dat. pl. demonstrative pronoun/definite article *der* shows diphthong in dat. pl. (Bav. *dem* ~ Alem. *dîen*).

Alemannic Text

Notker, Prologue to his Boethius Translation [Braune (1874–5/1979), No. xxiii, p. 61, lines 7–10].[4]

Tánnân geskáh pi des chéiseres zîten *Zenonis*, táz zuêne chúninga nórdenân chómene, éinêr ímo den stûol ze Romo úndergîeng únde álla *Italiam*, ánderêr nâhor ímo *Greciam* begréif únde díu lánt tíu dánnân únz ze Tûonouuo sínt: énêr hîez in únsera uuîs Ôtacher, tíser hîez Thioterih.

Afterwards, it happened in the days of the emperor Zeno that two kings (having) come from the North, the one took possession of the throne at Rome and of all Italy, the other, closer to him [Zeno], seized Greece and all the lands stretching from it as far as the river Danube: that [= *jener*] king was called in our fashion Otacher, this one was called Thioterih.

2. Bavarian

Centres, with approximate date of foundation.[5] [Augsburg (fifth century)]; Freising (724–30); [Wessobrunn (753)]; Tegernsee (*c.*756); Benediktbeuern (752); Regensburg (St Emmeram) (739); Passau (739); Salzburg (St Peter) (798); Mondsee (738). *Main Features.* There is more extreme shift of mediae *b, d, g* > voiceless stops *p, t, k*. There is a tendency for unstressed final vowels to appear as $\langle$a$\rangle$ in later texts, e.g. Otloh's Prayer (*unta, uppigas, unsûbras*, etc.).

Bavarian Texts

(1) *Muspilli* [Braune (1874–5/1979), No. xxx, p. 87, lines 31–6][6]

So denne der mahtigo khuninc daz mahal kipannit,
dara scal queman chunno kilihaz:
denne ni kitar parno nohhein den pan furisizzan,
ni alero manno uuelih ze demo mahale sculi.
dar scal er uuora demo rihcche az rahhu stantan,
pi daz er in uuerolti *eo* kiuuerkota hapeta.

When the mighty king appoints that Judgement Day each individual clan shall come there: then no single warrior ever born shall dare to disregard the summons, nor any man what ever who should attend that tribunal. There he shall stand before the Kingdom and give an account of everything that he has done in this world [*in uuerolti*].

(2) *From Otloh's Prayer* [Braune (1874–5/1979), No. xxvi, p. 80, lines 5–8].[7]

Leski, trohtin, allaz daz in mir, daz der leidiga vīant inni mir zunta uppigas unta unrehtes odo unsūbras, unta zunta mih ze den giriden des ēuuigin lībes, daz ich den alsō megi minnan unta mih dara nāh hungiro unta dursti alsō ih des bidurfi.

Extinguish, Lord, in me everything immoderate and unjust or unclean that the wicked devil kindled in me, and inflame me instead with desire for eternal life, so that I may love it and hunger and thirst after it as I should (need).

3. *Langobardic*

Lgb. is preserved only in isolated glosses in Latin manuscripts, e.g. in the legal code *Edictum Rothari* (634) with *plodraub* (NHG *Blutraub*) and *marhuorf* (*Herabwerfen vom Pferde*); Lgb. personal names and some Runic inscriptions also survive.

(Thuringian is virtually lost, represented only by four Runic inscriptions and possibly by glosses in the *Lex Thuringorum*, whose manuscript is post-800.)

MIDDLE GERMAN: EAST FRANKISH, SOUTH RHENISH FRANKISH, RHENISH FRANKISH, MIDDLE FRANKISH

A. GENERAL

All Frk. dialects of the shifted variety show HG consonantism to a lesser degree than UG, for the affricates are incompletely represented. All forms of Frk. lack the velar affricate ($/k\chi/$); note that the graphy ⟨ch⟩ denotes a voiceless stop /k/ or (less commonly) the voiceless spirant /hh/.

EFrk. is close to Alem. and Bav., being distinguished from them mainly by the absence of the velar affricate. Moreover, the UG voiceless lenes *p* and *k* (from pre-OHG *b* and *g*) seem to revert—in the spelling at least—to *b* and *g* as in EFrk., and this has been plausibly interpreted as Frk. influence on the written traditions of the UG areas. Finally, much of Bav. has also lost the velar affricate, which survives only in Alem. and in adjacent Bav. dialects.

The other Frk. dialects apparently show a progressive reduction in the labial and dental affricates from south to north, resulting in the curious dialectal gradation known as the 'Rhenish Fan' (see Appendix A).

Frk. dialects show early diphthongization of the pre-OHG vowels /ô/ and /ê²/, marked usually by the graphies ⟨uo⟩ (but in SRh.Frk. ⟨ua⟩) and ⟨ia⟩ respectively. The diphthongs are traditionally held to have spread from Frk. dialects to affect the southern, UG ones; the assimilatory change known as 'I-Mutation' or 'umlaut' may well also have travelled in this direction (see Chapter II). Although the diphthongization has been thought of as an internal development in terms of 'push-and-pull' chains, it remains conceivable that Frk. influence could have triggered diphthongizing tendencies already present in UG; Frk. influence is attested at the orthographical level.[8] Thus, as a quid pro quo, Frk. dialects may have provided innovations to the UG vocalic systems, having themselves received consonantal innovations resulting from the HG Sound Shift. In the Early German Frk. dialects, then, the conflicting internal, 'structuralist', autochthonic or polygenetic approach to language contrasts with an external, socio-linguistic view which looks to the interaction of speakers to explain certainly the geographical distribution, and possibly also the initial stimulus for the sound changes concerned.

B. INDIVIDUAL DIALECTS

1. *East Frankish*

Centres, with approximate date of foundation. Würzburg (741); Fulda (744); Bamberg (ninth century). *Main Features.* The consonant shift of voiceless stops is complete except for *k* > *kχ*. Voiced stops *b*, *g* remain unshifted, but *d* > *t*. Diphthongization of pre-OHG *ô* appears as ⟨uo⟩. Diphthongization of *ê²* as ⟨ia⟩; *th* becomes *d* in the ninth century.

East Frankish Text

The OHG Tatian *translation*, 199. 13–201. 2 [ed. Sievers (1892), 266].[9]

Thō forliez her in Barabban; then heilant thō bifiltan saltan in, thaz her uuāri erhangan. Thie kenphon thes grāuen intfiengun then heilant in themo thinchūs, gisamanōtun zi imo alla thia hansa, inti inan intuuātenti giuuātitun inan mit gotouuebbīneru tūnihhūn inti rōt lahhan umbibigābun inan. Inti flehtenti corōna fon thornon saztun ubar sīn houbit inti rōra in sīna zesauūn, inti giboganemo kneuue fora imo bismarōtun inan sus quedenti: heil, cuning Iudeōno!

Then he released Barabbas to them, the Saviour, however (having been) scourged, he handed him over [*salta 'n*] to them that he might be crucified. The soldiers of the governor received the Saviour in the assembly hall, gathered to him the whole band (of the soldiers) and, stripping him, dressed him in a purple [lit. 'of god-weave'] tunic and draped a red cloak round him. And, plaiting a crown of thorns, they set (it) on his head and a reed in his right hand, and with bended knee before him, they mocked him, saying thus: 'Hail, King of the Jews!'

2. *South Rhenish Frankish*

Centre, with approximate date of foundation. Weissenburg (seventh century). *Main Features.* The shift of voiceless stops is incomplete: there is no velar affricate, and initially *p-* remains (but this phoneme is rare outside loan-words), e.g. *plegan* (NHG *pflegen*, cognate with English *play*), *pad* (NHG *Pfad*, English *path*). Medially and finally after consonants the affricate occurs, e.g. *aphul* (NHG *Apfel*). The reflex of pre-OHG *ô* is written ⟨ua⟩, as in Alem. Initial ⟨th-⟩ remains.

South Rhenish Frankish Text

Otfrid's Gospel Harmony, i. 5. 3–12 [Braune (1874–5/1979), No. xxxii, pp. 103–4].[10]

> Tho quam bóto fona góte, engil ir himile.
> bráht er therera uuórolti diuri árunti.
> Floug er sunnun pad, stérrono stráza,
> uuega uuólkono zi deru ítis frono,
> Zi édiles fróuun, sélbun scā [= *sancta*] Máriun:
> thie fórdoron bi barne uuarun chúninga alle.
> Gíang er in thia pálinza, fand sia drúrenta,
> mit sálteru in hénti, then sáng si unz in énti:
> Vuáhero dúacho uuérk uuírkento,
> díurero gárno, thaz déda siu io gérno.

Then an emissary from God came, an angel from heaven. He bore a precious message for [lit. 'of'] the world. He flew along the path of the sun, the streets of the stars, the ways of the clouds to that noble lady, the queen of nobility, Saint Mary herself, whose ancestors were all of royal blood. He went into the palace and found her with downcast eyes, with a psalter in her hand singing it through as she worked at embroidering with exquisite cloths and rare threads. That was always one of her favourite occupations.

3. *Rhenish Frankish*

Centres, with approximate date of foundation. Mainz (747); Frankfurt; Lorsch (763); Worms (*c.*340); Speyer (610). *Main Features.* Incomplete shift of voiceless stops: there is no velar affricate; *p* shifts > *pf* only after *l* and *r*; *th-* > *d-* in the tenth century; pre-OHG *b*, *d*, *g* remain, but *d* > *t* in final position. Pre-OHG *ô* appears as ⟨uo⟩.

Rhenish Frankish Text[11]

Strasburg Oaths, 842 [Braune (1874–5/1979), No. xxi, p. 57, lines 16–19].

In godes minna ind in thes christānes folches ind unsēr bēdhero gehaltnissī, fon thesemo dage frammordes, sō fram sō mir got geuuizci indi mahd furgibit, sō haldih thesan mīnan bruodher, soso man mit rehtu sīnan bruodher scal . . .

For the love of God and for the preservation of Christian people and of us both, from this day forth, inasmuch as God shall give me understanding and power, I shall preserve this my brother, as a man ought properly to do . . .

4. *Middle Frankish*

Centres, with approximate date of foundation. Cologne; Trier (bishopric *c.*250); Echternach (698). *Main Features.* The dental /t/ shifts to affricate and spirant, but labials and velars /p/ and /k/ shift only to the spirants /ff/ and /hh/. Orthographically *b*, *d*, and *g* remain, but medial -*b*- is a voiced spirant, and *g* sometimes > *j*. Long *ô* > *uo*. Certain individual monosyllabic words appear with unshifted consonants, probably because they were unstressed (NHG forms are given in parentheses): *wat* (*was*), *dit* (*dies*), *dat* (*das*), *it* (*es*), and *up* (*auf*).

Middle Frankish Texts

(1) *Glosses from the* Maihinger Evangeliar [ed. Bergmann (1966), 90–2][12]

gan:os: ~ *Genosse*, cf. *ginôzo* (Otfrid), *ginôz* (*Tatian*).

hase ~ *mit Haß* (dat. sg.); cf. *haz* (Otfrid, *Tatian*).

nodi ~ *mit Notwendigkeit*, cf. *nôtî* (Otfrid, *Tatian*).

(2) *Trier Charm* (tenth-century manuscript) [Braune (1874–5/1979), No. xxxi, p. 92].

Quam Krist endi sancte Stephan zi ther burg zi Saloniun: thar uuarth sancte Stephanes hros entphangan. Soso Krist gibuozta themo sancte Stephanes hrosse thaz entphangana so gibuozi ihc it mid Kristes fullesti thessemo hro*ss*e. Pater noster. Uuala Krist, thu geuuertho gibuozian thuruch thina gnatha thessemo hrosse thaz antphangana atha thaz spurialza, soso thu themo sancte Stephanes hrosse gibuoztos zi thero burg Saloniun. Amen.

Christ and St Stephen came to the town of Salonium. St Stephen's horse went lame. Just as Christ healed St Stephen's horse that was spavined, so may I heal (it) this one with Christ's aid. Pater noster. Thus, O Christ, may you deign to heal through your mercy this lamed or spavined horse, just as you healed St Stephen's horse at the town of Salonium. Amen.

NOTES

INTRODUCTION

1. On the weaknesses and contradictions of some schools of linguistics in their rejection of 'scriptism'—'the assumption that writing is a more ideal form of linguistic representation than speech'—see Harris (1980), esp. 6 ff.
2. e.g. *die Saite* 'string' (of musical instruments) vs. *die Seite* 'side'; or even *der gefangene Floh* 'the captive flea' vs. *der Gefangene floh* 'the captive fled'. Such examples figure all too prominently in the continual discussions on orthographical reform; see Garbe (1978).
3. See Labov, (1978), 94 ff.
4. Sex may be important: in certain cultures, at certain times and for certain purposes the language of women differs from that of men. Age too affects language: recently the language of young people has differed radically from that of their parents on a hitherto unknown scale, probably because of the existence of an international youth culture commercially exploited (and created).
5. For the terms High German (HG) and Low German (LG), see pp. 40–4.
6. For more comprehensive treatment, see Bynon (1977); Robins (1979), esp. chaps. 7 and 8, pp. 164 ff.; Arens (1979) (contains selections of major theoretical writings); Lyons (1981), esp. chap. 7, pp. 216 ff.
7. See Lockwood (1969).
8. For Paul, Braune, and Sievers, see Reis (1978), Fromm (1978), and Ganz (1978).
9. See the histories by Kluge, Rückert, and Socin listed in the Select Bibliography (p. 29). Kluge (1888), 126–7, showed little sympathy for Romance influence, while Socin (1888), 519, had no ear for the urban colloquial of his day.
10. See, for example, Lichtenberger (1895).
11. See Schmidt (1872), esp. 27 ff.
12. See the critical edition of the *CLG* by Tullio de Mauro (1967; French version, Payot: Paris, 1973). The *CLG* was compiled by Saussure's pupils from lecture-notes.
13. 'Parole' comprises writing as well as speaking: 'output' from the system in actual situations.
14. See Chapter X for the semantic implications of the arbitrariness of the linguistic sign.
15. Paul (1880/1968), 2nd edn. (1886), 21–34, esp. 22, 25–7; Saussure knew Paul's work (*CLG* 36 f.), though his library may not have contained a copy of the *Principien*.
16. See his article 'La linguistique et les savants allemands', in Meillet (1921–38), ii. 152–9, esp. 158: 'chaque langue est un système rigoureusement agencé, où tout se tient.'
17. 'Un ensemble de plusieurs systèmes partiels'; see Trubetskoy (1949), 3, and also Firth (1968), 43. Firth also prefers a polysystemic approach to language.
18. See Chomsky (1957), esp. 49 ff., and (1965).
19. See King (1969), esp. 14.
20. Chomsky (1957), 49 f.

21. The rules mediating between deep and surface structure syntax (i.e. not those belonging to phonological or semantic interpretation or to the obligatory base or deep structure) are known as transformational rules, hence the label 'transformational–generative grammar', or TG. See King (1969), 16 ff.
22. See esp. Chomsky (1967), 17 ff.; (1965), 4.
23. Von Humboldt (1836), p. lvii.
24. Humboldt (1836), p. cxxii; Chomsky (1967), 17.
25. Watkins (1975), 88.
26. Rule reordering presupposes that rules are ordered, which is disputed; see Vennemann (1977), 24–42. For discussion of diachronic generative rules, see Bynon (1979), esp. 108 ff.
27. See King (1969), 65.
28. See King (1969), esp. 71 ff. and model on p. 85.
29. See Aitchison (1981), 173–190.
30. Aitchison (1981), 177, objects that sound change affects *less common* forms, not common ones as produced by the child. Nevertheless, perhaps the child's over-generalizations are 'ironed out', i.e. corrected, where they are common, while less common generalizations slip through the social net as less exceptionable.
31. See Götze (1928).
32. 'Conventional' here means 'binding upon the speakers', for individuals cannot arbitrarily alter the conventions of their language to any sudden or massive extent without being misunderstood. At the same time, except in a few instances (such as onomatopoeia), the signs of language are themselves arbitrary.
33. Labov (1978), p. xix.
34. Harris (1981), 165.
35. Weinreich, Labov, and Herzog (1968), 100.
36. For the role of grammarians and lexicographers in creating artificially uniform and limited language systems irrespective of the variation which actually occurs, see Harris (1980), esp. chap. 6.
37. Lerchner (1974).
38. Schildt (1976).
39. See especially Labov (1972), esp. 296 ff., and (1978), discussed by Aitchison (1981), esp. 53 ff.
40. e.g. Franz Xaver Kroetz expressly requires a stronger dialectal colouring than the orthography suggests: see his south German play *Wildwechsel*, (Georg-Lentz-Verlag, Vienna, 1973), p. (7). For problems of dialect notation, see Chapter IX.
41. Wolf (1971), and also Wellmann (1972). Most recently Schildt (1982) (this appeared too late to be used here).
42. 'High German' is a technical term denoting here a form of German whose consonantal structure is generally similar to that of the modern standard language: see pp. 40–4.
43. See Scherer (1878), 13–15.
44. A helpful outline of ENHG grammar is provided by Betzinger, Bock, and Langner (1969), 281–358, produced under the supervision of Wilhelm Schmidt. See also the Select Bibliographies to Chapters V and VI.
45. Recently, Eggers, (1963–77), iii. 16–19, 56–62.
46. For a successful and stimulating attempt at this pattern of historiography, see Strang (1970).

CHAPTER I

1. For the major contributions see Eggers (1970). More recently, see Worstbrock (1978). For a useful summary including the later developments of the term, see Sonderegger (1979), chap. 2.

2. In this book 'Frankish' will be preferred: the tribe on which the name is based is attested in late classical sources in two forms, viz. *Franci* and *Francones*; here 'Franconian' is the adjective for the German province *Franken*, Franconia.

3. *Walh, wälhisk* are cognate with English *Wales, Welsh*. They preserve in Gmc. form the name of an old Celtic tribe attested as *Volcae*. English *walnut*, OE *wealh-hnutu*, shows the name in its first element; cf. also Neth. *waals*, Fr. *wallon*.

4. In the early period, linguistic remains of LG are often called Old Saxon (OS) to distinguish them from other LG dialects, notably the ancestors of Dutch, which are labelled Old Low Frankish (OLF). See pp. 37, 39. The Frisian dialects (earliest forms OFris.), while 'LG' in the sense that they lack the HG Consonant Shift, share several features with Old English (OE) and are best kept separate from the other LG dialects. Frisian contributes little to modern standard German—which, in examples, we abbreviate to the traditional but inaccurate NHG = 'New High German'.

5. The *Evangeliar*'s German glosses antedate the traditional starting-point for OHG: the Bavarian (?) glossary known after the first entry as *Abrogans* (*c*.750).

6. See Bergmann (1977), 325 ff.; (1966–7).

7. Moulton (1941), suggests convincingly that the preservation of the final full vowels of certain, largely southern Swiss dialects results from the influence of Franco-Provençal intonation: specifically, the consequent weakening of the stress accent has preserved the qualities in inflexional syllables.

8. The *-en* ending (< *-jan*) was causative, the *-ēn* ending was often durative, and the *-ōn* ending marked verbs formed from nouns. For aspectual distinctions, see Chapter VI.

9. As we might expect, the weakening seems to have begun earlier and more extensively in speech as the spellings of words and names in draft documents from St Gall show (early ninth century). See Sonderegger (1961).

10. See Lockwood (1972), and the companion volume (1969).

11. For further details of the proto-language and its problems, see Prokosch (1939); Krahe (1969); the collection of essays in van Coetsem and Kufner (1972); and, most recently, Markey *et al.* (1977–   ).

12. For a definition of LG, see p. 42.

13. See Campbell (1959/1974), 45–9, §§ 120 ff.

14. West-Saxon (*ge*)*triewe*, non-West-Saxon (*ge*)*trīowe*/(*ge*)*trēowe*; see Wright (1925), 52, § 90; Campbell (1959/1974), 15 f. §§ 37 f.

15. Gordon (1957), 282, § 74.

16. Mutation or 'umlaut' involves the change in the articulation of a stressed syllable in the direction of the articulation of a following unstressed one. In this case, the raising and fronting of a long /â/ to a long open *e*-sound ([ɛ:]) under the influence of following /i/; the change is not shown in the orthography in this instance. See Chapter II.

17. Maurer (1954).

18. *Germania*, 2: 'Manno tris filios assignant, e quorum nominibus proximi Oceano Ingvaeones, medii Herminones, ceteri Istvaeones vocentur.' The manuscript forms are actually *Ingaevones, Hermiones, Istaevones*, and variants, but are generally emended. See Schönfeld (1910). The *Germania* was written *c*.AD 98.

19. See Antonsen (1965), 19–36; Bahnick (1973); Markey (1976*a*), introduction, (1976*b*). These writers survey the earlier literature on the 'macro-dialectal' relationships of Germanic languages; see also Herbert Kufner in van Coetsem and Kufner (1972), 71–97.

20. Called also the 'Second Sound Shift' (or, more correctly 'Second Consonant Shift'), to distinguish it from the 'First or Germanic Sound Shift' which is the hallmark of all Gmc. languages and separates their consonantism from that of

all other IE languages. Indeed, O. Höfler prefers 'zweite Lautverschiebung', since he detects some features of the shift in Gmc. dialects other than those HG ones considered here, e.g. in Gothic, Vandal, and Burgundian (see Appendix A). The largely onomastic evidence is controversial, and certainly the shift in other dialects is more limited than in the HG ones.

21. $k\chi$ is a combination of the stop k and a voiceless velar spirant similar to *ch* in mod. German *Acht* or Scots *loch*. The double spirant $/zz/$ was distinct from voiceless $/ss/$ but later merged with it: cf. *Tatian uuîs* 'wise' and *uuîz* = 'white'; medieval German *wazzer* and mod. German *Wasser*. For fuller treatment, including the apparently complementary shift of voiced stops and spirants, see Appendix A.

22. Schatz (1927), §§ 89, 63.

23. Braune and Eggers (1975), § 283 n. 1 (*a*), pp. 239–40.

24. Frings and Lerchner (1966), 42.

25. Lasch (1974), § 419, p. 226. The LG dialects in the narrow sense of the term 'LG' are also known as 'Platt-Deutsch'.

26. 'Isogloss' is used here to mean a line drawn on a map marking off from each other dialect areas which share the same linguistic feature, whether phonological, morphological, syntactic, or lexical. The Benrath Line is not the most northerly isogloss separating HG from LG—north of it runs the *ik/ich* line crossing the Rhine at Ürdingen—but it serves rather as the northernmost baseline which other isoglosses come to join. The age of the Benrath Line and other HG isoglosses is in dispute: nineteenth-century scholars viewed them as the demarcations of ancient tribal 'seats', while dialect geographers, notably Theodor Frings, attributed their present-day positioning to the political and administrative influence of great ecclesiastical and aristocratic territories in the post-medieval period. However, nothing in the OHG material suggests any significant geographical displacement since the earliest evidence.

27. Wenskus (1961).

28. Their first king, Meroveus, was supposedly cast up by the sea; sometimes the Franks were provided with an eponymous hero, *Francio* (Isidore, *Etym.* ix, 2. 101); Otfrid had read that they were of Alexander's race ('Alexandres slahtu', *Evangelienbuch* i, 1, 88); frequently they were held to come from Troy (Fredegar), (perhaps a misinterpretation of the Colonia Trajana (= Xanten) on the Rhine as 'Colonia Trojana') and they even assumed the names of Trojan heroes, e.g. Antenerus (< Antenor) and Hector (Ebeling (1974), 57, 172).

29. See Wallace-Hadrill (1962), 2.

30. See esp. Gamillscheg (1970).

31. See Rauch (1967). Both the OFr. and OHG diphthongized forms are assumed to derive from V.Lat. forms whese vowels differed in quantity and quality from the pronunciation regarded as classical. See now Jones (1979).

32. See Schützeichel (1976).

33. See Wells (1972).

34. Matzel (1970); also Haubrichs (1975).

35. The manuscript is remarkable in preserving—in the same hand—the OFr. *Sequence of St Eulalia*. See Harvey (1945); Schützeichel (1966–7).

36. The later onomastic material is particularly promising: see Knoch (1969).

37. Bergmann (1973).

38. Steinmeyer und Sievers (1879–1922).

39. This remains uncertain: see Ganz (1969), but Bernard Bischoff (1971) still attributes the text to Fulda/Mainz scriptorial traditions on palaeographical grounds; Geuenich (1976), 260–2, opts for Fulda because of spelling.

40. A recently discovered (1978) fragmentary manuscript of the *Hêliand*, the

Straubing fragment (S), has revived speculation about the poem's origins. According to Bernard Bischoff, MS M might have been written at Corvey; see Bischoff (1979*b*). The new fragment has been edited by Bischoff (1979*c*) and discussed by Taeger (1979).

41. Sonderegger (1971).
42. Keller (1978), 140.
43. Little is known of conditions in early German chanceries and scriptoria. While chanceries deal mainly with legal and administrative matters, have different grades of staff, and a bureaucratic tradition of classical origin, monastery scriptoria are primarily centres of learning, whose activities included transcription of patristic, historical, and biblical texts and the compilation of glossaries. But 'clerks' for secular administration were also trained in monastery schools, and charters and documents were produced and even forged there.
44. For the importance of Fulda in German linguistic history, see Geuenich (1976), esp. 213–74. Undoubtedly Bavarians occupied some key positions in the monastery—the first abbot, Sturmi, the fourth abbot, Eigil (*c.*818–22), and at least four scribes, Abraham, Asger, Uuolfram, and Uueliman—but their work shows only a few deviations from the scriptorial traditions. Similarly, OE and OS influence seems restricted to some personal names copied into Fulda necrologies. According to Geuenich the change in spelling traditions at Fulda is less radical than had been thought. Nevertheless, the mixed character of Fuldese, however slight, is noteworthy. At St Gall, where some OIr. manuscripts were written, we find an even crasser distinction between language inside and outside the scriptorium.
45. Braune and Eggers (1975), § 6 n. 2, p. 10.
46. Moulton (1944).
47. Similar problems of establishing 'purified', i.e. homogeneous, data for linguistic analysis beset investigation of medieval and post-medieval chancery documents. The origins and practice of editors, printers, compositors, and correctors all bear on the final linguistic form of early printings too—as does the language of the original or the language of the destined readership.
48. The *Conversations* unfortunately show a phonetics 'refracted' in its transcription by Romance scribes: the first person pronoun 'I' (= EFrk. *ih*) appears as $E \sim Eh \sim Hi \sim Hiih \sim ich$ and (when it precedes the negative particle *ne*) also as $Gne \sim En$ and perhaps *in*. Another awkward text, the *Georgslied*, 'verges on the dyslexic' (Ruth Harvey, pers. comm.).
49. A fuller account of language contact, particularly the main types of borrowing, will be found in Chapter VII, dealing with seventeenth century German. See Fig. 6, p. 276. For further information, see especially Maurer and Rupp (1974); the etymological details, earlier forms, etc. of words treated here can be found in Kluge (1883/1967).
50. See Krahe (1954), 122–43.
51. Early German *ambaht* had two forms: (1) masc. noun = 'servant', with variants *ambahtio/-eo* from a weak verb *ambahten* (NHG *dienen*); *ambahtman* (pl. *ambahtliuti*) replaced these; (2) neut. noun = 'service', 'office'. See Voetz (1977), 40–53. The English words *ambassador*, *embassy*, and *ombudsman* are cognates.
52. *Tonne* lacks the HG Consonant Shift and may therefore have been borrowed after it was complete.
53. See Frings and Müller (1968), vol. ii esp. pp. 137–8.
54. See Frings (1957), 25–6, and Map 21 on p. 111.
55. Masser (1966).
56. In *Bischof* the loss of initial *e-* and substitution of voiced *b-* for *p* suggest Gallo-Roman pronunciation, cf. *Büchse*. The word *opfern* was once restricted to

southern German dialects; other Gmc. and Romance languages preserve reflexes of the totally unrelated Lat. word *offerre* in the same sense: Fr. *offrir*, English *offer*, OFris. *offria*, ON *offra*.

57. NB, *papa* derives from Gk. *papās* 'priest' with short first vowel, as opposed to *pāpas* 'pope', which goes via Lat. *pāpa* to OHG *bābes* to mod. German *Papst*.

58. Today *weih-* is restricted to south German place-names and churches, e.g. Weihenstephan, a Benedictine abbey near Freising, Weihenbronn, near Schwäbisch Hall; otherwise it is choice style: *weihen*, *einweihen*, etc., see below, n. 65.

59. The South Tirolean Pustertal has the week as follows: *mǫntă, ērtă, mită, pfinztă, freită, sanstă*. The meaning of *Ertag* is uncertain, surely not reinterpretation of Gk. *Areōs hēmerā* (Ares, god of war) with Gothic bishop Arius (d. 636)? If *Pfinztag* comes from Gk. 'fifth day', no Gothic **pinte dags* is attested; similarly, if *Samstag* reflects a Vulgar Gk. form **samboton* for normal *sabbaton*, this is not the attested Gothic form (which is *sabbato dags*); but forms in *-m-* occur in Gaul: Fr. *samedi*. See Knobloch. (1961).

60. OHG *munistiri*, V.Lat. *monisterium* (attested in Merovingian Lat.), Graeco-Lat. *monasterium* 'hermitage'. The meaning changes to 'monastery', also 'monastery church', 'large church'. Today, *Münster* in the sense 'cathedral' occurs more in south Germany, as opposed to northern *Dom* (< Lat. *domus*). See Masser (1966), 13 f., 70–1.

61. Columban, Gallus, and their acolytes established great monastic centres at Luxeuil (590), Bobbio (612–13), and St Gall (613–14), and the tradition of Irish foundation persisted into the twelfth century, for example at Vienna, the Schottenkloster.

62. Weisgerber (1952).

63. Reiffenstein (1958), 22–3.

64. See Braune (1919).

65. The picture is complicated by stylistic and contextual considerations: some OHG texts have both *heilag* and *wīh* for Lat. *sanctus* and both *geist* and *ātum* (NHG *Atem*) for Lat. *spiritus*, e.g. the ninth-century Frk. catechism attributed to Weissenburg: 'Gilaubiu [= 'ich glaube'] . . . in heilenton Christ . . . ther intfangener ist fona *heilegemo geiste* [= 'conceived of the Holy Ghost'] . . . gilaubiu in *atum uuihan*.' The St Gall Paternoster and Creed (Alem. late eighth century) has *uuihan keist*, while Notker uses *heiligo geist* for *spiritus sanctus*, but translates *spiritus* as *ātem* when it means 'breath'; the Vorau manuscript of *Ezzo's Song* (Bav. twelfth century), on the other hand, has *der heilige atem* but renders 'breath' as *geist* (lines 412 and 73). See Becker (1964), 139 f., and Tschirch (1966–9), i. 136.

66. See Stenton (1971), chaps. V and VI; Levison (1946).

67. For a series of studies on Fulda in the light of the names of monks commemorated there, see K. Schmid *et al.* (1978). See also Geuenich (1976).

68. These lists are taken from Gutmacher (1914).

69. Bostock, King, and McLintock (1976), 167.

70. For example *chiliih* (= EFrk. *glīch*, NHG *gleich*) translates Lat. *ad similitudinem*, with the variant *in chiliihhnissu*, whereas *anachiliih* translates *ad imaginem* and *anaebanchiliih* renders *aequalem imaginem habere/una imago cum deo esse* (*Isidor* III. 4–5). The distinction is admittedly not thoroughly consistent, but the differentiated vocabulary to separate *similis* from *aequalis* exists.

71. B. Bischoff, reported in Fischer (1966), p. 20*.

72. McLintock (1966).

73. Behaghel (1923–32), vol. i, §§ 460–70, pp. 663–74. The instrumental case becomes ever rarer and by the thirteenth century has become fossilized in a few formulas.

74. Sonderegger (1965).

75. For the definitive edition and further bibliography, see Eckhardt (1953–7). See esp. i (1954), 93 and 179, and ii/1 (1955), 73–89.
76. See Kluge (1883/1967); PGmc. *maþla-/*maðla- > OHG mahal; cf. ON māl, Gothic maþl. It underlies place-names like Detmold (eighth-century Theotmalli 'Volksversammlung(sstätte)') and Mechelen/Malines in Belgium.
77. Sonderegger (1965a).
78. Van Helten (1900), § 163, 482 ff. This article and Baesecke (1935) remain basic for the early Gmc. legal vocabulary.
79. Schwarz (1977) examines Otfrid's glosses to Priscian's Institutiones Grammaticae in their educational function.
80. e.g. ⟨qu⟩ for Gmc. /w/, /hw/, e.g. quaren = waren; use of is-/es- for Gmc. s+consonant initially, e.g. esconae = skoni 'schön'; frequent loss of initial /h/; irregularity in rendering the undoubtedly shifted consonants. For an excellent analysis of the text, see Huisman (1969).
81. Cf. Otfrid, Evangelienbuch i. 5. 28 drof ni zuivolo thu thes, Gabriel addressing the Virgin Mary!
82. Sonderegger (1971), 176–92. However, Sonderegger is over-quick to evaluate deviations between the German text of the Tatian and its Latin source as evidence of German native syntax struggling to emancipate itself from Latin: the text-critical basis is complicated. See Ganz (1969).

CHAPTER II

1. See Appendices A and B.
2. Note the further problem, that of localizing even well-written and regular texts.
3. The extent to which languages borrow 'sounds' or even words, is hard to assess. Often foreign influence seems to be indirect and catalytic, triggering shifts in the structure of the recipient language which were always potentially likely; see Chapter VII. Links between phonological developments and social ones are not improbable per se, but are seldom susceptible of proof.
4. The monophthongization of PGmc. /ai/ to /ē/ in early German seems to have begun in the north, and northern dialects (e.g. OS) show it fully. In Frk. dialects the shift was restricted to positions before /r/, /h/, or /w/, or in final position or unstressed syllable. Weinhold implies that the change occurred more fully in speech but was adopted only later in other environments: MG scribes of the twelfth and thirteenth centuries still considered it vulgar, but in the course of the fourteenth century it spread over the whole MG area, as spoken forms gained entry to the written norms. See Weinhold (1883), § 98, pp. 91–2.
5. See Reis (1974).
6. Palmer (1972), 228
7. Paul (1880/1968), 58–9.
8. The history of the speech-community and the history of their 'sounds' were thus related at best 'subliminally', and the split between historical grammar and linguistic history is implicit in this approach.
9. 'Spontan' and 'kombinatorisch' (Sievers (1876), 125 ff.). In fact, Sievers was not strictly a Neogrammarian: he expressly stated that sounds changed not individually but in series, involving necessarily change to the system, and he also affirmed that phonetic analysis must begin with the examination of the sentence—but it was left to others to develop the implications of these views. See Ganz (1978).
10. See Kluge (1883/1967), 291–2.
11. Alternations explained by Verner's Law which persist in mod. German are f ~ b

(*Hefe, erhaben*); *d* ~ *t* (*schneiden, geschnitten*); *h* ~ *g* (*gedeihen, gediegen*); *s* ~ *r* (*genesen, ernähren*).

12. See also Fr. subj. *que je fásse* vs. *nous faisions* [s] ≠ [z]). The alternation in mod. German *Hannóver* ([ha¹nofɒ] vs. *Hannoveráner* [hanove¹ranɒ] is a disputed example: see Kuhn (1964).

13. The new /ā/ merges with another long /ā/ phoneme which derives from the PGmc. vowel /ǣ/, sometimes called, /ē¹/; cf. Gothic *nēmun* vs. OHG *nāmun* 'they took'.

14. OE *þencan*/*þōhte*; Campbell (1959/1974), § 753 (*b*) (5).

15. Saussure (1916/1973), 125 ff. (pp. 186 ff. of the original edition).

16. Lyons (1968), 60.

17. [ß] indicates a voiceless dental or alveolar spirant distinguished from /s/, perhaps, by being more fortis. In the editions of MHG poems, although not in the manuscripts themselves, it is often shown as <z> e.g. *wazzer* (NHG *Wasser*).

18. See Fudge (1970). In what follows an essentially physical view of the phoneme is adopted: this reflects our concern with written rather than spoken German.

19. The variations in the pronunciation of a speaker, especially where he speaks a dialect beside the standard language, may be termed 'free variation' or 'variphones'—e.g. *something* may occasionally be pronounced as *sumfink*: there is no change of meaning. However, a stylistic shift has occurred.

20. The phonetic identity of these phonemes /p, b/, /t, d/, and /k, g/ remains uncertain: it might be an alternation of voiceless (= fortis) stop and voiced (= lenis) stop; or it might be voiceless and voiced lenis—voiceless lenes occur today in southern German dialects. See Penzl (1955-6). A useful mnemonic: t*er* br*ûoder unde des* pr*ûoder sun* 'the brother and his brother's son'.

21. In late OHG the opposition between voiced ≠ voiceless consonants was lost in final position, hence the change in spelling from OHG *līb, tōd, lag* to MHG *līp, tôt, lac*. The phoneme inventory for this position was thus radically reduced, and remains so, although mod. German obscures this by regularizing the voiced medial consonant symbols into final position—*Leib, Tod, lag*.

22. For mod. German the opposition of tenseness and laxness is more important than length in differentiating some vowel phonemes: 'long' vowels are all tense (with the exception of [ɛː] in *wäre, gäbe, Ähre*, etc.), while all 'short' vowels are lax, but in MHG a number of short *e*-phonemes were distinguished by the tense ≠ lax opposition; see below on 'umlaut' (p. 88).

23. For details of structuralist and generativist studies, see the Select Bibliography to this Chapter.

24. For full and useful tables for the dialectal distribution of all three phonemes, see Sonderegger (1974), 159, 162, 172.

25. In this book, the macron usually indicates long vowel, except (1) where the manuscripts have circumflex, as in some diphthongs in Notker, (2) in normalized MHG.

26. Klopstock uses *Umlaut* as a German technical term both for *Strom*/*Ströme* and *sang*/*singen*—i.e. for mutation and apophony or 'ablaut' (see pp. 161-3): Klopstock (1774), ed. (1855), 169.

27. Triadic oppositions in the long vowel system in MHG are hard to find: OHG *sīgan* 'sink'/*sūgan* 'suck'/*sūgis* 'you (sg.) suck'. The short vowel oppositions are more important: *kinde* (dat. of *kind*)/*kundî* (cf. OHG *gotkundî*) = Lat. *divinitas*/*kunda* (pret. of *kunnan*, NHG *können*). Nevertheless, triadic arrangements of vowel systems are part of the description of older forms of German, not of the way it functioned. Binary oppositions (between pairs of 'phonemes') remain fundamental, and most if not all medieval dialects reduced the threefold distinction in the short *e*-phonemes, either retaining two or sometimes (as in standard NHG) only one short *e*- phoneme.

28. Martinet (1955), 59–62.
29. We should note in passing that many languages tolerate a large number of homonyms in speech and these can be distinguished by context: Fr. provides the classic example: *ô, haut, hauts, eau, eaux, au, aux, o* (= the letter of alphabet) are all homonyms pronounced [o].
30. Munich manuscript.
31. The change of /p, t, k/ to spirants and affricates also removed any function the correlation of voice may previously have had, making changes to the voiced stops possible.
32. All approaches have to cope with the difficulties of the data for OHG; the apparent inadequacy of some generative studies in handling dialect, style, and external factors reflects simply the preoccupation of most generativists with logical or philosophical rather than 'pragmatic' issues.
33. Fourquet (1948).
34. Braune and Eggers (1975), § 51, pp. 54–6.
35. Palatalization concerns the shift in articulation of vowels and consonants to the hard palate just behind the alveolar ridge. Vowels produced here are high and closed, palatalized consonants tend to be affricated. It has been argued that the consonants in OHG palatalize first, which subsequently affects the vowel—since Romance consonants also palatalize before high vowels, there might again be some catalytic interaction between German and Romance. Note that umlaut can cover other types of modification than palatalization ('raising and fronting'): vowels may also be lowered under the influence of a following low vowel. This process is supposed to resupply the Gmc. languages with a short *o* vowel to replace that lost when PIE *o* > PGmc. *a*, e.g. PGmc. **wulfaz* gives rise to OHG *wolf*, PGmc. **duχtēr* > OHG *tohter* (NHG *Tochter*).
36. Even with primary umlaut, there is much irregularity between ⟨a⟩ and ⟨e⟩ in the texts: see Schatz (1927), §§ 47–50. Factors cutting across the purely phonetic/ phonemic development include (*a*) traditional spellings—deviation between written and spoken language; (*b*) dialectal variation—umlaut is less marked in southern dialects; (*c*) paradigmatic analogy—non-mutated forms from other parts of a verb/noun paradigm are extended into forms which ought to show mutation, e.g. *henin* → *hanin* by virtue of *hano* (nom.) (NHG *Hahn*).
37. Sometimes a mutated form of the diphthong *iu* is also postulated, as in Table 2 above (p. 79), e.g. in *liuti* = *Leute*; but there is no orthographical evidence for this sound, nor does its subsequent development impinge on the modern standard language. However, if mutation is at one stage a purely phonetic process, it is plausible to reconstruct such a sound: it lacks any obvious structural role, unless to facilitate the merging of the 'old' diphthong *iu* with the 'new' mutated long *ṻ*.
38. Waterman (1966), 86, adduces this word, but we are dealing with sound-substitution: *Grenze* shows ⟨e⟩ for unstressed Polish *a* and ⟨z⟩ for Polish *č*, since the source is Polish *graníča*, probably with stress on the second syllable. As the loan was established in German, it adopted stress on the first syllable.
39. Twaddell (1938); Penzl (1949).
40. Where OHG /ë/ does occur before /i/ this is largely the result of morphological interference in the phonology, e.g. OHG *sëhs* 'six', inflected pl. *sẹhsi* with a closed [e] (Paul (1881/1969), 18 n. 3). Some loan-words also show /e/ before an /i/ in the next syllable, although, as we have seen, they are sometimes poor guides to phonology, e.g. OHG *belliz* < MLat. *pellicia* 'fur (coat)'. If such loan-words had a higher *e* allophone than those normally representing *ë*, this would make the merger of the raised *ẹ* allophones of /a/ with the phoneme /ë/ all the more probable.

41. A convenient minimal pair (two words distinguished by only one phonemic opposition) illustrating the 'primary' and 'secondary' umlaut is:

    pre-OHG *salida 'lodging'   → OHG selida → MHG selde
    *sālida 'blessedness' →   sālida →   sælde

    (where the graphy ⟨æ⟩ indicates long, open, mutated).
42. Antonsen (1964). Phonetic (i.e. purely allophonic) umlaut probably still operated during the OHG period, however, since new analogical plurals (e.g. old pl. hūs > new pl. hūsir) do show mutated phonemes in late OHG (Notker hiuser, MHG hiuser).
43. But note that this implies that morphological considerations were important in the phonemicization of umlaut.
44. See Wiesinger (1970), 22-3.
45. See Kiparski (1968); King (1969); Vennemann (1972a, b); Voyles (1974), (1976).
46. For 'morpheme' and the symbol ∅ meaning 'zero-morpheme', the absence of classifying element and of inflexion, see pp. 145-7.
47. Russ (1975).
48. In practice we cannot separate these two linked phases: morphological function accords the mutated vowels their phonemic status, at least, in inflexional morphology.

CHAPTER III

1. For periodization, see also pp. 22 ff.
2. Grimm (1819/1822-37), i (2nd edn., 1822), Preface, p. xi. For Grimm, languages increasingly lost formal perfection, becoming analytical in structure and relying not on morphology but on particles, word order, and periphrasis to convey syntactic relationships. But the impoverishment of poetic expression this entailed was compensated by their increased capacity to express abstract thought and by precision: see Grimm (1848), i. 5f., (1819/22-37), i (2nd edn., 1822), 19-20.
3. Broadly speaking UG, i.e. Alem., Bav., and E. Frk. Note also that Grimm's much more general view of the Germanic languages and their development inevitably led him to play down the dialectal variants found in German, while his desire to link language with literature unfortunately permitted both to be seen as 'decaying' after about 1250: Verfall implies decline and decadence but in respect of morphology the more neutral term 'erosion' is more appropriate.
4. Details below, pp. 112-15.
5. As in the best authority on the language of ENHG, Moser (1929-51), i/1 (1929), 1, i/3 (1951), 301-2.
6. The misnomer 'Saxons' for Frk.-speakers arises from their having adopted a Saxon legal code during the Reformation.
7. See Wiesinger (1973); Kloss (1973). For a map of the expansion, see König (1978), 74. Migrations of German speakers reached their highpoint in the eighteenth and early nineteenth centuries, but slackened off with the political unification and the economic rise of Germany. At first America and Canada were favoured as destinations, then in the nineteenth century South America and later Australia; German-speaking minorities survive there to this day.
8. See Bosl (1975); Bosl and Weis (1976), 64-130; Bumke (1977), with an appendix covering studies until 1976; Schröder (1972); Fleckenstein (1975).
9. Bumke (1976).
10. Bumke (1977), 77.

11. Konrad von Würzburg has patrician patrons at Basel in the late thirteenth century: his *Partonopier und Meliur* was commissioned by Peter Schaler, sometime burgomaster. Much courtly literature was preserved in later medieval manuscripts apparently produced for such an audience.
12. The wildest aspirations of the 'bourgeoisie' are celebrated *c*.1230 by the Vorarlberg poet Rudolf von Ems, whose merchant hero 'der gute Gerhart' consorts with the Emperor, has a son who is knighted (3588 ff.), and almost marries a princess, while Gerhart himself refuses a crown (5510 ff.) (*Der gute Gerhart*, ed. Asher (1962)). Gerhart's town, Cologne, was the biggest commercial centre in Germany. In the fifteenth century commoners could rise to high office: Caspar Schlick (d. 1449) was Chancellor to three emperors; Gregor Heimburg (d. 1472) was a jurist and diplomat; the famous Humanist Konrad Celtis (1459–1508) was a vintner's son.
13. See Planitz (1954); Cipolla (1972–4).
14. See Bechtel (1951), 255 ff.
15. The spelling *stadt* is a variant which becomes established in the sense 'town'; mod. German *Stätte* and (*Werk*)*Statt* show morphologically related forms.
16. *Vorrede zu Justus Menius' Oeconomia Christiana* (1529), in *Werke* (Weimar edn.), vol. xxx/2 (1909), 62. 9 f.
17. Planitz (1954), 123, cf. also ibid. 394 n. 41. Paul (1880/1968), 289, notes a functional shift in name structure: the second names originally identified the bearer by qualifying his forename, but increasingly the second name becomes a fixed, family name and the forename itself becomes the qualifying or identifying element.
18. The two last are regional variants from Ulm and Freiburg meaning 'potter'.
19. Besch (1965). Only as late as the seventeenth and eighteenth centuries are names officially fixed: Bavaria 1677, Austria 1776, Prussia 1794.
20. Fleischer (1964), 82, 86. See also Bach (1952–6); Schwarz (1949–50).
21. The word *chancery* (or *chancellery*) originally denoted a place with barriers (cf. 'barrister', 'the Bar') or *cancelli*, where legal decisions were made known and documents issued. Early (e.g. Merovingian) chanceries were, like the courts, peripatetic, but with the establishment of fixed local chanceries Emperors could travel about the realm making use of local chancery staff where necessary.
22. Studies of imperial chanceries, although they are not typical, provide a guide to the officials and procedures: see Moser (1977); also Schmitt (1966).
23. De Boor (1971*b*).
24. Kleiber (1965).
25. Ottokar von Steiermark (*c*.1300–10), ed. Seemüller (1890–3), 172. 13098 ff.
26. Comparisons with the poorly preserved chivalric texts, like Hartmann von Aue's *Erec*, are instructive: it is preserved virtually entire in only one (sixteenth-century) manuscript, and in short fragments of three others.
27. For medieval technical languages generally see Eis (1967).
28. Mechthild von Magdeburg (*c*.1207–*c*.1282) wrote down a series of mystical visions in LG rhythmical prose which shows the influence of the *Minnesang*. The original is unfortunately lost, the work being preserved in an Alem. version about a century after its composition and in a Latin version. Several other German nuns wrote mystical works, although none achieved Mechthild's expressiveness.
29. See the *Tobias*, ed. Degering (1916) and Müller (1923); the *Alexander*, ed. Kinzel (1884) and Müller (1923).
30. These sections are indebted to Guchmann (1964), (1969), esp. (1964), 60 ff.
31. *König Rother*, edd. Frings and Kuhnt (1954).
32. Paul (1881/1969), § 146A, note 6; the pronoun functioned as a plural, not a dual.

33. The Humanist Niclas von Wyle (d. 1478), town clerk at Esslingen, an author much concerned with chancery practice and a translator of late classical and Renaissance literature, rails against scribes who ape fashions from other, especially princely, chanceries, identifying certain Rhenish, Flemish, and Austrian habits. See *Translationen des Niclas von Wyle*, ed. Keller (1861), esp. the eighteenth *Translatze*.

34. In what follows, 'MHG' represents the grammarians' normalized language based on texts from the UG area. It is an essential reference point, but does not imply that such a language existed in this regular form. Phonetic interpretations (and notations) vary slightly, hence the alternative forms given under *diphthongization*.

35. Both monophthongization and diphthongization illustrate change in series— *Reihenschritte*: sounds with distinctive features in common, in this instance tongue height, shift together. For a detailed discussion of serial changes, see Wiesinger (1970), i. 29 ff. See now Jones (1984).

36. See Penzl (1975a), 113–18 (also for a full treatment of the other changes mentioned here).

37. Paul (1881/1969), § 24, pp. 55–9. See also below, pp. 153–5.

38. Schulze, (1967), esp. 373 ff.

39. *Der Renner von Hugo von Trimberg*, ed. Ehrismann, (1909).

40. Ehrismann (1920), esp. 225 ff. Line 22272 is disputed, since some scholars read 'wol schürgent', not 'vol schürgent'; see Eichler and Bergmann (1967), 5.

41. The circumflex to indicate long vowel, e.g. *sîn = NHG sein* vs. *sin = NHG Sinn*, occurs sporadically in OHG, as do the diphthongal graphies ⟨uo⟩ (*truoc = NHG trug*) and ⟨ou⟩ (*boum = NHG Baum*). But ⟨ä⟩ (*mähte = NHG Mächte*) is post-fourteenth-century, as are ⟨ö⟩ and ⟨ü⟩ (the actual manuscripts sometimes show superscribed symbols, ⟨ô⟩ and ⟨û⟩, which are ambiguous—diphthongal or mutation markers). Positional distinctions (allographs) made in manuscripts like long and short ⟨ſ⟩ and ⟨s⟩, or initial ⟨v⟩, medial ⟨u⟩, are ignored. Finally, Lachmann's successors distinguished dental affricates ⟨z⟩ and ⟨tz⟩ from spirants ⟨zz⟩ against the common manuscript practice. So, standard MHG orthography is a somewhat artificial, neo-Gothic edifice.

42. Lachmann (1820), Preface, p. xii. See also Ganz (1968); Lutz-Hensel (1975), 328.

43. Wolff (1973).

44. For the reconstruction, see Schieb and Frings (1964–5); also Schieb (1965), esp. 16–17.

45. Guchmann (1964), 112–16.

46. *Thomasin von Zerclaere* (1216), ed. Rückert (1852), lines 32–54, esp. 45.

47. *Deutsche Liederdichter des 12. bis 14. Jahrhunderts*, ed. Bartsch (1864), 245. The poem is a pastoral parody, and hence atypical.

48. Wilhelm (1920), i. 31.

49. Hartmann von Aue, *Gregorius*, ed. Neumann (1968), 118. 1575 ff.

50. For fuller treatment of the types of linguistic influence, see pp. 272 ff.

51. See Öhmann (1974).

52. *Tristan*, ed. Ganz (1978), lines 2292 f., 8073 f. (music) 2786–3055 (hunting). See also Hatto's translation (1960), 78 ff. and 147–8.

53. NHG *hübsch* is formally the reflex of either an old form OHG* *hubisk* or else a dialectal, possibly MFrk. form. Note the semantic change 'courtly' to 'pretty'. The form *hövesch* is north-western/Flemish. NHG *höfisch* 'courtly' and *höflich* 'polite' (from *hovelich*) have become differentiated in meaning over the centuries.

54. Suolahti (1929), esp. 39–40.

55. It survives as *Tölpel* 'oaf', with dissimilation of /r/ to /l/.

56. See Bumke (1977), 19 ff. The form *rit(t)er* is attested in HG before other 'Flemish' forms and is likely to be native; no forms *ridder* occur in HG.
57. *Meier Helmbreht*, ed. Gough (1957), 30–2. The form **sakent* (some editors have *snaket*) is an emendation; MS B has *sagt*. But Helmbrecht mixes LG and HG, and there is perhaps no need to alter the text. LG *parit, wîf, lîf, grîpen* correspond to MHG *pferit, wîp, lîp, grîfen*.
58. See Straßner (1968); Catholy (1966).
59. *Rudolfs von Ems Willehalm von Orlens*, ed. Junk (1905), lines 2279 ff.
60. The parallelism can be enhanced by rhythmical codas of stressed and unstressed syllables at the end of sentences and clauses, modelled on the Latin *cursus* developed in the papal chancery—but in Latin the alternation is between long and short syllables.
61. Text after Walshe (1951), based on Bernt (1917).
62. Burdach (1920); Burdach and pupils devoted a series of studies to clarifying the relationship between Bohemia and Italy in the late fourteenth and fifteenth centuries, and Bernt (1917), an edition of the *Ackermann*, forms part of this endeavour.
63. See Kluge (1883/1967); Schirmer (1911*a, b*).
64. Hase (1885). The first letters date from the 1490s.
65. Ed. Steinhausen (1895).
66. Both accounts were translated into German: see von Tscharner (1935); Strasmann (1968).
67. See Stammler (1953). For further bibliography see Kunisch (1974), esp. 298–322.
68. Rudolf IV founded Vienna University in 1365, and the Habsburg court remains associated with works from it. A Viennese circle of scholastic/theological writers includes, beside Langenstein, Niklaus von Dinkelsbühl (1360–1433), Ulrich von Pottenstein (1360–1420), Thomas Peuntner (1360/80–1439), Stephan von Landskron (d. 1477), and a number of other university men. See Weidenhiller (1965), esp. 206 ff. Catechetic vernacular tracts become extremely common after 1370, and some authors are prolific: Langenstein wrote well over a hundred works, Niklaus von Dinkelsbühl's sermons, especially Latin versions, occur in more than 600 manuscripts.
69. Thanks to Stammler (1953) and Ruh (1956), esp. 78–90.
70. Examples from Buijssen (1966): exceptions are common and reflect other, perhaps older, terminological traditions.
71. Ruh (1956), 87 n. 5, calls this 'indirect loan translation'.
72. Kloocke (1974). Eckhart seems closer to chivalric literature, where *-unge* formations are rarer than the dynamic infinitive nouns.
73. Ruh (1953), esp. 34, 39 f. Apparently the German terms reflect different Latin traditions: scholastic texts show Aristotelian–Thomistic vocabulary, mystic ones use Platonic and Neoplatonic terms.
74. See Burdach (1884); (1893), esp. 136–9; (1920), esp. 206 f.
75. Schmitt (1966).
76. von Bahder (1890), 3; Guchmann (1964–9), i. 141.
77. Guchmann (1964–9), i. 146 f.; Skála (1964), (1967); Bach (1937–43). See also Kettmann (1967*c*).
78. Adelung (1787), 50 ff., already talks of a colonial German, but attributed some phonetic features to Slav influence.
79. See Bach (1965), § 122a, p. 249; Henzen (1954), 75 ff.
80. Besch (1967), 16–17.
81. Henzen (1954), 76; Grosse (1955).
82. Schützeichel (1967).

83. This approach returns to the written language, *inter alia*, of chanceries; it does not overemphasize the role of any single chancery, but establishes where possible regions within which orthographical and other linguistic features are used, then attempts to show the influence of one *Schreiblandschaft* on another.
84. Guchmann, (1964–9), i. 102 ff.
85. Otto's *Die 24 Alten oder der goldene Thron der minnenden Seele* (title modernized) was written in 1386. Besch (1967) analyses two chapters from sixty-eight of the *c.*120 manuscripts.
86. Besch (1967), esp. 340–63. Without wishing to deny Luther's importance, via his Wittenberg printers, for the German language of his day, the persistence of this influence requires further examination and is often more celebrated than demonstrated.
87. Schützeichel (1960).
88. Wolf (1975), esp. 324. Wolf's material is not strictly from chancery sources: he examines late fifteenth-century German manuscripts of the Franciscan Rule (*Regula bullata*, 1227) written in Bav., Swabian, EMG, and LG.
89. Guchmann, (1964–9), ii. 53–7; 61, 74, 110–11 tries to link the Imperial Chancery and the printing centre of Augsburg.
90. See Werbow (1963); Josten (1976), esp. 91 ff.
91. See Hans Moser (1977); Kettmann (1967c).
92. Paradoxically, Luther claimed to follow chancery norms, but the importance of his writings enabled his printers, in particular Hans Lufft, to gain a temporary advantage over competitors and their printed forms became widely known.
93. Hans Moser (1977) distinguishes between a 'norm' within a chancery and the fluctuations of practice within a norm, the *Usus*. Anyway, the orthography, and to a lesser extent morphology, of the fifteenth to early seventeenth centuries were still 'open' systems subject to individual variation.

CHAPTER IV

1. Lyons (1968), 96.
2. Bynon (1977), 40.
3. Morphology and syntax merge into one another: Saussure (1916/1973), 185, views them as inseparable.
4. Humboldt (1836), p. ccx.
5. Lyons (1968), 181.
6. Nida (1949), 6. Morphemes have some identifiable meaning or function, whereas phonemes simply distinguish words as being different.
7. This approach derives from Bloomfield (1933), 160; bound morphs can sometimes be quoted, e.g. an '-ism'.
8. Since acoustic images of morphs must exist in the *listener's* mind, to enable him to interpret utterances, morphs also exist at some level of abstraction.
9. For various approaches to the disparity between morphemic and morph levels, see Matthews (1970).
10. Strong verbs form their past tenses by means of vowel gradation, or 'apophony' ('ablaut'); see below, pp. 161 ff.
11. But other grammatical categories are probably also involved, e.g. *ist* reflects (1) *indicative mood*, (2) *third person*, (3) *singular*; while *-en* classifies the verb as belonging to the strong conjugation. Grammatical categories like tense, number, person, etc. are also indicated by 'colligation', i.e. their interrelation in syntax. To some extent, then, the concepts 'grammatical category' and 'morpheme' will be conflated. To put the problem more clearly: in mod. German, the pret. and perfect verb forms are often used interchangeably, but, whereas the actually

occurring morphs in *liebte* are susceptible to morphemic analysis, those in *hat geliebt* involve colligation and discontinuity, which prevent our establishing an underlying, abstract 'morphemic shape'. In the present chapter the problem will be brushed under the carpet of overlapping morphological and syntactical levels. See Firth (1957), 183 ff.

12. A proliferation of zero morphs representing morphemes evident only from context (e.g. tense) or in the syntax (e.g. case) would be absurd; see Nida (1949), 46.

13. The root vowels in column (b) have all lengthened in open syllables in the modern standard language; see p. 113.

14. *Bögen* is common in southern Germany; for other 'sub-standard' mutated plurals, see below, p. 157.

15. The vowel is long; contrast pret. subj. *flösse* from *fließen* 'flow'.

16. Kern and Zutt (1977), 7–8.

17. Braune and Eggers (1975), § 214 n. 2: *meri* (NHG *Meer*) and *bini* (NHG *Biene*), old neut. *i* stems?

18. Braune and Eggers (1975), §§ 223, 226, 227.

19. Some forms of the adj. declension are pronominal, hence they differ from those of the noun: see below, pp. 157–8.

20. Reis (1974).

21. Grimm (1819/22–37), i (2nd edn., 1822), 597, distinguished nouns as strong and weak: the weak class reflect the old -*n*-stem class mentioned above (p. 150, No. (6)). With loss of unstressed final syllables, the weak nouns appeared in MHG texts with oblique cases ending predominantly in -(*e*)*n*.

22. See Franck (1909), 200 ff., § 154; Schatz (1927), §§ 321, 359–75.

23. Braune and Eggers (1975), 58 ff. For the implications for periodization, metre, and linguistic structure, see also pp. 34–5.

24. See Kauffmann (1890), 121 ff., esp. 135, § 117. Kauffmann stresses written traditions, but some southern Swiss dialects, e.g. in the Valais (*im Wallis*), have differentiated inflexional qualities in speech.

25. Paul (1881/1969), 141, § 120.

26. From Wilhelm (1932–63), vol. i, No. 20. Note the forms *wagenere*, *wagene*, and *andimi* (OHG *an demu*, MHG *an dem*(*e*)), and also the rendering of unstressed syllables with ⟨i⟩ and ⟨u⟩: *bidorfint*, *machinde*, *michilun*, etc.

27. Lindgren (1953), 209 (map).

28. For the functions of adverb and inflected and uninflected predicative adj., see Marache (1972), 217–34. Through apocope some old *i*/*j* stem adjs. which did not mutate or geminate (e.g. MHG *milte*, *reine*) merged with the rest.

29. August Schleicher held that all languages were organic and their history was a process of decay: the effects of the sound /j/ on consonantal structure he once described as 'dry rot in the joists of the word' (!): 'ein wahrer Hausschwamm (*merulius vastator* L.) in den Gebälken des Wortes' (Schleicher (1869), 56).

30. Paul (1880/1968). See esp. chaps. V, X, and XI.

31. 'Sobald eine Form ihrer Gestalt nach mehreren Klassen angehören kann, so ist es auch möglich von ihr aus die andern zugehörigen Formen nach verschiedenen Proportionen zu bilden. Welche von den verschiedenen anwendbaren Proportionen dann sich geltend macht, hängt durchaus nur von dem Machtverhältnis ab, in welchem sie zu einander stehen' (Paul (1880/1968), 113–14).

32. Unmarked classes include masc. *ja* stems (*hirte*), neut. *a*, *ja*, and *wa* stems (*wort*, *künne*, *knie*), fem. *ō* and *jō* stems (*gebe*, *sünde*), some consonantal stems, and more recent apocopated forms, e.g. masc. *a*-stem nom. sg. *nagel*, nom. pl. *nagel*(*e*); see Paul (1881/1969), §§ 119 ff. NHG retains unmarked plurals in some masc. and neut. nouns, e.g. *Lehrer*, *Schüler*, *Wagen*, *Mädchen*.

33. Some forms are acceptable variants in the standard, e.g. *Generäle*, *Herzöge*.

34. Hotzenköcherle (1962) (examples from p. 330).

35. Dal (1940).

36. A comparable example from the weak noun paradigm: the printers of Luther's *Sendbrief vom Dolmetschen* (1530) use the weak gen. form after a marked particle (*des herzen*), but analogical forms after an unmarked particle (printer A *zu vil herzes*, printer B *zu vil herzens*), since the weak form *herzen* could be confused with the plural—'too many hearts' instead of the required 'too much heart'. See Luther (1530), ed. Bischoff (1909), 16–19.

37. *Lancelot*, ed. Kluge, ii (1963), 320. The work was originally translated in the thirteenth century, but most manuscripts are later. This passage is from MS P (Heidelberg, *c*.1430), in Rh.Frk. or SRh.Frk. dialect.

38. As noted on p. 138, Besch (1967) has studied the forms used in manuscripts of a popular text by Otto von Passau; see his Map 73, pp. 242–5.

39. Besch (1967). Map 80, pp. 257 ff.

40. The *-er* pl., originally from a minor declension of neut. nouns, has been extended to masc., but not to fem., nouns. Hence, masc. and neut. nouns retain their declensional similarity; more than one pl.-marking is necessary.

41. See Besch (1967), 287–9.

42. In this instance Justus Georg Schottel (1663), 297. Cf. also *Rheinlande, Niederlande* with political and geographical unity, vs. *Bundesländer* as discrete, autonomous, and often stubbornly independent entities.

43. For general discussion of variant forms in NHG see *Duden Grammatik* (1973), §§ 411, 413, 415, 425; Wright (1907), §§ 346 ff., lists examples of gender and pl. changes under the old stem forms, and remains useful.

44. Schuster and Schikola (1956), 119.

45. Grimm (1819/22–37), i (2nd edn., 1822), 836, 839.

46. Strong verbs and secondary causatives remaining in mod. German include *sitzen/setzen, liegen/legen, fallen/fällen, hangen/hängen, sinken/senken*.

47. The old preterite-presents *wissen* and *gönnen* have not become modals, and MHG *tar/türren* 'dare' (with which it is cognate) has died out.

48. These alternations appear in nouns too: e.g. *Schneide, Schnitt*.

49. The mutation was caused by /i/ in the inflexions in the pre-textual period, e.g. OHG *er nimit, gibit, biutit* from earlier hypothetical **nemit, *gebit, *beutit*.

50. The pret. sg. forms *sluoc, fienc*, with devoiced final stops, show analogical levelling from the pl. and past part. even in medieval times: the original form should have been *sluoch*, while the form from *fâhen* is problematic.

51. Moser (1909), 195 ff.

52. As late as the mid-eighteenth century Gottsched tries vainly to promote these forms: Gottsched (1748, 1762), 5th edn. (1762), 344–5 (see Chapter VIII).

53. Augst (1975).

54. For causatives, see *trenken, brennen*, etc. (above, p. 161).

55. The past participles had two forms: (1) with umlaut when used as verb, e.g. *schenden/geschendet* (NHG *schänden*); (2) without mutation if used adjectivally —*ein geschanter ritter*—'a dishonoured knight'. However, *geschant* also occurs in uninflected form: *tavelrunder ist gesehant* (*Parzival* 284. 21); see also Walther von der Vogelweide's *Spruch* on the papal *Opferstock* (L. 34. 14), where both *gesendet* and *gesant* (from *senden*) occur.

56. Weinhold (1883), 412 f., § 384, lists some 150 verbs with *Rückumlaut*.

57. Werner (1965).

58. The 'new' *-st* ending in ind. and subj. is found in the ninth and tenth centuries: Braune and Eggers (1975), § 306 (*b*).

59. Orthographically, the EUG texts distinguish *ich rait* (MHG pret. sg. *reit*) from *ich reit*' (MHG *ich rîte*) with diphthongization.

60. Besch (1967), 299–301; 310–314; and maps 91 and 95.
61. See Rein (1915), who believes that the weak pret. ind. and subj. forms must also be adduced: these both ended in *-e* in the first and third person sg. before apocope; so did the strong verb pret. subj.; only the strong pret. ind. shows -∅, and parallelism is restored by extending final *-e* to these forms. This presupposes that speakers were aware of separate though phonetically identical ind. and subj. paradigms in the weak verb. Whatever their origin, the mixed preterites enjoyed considerable vogue in the sixteenth century, reaching their heyday in the seventeenth and eighteenth centuries before being eradicated as a result of the pronouncements of eighteenth-century grammarians, led by Gottsched see (1748, 1762), 306 n.
62. *Lancelot*, ed. Kluge (1963), 90.
63. See Lindgren 1957. Lindgren remains sceptical of the morphological explanation of the pret. loss. Since the pret. subj. forms remain in southern dialects but are indistinguishable formally from the pret. ind. (because of the apocope) in many instances, it may be the needs of modal marking that have predominated over those of tense: see below, pp. 247–8, and Schenker (1977), 51–3.
64. In the German version, randomly selected passages did not yield any unambiguous present forms: further linguistic studies treating the thorny question of the immediate original(s) of the German text are necessary.
65. The athematic verb *stehen*, in normal MHG *stân/stên*; it has strong pret. forms, MHG *stuont/stuonden* (cf. Class VI); the form *stände* is by analogy with Class III (*binden*).
66. See *Duden Grammatik* (1973), § 295.
67. See Moulton (1962), (1961).
68. Only the six remaining *Rückumlaut* verbs *brennen, nennen*, etc. have mutated forms (*brennte, nennte*, etc.), which are perhaps best explained by levelling of the present stem. The southern form *bräuchte*, for *brauchte*, though frequent, is still frowned upon.
69. In some dialects, e.g. Viennese, a pret. subj. with apocope but without syncope remains. Because of the loss of the pret. ind. (replaced by the perfect), no confusion arises: OHG *er sagēti* → MHG *er sagete* → Viennese *ea sǫgat*. No confusion with the pres. ind. (*ea sǫkt*) arises either. The *-at* subj. ending is even added to the pret. subj. of strong verbs, with or without mutation: *ea kamat* (NHG *er kämet*). Cf. H. C. Artmann's poem 'waun e schdeam soit': *waun i den aufwaund sechad* = 'wenn ich den Aufwand sähe' (Artmann (1958), 84, line 11).
70. As in the old form of the Class (2) weak past part. in the rhyme *ermorderôt/tôt* (*Nibelungenlied* 1012. 3).
71. Since similar changes from synthetic morphology to analytic occur in other languages (English and Fr.) the problem is of considerable interest to the linguistic historian. Comparative studies of the interrelation of phonology and syntax and of the differing intonational patterns of mod. dialects and standard languages might provide insights into processes imperfectly understood in the context of any individual language.
72. In OHG, see Braune and Eggers (1975), §§ 58–9, pp. 60–2.
73. Van Coetsem (1964).
74. Grimm (1819/22–37), i (2nd edn., 1822), preface, p. xi (quoted above, p. 95).

CHAPTER V

1. Ulrich Han, printer at Rome between 1465 and 1478, used a colophon which stated 'imprimit ille die quantum non scribitur anno' ('he prints in a day a quantity which is not written in a year').

2. Joined to Hieronymus Hornschuch's *Orthotypographia* in a German translation published at Leipzig in 1634 (Wolfenbüttel, HAB, Q.180, Helmstedt 8º, pp. 62, 69).

3. Laurentius Albertus, in the earliest(?) full grammar of German (Albertus (1573)), observes (p. Bviii b) 'Idioma vero, quo in his institutionibus utimur, commune et intelligibile erit omnibus superioris Germaniae populis, quo etiam scripta constant ex praecipuis typographiis edita, quae sunt Moguntiae, Ingolstadii, Norinbergae, Augustae, Basileae, Francofurti, Witebergae' ('The idiom, indeed, which we use in these precepts, will be common and intelligible to all peoples of Upper Germany, for the writings published by the foremost printers are based on it, who are at Mainz, Ingolstadt, Nuremberg, Augsburg, Basle, Frankfurt, and Wittenberg'). If a foreigner learns this he will at a pinch be understood even by Low Germans.

4. In China movable pottery characters were used in the mid-eleventh century, in Korea metal or alloy in the fourteenth century. Paper is attested in China around AD 105, and in Spain in the twelfth century; the first German paper-mill was set up by Ulman Stromer at Nuremberg in 1389-90.

5. Hence the term *Presse*; in some German dialects the winepress is called *Torkel* < Lat. *torcular*, and in 1476 Johann Veldener, a printer, uses *intorculare* to mean 'print'; It. *torchio* still means both 'winepress' and 'printing-press'.

6. From Lat. *incunabula* (neut. pl.) 'swaddling-clothes'; *Inkunabel* is attested in German in 1677, rendered as *Wiegendruck* in the nineteenth century.

7. For illustrations of these, see Kapr (1977).

8. Hase (1885), 445-62. For further examples see Schirokauer (1940), esp. 327-8.

9. *Format* occurs in a letter of 1524, see Hase (1885), p. cxxxv, No. 113.

10. The colophon was a concluding section of a book giving details of author, date, printer, etc., now usually called an *impressum*; the development of title-pages made it redundant.

11. Rubric < Lat. *rubrica terra*—additions made in red pigment (*Rötel*).

12. Various forms exist: UG dialects show less mutation, and thus *drucken* 'print' may reflect the early importance of southern printing centres. In distinguishing this form from *drücken* 'squeeze' the modern standard language has lexicalized a regional difference. Schottel's grammar has the variants *Trukk, trukken, drüken, Drükkereyen, die Trükkere*, etc. (Schottel (1663), 189, 221, 1435.

13. Before being folded and cut into quarto, octavo (etc.) pages, the sheet was printed; the side printed first was known as the first forme, or 'prototype'.

14. For language and customs, see Klenz (1900), e.g. s.v. *Kornut* 'the just-qualified journeyman'.

15. Hase (1885), 54, quoting one Johann Neudörffer, a contemporary.

16. Kurrelmeyer (1904), pp. ix ff.

17. The pl. of the verb ended in -*nt* in Strasburg written traditions, but this is not consistent in the Mentelin Bible.

18. See also Guchmann (1964-9), ii. 12 ff.

19. Huffines (1974).

20. These works sometimes contain advice on orthography and grammar; early printed examples were produced by Moritz Breunle (1529), Fabian Frangk (1531), and Johann Elias Meichsner (1538). The tradition blends into the epistolary guides (*Briefsteller*) of the seventeenth and eighteenth centuries.

21. The 1532 edn. has the following title-page: *Spiegel der artzney/ vorzeyten zunutz vnnd trost den Leyen gemacht/ durch Laurentium Friesen/aber offt nun gfälscht/ durch vnfleiß der Bůchtrucker/ yetzundt durch den selbigen Laurentium widerumb gebessert . . .* (Strasburg, 1532). The preface contains an interesting vindication of German: 'Auch bedunckt mich Teütsche zung nit minder würdig/ das alle ding

darinn beschriben werden/ dann Griechisch/ Hebreisch/ Latinisch/ Italianisch/ Hispanisch/ Frantzôsisch etc. in welchen man doch garbey (NHG *fast*) alle ding vertolmetscht findet/ Solt vnser sprach minder sein? Nein/ Jha wol vil mehr/ vrsach/ daz (NHG *weil*) sy ein vrsprünckliche sprach ist/ nitt zůsamen gebetlet . . . als Frantzôsisch/ auch mehr reguliert' (1546 edn., p. Aii (b) = Wolfenbüttel, HAB, Mf 4⁰ 9).

22. See Henzen (1954), 110 ff. Today Swiss regional printing language persists for local purposes—e.g. dialect columns in newspapers, novels, satirical squibs during *Fastnacht*—but HG forms current in central Germany effectively superseded it late in the eighteenth century. See Chapter VIII for Gottsched's controversy with the Swiss.

23. Sattler (1607), 24; the work shows a very 'modern' orthography and often cites printers' practice, e.g. in the use of capital letters.

24. After Luther's death Christoph Walther, corrector at Lufft's, claimed that Luther had devised the orthographical practice in that printing-house (see below, pp. 196-7). Study of the form of Luther's writings seldom considers the printing-house for its own sake, however: much of the credit for regularity has been given to Luther instead of Lufft.

25. Moser (1951), 300-3.

26. Stopp (1978).

27. See the edition of Roethe (1882), esp. 24 ff. Helber does not consider the first three types (Cölnisch or Gülisch, Sächsisch, and Flämmisch or Brabantisch) in detail, being mainly concerned with HG. Gottsched knew Helber's little work: see Gottsched (1748, 1762), 66-7, note (d).

28. A full survey is in Josten (1976). See also Eichler and Bergmann (1967).

29. Perhaps three distinct models for different regions are implied.

30. Letter of 4 July; see Reifferscheid (1889*a*), i. 321: 'hoc tamen nunc habe, veluti ego Silesiaca dialecto non utor, ita neque vestra Alsatica uti te posse. Est quoddam, quasi Atticum apud Graecos, genus quod Lutheranum vocitare per me potes: hoc nisi sequaris, erres necesse est' ('Now, however, consider that, just as I do not use the Silesian dialect, so you are not able to employ your Alsatian dialect either. There exists something rather like the Attic dialect among the Greeks—so far as I'm concerned you can call it 'Lutheran' if you like: if you don't follow it you are bound to make mistakes.').

31. Rebhun's grammar failed to materialize; see the preface to the 1544 edn. of his play *Susanna*, ed. Roloff (1967), 87-8. Note the title of Clajus' *Grammatica Germanicae Lingvae . . . Ex Bibliis Lvtheri Germanicis et aliis eius libris collecta* (Leipzig, 1578). See Reichard (1747), 16, 20 f.

32. For further statistics, see Rupprich (1973), 33; Tschirch (1966-9), ii. 99 f.

33. See Luther's *Biblia. Das ist die gantze Heilige Schrifft Deudsch auffs new zugericht* (1545), ed. Volz (1974), pp. 118*ff. and Appendix, pp. 259*-266*, where Petri's glossary is reproduced. See also Volz (1954), (1962).

34. Eleven LG Bibles and two bilingual Latin-German ones were also printed at Wittenberg between 1541 and 1607.

35. Johann Dietenberger in 1534 and Johann Eck in 1537 ('Ingolstadt Bible') were the other Catholic revisors of Luther's translation.

36. *Sendbrief vom Dolmetschen* (1530), ed. Bischoff (1957), 9.

37. Franke (1913-22), i, 1-22. A famous example is Luther's reduction of his fourteen variants of *Wittenberg*, first to six, then to two (*Wittemberg/Vittenberg*).

38. Franke (1913-22), i. 78, 106 ff.

39. Bach (1974). The introduction is planned for a subsequent volume, but see pp. vi-vii.

40. The texts derive from Reifferscheid (1889*b*) checked by Ulrich Kopp. Long *s*,

a positional variant, has been removed, but not the alternation of ⟨v⟩ and ⟨u⟩, which gives clues as to when *zu* is joined to the infinitive, cf. (1), (2), (4) *zu verderben* vs. (3) *zuuerderben*. Commas replace virgules; *vñ* is expanded.

41. The long [i:] (written ⟨y⟩) in *schry* shows the long vowel in open syllable from MHG *schri(r)en/geschri(r)en*: both are strong verbs of Class I. For Wolff's text, see Reifferscheid (1889*b*), 96.

42. With forms like *gottis*, *vbir*, *hirschen* (NHG *herrschen*), *wilch* (NHG *welch*), *zurtretten* (NHG *zertreten*), *menlin* (NHG *Männlein*), *nach* (NHG *noch*), etc. The progressive sloughing of these forms in Lufft's officine may be Luther's contribution. But how can we prove it?

43. *Bericht von vnterscheid der Deudschen Biblien vnd anderer Büchern der Ehrnwirdigen vnd seligen Herrn Doct. Martini Lutheri/ so zu Wittemberg gedruckt/ vnd an andern enden nachgedruckt werden* (Wittenberg, 1563). Corroboration for Luther's part in the orthography is lacking. Caspar Cruciger (1504–48) was assisted as corrector by Georg Rörer (1492–1557), whom Christoph Walther (*c.*1515–74) succeeded. See Albrecht (1929) for Luther's correcting.

44. *Antwort Auff Sigmund Feyerabends vnd seiner Mitgeselschafft falsches angeben vnd Lügen . . .* (Wittenberg, 1571). Between 1569 and 1571 Walther waged a minor pamphlet war against Feyerabend. See now Wolf (1984).

45. Moser (1923).

46. Bach (1974), 19f., 169, 226ff. Lufft had no ⟨å⟩ type in his fount.

47. Wolfenbüttel, HAB, Bibel S 2° 39; stylistically the repeated reading would have been important, however.

48. This mixed text is from a manuscript of Konrad Cordatus produced *c.*1536–7; see *D. Martin Luthers Werke. Tischreden*, ii (Weimar, 1913), 639–40. A German version, usually taken from Johannes Aurifaber's collection of the table-talk (1566), sounds like a translation (*certam* is glossed by *gewiß, sonderlich, eigen*, blurring the distinction between *certam* and *communem*): 'Ich habe keine gewisse sonderliche, eigene Sprache im Deutschen, sondern brauche der gemeinen deutschen Sprache, daß mich beide, Ober- und Niederländer verstehen mögen. Ich rede nach der sächsischen Canzeley, welcher nachfolgen alle Fürsten und Könige in Deutschland; alle Reichsstädte, Fürsten-Höfe schreiben nach der sächsischen und unsers Fürsten Canzeley, darum ists auch die gemeinste deutsche Sprache. Kaiser Maximilian und Kurf. Friedrich, H. zu Sachsen etc. haben im römischen Reich die deutschen Sprachen also in eine gewisse Sprache gezogen' (*Tischreden*, i (Weimar, 1912), 524–5).

49. See Kettmann (1967*a*, *b*).

50. For the various reactions to HG influence, see Josten (1976), 55–67; see also Gabrielsson (1932–3); Socin (1888), 220f.

51. Kluge (1918), 132.

52. Despite the LG Bible and LG church and school ordinances, no LG standard language survived. Possibly the reformers envisaged LG as a transitional stage in leading the faithful to Luther's HG original—if they considered the linguistic problem at all. Perhaps the HG Bible has been overemphasized in promoting HG, since the LG form could not of itself save LG.

53. Gabrielsson (1932–3), 61; Eichler and Bergmann (1967), 8.

54. Franciscus Omichius was a schoolmaster at Güstrow who dedicated his play, printed at Rostock, to King Frederick II of Denmark.

55. Stopp (1978), 250.

56. Kluge (1918), 125 n. 1; Moser (1909), 59; see also Socin (1888), 222.

57. Curious hybrid LG–HG mixtures, later known as *Missingsch* (from *Meißnisch*), represent initially unsuccessful attempts by LG-speakers to produce HG forms: the resultant 'mesolect' (a half-way house between dialect and standard) was

spoken as a creole by later generations—i.e. it became established as a recognizable and accepted language and did not arise *ad hoc* (see p. 362). The most-cited linguistic patterns in the seventeenth century are 'Meißen' and 'Luther'; see Josten (1976) and Eichler and Bergmann (1967).

58. Johannes Cochlaeus, *An expediat laicis, legere novi Testamenti libros lingua vernacula . . . (sineloco, 1533). He complains that cobblers, furriers, tailors, butchers, shepherds, farm labourers, and other most vile and sordid artisans 'ex infima plebe', who can scarcely read German, dispute the Bible with their priests and monks (p. D2 (b)); the Scriptures should be banned, not in Church, but at home and in German—'domi et in angulo secundum idioma vernaculum'— where speech is cruder and sense duller than 'in lingua regulata qualis Latina est et Graeca' (p. G1 (a)).

59. Bernstein (1978); also Tisch (1971).

60. Niclas von Wyle, *Translationen*, ed. Keller (1861) (page references are to the original edition).

61. Print J of the *Ackermann* (1477) has been attributed to Eßlingen, where Wyle's *Translatzen* were printed by Konrad Fyner in 1478; alternatively to Strasburg, where versions of Eyb's and Steinhöwel's works appeared.

62. Bernstein (1978), 73.

63. *Steinhöwels Äsop*, ed. Österley (1873), 4.

64. *Briefe*, v (Weimar, 1934), 309 (letter to Wenceslaus Linck, 8 May 1530), 13 ff.

65. *Sendbrief vom Dolmetschen*, ed. Bischoff (1957), 22.

66. Meinhold (1958), shows how Luther draws on scholastic tradition but also harnesses Humanistic 'philological' method to his religious purpose.

67. *An die Radherren aller stedte deutsches lands: das sie Christliche schulen auffrichten vnd hallten sollen* (Wittenberg, 1524). Luther borrowed the sword metaphor from Emser, who claimed that by rejecting patristic, expert interpretation of the Bible Luther was leaving the sword (= God's word) in its scabbard— the mere literal sense, regardless of a deeper significance. See also Ephesians 6.

68. *Sendbrief*, print B (Wittenberg, 1530); print A reads *an einem ort*. For Luther's approach to translation, including detailed discussion of the examples raised in the *Sendbrief*, see Bluhm (1965); Schwarz (1955); and various articles in *PBB* (H) 92 (1970).

69. 1 Corinthians 14: 11: 'Therefore if I know not the meaning of the voice I shall be unto him that speaketh a barbarian, and he that speaketh (shall be) a barbarian unto me.' Luther renders the Vulg. *barbarus* by *vndeudsch* at this point.

70. Dietenberger's Bible (1534), dedicatory preface to Archbishop Albrecht of Mainz (1564 copy from Cologne in the Bodleian Library, Mason KK 148, p. *a5ʳ).

71. *Sendbrief*, ed. Bischoff (1957), 17.

72. See Franke (1913–22), iii. 18 ff.: some of the approximately 301 syntactic alterations between the 1522 *September-Testament* and the 1545 version produced frames (see again December 1522). While the clausal frame is common in modern spoken German, only comparatively short dependent items are inserted into it.

73. Bluhm (1965), 138 ff.; Luther ridicules Emser's rendering in the *Sendbrief vom Dolmetschen*, ed. Bischoff (1957), 16–17.

74. *Sendbrief*, 14: the translator's handiwork is compared with clearing the ground of tree-stumps and rocks, preparing the field for ploughing (an old rhetorical image), and planing knots out of a plank of wood.

75. For both letters see *Briefe*, ii (Weimar, 1931), 489–90, 630–2.

76. Preface to the Old Testament (1523), WA, *Deutsche Bibel*, viii (1954), p. 32.

77. See esp. Arndt (1962), 86. Another preaching reformer, Huldrych Zwingli (1484–1531), was also slangy on occasion: *fressen, prassen* for *essen, suffen* for *trinken*, etc. Zwingli was, however, less concerned with producing a consistent,

natural, and economical style. He wanted to bring his Swiss audience to the full meaning of the text, whether by literal translation or colloquial expression: the form is subordinate to the content. See Schenker (1977). Luther called Zwingli's German 'filzicht, zottict deüdsch' (Schenker (1977), 8).

78. Quoted from his revision of Emser's New Testament which appeared in 1529.
79. Franke (1913–22), ii. 77–82.
80. Petri's 1522 reprint already has marginal glosses from 1 Corinthians 4 until the end (thirty-two in all); his 1523 glossary has 199 items.
81. Examples from Lindmeyr (1899).
82. Ising (1968), Maps 3 and 27.
83. See Reinitzer (1982), also Otte (1982).
84. Teller (1794–5), from which (i. 66 ff.) the above examples are drawn; for Adelung see Chapter VIII.
85. Guchmann (1974); also Hoyer and Rüdiger (1975) (with linguistic introduction by Guchmann).
86. Mod. German *Flugblatt/Flugschrift* 'pamphlet', 'squib', 'tract' conveys well the slight size of most of the productions. Some are even *Einblattdrucke*.
87. See Rupprich (1973), 116 f. The *Karst* is an agricultural tool, 'hoe', 'mattock'.
88. For the semantics of political polemic, see Chapter X. For the importance of the sermon in the history of spoken German, see Weithase (1961).
89. Rupprich (1973), 68 ff., distinguishes the various spiritual movements beside the Reformation—anabaptists, the *Geistkirche*, and so forth. Luther reduced them to the collective label *Schwärmer* (though this also means specifically 'enthusiasts' who communicate directly with God, without language).
90. After a satire by Friedrich Dedekind, *Grobianus*, translated into German by Kaspar Scheidt (1551).
91. For Humanism and the Renaissance, esp. the Italian beginnings, see Rupprich (1970), 425–60.
92. For the translations, see Worstbrook (1976).
93. *Teutsche Grammatica* (Augsburg, *c.*1535), p. B3.
94. Valentin Boltz, *Publij Terentij Aphri sechs verteutschte Comedien ausz eygen angeborner Lateinischen spraach auffs trewlichst transferiert . . .* (Tübingen, 1540), p. A3 b.
95. Weithase (1961), i. 56 ff.
96. The two commonest school and university grammars in the Middle Ages were those by Aelius Donatus (fourth century AD) and Priscianus Caesariensis (fifth/sixth century AD). Priscian's work survives in over 1,000 manuscripts. For the influence of Donatus on vernacular grammar, see esp. Ising (1966), (1970).
97. See Rupprich (1970), 136; Socin (1888), 165; Kluge (1918), 30.
98. *Teutsche Grammatica* (*c.*1535), pp. A1 b–A2 b; Müller (1882), 120–1.
99. For the linguistic problems of Dasypodius, see Guchmann (1964–9), ii. 168 f. Dasypodius culled his Latin lemmata from Italian Humanists, Cholevius drew on the French Humanist Robert Estienne.
100. See Ising (1956), 121.
101. Universities were originally theological in character, but soon became centres of Humanist studies. Towards the end of the fifteenth century the number of foundations increased and continued under the particularism after the mid-sixteenth century. The earliest 'German' universities are Prague (1348), Vienna (1365), Heidelberg (1385), Cologne (1388), Erfurt (1392), Leipzig (1409), Rostock (1419), Greifswald (1456), Freiburg im Breisgau (1460), Basle (1460), Ingolstadt (1472), Trier (1473), Mainz (1477), Tübingen (1477), Wittenberg (1502), Frankfurt-on-Oder (1506).
102. Fuchsperger's *Dialectica* (Wolfenbüttel, HAB, 461 Qu. (2)), pp. A2 b, B6 b.

103. e.g. Kluge (1918), 51; Bach (1965), § 117.
104. Cf. also the Ripuarian *Schryfftspiegel* (1527) from Cologne: 'Das *Radt* had der *Rath* wail (NHG *wohl*) machen laissen, das ghein (NHG *kein*) *Ratt* (NHG *Ratte*) dair in komen kann' (Müller (1882), 384). In the printing context, Christoph Walther's strictures on Frankfurt printers belong here too (see pp. 196–7 above).
105. Sattler also notes (p. 17) that 'alte, erfahrne vnd wohlgeûbte Setzer' print loanwords in *Antiqua* or *Fraktur* type depending on whether their endings are foreign, e.g. 'Commissio' or native (!) Commiſſion.
106. Müller (1882), 168, n. 10.
107. *Teutsche Grammatica | Daraus ainer von jm selbs mag lesen lernen* . . . (*c.*1535), p. A4 a; note the title—but God was the true teacher. For the religious conception of language in the sixteenth century, see Hankamer (1927), esp. 61 ff.
108. Op. cit., p. B2 a; cf. *Ackermann aus Böhmen*, xxii: 'Ga! ga! ga! schnatert die gans . . .'; the phonetic tradition goes back to classical grammarians.
109. *Deutsche Sprachkunst* . . . (Halle, 1630), preface signed T.O.M.H.S.
110. See Jellinek (1913–14), i. 60 ff.
111. Pp. B7 b–8 b; this, perhaps the first such table, was later copied by Schottel in the *Ausführliche Arbeit* (1663), 153–4.
112. See Guchmann (1964–9), ii. 170–1; she overemphasizes the rivalry between UG and MG forms at this period, however, implying links between Albertus' language and Augsburg printed usage.
113. Johannes Kromayer reports that of some 10,000 adults in the principality of Weimar, less than a third could read: Kromayer (1629), p. A2a (Wolfenbüttel, HAB, 240.61 Quodl.).
114. See Ratke's memorandum on educational reform placed before the imperial diet at Frankfurt in 1612: *Memorial. Welches zu Franckfort Auff dem Wahltag Ao. 1612 den 7. Maij dem teutschen Reich vbergeben*, ed. Ising (1959), 101–4 (at p. 101).
115. Ratke's theoretical grammatical writings were not published until recently, in Ising (1959).
116. p. A1a; in the list of some ninety-seven *Technica/Kunstwörter* (pp. 122–5) *dienstfertigkeit* glosses *habitus instrumentalis*!
117. See Gueintz (1641), 45, and Schottel (1641), 280ff., with the minor changes *Nennendung, Geschlechtendung*; Lat. forms are nom., gen., dat., acc., voc., and abl. For grammatical terminology at this period, see now Barbarić (1981).
118. See esp. his *Der Teutschen Sprache Einleitung/ Zu richtiger gewisheit und grundmeßigem vermügen der Teutschen Haubtsprache* . . . (Lüneburg, 1643), pp. B4 b–B5 b. Schottel sees his task as to search out the beauties of the language, and he was taken into the Fruchtbringende Gesellschaft as 'Der Suchende': an engraving shows him with a net and waders, as a pearl-fisherman; see Schottel (1645).
119. Schottel (1663), 152: 'Die Hochteutsche Sprache ist kein *Dialectus*, auch nicht die Niederteutsche Sprache/ sondern haben jhre *Dialectos* . . .'. He expressly rejects the claims of Meissen (§ 15, pp. 158–9).

CHAPTER VI

1. Notably for Martin Luther: Franke (1913–22); Erben (1954). For basic syntactic studies used in this chapter, see the Select Bibliography, p. 262.
2. e.g. the plays of Duke Heinrich Julius of Brunswick (1564–1613), which display a remarkable range of dialect-speakers who are roughly differentiated as speaking Ripuarian, Thuringian, Misnian, Frankish, Saxon, and Dutch.
3. The distinction between sentence and utterance corresponds to those between phoneme and phone, morpheme and morph; in another guise it occurs also in

Paul (1880/1968), chap. 6, which discusses discrepancies between grammatical (i.e. 'surface structure') subject/predicate and logical or psychological (i.e. underlying, 'deep structure') subject/predicate.

4. The above devices are based on Paul (1880/1968), 123–4; see also Paul (1916–20), iii. 4 ff.

5. Inferences may be drawn from word-order patterns, especially in verse, and from the coexistence of stressed forms *zuo, -lîch, daz ist* beside unstressed *ze, -lich,* and *deist.* Moreover, in the medieval period, the spoken language was rich in contracted forms which appear sporadically in writing, especially for metrical reasons. See Grimm (1819/22–37), Part IV, pp. 368 ff. Such forms remind us of the discrepancy between the regularized literary usage and speech: they remained current in the fifteenth and sixteenth centuries. See Kehrein (1854–6), iii. 76–9, § 119: *abem = ab dem, vorm = vor dem, gegem = gegen dem, beir nasen = bei der Nase, zun füssen = zu den Füßen; ans keisers statt = anstatt des Keisers; ubert = über die (biß uberd Ohren).*

6. Meillet (1922), 187 ff.

7. Paul (1916–20), iii. 162 ff.; the WGmc. languages share this development, and Lockwood (1968), 86 ff., suggests that the articles originate as calques on V.Lat. and the emergent Romance languages during the Merovingian period and perhaps even earlier.

8. Tschirch (1955), 16–17.

9. Gueintz (1641), 117, § 5, notes that the closing formulae in letters omit pronouns and auxiliaries: 'Wollest derhalben . . .', 'Es ist also/wie geschrieben', etc.

10. Paul (1916–20), iii. 167: the article is omitted in formulae like *Mann und Frau, Weib und Kind, in See stechen* 'put to sea', *unter Dach und Fach* 'home and dry', and also in special contexts, e.g. military commands, telegrams, baby language. See also Behaghel (1923–32), i. 131, §§ 83 ff.

11. Kiechel (1585) ed. Haszler (1866), 26–7.

12. See Kehrein (1854–6), iii. 79, § 125; Grimm (1819/22–37), iii. 415 ff. Clajus (1578), 213, will not accept the article with proper names, e.g. *Johannes,* not *der Johannes.*

13. This marking was already familiar to early grammarians, e.g. Clajus (1578), 55: 'Casus Nominum sunt sex: Nominativus, Genitivus, Dativus, Accusativus, Vocativus, Ablativus, qui discernuntur magis articulis quàm terminationibus'— ('Cases . . . distinguished rather by articles than by endings').

14. A few examples of *ein* used in the pl. occur, e.g. MHG 'ze einen sunewenden' (*Nibelungenlied* 31. 4), 'in einen zîten' (ibid. 1143. 1).

15. Of the early grammarians, Clajus seems to restrict the use of 'endingless' forms, not listing them in his adj. paradigms at all (Clajus, (1578), 69–71), although he does use them in examples—*ein fein gut hertz* (p. 219). See also Jellinek (1913–14), ii. 383–4. Apocope may account for endingless (strong) adj. forms in the pl.

16. Full appraisal of the EMG contribution here is possible only after further study of WMG in the late fifteenth and sixteenth centuries. Even UG, Augsburg printers have some weak endings after definite article, despite apocope (Guchmann (1964–9), ii. 89). The MHG weak adj. ended in *-en* in the fem. acc. sg. but was later remodelled.

17. For Adelung, see Chapter VIII.

18. *Duden Grammatik* (1973), 324, § 802. The oldest prepositions indeed develop from local adverbs, and the adverbial usage may remain in the form of verbal prefixes: *bei jemanden stehen* and *jemandem beistehen* 'support someone'.

19. This is the instr. case-form of the masc./neut. definite article; *wiu* from the interrogative pronoun *wer* is occasionally found.

20. Many kinds of gen. can be distinguished—objective, adverbial, possessive, partitive, etc.—for most of which competing prepositional constructions with other

case-forms can be found. While genitival relationships between nouns remain common (*Tag der Arbeit, Anfang der Woche, Sturz des Ministers*, etc.), the gen. now seldom follows verbs or adjectives: *Freut Euch des Lebens, Großmutter wird mit der Sense rasiert* would now be *Freut Euch über das Leben . . .*; or cf. *des bin ich froh* (Luther, Psalm 60: 8). See Erdmann (1886–98), ii. 177–232; Paul (1916–20), iii. 284–378.

21. Letter of 1 January 1592, ed. Steinhausen (1895), No. 92, p. 153 (NB. The text has been slightly modernized). For Luther's use of the gen. see Franke (1913–22), iii. 5.

22. It overemphasizes the role of paradigmatic morphology. The phonological merger is attested in documents of the thirteenth century, but the gen. remains frequent in ENHG texts even in the sixteenth century. The neut. definite article retains oppositions in many areas between nom./acc. forms in ⟨a⟩ and gen. ones in ⟨e⟩: *das* ≠ *des*. In the sixteenth century strong endingless neut. adj. forms in the nom./acc. would still contrast with the gen. by an opposition: *gut* ≠ *gutes*.

23. For this approach, see Fillmore (1968). Unfortunately, identifying basic semantic case relations proves difficult. For a case-grammar approach to the gen. in English, see Baron (1974).

24. See Jellinek (1913–14), ii. 190 ff., § 349.

25. e.g. Alsatian, and the Swiss dialect of Zurich (*Züritüütsch*)—see Keller (1961), 34, 66, 143; but not Bernese (*Bärndütsch*)—Keller (1961), 100.

26. Letter No. 27 (8 August 1584), ed. Steinhausen (1895), 59.

27. See Erdmann (1886–98), i. 2–6, §§ 3–5; Behaghel (1923–32), i. 274, § 165; fossilized pronounless forms in NHG include *bitte, danke, geschweige denn* 'let alone . . .', 'to say nothing of . . .'.

28. Hockett (1958), 237; Lyons (1968), 315.

29. The distinction between *Aspekt* and *Aktionsart* will be ignored: possibly *Aspekt* should denote a purely morphological aspectual system on Slavonic lines, whereas syntactic, suppletive, and lexical aspectual marking could be termed *Aktionsarten*. The competing aspectual devices in German make distinguishing 'subjective' from 'objective' aspect difficult.

30. Fischart (1575), 1590 edn., ed. Nyssen (1963), 102. See also Spengler (1969); Nyssen (1964), 71.

31. The more and less close associations of particle and verb can be illustrated from English as well as German. Compare (*a*) *The car backfired/Das Kind wiederholte die Noten* ('repeated'); (*b*) *The soldiers fired back/Das Kind holte die Noten wieder* ('retrieved'—the music had been thrown in the dustbin); (*c*) *Back he came again/ Und wieder holte das Kind die Noten* ('fetched the music again; i.e. on another occasion)—although (*b*) and (*c*) are admittedly difficult to separate in German. In English prepositions do not 'govern' cases, since these are not marked, and they have often become virtually postpositioned after verbs to create set phrases that are akin to German separable prefixes. Compare 'to *run out of* breath, steam, etc.' with 'to *run* | out of the house, cinema, etc.' (Leisi (1967), 107 ff.).

32. Paul (1881/1969), 359, § 297.

33. These defective verbs were past in form but used as though present to qualify the action of a dependent infinitive. They become modal auxiliaries in mod. German.

34. Behaghel (1923–32), ii. 101, § 597.

35. Behaghel (1923–32), ii. 100, §§ 596 f.; cf. *zusammenhauen, zusammenschlagen* 'beat up', and even *zusammenbrechen* 'break up', where *zusammen* has aspectual force; even *zusammenbetteln* means primarily 'to cadge out of people', not 'to accumulate by begging' (NHG *erbetteln*).

36. See Henzen (1957), 210–29.

37. See Paul (1881/1969), 369–72, §§ 307ff.; Behaghel (1923–32), ii. 111–12, § 611. Periphrasis with *werden*, a true auxiliary, also marks inchoative aspect; see below, p. 242. The periphrastic constructions are attested early and compete with synthetic, suffixal aspect, providing stylistic variation.
38. Polenz (1963).
39. Examples are from *DWB*, s.v. *geraten*: Geiler's are from sermons published in 1514 and 1522 and are tautologous (popular, emphatic style?).
40. Consider 'Now you've *been* and *gone* and *made* a right *cock-up* there!' and 'What did you *want* to *go* and tell her that for?' Both are emphatic as well as perfective.
41. Paul (1881/1969), 363, § 299 n. 6, with further bibliography. The 'replacement' of pres. part. by infinitive in the progressive constructions is attested since the thirteenth century in Alem.
42. Letter No. 92 (1 January 1592), ed. Steinhausen (1895), 153. See Behaghel (1923–32), ii. 380f., § 762; for Luther see Franke (1913–22), ii. 312, § 139. The pres. part. plus *sein* seems rare, even in MHG.
43. Letter No. 1 (*a*) (7 May 1572), ed. Steinhausen (1895), 3.
44. Niclas von Wyle's *Translatzen*, ed. Keller (1861), 202, and Strauss (1912), 33.
45. In English the progressive form competes with the 'normal' synthetic verb form (*I am going*/*I go*), often emphasizing an activity as a *process*, where the synthetic form states it as a *fact*. See Leisi (1967), 117. A similar distinction may account for the MHG/ENHG variants of participial and synthetic forms. In mod. German English progressive forms are sometimes translated by different words, i.e. aspect has been 'lexicalized'; 'think' = *der Meinung sein*, 'be thinking' = *überlegen*; 'fly' = *fliegen*, 'be flying' = *wehen*, etc.
46. See Glinz (1969), 53: the verb form alone of a main verb in the pres. does not of itself determine the verb's temporal value.
47. This example is from Fourquet (1969). The use of subj. for hypothetical/unreal conditions or statements, and as a formal device indicating dependent clauses, also cuts across this pattern.
48. Franke (1913–22), ii. 364, § 163; some of the examples imply that for Luther the *sollen*/*wollen* periphrasis already had primarily modal, not temporal, force. For the grammarians, see Jellinek (1913–14), ii. 330ff.
49. Clajus (1578), 115–16, gives both auxiliaries for his future ind. paradigms: 'Amabo, Ich will/oder werde lieben etc.'.
50. Gottsched (1748, 1762), 294; he also treats the conditional periphrasis with *würde* as the *bedingt zukünftige Zeit* (*tempus futurum conditionatum*).
51. Letter No. 36 (8 September 1585), ed. Steinhausen (1895), 73 (spelling modernized). Example (1) seems to be modal as well as temporal (*noch endlich*).
52. The perfect infinitive was rare in medieval German, occurring particularly after modal verbs; again, *werden* competed with *wollen* and *sollen*. In NHG 'er sollte es gemacht haben' means 'he was held to have done it', but occasionally speakers use it in colloquial non-standard to mean 'he ought to have done it'.
53. Lindgren (1957).
54. For the problems of attempting to establish complementary distribution along these lines for perfect and pret. in mod. German, see Hauser-Suida and Hoppe-Beugel (1964).
55. Morphological confusion in the strong verbs and the effects of southern German apocope are contributing factors in the loss of the pret. in speech; see above, p. 172.
56. Naumann (1915), 113–15.
57. See *Muspilli*, 36 *pi daz er . . . kiuerkota hapeta* 'according to what he has done'; *kiuerkota* is the neut. weak adj. ending. Similarly, Notker's translation of Psalm 7

has *er habet . . . gispannenen sînen bogen* 'he has drawn his bow' (Lat. *Arcum suum tetendit*).

58. See Gelhaus (1966), esp. 226–7.
59. In spoken German, the frames are often avoided, especially in dependent clauses, where demonstratives are preferred to relative pronouns. Also, in speech long lists of objects or modifiers governed by one verb are frequently placed outside the frame: 'Er hat gekauft: 3 Pf. Weizen, 6 Eier, 2 Fl. Wein . . .'. See also below, pp. 257 ff.
60. Gelhaus (1966), 223.
61. At times apparently (because the force is aspectual) pluperfect denotes posterior action: e.g. 'Er schlug seinen Gegner nieder und *hatte* damit den Sieg *errungen*.'
62. *Lancelot*, ed. Kluge (1948–74), i. 301: the final *-e* of *gaße* is by analogy with the weak conjugation pret.
63. Behaghel (1923–32), ii. 290, § 708, cites comparable examples where the pret. is used in semi-literate UG (Alsace, southern Baden, and Swabia) to replace the pres. tense: 'es *war* gottlob heut' ein schöner Tag' = '*ist* ein schöner Tag'.
64. Ölinger (1573–4), 154, seems to be the only sixteenth-century grammarian to mention the forms which have analogues in Fr. of the period: '*I' ay eu escrit* [= *J'ai eu écrit*], ich hab geschrieben gehabt'; but he observes that not everyone accepts this usage.
65. Letter No. 2 (15 December 1582), ed. Steinhausen (1895), 6; 9.
66. Geographical studies for the ENHG period are lacking. In mod. German the past anterior is attested in central as well as southern areas; it is generally regarded as substandard, even incorrect.
67. For example, Robert Musil and Thomas Bernhard.
68. In this book 'mood' will be restricted to formal changes in verb morphology, as opposed to 'modality', the more general term.
69. Note that in English the pret. ind. and subj. are not formally distinct, and in ENHG the context also 'disambiguates' e.g. Luther, Matth. 22: 15 (1522), '. . . und hielten einen radt, wie sie yn [NHG *ihn*] *bestrickten* ynn seyner rede,' (1545), '. . . wie sie jn *fiengen* in seiner rede', where NHG would require *bestricken könnten, fangen könnten*.
70. See Glinz (1968). The terms 'conjunctive' and 'subjunctive' relate to the use of verb forms in dependent or subordinate clauses or sentences in other, notably classical, languages. *Konjunktiv* and KI, KII are equivalent to the terms 'subjunctive', 'SI, SII', used here.
71. See Erdmann (1886–98), i. 180, for this example, and see generally his section on pp. 113–81.
72. The use of subj. rather than ind. depends on the relationship of the clauses, attitude of the speaker, etc., while the sequence of tenses determines only *which* subjunctive form is most likely to occur.
73. See Behaghel (1923–32), iii. 675 ff.
74. The Paumgartner letters, for example, were written at Nuremberg, i.e. in an area which should show SII marked forms, but SI is regularly used in them for reported speech, e.g. in Letters Nos. 117–18.
75. See Jellinek (1913–14), ii. 312 ff.
76. Schottel eventually dispensed with the optative mood altogether, removed the introductory conjunctions from the paradigms, and listed only true subj. forms; see Jellinek (1913–14), ii. 318 f.
77. Ölinger (1573–4), 151–2, apparently regards some SII forms (*würde*) as future perfect.
78. Bech (1951).
79. See Bergmann and Pauly (1975).

80. For example, in informal speech, where emphasis is more important than the modal chosen: e.g. 'Hasso, du kannst (darfst/sollst/möchtest/solltest/mußt) die Badezimmertür nicht immer so auf lassen!'
81. Stammler (1931), esp. 42.
82. Schottel (1641), 650 ff., does distinguish *Vorsatz* and *Nachsatz*, and Kaspar Stieler includes a brief section on sentence structure in his dictionary of 1691.
83. See also Burdach (1886/1914), esp. 29–33. Burdach sought the origins of mod. German word order not in the direct influence of classical Latin syntax, but rather in the effects of Latin chancery language based on the Italian Humanist model from the later Middle Ages (ibid. 31). This was a further link in the chain of development from the Middle Ages to the Reformation.
84. The fem. weak noun and weak adj. declension shows a similar syncretism by different means; for example, MHG *diu zunge* (nom.) and *die zungen* (acc.) have coalesced as NHG *die Zunge*.
85. Examples are from Leisi (1967), 147.
86. The traditional 'main' and 'subordinate' clauses are also known as 'matrix' and 'constituent' clauses respectively: see Schieb (1972). For 'subordinate clause' the term *Gliedsatz* has become normal. In this chapter the designation 'dependent clause' is preferred, subordinate clauses being understood as dependent clauses where the finite verb would nowadays stand in final or near-final position. In the sixteenth century, not all dependent clauses are subordinate clauses, i.e. they do not have subordinating word order; but all subordinate clauses are dependent clauses.
87. For other examples see Schröbler in Paul (1881/1969), § 334. 3, pp. 410–11, §§ 336 ff., esp. § 340, p. 417.
88. See Moser (1929–51), i/1, § 30. 17, pp. 54–5; Moser (1977); Fleischmann (1973), 165 ff., 203 ff. For the uses of *daß* see Behaghel (1923–32), iii. 128–52.
89. Archaic English has similar compound conjunctions: 'o, pardon *if that* I descend so low' (*1 Henry IV*, i. iii. 167).
90. In origin *können* is a past part. form without *ge-* prefix.
91. It seems that final position is possible in the earliest forms of Germanic dependent clause. Moreover, even the cautious theory that Lat. influence only encourages the final position in later German has been rejected. First, classical Lat. does not always relegate the verb to the end in dependent clauses; secondly, in Luther's bilingual *Tischreden* German phrases introduced by *dass* and *wie* have a higher percentage of finite verbs in final position than otherwise, whereas the Lat. equivalents *quod* and *sicut* show predominantly the main-clause word order with the verb in second position. See Stolt (1964), esp. 160 ff.; Fleischmann (1973), 50–1.
92. See Ebert (1981).
93. See Jellinek (1913–14), i. 248 ff., ii. 451, for Aichinger, and i. 257, ii. 453, for Basedow.
94. The *Relieftheorie* developed by Weinrich (1964), has been applied to subordinate dependent clauses by Fleischmann (1973).
95. See Hartmann (1969).
96. 'Distance-position' as opposed to 'contact-position' (*Kontaktstellung*).
97. Other combinations which create 'distance-positioning' include the periphrastic aspectual constructions (*Funktionsverbgefüge*), such as *zur Erörterung stellen, in Gang setzen*, etc. (see above).
98. Bolli (1975), esp. 160–2.
99. Clajus (1578), 256, notices the frame: 'Casus qui à verbo reguntur, item adverbia & praepositiones cum suis casibus, interjiciuntur inter particula Praeteriti & Futuri ac passiui Ich habe/ Ich bin/ Ich will/ Ich werde/ & inter participium ex

quo formatur praeteritum, aut infinitiuum, ex quo formatur futurum, vt: Ich habe dir meine meinung im nechsten schreiben angezeigt . . . etc.' ('The cases which are governed by the verb, and similarly adverbs and prepositions with their cases, are interposed between the particles of the Preterite & Future and passive, Ich habe/Ich bin/ Ich will/ Ich werde/ & between the participle from which the preterite is formed, or the infinitive from which is formed the future, as: Ich habe . . . angezeigt . . . etc.'). But he regards them as irregular: 'Sunt etiam quaedam peculiares phrases linguae Germanicae, quae non regulis Syntaxeos comprehendi possunt, sed usu discendae sunt' ('But these are also certain special locutions of the German language which cannot be captured by the rules of Syntax, but have to be learned by usage').

100. See Schildt (1968), (1972).
101. Ebert (1980).
102. Some caution is necessary in taking this view: there is apparently a tendency for verbs to gravitate towards the end of clauses in classical Latin. Nevertheless, much may depend on the kind of Latin under consideration—certainly medieval and post-medieval Latin was far from classical in construction. The chancery type was also shaped by the *cursus*. Nor do other European languages perhaps equally dominated by Latin show characteristic verb-final position in dependent clauses, and this applies not only to English but also to Romance languages like French and, more important still, Italian.
103. Ebert (1980) 382. The frame must, then, have had some basis in the spoken language of educated circles close to the town administration—not, however, necessarily in general colloquial or dialect speech at Nuremberg.
104. Ebert (1980), 367.
105. Ebert (1981). esp. 230 ff., refutes theories of Lat. influence on the positioning of the auxiliary verb, and considers unstressed and stressed alternations.
106. See above, p. 186.
107. Developments in punctuation confirm this trend: in the sixteenth century the comma and virgula (/) split up the utterance into speech pauses, more appropriate to the demands of rhythmical oral delivery. Mod. German punctuation introduced by later grammarians divides sentences into logical units, more in keeping with private reading. For the development of the theory of punctuation in German-speaking areas, see Höchli (1981): again, the early theorists at first modelled themselves on Latin.
108. Hildebrand (1889) gives examples of multiple negation from eighteenth-century literary language, as well as from speech, and even from an early legal text from the Alem. area which restricts the right of inheritance under one title with a six-fold negation: 'und sol *kain* herr *kain* ligen gut noch *kain* hus von *kainem* [man] noch *kainer* [frau] ze Nuwkilch erben in *kainem* weg.'

CHAPTER VII

1. See Moser (1929-51), vol. i, pp. xxxii-xxxiii (1936, 1948, 1949). The very term *Orthographiereform* used by Moser implies some already extant norms to be altered. For Philipp von Zesen, one of the most notorious reformers, see below, pp. 292 ff.
2. *Forelle* from OHG *forhila* 'trout' sounds more foreign (cf. *Zitadelle, Frikadelle, Libelle,* etc.) than does *Büchse* from Graeco-Latin *buxis/puxis* (cf. *Füchse, Auswüchse*).
3. See Jones (1978), esp. 153-4, and (1976), on which the statistics are based.
4. *Andreas Gryphius. Horribilicribrifax Teutsch, Scherzspiel,* ed. Dünnhaupt (1976); the work was written about 1650.

5. Sagarra (1977), 5, states that Germany lost some 40 per cent of the rural and 33 per cent of its urban population.
6. Sagarra (1977), 23 f., and see 22–36 for court life generally.
7. Schultz (1888), chap. 3. The membership of twenty included ten princesses and seven countesses.
8. Laudismann (1618), 44.
9. Voltaire, in a letter to the Marquis de Thibouville, 1750 (ed. Thiériot (1878), 66), see Brunt (1983), 76.
10. See Brunt (1978), 7 ff., and (1983), 1–12.
11. Brunt (1978), 17, 64 f. = (1983), 20–2 and 76–80.
12. See Chapter V above, and Ising (1959), 14.
13. 'Macaronic'—specifically Latin comic poetry with an admixture of foreign elements, more loosely used for linguistic mixture characterized by outlandishness.
14. See Harsdörffer's *Teutscher Sekretarius* (1656), iii, No. 30; for scholarly bombast, see Meyster Janotus von Pragamado's parodistic address in Fischart's *Geschicht-klitterung* (Fischart (1575)), cap. 22. For the uses of Latin see also Wehrli (1976).
15. Hope (1971), i. 578–9. This is not true bilingualism but rather 'functional diglossia', i.e. the stylistic use of foreign borrowing within a native setting.
16. On Thomasius, see Blackall (1978), chap. I. The vindication of German for a wide range of uses undoubtedly occurred in the seventeenth century, and others before Thomasius had lectured in German even in the sixteenth century. He was forced to leave Leipzig, but lecturing in German was probably not the only or even the main reason.
17. See *Thomasius* (1687/1701), ed. Sauer (1894), esp. 6, 12–16, 19–20.
18. Paulsen (1896–7), i. 513 f. and 524.
19. See Leibniz (*c*.1697), paragraph 17, ed. Schmarsow (1877), 55–7. Leibniz's influence works through his voluminous correspondence and via personal contacts: the *Unvorgreiffliche Gedancken* were first published in 1717 after his death. For a recent edition see Pörksen and Schiewe (1983).
20. See Hechtenberg (1903), esp. 42 ff. Of the minor donor languages, Italian, then Greek, outweigh English, Spanish, and LG, while Bohemian, Hungarian, and Turkish gave only isolated words in the material examined.
21. For *Alamode* itself, see Schramm (1914), 16–29.
22. See Jones (1976), 31 ff.
23. Jones (1978), 160.
24. See especially Weinreich (1953) for basic problems; but in the seventeenth century we are not concerned with 'the flowing speech of bilinguals in the natural setting of language contact' (Weinreich (1953), 44).
25. See Brunt (1978), 83–5 = (1983), 99–101; Penzl (1961); Russ (1978), 85–6. In voiceless environments, uvular [R] can merge with the voiceless spirant [χ], leading to homonymic merger: for example, *Docht* and *dort* coincide phonetically in informal speech.
26. See Moulton (1962), 65–7; for example in the prescriptions of *Siebs* (1898/1969), 18th edn. (1961) [entitled *Deutsche Hochsprache. Bühnenaussprache*], which gives *Radius* = [ˈraːdĭus] with open [ĭ] but *Radium* = [ˈraːdi̯um] with closed [i].
27. Jones (1976), 49 f.
28. Brunt (1978), 87 = Brunt (1983), 102–3.
29. Nickisch (1969). Translation of the French manuals of De la Serre in 1638 and 1645 is discussed ibid. 63 ff. According to Steinhausen (1893), men wrote four kinds of letters: fluent Latin epistles; turgid and convoluted chancery missives; over-elaborated and would-be poetic outpourings; and gallant *Alamode*-letters.

full of lies and compliments. Women, protected by ignorance, wrote simply and directly if somewhat woodenly!

30. See Vennemann and Wagener (1970), esp. 79-82.
31. See Fig. 6. The diagram modifies that of Betz, see Maurer and Rupp (1974), 137.
32. Zesen's attacks on certain 'letters' in the German alphabet—c, q, and ph—are intended to purify it, not adapt foreign words and phrases.
33. Harsdörffer (1641-9), Part II, 2nd edn. (1657), 178-9.
34. Performed in 1642 (ed. Koldewey (1900)).
35. Scheraeus (1619), 162. It derives, of course, from Fr. *baiser la main*. Derivation from Spanish *beso las manos* is claimed by Schramm (1914), 82-6.
36. Scheraeus (1619), 152.
37. Brunt (1978), 81 = (1983), 95-6, for the period 1650-1735. Similar figures hold for the period to 1650 (see Jones (1978)), although adjectives were markedly less common in the first half of the century (*c*.8 per cent).
38. The loan-word *dame* occurs already in medieval texts, but seems to have been borrowed again in the seventeenth century: early forms (e.g. *Dama*) suggest the influence of Italian and Spanish. For details, see esp. Schramm (1914), 57-69, with an illustration of, and attack on, various kinds of *alamode* female dress from a print of *c*.1629 (pp. 105-9 and Plate III).
39. The forms here given are generally modernized.
40. See Gottsched (1748, 1762), 195-7, ed. Penzl (1978), i. 239-41. As many as one-third of all loans listed by Jones for the period 1648 are military terms, and many have survived. Jones (1978), 154.
41. Ullmann (1962), 204 ff.
42. See Jones (1976), 440 ff; Schramm (1914), 16-29.
43. Weise (1672), ed. Braune (1878), chaps. 4 and 20. See also Schramm (1914), 32-57, 104-20, and Plates I and II.
44. Compounds with *Lust-* from Philip von Zesen's *Adriatische Rosemund* (1645) include *Lustbrunnen, Lustfall, Lustfahrt, Lustgang/-gänge, Lustgarten, Lust-gebüsche, Lustgespräche, Lustgezänke, Lusthöhle* (= *Grotte*), *Lustlaube, Lustort, lustrieseln, Lustschifflein, Lustwall, lustwandeln, Lustwandel, Lustwaltung, Lust-spiele,* and *lustig, sich erlustigen.*
45. The title (see the General Bibliography) is significant.
46. His influential treatise, *Buch von der Deutschen Poeterey* (1624) (some thirteen editions down to 1690) sought to emulate foreign verse-forms in clear and elegant German free from unnecessary foreign words. For a facsimile of the *Aristarchus,* see Fechner (1970).
47. Moscherosch (1643), ed. Bobertag (1883), 184. The work was inspired by a foreign (Spanish) source: the *Sueños* of Quevedo, hence also Moscherosch's sobriquet 'Der Träumende' when he joined the Fruchtbringende Gesellschaft in 1645. The genesis of his *Gesichte* is complex: see Dünnhaupt (1980-1), ii. 1240-63, for details. The second part of Philander's visions contains as its first section the 'A la Mode Kehraus' (1643); the so-called 'Soldatenleben' vision appeared in 1646. Bobertag's reprint is based on an edition of 1650.
48. The author and date are unknown. A version is reprinted in Kluge (1918), 172-8. The work may even be as early as 1617: see Jones (1976), 688.
49. The *Sprachverderber* may also have been Moscherosch, perhaps subsequently reworked by Christoph Schorer (1618-71). The later title is significant: *C.S.* [= Christoph Schorer?] *Teutscher vnartiger Sprach-Sitten vnd Tugend verderber* . . . (1644): language and morals have been corrupted. See Brunt (1978), 44 = (1983), 49.
50. See Moscherosch (1643), ed. Bobertag (1883), 183.
51. These etymologies were copied, but few attained Friedrich von Logau's

(1604–55) elegance: 'Was Dame sey, und denn was Dama, wird verspüret | Dass jene Hörner macht, und diese Hörner führet' (i. 1. 66). Similarly, Lauremberg, Moscherosch, and Schupp: see Schramm (1914), 67.

52. Tailors are repeatedly mentioned; probably they needed to know technical/ fashionable terms for foreign dress (see Brunt (1978), 67 = (1983), 78–9). As the *Teutscher Michel* has it:

> Ein jeder Schneyder will jetzund leyder
> Der Sprach erfahren sein und redt Latein,
> Welsch und Frantzösisch, halb Japonesisch,
> Wann er ist voll und doll, der grobe Knoll.

See Kluge (1918), 204.

53. Rachel (1664), ed. Drescher (1903), No. VIII, *Der Poet* (pp. 104–24), lines 357–64.

54. 'Ach, man wird ja zutiefst geplagt; ich überlege mir, wie ich eine Bitte an den Major richten werde, der sein Quartier und seine Wohnung hier in der Nähe hat. Denn man spricht davon, daß Soldaten im Anmarsch seien: und diesen [Offizier] wollen sie bei uns einquartieren' (Schottel (1648), ed. Koldewey (1900), 70–1).

55. See Kluge (1918), 215.

56. p. 36; compare also Brunt (1983), 30 n. 30.

57. Weise (1676), 31; later apparently translated into German by Christian Juncker as *Curieuse Gedanken von den Nouvellen oder Zeitungen* . . . (1703), with an appendix listing foreign words. See Brunt (1978), 38 = (1983), 41.

58. In the poet Neidhart von Reuental's parodies of peasant pretensions and Werner der Gartenære's *Meier Helmbrecht*; see p. 122.

59. See Otto (1972*a*); Stoll (1973); Engels (1983). Still useful is Schultz (1888).

60. For a readable account of the Fruchtbringende Gesellschaft's dissensions in the 1640s, see Jellinek (1913–14), i. 160–84.

61. Moscherosch (1643), ed. Bobertag (1883), 138.

62. Schottel (1648), ed. Koldewey (1900), 77 ff.

63. The Dutch *Rederijkerskamers* ('chambers of rhetors') since the fifteenth century and in Italy the famous *Academia della Crusca* ('Clover Academy'), founded at Florence in 1582/3.

64. See Goedeke (1887), 5 ff., for names and details of the membership.

65. Gueintz was said to have had 35,000 pupils, his orthographical guide (see Gueintz (1645)) was reprinted, and its recommendations seem 'modern'. Indeed, the problematic reprinting of Grimmelshausen's *Simplicissimus* known as E3a (Formerly A) appears to have replaced the author's Alem./Upper Rhine spelling by a form which agrees with Gueintz's prescriptions. See Weydt (1971), 16 f., 57 f.

66. Hankamer (1927), 124.

67. Harsdörffer (1641–9), Part I (*Schutzschrift für die Teutsche Spracharbeit*), 2nd edn. (1644), 12 (compare also Part III (1643), 288–95); Schottel holds the same view: see the *Sprachkunst* (1641), 74–95, and especially the second edition (1651), fourth 'Lobrede', pp. 120–1.

68. See Blume (1978*a*, *b*).

69. Schottel (1663), 455, 1245–8.

70. Sacer (1673); see esp. his chaps. 33–4. Sacer belonged to the Elbschwanen as 'Hierophilo'.

71. Sacer (1673), 80.

72. See Kirkness (1975), i. 30 ff.

73. Birken, in Neumark (*c.*1668), pp. b6ʳ–b6ᵛ, lines 21–4; see Stoll (1973), 20.

74. The logic is unintentionally comic in that without foreign borrowings the German language is naked!

75. See Van Ingen (1970); Blume (1967).
76. Blume (1972).
77. Cholevius (1866), 18; and see Schultz (1888), 96–7. The second element of 'clavichord' derives from Lat. c(h)orda (fem.) 'cord', 'string', not from Lat. cor (neut.) 'heart'.
78. Rachel (1664), ed. Drescher (1903), No. VIII, Der Poet (pp. 104–24), lines 254–64; see also Rachel's remarks, lines 369–96 (pp. 119–20 in Drescher). Rachel, Lauremberg, Sacer, and others attack three striking poetic styles: the Alamode mixture of the 'Sprachenmenger'; the curious neologisms of the purists; and the far-fetched emblematic and metaphorical diction of the baroque (Schwulst).
79. Schottel (1663), 1368.
80. See the Liber Vagatorum (c.1510–11) edited by Luther (1528), (WA, vol. xxvi, pp. 634 ff.); also Moscherosch, 'Soldatenleben' (1646), ed. Bobertag (1883), 290.
81. The 'etymological' approach concerned native, not non-Germanic, words, and is thus a further factor in Zesen's purism: indeed, he rejected as 'foreign' letters c, ph, etc., which might otherwise have marked Fremdwörter.
82. See Zesen, Adriatische Rosemund (1645), ed. Jellinek (1889), for differences in the use of the symbols: ⟨ö⟩ = closed /ẹ/; ⟨ä⟩ = open /ę/; whereas ⟨e⟩ could be used for both.
83. Zesen's contemporaries had curious enough theories, especially concerning the lingua adamica and its links with Celtic or Hebrew.
84. For some of the neologisms, see p. 299.
85. The term 'baroque' here relates to a specific literary/linguistic epoch, while 'mannerism' applies to a particular emphatically formal style. See Barner (1975).
86. Conrady (1962), 465.
87. Political and advertising styles are also emblematic. See Schottel (1663), 84–7.
88. 'Auf die Fruchtbringende Herbst=Zeit' (Conrady (1962), 465–6); the poetess was a member of Zesen's Teutschgesinnte Genossenschaft.
89. 'Lob-rede an das liebwertheste Frauen-zimmer', in Gedichte, ed. Windfuhr (1969), 26–9, lines 13, 65–72.
90. Suter (1664), vi. 48, quoted by Nickisch (1969), 87.
91. Sacer (1673), 89.

CHAPTER VIII

1. See pp. 2–4. The fourth factor, the purpose or function of language, was seldom considered outside the dichotomy between the use of German for literature, especially poetry, and in everyday polite discourse. In general at this period, even in literature, people are held to speak according to the patterns of the social class to which they belong and do not have different styles at their disposal. Some concessions were made in the choice of words for technical or poetic purposes, but on the whole it was left to later writers, especially writers like Fritz Reuter and Gerhart Hauptmann, who used dialect and regional colloquial language, to introduce figures whose usage fluctuates according to their situation.
2. For the development of literary style, see especially Blackall (1978), and the new bibliographical essay it contains.
3. The history of grammatical codification and accounts of individual grammarians are treated by Jellinek (1913–14), esp. i. 184–385.
4. For a detailed examination of the criteria for identifying the best language in the sixteenth and seventeenth centuries, see Josten (1976). Josten discusses the distinction between the analogical and anomalist argument in classical authorities including Varro, Gellius, and Quintilian (pp. 211–14).

5. They were the subject of a heated epistolary argument within the Fruchtbringende Gesellschaft during the 1640s and 1650s, with Schottel and Harsdörffer defending the analogist position against Prince Ludwig of Anhalt-Köthen and Gueintz. See Jellinek (1913–14), i. 160–84.

6. Adelung (1782–4*b*). He claims to speak this form of German himself and sees it as US taken over into other dialect areas. The term *Niederhochdeutsch* was first used by the anonymous author of an article on German dialects, 'Etwas von deutschen Mundarten', *Deutsches Museum*, vol. vi, 3. Stück (March 1782), No. 9, pp. 276–84 (at p. 278); see Adelung (1782–4*b*), 32. The author of the *Deutsches Museum* article claims that *Niederhochdeutsch* represents 'den obersächsischen Dialekt in einem niedersächsischen Munde' (p. 277). The result is a much purer form of language than US itself. Adelung, however, claims that US alone is 'Hochdeutsch', without error when spoken properly by the right people.

7. See p. 224.

8. Herder for one was well aware of the inadequacy of orthography for rendering the multifarious variations of pronunciation and the richness of speech: 'Keine einzige lebendigtönende Sprache läßt sich vollständig in Buchstaben bringen . . .' (Herder (1770), ed. Pross (1979?), 13 f.) The problems of comprehensibility vs. phonetic accuracy recur in Naturalist drama (see Chapter IX). For imprecise regional orthography for transcribing dialect poetry, see the section on J. P. Hebel, pp. 360–1).

9. See pp. 270–1, and Leibniz (*c*.1697), edd. Pörksen and Schiewe (1983), 17–19, §§ 32–5. One of the best such dialect dictionaries is Richey (1743). For others see Adelung's review in Adelung (1782–4*d*), and Adelung (1806–17), ii. 201–82.

10. In particular Bodmer, Haller, Klopstock, and Lessing saw the value of regional and archaic forms in the language of poetry: Lessing actually produced a word-list of the works of the seventeenth-century poet Logau, whom he co-edited with Karl Wilhelm Ramler (1725–98).

11. Compare the dispute between Klaus Groth and Fritz Reuter (below, Chapter IX). Groth distinguishes between *Mundart* in the idealized sense of *Sprachart*, a particular manifestation of language with its own tradition and rules, and *Dialekt*, which is pronunciation and speech. Groth looks back to older forms of LG tradition, while Reuter listens to the language he hears around, and presents its vulgar features and the curious mixed forms (*Missingsch*) arising from LG-speakers trying to upgrade themselves and speak HG; Reuter treats serious social problems in his writing, while Groth does not.

12. For the sociological background, see Schenda (1977), and Engelsing (1973), esp. chaps. 9–13, both with further bibliography.

13. By 1739 the first such society, founded by Freiherr Karl Hildebrand von Canstein (1667–1719), had distributed some 340,000 New Testaments and nearly half a million 'Canstein Bibles'(on which see Reinitzer (1983*a*), 278). Luther's NT cost 1½ gulden in 1522—the price of a horse; see Rosenzweig (1926), 25.

14. See Engelsing (1973), 52 f., and Currie (1968).

15. Technical books, particularly in law, remained in Latin for some time; by the mid-eighteenth century German publications had overtaken Latin ones in science, philosophy, and medicine; Protestant theological studies tended from the outset to be published in German. See Paulsen (1896–7), ii. 688–91.

16. Justus Möser averred in 1771: 'Ich fühle, daß das viele Buchstaberei und Schulgehen unsere Jugend vom Spinnrocken zieht . . . Was die Mädchen betrifft — ich möchte keines heirathen, das lesen und schreiben kann!' (cited by Schenda (1977), 54). In 1772 a village schoolmaster (NB) equates literacy with billets-doux: 'Bei den virginibus ist das Schreiben nur ein vehiculum zur Lüderlichkeit'

(cited by Engelsing (1973), 69). This opinion goes back at least to the seventeenth century: in Gryphius's *Verlibtes Gespenste/Die gelibte Dornrose* (1660) the rebuffed peasant Matz Aschewedel complains of the HG-speaking Dornrose: 'doß hot ma dervon/we me [NHG *man*] de Maidlen lest in die Schule gihn/ unde buchstabiren lärnen. Do machen se denn Buler Brife und singen Zschäntscher Lider [i.e. *Liebeslieder*] vum schine Schaffer [= vom schönen Schäfer] und der falschen Sylviges [= *Silvia*] (Act II) (ed. Powell (1972), 204).

17. See Gräf (1956), esp. p. xx n. 1. Goethe's mother was also not sound in 'das Bustawiren und gerade Schreiben' and blames her schoolmaster (letter of 16 May 1807). Goethe (1826), observes that friends and colleagues have helped him to attain orthographical consistency: as is well known, he dictated much of his work. The letters of Lessing's mother and sister offer a similar illustration, contrasting sharply with those of his father and brothers.

18. Kaiser (1930), 240–1. See also Friedrich Wilhelm I's letters to Prince Leopold of Anhalt-Dessau, ed. Krauske (1905).

19. Gottsched (1748, 1762), 2, note (*b*), ed. Penzl (1978), i. 38.

20. Such language undoubtedly occurred even in the eighteenth century, given the existence of towns of 10,000 inhabitants and more, but *Umgangssprache* as such is neglected until the late nineteenth century, when the lower urban social classes ('proletariat') generally engaged the attention of scholars, at first in the large metropolitan agglomerations, particularly Berlin. We shall argue (pp. 319–20) that Frau Gottsched's play *Der Witzling* exemplifies some features of Leipzig *Umgangssprache*.

21. This written 'EMG' is no direct reflection of the speech of the area, as will be seen shortly. Ultimately the grammatical and orthographical consensus of printers from a wide area, including particularly the WMG towns, notably Frankfurt, may have contributed more to the stabilization of the written koine than the seventeenth-century grammarians.

22. Kandler (1736), 74.

23. Recognizing the ambiguity of the term *Mundart*, Kaiser uses it to mean what would now be called *Umgangssprache*, and so arrives at a closer understanding of the eighteenth-century controversies by arguing in eighteenth-century terms. However, the lack of clear distinction between colloquial and dialect deserves more emphasis (Kaiser (1930), 3–21).

24. Louise Adelgunde Viktorie Gottsched, née Kulmus (1713–62).

25. *Hauptaktionen* in contrast to 'preludes' or humorous 'postludes'; *Staatsaktionen* because of the pseudo-historical and 'political' subject-matter of these blood-and-thunder melodramas.

26. Bodmer's 'Persönliche Anekdoten', ed. Vetter (1892), 37. For the many societies on the Gottschedian model, see Kaiser's diagram 'Gottschedkreis und Gott-schedgegner' in Lüdtke and Mackensen (1928–38), iii, No. 76.

27. One of the French grammars, *Le Maître de la langue allemande . . . composée sur le modèle des meilleurs auteurs de nos jours, et principalement sur celui de Mr. le professeur Gottsched* (Lausanne, 1754), reached its sixth edition in 1771.

28. Third edition, published in London. Wendeborn was preacher at Ludgate Hill.

29. Johann Bödiker (1641–95). His *Grundsätze der deutschen Sprache* (1690) was probably the most important pre-Gottsched school grammar, reprinted 1701, 1709, and in 1723 and 1729 with important additions by Johann Leonhard Frisch, then in 1746 further enlarged by J. J. Wippel. The emphasis lies on *Gebrauch*, which is equated with the written traditions, and LG-speakers are credited with the best pronunciation of this HG. Frisch especially rejects pronunciation as a guide to spelling and argues instead for a pronunciation based

on written traditions; Luther's language is no longer 'modern', and a list of archaisms is given which Wippel expands to some fifty pages; see Socin (1888), 360 ff., and Bödiker (1690, 1746), repr. (1977), 290–348.

30. For the most important individual grammarians, see Jellinek (1913–14) and Nerius (1967).

31. Supposedly, among others, the following: Christoph Heinrich Amthor (1678–1721), Johann von Besser (1654–1729), Heinrich von Bünau (1697–1762), Friedrich Rudolf Ludwig von Canitz (1654–99), Nicolaus Hieronymus Gundling (1671–1729), Johann Christian Günther (1695–1723), Friedrich von Hagedorn (1708–54), Johann Jacob Mascov (1689–1761), Johann Lorenz Mosheim (1694–1755), Benjamin Neukirch (1665–1729), and Johann Valentin Pietsch (1690–1733). See Gottsched (1748, 1762), 485, 489, and Frau Gottsched's play *Der Witzling* (Scene 5), written before 1744 to defend her husband's aesthetic and grammatical theory. Some of the writers are statesmen, historians, and jurists; Pietsch was Gottsched's teacher. In fact, in keeping with his interest in poetry, Gottsched mostly cites Opitz, who does not appear in his list of model authors; see Penzl (1980), 171, 227–8.

32. Cf. the ambiguity of the term *Mundart*: 'diejenige Art zu reden [*from* 'façon de parler'], die in einer gewissen Provinz eines Landes herrschet' (Gottsched (1748, 1762), 2, § 2, ed. Penzl (1978), 38), yet also the supra-regional 'language' of scholars and courts, where 'Art zu reden' clearly implies style as well as external form.

33. Gottsched (1748, 1762), 2–3, ed. Penzl (1978), 37–8. This closely resembles Bödiker's statement: 'Die hochteutsche Sprache ist keine Mundart eines einige[n] Volks oder einer Nation der Teutschen, sondern aus allen durch Fleis der Gelehrten zu solcher Zierde erwachsen, und in ganz Teutschland im Schreiben der Gelehrten wie auch im Reden vieler vornehmer Leute üblich' (Bödiker (1746), 351). It is contrasted with the various dialects belonging to the two major groups, *Niederteutsch* and *Oberteutsch*.

34. Gottsched (1748, 1762), 68 n., broadens his US dialectal basis to include Thuringia, the Voigtland, Anhalt, Mansfeld, Lusatia ('die Lausitz'), and Lower Silesia—(see Map 4, p. 305).

35. Gottsched (1748, 1762), 402, ed. Penzl (1978), ii. 460.

36. Gottsched (1748, 1762), 331, note (*b*), ed. Penzl (1978), 381.

37. Gottsched (1730), 3rd edn. (1742), 743, 747. Gottsched clearly recognizes an informal, colloquial language, 'Umgangssprache', although he focuses on defining its upper and lower limits; nor must the stage language be 'pöbelhaft' etc. Similarly, commenting on Horace, *Ars Poetica*, Gottsched distinguishes two types of *usus* ('Gewohnheit')—one current amongst the most polished courtiers, the best authors, and the most enlightened sectors of the aristocracy and bourgeoisie, the other predominating among the plebs ('Pöbel'), feeble-witted authors, untutored aristocrats, and affected courtiers. The former is the model for poets, the latter for vulgar rhymesters (Gottsched (1730), 3rd edn. (1742), 16).

38. Socin (1888), 400; the page reference to Sonnenfels is from the reprint (1884).

39. Gottsched (1725), No. 23.

40. Some LG dialects also have diphthongal forms for HG monophthongs, e.g. *geihn* (NHG *gehen*), *graut/chraut* (NHG *groß*); the LG dialects to the north of the EMG area must be examined to ascertain possible influence of their phonology. Among other forms deplored by Gottsched are the regional interjections (*unnütze Zwischenwörter*) which make a discourse ludicrous; he cites Austrian *halt*, *halter* [< ich halte dafür/halt ich], and from Meissen 'das pöbelhaft gleech, oder meech' [*from glaube ich, meine ich*]: Gottsched (1748, 1762), 530–1, ed. Penzl (1978), ii. 597.

41. Gottsched (1748, 1762), 114–50, ed. Penzl (1978), i. 153–90.
42. See Becker (1937); Franke (1884); Wahl (1725), 18; and, for EMG dialects generally, Putschke (1973).
43. The play was printed in the first edition of *Die deutsche Schaubühne nach den Regeln und Exempeln der Alten* (Breitkopf: Leipzig, 1741–5), in the sixth part (1745): Gottsched (1748, 1762), 455, note (*a*), ed. Penzl (1978), ii. 518 (this section appears in the third edition of the *Sprachkunst* (1752)), and 515 ff., ed. Penzl (1978), ii. 581–2 (again, the references to the *Witzling* are absent from the first two editions).
44. LG dialects lack differentiated acc. and dat. forms of the first person pronoun, having only *mi/me*; confusion of final nasals -*m* and -*n* (e.g. 'mit *den* Hut auf *den* Kopf') reinforces the uncertainty in the use of these cases.
45. Sinnreich, Jambus, and Vielwitz deny that German has any rules, declare rules to be detrimental to poetry, and propose a new journal, *Der Lustigmacher*, an allusion to the defectors' 'Beiträge zum Vergnügen des Verstandes und Witzes' (*Bremer Beiträge*), 1744–57.
46. For Haller and further bibliography, cf. Siegrist (1967), esp. 18 ff.
47. See Bender (1973), with bibliography.
48. Haller (1748), preface to 4th edition.
49. See Breitinger (1740), preface.
50. This unstressed -*e* was also added to adjectives.
51. Gottsched (1748, 1762), 332 f., ed. Penzl (1978), i. 381–2. There is evidence that the Gottscheds used such forms in speech: Frau Gottsched told a visitor enquiring for her husband 'Er ist auf der Jagd, er scheußt Hasen'—unfortunate in view of the Leipzig colloquial unrounding (quoted by Penzl (1977), 77). Gottsched, loc. cit., recognized that 'im gemeinen Gebrauch' the *eu* forms were not used in Meissen, although he claims they were still known there.
52. Gottsched (1748, 1762), 14–15, ed. Penzl (1978), i. 50–1 n.; but he later denies this: p. 63, note (*b*), ed. Penzl (1978), i. 101.
53. Gottsched (1758), Preface.
54. As an example of Gottsched's 'binary' distinctions, see the opposition between *Pasquill* 'an immoral, personal, illegal, and usually anonymous attack on an honest man' and *Satire* 'a moral, open castigation of viciousness for philanthropic reasons': see Gottsched (1725–7), ii. 30. Stück, p. 270; (1730), 3rd edn. (1742), 116, 570 f., and (1758), 229–30, ed. Slangen (1955), 162–3. Herder was to observe that synonyms are a blessing for the poet but the bane of the philosopher: Herder (1767), ed. Matthias (1903), i. 37 (see also ibid. 23–4, Herder's attack on Johann Georg Sulzer).
55. Bodmer (1746); see Blackall (1978), 114 n. 1.
56. See especially Blackall (1978), 139 ff., 173 ff., 183 ff. and (1955). See the General Bibliography for the title of Dornblüth's work.
57. For these men, see Jellinek (1913–14), i. 274 ff., 282 ff.; Nerius (1967), 48 ff.
58. Antesperg did not discuss the relationship to each other of the thirty-seven German dialects he believed to exist (Antesperg (1747), preface, § 21, and p. 243). Individual words or forms are dismissed as 'rusticè' or 'bäuerisch', e.g. the diminutive suffix -*el* rather than -*lein* (p. 34); pronunciation is occasionally criticized, e.g. *Eâ laft a mid, Sô kemâ scho, J sag enks, gehts nôt aba*, for *Er lauft auch mit, sie kommen schon, ich sage es euch, gehet nicht hinab* (p. 240).
59. Popowitsch (1750), 312–14 and n., and 399. Prominent Austrian orators and writers are taken to task for their linguistic slips. For attacks on Gottsched see esp. pp. 286 ff., 398 ff.
60. Popowitsch (1750), 426 n.
61. Goethe (1810–31), Part II, Book 6, in Jubiläums-Ausgabe, xxiii. 44. For Goethe,

altering even his pronunciation involved the sacrifice of his own cast of thought ('Denkweise'), powers of imagination, feeling, and sense of identity ('vaterländischer Charakter'). The first three parts of *Dichtung and Wahrheit* were written between 1809/10 and 1814, and the fourth part, begun in 1813, was completed only in 1830-1. The passage quoted here dates from around 1812.

62. Immanuel Jakob Pyra (1715-44). The various manifestos and polemics cannot concern us here; see Schneider (1960).

63. His very name was a watchword ('Losung') for poetic feeling: '. . . sie legte ihre Hand auf die meinige, und sagte — Klopstock! — Ich erinnerte mich sogleich der herrlichen Ode, die ihr in Gedanken lag, und versank in dem Strome von Empfindungen, den sie in dieser Losung über mich ausgoß' (Goethe (1774), edd. von der Hellen *et al.* (1902), xvi. 28).

64. Klopstock (1758), ed. 1854-5), x. 202: 'Soviel ist unterdeß gewiß, daß keine Nation weder in der Prosa noch in der Poesie vortrefflich geworden ist, die ihre poetische Sprache nicht sehr merklich von der prosaischen unterschieden hätte.' Contrast in this connection the dictum of Christian Weise: 'Welche *Construction* in *prosâ* nicht gelitten wird/ die soll man auch in Versen davon lassen' (Weise (1693), i. 141, quoted from Blackall (1978), 214).

65. Schneider (1960), 36-7.

66. Schönaich (1754), ed. Köster (1900). The work is dedicated to 'Dem Geist-Schöpfer, dem Seher, dem neuen Evangelisten, dem Träumer, dem göttlichen St. Klopstocken . . .', and to Bodmer in similar terms. Schönaich mocks Haller's use of *Abtritt*—'man vermenge nicht dieß Wort mit einem heimlichen Gemache' (p. 4)—and lampoons other authors with scurrilous neologisms of his own, e.g. Naumann's *Altvordern* prompts the suggestion *Junghintern* for 'grandchildren'. See Schönaich (1754), ed. Köster (1900), 18, 27.

67. Klopstock (1779), ed. (1855), 196.

68. Christoph Martin Wieland (1733-1813); see Wieland (1783), 320, ed. Kurrelmeyer (1954), p. A 113.

69. For much of what follows, see Baudusch-Walker (1958), and King (1967). Curiously, Klopstock does not consider the needs of the stage, nor was a standard pronunciation codified until over a century later, based on theory a good deal less clear than Klopstock's.

70. Klopstock (1774), ed. (1855), 174 ff. The *Gelehrtenrepublik* is again reminiscent of the seventeenth-century whimsy found in Harsdörffer's *Frauenzimmer-Gesprächspiele* (1641-57), for example, though it is intellectually more substantial, clear, and urbane. Contemporary readers failed to appreciate it, however. In 1779, 'Über die deutsche Rechtschreibung' appeared in the orthography it was defending.

71. An open syllable is a syllable which ends in a vowel; closed syllables end in a consonant. The disyllabic examples used (*Kahne, Kanne*) must be analysed phonetically, not orthographically, i.e. as [ˈkaːnə] and [ˈkanə] respectively. In each case the medial consonant /n/ begins the next syllable, so the first syllables are open. Consonantal clusters like /ft/ in *prüfte* [ˈpryːftə] are split so that the first element closes the initial syllable and the second opens the subsequent one: *prüf-te*. Note that in *Kanne* the geminated ⟨nn⟩ has the phonetic value of a single /n/. However, metrical and morphological variation supervenes to spoil the system (e.g. 'Im Bạd' erkeltet'; 'ịr' vs. 'ire Augen'; 'geblịbnen' (for 'geblibenen')), and Klopstock himself was misled by spelling: 'Aussprạche' has a long vowel in an open syllable and should not have the loop.

72. Lichtenberg (1799-83), 139 [*fürzen* (wk. vb.) 'to fart'; *schatz = schadet es*]. Lichtenberg assumes elsewhere that Klopstock's 'Ordokrafi' (!) is based simply on the principle of writing as one speaks: see Lichtenberg (1766-99), 387 (letter

of 20 March 1780 to Johann Christian Ehrmann, No. 255 in Promies), 455 (letter of 1 August 1782 to Franz Ferdinand Wolff, No. 322 in Promies).

73. See Baudusch-Walker (1958), 234–5; for photographs of pages from this extremely rare printing, see plates after p. 254.

74. '*Adelung*, m. vir nobilis, ahd. *adalunc*, und gangbarer mannesname, der wohlklingende eigenname eines mannes, der vor uns durch sein wörterbuch ein hohes verdienst um unsere sprache sich errungen hat' (Grimm (1854), col. 178).

75. Adelung (1782–4*e*).

76. Adelung (1782–4*c*), 23.

77. Adelung (1782–4*c*), 25. The imagery of these essays in the *Magazin* reveals Adelung as an Enlightenment grammarian: 'klar', 'sich aufklären', 'sich aufhellen' contrast with 'dunkel' etc., even 'in Dichtung eingehüllet'.

78. Adelung (1782–4*f*), 83. This is perhaps the most extreme formulation of Adelung's position: see Henne (1968*a*), esp. 116 ff.

79. Adelung (1774–86), i, preface, p. vi. Cf. also the article s.v. 'Hochdeutsch', ibid. ii, col. 1221, esp. '. . . ist die hochdeutsche Mundart die obersächsische oder vielmehr meißnische Mundart so wie sie durch Schriftsteller theils erweitert, theils aber auch eingeschränket und seit der Reformation die herrschende Büchersprache des ganzen gelehrten Deutschlandes geworden ist.'

80. Nineteenth- and twentieth-century models for German linguistic history remain indebted to Adelung's scheme with its shifting emphasis from Frk. to the 'Swabian' (or at least UG) of the Minnesinger, and then the gradual growth of EMG. More work needs to be done on the linguistic historiography from seventeenth- and eighteenth-century theorists onwards. The studies of Scherer and Burdach on chancery language, and especially on the Imperial Chancery at Prague, can be viewed as attempts to overcome the chronological and geographical hiatus between the end of 'MHG' and the beginning of 'NHG'. Scherer in particular was scathing about Adelung's scholarship—see Scherer (1875)—but his own view of linguistic history is less adequate than Adelung's, amounting primarily to historical grammar and comparative philology. Without denying Scherer's importance, his alternating more masculine/manly and more feminine/womanly periods in language and literature—a kind of linguistic yin and yang—are at least as irrational and tendentious as Adelung's genealogy of taste (Scherer (1878), 14).

81. Adelung (1782), i. 113 f.

82. Johann Andreas Cramer (1723–88), theologian, preacher, and hymn-writer; Johann Arnold Ebert (1723–95), English scholar and translator of Young's *Night Thoughts*; Nicolaus Dietrich Giseke (1724–65), poet; Christian Felix Weisse (1726–1804), poet and translator. Details in the *Allgemeine Deutsche Biographie*. See Müller (1903), esp. 22 f. Adelung always distances himself from Gottsched, whose contribution to German grammar he nevertheless acknowledged, and whose projected dictionary of German he so successfully took over.

83. Adelung (1774–86), i, preface, p. xi.

84. Adelung (1782–4*f*). In another essay (1782–4*g*) Adelung describes the loss of artistic unity after 1760 with the new-fangled 'Barden- und Druiden-Geschmack, Minnegesang, Volkston, Vernachläßigung der Reinigkeit und Richtigkeit der Sprache'—all indicative of the weakening of the influence of good taste, prejudicial to the establishment of a 'National-Litteratur' which should incorporate unity.

85. Adelung (1782–4*h*), 140.

86. Johann Christian Christoph Rüdiger (1751–1822), a clear-headed and impressive critic; see Rüdiger (1783); (an interesting essay entitled 'Ueber das Verhältniß der hochteutschen Sprache und obersächsischen Mundart').

87. Rüdiger notes: 'Kuttentoll hört man in Obersachsen selbst vom Frauenzimmer für übermüthig lustig, da es hingegen in Niedersachsen ein äußerst unanständiger Ausdruck ursprünglich von der Nymphomanie ist' (Rüdiger (1783), 96). See also p. 41.

88. The monophthongization *ei > ē*, e.g. *Kleeder*: note that Adelung prescribes that the diphthong be pronounced as [ei], not as [ai], so that the difference between diphthongal and monophthongal pronunciation was less marked; see Adelung (1774–86), i, s.v. *Ei*, col. 1523. Rüdiger (1783), 136, notes that *Sohn* is pronounced like *saun*, evidence for what has been treated above (p. 319) as hypercorrection.

89. See Henne (1968a), 127, for this 'Dresdenerei', and Adelung (1774–86), i, cols. 1489 f.

90. Rüdiger (1783), 54, argues that the educated and upper classes *in all areas* use a form of language which differs from provincial habits, and in fact they attempt to practise the 'book language'. Contrast, however, Sonnenfels (1768), 97–103, No. 17, 1 April 1768.

91. See Henne (1968a), 125.

92. See Henne (1975), 109–42.

93. Adelung (1785–9), published anonymously; *inter alia*, it treats Paracelsus, Quirinus Kuhlmann, and Faust.

94. Adelung (1774–86), i, p. xiv.

95. Compare Adelung (1787), i, chap. 7, 'Von der Würde des Styles', 209–23. Jacob Grimm remarked: 'Die sprache überhaupt in eine erhabne, edle, trauliche, niedrige und pöbelhafte zu unterscheiden taugt nicht, und Adelung hat damit vielen wörtern falsche gewichte angehängt', and in general: 'Das wörterbuch ist kein sittenbuch, sondern ein wissenschaftliches, allen zwecken gerechtes unternehmen' (Grimm (1854), cols. 32, 34).

96. Curiously, *schmeißen* is also vulgar by association with *scheißen*, and Adelung cites the example 'Das Kind hat ins Bett geschmissen' (Adelung (1774–86), iv, cols. 178–9). Perhaps an instance of euphemism itself having become taboo.

97. Lessing already used the word in this archaic (revived?) sense in *Emilia Galotti* (1772), I. 4: 'ein alter Degen, stolz und rauh.'

98. Adelung (1782–4d), esp. p. 59.

99. See Müller (1903).

100. Campe (1801). Wieland and Adelung objected to Campe's extreme eradication of foreign words—Wieland speaks of 'Sprach-Jakobinismus' (letter of 26 January 1801). While Campe's replacements were often successful, perhaps a testimony to the importance of his and Theodor Bernd's large dictionary of 1807–11, he probably helped to promote the understanding and use of the very foreign words he was anxious to replace. For Campe's purist influence, see also Chapter X, on the Allgemeiner Deutscher Sprachverein.

101. See Adelung (1774–86), i, col. 145, s.v. 'Adelig'; but under 'Buckelig' (ibid., col. 1121), Adelung proposes changing the form to *buckelich, buckellicht*, etc. when it denotes 'einem Buckel gleich oder ähnliches', rather than 'possessing a hump': 'Doch wer beobachtet wohl alle diese Kleinigkeiten?'

102. Letter to Goethe, 26 January 1804.

103. Klopstock (1794), ed. (1855), 92: 'Denn du verlangst z.B. doch wohl gewiß nicht von mir, daß ich begreifen soll, warum sich Wieland das mundartische Wörterbuch auf den Tisch nagelte.'

104. Voss (1804); quotations from cols. 205 and 317.

105. Rüdiger (1783), 52.

CHAPTER IX

1. Hartig (1981), 67.
2. See esp. Sütterlin (1897–9), preface, and Eggers (1977), 21 ff.
3. Words, expressions, and catch-phrases do mark changes in the individual varieties and styles of German, however.
4. See esp. Sagarra (1980), chap. 1.
5. See Wagner (1974).
6. See Ramm (1967), 391 ff., quoting figures from the *Statistisches Jahrbuch des deutschen Reiches*. Industrial output increased massively in the same period, e.g. coal from 34m. tons in 1870 to 149m. in 1900 and 277m. in 1914; between 1883 and 1913 German trade increased fourfold. Some population increase may be accounted for by a falling off of emigration, which was running at as high as a quarter of a million per year in the 1850s; see Taylor (1954), 87–8.
7. Mackensen (1971), 80.
8. Mauersberg (1960), 72 f., 75–8. (Some growth is explained by the incorporation of suburbs.)
9. Sagarra (1980), 57–8, states that in 1891 the urban population had outstripped the rural populace for the first time.
10. Hickmann (1896–8?), vol. ii, Table 32.
11. Schenda (1977), 456 ff.
12. *Der Große Brockhaus* (1958), xii. 174–5.
13. The influence of Adelung is plain, but detailed studies showing the main traditions of nineteenth-century school grammars are scarce; see Vesper (1979), Schieb (1981), Chorley (1984). Normative morphology and syntax cannot be treated here.
14. See Grimm (1819/22–37), vol. i (1st edn. 1819), preface, repr. in Grimm (1864–90), viii. 29–45, esp. 30–1, 37.
15. See Lockwood (1969).
16. In the preface to the 12th edition of Heyse (1816), which appeared in 1840, Heyse's son Karl warns that the modest and practical purpose of school grammar must not be lost sight of: 'Der Schüler soll seine Muttersprache in ihrem gegenwärtigen Zustande verstehen und mit Sicherheit und Freiheit handhaben lernen.' For the Heyses, see now Chorley (1984).
17. Grimm was more interested in correcting current usage in accordance with historical practice, so he avoided capital letters for nouns and also rejected the 'Gothic' or *Fraktur* type as being neither German in origin nor aesthetically pleasing. The great lexicographical works of German philology are all printed in roman or *Antiqua* type-founts (Graff (1834–46), Benecke, Müller, and Zarncke (1854–61), Grimm (1854), and Lexer (1872–8)); and so are some learned journals. Despite claims that it induced myopia (e.g. *Zeitschrift für deutsche Orthographie*, 3 (1883), 14–16—notice of findings of a commission of medical experts on the condition of high schools in Alsace-Lorraine), German publishers remained faithful to *Fraktur*, and Bismarck staunchly defended it. The National Socialists at first cultivated it, but eventually they introduced roman to further the use of German in occupied territory, and in 1941 the newspapers *Angriff* and *Völkischer Beobachter* dropped 'Gothic' type. See Priebsch and Collinson (1968), 420.
18. Very few primary-school children went on to higher schools—still only 7.2 per cent of the population in 1906 (Sagarra (1980), 33). Schoolmasters at the Gymnasium can perhaps not be blamed for their prejudice against the spoken usage of those who did not attend their schools.
19. Examples drawn from Leistner (1880).

20. See Eisen (1880), 48–51. The material mostly derives from dictionaries. Note the title of Wolke (1812)!
21. See Schlaefer (1980*b*) and in general Schlaefer (1980*a*).
22. Reissued as Duden (1872). The preface expresses a patriotic desire for a uniform national orthography matching the new unity: practical activities—even spelling —acquire a political veneer. The book presents controversial points, distinguishing carefully between equally justifiable alternatives, where both sounds and spelling differ (e.g. *Hülfe*/*Hilfe* or *gültig*/*giltig*), and mere variations in spelling the same sound (e.g. *Theil*/*Teil*), which could be eradicated (in this case by dropping the ⟨h⟩). For Duden's biography see Wurzel (1979).
23. Wilhelm Scherer has left several interesting accounts of the conference, especially Scherer (1876*a*–*c*).
24. At least six devices were used, including (1) doubling (*Aar*, *Meer*); (2) use of ⟨e⟩ (*Sieg*, MHG *sic*/*siges*); (3) use of ⟨h⟩ after vowel (*Jahr*); (4) use of ⟨h⟩ after ⟨t⟩ (*Thal* or *Rath*, now *Tal*, *Rat*); (5) use of ⟨ß⟩ after long vowel but ⟨ss⟩ after short; (6) no marking before single consonant (*wir*, *wider*).
25. Factors combining in differing degrees involve phonetic, phonemic, morphophonemic (cf. *Rad* = ['ra:t] ∼ *Rades* = ['ra:dəs]), historical, etymological, graphemic (cf. *Seite* ≠ *Saite* separating homonyms), grammatical (cf. capital letters for nouns), and extra-linguistic (e.g. socio-linguistic) considerations. These interact, cutting across the rational principle of a minimum set of distinct symbols distributed so that one sound is consistently represented by one symbol.
26. See especially the preface to the *DWB* (Grimm (1854)), 52–63, with many examples of inconsistent spelling, esp. regarding vowel length; also Grimm's letter of April 1849 to the Weidmann publishing house, in which he rejects the 'graphemic' approach to orthography since context will always separate homonyms, pointing out that medieval manuscripts seldom indicate vowel length and capital letters are rare (reprinted in *ZfdPh* 1 (1869), 227–230, and in Garbe (1978), 51–3).
27. Weinhold's 'Über deutsche Rechtschreibung' in the *Zeitschrift für die österreichischen Gymnasien* (Vienna, 1852) so shocked the editor, Professor Bonitz, that he got von Raumer to reply in the same journal in 1855. For this and other articles on the same subject, see von Raumer (1863).
28. *Verhandlungen der zur Herstellung größerer Einigung in der deutschen Rechtschreibung berufenen Konferenz . . .*, 2nd edn. (Halle, 1876), 83, 94.
29. Blatz (1895–6), i. 174.
30. The Allgemeiner Deutscher Sprachverein, founded in 1885, expressly forbade questions of orthography to be raised for fear that the dissent and acrimony would split the society even at its inception (Article 3 of the constitution, repealed in 1901).
31. But not from foreign words—'Am *Th*ron wurde nicht gerüttelt', as some wit observed.
32. The orthographical debate continues to surface at intervals, and centres on the inconsistencies, for example in the indication of vowel length and in the use of capital letters for nouns—*Auto fahren* beside *radfahren* etc. In 1974 the editor of the West German Duden commented: '. . . unsere rechtschreibung ist seit 1901 nicht besser geworden, sie weist wenig logisch-systematische züge auf und steckt voller ungereimtheiten, ihr regelwerk ist schwer durchschaubar'; see Garbe (1978), 221. Yet in 1955 the various education ministers of the states in the Federal Republic of Germany made the Duden authoritative. The prime concern remains what it was at the end of the nineteenth century: to preserve uniformity throughout the German-speaking area, even if the spelling system has its faults. Political problems, principally the differences between the Federal and

Democratic German states, stand in the way of a rational and thorough orthographical reform. Recently, the so-called 'gemäßigte Kleinschreibung' has been much ventilated—a modified spelling that would dispense with capital letters for most nouns. This might actually gain acceptance: compare articles in *Der Spiegel*, 1973/14, 176–7, and ibid. 1982/26, 142–8.

33. Goethe (1803), 197, § 1.
34. For example, Heyse (1816), 23rd edn. (1878), 2–3: 'man befleißige sich einer r e i n e n und d e u t l i c h e n hochdeutschen A u s s p r a c h e, vermeide zu dem Ende jede fehlerhafte Lauteigenheit einzelner Provinzen und bemühe sich, jeden Buchstaben im Sprechen und Lesen so auszudrücken, wie es seine Natur und der hochdeutsche Sprachgebrauch erfordern.' The term *Buchstabe* stems from a period when phonetic analysis was based on classical tradition rather than observation; 'a sound' and 'its' symbol were held to be in a one-to-one relationship, and *Buchstabe* may often be translated as 'phoneme'.
35. Paul (1880/1968), 2nd edn. (1886), 352: 'Die mustergültige sprache . . . ist vielmehr die auf dem theater im ernsten drama übliche, mit der die herrschende aussprache der gebildeten an keinem orte vollständig übereinkommt.' Paul observes that actors are specifically schooled in declamation.
36. Blatz (1895–6), i. 154.
37. The conference included theatre managers from Berlin, Schwerin, and Coburg and the noted phoneticians Eduard Sievers and Karl Luick (1865–1935).
38. Wilhelm Braune reiterated this view in an inaugural lecture in 1904 (Braune (1905)).
39. Braune (1905) suggested that after the Prussian victories of 1870–1 a Prussian officer caste might conceivably have made fashionable the pronunciation of /g/ initially as [j] in words like *jut, Jott, Jarde* (= *gut, Gott, Garde*), but was unsuccessful because of spelling tradition.
40. See Siebs (1901).
41. Siebs (1905).
42. Curme (1904), 2nd edn. (1922), preface, pp. vii–viii.
43. See the title in the General Bibliography, s.v. *Siebs* (1898/1969). The new *Siebs* has made greater concessions to common educated colloquial speech, partly under the influence of the excellent East German *Wörterbuch der Deutschen Aussprache* (1964). Thus, *Siebs* (1969) now accepts both the apico-dental trilled /r/ ([r]), and the uvular trill ([R]) as part of the 'reine Hochlautung', while the commonly heard velar fricative realization of /r/ as [ʁ] belongs to the 'gemäßigte Hochlautung', and the vocalization of /r/ in words like *Heer* (['heːɐ]) and *Moor* (['moːɐ]) is 'Alltagssprache'. Originally, only the apico-dental trill was accepted as 'Bühnenaussprache'; in 1933 the uvular trill became a permissible variant.
44. For details of the individual dialects and important writers in them, see the Select Bibliography (p. 387). Here we are concerned with the use rather than with the description of dialects.
45. See below, pp. 364 ff. We have already seen the mixed language of towns in the Leipzig colloquial of the eighteenth century (Chapter VIII).
46. For 'register' see Turner (1973), 165 ff. Register involves such factors as degree of technicality and formality and the choice of writing or speech, depending on the speaker's situation, status, intentions, and subject-matter, and his relationship to his interlocutors.
47. See p. 200; there was a marked difference between LG dialects and the HG book language. Still, Duke Heinrich Julius of Brunswick introduced speakers from several dialect areas into his plays, e.g. *Susanna* (*c*.1594): they are convincingly, if not always consistently, marked out by their language.
48. Herder's *Volkslieder* appeared in 1778–9 and stimulated other collectors.

49. The same holds for nineteenth-century *Volksschriftsteller*, whose works were also mostly escapist, apolitical, or else nationalistic. They propounded a positive, passive view of social conditions, taught patience in adversity rather than social change, and reassured their essentially middle-class readership. See Schenda (1977), 160–73. The works of more controversial authors were in any case subject to censorship as obscene, as socialist revolutionary propaganda, or as nihilistic materialism.

50. The artificiality of this writing was already recognized at the time, e.g. by Rückert (1864). See Socin (1888), 490–3.

51. Jaeger (1964) distinguishes popular *Volkspoesie*, written for and in the idiom of the people, from cultivated *Mundartdichtung*, produced by educated writers for educated readers. A debased sentimental attitude to dialect poetry has filtered down from the highest intellectual circles around 1800, via the bourgeoisie in the mid-nineteenth century, to the mass of the working population in the twentieth (Jaeger (1964), 74–5).

52. But sometimes classical plays with dialect or polyglot scenes were transposed into German dialects: Plautus' Punic-speaker in *Poenulus* eventually crops up as a LG-speaker in Jacob Ayrer's sixteenth-century version.

53. The 'dialect' in some plays, e.g. *Frühere Verhältnisse* (1862), shows social differentiation within a town colloquial (*Umgangssprache*), though it probably strikes North Germans as uniformly dialectal in that it differs in sounds and forms from the standard language.

54. See Bichel (1974); Voss actually moved away from the dialect for metrical reasons and aimed to echo the MLG written language of the Middle Ages ('einen schüchternen Nachhall der sassischen Buchsprache'), free from archaic, vulgar, or narrowly local features—a literary LG 'standard', in fact.

55. For Hebel see Kully (1969); Däster (1973).

56. See Hebel's letter of 3 October 1804 to his friend F. W. Hitzig, ed. Zentner (1939), 207 f.

57. Hebel (1803), preface, ed. Sütterlin (*c*.1910), i. 141.

58. By the Tübingen Professor Moritz Rapp (1803–83); see Jaeger (1964), 56–7.

59. However, the Swabian Sebastian Sailer wrote a harmless dialect play, his *Creatio*, which was banned by the censor Osiander in 1811 as '. . . eine im niedrigsten schwäbischen Volkstone verfaßte dramatische Darstellung der Geschichte der Schöpfung und des Sündenfalls. Die Absicht ist, die biblische Erzählung also einen Theil der Religion lächerlich zu machen . . .'. See Schenda (1977), 92. Doubtless this indicates once more that dialect could be tolerated in the salons of the cultivated classes, but was seen as subversive in more popular contexts.

60. The sincere but amateurish dialectological journal known as *Fromanns Zeitschrift* (founded 1854) contains reviews and selections of such poetry and interesting attempts to turn literature in other languages—including Portuguese sonnets—into German dialects, as well as polyglot transpositions of dialect poems from one dialect into others. One 'Jovialis' proffers part of a translation of Schiller's *Wilhelm Tell* turned into Swiss: 'Dän bravo man denχt â siχ sälb zi letzist . . .' (*Fromanns Zeitschrift*, 3 (1856), 198–209).

61. Groth's more important theoretical linguistic writings, including the *Briefe über Hochdeutsch und Plattdeutsch* (1858), are conveniently available in Braak and Mehlem (1961).

62. See esp. Socin (1888), 521 ff. and Jaeger (1964), 49–50.

63. Prutz (1857) praises Reuter as a 'gesunder Volksdichter', while Groth's poetry is HG in LG dress. Reuter (1858) reveals Groth's own linguistic inconsistency and mocks him as concerned only with the 'höhere Kultur der Feldblumen', not with 'growing corn' and the practical necessity of dunging the fields which this required.

64. See Groth (c.1877).
65. Groth (1858), 169.
66. For an early use of the term in German see Groth (1858), 165: 'Die Naturalisten glauben zu schreiben, wie man spricht. Es geht mit dieser einfachen Regel wie mit der Maxime: handle wie du sollst, die auch sehr einfach ist, und die Niemand befolgen kann.'
67. Groth (1858), 156 f.: The tenor of Groth's language is typical of later popular linguistic theorists. In keeping with the ideal view of 'Volk', he is anxious to present what is 'echt' and 'gesund'; Platt-Deutsch is said to lack some of the sicknesses which afflict the standard language. Such pathological imagery recurs much later in the Allgemeiner Deutscher Sprachverein, and in National Socialist writing on society and literature.
68. See Borchling (1916) and Teuchert (1961). The term *Missingsch* may originate in Mecklenburg, where it is attested from the early eighteenth century onwards; it probably derives from *Meißnisch*, so indicating the influence of the southern HG book language on Mecklenburg Platt. Popular association with *Messing* 'bronze' also takes place, since this metal is an alloy, i.e. a mixture.
69. See the many entries under 'Mundartdichtung' in Merker and Stammler (1958-84), vol. ii, 2nd edn. (1965), 442-538. Reuter did treat social injustice, unlike Groth, in his verse epic *Kein Hüsung* (1858), written 'mit meinem Herzblute im Interesse der leidenden Menschheit' (letter to Frl. Tiessen, 11 January 1865). In this Reuter was close to Charles Dickens, whom he admired and by whom he was influenced.
70. Hauptmann (1937), chap. 41, ed. Hass (1962), 1079.
71. Wenker did not live to edit the 44,251 questionnaires that were returned to him; his assistant Ferdinand Wrede (1865-1934) began publication in 1926. After the Second World War, the *Deutscher Sprachatlas* was continued under Walther Mitzka and Ludwig Erich Schmitt, and provisionally completed in 1956. Not surprisingly, the material on which it was based was no longer accurate, economic, cultural, and especially political changes having occurred in the intervening seventy years. Mitzka produced a preliminary *Deutscher Wortatlas*, recommenced in 1951, to illustrate the regional differences in vocabulary.
72. The fourth of the forty-odd 'Wenkersätze', 'Der gute alte Mann ist mit dem Pferde durch's Eis gebrochen und in das kalte Wasser gefallen', was designed to elicit information about the shifted consonants and the use of unstressed dative -e (*Pferde*), but also showed dialect differentiation in the words for 'horse'—*Roß, Pferd, Gaul, Hengst*—which in the standard language are stylistic variants (*Roß, Gaul*) or gender-determined (*Hengst*).
73. Socin (1888), 519.
74. Apparently there is evidence to show that factory-workers at Magdeburg had given up dialect in favour of a regional colloquial as early as 1830: see Schönfeld (1977); Schildt (1977).
75. In parts of Swabia the language of the educated and professional classes known as *Honoratiorenschwäbisch* occurs, a refined form based, perhaps, on the *Umgangssprache* of Stuttgart. But see Bynon (1970).
76. See Henzen (1954), 19 f.
77. No separate symbol is reserved for it, and the English section regards it as part of the 'common literary and conventional style'. Instead, F (= *familiär*) is equated with 'informal', e.g. *abmurksen* 'kill'; P (= *popular*), is equated with 'uneducated'; but quite vulgar expressions are graced with it (*Aas, ficken*); ⌐ (= *Gaunersprache*, 'gallows', 'criminal classes') is reserved for this specific group language, e.g. *dufte* 'fine', 'great'.
78. Sütterlin, (1897-9), 5th edn. (1923), 19-20.

79. For discussion, see Bichel (1973).
80. The Naturalists were the first to explore the possibilities of speech consistently, and Arno Holz (1863-1929) coined the term 'Sekundenstil' for his and Johannes Schlaf's (1862-1941) attempts to render conversations with phonographic fidelity. Their short narrative, *Papa Hamlet* (1889), abounds in dashes, exclamation marks, series of dots, inarticulate particles, and question marks. See the edition by Martini (1963), and also Hamann and Hermand (1972), 250-7. As early as 1894 the grammarian Herman Wunderlich (1858-1916) produced an excellent preliminary study of speech acts (Wunderlich (1894)), which treated the main differences between speech and writing ('Umgangsprache' (*sic*) is here understood as speech, and so covers dialect material too), ways of opening conversations, the compression and redundancy in speech, formulaic elements and their interchangeability, and patterns of word order. Unfortunately, this break with traditional grammar seems largely to have been neglected in its day.
81. By contrast, English regional varieties are less important in Britain than are 'class' varieties; see Brook (1979), 37 ff.
82. For 'group' and 'technical' languages (*Gruppensprachen, Sondersprachen,* and *Fachsprachen*) in our period, see below, pp. 374 ff.
83. Fig. 9 (from König (1978), 132, modified from Bausinger (1972), 35) illustrates the intermediate stylistic character of colloquial language in present-day Austria. The geographical area covered by dialects in the Innsbruck and Vienna regions is small in comparison with the much greater communicative range of the regional colloquials based on the language of these important urban centres. The standard language covers the whole country and overlies both dialects and colloquials. The higher up the social scale a speaker is situated, the closer his language to the standard, the wider his communicative powers. However, the diagram does not cope with social mobility upwards or downwards, nor does it take cognizance of the overlapping of dialects or of regional colloquials; an individual speaker may have all three levels (and their variants) available to him and these will, again, overlap.
84. See Eichhoff (1977-8), Maps 6 and 19, and introduction, pp. 10 ff.
85. See Kretschmer (1918). He regards the 'Umgangssprache' as primarily spoken, and as the 'Gemeinsprache der Gebildeten' with a band of variation from formal public speaking ('Öffentlichkeitssprache') through everyday communication ('Verkehrssprache') to familiar language ('familiäre Sprache'); slang and vulgarity are not considered, being relegated instead to the 'Halbmundart des Volkes' (10-11). Kretschmer, whose material dates from about 1910, provides no maps, but Eichhoff's (1977-8) can be consulted for modern conditions.
86. *Straßenbahn* is the official term, and is replacing *Trambahn* in Bavaria, to the annoyance of local patriots; see, for example, Bekh (1973), 21.
87. Schoolboy slang (*Pennälersprache*) and students' language have been studied, but otherwise it is only after 1945 that the language of young people has made considerable, if ephemeral, contributions to the speech-community, both directly and indirectly through commercial exploitation: teenagers' language, *Twensprache*, the language of 'hippies' or *Gammler*, of the drug-using alternative society (*Drogenszene* or *Szien*), and of *Punker, Popper*, or the *Diskothek*, to name a few of the most striking examples of youth culture. For the bewildering range of youth groups, see the article 'Die Neue Boheme. Jugend-Stil '82' in *Der Spiegel*, 1982/17, 234-49.
88. See Lasch (*c*.1928).
89. Lasch (*c*.1928), 70 ff. Berlin phonology is explicable on the basis of spoken EMG forms.
90. Lasch (*c*.1928), 120-2.

91. See Lasch (*c*.1928) and Meyer (1878/1965). Some examples are taken from Fontane's *Irrungen Wirrungen*.
92. See Büchmann (1864), 203. Rüthling's poem is entitled 'Mir und Mich'.
93. See also the purist Eduard Engel's book (Engel (1916)), 75 ff., 'Das Berlin-französisch'.
94. But a surprising number of workers read, or claimed to read, literary, scientific, and political books and pamphlets; see Basler (1914), esp. 247. Metal-workers seem to have been more enterprising than miners or textile workers on the figures given.
95. The term *Sondersprache* sometimes covers specialist registers as a whole, sometimes only group languages, as here. See Fluck (1980); Möhn (1980); Hahn (1980).
96. Spirited attempts were made to use *Flieger* for the vehicle itself, but *Flugzeug* was adopted after the '8. Deutscher Luftschiffertag', held in 1910, and *Flieger* was used for the agent noun; passengers were *Fluggäste*.
97. Relatively few technical military terms are borrowed into the colloquial, but one example shows progressive change in step with developments in the technical sphere: *Zündnadelschnauze* was a sobriquet applied to Prussian soldiers after 1866, characterizing them as quick-tongued; about 1870 the term *Mitrailleusen-schnauze* is applied to a 'freches, schamloses Maul'; while *Revolverschnauze* in Muret–Sanders (1891–1901) means having a 'ready jaw', for 1939–45 cf. also *MG-Schnauze* = 'unüberbietbare Redefertigkeit', Küpper (1970), 136.
98. See particularly Horn (1905); Loose (1947); Stern (1960); and Mechow (1971).
99. Some LG words may reflect the high reputation of the Prussian army, e.g. *stramm*, *schlapp*, *Kopp* (NHG *Kopf*: *Bumsköppe* 'artillery'), *Pott* 'helmet', etc. See Hübner (1919), esp. 83.
100. *Landser* 'private soldier' (from sixteenth-century *Landsknecht*?) remained in the Second World War; other nineteenth-century terms failed to survive the First World War: *Latschenpatscher*, *Furchen-/Kartoffelhopser*, *Dreckstampfer*, *Kilometerschwein*, *Backzahn*, *Kanonenfutter*, *Hurrahkanaille*, *Feldratten*, *Schaschke*, *Fußlappenindianer* (Austria), *Fußfantrakt* (Austria); see Horn (1899), 32. Horn lists some thirty compounds with *Kommiß* (from *in Kommission* 'military'); only *Kommißbrot* 'poor-quality (army) bread' and *Kommißanzug* 'fatigues', 'undress uniform' survive. In West Germany *beim Bund sein*, *zum Bund gehen* have replaced older expressions with *Kommiß*.
101. See Sagarra (1980), 163: in 1865 65 per cent of all officers had been noblemen; in cavalry regiments in 1913 some 80 per cent still were.
102. See *A Supplement to the Oxford English Dictionary* s.v.v. 'blitz', 'flak'.
103. Some expressions passed on are technical, at least in origin, others e.g. *sich verfranzen* ('lose one's way') are slang: the navigator/observer in an aircraft was nicknamed *Franz*.
104. Sperber (1923), 45 ff. quotes the following for machine-gun: *Stottertante*, *Steinklopfer*, *Dengelmaschine*, *Stotterkasten*, *Tak-tak(-tak)*, *Mähmaschine*, *Fleischhackmaschine*, *Durchfallkanone*, *alte Weibergosche*, *Drehorgel*, *Nähmaschine*, *Tippmamsell*, *Kaffeemühle*, *Fässlesklopfer*, *Dachdecker*, *Gaisbock*, *Kettenhund*, *Stotterbüchse*, *Schuster*, *sanfter Heinrich* (all from the First World War).
105. Originally = 'rubble', 'broken bricks'; cf. English *heap*.
106. *Stuka* (masc.) must come from *Sturzkampfflieger*, with agent noun transferred to the vehicle (cf. dive-bomber); cf. also *der Jabo* = *Jagdbomber*, but *die Wabo* = *Wasserbombe* 'depth-charge'.
107. See Hübner (1919), esp. 79–83.
108. See Küpper (1970), and, for the modern soldiers' language in the Federal Republic, Hauschild and Schuh (1981).

109. For functions and features of technical and scientific languages see Mackensen (1959). For relations between scientific and standard, see Pörksen (1977).
110. The Deutscher Normenausschuß, founded in 1917, established norms for terminology too; it was not a State body. The modern title is Deutsches Institut für Normung, abbreviated to DIN. See Ischreyt (1965).
111. The 1891 English–German vol. i does not list *Birne*, preferring *Glühlampe* (see s.v. *bulb*, p. 336), nor *gas mantle*; but the German–English vol. iii (1899), p. 903, gives *Birne* and *Glühstrumpf* under *Glüh-*. See also Ischreyt (1965), 238 ff.
112. Twain (1880), Appendix D, 545–6: *Zug* means 'Pull, Tug, Draught, Procession, March, Progress, Flight, Direction, Expedition, Train, Caravan, Passage, Stroke, Touch, Line, Flourish, Trait of Character, Feature, Lineament, Chess-move, Organ-stop, Team, Whiff, Bias, Drawer, Propensity, Inhalation, Disposition . . .'. And he might have added that, even if context and situation usually clarify the meaning in German itself, such polysemy creates problems for the German learning English.
113. For example, *Antrieb* 'goad', 'stimulus' and *Auftrieb* (1) 'buoyancy', (2) 'driving cattle up to summer pasture' were already in the language but have been overlaid by their new mechanical associations (*Antrieb* 'motor (force)', *Auftrieb* 'upthrust', etc.); and even when used figuratively, the technical meanings are probably foremost: *neuen Antrieb bekommen*, *die Wirtschaft erhielt einen Auftrieb*, etc. See also Pörksen (1978), who considers Goethe's *Die Wahlverwandtschaften*, Darwin's *On the Origin of Species*, and Freud's psycho-analytical writings in terms of this metaphorical interchange between technical terminology and everyday usage.
114. See esp. Moser (1974); Bauermeister (1960).

CHAPTER X

1. Fishman (1972), 216, talks of the 'societal function' of linguistic behaviour, and the abandoning of simplistic concepts like 'The X [German] language' in favour of the construct 'the repertoire of societally allocated varieties of X'. Gottsched in his dramatic theory (see Chapter VIII) was still working with a classical theory of three styles linked to social status. While class and status naturally attach to varieties of German, they are no longer the determining factors for most users (although they retain an attraction for would-be users).
2. See Frühwald (1973) and Dieckmann (1964), 22 ff. It should be noted that Austrian authors, for example Franz Grillparzer, and especially Hugo von Hofmannsthal, were also affected by the 'language crisis'.
3. This is not to imply that purism and National Socialism were causally linked: the National Socialist leaders were not sympathetic to the aims of the Allgemeiner Deutscher Sprachverein (see below).
4. Humboldt (1836), p. lxxiv.
5. See Ullmann (1962), 54 f.; Lyons (1968), 404 f. For the weaknesses of this semantic triangulation, especially from the thought angle, see Palmer (1976), 25 ff.; Lyons (1977), 95–9.
6. Stylistic and emotive factors ·will be disregarded in the sketch of sense-relationships presented here.
7. Translation errors, in particular those of partial bilingualism, can make one conscious of polysemy: 'Daddy, please take your pocket off the seat, I want to sit down.'
8. For this whole topic, see esp. Kirkness (1975).
9. See Dieckmann (1964), 138 ff.
10. Campe regrets not being able to think of a suitable replacement for *Electricität*,

electrisch, electrisieren, etc. (see Campe (1801), 324). Adelung added the word in the second edition of his dictionary, without, of course, wanting to replace it.

11. They mocked Campe as the 'furchtbare Waschfrau, / Welche die Sprache des Teut säubert mit Lauge und Sand', asking how to render *Pedant* in German: Campe lamely suggested *Schulfuchs,* or *Steifling* (Goethe and Schiller (1795-7), edd. von der Hellen *et al.* (1902), 164, 169). Schottel (1663), 1272, proposed *Strengling.*

12. See Leyser (1896), ii. 92 ff., a letter from Wieland (26 January 1801). Wieland rightly observes that time alone will tell which loans survive and which do not.

13. *Schmollzimmer* was originally proposed, but August von Kotzebue suggested *Schmollwinkel*; see Campe (1801), 196.

14. Kirkness (1975), 222 ff. and 228 ff. Individual words may yet derive from Wolke (*Fernsprecher* for *Telegraph, Volkheit* for *Nation*) and Krause (*Fremdwort?*), despite their otherwise impressive failure.

15. Sarrazin (1889), p. viii.

16. Words like *Hantel, Reck, Riege, Holm,* and of course *turnen* and derivatives. Jahn was also responsible for *Reichswehr* (= *Militär*), *Eilbrief* (= *Kurier*), and *Volkstum* (= *Nationalität*), and drew widely on provincial and dialectal forms; see Kirkness (1975), 196 ff. Jahn's wilder flights include *Hungerleidenschaft* (= *Familie*) (!), and the charming etymologies *Kater* from *kat + er* and *Katze* from *kat + sie.*

17. Arndt (1813*a*), 34.

18. Arndt (1813*b*), 148; see Kluckhohn (1934), 150-1. Kluckhohn, p. 223, sees Arndt and others as forerunners of National Socialism.

19. See Ganz (1957), Stiven (1936); and for the reaction Dunger (1909) (examples above are from pp. 46 ff.).

20. Engel (1911), 159.

21. In 1841, Friedrich Wilhelm IV had advocated replacing *Kapitän* by *Hauptmann.* For the 1899 Edict, see *ZADS* 14 (1899), No. 2.

22. See Kirkness (1975), 360 ff. A similar purism—somewhat more moderate in extent—is found in legal language from 1871 onwards.

23. Incidentally, for telephone use the form *zwo* (originally the fem.) of the numeral *zwei* was perhaps prescribed by Stephan, as more distinctive acoustically. See DWB, 16, col. 973: 'durch amtliche bestimmung im fernsprechwesen'.

24. See Leisi (1967), 54-5, who cites colloquial *Kino* vs. official *Lichtspielhaus,* and similarly *Photo* vs. *Lichtbild, Champagner/Sekt* vs. *Schaumwein, Telephon* vs. *Fernsprecher,* etc.

25. The official abbreviations *Pkw, Lkw* have not become colloquial either; the common terms are *Wagen/Auto* or *Laster.*

26. See the funeral elogy by Hermann Dunger, *ZADS* 16 (1901), Nos. 3-4.

27. *ZADS* 16 (1901), cols. 43-4, 273 ff., 327; ibid. 17 (1902), col. 88; ibid. 24 (1909), cols. 343-4. Other suggestions for automobile included *Kraftwagen, Selbstfahrer, Selbster, Schnauferl* (dialectal), *Krafter,* etc.; the form *Kraftfahrzeug* was probably officially established in 1909 in the 'Gesetz über den Verkehr mit Kraftfahrzeugen'.

28. All figures from *ZADS* for the relevant years (Nos. 7-8 and the 'Jahresbericht' in No. 9). Figures for Vienna must be seen also in relation to the branches at Graz, Innsbruck, Krems, Klagenfurt, Linz, which in 1910 totalled 488; there were in addition individual members.

29. See, for example, *ZADS* 16 (1901), No. 9, cols. 257-60; Austro-Hungarian customs tariffs are reformed, but not their language, whereas the German customs tariffs are purified, thanks to the Sprachverein's influence. Presumably neither Switzerland nor Austria-Hungary, as polyglot states, could afford to espouse German purism, for political reasons.

30. See *ZADS* 17 (1902), No. 5, cols. 129 ff., and ibid. 18 (1903), Nos. 7–8, col. 256.
31. The journal still exists. See further Bernsmeier (1977), (1980), (1983).
32. See Polenz (1967). Goebbels, indeed, declared that those with nothing better to do than seek about for German translations of common words like *Akkumulator* should be among the first sent to the front (speech in the Sportpalast, 18 February 1943).
33. Dieckmann (1969), 12.
34. For such analysis see Horst Grünert's study of the first German National Parliament, 1848–9 (Grünert (1974)).
35. Further justification of this restricted view rests in the fact that any activity of the individual or in society may become a political issue, so that 'political language' in its dynamic, rhetorical sense draws upon vocabulary and terminology from all walks of life as they become politically relevant.
36. Dieckmann (1964), 21 ff. Many of the revolutionary terms were originally historical or technical terms without political significance, and are drawn from spheres as distinct as astronomy (*Revolution*), medicine (*Régime*), natural science (*Organisation, organisieren*), chemistry/physics (*Koalition, Reaktion*), and the Catholic Church (*Propaganda*).
37. See Feldmann (1911–12).
38. See Wagner (1974); Römer (1962).
39. See Ladendorf (1906) and Meyer (1900). The first attestations of such key- and catchwords are, of course, less important and less ascertainable than the time at which they become current: again, the revolutions of 1830 and 1848 promote many political catchwords.
40. The term 'connotation' (also 'affective, emotive meaning' etc.) has a wide range of meanings; see Dieckmann (1979).
41. See Ullmann (1962), 131, who talks of 'perversions of meaning', citing C. S. Lewis, who called this 'verbicide'.
42. 'Wo ist die Oppositionspartei, die nicht von ihren regierenden Gegnern als kommunistisch verschrien worden wäre, wo die Oppositionspartei, die den fortgeschritteneren Oppositionsleuten sowohl wie ihren reaktionären Gegnern den brandmarkenden Vorwurf des Kommunismus nicht zurückgeschleudert hätte?' (Marx and Engels (1847–8), 19).
43. Mackensen (1971), 209 f.
44. Actually a loan from French *electriser*, attested since the 1730s in the sense of 'charge up', 'fill with enthusiasm'.
45. See Dieckmann (1964), 126 ff., 138 ff. Cf. the recent use of pej. *-ant: Querulant, Simulant, Sympathisant.*
46. Sternberger, Storz, and Süskind (1945), preface. The authors changed their views by the time of the second edition (1957).
47. Klemperer (1946), 3rd edn. (1969), 10.
48. Two main types of abbreviation occur: 'initial words' (e.g. *NSDAP* itself, pronounced as letters of the alphabet, [ɛnɛs'dea'pe]) and 'syllable words', where (usually initial) syllables are combined, as in *Persil = Perborat + Silikat.* Klemperer (1946), 3rd edn. (1969), 96, sees in abbreviated forms in National Socialist usage a tendency to dehumanize and mechanize; they can also be regarded as group symbols, relished by insiders.
49. Winckler (1970), 23.
50. Mann (1947), 10.
51. See Dieckmann (1969), 111.
52. See the documentation in Wulf (1964–6) and Zeman (1964). In 1933 the National Socialists controlled only 121 out of approximately 4,700 German newspapers (about 7.5 per cent); by late 1934 3,298 papers had been closed down, and the

National Socialists controlled 434 papers directly and the whole press indirectly. In 1944 they controlled 82 per cent of the 970 papers directly.
53. See Wulf (1964–6); Sündermann (1973).
54. Propaganda directives sometimes changed tack: the enemy troops are not to be underestimated; a directive of 13 September 1940 simultaneously permits English airmen to be called *Nachtpiraten* and forbids that they should be branded *feig* (Sündermann (1973), 47).
55. See Glunk (1966–71), *ZfdS* 23 (1967), 100–7, esp. 103. While the older meaning of *Propaganda* as 'advertising' was successfully ousted, the pejorative associations attaching to the word eventually predominated.
56. Hitler (1925–7), preface to vol. i of 1st edn.
57. Hitler (1925–7), 533–4; for the superiority of *Rede* over *Schrift* see also ibid. 116 and 525 ff.
58. See Schnauber (1972), esp. 49–53, 77 ff. (to be treated with caution). On pp. 8–10 Hitler's private secretary's account of how Hitler composed his speeches is discussed.
59. See Winckler (1970), 31 ff. Cf. Chaplin's brilliant parody (in gibberish) in *The Great Dictator*.
60. Klemperer (1946), 29.
61. Hitler (1925–7), 452.
62. Hitler (1925–7), 287.
63. Hitler (1925–7), 285.
64. Hitler (1925–7), 385.
65. A nineteenth-century distinction between 'community' and 'class society', drawn by Ferdinand Tönnies; see Sagarra (1977), 201.
66. Much in these sections is indebted to Berning (1964), and particularly to Berning (1960, 1961, 1962, 1963).
67. See especially Korn (1959).
68. Diary entry for 31 January 1942, ed. Lochner (1948), 67. The electrical imagery was appreciated by the population at large: a contemporary joke playing on Hitler's complicity in the Röhm-putsch affair runs as follows: 'Wer ist der größte Elektriker Europas?' 'Hitler. Er hat Deutschland gleichgeschaltet, Polen ausgeschaltet und Röhm geerdet!'
69. Religious language is often used in politics because religious ideology presents a systematic (although invariably simplified) view of social reality and the human condition, the National Socialists cannot be blamed for following this tradition. However, their use of religious terms seems particularly cynical and offensive, as when an old word for martyr, *Blutzeuge*, acquires eugenic associations. (*Blutzeuge* is attested since the seventeenth century (Gryphius); see *DWB* ii. 198.)
70. For these documents from the so-called *Kirchenkampf*, see Michaelis, Schraepler, and Scheel (c.1964), documents Nos. 2524, 2531, and 2524 respectively.
71. Cobet, (1973); see also Sagarra (1977), 304–23.
72. Chamberlain seems less virulently anti-Semitic than he is painted, but he misguidedly asserted the superiority of the Aryans: see Chamberlain (1903).
73. *Art* 'way', 'manner', 'kind' and *Erbe* 'inheritance', 'succession', 'estate' were already widely used, especially in compounds, and speakers easily assimilated the newer biological technical meanings—a process of polysemy (see p. 383).
74. Possibly the Hitler-Gruß and the swastika emblem derive from the followers of List. See esp. List (1912), 14: '"Heil und Sieg!" — Dieser vieltausendjährige urarische Gruß- und Kampfruf . . .' (the origin of *Sieg Heil!*?); and also p. 20, where the eighteenth 'rune' discussed is the *Fyrfos* or *Hakenkreuz*. For these obscure ideas, see the recent thesis by Goodrick-Clarke (1982), but note esp. 302 ff.

75. Hitler (1925-7), 395-6.
76. See especially Berning (1962). In modern German its appropriate form would have been *Udel*, from OHG *uodal*; cf. the name *Ulrich*.
77. Chamberlain (1903), 121, 267 ff.; Hitler (1925-7), 317.
78. See Glunk (1966-71), *ZfdS* 22 (1966), 59-62; Polenz (1967), 137-8.
79. See Berning (1962), 113 ff.; Wulf (1963).
80. Many critics of modern German style have been worried by what they see as the persistence of National Socialist language. Others have sought pointedly for links with the nineteenth century nationalist movements, which share the rhetoric but not the aims or methods of National Socialism. Attempts to prove 'unbewältigte Vergangenheit' in the Federal Republic or the GDR reflect the same continuity of linguistic development, which may be aesthetically displeasing, but is not necessarily 'malignant'.

APPENDIX A

1. Only an outline of the shift and its attendant problems can be attempted here. The most detailed recent studies are Lerchner (1971) and Simmler (1981).
2. Otto Höfler (1957) has claimed that the shift affects other Gmc. languages, notably EGmc., since personal names in Spain and Italy appear to show it. However, the largely onomastic evidence poses problems of textual criticism, and Romance scribal practice distorts it.
3. Spirants (or fricatives) are frictional consonants formed by constriction of the breath-flow at some point of articulation in the mouth or throat. Affricates are combinations of stops (where the air-flow is momentarily entirely blocked) and spirants formed at approximately the same point ('homorganic spirants'), e.g. $[p] + [f] \rightarrow pf$, $[t] + [s] \rightarrow ts$, $[k] + [\chi] \rightarrow k\chi$. Only voiceless sounds concern us here, namely the affricates, /pf/, /ts/ (written ⟨z⟩), and /kχ/ (written variously ⟨ch⟩, ⟨cch⟩ and the double (i.e. long) spirants /ff/, /zz/ (not always distinguished in OHG spelling from the affricate, and phonetically different from the voiceless /s/ phoneme with which it subsequently merged), and /χχ/ (written ⟨hh⟩ or ⟨ch⟩).
4. This presupposes that the opposition voiced ≠ voiceless remained important within the German consonantal system. Admittedly, this correlation of voice was quantitatively reduced in favour of oppositions based on the distinctions between stop vs. affricate vs. spirant.
5. For these 'exceptions' to the sound shift, compare OS *springan*, OHG *springan*; OE *stān*, OHG *stein*; OE *scīnan* 'shine', OHG *skīnan*; OE *cræft* 'craft', OHG *kraft*; OE *eahta* 'eight', OHG *ahto*; OE *trëdan* 'tread', OHG *trëtan*. In all these clusters no build-up of breath is possible before the release of the stops, hence no strong aspiration and no development to affricate.
6. The dialectal development of *pf* to *f* after consonant, as in *werpfan > werfan*, *helpfan > helfan*, which in these forms is widespread in the ninth century, may support this interpretation: Braune and Eggers (1975), § 131 n. 5.
7. For a more complex view, see Lerchner (1971), 142-6; those who argue for an independent Frk. sound shifting need to postulate that stops can develop directly into spirants without intermediate affricate stages, since affricates (and, indeed, aspiration) are rare in Frk. dialects.
8. These rules are taken from Bahnick (1973), 114, 116. (Bahnick does not discuss UG and thus does not include the shift to affricates in full, which is supplied under (A) in the following diagram.)
9. For emotive or expressive changes to consonants, see Henzen (1957), 20 f., § 7. In origin, the name *Attila* could be Hunnish, or else from another non-Gmc. language: Hungarian *atya*, Turkish *ata* also mean 'father'. See Hoops (1973).

10. Taken from Sonderegger (1979), 130.
11. Lerchner (1971), 270-3, combines horizontal and vertical axes: a Frk. warrior and administrative stratum overlaid the UG areas, but was itself influenced by their consonantism. This influence spread to members of the same caste in Franconia, and then filtered down in varying degree to the common folk of those regions.
12. Schützeichel (1976).
13. For the controversy see Kuhn (1976); Goossens (1978), (1979), (1980); Schützeichel (1979); Bergmann (1980), (1983).

APPENDIX B

1. 'Voiceless lenes', in this instance /b̦/, /d̦/, /g̦/, are voiceless stops with a weaker articulation than the fortes /p/, /t/, /k/, i.e. with less aspiration.
2. This lenition has not much affected standard modern German, although it is a factor in southern dialects. For a fuller treatment of these problems, see the literature in Paul (1881/1969), 91 ff.
3. Notker's 'law of initial consonantal alternation' affects only the reflexes of PGmc. /b/, /g̦/, and /b̦/, not those of PGmc. /ð/, which had become /d/ in pre-OHG and was then devoiced to give /t/ in UG (e.g. PGmc. *faðar > OHG vater).
4. Variant forms (Tánnân ~ dánnân; díu ~ tíu, etc.) are explained by Notker's Anlautgesetz).
5. Although not in Bav.-speaking territory, Augsburg and Wessobrunn have been credited with Bav. texts.
6. An alliterative poem on the Last Judgement, written down in the late ninth century, attributed to the court of Louis the German at Regensburg.
7. Post-1060, from St Emmeram.
8. The debate on the diphthongization continues: see Jones (1979).
9. Written down c.825-50, probably at Fulda. Accents supplied. Morphologically, the forms her beside er for the third pers. sg. masc. personal pronoun and the forms the, thie for the dem. pron./definite article are characteristic of this text.
10. Composed c.868-70 at Weissenburg (Wissembourg) in Alsace.
11. Rh.Frk. and SRh.Frk. differ from each other only minimally, notably in the (purely orthographical?) distinction Rh.Frk. ⟨uo⟩ vs. SRh.Frk. ⟨ua⟩, and in the distribution of p/pf and th/d.
12. There are sixteen OHG glosses in the manuscript, only some of which seem to be from the early eighth century. The spelling ⟨s⟩ for shifted t in gan:os: and hase, and the spelling ⟨d⟩ (= đ?) for usual MFrk. th (e.g. in bidarf, NHG bedarf), have been explained as OE orthographical influence—Echternach was founded in 698 by the Anglo-Saxon missionary Willibrord (d. 739). The same manuscript contains fourteen OE glosses, and OE must have been spoken there during Willibrord's time.

GENERAL BIBLIOGRAPHY

The entries in the General Bibliography are usually presented under the date of first publication, except that, in the case of certain regularly reissued handbooks and grammars, composite dates are given to indicate the actual edition used. In the references in the notes, and in the Select Bibliographies, composite dates for authors are also sometimes given: the first date indicates the original or main date of publication, the second marks the edition actually used.

The entries in the General Bibliography have been slightly simplified in that umlaut and short *s* generally replace superscript *e* and long *s* respectively (whereas quotations and titles in the text appear in older style where I have had access to original texts or facsimiles).

For further bibliography, see in particular:

(1) *Bibliographie der deutschen Literaturwissenschaft* (Vittorio Klostermann: Frankfurt-on-Main, 1945–) [in progress].

(2) *Germanistik. Internationales Referatenorgan mit bibliographischen Hinweisen* (Niemeyer: Tübingen, 1960–) [in progress] (appears quarterly).

ADELUNG, JOHANN CHRISTOPH (1774–86), *Versuch eines vollständigen grammatisch-kritischen Wörterbuches der Hochdeutschen Mundart mit beständiger Vergleichung der übrigen Mundarten, besonders aber der Oberdeutschen . . .*, i (A–E) (1774); ii (F–K) (1775); iii (L–Scha) (1777); iv (Sche–V) (1780); v (W–Z) (1786) (Breitkopf: Leipzig, 1774–86; 2nd edn., *Grammatisch-kritisches Wörterbuch der Hochdeutschen Mundart . . .*, i (1793); ii (1796); iii (1798); iv (1801), Breitkopf: Leipzig, 1793–1801; 3rd edn., with contributions by D. W. Soltau, rev. Franz Xaver Schönberger, four parts, Anton Pichler: Vienna, 1808, repr. B. Ph. Bauer: Vienna, 1811).

—— (1781*a*), *Deutsche Sprachlehre. Zum Gebrauche der Schulen in den Königlichen Preußischen Landen . . .* (Voß: Berlin, 1781).

—— (1781*b*), *Über die Geschichte der deutschen Sprache, über deutsche Mundarten und deutsche Sprachlehre* (J. G. Breitkopf: Leipzig, 1781).

—— (1782), *Umständliches Lehrgebäude der deutschen Sprache, zur Erläuterung der deutschen Sprachlehre für Schulen*, two vols. (Breitkopf: Leipzig, 1782).

—— (1782–4), *Magazin für die deutsche Sprache*, two vols. containing various 'Stücke' (Breitkopf: Leipzig, 1782–4) [details in Henne (1975), 139–40, bibliography, Nos. 55–6; facsimile: Olms; Hildesheim and New York, 1969]. Note especially:

(*a*) vol. i, 1. Stück (1782), 1, pp. 1–31, 'Was ist Hochdeutsch?'

(*b*) vol. i, 1. Stück (1782), 2, pp. 32–40, 'Von der Nieder-Hochdeutschen Mundart, und von Obersächsischen Sprachfehlern'.

(*c*) vol. i, 2. Stück (1782), 1, pp. 3–28, 'Beweis der fortschreitenden Cultur des menschlichen Geistes an der Vergleichung der ältern Sprachen mit den neuern'.

(*d*) vol. i, 2. Stück (1782), 3, pp. 44–60, 'Litteratur der Deutschen Mundarten'.

(*e*) vol. i, 3. Stück (1782), 4, pp. 45–57, 'Sind es die Schriftsteller, welche die Sprache bilden und ausbilden?'

(*f*) vol. i, 4. Stück (1783), 4, pp. 79–111, 'Über die Frage: was ist Hochdeutsch? Gegen den Deutschen Merkur'.

(*g*) vol. i, 4. Stück (1783), 5, pp. 112–26, 'Über die schöne Litteratur der Deutschen; auch gegen den Deutschen Merkur'.

(*h*) vol. ii, 4. Stück (1784), 4, pp. 138–63, 'Fernere Geschichte der Frage Was ist Hochdeutsch?'

—— (1783–96), *Neues grammatisch-kritisches Wörterbuch der englischen Sprache für die Deutschen; vornehmlich aus dem größern englischen Werke des Hrn. Samuel Johnson nach dessen vierten Ausgabe gezogen, und mit vielen Wörtern, Bedeutungen und Beyspielen vermehrt* . . . (first part (A–J), Schwickert: Leipzig, 1783; second part (K–Z), 1796).

—— (1785–9), *Geschichte der menschlichen Narrheit oder Lebensbeschreibungen berühmter Schwarzkünstler, Goldmacher, Teufelsbanner, Zeichen- und Liniendeuter, Schwärmer, Wahrsager, und anderer philosophischer Unholden*, seven vols. (Weygand: Leipzig, 1785–9) [issued anonymously].

—— (1787), *Über den deutschen Styl* (1785, 2nd rev. edn., Bey Ch. Fr. Voß & Sohn: Berlin, 1787).

—— (1788), *Vollständige Anweisung zur Deutschen Orthographie, nebst einem kleinen Wörterbuche für die Aussprache, Orthographie, Biegung und Ableitung* . . ., two parts (Weygand: Leipzig, 1788).

—— (1806–17), *Mithridates oder allgemeine Sprachenkunde mit dem Vater Unser als Sprachprobe in bey nahe fünfhundert Sprachen und Mundarten* (first part, Voß: Berlin, 1806; second part by Adelung and J. S. Vater, 1809; third and fourth parts, 1812–17).

ADMONI, VLADIMIR G. (1979), *Zur Ausbildung der Norm der deutschen Literatursprache im Bereich des neuhochdeutschen Satzgefüges (1470– 1730)* (Akademie-Verlag: Berlin, 1980) [= Bausteine zur Sprachgeschichte des Neuhochdeutschen, ed. G. Feudel, 56/4].

Adolf Hitler spricht. Ein Lexikon des Nationalsozialismus (Leipzig, 1934).

AITCHISON, JEAN (1981), *Language Change: Progress or Decay?* (Fontana: Bungay, Suffolk, 1981).

ALBERTUS, LAURENTIUS (OSTROFRANCUS) (1573). *Teutsch Grammatick oder Sprach-Kunst.| CERTISSIMA RATIO| discendae| augendae| ornandae| propagandae| conservandaeq(ue) linguae Alemanorum| sive Germanorum| GRAMMATICIS REGULIS ET exempla comprehensa & conscripta* . . . (Manger: Augsburg, 1573); ed. Carl Müller-Fraureuth, *Die deutsche Grammatik des Laurentius Albertus* (Trübner: Strasburg, 1895) [= Ältere deutsche Grammatiken in Neudrucken, ed. John Meier, 3].

ALBRECHT, OTTO (1929), 'Luthers Mitwirken bei der Druckkorrektur', in *Deutsche Bibel*, WA 6 (1929), 86–9.

Allgemeine Deutsche Biographie (1875–1912) (Verlag von Duncker und Humblot: Leipzig, 1875–1912).

ALTHAUS, HANS PETER (1980), 'Orthographie/Orthophonie', in *LGL* (1980), 787–92.

An die Versammlung gemeiner Bauernschaft (1525); edd. Siegfried Hoyer and Bernd Rüdiger, *An die Versammlung gemeiner Bauernschaft. Eine revolutionäre Flugschrift aus dem Deutschen Bauernkrieg (1525)*, with introduction by Mirra M. Guchmann (VEB Bibliographisches Institut: Leipzig, 1975).

ANTESPERG, JOHANN BALTHASAR VON (1747), *Die Kayserliche Deutsche Grammatik* (Vienna, 1747; repr. 1749).

ANTONSEN, ELMER H. (1964), 'Zum Umlaut im Deutschen', *PBB* (T) 86 (1964), 177–96.

—— (1965), 'On Defining Stages in Prehistoric Germanic', *Language*, 41 (1965), 19–36.

—— (1972), 'The Proto-Germanic Syllabics [= Vowels]', in Van Coetsem and Kufner (1972), 117–40.

ARENS, HANS (1974), *Sprachwissenschaft. Der Gang ihrer Entwicklung von der Antike bis zur Gegenwart* (Fischer Athenäum Taschenbücher, 2077; Frankfurt-on-Main, 1974; repr. 1979).

ARNDT, ERNST MORITZ (1813*a*), *Über Volkshaß und über den Gebrauch einer fremden Sprache (sine loco*, 1813).

—— (1813*b*), *Der Rhein, Deutschlands Strom aber nicht Deutschlands Grenze* (Rein: Leipzig, 1813); in *Ernst Moritz Arndts ausgewählte Werke in sechzehn Bänden*, edd. Heinrich Meisner and Robert Geerds, xiii. *Kleine Schriften*, Part I (Max Hesse's Verlag: Leipzig, n.d. [after 1904]), 145–97.

ARNDT, ERWIN (1962), *Luthers deutsches Sprachschaffen* (Akademie-Verlag: Berlin, 1962).

—— and BRANDT, GISELA (1983), *Luther und die deutsche Sprache. Wie redet der Deudsche man jnn solchem Fall?* (VEB, Bibliographisches Institut: Leipzig, 1983).

ARTMANN, HANS CARL (1958), *Med ana schwoazzn dintn. gedichta r aus bradnse* (Otto Müller Verlag: Salzburg, 1958).

ASHER, JOHN A. (1962), ed. Rudolf von Ems (*c.*1220) [q.v.].

—— (1967), *A Short Descriptive Grammar of Middle High German, with Texts and Vocabulary* (Oxford University Press: Auckland, 1967; repr. 1968).

AUGST, GERHARD (1975), 'Wie stark sind die starken Verben? Überlegungen zur Subklassifizierung der neuhochdeutschen Verben', in *Untersuchungen zum Morpheminventar der deutschen Gegenwartssprache* (Tübingen, 1975), 231–81 [= IDS 25].

BACH, ADOLF (1950), *Deutsche Mundartforschung*, 2nd edn. (Carl Winter: Heidelberg, 1950) [= Germanische Bibliothek, R 3].

—— (1952–6), *Deutsche Namenkunde*, five parts, 2nd edn. (Carl Winter: Heidelberg, 1952–6) [= Grundriß der germanischen Philologie, 18; vol. i/1 and 2 = *Die deutschen Personennamen*].

—— (1965, 1970), *Geschichte der deutschen Sprache*, 8th edn. (1965; 9th edn., Quelle & Meyer: Heidelberg, 1970).

BACH, HEINRICH (1934), *Laut- und Formenlehre der Sprache Luthers* (Levin & Munksgaard: Copenhagen, 1934).

—— (1937–43), *Die thüringisch-sächsische Kanzleisprache bis 1325*, two vols. (Levin & Munksgaard/Ejnar Munksgaard: Copenhagen, 1937, 1943).

BACH, HEINRICH (1974), *Handbuch der Luthersprache. Laut- und formenlehre in Luthers Wittenberger drucken bis 1545*, Part I, *Vokalismus* (Gad: Copenhagen, 1974).

BAESECKE, GEORG (1921-52), *Kleinere Schriften zur althochdeutschen Sprache und Literatur*, ed. Werner Schröder (Francke Verlag: Berne and Munich, 1966).

—— (1935), 'Die deutschen worte der germanischen gesetze', *PBB* 59 (1935), 1-101.

BAHDER, KARL VON (1890), *Grundlagen des neuhochdeutschen Lautsystems. Beiträge zur Geschichte der deutschen Schriftsprache im 15. und 16. Jahrhundert* (Trübner: Strasburg, 1890).

—— (1925), *Zur Wortwahl in der frühneuhochdeutschen Schriftsprache* (Carl Winter: Heidelberg, 1925) [= Germanische Bibliothek, 19].

BAHNICK, KAREN R. (1973), *The Determination of Stages in the Historical Development of the Germanic Languages by Morphological Criteria: An Evaluation* (Mouton: The Hague, 1973) [= Janua Linguarum, ser. pract. 139].

BARBARIĆ, STJEPAN (1981), *Zur grammatischen Terminologie von Justus Georg Schottelius und Kaspar Stieler, mit Ausblick auf die Ergebnisse bei ihren Vorgängern*, two vols. (Peter Lang: Berne, Frankfurt-on-Main, and Las Vegas, 1981) [= Europäische Hochschulschriften, Reihe 1: Deutsche Sprache und Literatur, 396].

BARBER, CHARLES CLYDE (1951), *An Old High German Reader. With Notes, List of Proper Names, and Vocabulary* (Blackwell: Oxford, 1951).

BARNER, WILFRIED (1975), ed. *Der literarische Barockbegriff* (WBG: Darmstadt, 1975) [= Wege der Forschung, 358].

BARON, DENIS E. (1974), *Case Grammar and Diachronic English Syntax* (Mouton: The Hague, 1974).

BARTHOLMES, HERBERT (1970), *Bruder, Freund, Genosse und andere Wörter der sozialistischen Terminologie* (Peter Hammer: Wuppertal, 1970).

BARTSCH, KARL (1864), ed. *Deutsche Liederdichter des zwölften bis vierzehnten Jahrhunderts* (1864; 4th edn. 1900; repr. Behr/Feddersen: Berlin, 1928).

BASLER, OTTO (1914), 'Die Sprache des modernen Arbeiters', *ZfdW* 15 (1914), 246-70.

BAUDUSCH-WALKER, RENATE (1958), *Klopstock als Sprachwissenschaftler und Orthographiereformer* (Akademie-Verlag: Berlin, 1958) [= DAdWB, VdSK 2].

BAUERMEISTER, OTTO (1960), 'Die Ausbreitung technisch-wissenschaftlicher Fachwörter in der Gemeinsprache', *Muttersprache*, 70 (1960), 169-76, 217-25.

BAUSINGER, HERMANN (1972), *Deutsch für Deutsche. Dialekte, Sprachbarrieren, Sondersprachen* (Fischer Taschenbuch 6145; Fischer Verlag: Munich, 1972).

BECH, GUNNAR (1951), *Grundzüge der semantischen Entwicklungsgeschichte der hochdeutschen Modalverba* (Copenhagen, 1951) [= Det Kongelige Danske Videnskabernes Selskab, Historisk-filologiske Meddelelser, 32/6].

BECHSTEIN, REINHOLD (1862), ed. *Der Vnartig Teutscher Sprachverderber* [q.v.].

BECHTEL, HEINRICH (1951), *Wirtschaftsgeschichte Deutschlands von der Vorzeit bis zum Ende des Mittelalters* (1st edn., Vittorio Klostermann: Frankfurt-on-Main, 1941; 2nd edn., Georg D. W. Callwey: Munich, 1951).

BECKER, GERTRAUD (1964), *Geist und Seele im Altsächsischen und im Althochdeutschen* (Carl Winter: Heidelberg, 1964).

BECKER, HENRIK (1944), *Deutsche Sprachkunde*, ii. *Sprachgeschichte* (Philipp Reclam jun.: Leipzig, 1944).

BECKER, HORST (1939–40), *Sächsische Mundartenkunde. Entstehungsgeschichte und Lautstand der Mundarten Sachsens und Nordböhmens* (Dresden, n.d. [1939–40]; new edn. by G. Bergmann, 1969).

BEHAGHEL, OTTO (1923–32), *Deutsche Syntax. Eine geschichtliche Darstellung*, four vols. (Carl Winter: Heidelberg, 1923–32).

—— (1968), *Die deutsche Sprache*, 14th edn. (VEB Max Niemeyer: Halle a/S., 1968).

BEKH, WOLFGANG JOHANNES (1973), *Richtiges Bayerisch. Ein Handbuch der bayerischen Hochsprache. Eine Streitschrift gegen Sprachverderber* (Bruckmann: Munich, 1973) [with a preface by Franz-Josef Strauß].

BENDER, WOLFGANG (1966), ed. Breitinger (1740) [q.v.].

—— (1973), *Johann Jacob Bodmer und Johann Jacob Breitinger* (Sammlung Metzler, M 113; Metzler: Stuttgart, 1973).

BENECKE, GEORG FRIEDRICH, MÜLLER, WILHELM, and ZARNCKE, FRIEDRICH (1854–61), *Mittelhochdeutsches Wörterbuch. Mit Benutzung des Nachlasses von Georg Friedrich Benecke, ausgearbeitet von Wilhelm Müller und Friedrich Zarncke*, three vols. in four parts (S. Hirzel: Leipzig 1854–61; repr. Hildesheim, 1963) [= BMZ].

BERGER, ARNOLD (1943), 'Luther und die neuhochdeutsche Schriftsprache', in F. Maurer and F. Stroh (edd.), *Deutsche Wortgeschichte*, ii (de Gruyter: Berlin, 1943), 37–132 [= 1st edn.; replaced in 3rd edn. by Erben (1974), q.v.].

BERGMANN, ROLF (1966), *Mittelfränkische Glossen. Studien zu ihrer Ermittlung und sprachgeographischen Einordnung* (Ludwig Röhrscheid: Bonn, 1966; 2nd edn. 1977). [= *Rh. Archiv*, 61].

—— (1966–7), 'Zur Stellung der Rheinlande in der althochdeutschen Literatur aufgrund mittelfränkischer Glossen', *Rheinische Vierteljahrsblätter*, 31 (1966–7), 307–21.

—— (1973), *Verzeichnis der althochdeutschen und altsächsischen Glossenhandschriften* (de Gruyter: Berlin and New York, 1973) [= Arbeiten zur Frühmittelalterforschung. Schriftenreihe des Instituts für Frühmittelalterforschung der Universität Münster, 6].

—— (1980), 'Methodische Probleme der Lautverschiebungsdiskussion', *Sprachwissenschaft*, 5 (1980), 1–14.

—— (1983), 'Froumund von Tegernsee und die Sprachgeschichte in Köln. Zur Diskussion der 2. Lautverschiebung', *ZDL* 50 (1983), 1–21.

—— and PAULY, PETER (1973), *Alt- und Mittelhochdeutsch. Arbeitsbuch zum linguistischen Unterricht* (Vandenhoeck & Ruprecht: Göttingen, 1973).

BERGMANN, ROLF and PAULY, PETER (1975), *Neuhochdeutsch. Arbeitsbuch zum linguistischen Unterricht* (Vandenhoeck & Ruprecht: Göttingen, 1971; 2nd edn. 1975; 3rd edn. 1983).

BERNING, CORNELIA (1960, 1961, 1962, 1963), 'Die Sprache des Nationalsozialismus', *ZfdW* 16 (1960), 71–118, 178–88; ibid. 17 (1961), 83–121, 171–82; ibid. 18 (1962), 108–18, 160–72; ibid. 19 (1963), 92–112.

—— (1964), *Vom 'Abstammungsnachweis' bis zum 'Zuchtwart'. Vokabular des Nationalsozialismus* (de Gruyter: Berlin, 1964).

BERNSMEIER, HELMUT (1977), 'Der Allgemeine Deutsche Sprachverein in seiner Gründungsphase', *Muttersprache*, 87 (1977), 369–95.

—— (1980), 'Der Allgemeine Deutsche Sprachverein in der Zeit von 1912 bis 1932', *Muttersprache*, 90 (1980), 117–40.

—— (1983), 'Der Deutsche Sprachverein im "Dritten Reich"', *Muttersprache*, 93 (1983), 31–58.

BERNSTEIN, ECKHARD (1978), *Die Literatur des deutschen Frühhumanismus*, (Sammlung Metzler M 168; Metzler: Stuttgart, 1978).

BERNT, ALOIS (1917), ed. Johannes von Tepl (*c.*1400) [q.v.].

BERTAU, KARL (1972–3), *Deutsche Literatur im europäischen Mittelalter*, two vols. (C. H. Beck: Munich, 1972, 1973) [vol. i: 800–1197; vol. ii: 1195–1220].

BESCH, WERNER (1965), 'Das Villinger Spitalurbar von 1379 f. als sprachliches Zeugnis', in Friedrich Maurer (ed.), *Vorarbeiten und Studien zur Vertiefung der südwestdeutschen Sprachgeschichte* (Eberhard Albert Verlag: Freiburg im Breisgau, 1965), 260–88.

—— (1967), *Sprachlandschaften und Sprachausgleich im 15. Jahrhundert* (Francke Verlag: Munich, 1967) [= Bibliotheca Germanica, 11].

—— (1973), 'Frühneuhochdeutsch', *LGL* (1973), 421–30 (2nd edn. (1980), 588–97).

BETZ, WERNER (1974), 'Lehnwörter und Lehnprägungen im Vor- und Frühdeutschen', in Maurer and Rupp (1974), i. 135–63 [diagram on p. 137].

BICHEL, ULF (1973), *Problem und Begriff der Umgangssprache in der germanistischen Forschung* (Niemeyer: Tübingen, 1973) [= Hermaea, NF 32].

—— (1974), 'Über Urfassung und Spätfassung der plattdeutschen Idyllen von Johann Heinrich Voß und deren Bedeutung für die Mundartliteratur', in *Klaus Groth Gesellschaft. Jahresgabe 1973–4* (1974), 84–97.

BIRKE, JOACHIM, and BIRKE, BRIGITTE (1968–), edd. Johann Christoph Gottsched, *Ausgewählte Werke*, twelve vols. (de Gruyter: Berlin and New York) [= Ausgaben Deutscher Literatur des XV. bis XVIII. Jahrhunderts, edd. Hans-Gert Roloff and Käthe Kahlenberg; see the entries under Gottsched (1730, 1742, 1751), (1748, 1762)].

BIRLO, HANS (1908), *Die Sprache des Parnassus Boicus* (Diss. Munich; K. B. Hof buchdruckerei Gebrüder Reichel: Augsburg, n.d. [1908]).

BISCHOFF, BERNHARD (1971), 'Paläographische Fragen deutscher Denkmäler in der Karolingerzeit', *FMSt* 5 (1971), 101–34.

—— (1979a), *Paläographie des römischen Altertums und des abendländischen Mittelalters* (Erich Schmidt Verlag: Berlin, 1979).

—— (1979b), 'Die Schriftheimat der Münchener Heliand-Handschrift', *PBB* (T) 101 (1979), 161–70.

—— (1979*c*), 'Die Straubinger Fragmente einer Heliand-Handschrift' *PBB* (T) 101 (1979), 171-80 [an edition of the manuscript].

BISCHOFF, KARL (1957), ed. Luther (1530) [q.v.].

BLACKALL, ERIC A. (1955), 'The Observations of Father Dornblüth', *MLR* 50 (1955), 450-63.

—— (1978), *The Emergence of German as a Literary Language 1700-1775* (Cambridge University Press, 1959; 2nd edn. [with a new bibliographical essay], Cornell University Press: Ithaca and London, 1978).

BLATZ, FRIEDRICH (1895-6), *Neuhochdeutsche Grammatik mit Berücksichtigung der historischen Entwickelung der deutschen Sprache* (1880; 3rd edn., two vols., J. Lang: Karlsruhe, 1895-6).

BLOOMFIELD, LEONARD (1933), *Language* (Holt, Rinehart, & Winston: New York, 1933).

BLUHM, HEINZ (1965), *Martin Luther, Creative Translator* (Concordia Publishing House: St Louis, 1965).

BLUME, HERBERT (1967), *Die Morphologie von Zesens Wortneubildungen* (Diss. Gießen, 1967).

—— (1972), 'Zur Beurteilung von Zesens Wortneubildungen', in F. van Ingen (ed.), *Philipp von Zesen, 1619-1969. Beiträge zu seinem Leben und Werk* (Wiesbaden, 1972), 253-73.

—— (1973), 'Deutsche Literatursprache des Barock', in *LGL* (1973), 523-30 (2nd edn. (1980), 719-25).

—— (1978*a*), 'Sprachgesellschaften und Sprache', in *Sprachgesellschaften, Sozietäten, Dichtergruppen* (Hamburg, 1978), 39-52 [= Wolfenbütteler Arbeiten zur Barockforschung, 7 (1977)].

—— (1978*b*), 'Sprachtheorie und Sprachenlegitimation im 17. Jahrhundert in Schweden und in Kontinentaleuropa', *Arkiv för Nordisk Filologi*, 93 (1978), 205-18.

BOBERTAG, FELIX (1883), ed. Moscherosch (1643), (1646) [qq.v.].

BÖDIKER, JOHANN (1690, 1746), *Grundsätze der deutschen Sprache*, rev. by Johann Leonhard Frisch and again by Johann Jacob Wippel (Nicolai: Berlin, 1746) [repr. Zentralantiquariat der DDR: Leipzig, 1977].

BODMER, JOHANN JACOB (n.d.), 'Persönliche Anekdoten'; ed. Theodor Vetter, *Zürcher Taschenbuch* (1892).

—— and BREITINGER, JOHANN JACOB (1721-3), *Discourse der Mahlern* (Bodmersche Druckerey: Zurich, 1721-3).

—— and —— (1746), *Der Mahler der Sitten* (Orell: Zurich, 1746).

BOLLI, ERNST (1975), *Die verbale Klammer bei Notker. Untersuchungen zur Wortstellung in der Boethius-Übersetzung* (de Gruyter: Berlin and New York, 1975).

BOLTZ, VALENTIN (1540), *Publij Terentij Aphri sechs verteutschte Comedien ausz eygen angeborner Lateinischen spraach auffs trewlichst transferiert . . .* (Tübingen, 1540).

BORCHLING, CONRAD (1916), 'Sprachcharakter und literarische Verwendung des sogenannten Missingsch', *Wissenschaftliche Beihefte des Allgemeinen Deutschen Sprachvereins*, 37 (1916), 193-222.

BORK, SIEGFRIED (1970), *Mißbrauch der Sprache. Tendenzen nationalsozialistischer Sprachregelung* (Francke: Berne and Munich, 1970).

BOSL, KARL (1966), *Die Gesellschaft in der Geschichte des Mittelalters* (1966; 3rd edn., Vandenhoeck & Ruprecht: Göttingen, 1975).

—— and WEIS, EBERHARD (1976), *Die Gesellschaft in Deutschland,* i (Lurz: Munich, 1976).

BOSTOCK, J. KNIGHT, KING, KENNETH C., and McLINTOCK, DAVID ROBERT (1976), *A Handbook on Old High German Literature* (Clarendon Press: Oxford, 1976 [first edn. 1954]).

BRAAK, IVO, and MEHLEM, RICHARD (1961), edd. Groth (1858), (*c.*1877) [qq.v.].

BRANDT, WOLFGANG (1971), 'Mittelhochdeutsche Literatur: Epik', in Schmitt (1971), 384–463.

BRAUN, PETER (1979), *Tendenzen in der deutschen Gegenwartssprache* (Urban Taschenbuch 297; Kohlhammer: Stuttgart, Berlin, Cologne, and Mainz, 1979).

BRAUNE, WILHELM (1874–5/1979), *Althochdeutsches Lesebuch* (1874–5; rev. Karl Helm; 16th edn. rev. Ernst A. Ebbinghaus, Niemeyer: Tübingen, 1979).

—— (1878), ed. Weise (1672) [q.v.].

—— (1886/1975), *Althochdeutsche Grammatik* (1886; 13th edn. rev. Hans Eggers, Niemeyer: Tübingen, 1975).

—— (1891/1977), *Abriß der althochdeutschen Grammatik. Mit Berücksichtigung des Altsächsischen* (1891; 14th edn. by Ernst A. Ebbinghaus, Niemeyer: Tübingen, 1977).

—— (1905), *Über die Einigung der deutschen Aussprache* (Halle, 1905).

—— (1919), 'Althochdeutsch und Angelsächsisch', *PBB* 43 (1919), 361–445.

—— (1966), ed. Opitz (1624) [q.v.].

—— and EBBINGHAUS (1977). See Braune (1891/1977).

—— and —— (1979). See Braune (1874–5/1979).

—— and EGGERS (1975). See Braune (1886/1975).

BREITINGER, JOHANN JACOB (1740), *Critische Dichtkunst,* 2nd edn. (Orell & Co.: Zurich, 1740); ed. Wolfgang Bender (Metzler: Stuttgart, 1966).

BREUNLE, MORITZ (1529), *Ein kurtz Formular vnnd Cantzleybüchlin/ darynn begriffen wirdt/ wie man einem yeglichen/ wz Standts/ wirde/ eheren vñ wesen er ist/ schreyben soll . . .* (Stainer: Augsburg, 1529).

BRINKMANN, HENNIG (1931), *Sprachwandel und Sprachbewegungen in althochdeutscher Zeit* (Frommann/W. Biedermann: Jena, 1931).

BROOK, GEORGE LESLIE (1979), *Varieties of English* (1973; 2nd edn., Macmillan: London and Basingstoke, 1979).

BROOKE, KENNETH (1955), *An Introduction to Early New High German* (Blackwell: Oxford, 1955).

BRUNT, RICHARD J. (1978, 1983), 'The Influence of the French Language on the German Vocabulary (1649–1735)' (Diss. Oxford 1978; published by de Gruyter: Berlin and New York, 1983) [= Studia Linguistica Germanica, 18].

BÜCHMANN, GEORG (1864), *Geflügelte Worte. Der Zitatenschatz des deutschen Volkes* (Berlin, 1864; often repr.) [cited from the Atlas-Verlag edn., Cologne, n.d.].

BUIJSSEN, GERARD H. (1966), *Durandus' Rationale in spätmittelhochdeutscher Übersetzung* (Van Gorcum/Prakke: Assen, 1966).

BUMKE, JOACHIM (1976), *Ministerialität und Ritterdichtung. Umrisse der Forschung* (C. H. Beck: Munich, 1976).

—— (1977), *Studien zum Ritterbegriff im 12. und 13. Jahrhundert* (1964; 2nd edn. with supplement [*Zum Stand der Ritterforschung* (1976)], Carl Winter: Heidelberg, 1977).

BURDACH, KONRAD (1884), 'Die Einigung der neuhochdeutschen Schriftsprache. Einleitung: Das sechzehnte Jahrhundert'; repr. in *Vorspiel. Gesammelte Schriften zur Geschichte des deutschen Geistes*, i/2 (Niemeyer: Halle a/S., 1925), 1–33 [first printed as a Halle Habilitationsschrift (J. B. Hirschfeld: Leipzig, 1884)].

—— (1893), 'Vom Mittelalter zur Reformation. Forschungen zur Geschichte der deutschen Bildung'; repr. ibid. 127–40 [first printed as the preface to vol. i of Burdach *et al.* (1893–1934)].

—— (1886/1914), 'Über deutsche Erziehung', with addition 'Nebst einem Nachwort und Ausblick'; repr. ibid. i/1. *Mittelalter* (Niemeyer: Halle a/S., 1925), 20–45 [first printed in *Anzeiger für deutsches Altertum*, 12 (1886), 156–63; repr. with the addition in *Zeitschrift für den deutschen Unterricht*, 28 (1914), 657–78].

—— (1920), 'Bericht über die Forschungen zur neuhochdeutschen Sprach- und Bildungsgeschichte'; repr. ibid. i/2. 203–22 [first printed in *Sitzungsberichte der Berliner Akademie der Wissenschaften* (1920), 71–86].

—— *et al.* (1893–1934), *Vom Mittelalter zur Reformation. Forschungen zur Geschichte der deutschen Bildung* [*VMzR*].

BURGER, HARALD (1980), 'Deutsche Literatursprache des Mittelalters', in *LGL*, 2nd edn. (1980), 707–12.

BYNON, THEODORA (1970), 'Swabian Umgangssprache', *TPS 1970* (1971), 25–61.

—— (1977), *Historical Linguistics* (Cambridge University Press, 1977; repr. 1979).

CAMPBELL, ALISTAIR (1959/1974), *Old English Grammar* (Clarendon Press: Oxford, 1959; corr. repr. 1974).

CAMPE, JOACHIM HEINRICH (1801), *Wörterbuch zur Erklärung und Verdeutschung der unserer Sprache aufgedrungenen fremden Ausdrücke. Ein Ergänzungsband zu Adelungs Wörterbuche* (In der Schulbuchhandlung: Brunswick, 1801).

—— and BERND, THEODOR (1807–11), *Wörterbuch der Deutschen Sprache* (In der Schulbuchhandlung: Brunswick, 1807–11).

CATHOLY, ECKEHARD (1966), *Fastnachtspiel* (Sammlung Metzler, M 56; Metzler: Stuttgart, 1966)

CHAMBERLAIN, HOUSTON STEWART (1903), *Die Grundlagen des neunzehnten Jahrhunderts* (1898), 4th edn. (F. Bruckmann: Munich, 1903).

CHAMBERS, WILLIAM WALKER, and WILKIE, JOHN (1970), *A Short History of the German Language* (Methuen: London, 1970).

CHERUBIM, DIETER (1980), 'Grammatikographie', in *LGL*, 2nd edn. (1980) 768–78.

CHERUBIM, DIETER and OBJARTEL, GEORG (1981), 'Historische Sprachwissenschaft', *Studium Linguistik*, 10 (1981), 1-19.

CHOLEVIUS, CARL LEO (1866), *Die bedeutendsten deutschen Romane des siebzehnten Jahrhunderts. Ein Beitrag zur Geschichte der deutschen Literatur* (B. G. Teubner: Leipzig, 1866).

CHOMSKY, NOAM (1957), *Syntactic Structures* (Mouton: The Hague, 1957).

—— (1964), *Current Issues in Linguistic Theory* (Mouton: The Hague, 1964; repr. 1967).

—— (1965), *Aspects of the Theory of Syntax* (MIT: Cambridge, Mass. 1965).

CHORLEY, JULIE A. (1984), 'J. C. A. Heyse (1764-1829) and K. W. L. Heyse (1797-1855) and German School Grammar in the First Half of the Nineteenth Century' (M.Litt. thesis, Oxford, 1984).

CHRISTIANSEN, HEINZ C. (1975), *Fritz Reuter* (Sammlung Metzler, M 134; Metzler: Stuttgart, 1975).

CIPOLLA, CARLO M. (1972-4), ed. *The Fontana Economic History of Europe*, i. *The Middle Ages* (Collins/Fontana Books: London, 1972); ii. *The Sixteenth and Seventeenth Centuries* (1974).

CLAES, FRANZ (1977), *Bibliographisches Verzeichnis der deutschen Vokabulare und Wörterbücher (gedruckt) bis 1600* (Olms: Hildesheim and New York, 1977).

CLAJUS, JOHANNES (1578), *Grammatica GERMANICAE LINGVAE M. Johannis Claij Hirtzbergensis: EX BIBLIIS LVTHERI GERMANICIS ET ALIIS EIVS LIBRIS COLLECTA* (Rhamba: Leipzig, 1578; often reprinted); ed. Friedrich Weidling, *Ältere deutsche Grammatiken in Neudrucken*, ed. John Meier, ii (Trübner: Strasburg, 1894) [Note the title of the 5th edn., *Grammatica GERMANICAE LINGVAE EX OPTIMIS quibusque Autoribus collecta . . .* (Grosius: Leipzig, 1610)].

COBET, CHRISTOPH (1973), *Der Wortschatz des Antisemitismus in der Bismarckzeit* (W. Fink: Munich, 1973) [= Münchener Germanistische Beiträge, 11].

COCHLAEUS, JOHANNES (1533), *An expediat laicis/ legere novi Testamenti libros lingua vernacula . . . (sine loco*, 1533).

COLETSOS BOSCO, M. SANDRA (1977-80), *Storia della lingua tedesca*, 3 vols., i. *Origini e alto tedesco antico* (Bottega d'Erasmo: Turin, 1977); ii. *Alto tedesco medio e moderno* (Giappichelli: Turin, 1979); iii. *Scelta antologica* (Giappichelli: Turin, 1980).

CONRADY, KARL OTTO (1962), 'Vom "Barock" in der deutschen Lyrik des 17. Jahrhunderts', in Barner (1975), 460-87 [first printed in *Lateinische Dichtungstradition und deutsche Lyrik des 17. Jahrhunderts* (Bonner Arbeiten zur deutschen Literatur, 4; H. Bouvier & Co.: Bonn, 1962), 243-63].

CORDES, GERHARD (1980), 'Altniederdeutsch', in *LGL*, 2nd edn. (1980), 576-80.

COUPE, WILLIAM A. (1972), *A Sixteenth-century German Reader* (Clarendon Press: Oxford, 1972).

CRAMER, DANIEL (1634), *Folget nun des heiligen Jobs Bleyern Schreib-Täfflein/ zu der edlen Drucker-Kunst/ Erkläret durch Danielen Kramern/*

H. Schrifft Doctorn vnd Superintendenten zu alten Stetin [appended to Hornschuch (1634), q.v.].

CURME, GEORGE (1904), *A Grammar of the German Language*, 2nd edn. (Frederick Ungar: New York, 1922; 9th impr. 1964).

CURRIE, PAMELA (1968), 'Moral Weeklies and the Reading Public in Germany, 1711-1750', *OGS* 3 (1968), 69-86.

DAL, INGERID (1940), 'Systemerhaltende Tendenzen in der deutschen Kasusmorphologie' (1940); repr. in Hugo Moser (ed.), *Das Ringen um eine neue deutsche Grammatik* (WBG: Darmstadt, 1962), 74-88 [= Wege der Forschung, 25].

—— (1966), *Kurze deutsche Syntax auf historischer Grundlage* (1952; 3rd edn., Niemeyer: Tübingen, 1966).

—— (1967), 'Über den I-Umlaut im Deutschen', *Neuphilologische Mitteilungen*, 68 (1967), 47-65.

DÄSTER, ULI (1973), *Johann Peter Hebel in Selbstzeugnissen und Bilddokumenten* (rowohlt monographie, 195; Rowohlt: Hamburg, 1973).

DE BOOR, HELMUT (1949/1979), *Die deutsche Literatur von Karl dem Großen bis zum Beginn der höfischen Dichtung. 770-1170* (1st edn. 1949; 9th edn., rev. H. Kolb, C. H. Beck: Munich, 1979) [= de Boor, Newald, *et al.*, vol. i].

—— (1953/1979), *Die höfische Literatur. Vorbereitung, Blüte, Ausklang. 1170-1250* (1st edn. 1953; 10th edn., rev. Ursula Hennig, C. H. Beck: Munich, 1979) [= de Boor, Newald, *et al.*, vol. ii].

—— (1959), ed. *Das Nibelungenlied (c.*1200) [q.v.].

—— (1962/1973), *Die deutsche Literatur im späten Mittelalter. Zerfall und Neubeginn*, Part I. *1250-1350* (1st edn. 1962; 4th repr. C. H. Beck: Munich, 1973) [= de Boor, Newald, *et al.*, vol. iii/1].

—— (1965), ed. *Mittelalter: Texte und Zeugnisse*, two vols. (C. H. Beck: Munich, 1965) [= *Die deutsche Literatur. Texte und Zeugnisse*, i/1 and 2].

—— (1971), 'Das Corpus der altdeutschen Originalurkunden', *Jahrbuch für internationale Germanistik*, 3 (1971), 199-217.

—— Newald, Richard, *et al.*, *Geschichte der deutschen Literatur von den Anfängen bis zur Gegenwart* (C. H. Beck, Munich) [for individual volumes see de Boor (1949/1979), (1953/1979), (1962/1973), Glier (forthcoming), Newald (1967), Rupprich (1970), (1973)].

—— and WISNIEWSKI, ROSWITHA (1969), *Mittelhochdeutsche Grammatik*, 7th edn. (Sammlung Göschen, 1108; de Gruyter: Berlin and New York, 1969).

DEGERING, HERMANN (1916), ed. Lamprecht (12th cent., *b*) [q.v.].

Der Große Brockhaus (1958), 16th edn. (Wiesbaden, 1958).

Deutscher Kulturatlas (1928-38), edd. Gerhard Lüdtke and Lutz Mackensen, five vols. (de Gruyter: Berlin and Leipzig, 1928-38).

Deutscher Sprachatlas (1926-56), edd. Ferdinand Wrede, Walther Mitzka, and Bernhard Martin (N. G. Elwert: Marburg, 1926-56).

Deutscher Wortatlas (1951-80), twenty-two vols., edd. Walther Mitzka and Ludwig Erich Schmitt (Wilhelm Schmitz Verlag: Gießen, 1951-80).

DIECKMANN, WALTHER (1964), *Information oder Überredung? Zum Wortgebrauch der politischen Werbung in Deutschland seit der französischen Revolution* (Marburg, 1964) [= Marburger Beiträge zur Germanistik, 8].

DIECKMANN, WALTHER (1969), *Sprache in der Politik. Einführung in die Pragmatik und Semantik der politischen Sprache* (Carl Winter: Heidelberg, 1969; repr. 1975).

—— (1979), 'K. O. Erdmann und die Gebrauchsweisen des Ausdrucks "Konnotationen" in der linguistischen Literatur', in K. Grotsch, Hans-H. Lieb, and A. Lundt (edd.), *Aufsätze zum Konnotationsbegriff und zur Sprachkritik* (LAB 13: Berlin, 1979; repr. in Dieckmann (1981), 78–136).

—— (1981), *Politische Sprache. Politische Kommunikation* (Carl Winter: Heidelberg, 1981).

DORNBLÜTH, R. P. AUGUSTINUS (1755), *OBSERVATIONES oder Gründliche Anmerckungen über die Art und Weise eine gute Ubersetzung besonders in die teutsche Sprach zu machen. Wobey die Fehler der bisherigen teutschen Ubersetzungen samt denen Ursachen solcher Fehleren, und daraus erfolgten Verkehrung der teutschen Sprach, aufrichtig entdeckt werden. Nebst einer zu disem Vorhaben unentpärlichen Critic über Herrn Gottschedens sogenannte Redekunst, und teutsche Grammatic, oder (wie er sie nennt) Grundlegung zur teutschen Sprache. Aus patriotischem Eyfer zur Verhütung fernerer Verkehrung und Schändung der ausländischen Bücheren, ans Tagliecht gegeben von R. P. AUGUSTINO DORNBLÜTH . . .* (Rieger: Augsburg, 1755).

DRESCHER, KARL (1903), ed. Rachel (1664) [q.v.].

Duden Grammatik (1973), 3rd edn. (Duden, Bibliographisches Institut: Mannheim, 1973; 4th edn. 1983).

DUDEN, KONRAD (1872), *Die deutsche Rechtschreibung. Abhandlung, Regeln und Wörterverzeichnis mit etymologischen Angaben. Für die oberen Klassen höherer Lehranstalten und zur Selbstbelehrung für Gebildete* (Teubner: Leipzig, 1872).

—— (1876), *Die Zukunftsorthographie nach den Vorschlägen der zur Herstellung größerer Einigung in der deutschen Rechtschreibung berufenen Konferenz . . .* (Bibliographisches Institut: Leipzig and Vienna, 1876).

—— (1880), *Vollständiges orthographisches Wörterbuch für die Schule. Nach den amtlichen Regeln der neuen Orthographie* (Verlag des Bibliographischen Instituts: Leipzig 1880; repr. 1883).

—— (1902), *Die deutsche Rechtschreibung nebst Interpunktionslehre und ausführlichem Wörterverzeichnis nach den für Deutschland, Österreich und die Schweiz gültigen Regeln zum Gebrauch für Schulen und zur Selbstbelehrung neu bearbeitet*, 7th edn. (C. H. Beck: Munich, 1902).

DUNGER, HERMANN (1909), *Engländerei in der deutschen Sprache*, 2nd edn. (Verlag des Allgemeinen Deutschen Sprachvereins (S. Berggold): Berlin, 1909).

DÜNNHAUPT, GERHARD (1976), ed. Gryphius (1663) [q.v.].

—— (1980–1), *Bibliographisches Handbuch der Barockliteratur. Hundert Personalbibliographien deutscher Autoren des 17. Jahrhunderts*, three vols. (Anton Hiersemann Verlag: Stuttgart, 1980–1; i (A–G), 1980, ii (H–P), 1981, iii (R–Z), 1981).

EBELING, HORST (1974), *Prosopographie der Amtsträger des Merowinger-reiches. Von Chlothar II. (613) bis Karl Martell (741)* (Wilhelm Fink Verlag: Munich, 1974).

EBERT, ROBERT PETER (1978), *Historische Syntax des Deutschen* (Sammlung Metzler, M 167; Metzler: Stuttgart, 1978).

—— (1980), 'Social and Stylistic Variation in Early New High German Word Order: the Sentence Frame (Satzrahmen)', *PBB* (T) 102 (1980), 357–98.

—— (1981), 'Social and Stylistic Variation in the Order of Auxiliary and Non-finite Verb in Dependent Clauses in Early New High German', *PBB* (T) 103 (1981), 204–37.

ECKHARDT, KARL AUGUST (1953–7), ed. *Lex Salica* (6th cent.) [q.v.].

EGGERS, HANS (1963–77), *Deutsche Sprachgeschichte* (Rowohlt, Reinbek), i. *Das Althochdeutsche* (1963); ii. *Das Mittelhochdeutsche* (1965); iii. *Das Frühneuhochdeutsche* (1969; 2nd edn. 1973); iv. *Das Neuhochdeutsche* (1977) [= rowohlts deutsche enzyklopädie, Nos. 185-6, 191-2, 270-1, 375].

—— (1970), ed. *Der Volksname Deutsch* (WBG: Darmstadt, 1970) [= Wege der Forschung, 156].

—— (1973a), *Deutsche Sprache im 20. Jahrhundert* (Munich, 1973; 2nd edn. 1978).

—— (1973b), 'Deutsche Standardsprache des 19./20. Jahrhunderts', in *LGL* (1973) 437-42 (2nd edn. (1980), 603-9).

—— (1977), 'Was ist "deutsche Gegenwartssprache"?', in Karl Hotz (ed.), *Deutsche Sprache der Gegenwart* (Reclam U-B 9531; Reclam: Stuttgart, 1977), 7-23.

EHRISMANN, GUSTAV (1909), ed. Hugo von Trimberg (1300) [q.v.].

—— (1920), 'Hugo von Trimbergs *Renner* und das mittelalterliche Wissenschaftssystem', in *Aufsätze zur Sprach- und Literaturgeschichte* [Festschrift for Wilhelm Braune] (Ruhfus: Dortmund, 1920), 211-36.

—— (1932), *Geschichte der deutschen Literatur bis zum Ausgang des Mittelalters*, i. *Die althochdeutsche Literatur*, 2nd edn. (C. H. Beck: Munich, 1932; repr. 1954).

EHRISMANN, OTFRID, and RAMGE, HANS (1976), *Mittelhochdeutsch. Eine Einführung in das Studium der deutschen Sprachgeschichte* (Niemeyer: Tübingen, 1976) [= Germanistische Arbeitshefte, 19].

EIBL, KARL (1973), 'Deutsche Literatursprache der Moderne', in *LGL* (1973), 545-51 (2nd edn. (1980), 746-52).

EICHHOFF, JÜRGEN (1977-8), *Wortatlas der deutschen Umgangssprachen*, two vols. (Francke: Berne and Munich, 1977-8).

EICHLER, INGRID, and BERGMANN, GUNTHER (1967), 'Zum Meissnischen Deutsch. Die Beurteilung des Obersächsischen vom 16. bis zum 19. Jahrhundert', *PBB* (H) 89 (1967), 1-57.

EIS, GERHARD (1967), *Mittelalterliche Fachliteratur*, 2nd edn. (Sammlung Metzler, M 14; Metzler: Stuttgart, 1967).

—— (1971), 'Mittelhochdeutsche Literatur: Fachprosa', in Schmitt (1970-1), ii. 528-72.

EISEN, PAUL (1880), *Herr Professor von Raumer und die Deutsche Rechtschreibung. Ein Beitrag zur Herstellung einer orthographischen Einigung* (Friedrich Wreden: Brunswick, 1880).

EISENSTEIN, ELISABETH, L. (1979), *The Printing Press as an Agent of Change* (Cambridge University Press, 1979).

ENGEL, EDUARD (1911), *Deutsche Stilkunst* (F. Tempsky: Vienna, and G. Freytag: Leipzig, 1911).

—— (1916), *Sprich Deutsch! Ein Buch zur Entwelschung* (Hesse & Becker: Leipzig, 'Im dritten Jahr des Weltkrieges ums deutsche Dasein' [1916]).

ENGELS, HEINZ (1983), *Die Sprachgesellschaften des 17. Jahrhunderts* (W. Schmitz: Giessen, 1983) [= Beiträge zur deutschen Philologie, 54].

ENGELSING, ROLF (1973), *Analphabetentum und Lektüre. Zur Soziologie des Lesens in Deutschland zwischen feudaler und industrieller Gesellschaft* (Metzler: Stuttgart, 1973).

ERBEN, JOHANNES (1954), *Grundzüge einer Syntax der Sprache Luthers* (Akademie-Verlag: Berlin, 1954) [= DAdWB, VdIfdSuL 2].

—— (1961), *Ostmitteldeutsche Chrestomathie. Proben der frühen Schreib- und Druckersprachen des mitteldeutschen Ostens* (Akademie-Verlag: Berlin, 1961) [= DAdWB, VdIfdSuL 24].

—— (1970), 'Frühneuhochdeutsch', in Schmitt (1970–1), i. 386–440.

—— (1974), 'Luther und die neuhochdeutsche Schriftsprache', in Maurer and Rupp (1974), i. 509–81.

ERDMANN, OSCAR (1886–98), *Grundzüge der deutschen Syntax*, i (Verlag der J. G. Cotta'schen Buchhandlung: Stuttgart, 1886); ii, rev. O. Mensing (1898).

FEIST, SIGMUND (1933), *Die deutsche Sprache*, 2nd rev. edn. (Max Hueber Verlag: Munich, 1933).

FELDMANN, WILHELM (1911–12), 'Die Große Revolution in unserer Sprache', *ZfdW* 13 (1911–12), 245–82.

FILLMORE, CHARLES (1968), 'The Case for Case', in E. Bach and R. Harms (edd.), *Universals in Linguistic Theory* (Holt, Rinehart, & Winston: New York, 1968).

FIRTH, JOHN RUPERT (1955), 'Structural Linguistics', in *Selected Papers of J. R. Firth 1952–59*, ed. F. R. Palmer (Longmans: London and Harlow, 1968), 35–52.

—— (1957), 'A Synopsis of Linguistic Theory, 1930–55', ibid. 168–205.

FISCHART, JOHANNES (1575), *Affentheuerlich Naupengeheurliche Geschicht-klitterung* . . . [= *Gargantua*]; later edn. (1590), ed. Ute Nyssen (Karl Rauch Verlag: Düsseldorf, 1963) [*Glossar*: id. (Düsseldorf, 1964)].

FISCHER, HANNS (1966), ed. *Schrifttafeln zum althochdeutschen Lesebuch* (Niemeyer: Tübingen, 1966).

FISHMAN, JOSHUA A. (1972), *The Sociology of Language* (Newbury House: Rowley, Mass., 1972).

FLECKENSTEIN, JOSEF (1975), 'Zur Frage der Abgrenzung von Bauer und Ritter', in R. Wenskus, H. Jankuhn, and Kl. Grinda (edd.), *Wort und Begriff 'Bauer'* (Vandenhoeck & Ruprecht: Göttingen, 1975), 246–53 [= Abhandlungen der Akademie der Wissenschaften in Göttingen, phil.-hist. Klasse, 3, No. 89].

FLEISCHER, WOLFGANG (1964), *Die deutschen Personennamen: Geschichte, Bildung und Bedeutung* (Akademie-Verlag: Berlin, 1964).

FLEISCHMANN, KLAUS (1973), *Verbstellung und Relieftheorie. Ein Versuch zur Geschichte des deutschen Nebensatzes* (Fink: Munich, 1973) [Münchener Germanistische Beiträge, 6].

FLEMING, WILLI, and STADLER, ULRICH (1974), 'Barock', in Maurer and Rupp (1974), ii. 1-30.

FLUCK, HANS-RÜDIGER (1980), *Fachsprachen. Einführung und Bibliographie* (1976); 2nd edn., Francke: Munich, 1980) [= UTB 483].

FOURQUET, JEAN (1948), *Les Mutations consonantiques du germanique* (Société d'Édition: Les Belles Lettres: Paris, 1948; 2nd edn. 1956) [= Publications de la Faculté des Lettres de l'Université de Strasbourg, 111].

——— (1969), 'Das Werden des neuhochdeutschen Verbsystems', in U. Engel, P. Grebe, and H. Rupp (edd.), *Festschrift für Hugo Moser* (Schwann: Düsseldorf, 1969), 53-65.

FRANCK, JOHANNES (1909), *Altfränkische Grammatik, Laut- und Flexionslehre* (Vandenhoeck & Ruprecht: Göttingen, 1909; 2nd edn., rev. R. Schützeichel, 1971).

FRANGK, FABIAN (1531), *Ein Cantzley- vnd Titelbüchlin/ Darinnen gelernt wird/ wie man Sendebriefe förmlich schreiben/ vnd einem jdlichen seinen gebürlichen Titel geben sol* [printed with his *Orthographia Deutsch/ Lernt recht buchstäbig schreiben . . .*] (Schirlentz: Wittenberg, 1531).

FRANKE, CARL (1913-22), *Grundzüge der Schriftsprache Luthers in allgemein verständlicher Darstellung*, three vols., 2nd edn. (Buchhandlung des Waisenhauses: Halle, 1913-22).

FRANKE, C. G. (1884), *Der obersächsische Dialekt* (Programm der Realschule Leisnig, 1884).

FRIEDRICH WILHELM I, Letters to Prince Leopold of Anhalt-Dessau; ed. O. Krauske, *Die Briefe König Friedrich Wilhelms I. an den Fürsten Leopold zu Anhalt-Dessau* (P. Parey: Berlin, 1905) [= *Acta Borussica*, Supplement].

FRIES, LAURENTIUS (1518), *Spiegel der artzeney . . .* (Colmar, 1518) [2nd edn. with title *Spiegel der artzney/ vorzeyten zunutz vnnd trost den Leyen gemacht/ durch Laurentium Friesen/ aber offt nun gfälscht/ durch vnfleiß der Buchtrucker/ yetzundt durch den selbigen Laurentium widerumb gebessert . . .* (Brunfelß: Strasburg, 1532; repr. Beck: Strasburg, 1546)].

FRINGS, THEODOR (1957), *Grundlegung einer Geschichte der deutschen Sprache*, 3rd edn. (VEB Max Niemeyer: Halle a/S., 1957).

——— and KUHNT, JOACHIM (1954), edd. *König Rother* (c.1150) [q.v.].

——— and LERCHNER, GOTTHARD (1966), *Niederländisch und Niederdeutsch. Aufbau und Gliederung des Niederdeutschen* (Akademie-Verlag: Berlin, 1966).

——— and MÜLLER, GERTRAUD (1966-8), *Germania Romana*, two vols. (VEB Max Niemeyer: Halle a/S., 1966, 1968), [= Mitteldeutsche Studien, 19/1 and 2].

FROMM, HANS (1978), 'Wilhelm Braune', *PBB* (T) 100 (1978), 4-39.

FRÜHWALD, WOLFGANG (1973), 'Deutsche Literatursprache von der Klassik bis zum Biedermeier', in *LGL* (1973), 531-8 (2nd edn. (1980), 732-40).

FUCHSPERGER, ORTOLPH (1556), *Ein grundtlicher klarer anfang der natürlichen vnd rechten kunst der waren Dialectica/ durch Ortholphen Fuchsperger von Ditmoning/ keiserlicher rechten Licentiatē/ auß dē Latein ins Teutsch transferiert vnd zůsamen gefaßt/ so allen denen die mit gschrifftlichen künsten vmbgehend| nicht weniger nutz dann not ist zů wüssen* . . . (1556) [copy in Wolfenbüttel, HAB, 461 Qu. (2)].

FUDGE, ERIK C. (1970), 'Phonology', in Lyons (1970), 76–95.

GABRIELSSON, ARTUR (1932–3), 'Das Eindringen der hochdeutschen Sprache in die Schulen Niederdeutschlands im 16. und 17. Jahrhundert', *Jahrbuch des Vereins für niederdeutsche Sprachforschung*, 58–9 (1932–3), 1–79.

GAMILLSCHEG, ERNST (1934), *Romania Germanica. Sprach- und Siedlungsgeschichte der Germanen auf dem Boden des alten Römerreichs*, i. *Die Franken* (de Gruyter: 1934; 2nd edn. Berlin, 1970) [= Grundriß der germanischen Philologie, 11/1].

GANZ, PETER FELIX (1955), 'Seventeenth-Century English Loan Words in German', *JEGP* 54 (1955), 80–90.

—— (1957), *Der Einfluß des Englischen auf den deutschen Wortschatz 1640–1815* (Erich Schmidt: Berlin, 1957).

—— (1968), 'Lachmann as an Editor of Middle High German Texts', in P. F. Ganz and W. Schröder (edd.), *Probleme mittelalterlicher Überlieferung und Textkritik. Oxforder Colloquium, 1966* (Erich Schmidt Verlag: Berlin, 1968), 12–30.

—— (1969), 'Ms. Junius 13 und die althochdeutsche Tatianübersetzung', *PBB* (T) 91 (1969), 28–76.

—— (1978), ed. Gottfried von Straßburg (*c*.1210) [q.v.].

—— (1978), 'Eduard Sievers', *PBB* (T) 100 (1978), 40–85.

GARBE, BURCKHARD (1978), *Die deutsche rechtschreibung und ihre reform 1722–1974* (Niemeyer: Tübingen, 1978).

GÄRTNER, KURT, and STEINHOFF, HUGO H. (1976), *Minimalgrammatik zur Arbeit mit mittelhochdeutschen Texten* (Kümmerle: Göppingen, 1976; 3rd edn. 1979) [= GAG 183].

GASKELL, PHILIPP, and BRADFORD, P. (1972), edd. Hornschuch (1634) [q.v.].

GELHAUS, HERMANN (1966), 'Zum Tempussystem der deutschen Hochsprache', *WW* 16 (1966), 217–30.

GEUENICH, DIETER (1976), *Die Personennamen der Klostergemeinschaft von Fulda im früheren Mittelalter* (Wilhelm Fink: Munich, 1976) [= Münstersche Mittelalter-Schriften, 5].

GLIER, INGEBORG (forthcoming): Part II of de Boor (1962/1973) [q.v.].

GLINZ, HANS (1967), *Deutsche Syntax*, 2nd edn. (Sammlung Metzler, M 43; Metzler: Stuttgart, 1967).

—— (1968), *Die innere Form des Deutschen* (1952, 5th edn., Francke: Berne and Munich, 1968).

—— (1969), 'Zum Tempus- und Modussystem des Deutschen', in *Der Begriff Tempus — eine Ansichtssache?* (*WW* Beiheft 20, 1969), 50–8.

GLUNK, ROLF (1966–71), 'Erfolg und Mißerfolg der nationalsozialistischen Sprachlenkung', *ZfdS* 22 (1966), 57–73, 146–53; ibid. 23 (1967), 83–113, 178–88; ibid. 24 (1968), 72–91, 184–91; ibid. 25 (1969), 116–28, 180–3; ibid. 26 (1970), 84–97, 176–83; ibid. 27 (1971), 113–23, 177–87.

GOEBBELS, JOSEPH (1932–45), Speeches; ed. Helmut Heiber, *Goebbels Reden*, two vols. (Droste Verlag: Düsseldorf, 1971, 1972) [i: 1932–9; ii: 1939–45].

—— (1942–3), *Tagebücher*; ed. Louis Lochner, *Goebbels Tagebücher. Aus den Jahren 1942–43* (Atlantis Verlag: Zurich, 1948).

—— (1943), *Das Eherne Herz. Reden und Aufsätze aus den Jahren 1941–42* (Zentralverlag der NSDAP: Munich, 1943).

GOEBEL, ULRICH (1974). See Wilhelm (1932–63).

GOEDEKE, KARL (1887), *Grundrisz zur Geschichte der deutschen Dichtung aus den Quellen*, iii, 2nd edn. (Ehlermann: Dresden, 1887) [1st edn. 1881].

GOETHE, JOHANN WOLFGANG VON (1774), *Die Leiden des jungen Werthers*; edd. Eduard von der Hellen *et al.* (J. G. Cotta'sche Buchhandlung Nachfolger): Stuttgart and Berlin [1902]) [= Jubiläums-Ausgabe, vol. xvi].

—— (*c.*1795), 'Physiologie und ihre Hülfswissenschaften. Betrachtung über Morphologie überhaupt', in *Goethe. Gesamtausgabe der Werke und Schriften . . . Zweite Abteilung. Schriften*, xviii. *Schriften zu Natur und Erfahrung. Schriften zur Morphologie*, I (J. G. Cotta'sche Buchhandlung Nachfolger: Stuttgart, 1959), 653–62.

—— (1803), *Regeln für Schauspieler*, in the Jubiläums-Ausgabe, edd. Eduard von der Hellen *et al.*, xxxvi (J. G. Cotta'sche Buchhandlung Nachfolger: Berlin, [1902]), 197–214.

—— (1810–31), *Dichtung und Wahrheit*; ibid., vols. xxii–xxv (1902).

—— (1826), *Anzeige der Ausgabe letzter Hand*, ibid., vol. xxxviii (Cotta: Stuttgart, 1826), 47–8.

—— and SCHILLER, FRIEDRICH VON (1795–7), *Xenien*; edd. Eduard von der Hellen *et al.*, in Jubiläums-Ausgabe, vol. iv. *Gedichte* (J. G. Cotta'sche Buchhandlung Nachfolger: Stuttgart and Berlin, [1902]), 156–90.

GOODRICK-CLARKE, NICHOLAS (1982), 'The Ariosophists of Austria and Germany 1890–1935. Reactionary and Political Fantasy in Relation to Social Anxiety' (D.Phil. thesis, Oxford, 1982).

GOOSSENS, JAN (1977), *Deutsche Dialektologie* (de Gruyter: Berlin and New York, 1977).

—— (1978), 'Das Westmitteldeutsche und die zweite Lautverschiebung. Zur zweiten Auflage von Rudolf Schützeichels Buch "Die Grundlagen des Westmitteldeutschen" (1976)', *ZDL* 45 (1978), 281–9.

—— (1979), Über Dialektologie und eine angeblich merovingische Laut-verschiebung', *Niederdeutsches Wort*, 19 (1979), 198–213.

—— (1980), 'Lautverschiebung', *ZDL* 47 (1980), 77.

GORDON, E. V. (1957), *An Introduction to Old Norse*, 2nd edn., rev. A. R. Taylor (Clarendon Press: Oxford, 1957).

GOTTFRIED VON STRASSBURG (*c.*1210), *Tristan*; ed. P. F. Ganz, two vols. (F. A. Brockhaus; Wiesbaden, 1978) [= Deutsche Klassiker des Mittel-alters, NF 4].

GOTTSCHED, JOHANN CHRISTOPH (1725–7), ed. *Die Vernünftigen Tadlerinnen* [a weekly publication] (Leipzig, 1725–7; 3rd edn., Hamburg, 1748).

—— (1727–9), ed. *Der Biedermann* [a weekly publication] (Leipzig, 1727–9).

—— (1730, 1742, 1751), *Versuch einer Critischen Dichtkunst durchgehends mit den Exempeln unserer besten Dichter erläutert . . .* (1730; 3rd edn. 1742; 4th edn., B. C. Breitkopf: Leipzig, 1751); edd. Joachim Birke and Brigitte Birke in Birke and Birke (1968–   ), vi/1–3 (1973), based on 3rd edn.; repr. of 4th edn., WBG: Darmstadt, 1982 [Commentary: P. M. Mitchell in Birke and Birke (1968–   ), vi/4 (1978); Index: Hans Otto Horch, *Register zu Gottscheds 'Versuch einer Critischen Dichtkunst'* (WBG: Darmstadt, 1978)].

GOTTSCHED, JOHANN CHRISTOPH (1736), *Ausführliche Redekunst Nach Anleitung der alten Griechen und Römer, wie auch der neuern Ausländer . . .* (Breitkopf: Leipzig, 1736; repr. Olms: Hildesheim and New York, 1973).

—— (1748, 1762), *Grundlegung einer deutschen Sprachkunst, nach den Mustern der besten Schriftsteller des vorigen und jetzigen Jahrhunderts* (Breitkopf: Leipzig, 1748; 5th edn. 1762); ed. Herbert Penzl in Birke and Birke (1968–   ), viii/1–2 (1978); facsimile of 5th edn. [*Vollständigere und neu erläuterte Deutsche Sprachkunst*], Olms: Hildesheim and New York, 1970 [Commentary: Herbert Penzl in Birke and Birke (1968–   ), viii/3 (1980)].

—— (1758), *Beobachtungen über den Gebrauch und Misbrauch vieler deutscher Wörter und Redensarten* (1758); ed. Johannus Hubertus Slangen (Diss. Utrecht, Winants: Heerlen, 1955).

GOTTSCHED, LUISE VIKTORIE ADELGUNDE (1740–4), *Der Witzling. Ein deutsches Nachspiel in einem Aufzug*; ed. Wolfgang Hecht, *Gottsched, Luise A./Schlegel, Johann E.: Der Witzling. Ein deutsches Nachspiel in einem Aufzug.— Die stumme Schönheit* (de Gruyter: Berlin and New York, 1962) [= Komedia, 1].

GÖTZE, ALFRED (1912), *Frühneuhochdeutsches Glossar*, 7th edn. (de Gruyter: Berlin, 1977).

—— (1928), *Deutsche Studentensprache* (Verlag des Deutschen Sprachvereins: Berlin, 1928).

—— and VOLZ, HANS, *Frühneuhochdeutsches Lesebuch*, 6th edn. (Vandenhoeck & Ruprecht: Göttingen, 1976).

GOUGH, CHARLES E. (1942), ed. Wernher der Gartenaere (13th cent.) [q.v.].

GRÄF, HANS GERHARD (1956), ed. *Goethes Ehe in Briefen* (Insel Verlag: Leipzig, 1956).

GRAFF, EBERHARD G. (1834–46), *Althochdeutscher Sprachschatz oder Wörterbuch der althochdeutschen Sprache*, six vols. (Nikolai: Berlin, 1834–46; repr. Hildesheim, 1963, in seven vols.) [vol. vi contains the indispensable index by H. F. Massmann, *Gedrängtes althochdeutsches Wörterbuch oder vollständiger Index zu Graff's althochdeutschem Sprachschatze* (Berlin, 1846)].

GRAVIER, MAURICE (1948), *Anthologie de l'allemand du XVIᵉ siècle* (Aubier: Paris, 1948) [= Bibliothèque de Philologie Germanique, 11].

GREBE, PAUL (1963), ed. *Akten zur Geschichte der deutschen Einheitsschreibung 1870–1880* (Sammlung Duden; Bibliographisches Institut: Mannheim, 1963).

GRIMM, JACOB (1819/22–37), *Deutsche Grammatik*, four vols. (Dieterich: Göttingen, 1819–37) [Part I (1819; 2nd edn. 1822), Book 1. *Von den Buchstaben*; Book 2. *Von den Wortbiegungen*; Part II (1826), Book 3. *Von der Wortbildung*; Part III (1831), Book 3, chap. 4. *Pronominalbildungen*; Part IV (1837), Book 4. *Syntax*; repr. 1967].

—— (1848), *Geschichte der deutschen Sprache*, two vols. (1848; 4th edn., Hirzel: Leipzig, 1880).

—— (1854), *Deutsches Wörterbuch*, i (A–Biermolke) (Hirzel: Leipzig, 1854) [= *DWB*].

—— (1864–90), *Kleinere Schriften*, eight vols., edd. Karl Müllenhoff and Eduard Ippel (F. Dümmler: Berlin, 1864–90 and C. Bertelsmann: Gütersloh, 1890).

GROSSE, RUDOLF (1955), *Die Meissnische Sprachlandschaft. Dialektgeographische Untersuchungen zur obersächsischen Sprach- und Siedlungsgeschichte* (VEB Max Niemeyer: Halle, 1955) [= Mitteldeutsche Studien, 15].

—— (1981), 'Zu den Prinzipien der Sprachgeschichtsschreibung heute', *Beiträge zur Erforschung der deutschen Sprache*, 1 (1981), 125–31.

GROTH, KLAUS (1855), *Quickborn* (1st edn. 1852; 4th edn. 1855; repr. Lipsius and Tischer: Kiel, 1892).

—— (1858), *Briefe über Hochdeutsch und Plattdeutsch* (Schwersche Buchhandlung: Kiel, 1858); edd. Ivo Braak and Richard Mehlem, in *Klaus Groth. Sämtliche Werke*, vi. *Über Sprache und Dichtung. Kritische Schriften* (Christian Wolff Verlag: Flensburg and Hamburg, 1961), 67–137.

—— (*c*.1877), 'Sophie Dethlefs un ik' (first published 1893); edd. Ivo Braak and Richard Mehlem, *Klaus Groth. Sämtliche Werke*, iv (Christian Wolff Verlag: Flensburg, 1959), 430–7 (with notes, pp. 465–9).

GRÜNERT, HORST (1974), *Sprache und Politik. Untersuchungen zum Sprachgebrauch der 'Paulskirche'* (de Gruyter: Berlin and New York, 1974) [= Studia Linguistica Germanica, 10].

GRYPHIUS, ANDREAS (1660), *Verlibtes Gespenste/Die gelibte Dornrose*; ed. Hugh Powell, *Andreas Gryphius, Lustspiele*, ii (Niemeyer: Tübingen, 1972) [= Gesamtausgabe, edd. M. Szyrocki and Hugh Powell, vol. viii].

——(1663), *Horribilicribrifax Teutsch, Scherzspiel*; ed. Gerhard Dünnhaupt (Reclam U-B 688; Reclam: Stuttgart, 1976).

GUCHMANN, MIRRA M. (1964–9), *Der Weg zur deutschen Nationalsprache* [trans. from the Russian by G. Feudel], two vols. (Akademie-Verlag: Berlin, 1964, 1969).

—— (1974), *Die Sprache der deutschen politischen Literatur in der Zeit der Reformation und des Bauernkrieges* (Akademie-Verlag: Berlin, 1974) [= Bausteine zur Sprachgeschichte des Neuhochdeutschen, ed. Günter Feudel, 54].

—— (1975). See *An die Versammlung gemeiner Bauernschaft* (1525).

—— and SEMENJUK, N. N. (1981), *Zur Ausbildung der Norm der deutschen Literatursprache im Bereich des Verbs (1470–1730). Tempus und Modus* (Akademie-Verlag: Berlin, 1981) [= Bausteine zur Sprachgeschichte des Neuhochdeutschen, ed. G. Feudel, 56/5].

GUEINTZ, CHRISTIAN (1641), *Christian Gueintzen/ Deutscher Sprachlehre Entwurf* (Cöthen, 1641).

—— (1645), *Die Deutsche Rechtschreibung Auf sonderbares gut befinden Durch den Ordnenden verfasset/ Von der Fruchtbringenden Geselchaft übersehen/ und zun nachricht an den tag gegeben* (Salfelden: Halle, 1645).

GUTMACHER, ERICH (1914), 'Der Wortschatz des althochdeutschen Tatian in seinem Verhältnis zum Altsächsischen, Angelsächsischen, und Altfriesischen', *PBB* 39 (1914), 1–83, 229–89, 571–7.

HAHN, WALTHER VON (1980), 'Fachsprachen', in *LGL*, 2nd edn. (1980), 390-5.

HALLER, ALBRECHT VON (1732, 1748), *Versuch schweizerischer Gedichten* (Niclaus Haller: Berne, 1732; 4th edn. 1748).

HAMANN, RICHARD, and HERMAND, JOST (1972), *Epochen deutscher Kultur von 1870 bis zur Gegenwart*, ii. *Naturalismus* (1959; new edn., Munich, 1972).

HANDT, FRIEDRICH (1964), ed. *Deutsch — Gefrorene Sprache in einem gefrorenen Land. Polemik — Analysen — Aufsätze* (Literarisches Colloquium: Berlin, 1964).

HANKAMER, PAUL (1927), *Die Sprache. Ihr Begriff und ihre Deutung im 16. und 17. Jahrhundert* (F. Cohen: Bonn, 1927; repr. Olms: Hildesheim, 1965).

HÄRD, JOHN EVERT (1973), 'Mittelniederdeutsch', in *LGL* (1973), 418-21 (2nd edn. (1980), 584-8).

HARRIS, ROY (1980), *The Language Makers* (Duckworth: London, 1980).

—— (1981), *The Language Myth* (Duckworth: London, 1981).

HARSDÖRFFER, GEORG PHILIPP (1641-9), *Frauenzimmer-Gesprächspiele*, Parts I (1641; 2nd edn. 1644), II (1642; 2nd edn. 1657), III-VIII (1643, 1644, 1645, 1646, 1647, 1649 respectively); facsimile repr. by Irmgard Böttcher, eight volumes [reprinting the second editions of Parts I and II] (Niemeyer: Tübingen, 1968-9).

—— (1656), *Der Teutsche Secretarius* (1656; facsimile repr. in two vols., Olms: Hildesheim and New York, 1971).

HARTIG, MATTHIAS (1981), *Sprache und sozialer Wandel* (Urban Taschenbuch, 327; Kohlhammer: Stuttgart, Berlin, Cologne, and Mainz, 1981).

HARTMANN, WALTHER (1969), *Zur Verbstellung im Nebensatz nach frühneuhochdeutschen Bibelübersetzungen* (Diss. Heidelberg, 1969).

HARTMANN VON AUE (*c.*1190), *Gregorius. Der 'Gute Sünder'*; ed. Friedrich Neumann (5th edn., F. A. Brockhaus: Wiesbaden, 1968; rev. (with bibliographical supplement, Christoph Cormeau, 1981) [= Deutsche Klassiker des Mittelalters, NF 2].

HARVEY, RUTH CHARLOTTE (1945), 'The Provenance of the Old High German *Ludwigslied*', *Medium Aevum*, 14 (1945), 1-20.

HASE, OSCAR (1885), *Die Koberger. Eine Darstellung des buchhändlerischen Geschäftsbetriebes in der Zeit des Überganges vom Mittelalter zur Neuzeit*, 2nd edn. (Breitkopf & Härtel: Leipzig, 1885).

HASZLER, K. D. (1866), ed. Kiechel (1585) [q.v.].

HATTO, ARTHUR T. (1960), *Gottfried von Strassburg*, Tristan, *with the* Tristran *of Thomas* [trans. into English prose] (Penguin: London, 1960).

HAUBRICHS, WOLFGANG (1975), 'Zum Stand der Isidorforschung', *ZfdPh* 94 (1975), 1-15.

HAUGEN, EINAR, and BLOOMFIELD, MORTON (1975), edd. *Language as a Human Problem* (Lutterworth Press: Guildford and London, 1975).

HAUPTMANN, GERHART (1937), *Das Abenteuer meiner Jugend* (1937) [*Sämtliche Werke*, ed. Hans-Egon Hass, vii (Propyläen Verlag: Frankfurt-on-Main and Berlin, 1962)].

HAUSCHILD, REINHARD, and SCHUH, HORST (1981), *Ich glaub, mich knutscht ein Elch! Sprüche aus der Bundeswehr* (5th impr. E. S. Mittler & Sohn: Herford, 1981).

HAUSER-SUIDA, ULRIKE, and HOPPE-BEUGEL, GABRIELE (1964), *Die Vergangenheitstempora in der deutschen geschriebenen Sprache der Gegenwart* (Hueber: Munich, and Schwann: Düsseldorf, 1964; repr. 1972) [= *Heutiges Deutsch*, i/4].

HEBEL, JOHANN PETER (18th–19th cent.), *Briefe*; ed. Wilhelm Zentner (C. F. Müller: Karlsruhe, 1939).

—— (1803), *Alemannische Gedichte* (1803); ed. Adolf Sütterlin, as Part I of *Hebels Werke*, two vols. [with *Alemannisches Wörterbuch* as suppl.] (Deutsches Verlagshaus Bong & Co.: Berlin, Leipzig, Vienna, and Stuttgart, c.1910).

HECHT, WOLFGANG (1962), ed. L. V. A. Gottsched (1740–4) [q.v.].

HECHTENBERG, KLARA (1903), *Der Briefstil des 17. Jahrhunderts. Ein Beitrag zur Fremdwörterfrage* (Berlin, 1903).

HEIBER, HELMUT (1971–2), ed. Goebbels (1932–45) [q.v.].

HEINRICH VON VELDEKE (c.1189), *Eneit*; edd. Gabriele Schieb and Theodor Frings, *Henric van Veldeken, Eneide*, i. *Einleitung und Text* (Akademie-Verlag: Berlin, 1964), ii. *Untersuchungen von Gabriele Schieb unter Mitwirkung von Theodor Frings* (Berlin, 1965) [= DTM 58–9].

HELBER, SEBASTIAN (1593), *Teutsches Syllabierbüchlein/ Nemlich/ Gedruckter Hochteütscher sprach Lesenskunst . . .* (Gemperle: Freiburg in Vchtland [= Fribourg], 1593); ed. Gustav Roethe (Akademische Verlagsbuchhandlung von J. C. B. Mohr (Paul Siebeck): Freiburg im Breisgau and Tübingen, 1882).

HELM, KARL (1980), *Abriß der mittelhochdeutschen Grammatik*, 5th edn., rev. E. A. Ebbinghaus (Niemeyer: Tübingen, 1980).

HENNE, HELMUT (1965), 'Punktuelle und politische Sprachlenkung. Zu 13 Auflagen von Gustav Wustmanns "Sprachdummheiten"', *ZfdS* 21 (1965), 174–84.

—— (1968a), 'Das Problem des meißnischen Deutsch oder "Was ist Hochdeutsch" im 18. Jahrhundert', *ZMF* 35 (1968), 109–29.

—— (1968b), 'Deutsche Lexikographie und Sprachnorm im 17. und 18. Jahrhundert', in W. Mitzka (ed.), *Wortgeographie und Gesellschaft. Festgabe für L. E. Schmitt* (Berlin, 1968), 80–114.

—— (1975), ed. *Deutsche Wörterbücher des 17. und 18. Jahrhunderts. Einführung und Bibliographie* (Olms: Hildesheim and New York, 1975).

HENZEN, WALTER (1954), *Schriftsprache und Mundarten*, 2nd rev. edn. (Francke Verlag: Berne, 1954) [= Bibliotheca Germanica, 5].

—— (1957), *Deutsche Wortbildung*, 2nd edn. (Niemeyer: Tübingen, 1957).

HERDER, JOHANN GOTTFRIED (1767), *Fragmente über die neuere deutsche Litteratur* (Hartknoch: Riga, 1767); ed. Theodor Matthias, *Herders Werke*, i (Bibliographisches Institut: Leipzig and Vienna, 1903), 1–198.

—— (1770), *Abhandlung über den Ursprung der Sprache*; ed. Wolfgang Pross (Hanser Verlag: n.d. [1979?]).

HEYSE, JOHANN CHRISTOPH AUGUST (1816/1908), *Deutsche Schulgrammatik oder kurzgefasstes Lehrbuch der deutschen Sprache* (1816; 12th edn. by K. Heyse, 1840; 23rd edn., Hanover, 1878; 24th edn. by Otto Lyon, 1886; 27th edn. 1908).

HICKMANN, A. L. (1896–8?), ed. *Geographisch-statistischer Taschen-Atlas des Deutschen Reichs*, three vols. (G. Freytag & Berndt: Leipzig and Vienna, 1896–8?).

HILDEBRAND, RUDOLF (1889), 'Gehäufte Verneinung', *Zeitschrift für den deutschen Unterricht*, 3 (1889), 149 ff.; in *Gesammelte Aufsätze und Vorträge zur deutschen Philologie und zum deutschen Unterricht* (B. G. Teubner: Leipzig, 1890), 214–24.

HIRSCH, RUDOLF (1967), *Printing, Selling and Reading 1450–1550* (Otto Harrassowitz: Wiesbaden, 1967; 2nd edn. with bibliographical supplement, Otto Harrassowitz: Wiesbaden, 1974).

HIRT, HERMANN (1925), *Geschichte der deutschen Sprache*, 2nd edn. (C. H. Beck: Munich, 1925).

HITLER, ADOLF (1925–7), *Mein Kampf*, two vols. (1925, 1927; repr. in one vol. 1943, Zentralverlag der NSDAP: Munich, 1943) [cited by page of the 1943 edition].

HÖCHLI, STEFAN (1981), *Zur Geschichte der Interpunktion im Deutschen. Eine kritische Darstellung der Lehrschriften von der zweiten Hälfte des 15. Jahrhunderts bis zum Ende des 18. Jahrhunderts* (de Gruyter: Berlin and New York, 1981) [= Studia Linguistica Germanica, 17].

HOCKETT, CHARLES F. (1958), *A Course in Modern Linguistics* (Macmillan: New York, 1958; 9th repr. 1965).

HÖFLER, OTTO (1955, 1956), 'Stammbaumtheorie, Wellentheorie, Entfaltungstheorie', *PBB* (T) 77 (1955), 30–66, 424–76; ibid. 78 (1956), 1–44.

—— (1957), 'Die zweite Lautverschiebung bei Ostgermanen und Westgermanen', *PBB* (T) 79 (1957), 161–350 [repr. separately, 1958].

HOFMANN VON HOFMANNSWALDAU, CHRISTIAN (17th cent.), *Gedichte*; ed. Manfred Windfuhr (Reclam U-B 8889; Reclam: Stuttgart, 1969).

HOLZ, ARNO, and SCHLAF, JOHANNES (1899), *Papa Hamlet*; ed. Fritz Martini (Reclam, Nos. 8853–4; Reclam: Stuttgart, 1963).

HOOPS, JOHANNES (1911–19), *Reallexikon der germanischen Altertumskunde*, four vols. (Trübner: Strasburg, 1911–19; 2nd edn., de Gruyter: Berlin and New York, 1973–).

HOPE, T. E. (1971), *Lexical Borrowing in the Romance Languages. A critical study of Italianisms in French and Gallicisms in Italian from 1100–1900*, two vols. (Blackwell: Oxford, 1971).

HORN, PAUL (1899, 1905), *Die deutsche Soldatensprache* (1899; 2nd edn., J. Rickers: Gießen, 1905).

HORNSCHUCH, HIERONYMUS (1634), *(Orthotypographia)/ Das ist:/ Ein kurtzer Vnterricht/ für die jenigen/ die gedruckte Werck/ corrigiren wollen . . .*, trans. into German by T.H.D. (Ritzsch: Leipzig, 1634) (= Wolfenbüttel, HAB Q. 180 Helmstedt 8) [originally published in Latin (Lantzenberger: Leipzig, 1608)]; English edn. and trans. by Philipp Gaskell and P. Bradford (Cambridge, 1972).

HOTZENKÖCHERLE, RUDOLF (1962), 'Entwicklungsgeschichtliche Grundzüge des Neuhochdeutschen', *WW* 12 (1962), 321–331.

HOYER, SIEGFRIED, and RÜDIGER, BERND (1975), edd. *An die Versammlung gemeiner Bauernschaft* (1525) [q.v.].

HÜBNER, ARTUR (1919), 'Zur Charakteristik der Soldatensprache', repr. in

Kleinere Schriften, edd. Hermann Kunisch and Ulrich Pretzel (E. Ebering: Berlin, 1940), 77–88.

HUFFINES, MARION LOIS (1974), 'Sixteenth-century Printers and Standardization of New High German', *JEGP* 73 (1974), 60–72.

HUGO VON TRIMBERG (1300), *Der Renner*; ed. Gustav Ehrismann (Tübingen, 1909) [= BLVS 252].

HUISMAN, JOHANNES A. (1969), 'Die Pariser Gespräche', *Rheinische Vierteljahrsblätter*, 33 (1969), 272–96.

HUMBOLDT, WILHELM VON (1836), *Über die Verschiedenheit des menschlichen Sprachbaues, und ihren Einfluß auf die geistige Entwickelung des Menschengeschlechts* (Berlin, 1836; repr. Dümmler: Bonn, 1967–8).

HURLEBUSCH, ROSE M. (1975), ed. Klopstock (1774a) [q.v.].

ICKELSAMER, VALENTIN (c.1535), *Teutsche Grammatica. Darauß ainer von jm selbs mag lesen lernen/ mit allem dem/ so zum Teütschen lesen vnnd desselben Orthographian mangel vnd überfluß . . . zu wissen gehört . . .* (Ph. Ulhart d. Ä.: Augsburg, c.1535) [see also Müller (1882), 120].

Inter Nationes (*1979*). *Kultureller Tonbanddienst. Der Nationalsozialismus. Eine Dokumentation über die zwölf dunklen Jahre deutscher Geschichte*, 2nd edn. by M. Fischer, S. Hügli, B. Ischi, D. Schärer (Bonn, 1979) [with eight tapes].

ISCHREYT, HEINZ (1965), *Studien zum Verhältnis von Sprache und Technik* (Schwann: Düsseldorf, 1965).

ISING, ERIKA (1959), ed. Ratke (1612–30) [q.v.].

—— (1966), *Die Anfänge der volkssprachlichen Grammatik in Deutschland und Böhmen* (Akademie-Verlag: Berlin, 1966) [= DAdWB, VdSK, No. 6].

—— (1970), *Die Herausbildung der Grammatik der Volkssprachen in Mittel- und Osteuropa* (Akademie-Verlag: Berlin, 1970) [= DAdWB, VdIfdSuL, No. 47].

ISING, GERHARD (1956), *Die Erfassung der deutschen Sprache des ausgehenden 17. Jahrhunderts in den Wörterbüchern Matthias Kramers und Kaspar Stielers* (Akademie-Verlag: Berlin, 1956).

—— (1968), *Zur Wortgeographie spätmittelalterlicher deutscher Schriftdialekte. Eine Darstellung auf der Grundlage der Wortwahl von Bibelübersetzungen und Glossaren*, in two parts. I. *Untersuchungen*; II. *Karten* (Akademie-Verlag: Berlin, 1968) [= DAdWB, VdIfdSuL, No. 38/1 and 2].

JAEGER, MONIKA (1964), *Theorien der Mundartdichtung* (Tübinger Vereinigung für Volkskunde: Tübingen, 1964) [= *Volksleben*, vol. iii].

JELLINEK, MAX HERMANN (1899), ed. Philipp von Zesen (1645) [q.v.].

—— (1913–14), *Geschichte der neuhochdeutschen Grammatik von den Anfängen bis auf Adelung*, two vols. (Carl Winter: Heidelberg, 1913, 1914) [= Germanische Bibliothek, 7].

JOHANNES VON TEPL (c.1400), *Der Ackermann aus Böhmen*; ed. (1) Alois Bernt (Weidmann: Berlin, 1917) [*VMzR* 3/1], (2) Maurice O'Connor Walshe (Duckworth: London, 1951).

JONES, WILLIAM JERVIS (1976), *A Lexicon of French Borrowings in the German Vocabulary* (*1575–1648*) (de Gruyter: Berlin and New York, 1976) [= Studia Linguistica Germanica, 12].

JONES, WILLIAM JERVIS (1978), 'A Quantitative View of Franco-German Loan-Currency (1575–1648)', *ZDL* 45 (1978), 149–60.

—— (1979), 'Graphemic evidence for the diphthongisation of /ê/ and /ô/ in Old High German: the case re-opened', *Neophilologus*, 63 (1979), 250–9.

—— (1984), 'The Central German Monophthongization in Synchronic and Diachronic Perspective', *TPS* (1984), 58–116.

JOSTEN, DIRK (1976), *Sprachvorbild und Sprachnorm im Urteil des 16. und 17. Jahrhunderts. Sprachlandschaftliche Prioritäten, Sprachautoritäten, Sprachimmanente Argumentation* (P. Lang: Frankfurt-on-Main, and H. Lang: Berne, 1976) [= Arbeiten zur Mittleren Deutschen Literatur und Sprache, 3].

JUNGANDREAS, WOLFGANG (1947, 1949), *Geschichte der deutschen und der englischen Sprache*, two vols. (Vandenhoeck & Ruprecht: Göttingen; vol. i, 2nd rev. edn., 1949; vol. ii, 1947).

JUNK, VICTOR (1905), ed. Rudolf von Ems (*c*.1240) [q.v.].

KAISER, KÅRE (1930), *Mundart und Schriftsprache. Versuch einer Wesensbestimmung in der Zeit zwischen Leibniz und Gottsched* (Eichblatt: Leipzig, 1930).

KANDLER, AGNELLUS (1736), 'Einige Anmerckungen über die Teutsche Sprach', in *Neu-fortgesetzter PARNASSUS BOICUS — Oder Neueröffneter Musen-Berg/ Worauff Verschiedene Denck- vnd Leßwürdigkeiten auß der gelehrten Welt/ zumahlen aber auß denen Landen zu Bayrn/ abgehandlet werden* (Strötter, Gastel, und Ilgers: Augsburg and Stadt am Hof nächst Regenspurg, 1736), vol. v, 30. B(ericht) [for vols. i–iv (1722–7) and vol. vi (1737), see Birlo (1908)].

KAPR, ALBERT (1977), *Johannes Gutenberg. Tatsachen und Thesen* (Insel: Leipzig, 1977).

KARG-GASTERSTÄDT, ELISABETH, and FRINGS, THEODOR (1952–), *Althochdeutsches Wörterbuch auf Grund der von Elias von Steinmeyer hinterlassenen Sammlungen* (Akademie-Verlag: Berlin, 1952–) [vol. i (A–B), 1968; vol. iii (E–F), fasc. 12 and 13, 1982].

KAUFFMANN, FRIEDRICH (1890), *Geschichte der Schwäbischen Mundart im Mittelalter und in der Neuzeit* (Trübner: Strasburg, 1890).

KEHREIN, JOSEPH (1854–6), *Grammatik der deutschen Sprache des fünfzehnten bis siebenzehnten Jahrhunderts* (Otto Wigand: Leipzig, 1854–6; 2nd edn. 1863; repr. Olms: Hildesheim, 1968) [vol. iii, *Syntax des einfachen und mehrfachen Satzes*].

KELLER, ADALBERT (1861), ed. Wyle (15th cent.) [q.v.].

KELLER, RUDOLF E. (1961), *The German Dialects* (Manchester University Press, 1961).

—— (1978), *The German Language* (Faber: London and Boston, 1978).

KERN, PETER CHRISTOPH, and ZUTT, HERTA (1977), *Geschichte des deutschen Flexionssystems* (Niemeyer: Tübingen, 1977) [= Germanistische Arbeitshefte, 22].

KETTMANN, GERHARD (1967*a*), 'Zur schreibsprachlichen Überlieferung Wittenbergs in der Lutherzeit', *PBB* (H) 89 (1967), 76–120.

—— (1967*b*), 'Aufbau und Entwicklung der kursächsischen Kanzleisprache in der Lutherzeit', *PBB* (H) 89 (1967), 121–9.

—— (1967c), *Die kursächsische Kanzleisprache zwischen 1486 und 1546. Studien zum Aufbau und zur Entwicklung* (Akademie-Verlag: Berlin, 1967) [= DAdWB, VfdSuL, 34].

—— (1971), *Frühneuhochdeutsche Texte* (VEB Bibliographisches Institut: Leipzig, 1971).

—— and SCHILDT, JOACHIM (1976), edd. *Zur Ausbildung der Norm der deutschen Literatursprache auf der syntaktischen Ebene (1470–1730). Der Einfachsatz* (Akademie-Verlag: Berlin, 1976) [= Bausteine zur Sprachgeschichte des Neuhochdeutschen, ed. G. Feudel, 56/1].

KIECHEL, SAMUEL (1585), *Die Reisen des Samuel Kiechel* (1585); ed. K. D. Haszler (Stuttgart, 1866) [= BLVS 86].

KING, ROBERT D. (1967), 'In Defense of Klopstock as Spelling Reformer. A Linguistic Appraisal', *JEGP* 66 (1967), 369–82.

—— (1969), *Historical Linguistics and Generative Grammar* (Prentice-Hall: Englewood Cliffs, 1969).

KINNE, MICHAEL (1981), ed. *Nationalsozialismus und deutsche Sprache. Arbeitsmaterialien zum deutschen Sprachgebrauch während der nationalsozialistischen Herrschaft* (Moritz Diesterweg: Frankfurt-on-Main, 1981).

KINZEL, KARL (1884), ed. Lamprecht (12th cent., *a*) [q.v.].

KIPARSKY, PAUL (1968), 'Linguistic Universals and Linguistic Change', in E. Bach and R. T. Harms (edd.), *Universals in Linguistic Theory* (Holt, Rinehart & Winston: New York, 1968), 171–205.

KIRK, ARTHUR (1923), *An Introduction to the Historical Study of New High German* (Manchester University Press: London and New York, 1923).

KIRKNESS, ALAN (1975), *Zur Sprachreinigung im Deutschen 1789–1871*, two vols. (Narr: Tübingen, 1975) [= Forschungsberichte IDS, 26/1 and 2].

KLEIBER, WOLFGANG (1965), 'Urbare als sprachgeschichtliche Quelle. Möglichkeiten und Methoden der Auswertung', in Friedrich Maurer (ed.), *Vorarbeiten und Studien zur Vertiefung der südwestdeutschen Sprachgeschichte* (Eberhard Albert Verlag: Freiburg im Breisgau, 1965), 151–243.

Kleine Enzyklopädie (1969–70). *Die deutsche Sprache.* Edd. Erhard Agricola, Wolfgang Fleischer, Helmut Protze, and Wolfgang Ebert, two vols. (VEB Bibliographisches Institut: Leipzig, 1969, 1970).

Kleine Enzyklopädie (1983). *Deutsche Sprache.* Recast in one vol. by Wolfdietrich Hartung, Wolfgang Fleischer, Joachim Schildt, Peter Suchsland, *et al.* (VEB Bibliographisches Institut: Leipzig, 1983).

KLEMPERER, VIKTOR (1946), '*LTI*'. *Die unbewältigte Sprache. Aus dem Notizbuch eines Philologen* (1946; 3rd edn. (dtv 575), Deutscher Taschenbuch Verlag: Munich, 1969).

KLENZ, HEINRICH (1900), *Die deutsche Druckersprache* (Trübner: Strasburg, 1900).

KLOOCKE, HELLA (1974), *Der Gebrauch des substantivierten Infinitivs im Mittelhochdeutschen* (Kümmerle: Göppingen, 1974) [= GAG 130].

KLOPSTOCK, FRIEDRICH GOTTLIEB (1748–73), *Der Messias* [first three cantos published in the *Bremer Beiträge*; 1780 edn. (Altona) in Klopstock's own orthography].

—— (1758), 'Von der Sprache der Poesie', in *Klopstocks Sämmtliche Werke*,

2nd edn. (Leipzig, 1854–5), x. 202–14 [first in the *Nordischer Aufseher*, ed. J. A. Cramer, vol. i, Stück 26 (1758)].

KLOPSTOCK, FRIEDRICH GOTTLIEB (1774), *Die deutsche Gelehrtenrepublik*; cited from *Sämmtliche Werke*, 2nd edn., vol. viii (Göschen: Leipzig, 1855); new edn. by Rose M. Hurlebusch (de Gruyter: Berlin and New York, 1975) [= Hamburger Klopstock-Ausgabe, vii/1].

—— (1779), 'Von der Darstellung', in *Klopstocks Sämmtliche Werke*, 2nd edn. (Leipzig, 1854–5), x. 193–201.

—— (1779–80), 'Über die deutsche Rechtschreibung', in *Klopstocks Sämmtliche Werke*, 2nd edn. (Leipzig, 1854–5), ix. 325–400.

—— (1794), *Grammatische Gespräche* (J. H. Kaven: Altona, 1794; repr. Göschen: Leipzig, 1855) [= *Sämmtliche Werke*, 2nd edn., ix. 3–305].

KLOSS, HEINZ (1973), 'Deutsche Sprache im Ausland', in *LGL* (1973), 377–87 (2nd edn., 'Deutsche Sprache außerhalb des geschlossenen deutschen Sprachgebiets', *LGL* (1980), 536–46).

KLUCKHOHN, PAUL (1934), *Die Idee des Volkes im Schrifttum der deutschen Bewegung von Möser und Herder bis Grimm* (Junker & Dünnhaupt: Berlin, 1934).

KLUGE, FRIEDRICH (1918), *Von Luther bis Lessing* (2nd edn., Strasburg 1888; 5th edn., Quelle & Meyer: Leipzig, 1918).

—— (1920), *Deutsche Sprachgeschichte. Werden und Wachsen unserer Muttersprache von ihren Anfängen bis zur Gegenwart* (Quelle & Meyer: Leipzig, 1920).

—— (1883/1967), *Etymologisches Wörterbuch der Deutschen Sprache*, 20th edn. by Walther Mitzka (de Gruyter: Berlin and New York, 1967; 21st edn. 1975).

KLUGE, REINHOLD (1948–74), ed. *Lancelot* (13th cent.) [q.v.].

KNOBLOCH, JOHANNES (1960), 'Recherches sur le vocabulaire de la mission mérovingienne', *Orbis*, 9 (1960) [published Louvain, 1961], 427–37.

KNOCH, HARTMUT (1969), *Möglichkeiten und Aspekte der Erforschung westfränkischer Personennamen in der karolingischen Nordgallia* (Carl Winter: Heidelberg, 1969).

KÖBLER, GERHARD (1971), *Lateinisch–althochdeutsches Wörterbuch* (Musterschmidt-Verlag: Göttingen, Zurich, and Frankfurt-on-Main, 1971).

KOHLHASE, JÖRG (1981), 'Aspekte der deutschen Sprachgeschichte', *Studium Linguistik*, 10 (1981), 20–41.

KÖNIG, WERNER (1978), ed. *dtv-Atlas zur deutschen Sprache* (dtv 3025; Deutscher Taschenbuch Verlag: Munich, 1978).

König Rother (c.1150); edd. Theodor Frings and Joachim Kuhnt (VEB Max Niemeyer: Halle, 1954; 2nd edn. 1961).

KORN, KARL (1959), *Sprache in der verwalteten Welt*, 2nd edn. (Walter-Verlag: Olten and Freiburg im Breisgau, 1959).

KÖSTER, A. (1900), ed. Schönaich (1754) [q.v.].

KRAHE, HANS (1954), *Sprache und Vorzeit* (Quelle & Meyer: Heidelberg, 1954).

—— (1969), *Germanische Sprachwissenschaft*, 7th edn. by Wolfgang Meid (Sammlung Göschen, 238, 780; de Gruyter: Berlin and New York, 1969).

KRAUSKE, OTTO (1905), ed. Friedrich Wilhelm I [q.v.].

KRETSCHMER, PAUL (1918), *Wortgeographie der hochdeutschen Umgangssprache* (Vandenhoeck & Ruprecht: Göttingen, 1918; 2nd edn. 1969).

KROETZ, FRANZ XAVER (1973), *Wildwechsel* (Georg-Lentz Verlag: Vienna, 1973).

KROMAYER, JOHANNES (1629), *Etliche Schul-Tractat zum Newen METHODO gehörig| Für die Schulen im Fürstenthumb Weymar . . .* (Weimar, 1629).

KUFNER, HERBERT L. (1972), 'The grouping and separation of the Germanic languages', in Frans Van Coetsem and Herbert L. Kufner (edd.), *Toward a Grammar of Proto-Germanic* (Niemeyer: Tübingen, 1972), 71–97.

KUHN, HANS (1964), 'Hannover und der grammatische Wechsel', *ZfdA* 93 (1964), 13–18.

—— (1976), 'Zur zweiten Lautverschiebung im Mittelfränkischen', *ZfdA* 105 (1976), 89–99.

KULLY, ROLF MAX (1969), *Johann Peter Hebel* (Sammlung Metzler, M 80; Metzler, Stuttgart, 1969).

KUNISCH, HERMANN (1974), 'Spätes Mittelalter (1250–1500)', in Maurer and Rupp (1974), i. 255–322.

KÜPPER, HEINZ (1955–70), *Wörterbuch der deutschen Umgangssprache*, six vols. (Claassen: Hamburg, 1955–70).

—— *Am A . . . . der Welt. Landserdeutsch 1939–1945* (Claassen: Hamburg and Düsseldorf, 1970).

KURRELMEYER, W. (1904), *Die erste deutsche Bibel*, i (Tübingen, 1904) [= BLVS 234].

LABOV, WILLIAM (1972), 'The Study of Language in its Social Context', in Pier Paolo Giglioli (ed.), *Language and Social Context* (Penguin: London, 1972), 283–307.

—— (1978), *Sociolinguistic Patterns* (Philadelphia, 1972; repr. Blackwell: Oxford, 1978).

LACHMANN, KARL (1820), *Auswahl aus den Hochdeutschen Dichtern des dreizehnten Jahrhunderts. Für Vorlesungen und zum Schulgebrauch* (Reimer: Berlin, 1820).

—— (1833), ed. Wolfram von Eschenbach (12th–13th cent.) [q.v.].

LADENDORF, OTTO (1906), *Historisches Schlagwörterbuch* (1906; repr., ed. H.-G. Schumann, Olms: Hildesheim and New York, 1968).

LAMPRECHT (12th cent., *a*), *Alexanderlied*; ed. (1) Karl Kinzel (Buchhandlung des Waisenhauses: Halle, 1884) [= Germanistische Handbibliothek, 6], (2) Hans Ernst Müller, *Die Werke des Pfaffen Lamprecht nach der ältesten Überlieferung* (Georg D. W. Callwey: Munich, 1923) [= Münchener Texte, 12].

—— (12th cent., *b*), *Tobias*; ed. (1) Hermann Degering, 'Neue Funde aus dem zwölften Jahrhundert', *PBB* 41 (1916), 513–53, at pp. 528–36, (2) Hans Ernst Müller, ed. cit. [see last entry] (1923).

Lancelot (13th cent.); ed. Reinhold Kluge, *Lancelot*, three vols. (Akademie-Verlag: Berlin; vol. i (1948), vol. ii (1963), vol. iii (1974)) [= DTM 43, 47, 63].

LANGEN, AUGUST (1957), 'Deutsche Sprachgeschichte vom Barock bis zur

Gegenwart', in W. Stammler (ed.), *Deutsche Philologie im Aufriß* (1952; 2nd edn., Erich Schmidt Verlag: Berlin, 1957), cols. 931–1395.

LASCH, AGATHE (1914), *Mittelniederdeutsche Grammatik* (1914; repr. Niemeyer: Tübingen, 1974).

—— (c.1928), 'Berlinisch'. *Eine berlinische Sprachgeschichte* (Reimar Hobbing: Berlin, n.d. [c.1928]).

LAUDISMANN, CASPAR (1618), *Consilium integrum, et perfectum de exoticis lingvis Gallica et Italica rectè et eleganter addiscendis, & ad usum transferendis* . . . (Stettin, 1618) [copy in Wolfenbüttel, HAB, 33, Gram.].

LEHMANN, WINFRIED P., and MALKIEL, YAKOV (1968), edd. *Directions for historical linguistics. A Symposium* (University of Texas Press: Austin, 1968).

LEIBFRIED, ERWIN (1973), 'Deutsche Literatursprache vom Jungen Deutschland bis zum Naturalismus', in *LGL* (1973), 539–45 (2nd edn. (1980), 740–6).

LEIBNIZ, GOTTFRIED WILHELM (c.1697), 'Unvorgreiffliche Gedanken betreffend die aufrichtung eines Teutsch gesinneten Ordens', first published as 'Unvorgreiffliche gedancken, betreffend die ausübung und verbesserung der teutschen sprache (De linguae germanicae cultu)', in *Illustris viri Godofr. Guilielmi Leibnitii Collectanea etymologica illustrationi linguarum veteris celticae, germanicae, gallicae aliorumque inservientia*, with preface by Johann Georg Eccard (Foerster: Hanover, 1717), 255–314; cited from A. Schmarsow (ed.), *Leibniz und Schottelius. Die Unvorgreiflichen Gedanken* (Strasburg, 1877) [= Quellen und Forschungen zur Sprach- und Culturgeschichte der germanischen Völker, 23]; modern edn. with commentary by Uwe Pörksen and Jürgen Schiewe, *Gottfried Wilhelm Leibniz. Unvorgreifliche Gedanken, betreffend die Ausübung und Verbesserung der deutschen Sprache. Zwei Aufsätze* (Reclam UB 7987; Philipp Reclam: Stuttgart, 1983).

LEISI, ERNST (1967), *Das heutige Englisch. Wesenszüge und Probleme* (Carl Winter: Heidelberg, 1955; 4th rev. edn. 1967).

LEISTNER, ERNST (1880), 'Ungeheuerlichkeiten in der deutschen Rechtschreibung', *Zeitschrift für Orthographie* [ed. W. Vietor], i/2 (1880), 37–40.

LERCHNER, GOTTHARD (1971), *Zur II. Lautverschiebung im Rheinisch-Westmitteldeutschen. Diachronische und diatopische Untersuchungen* (VEB Max Niemeyer: Halle, 1971) [= Mitteldeutsche Studien, 30].

—— (1974), 'Zu gesellschaftstheoretischen Implikationen der Sprachgeschichtsforschung', *PBB* (H) 94 (1974), 141–55.

LEVISON, WILHELM (1946), *England and the Continent in the Eighth Century* (Clarendon Press: Oxford, 1946).

LEXER, MATTHIAS (1872–8), *Mittelhochdeutsches Handwörterbuch. Zugleich als Supplement und alphabetischer Index zum Mittelhochdeutschen Wörterbuch von Benecke–Müller–Zarncke* (S. Hirzel: Leipzig, 1872–8; repr. Stuttgart, 1970).

—— (1879/1961), *Mittelhochdeutsches Taschenwörterbuch* (1st edn. 1879; 30th edn. by Ulrich Pretzel, S. Hirzel: Stuttgart, 1961).

Lexikon der Germanistischen Linguistik (1973; 2nd edn. by Hans-Peter

Althaus, Helmut Henne, and Herbert Ernst Wiegand, Niemeyer: Tübingen, 1980) [= *LGL*].

Lex Salica (6th cent.); ed. Karl August Eckhardt (1953–7): *Lex Salica*. *100 Titel-Text* (Verlag Hermann Böhlaus Nachfolger: Weimar, 1953); i. *Einführung und 80 Titel-Text*; i/2. *Systematischer Text*; ii/1. *65 Titel-Text*; ii/2. *Kapitularien und 70 Titel-Text* (Historisches Institut des Werralandes; Musterschmidt-Verlag: Göttingen, Berlin, and Frankfurt-on-Main, 1953–7) [Germanenrechte, NF: Abteilung Westgermanisches Recht].

LEYSER, J. (1896), *Joachim Heinrich Campe. Ein Lebensbild aus dem Zeitalter der Aufklärung*, 2nd edn., two vols. (Friedrich Vieweg & Sohn: Brunswick, 1896).

LICHTENBERG, GEORG CHRISTOPH (1766–99), *Briefe*; in *Schriften und Briefe*, vol. iv, ed. Wolfgang Promies (WBG: Darmstadt, 1967).

—— (1779–83), *Sudelbücher*; ibid., vol. ii. *Sudelbücher II, Materialhefte, Tagebücher* (WBG: Darmstadt, 1971).

LICHTENBERGER, HENRI (1895), *Histoire de la langue allemande* (A. Laisney: Paris, 1895).

LINDGREN, KAJ B. (1953), *Die Apocope des mittelhochdeutschen -E in seinen verschiedenen Funktionen* (Helsinki, 1953) [= Annales Academiae Scientiarum Fennicae, Ser. B, 78/2].

—— (1957), *Über den oberdeutschen Präteritumschwund* (Helsinki, 1957) [= Annales Academiae Scientiarum Fennicae, Ser. B, 112/1].

—— (1973), 'Mittelhochdeutsch', in *LGL* (1973), 415–18 (2nd edn. (1980), 580–4).

LINDMEYR, BERNHARD (1899), *Der Wortschatz in Luthers Emsers und Ecks Übersetzung des 'Neuen Testamentes'* (Trübner: Strasburg, 1899).

LIST, GUIDO VON (1912), *Das Geheimnis der Runen* (Winen: Verlag der Guido-von-List-Gesellschaft; in Kommision E. F. Steinacker, Leipzig, 1912) [= Guido-List-Bücherei, 1. Reihe, Forschungsergebnisse, No. 1].

LOCHNER, LOUIS P. (1948), ed. Goebbels (1942–3) [q.v.].

LOCKWOOD, WILLIAM BURLEY (1965), *An Informal History of the German Language* (1965; 2nd edn., André Deutsch: London, 1976).

—— (1968), *Historical German Syntax* (Clarendon Press: Oxford, 1968).

—— (1969), *Indo-European Philology: Historical and comparative* (Hutchinson University Library: London, 1969).

—— (1972), *A Panorama of Indo-European Languages* (Hutchinson University Library: London, 1972).

LOOSE, GERHARD, 'Zur deutschen Soldatensprache des zweiten Weltkrieges', *JEGP* 46 (1947), 279–89.

LOTZMANN, GEERT (forthcoming), *Bibliographie zur Orthoepie des Deutschen* (Niemeyer: Tübingen, forthcoming) [= Arbeitsmaterialien, 3].

LÜDTKE, GERHARD, and MACKENSEN, LUTZ (1928–36), edd. *Deutscher Kulturatlas*, five vols. (de Gruyter: Berlin and Leipzig, 1928–38).

LUTHER, MARTIN (1523), Preface to the Old Testament (1523); cited from *Die Deutsche Bibel* (Böhlaus Nachfolger: Weimar, 1954), viii. 10–32 [= WA].

—— (1524), *An die Radherrn aller stedte deutsches lands: das sie Christliche schulen auffrichten vnd hallten sollen* (Wittenberg, 1524); repr. in *Werke* (Böhlaus Nachfolger: Weimar, 1899), 9–53 [= WA, vol. xv].

LUTHER, MARTIN (1528), ed. *Von der falschen Bettler Büberey* [= *Liber Vagatorum*]; edd. E. Thiele and O. Brenner (Böhlaus Nachfolger: Weimar, 1909), 634–54 [= WA, vol. xxvi].

—— (1530), *Ein Sendbrief vom Dolmetschen*; ed. Karl Bischoff (2nd edn., Max Niemeyer: Halle, 1957) [= parallel text of A and B prints; see also WA, vol. xxx/2 (1909), 627–46].

—— (1545), *Biblia. Das ist die gantze Heilige Schrifft Deudsch auffs new zugericht*; ed. Hans Volz, three vols. (dtv 6031–3; Deutscher Taschenbuch Verlag: Munich, 1974).

—— *Tischreden*, WA edn., six vols. (Böhlaus Nachfolger: Weimar, 1912–26).

—— *Briefwechsel*, WA edn., sixteen vols. (Böhlaus Nachfolger: Weimar, 1930–80).

LUTZ-HENSEL, MAGDALENA (1975), *Prinzipien der ersten textkritischen Editionen mittelhochdeutscher Dichtung. Brüder Grimm — Benecke — Lachmann* (Erich Schmidt Verlag: Berlin, 1975) [= Philologische Studien und Quellen, 77].

LYONS, JOHN (1968), *Introduction to Theoretical Linguistics* (Cambridge University Press, 1968; repr. 1979).

—— (1970), ed. *New Horizons in Linguistics* (Penguin: London, 1970).

—— (1977), *Semantics*, two vols. (Cambridge University Press, 1977; repr. 1978, 1979).

—— (1981), *Language and Linguistics* (Cambridge University Press, 1981).

MACKENSEN, LUTZ (1954), *Sprache und Technik. 2 Vorträge* (Heliand Verlag: Lüneburg, 1954).

—— (1959), 'Muttersprachliche Leistungen der Technik', in *Sprache — Schlüssel zur Welt. Festschrift für Leo Weisgerber*, ed. Helmut Gipper (Schwann: Düsseldorf, 1959), 293–305.

—— (1971), *Die deutsche Sprache in unserer Zeit* (1956; 2nd edn., Quelle & Meyer: Heidelberg, 1971).

MCLINTOCK, DAVID ROBERT (1966), 'The Language of the *Hildebrandslied*', OGS 1 (1966), 1–9.

MANN, THOMAS (1947), *Doktor Faustus. Das Leben des deutschen Tonsetzers Adrian Leverkühn, erzählt von einem Freunde* (Berlin, 1947; repr. Fischer: Berlin, 1963).

MARACHE, MAURICE (1972), *Syntaxe structurale de l'allemand* (Aubier Montaigne: Paris, 1972) [= Bibliothèque de Philologie Germanique, 23].

Marco Polo (14th cent.). *Der mitteldeutsche Marco Polo, nach der Admonter Handschrift herausgegeben*; ed. Horst von Tscharner (Weidmann: Berlin, 1935) [= DTM 40].

MARKEY, THOMAS L. (1976a), *A North Sea Germanic Reader* (Wilhelm Fink Verlag: Munich, 1976).

—— (1976b), *Germanic Dialect Grouping and the Position of Ingvaeonic* (Institut für Sprachwissenschaft der Universität Innsbruck: Innsbruck, 1976) [= Innsbrucker Beiträge zur Sprachwissenschaft, 15].

—— et al. (1977–), *Germanic and its Dialects: A Grammar of Proto-*

Germanic, three vols.: i. *Text*; ii. *Maps and Commentaries*; iii. *Bibliography and Indices* (Amsterdam, 1977–).

MARTIN, BERNHARD (1939), *Die deutschen Mundarten* (Leipzig, 1939; 2nd edn., N. G. Elwert: Marburg, 1959).

MARTINET, ANDRÉ (1955), *Économie des changements phonétiques. Traité de phonologie diachronique* (A. Francke: Berne, 1955; 3rd edn. 1970).

MARTINI, FRITZ (1963), ed. Holz and Schlaf (1899) [q.v.].

MARX, KARL, and ENGELS, FRIEDRICH (1847–8), *Manifest der Kommunistischen Partei* (1847–8; repr. Moscow, 1945).

MASSER, ACHIM (1966), *Die Bezeichnungen für das christliche Gotteshaus in der deutschen Sprache des Mittelalters* (Erich Schmidt Verlag: Berlin, 1966) [= Philologische Studien und Quellen, 33].

MASSMANN, H. F. (1846). See Graff (1834–46).

MATTHEWS, PETER HUGOE (1970), 'Recent Developments in Morphology', in Lyons (1970), 96–114.

MATTHIAS, THEODOR (1892), *Sprachleben und Sprachschäden. Ein Führer durch die Schwankungen und Schwierigkeiten des deutschen Sprachgebrauchs* (Richard Richter: Leipzig, 1892).

MATZEL, KLAUS (1970), *Untersuchungen zur Verfasserschaft Sprache und Herkunft der althochdeutschen Isidor-Sippe* (Ludwig Röhrscheid: Bonn, 1970) [= *Rh. Archiv*, 75].

MAUERSBERG, HANS (1960), *Wirtschafts- und Sozialgeschichte zentraleuropäischer Städte in neuerer Zeit. Dargestellt an den Beispielen von Basel, Frankfurt am Main, Hamburg, Hannover, und München* (Vandenhoeck & Ruprecht: Göttingen, 1960).

MAURER, FRIEDRICH (1954), *Nordgermanen und Alemannen: Studien zur germanischen und frühdeutschen Sprachgeschichte, Stammes- und Volkskunde*, 3rd edn. (Francke Verlag: Berne, 1954) [= Bibliotheca Germanica, 3].

—— (1960), ed. Walther von der Vogelweide (12th–13th cent.) [q.v.].

—— (1965), ed. *Vorarbeiten und Studien zur Vertiefung der südwestdeutschen Sprachgeschichte* (Eberhard Albert Verlag: Freiburg im Breisgau, 1965).

—— and RUPP, HEINZ (1974), *Deutsche Wortgeschichte*, two vols., 3rd edn. (de Gruyter: Berlin and New York, 1974).

MAURO, TULLIO DE (1967), ed. Saussure (1916) [q.v.].

MECHOW, MAX (1971), 'Zur deutschen Soldatensprache des zweiten Weltkrieges', *ZfdS* 27 (1971), 81–100.

MEICHSNER, JOHANN ELIAS (1538), *Handbüchlin gruntlichs berichts/ recht vñ wolschrybens/ der Orthographie vnd Grammatic/ sampt kurtzer erzelung jrer anhangenden kräfften der wörter/ ouch etlichen compositis/ Deßglych von jrrtzen vnd tutzen aller graden/ von den clauibus der Missiuen/ vnder vnd ÿberschrifften/ mit jren eigenschafttē vnd exempeln/ Synonyma/ zierlichen vnd artlichen wörtern defs weidwercks/ Derglych vilerley höflicher send vnd offner brieffs formen/ von aller hand sachen sich in Fürsten Cantzlyen begeben/ zů schimpff vnd ernst/ in friden vnnd kriegen zů gebruchen . . . nit allein . . . allen jungen Schrybern vnnd liebhabern der waren kunst recht teutsch schrybens/ besonder ouch andern so sich der schrybery vnderfahen wöllen/ nutz vnnd lustig zů leßen* (Morhart: Tübingen, 1538;

c.10 reprints in the sixteenth century; repr. Olms: Hildesheim and New York, 1976).

MEILLET, ANTOINE (1921–38), *Linguistique historique et linguistique générale* (vol. i, Champion: Paris, 1921; vol. ii, Klincksieck: Paris, 1938).

—— (1922), *Caractères généraux des langues germaniques*, 2nd edn. (Hachette: Paris, 1922).

MEINHOLD, PETER (1958), *Luthers Sprachphilosophie* (Lutherisches Verlagshaus: Berlin, 1958).

MENTRUP, WOLFGANG (1980), ed. *Materialien zur historischen entwicklung der gross- und kleinschreibungsregeln* (Niemeyer: Tübingen, 1980).

MERKER, PAUL, and STAMMLER, WOLFGANG (1958–84), *Reallexikon der deutschen Literaturkunde*, four vols. (de Gruyter: Berlin, 1958–84).

MEYER, HANS (1878/1965), *Der richtige Berliner in Wörtern und Redensarten* (H. S. Hermann: Berlin, 1878; 10th edn. by Walther Kiaulehn, repr. Biederstein: Berlin and Munich, 1965).

MEYER, RICHARD M. (1900), *Vierhundert Schlagworte* (Teubner: Leipzig, 1900).

MICHAEL, WOLFGANG (1971), 'Deutsche Literatur bis 1500: Drama', in Schmitt (1970–1), ii. 573–607.

MICHAELIS, HERBERT, SCHRAEPLER, ERNST, and SCHEEL, GÜNTER (*c*.1964), *Das Dritte Reich. Innere Gleichschaltung. Der Staat und die Kirchen* (Berlin, n.d. [*c*.1964]) [= *Ursachen und Folgen vom deutschen Zusammenbruch 1918 und 1945 bis zur staatlichen Neuordnung Deutschlands in der Gegenwart*, vol. xi].

MICHELS, VICTOR (1912), *Mittelhochdeutsches Elementarbuch*, 2nd edn. (Carl Winter: Heidelberg, 1912).

MITCHELL, P. M. (1978), comm. Gottsched (1730, 1742, 1751) [q.v.].

MITZKA, WALTHER (1943), *Deutsche Mundarten* (Carl Winter: Heidelberg, 1943).

—— (1952), *Handbuch zum Deutschen Sprachatlas* (N. G. Elwert: Marburg, 1952).

—— (1957), 'Hochdeutsche Mundarten', in Wolfgang Stammler (ed.), *Deutsche Philologie im Aufriß*, 2nd edn., vol. i (Erich Schmidt Verlag: Berlin, 1957), cols. 1599–1728.

MÖHN, DIETER (1980), 'Sondersprachen', in *LGL* (1980), 384–90.

MOSCHEROSCH, JOHANNES MICHAEL (1643), 'A la Mode Kehraus', in *Visiones de Don Quevedo. Wunderliche und Wahrhafftige Gesichte Philanders von Sittewald . . . Zum andern mahl auffgeleget . . .*, Part II (Mülben: Strasburg, 1643), 20 ff.; ed. Felix Bobertag (Verlag von W. Spemann: Berlin and Stuttgart, [1883]).

—— (1646), 'Soldatenleben', in *Les Visions de Don Quevedo. Das ist: Wunderl. Satyrische Gesichte Philanders von Sittewaldt . . .*, five vols. (Adrian Weingarten: Leiden, 1646), vol. iv, No. 19; ed. Felix Bobertag (Verlag von W. Spemann: Berlin and Stuttgart, [1883]).

MOSER, HANS (1977), *Die Kanzlei Maximilians I. Graphematik eines Schreibusus*, two vols. (Innsbruck, 1977) [= Innsbrucker Beiträge zur Kulturwissenschaft, Germanistische Reihe, 5/1 and 2].

—— WELLMAN, HANS, and WOLF, NORBERT RICHARD (in progress),

Geschichte der deutschen Sprache (Uni-Taschenbücher; Quelle & Meyer: Heidelberg, in progress).

MOSER, HUGO (1962), ed. *Das Ringen um eine neue deutsche Grammatik* (WBG: Darmstadt, 1962) [= Wege der Forschung, 25].

—— (1968), *Annalen der deutschen Sprache*, 3rd edn. (Sammlung Metzler, M 5; Stuttgart, 1968).

—— (1969), *Deutsche Sprachgeschichte. Mit einer Einführung in die Fragen der Sprachbetrachtung*, 6th edn. (Niemeyer: Tübingen, 1969).

—— (1974), 'Neuere und neueste Zeit', in Maurer and Rupp (1974), ii. 529–645.

—— and STOPP, HUGO (1970–8), *Grammatik des Frühneuhochdeutschen*, i, Parts I–III, *Vokalismus der Nebensilben*: Part I, ed. K. O. Sauerbeck (1970); Part II, ed. H. Stopp (1973); Part III, ed. H. Stopp (1978) (Carl Winter: Heidelberg, 1970, 1973, 1978).

MOSER, VIRGIL (1909), *Historisch-grammatische Einführung in die frühneuhochdeutschen Schriftdialekte* (Niemeyer: Halle a/S., 1909; repr. WBG: Darmstadt, 1971).

—— (1923), 'Frühneuhochdeutsche Studien, 5: Zur Sprache der Lutherbibel im 17. Jahrhundert', *PBB* 47 (1923), 384–98.

—— (1929–51), *Frühneuhochdeutsche Grammatik*, i/1. *Lautlehre*, 1. Hälfte. *Orthographie, Betonung, Stammsilbenvokale*; i/3. *Konsonanten*, 2. Hälfte (Schluss) (Carl Winter: Heidelberg; i/1 (1929), i/3 (1951)) [continued as Moser and Stopp (1970–8)].

—— (1936, 1948, 1949), 'Deutsche Orthographiereformen des 17. Jahrhunderts', *PBB* 60 (1936), 193–258; ibid. 70 (1948), 467–96; ibid. 71 (1949), 386–465.

MOULTON, WILLIAM G. (1941), *Swiss German Dialect and Romance Patois* (*Language* Diss. 34; Linguistic Society of America, 1941).

—— (1944), 'Scribe Y of the OHG Tatian Translation', *PMLA* 59 (1944), 307–34.

—— (1961), 'Zur Geschichte des deutschen Vokalsystems', *PBB* (T) 83 (1961), 1–35.

—— (1962), *The Sounds of English and German* (University of Chicago Press; Chicago and London, 1962; 5th repr. 1968).

MÜLLENHOFF, KARL, and SCHERER, WILHELM (1892), *Denkmäler deutscher Poesie und Prosa aus dem viii.–xii. Jahrhundert* (1863; 3rd edn. in two vols., Weidmann: Berlin, 1892; repr. 1964).

MÜLLER, HANS ERNST (1923), ed. Lamprecht (12th cent., *a*, *b*) [q.v.].

MÜLLER, JOHANNES (1882), *Quellenschriften und Geschichte des deutschsprachlichen Unterrichtes bis zur Mitte des 16. Jahrhunderts* (Gotha, 1882; repr. WBG: Darmstadt, 1969).

MÜLLER, MAX (1903), *Wortkritik und Sprachbereicherung in Adelungs Wörterbuch* (Mayer & Müller: Berlin, 1903) [= Palaestra, 14].

MÜLLER-FRAUREUTH (1895), ed. Albertus (1573) [q.v.].

MURET-SANDERS (1891–1901), Eduard Muret and Daniel Sanders, *Encyklopädisches Englisch–Deutsches und Deutsch–Englisches Wörterbuch*, four vols. (Langenscheidt: Berlin, 1891–1901).

NAUMANN, HANS (1915), *Kurze historische Syntax der deutschen Sprache* (Karl J. Trübner: Strasburg, 1915).

—— and BETZ, WERNER (1962), *Althochdeutsches Elementarbuch. Grammatik und Texte*, 3rd edn. (Sammlung Göschen, 1111, 1111a; de Gruyter: Berlin and New York, 1962).

NERIUS, DIETER (1967), *Untersuchungen zur Herausbildung einer nationalen Norm der deutschen Literatursprache im 18. Jahrhundert* (VEB Max Niemeyer: Halle a/S., 1967).

NEUMANN, FRIEDRICH (1968), ed. Hartmann von Aue (*c*.1190) [q.v.].

NEUMARK, GEORG (*c*.1668), *Der Neu-Sprossende Teutsche Palmbaum. Oder Ausführlicher Bericht/ Von der Hochlöblichen Fruchtbringenden Gesellschaft Anfang/ Absehn/ Satzungen/ Eigenschaft/ und deroselben Fortpflanzung . . . hervorgegeben von dem Sprossenden* [= Georg Neumark] ('Zufinden bey Joh. Hoffman Kunsth. in Nürnb. Drukkts/ Joachim-Heinrich Schmid in Weinmar/ F.S. Hof-Buchdr.', [*c*.1668]; repr. Munich 1970 as vol. iii of Martin Bircher (ed.), *Die Fruchtbringende Gesellschaft. Quellen und Dokumente* (four vols.)).

NEWALD, RICHARD (1967), *Vom Späthumanismus zur Empfindsamkeit 1570–1750*, 6th edn. (C. H. Beck: Munich, 1967) [= de Boor, Newald, *et al.*, vol. v].

Nibelungenlied, Das (*c*.1200); ed. Helmut de Boor, *Das Nibelungenlied. Nach der Ausgabe von Karl Bartsch* (Brockhaus: Wiesbaden, 1959; 20th edn. 1972).

NICKISCH, REINHARD M. G. (1969), *Die Stilprinzipien in den deutschen Briefstellern des 17. und 18. Jahrhunderts. Mit einer Bibliographie zur Briefschreiblehre (1474–1800)* (Vandenhoeck & Ruprecht: Göttingen, 1969) [= Palaestra, 254].

NIDA, EUGENE A. (1949), *Morphology. The Descriptive Analysis of Words*, 2nd edn. (University of Michigan Press: Ann Arbor, 1949; repr. 1965).

NYSSEN, UTE (1963), ed. Fischart (1590) [q.v.].

OBJARTEL, GEORG (1980), 'Deutsche Literatursprache der frühen Neuzeit', in *LGL* (1980), 712–19.

ÖHMANN, EMIL (1936), ed. Roth (1571) [q.v.].

—— (1974), 'Der romanische Einfluß auf das Deutsche bis zum Ausgang des Mittelalters', in Maurer and Rupp (1974), i. 323–96.

OKSAAR, ELS (1965), *Mittelhochdeutsch* (Almqvist & Wiksell: Stockholm, Göteborg, and Uppsala, 1965).

OLEARIUS, TILEMANN (1630), *Deutsche Sprachkunst. Aus dem allergewissesten/ der Vernunfft vñ gemeinen brauch Deutsch zu reden gemässen gründen genommen. Sampt angehengten newen methodo, die Lateinische Sprache geschwinde vnd mit lust zu lernen* (Oelschlegel: Hall, 1630) [= Wolfenbüttel, HAB, 103.1 Gram. (4): the author signs 'T.O.M.S.'].

ÖLINGER, ALBERTUS (1573–4), *Vnderricht der HochTeutschen Spraach: GRAMMATICA SEV INSTITUTIO VERAE Germanicae linguae . . . IN VSVM IVVENTVTIS maximè Gallicae . . .* (Vvyriot: Strasburg, *c*.1573); ed. Willy Scheel in John Meier (ed.), *Ältere deutsche Grammatiken in Neudrucken*, No. 4 (Halle, 1897); repr. of the 1574 Strasburg edn., Olms: Hildesheim, 1975.

OLT, REINHARD (1981), 'Soldatensprache. Ein Forschungsbericht', *Muttersprache*, 91 (1981), 93–105.

OPITZ, MARTIN (1617), *Aristarchus sive de contemptu linguae Teutonicae* (Dörfer: Beuthen, 1617) [modern facsimile: Jörg-Ulrich Fechner (ed.), *Martin Opitz. Jugendschriften vor 1619* (Sammlung Metzler, M 88; Metzler: Stuttgart, 1970)].

—— (1624), *Buch von der deutschen Poeterey* (Müller: Breslau, 1624); ed. Wilhelm Braune, rev. R. Alewyn (Niemeyer: Tübingen, 1966).

ÖSTERLEY, H. (1873), ed. Steinhöwel (1477) [q.v.].

OTTE, WOLF-DIETER (1982), 'Herzog August und die Revision der deutschen Luther-Bibel', *Wolfenbütteler Beiträge*, 5 (1982), 53–82.

OTTO, KARL F., Jun. (1972a), *Die Sprachgesellschaften des 17. Jahrhunderts* (Sammlung Metzler, M 109; Metzler: Stuttgart, 1972).

—— (1972b), *Philipp von Zesen. A Bibliographical Catalogue* (Francke Verlag: Berne and Munich, 1972).

OTTOKAR VON STEIERMARK (c.1300–10), *Österreichische Reimchronik*; ed. Joseph Seemüller (Hanover and Leipzig, 1890–3) [= Monumenta Germaniae Historica, Deutsche Chroniken, 5].

PALMER, FRANK R. (1968), ed. Firth (1955, 1957) [qq.v.].

—— (1976), *Semantics. A New Outline* (Cambridge University Press, 1976).

PALMER, LEONARD R. (1972), *Descriptive and Comparative Linguistics. A Critical Introduction* (Faber: London, 1972).

PALMER, PHILIP M. (1950, 1960), *The Influence of English on the German Vocabulary to 1700* (University of California Press: Berkeley and Los Angeles, 1950; Supplement, 1960).

PAUL, HERMANN (1880/1968), *Principien der Sprachgeschichte* (1880; 2nd edn., Halle a/S., 1886; 8th edn. [repr. of 5th edn.], Niemeyer: Tübingen, 1968).

—— (1881/1969), *Mittelhochdeutsche Grammatik* (1881; 20th edn. by Hugo Moser and Ingeborg Schröbler, Niemeyer: Tübingen, 1969; 22nd edn., rev. Siegfried Grosse, 1982).

—— (1916–20), *Deutsche Grammatik*, five vols. (Niemeyer: Halle a/S., 1916–20; repr. Niemeyer: Tübingen, 1968) [i (1916), Part I. *Geschichtliche Einleitung*; Part II. *Lautlehre*; ii (1917), Part III. *Flexionslehre*; iii (1919), Part IV. *Syntax* (I); iv (1920), Part IV. *Syntax* (II); v (1920), Part IV. *Wortbildungslehre*].

PAULSEN, FRIEDRICH (1896–7), *Geschichte des gelehrten Unterrichts auf den deutschen Schulen und Universitäten vom Ausgang des Mittelalters bis zur Gegenwart . . .*, two vols., 2nd edn. (Veit & Co.: Leipzig, 1896–7).

PAUMGARTNER, BALTHASAR and MAGDALENA (1582–98), Letters; ed. Georg Steinhausen, *Briefwechsel Balthasar Paumgartners des Jüngeren mit seiner Gattin Magdalena, geb. Behaim (1582–98)* (Tübingen, 1895) [= BLVS 204].

PECHAU, M. (1935), *Nationalsozialismus und deutsche Sprache* (Diss. Greifswald, 1935).

PENZL, HERBERT (1949), 'Umlaut and secondary Umlaut in Old High German', *Language*, 25 (1949), 223–40.

—— (1955–6), 'Zur Erklärung von Notkers Anlautgesetz', *ZfdA* 86 (1955–6), 196–210.

PENZL, HERBERT (1961), 'OHG ⟨r⟩ and its phonetic identification', *Language*, 37 (1961), 488–96.
—— (1971), *Lautsystem und Lautwandel in den althochdeutschen Dialekten* (Hueber: Munich, 1971).
—— (1975a), *Vom Urgermanischen zum Neuhochdeutschen. Eine historische Phonologie* (Erich Schmidt Verlag: Berlin, 1975).
—— (1975b), 'Johann Christoph Gottsched und die deutsche Sprache in Österreich', *Michigan German Studies*, 1 (1975), 141–51.
—— (1977), 'Gottsched und die Aussprache des Deutschen im 18. Jahrhundert', *Sprachwissenschaft*, 2 (1977), 61–92.
—— (1978), ed. Gottsched (1748, 1762) [q.v.].
—— (1980), comm. Gottsched (1748, 1762) [q.v.].
—— (1984), *Frühneuhochdeutsch* (Peter Lang: Berne, Frankfurt-on-Main, Nancy, and New York, 1984) [= Germanistische Lehrbuchsammlung, 9].
PETZET, ERICH, and GLAUNING, OTTO (1910–30), *Deutsche Schrifttafeln des ix. bis xvi. Jahrhunderts aus Handschriften der K. Hof- und Staatsbibliothek in München*, sections 1–3 (C. Kuhn: Munich, 1910–12); sections 4–5 (Hiersemann: Leipzig, 1924–30) [title changed to . . . *Handschriften der Bayerischen Staatsbibliothek* . . .].
PHILIPP, GERHARD (1980), *Einführung ins Frühneuhochdeutsche: Sprachgeschichte, Grammatik, Texte* (UTB 822; Quelle & Meyer: Heidelberg, 1980).
PHONAI (1969), *Lautbibliothek der europäischen Sprachen und Mundarten*. Deutsche Reihe, No. 5. *Proben deutscher Mundarten*, edd. W. Bethge and G. M. Bonnin (1969) [with taped specimens of major German dialects].
PIIRAINEN, ILPO TAPANI (1980), *Frühneuhochdeutsche Bibliographie. Literatur zur Sprache des 14.–17. Jahrhunderts* (Niemeyer: Tübingen, 1980).
PLANITZ, HANS (1954), *Die deutsche Stadt im Mittelalter* (Böhlau: Graz and Cologne, 1954).
POLENZ, PETER VON (1963), *Funktionsverben im heutigen Deutsch* (1963) [= *WW*, Beiheft 5].
—— (1967), 'Sprachpurismus und Nationalsozialismus', in E. Lämmert, W. Killy, K. O. Conrady, and P. von Polenz, *Germanistik — eine deutsche Wissenschaft* (Suhrkamp 204; Suhrkamp Verlag: Frankfurt-on-Main, 1967), 111–65.
—— (1978), *Geschichte der deutschen Sprache*, 9th edn. (Sammlung Göschen, 2206; de Gruyter: Berlin and New York, 1978) [a recasting of Sperber and Fleischhauer (1963)].
POPOWITSCH, JOHANN SIEGMUND VALENTIN (1750), *Untersuchungen vom Meere* (Frankfurt-on-Main and Leipzig, 1750).
PÖRKSEN, UWE (1977), 'Einige Aspekte einer Geschichte der Naturwissenschaftssprache und ihrer Einflüsse auf die Gemeinsprache', in Hugo Moser *et al.* (edd.), *Sprachwandel und Sprachgeschichtsschreibung im Deutschen. Jahrbuch 1976 des Instituts für deutsche Sprache* (Schwann: Düsseldorf, 1977), 145–66 [= Sprache der Gegenwart, 41].
—— (1978), 'Zur Metaphorik der naturwissenschaftlichen Sprache', *Neue Rundschau*, 73 (1978), 64–82.
—— and SCHIEWE, JÜRGEN (1983), edd. Leibniz (c.1697) [q.v.].

POWELL, HUGH (1972), ed. Gryphius (1660) [q.v.].

PRIEBSCH, ROBERT, and COLLINSON, WILLIAM E. (1968), *The German Language*, 6th edn. (Faber: London, 1968).

PROKOSCH, E. (1939), *A Comparative Germanic Grammar* (Linguistic Society of America: Philadelphia, 1939).

PROMIES, WOLFGANG (1967), ed. Lichtenberg (1766–99) [q.v.].

—— (1971), ed. Lichtenberg (1779–83) [q.v.].

PROSS, WOLFGANG (1979?), ed. Herder (1770) [q.v.].

PRUTZ, ROBERT (1857), 'Über plattdeutsche Dichtung', *Deutsches Museum*, 7 (1857), 696–700.

PUTSCHKE, WOLFGANG (1973), 'Ostmitteldeutsch', in *LGL* (1973) 341–52 (2nd edn. (1980), 474–8).

PYRITZ, HANS, and PYRITZ, ILSE (1979–   ), edd. *Bibliographie zur deutschen Literaturgeschichte des Barockzeitalters* (Francke Verlag: Berne and Munich, 1979–   : i (1979), ii/4 (1981)).

RACHEL, JOACHIM (1664), *Teutsche Satyrische Gedichte* (Frankfurt-on-Main, 1664); ed. Karl Drescher (Niemeyer: Halle a/S., 1903) [= NDL 200–2].

RAMM, AGATHA (1967), *Germany 1789–1919. A Political History* (Methuen: London, 1967).

RATKE, WOLFGANG (1612–30), grammatical writings; ed. Erika Ising, *Wolfgang Ratkes Schriften zur deutschen Grammatik (1612–1630)* (Akademie-Verlag: Berlin, 1959) [= DAdWB, VdSk, No. 3].

RAUCH, IRMENGARD (1967), *The Old High German Diphthongization. A Description of a Phonetic Change* (Mouton: The Hague, 1967).

RAUMER, RUDOLF VON (1863), *Gesammelte sprachwissenschaftliche Schriften* (Frankfurt-on-Main and Erlangen, 1863).

—— (1870), *Geschichte der Germanischen Philologie, vorzugsweise in Deutschland* (R. Oldenbourg: Munich, 1870).

—— (1876), *Regeln und Wörterverzeichnis für die deutsche Orthographie* [contained in *Verhandlungen . . . 1876*, q.v.].

RAYNAUD, FRANZISKA (1982), *Histoire de la langue allemande* (Que sais-je?, 1952; Presses Universitaires de France: Paris, 1982).

REBHUN, PAUL (1536), *Susanna*; ed. Hans-Gert Roloff (Reclam U-B, 8787–8; Reclam: Stuttgart, 1967).

Regeln und Wörterverzeichnis für die deutsche Rechtschreibung zum Gebrauch in den preußischen Schulen (Weidmann: Berlin, 1880).

REICHARD, ELIAS CASPAR (1747), *Versuch einer Historie der deutschen Sprachkunst* (Martini: Hamburg, 1747).

REIFFENSTEIN, INGO (1958), *Das Althochdeutsche und die irische Mission im oberdeutschen Raum* (Sprachwissenschaftliches Institut der Universität Innsbruck: Innsbruck, 1958).

—— (forthcoming), *Geschichte der deutschen Sprache* (Peter Lang: Berne, forthcoming) [part of the 'Germanistische Lehrbuchsammlung', ed. Hans-Gert Roloff].

REIFFERSCHEID, ALEXANDER (1889a), *Quellen zur Geschichte des geistigen Lebens in Deutschland während des 17. Jahrhunderts*, i (Gebrüder Henninger: Heilbronn, 1889).

—— (1889b), *Marcus Evangelion Mart. Luthers nach der Septemberbibel*,

Mit . . . Proben aus den Hochdeutschen Nachdrucken des 16. Jahrhunderts (Gebrüder Henninger: Heilbronn, 1889).

REIN, O. P. (1915), *Mixed Preterites in German* (Vandenhoeck & Ruprecht: Göttingen and Johns Hopkins Press: Baltimore, 1915) [= Hesperia, 5].

REINITZER, HEIMO (1982), 'Auch in Psalmis ex bubonibus ranas gemachet. Herzog August der Jüngere und seine Revision der Luther-Bibel', *Vestigia bibliae. Jahrbuch des Deutschen Bibel-Archivs*, 4 (1982), 42–69.

—— (1983*a*), 'Die Bedeutung der Bibelübersetzung Martin Luthers', in *Martin Luther heute*, Themenheft 3 (Bundeszentrale für politische Bildung: Bonn, 1983).

—— (1983*b*), ed. *Biblia deutsch. Luthers Bibelübersetzung und ihre Tradition* (HAB Wolfenbüttel and Wittig: Brunswick, 1983) [= *Ausstellungskataloge der HAB*, No. 40; catalogue of an exhibition held at Wolfenbüttel 1983 and Hamburg 1983–4].

REIS, MARGA (1974*a*), *Lauttheorie und Lautgeschichte. Untersuchungen am Beispiel der Dehnungs- und Kürzungsvorgänge im Deutschen* (Wilhelm Fink Verlag: Munich, 1974) [= International Library of General Linguistics, 14].

—— (1974*b*), 'Phonologie des spätgemeingermanischen Vokalismus unter besonderer Berücksichtigung der Nebensilbenvokale', in *Probleme der historischen Phonologie* (1974), 23–68 [*ZDL*, Beiheft 12].

—— (1978), 'Hermann Paul', *PBB* (T) 100 (1978), 159–204.

REUTER, FRITZ (1858), *Abweisung der ungerechten Angriffe und unwahren Behauptungen, welche Dr. Klaus Groth in seinen Briefen über Plattdeutsch und Hochdeutsch gegen mich gerichtet hat* (1858; repr. in *Gesammelte Werke und Briefe*, ed. Kurt Batt, VEB Hinstorff Verlag: Rostock, 1967, vii. 567–93).

RICHEL, VERONICA (1973), *Luise Gottsched. A Reconsideration* (Lang: Berne and Frankfurt-on-Main, 1973) [= Europäische Hochschulschriften, 1/75].

RICHEY, MICHAEL (1743), *Idioticon Hambvrgense sive Glossarivm vocvm Saxonicarvm qvae popvlari nostra dialecto Hambvrgi maxime frequentantvr . . .* (Conr. Koenig: Hamburg, 1743).

RIECK, WERNER (1972), *Johann Christoph Gottsched. Eine kritische Würdigung seines Werkes* (Akademie-Verlag: Berlin, 1972).

RIEGEL, HERMANN (1891–3), ed. *Der Vnartig Teutscher Sprachverderber* [q.v.].

ROBINS, ROBERT HENRY (1967), *A Short History of Linguistics* (Longmans: London and Harlow, 1967; 2nd edn. 1979).

RÖMER, RUTH (1962), 'Die Entwicklung des Wortes Partei zum Bestandteil von Eigennamen', *Muttersprache*, 72 (1962), 326–32.

ROSENFELD, HANS-FRIEDRICH (1974), 'Humanistische Strömungen', in Maurer and Rupp (1974), i. 399–508.

ROSENZWEIG, FRANZ (1926), *Die Schrift und Luther* (Schocken-Verlag: Berlin, 1926).

ROT(H), SIMON (1571), *Ein Teutscher Dictionarius/ dz ist ein außleger schwerer/ vnbekanter Teutscher/ Griechischer/ Lateinischer/ Hebraischer/ Wälscher vnd Frantzösischer/ auch andrer Nationen wörter/ so mit der weil inn Teutsche sprach kommen seind/ vnd offt mancherley jrrung bringen:*

hin vnd wider auß manicherley geschrifften/ vnd gemainer Red zusamen gelesen/ außgelegt/ vnd also allen Teutschen/ sonderlich aber denen so zu Schreibereien kommen/ vnd Ampts verwaltung haben/ aber des Lateins vnerfarn seind/ zu gutem publiciert durch Simon Roten . . . (Michael Manger: Augsburg, 1571); ed. Emil Öhmann, *Mémoires de la Société Néophilologique de Helsinki (Helsingfors)*, 11 (1936), 225-370.

RÜCKERT, HEINRICH (1852), ed. Thomasin von Zerclaere (1216) [q.v.].

—— (1864), 'Die deutsche Schriftsprache der Gegenwart und die Dialekte', *Deutsche Vierteljahrsschrift*, 107 (1864), 90-137; repr. in *Kleinere Schriften*, edd. A. Sohr and A. Reifferscheid (Weimar, 1877), i. 283 ff.

—— (1875), *Geschichte der Neuhochdeutschen Schriftsprache*, two vols. (T. O. Weigel: Leipzig, 1875).

RÜDIGER, JOHANN CHRISTIAN CHRISTOPH (1783), 'Ueber das Verhältniß der hochteutschen Sprache und obersächsischen Mundart', in *Neuester Zuwachs der teutschen, fremden und allgemeinen Sprachkunde in eigenen Aufsätzen, Bücheranzeigen und Nachrichten*, four parts (1781-5), Part II (P. G. Kummer: Leipzig, 1783), 1-140.

RUDOLF VON EMS (c.1220), *Der gute Gerhart*; ed. John A. Asher (Niemeyer: Tübingen, 1962) [= ATB 56].

—— (c.1240), *Willehalm von Orlens;* ed. Victor Junk (Berlin, 1905) [= DTM 2].

RUH, KURT (1953), 'Die trinitarische Spekulation in deutscher Mystik und Scholastik', *ZfdPh* 72 (1953), 24-53.

—— (1956), *Bonaventura deutsch* (Francke Verlag: Berne, 1956) [= Bibliotheca Germanica, 7].

RUPPRICH, HANS (1970), *Vom späten Mittelalter bis zum Barock*, Part I. *Das ausgehende Mittelalter, Humanismus und Renaissance 1370-1520* (Beck: Munich, 1970) [= de Boor, Newald, *et al.*, vol. iv/1].

—— (1973), *Vom späten Mittelalter bis zum Barock*, Part II. *Das Zeitalter der Reformation 1520-1570* (Beck: Munich, 1973) [= de Boor, Newald, *et al.*, vol. iv/2].

RUSS, CHARLES V. J. (1975), 'Umlaut in German: the Development of a Phonological Rule', *York Papers in Linguistics*, 5 (1975), 51-65.

—— (1978), *Historical German Phonology and Morphology* (Clarendon Press: Oxford, 1978).

SACER, GEORG WILHELM VON (1673), *Reime dich/ oder ich fresse dich/ Das ist/ deutlicher zu geben/ ANTIPERICATAMETANAPARBEUGEDAM-PHIRRIBIFICATIONES POETICAE, oder Schellen- vnd Scheltenswürdige Thorheit Bœotischer Poeten in Deutschland/ Hans Wursten/ zu sonderbahren Nutzen vnd Ehren/ zu keinem Nachtheil der Edlen Poesie/ unsrer löblichen Muttersprache/ oder einiges rechtschaffenen/ gelehrten Poetens/ zu belachen und zu verwerffen vorgestellet von Hartmann Reinholden/ dem Franckfurter* . . . (Bey Barthold Fuhrmannen: Nordhausen, 1673).

SAGARRA, EDA (1977), *A Social History of Germany 1648-1914* (Methuen: London, 1977).

—— (1980), *An Introduction to Nineteenth Century Germany* (Longmans: Harlow, 1980).

SALMON, PAUL B. (1967), *Literature in Medieval Germany* (The Cresset Press: London, 1967).

SANDERS, DANIEL (1871), *Fremdwörterbuch*, two vols. (Leipzig, 1871).

SARAN, FRANZ (1930/1975), *Das Übersetzen aus dem Mittelhochdeutschen. Eine Anleitung für Studierende, Lehrer und zum Selbstunterricht*, rev. Bert Nagel, 6th edn. (Niemeyer: Tübingen, 1975).

SARRAZIN, OTTO (1889), *Verdeutschungs-Wörterbuch*, 2nd edn. (Ernst & Korn: Berlin, 1889).

SATTLER, JOHANN RUDOLPH (1607), *Teutsche Orthographey Vnd Phraseologey das ist/ die Kunst vnd wissenschafft Teutsche sprach recht vnd wohl zu schreiben* . . . (König: Basel, 1607).

SAUER, AUGUST (1894), ed. *Thomasius* (1687/1701) [q.v.].

SAUSSURE, FERDINAND DE (1916/1973), *Cours de linguistique générale*; ed. Tullio de Mauro (1967; French edn., Payot; Paris, 1973) [= *CLG*].

SCAGLIONE, ALDO (1981), *The Theory of German Word Order from the Renaissance to the Present* (University of Minnesota Press: Minneapolis, 1981).

SCHATZ, JOSEF (1907), *Altbairische Grammatik. Laut- und Flexionslehre* (Vandenhoeck & Ruprecht: Göttingen, 1907).

—— (1927), *Althochdeutsche Grammatik* (Vandenhoeck & Ruprecht: Göttingen, 1927).

SCHEEL, WILLY (1897), ed. Ölinger (*c.*1573) [q.v.].

SCHENDA, RUDOLF (1977), *Volk ohne Buch. Studien zur Sozialgeschichte der populären Lesestoffe 1770-1910* (1970; 2nd edn. [dtv 4282], Deutscher Taschenbuch Verlag: Munich, 1977).

SCHENKER, WALTER (1977), *Die Sprache Huldrych Zwinglis im Kontrast zur Sprache Luthers* (de Gruyter: Berlin and New York, 1977) [= Studia Linguistica Germanica, 14].

SCHERAEUS, BARTHOLOMAEUS (1619), [*Symmikta hierarchica.*] *MISCELLANEA HIERARCHICA. Geistliche/ Weltliche/ vnd Häusliche Sprachen Schule* . . . (Wittenberg, 1619).

SCHERER, WILHELM (1875), 'Johann Christoph Adelung', in *Allgemeine Deutsche Biographie*, i (1875), 80-4; repr. in *Kleine Schriften zur altdeutschen Philologie*, ed. Konrad Burdach (Weidmann: Berlin, 1893), i. 213-17.

—— (1876*a*), 'Die orthographische Guillotine', *Gegenwart*, 9 (12 Feb. 1876), 102-3; repr. ibid. i. 430-5.

—— (1876*b*), 'Die Berliner Conferenz zur Einigung über die Grundsätze der deutschen Rechtschreibung', *Deutsche Rundschau*, 6 (1876), 462-70; repr. ibid. i. 435-47.

—— (1876*c*), 'Orthographische Nachwehen', *Deutsche Rundschau*, 8 (1876), 460-2; repr. ibid. i. 447-51.

—— (1878), *Zur Geschichte der deutschen Sprache* (1868; 2nd edn., Weidmann: Berlin, 1878).

SCHIEB, GABRIELE (1965), *Henric van Veldeken* (Sammlung Metzler, M 42; Metzler: Stuttgart, 1965).

—— (1970), 'Mittelhochdeutsch', in Schmitt (1970-1), i. 347-85.

—— (1972), 'Zum System der Nebensätze im ersten deutschen Prosaroman

[= the *Prose Lancelot* translation]', in Günther Feudel (ed.), *Studien zur Geschichte der deutschen Sprache* (Akademie-Verlag: Berlin, 1972) [= Bausteine zur Geschichte des Neuhochdeutschen, 49].

—— (1981), 'Zu Stand und Wirkungsbereich der kodifizierten grammatischen Norm Ende des 19. Jahrhunderts', *BES* 1 (1981), 134–76.

—— and FRINGS, THEODOR (1964–5); edd. Heinrich von Veldeke (1189) [q.v.].

SCHILDT, JOACHIM (1968), 'Zur Ausbildung des Satzrahmens in Aussagesätzen der Bibelsprache 1350–1550', *PBB* (H) 90 (1968), 174–97.

—— (1972), 'Die Satzklammer und ihre Ausbildung in hoch- und niederdeutschen Bibeltexten des 14. bis 16. Jahrhunderts', in G. Feudel (ed.), *Studien zur Geschichte der deutschen Sprache* (Akademie-Verlag: Berlin, 1972), 231–42 [= Bausteine zur Geschichte des Neuhochdeutschen, 49].

—— (1976), *Abriß der Geschichte der deutschen Sprache. Zum Verhältnis von Gesellschafts- und Sprachgeschichte* (Akademie-Verlag: Berlin, 1976).

—— (1977), 'Deutsche Sprache und industrielle Revolution im 19. Jahrhundert', *Weimarer Beiträge*, 23 (1977), vi. 156–64.

—— (1978), *Zum Einfluß von Marx und Engels auf die deutsche Literatursprache. Studien zum Wortschatz der Arbeiterklasse im 19. Jahrhundert* (Akademie-Verlag: Berlin, 1978).

—— (1982), ed. *Zur Periodisierung der deutschen Sprachgeschichte. Prinzipien — Probleme — Aufgaben* (Akademie-Verlag: Berlin, 1982) [= AdWdDDR; ZIfS, Linguistische Studien, Reihe A, Arbeitsberichte, 88].

—— et al. (1981), edd. *Auswirkungen der industriellen Revolution auf die deutsche Sprachentwicklung im 19. Jahrhundert* (Akademie-Verlag: Berlin, 1981) [= AdWdDDR; ZIfS; Bausteine zur Sprachgeschichte des Neuhochdeutschen, 60].

SCHIRMER, ALFRED (1911a), *Zur Geschichte der deutschen Kaufmannssprache* Diss. Leipzig, 1911).

—— (1911b), *Wörterbuch der deutschen Kaufmannssprache* (Trübner: Strasburg, 1911).

SCHIRMUNSKI, VIKTOR MAKSIMOVICH (1962), *Deutsche Mundartenkunde* (Akademie-Verlag: Berlin, 1962) [DAdWB, VdIfdSuL, 25; trans. Wolfgang Fleischer from the Russian version, *Nemetskaja dialektologija* (Moscow, 1956)].

SCHIROKAUER, ARNO (1940), 'Der Anteil des Buchdrucks an der Bildung des Gemeindeutschen', *DVLG* 25 (1940), 317–50.

—— (1952), 'Frühneuhochdeutsch', in Wolfgang Stammler (ed.), *Deutsche Philologie im Aufriß* (1952; 2nd edn., Erich Schmidt Verlag: Berlin, 1957), vol. i, cols. 855–930.

SCHLAEFER, MICHAEL (1980a), *Kommentierte Bibliographie zur deutschen Orthographietheorie und Orthographiegeschichte im 19. Jahrhundert* (Carl Winter: Heidelberg, 1980).

—— (1980b). 'Grundzüge der deutschen Orthographiegeschichte vom Jahre 1800 bis zum Jahre 1870', *Sprachwissenschaft*, 5 (1980), 276–319 [with map].

SCHLEICHER, AUGUST (1860, 1869), *Die deutsche Sprache* (1860; 2nd edn., Cotta: Stuttgart, 1869).

SCHLOSSER, HORST DIETER (1970), *Althochdeutsche Literatur mit Proben aus dem Altniederdeutschen. Ausgewählte Texte mit Übertragungen und Anmerkungen* (Fischer-Taschenbuch, 6036; Frankfurt-on-Main, 1970; repr. 1976).

—— (1977), *Die literarischen Anfänge der deutschen Sprache: ein Arbeitsbuch zur althochdeutschen und altniederdeutschen Literatur* (Erich Schmidt Verlag: Berlin, 1977).

SCHMARSOW, A. (1877), ed. Leibniz (*c.*1697) [q.v.].

SCHMID, KARL, *et al.* (1978), *Die Klostergemeinschaft von Fulda im früheren Mittelalter*, three parts (de Gruyter: Berlin and New York, 1978) [= Münstersche Mittelalter-Schriften, 8].

SCHMIDT, JOHANNES (1872), *Die Verwantschaftsverhältnisse* [sic] *der Indogermanischen Sprachen* (Böhlau: Weimar, 1872).

SCHMIDT, WILHELM, *et al.* (1969), *Geschichte der deutschen Sprache* (Volk und Wissen Volkseigner Verlag: Leipzig, 1969; 2nd edn. 1976).

SCHMITT, LUDWIG ERICH (1966), *Untersuchungen zur Entstehung und Struktur der 'neuhochdeutschen Schriftsprache'*, i. *Sprachgeschichte des Thüringisch-Obersächsischen im Spätmittelalter. Die Geschäftssprache von 1300 bis 1500* (1966; 2nd edn., Böhlau: Cologne and Vienna, 1982) [= Mitteldeutsche Forschungen, 36/1].

—— (1970-1), ed. *Kurzer Grundriß der germanischen Philologie bis 1500*, two vols., i. *Sprachgeschichte*; ii. *Literaturgeschichte* (de Gruyter: Berlin, 1970, 1971).

SCHNAUBER, CORNELIUS (1972), *Wie Hitler sprach und schrieb. Zur Psychologie und Prosodik der faschistischen Rhetorik* (Athenäum Verlag: Frankfurt-on-Main, 1972).

SCHNEIDER, KARL LUDWIG (1960), *Klopstock und die Erneuerung der deutschen Dichtersprache im 18. Jahrhundert* (Carl Winter: Heidelberg, 1960).

SCHÖNAICH, CHRISTOPH OTTO VON (1754), *Die ganze Aesthetik in einer Nuß oder Neologisches Wörterbuch*; ed. Albert Köster (B. Behrs Verlag (E. Bock): Berlin, 1900) [= Deutsche Litteraturdenkmale des 18. und 19. Jahrhunderts, 70-81].

SCHÖNE, ALBRECHT (1968), ed. *Das Zeitalter des Barock. Texte und Zeugnisse*, 2nd edn. (Beck: Munich, 1968) [= Die deutsche Literatur: Texte und Zeugnisse, 2].

SCHÖNFELD, HELMUT (1977), 'Zur Rolle der sprachlichen Existenzformen in der sprachlichen Kommunikation', in W. Hartung *et al.* (edd.), *Normen in der sprachlichen Kommunikation* (Akademie-Verlag: Berlin, 1977), 163-208.

SCHÖNFELD, MORITZ (1910), *Wörterbuch der altgermanischen Personen- und Völkernamen* (Carl Winter: Heidelberg, 1910; repr. 1965).

SCHOTTEL(IUS), JUSTUS GEORG (1641), *Teutsche Sprachkunst/ Darinn die Allerwortreichste/ Prächtigste/ reinlichste/ vollkommene/ Uhralte Hauptsprache der Teutschen auß jhren Gründen erhoben/ dero Eigenschafften und Kunststücke völliglich entdeckt/ und also in eine richtige Form der Kunst zum ersten mahle gebracht worden . . .* (Gruber: Brunswick, 1641).

—— (1643), *Der Teutschen Sprache Einleitung/ Zu richtiger gewisheit und grundmeßigem vermügen der Teutschen Haubtsprache/ samt beygefügten Erklärungen . . .* (Dünckler: Lüneburg, 1643).

—— (1645), *Iusti-Georgii Schottelii Teutsche Vers- oder ReimKunst darin Vnsere Teutsche MutterSprache, so viel dero süßeste Poesis betrift, in eine richtige Form der Kunst zum ersten mahle gebracht worden . . .* (Johann Bismarck: Wolfenbüttel, 1645).

—— (1648), *Neu erfundenes FreudenSpiel genandt Friedens Sieg* (1648); ed. F. E. Koldewey (Neimeyer: Halle a/S., 1900) [= NDL 175].

—— (1663), *Ausführliche Arbeit Von der Teutschen HaubtSprache/ Worin enthalten Gemelter dieser HaubtSprache Uhrankunft/ Uhraltertuhm/ Reinlichkeit/ Eigenschaft/ Vermögen/ Unvergleichlichkeit/ Grundrichtigkeit/ zumahl die SprachKunst und VersKunst und guten theils Lateinisch völlig mit eingebracht . . .*, five vols. in one (Zilliger: Brunswick, 1663).

—— (1676), *Brevis & fundamentalis Manuductio ad ORTHOGRAPHIAM & ETYMOLOGIAM in Lingua Germanica. Kurtze und gründliche Anleitung Zu der RechtSchreibung Und zu der WortForschung In der Teutschen Sprache. Für die Jugend in den Schulen/ und sonst überall nützlich und dienlich* (Zilliger: Brunswick, 1676).

SCHOTTMANN, HANS (1971), 'Mittelhochdeutsche Literatur: Lyrik', in Schmitt (1970–1), ii. 464–527.

SCHRAMM, FRITZ (1914), *Schlagworte der Alamodezeit* (Karl J. Trübner: Strasburg, 1914) [= ZfdW 15 (Beiheft)].

SCHRIMPF, HANS JOACHIM (1980), *Karl Philipp Moritz* (Sammlung Metzler, M 195; Metzler: Stuttgart, 1980).

SCHRÖBLER (1969). See Paul (1881, 1969).

SCHRÖDER, WERNER (1972), 'Zum *ritter*-Bild der frühmittelhochdeutschen Dichter', *GRM* 53 (1972), 333–51.

SCHRÖTER, WALTHER (1973). See Steinbach (1734).

—— (1975), 'Einführung und Bibliographie zu Christoph Ernst Steinbach, Vollständiges Deutsches Wörter-Buch (1734)', in Henne (1975), 71–91.

SCHULTZ, HEINRICH (1888), *Die Bestrebungen der Sprachgesellschaften des XVII. Jahrhunderts für Reinigung der deutschen Sprache* (Vandenhoeck & Ruprecht: Göttingen, 1888; repr. Zentralantiquariat der DDR: Leipzig, 1975).

Schulz-Basler (1913–83). Deutsches Fremdwörterbuch, i (A–K), ed. Hans Schulz (Strasburg, 1913); ii (L–P), rev. Otto Basler (Berlin, 1942); iii. (Q–R), edd. Alan Kirkness et al. (de Gruyter: Berlin, 1977); iv (S) (1978); v (T) (1981); vi (U–Z) (1983).

SCHULZE, URSULA (1967), *Studien zur Orthographie und Lautung der Dentalspiranten 's' und 'z' im späten 13. und frühen 14. Jahrhundert durchgeführt aufgrund der ältesten deutschsprachigen Urkunden im nordbairisch-ostfränkischen und thüringisch-obersächsischen Sprachgebiet* (Niemeyer: Tübingen, 1967) [= Hermaea, NF 19].

SCHUSTER, MAURIZ, and SCHIKOLA, HANS (1956), *Sprachlehre der Wiener Mundart*, rev. edn. by Hans Schikola (Österreichischer Bundesverlag f. Unterricht, Wissenschaft und Kunst: Vienna, 1956).

SCHÜTZEICHEL, RUDOLF (1960), *Mundart, Urkundensprache und Schriftsprache. Studien zur Sprachgeschichte am Mittelrhein* (Ludwig Röhrscheid: Bonn, 1960) [= Rh. Archiv, 54].

SCHÜTZEICHEL, RUDOLF (1962), 'Zur Frage des Westfränkischen', in *Die Grundlagen des westlichen Mitteldeutschen* (Niemeyer: Tübingen, 1962; 2nd rev. edn. 1976), 94-134 [= Hermaea, 10].

—— (1966-7), 'Das Ludwigslied und die Erforschung des Westfränkischen', *Rheinische Vierteljahrsblätter*, 31 (1966-7), 291-306.

—— (1967), 'Zur Entstehung der neuhochdeutschen Schriftsprache', *Nassauische Annalen*, 78 (1967), 75-92.

—— (1969), *Althochdeutsches Wörterbuch* (1969; 2nd edn., Niemeyer: Tübingen, 1974; 3rd edn. 1980).

—— (1979), 'Nochmals zur merovingischen Lautverschiebung', *ZDL* 46 (1979), 204-30.

SCHWARZ, ALEXANDER (1977), 'Glossen als Texte', *PBB* (T) 99 (1977), 25-36.

SCHWARZ, ERNST (1949-50), *Deutsche Namenforschung*, two vols., i. *Ruf- und Familiennamen*; ii. *Orts- und Flurnamen* (Vandenhoeck & Ruprecht: Göttingen, 1949, 1950).

—— (1950), *Die deutschen Mundarten* (Vandenhoeck & Ruprecht: Göttingen, 1950).

SCHWARZ, WERNER (1944), 'Translation into German in the Fifteenth Century', *MLR* 39 (1944), 368-73.

—— (1945), 'The Theory of Translation in Sixteenth-Century Germany', *MLR* 40 (1945), 289-99.

—— (1955), *Principles and Problems of Biblical Translation* (Cambridge University Press: Cambridge, 1955).

SEEMÜLLER, JOSEPH (1890-3), ed. Ottokar von Steiermark (*c.*1300-10) [q.v.].

SEIDEL, EUGEN, and SEIDEL-SLOTTY, INGEBORG (1961), *Sprachwandel im Dritten Reich. Eine kritische Untersuchung faschistischer Einflüsse* (VEB Verlag Sprache und Literatur: Halle, 1961).

SICKEL, KARL E. (1934), *Johann Christoph Adelung* (Diss. Leipzig, 1934).

Siebs (1898/1969). *Deutsche Aussprache. Reine und gemäßigte Hochlautung mit Aussprachewörterbuch*, 19th edn. by H. de Boor, H. Moser, and Christian Winkler (de Gruyter: Berlin, 1969) [1st edn. by Theodor Siebs, *Deutsche Bühnenaussprache* (Ahn: Berlin, Cologne, and Leipzig, 1898); 8th, 9th edns., 1910; 18th edn. by H. de Boor and Paul Diels, *Deutsche Hochsprache. Bühnenaussprache* (1961)].

SIEBS, THEODOR (1901), 'Zur deutschen Bühnen- und Musteraussprache', *ZADS* 16 (1901), cols. 312-17.

—— (1905), 'Neues zur deutschen Bühnen- und Musteraussprache', *ZADS* 20 (1905), cols. 229-34.

SIEGRIST, CHRISTOPH (1967), *Albrecht von Haller* (Sammlung Metzler, M 57; Metzler: Stuttgart, 1967).

SIEVERS, EDUARD (1876), *Grundzüge der Lautphysiologie zur Einführung in das Studium der Lautlehre der indogermanischen Sprachen* (Leipzig, 1876) [= Bibliothek der indogermanischen Grammatiken, 1].

—— (1892), ed. *Tatian* (*c.*830) [q.v.].

SIMMLER, FRANZ (1981), *Graphematisch-phonematische Studien zum althochdeutschen Konsonantismus insbesondere zur zweiten Lautverschiebung* (Carl Winter: Heidelberg, 1981).

SITTA, HORST (1980), ed. *Ansätze zu einer pragmatischen Sprachgeschichte. Zürcher Kolloquium 1978* (Niemeyer: Tübingen, 1980).

SKÁLA, EMIL (1964), 'Die Entwicklung der Kanzleisprache in Eger (1310–1660)', *PBB* (H) 86 (1964), 35–68.

—— (1967), *Die Entwicklung der Kanzleisprache in Eger 1310 bis 1660* (Akademie-Verlag: Berlin, 1967) [= DAdWB, VdIfdSuL, 35].

SLANGEN, JOHANNUS HUBERTUS (1955), ed. Gottsched (1758) [q.v.].

SOCIN, ADOLF (1888), *Schriftsprache und Dialekte im Deutschen nach Zeugnissen alter und neuer Zeit* (Gebrüder Henninger: Heilbronn, 1888).

SONDEREGGER, STEFAN (1961), 'Das Althochdeutsch der Vorakte der älteren St. Galler Urkunden', *ZMF* 28 (1961), 251–86.

—— (1965*a*), 'Die ältesten Schichten einer germanischen Rechtssprache. Ein Beitrag zur Quellensystematik', in *Festschrift Karl Siegfried Bader* (Verlag Schulthess & Co. AG: Zurich, and Böhlau-Verlag: Cologne and Graz, 1965), 419–38.

—— (1965*b*), 'Frühe Übersetzungsschichten im Althochdeutschen', in W. Kohlschmidt and P. Zinsli (edd.), *Philologia Deutsch. Festschrift zum 70. Geburtstag von Walther Henzen* (Francke Verlag: Berne, 1965), 101–14.

—— (1971), 'Reflexe gesprochener Sprache in der althochdeutschen Literatur', *FMSt* 5 (1971), 176–92.

—— (1973), 'Althochdeutsch', in *LGL* (1980), 569–76.

—— (1974), *Althochdeutsche Sprache und Literatur. Eine Einführung in das älteste Deutsch* (Sammlung Göschen, 8005; de Gruyter: Berlin and New York, 1974).

—— (1979), *Grundzüge deutscher Sprachgeschichte. Diachronie des Sprachsystems,* i. *Einführung — Genealogie — Konstanten* (de Gruyter: Berlin and New York, 1979).

SONNENFELS, J. VON (1768), *Briefe über die wienerische Schaubühne aus dem Französischen übersetzt* (Kurtzböck, auf dem Hofe: Vienna, 1768; repr. C. Konegen: Vienna, 1884) [= Wiener Neudrucke, 7].

SPENGLER, WALTER E. (1969), *Johann Fischart gen. Mentzer. Studie zur Sprache und Literatur des ausgehenden 16. Jahrhunderts* (Kümmerle: Göppingen, 1969) [= GAG 10].

SPERBER, HANS (1923), *Einführung in die Bedeutungslehre* (Kurt Schroeder Verlag: Bonn and Leipzig, 1923).

—— (1929), 'Die Sprache der Barockzeit', *Zeitschrift für Deutschkunde,* 43 (1929), 670–84.

—— and FLEISCHHAUER, WOLFGANG (1963), *Geschichte der deutschen Sprache,* 4th edn. (Sammlung Göschen, 915; de Gruyter: Berlin and New York, 1963).

SPIRIDONOVA, L. F. (1963), 'Adelung i grammaticeskie i ortograficeskie normy nemeckogo jazyka', *Vestnik Moskovskogo Universiteta,* Serija 7. *Filologija,* 18/2 (1963), 40–50.

STAMMLER, WOLFGANG (1931), 'Sprachliche Beobachtungen an der Luther-Bibel des 17. Jahrhunderts', *Zeitschrift für Kirchengeschichte,* 50 (1931), 378–92; cited from W. Stammler, *Kleine Schriften zur Sprachgeschichte* (Erich Schmidt Verlag: Berlin, Bielefeld, and Munich, 1954), 36–47.

—— (1953), 'Deutsche Scholastik', *ZfdPh* (1953), 2–13.

STARCK, TAYLOR, and WELLS, J. C. (1972–), *Althochdeutsches Glossen-wörterbuch* (Carl Winter: Heidelberg, 1972–).

STECKEL, KONRAD (1359), trans. Odorico de Pordenone, *Travels to China* [into 'slechtew, vngereimtew vnd vngeziertew dewsch']; ed. Gilbert Stras-mann, *Konrad Steckels deutsche Übertragung der Reise nach China des Odorico de Pordenone* (Erich Schmidt Verlag: Berlin, 1968) [= Texte des späten Mittelalters und der frühen Neuzeit, 20].

STEINBACH, CHRISTOPH ERNST (1734), *Vollständiges Deutsches Wörterbuch* (*Vel Lexicon Germanico-Latinum cum Praefationibus et Autoris et Johannis Ulrici König S. R. M. Polon et Elect. Sax. Consiliarii Aulici*), two vols. (Breslau, 1734; repr. Olms: Hildesheim and New York, 1973) [with an introduction by Walther Schröter].

STEINHAUSEN, GEORG (1893) 'Die deutschen Frauen im siebzehnten Jahr-hundert', in *Kulturstudien* (Verlagsbuchhandlung, Hermann Heyfelder: Berlin, 1893), 66–83.

—— (1895), ed. Paumgartner (1582–98) [q.v.].

STEINHÖWEL, HEINRICH (1477), *Äsop* [trans.]; ed. H. Österley, *Steinhöwels Äsop* (Tübingen, 1873) [= BLVS 117].

STEINMEYER, ELIAS VON (1916), *Die kleineren althochdeutschen Sprach-denkmäler* (Weidmann: Berlin, 1916; repr. Berlin and Zurich, 1963, 1971).

—— and SIEVERS, EDUARD (1879–1922), *Die althochdeutschen Glossen*, five vols. (Weidmann: Berlin, 1879–1922; repr. 1969).

STENTON, Sir FRANK M. (1971), *Anglo-Saxon England*, 3rd edn. (Clarendon Press: Oxford, 1971).

STERN, H. H. (1960), 'The Language of the German Serviceman of World War II', *GLL* 13 (1960), 282–97.

STERNBERGER, DOLF, STORZ, GERHARD, and SÜSKIND, WILHELM EMANUEL (1945), *Aus dem Wörterbuch des Unmenschen* (1945; 2nd edn. [dtv 48], Deutscher Taschenbuch Verlag: Munich, 1957).

STEUERNAGEL, O. (1926), *Die Einwirkungen des Deutschen Sprachvereins auf die deutsche Sprache* (Wissenschaftliche Beihefte zur *Zeitschrift des Allgemeinen Deutschen Sprachvereins*, 41: Verlag Moritz Diesterweg: Frankfurt-on-Main, 1926).

STIELER, KASPAR (1691), *Der Teutschen Sprache Stammbaum und Fortwachs Oder Teutscher Sprachschatz* (*Worinnen alle und iede teutsche Wurzeln oder Stammwörter/ so viel deren annoch bekannt und ietzo im Gebrauch seyn/ nebst ihrer Ankunft/ abgeleiteten/ duppelungen/ und vornehmsten Redarten/ mit guter lateinischen Tolmetschung und kunstgegründeten Anmerkungen befindlich . . . gesamlet von dem Spaten*, three vols. (in Verle-gung Johann Hofmanns: Nuremberg, 1691; repr with an introduction and bibliography by G. Ising, Olms: Hildesheim, 1968–9).

STIVEN, AGNES BAIN (1936), *Englands Einfluß auf den deutschen Wortschatz* (Bernhard Sporn Verlag: Zeulenroda, 1936).

STOLL, CHRISTOPH (1973), *Sprachgesellschaften im Deutschland des 17. Jahr-hunderts* (List: Munich, 1973) [= LTW 1463].

STOLT, BIRGIT (1964), *Die Sprachmischung in Luthers Tischreden — Studien zum Problem der Zweisprachigkeit* (Uppsala, 1964) [= Acta Universitatis Stockholmiensis; Stockholmer Germanistische Forschungen, 4].

STOPP, HUGO (1974), 'Veränderungen im System der Substantivflexion vom Althochdeutschen bis zum Neuhochdeutschen', in *Studien zur deutschen Literatur und Sprache des Mittelalters. Festschrift für Hugo Moser zum 65. Geburtstag*, edd. Werner Besch *et al.* (E. Schmidt: Berlin, 1974), 324–44.

—— (1976), *Schreibsprachwandel. Zur großräumigen Untersuchung frühneuhochdeutscher Schriftlichkeit* (Ernst Vögel: Munich, 1976) [= Schriften der Philosophischen Fachbereiche der Universität Augsburg, 6].

—— (1978), 'Verbreitung und Zentren des Buchdrucks auf hochdeutschem Sprachgebiet im 16. und 17. Jahrhundert', *Sprachwissenschaft*, 3 (1978), 237–63.

—— and MOSER, HUGO (1967), 'Flexionsklassen der mittelhochdeutschen Substantive in synchronischer Sicht', *ZfdPh* 86 (1967), 70–101.

STRANG, BARBARA M. H. (1970), *A History of English* (Methuen: London, 1970).

STRASMANN, GILBERT (1968), ed. Steckel (1359) [q.v.].

STRASSNER, ERICH (1968), *Schwank* (Sammlung Metzler, M 77; Metzler: Stuttgart, 1968).

STRAUSS, BRUNO (1912), *Der Übersetzer Nicolaus von Wyle* (Mayer and Müller: Berlin, 1912) [= Palaestra, 118].

STRONG, H. A., and MEYER, KUNO (1886), *Outlines of a History of the German Language* (Swan Sonnenschein, Le Bas & Lowrey: London, 1886).

SÜNDERMANN, HELMUT (1973), *Tagesparolen: Deutsche Presseweisungen 1939–45. Hitlers Propaganda und Kriegsführung*, ed. G. Sudholt (Druffel: Leoni am Starnberger See, 1973).

SUOLAHTI, HUGO (1929), 'Der französische Einfluß auf die deutsche Sprache im 13. Jahrhundert', *Mémoires de la Société Néo-philologique de Helsingfors*, 8 (1929), 1–310.

SUTER, JOHANN KASPAR (1664), *Neu auffgerichtete Schreib-Kunst . . .* (Schaffhausen, 1664).

SÜTTERLIN, ADOLF (*c*.1910), ed. Hebel (1803) [q.v.].

SÜTTERLIN, LUDWIG (1897–9), *Die deutsche Sprache der Gegenwart* (R. Voigtländer: Leipzig, 1897–9; 2nd edn. 1907; 5th edn. 1923).

SZULC, ALEKSANDER (1974), *Diachronische Phonologie und Morphologie des Althochdeutschen* (Państwowe Wydawnictwo Naukowe: Warsaw, 1974).

SZYROCKI, MARIAN (1968), *Die deutsche Literatur des Barock* (Rowohlt: Hamburg, 1968).

TAEGER, BURKHARD (1979), 'Das Straubinger "Heliand"-Fragment. Philologische Untersuchungen', *PBB* (T), 101 (1979), 181–228.

Tatian (*c*.830) [OHG trans. of Tatian's Gospel harmony]; ed. Eduard Sievers, *Tatian. Lateinisch und altdeutsch mit ausführlichem Glossar* (1872; 2nd edn. 1892; repr. F. Schöningh: Paderborn, 1962).

TAYLOR, ALAN J. P. (1954), *The Course of German History. A Survey of the Development of Germany since 1815* (1945; 5th edn., Hamish Hamilton: London, 1954).

TELLER, WILHELM ABRAHAM (1794–5), *Vollständige Darstellung und Beurtheilung der deutschen Sprache in Luthers Bibelübersetzung*, two parts (Mylius: Berlin, 1794–5).

TEUCHERT, HERMANN (1961), 'Missingsch. Eine sprachliche Untersuchung', *PBB* (H) 82 [Sonderband] (1961), 245–61.

THIELE, E., and BRENNER, O., edd. Luther (1528) [q.v.].

THIÉRIOT, ALBERT (1878), ed. Voltaire (1750–3) [q.v.].

THOMASIN VON ZERCLAERE (1216), *Der Wälsche Gast*; ed. H. Rückert (Basse: Leipzig and Quedlinburg, 1852; repr. de Gruyter, 1965).

THOMASIUS, CHRISTIAN (1687/1701), *Christian Thomas eröffnet Der Studirenden Jugend zu Leipzig in einem* Discours *Welcher Gestalt man denen Frantzosen in gemeinem Leben und Wandel nachahmen solle? ein COLLEGIUM über des GRATIANS Grund-Reguln/ Vernünftig/ klug und artig zu leben* (Moritz Georg Weidemann: [Leipzig, 1687]); ed. August Sauer (based on edns. of 1687 and 1701) (Göschen: Stuttgart, 1894) [= Deutsche Litteraturdenkmale des 18. und 19. Jahrhunderts, NF 1].

TISCH, J. HERMANN (1971), *Fifteenth Century German Courts and Renaissance Literature* (University of Tasmania: Hobart, 1971).

TONNELAT, ERNST (1962), *Histoire de la langue allemande*, 6th edn. (Armand Colin: Paris, 1962).

TÖTEBERG, MICHAEL (1978), *Fritz Reuter in Selbstzeugnissen und Bilddokumenten* (Rowohlt: Reinbek bei Hamburg, 1978) [= rowohlt monographien, 271].

TRUBETSKOY, NIKOLAY SERGEJEVITSCH (1949), *Principes de phonologie*, trans. J. Cantinean (Klincksieck: Paris 1949) [originally published as *Grundzüge der Phonologie* (Prague, 1939; repr. Kraus, 1969)].

TSCHARNER, HORST VON (1935), ed. *Marco Polo* (14th cent.) [q.v.].

TSCHIRCH, FRITZ (1955), *1200 Jahre deutsche Sprache. Die Entfaltung der deutschen Sprachgestalt in ausgewählten Stücken der Bibelübersetzung vom Ausgang des 8. Jahrhunderts bis in die Gegenwart* (de Gruyter: Berlin, 1955).

—— (1966–9, 1971–5), *Geschichte der deutschen Sprache*, two vols. (1966, 1969; 2nd edn., Erich Schmidt Verlag: Berlin, 1971, 1975).

TURNER, GEORGE W. (1973), *Stylistics* (Penguin: London, 1973).

TWADDELL, W. FREEMAN (1938), 'A note on Old High German Umlaut', *Monatshefte für den deutschen Unterricht*, 30 (1938), 177–81; repr. in Martin Joos (ed.), *Readings in Linguistics*, i (University of Chicago Press: Chicago and London, 1957; 4th edn. 1966; repr. 1971).

TWAIN, MARK [Samuel L. Clemens] (1880), 'The Awful German Language', in *A Tramp Abroad* (1880; repr. Chatto & Windus: London, 1909), 538–53.

ULLMANN, STEPHEN (1962), *Semantics. An Introduction to the Science of Meaning* (Blackwell: Oxford, 1962; repr. 1972).

UNGEHEUER, GEROLD (1969), 'Duden, Siebs und WDA: drei Wörterbücher der deutschen Hochlautung', in U. Engel, P. Grebe, and H. Rupp (edd.), *Festschrift für Hugo Moser* (Schwann: Düsseldorf, 1969), 202–17.

VALENTIN, PAUL (1969), *Phonologie de l'allemand ancien. Les systèmes vocaliques* (Klincksieck: Paris, 1969).

VAN COETSEM, FRANS (1964), *Das System der starken Verba und die Periodisierung im älteren Germanischen*, 2nd edn. (Amsterdam, 1964) [= Mededelingen der koninklijke nederlandse akademie van wetenschapen, afd. Letterkunde, NF 19/2].

—— and KUFNER, HERBERT L. (1972), edd. *Toward a Grammar of Proto-Germanic* (Niemeyer: Tübingen, 1972).

VAN HELTEN, WILLEM LODEWIJK (1900), 'Zu den malbergischen Glossen', *PBB* 25 (1900), 225–542.

VAN INGEN, FERDINAND (1970), *Philipp von Zesen* (Sammlung Metzler, M 96; Metzler: Stuttgart, 1970).

VAN RAAD, A. A., and VOORWINDEN, N. TH. J. (1973), *Die historische Entwicklung des Deutschen*, i (Stam/Robijns: Culemborg and Cologne, 1973).

VENNEMANN, THEO (1972a), 'Sound Change and markedness theory: on the history of the German consonant system', in R. P. Stockwell and R. K. S. Macaulay (edd.), *Linguistic Change and Generative Theory* (Indiana University Press: Bloomington, 1972), 230–74 [= UCLA Conference on Historical Linguistics in the Perspective of Transformational Theory, 1969].

—— (1972b), 'Phonetic Detail in Assimilation: Problems in Germanic Phonology', *Language*, 48 (1972), 863–92.

—— (1977), 'Beiträge der neueren Linguistik zur Sprachgeschichtsschreibung', in Hugo Moser *et al.* (edd.), *Sprachwandel und Sprachgeschichtsschreibung. Jahrbuch 1976 des Instituts für deutsche Sprache* (Schwann: Düsseldorf, 1977), 24–42 [= Sprache der Gegenwart, 51].

—— and WAGENER, HANS (1970), *Die Anredeformen in den Dramen des Andreas Gryphius* (Fink: Munich, 1970).

Verfasserlexikon (1978–): *Die deutsche Literatur des Mittelalters, Verfasserlexikon*, five vols. (de Gruyter: Berlin and Leipzig, 1933–55; rev. edn. by Kurt Ruh *et al.*, de Gruyter: Berlin and New York, 1978–).

Verhandlungen der zur Herstellung größerer Einigung in der deutschen Rechtschreibung berufenen Konferenz, Berlin, den 4. bis 15. Januar 1876, 2nd edn. (Buchhandlung des Waisenhauses: Halle, 1876) [contains Rudolf von Raumer, *Regeln und Wörterverzeichnis für die deutsche Orthographie*, the basis for discussion].

VESPER, WILHELM (1980), *Deutsche Schulgrammatik im 19. Jahrhundert. Zur Begründung einer historisch-kritischen Sprachdidaktik* (Niemeyer: Tübingen, 1980).

VETTER, THEODOR (1892), ed. Bodmer, 'Persönliche Anekdoten' [q.v.].

Vnartig Teutscher Sprachverderber, Der [anon.] (*sine loco*, 1643); repr. (1) Reinhold Bechstein (ed.), *Der Unartig Teutscher Sprachverderber*, in *Deutsches Museum für Geschichte, Literatur, Kunst und Altertumsforschung*, NF 1 (1862), 295–320; (2) Hermann Riegel (ed.), *Der Vnartig Teutscher Sprachverderber*, in *ZADS*, Wissenschaftliche Beihefte, 1/1 (1891–3), 26–44.

VOETZ, LOTHAR (1977), *Komposita auf -man im Althochdeutschen, Altsächsischen und Altniederfränkischen* (Carl Winter: Heidelberg, 1977).

VOLTAIRE, FRANÇOIS-MARIE AROUET (1750–3), Letters, in Albert Thiériot (ed.), *Voltaire en Prusse. Lettres extraites de sa corréspondence (juillet 1750 à mars 1753)* (Sandoz, Fischbacher, Desrogis: Paris, Neuchatel, and Geneva, 1878).

VOLZ, HANS (1954), *Hundert Jahre Wittenberger Bibeldruck 1522-1626* (Häntzschel: Göttingen, 1954).

—— (1962), 'Aus der Druckpraxis der Nachdrucke der Lutherbibel', *Gutenberg Jahrbuch* (1962), 234-50.

—— (1974), ed. Luther (1545) [Q.V.].

VOSS, JOHANN HEINRICH (1804), 'Grammatische Gespräche von Klopstock. Eingeschlossen eine Urteil über Adelungs Wörterbuch', *Jenaische Allgemeine Literatur-Zeitung*, 24 (28 January 1804), cols. 185-208 and 305-43.

VOYLES, JOSEPH B. (1974), *West Germanic Inflection, Derivation and Compounding* (Mouton: The Hague and Paris, 1974).

—— (1976), *The Phonology of Old High German* (Steiner: Wiesbaden, 1976) [= *ZDL* Beihefte, NF 18].

WAAS, EMIL (1967), ed. *Kuckucksuhr mit Wachtel. Reklame der Jahrhundertwende* (dtv 448; Deutscher Taschenbuch Verlag: Munich, 1967).

WAGNER, KURT (1974), 'Das 19. Jahrhundert', in Maurer and Rupp (1974), ii. 493-528.

WAHL, JOHANN SAMUEL (1715), *Kurtze doch gründliche Einleitung zu der rechten, reinen und galanten Teutschen Poesie* (Chemnitz, 1715) [1st edn. (Jena, 1709) entitled *Poetischer Wegweiser*].

WALLACE-HADRILL, JOHN MICHAEL (1962), *The Long-haired Kings and other Studies in Frankish History* (Methuen: London, 1962).

WALSHE, MAURICE O'CONNOR (1951), ed. Johannes von Tepl (*c.*1400) [q.v.].

—— (1962), *Medieval German Literature: A Survey* (Routledge & Kegan Paul: London, 1962).

—— (1974), *A Middle High German Reader. With Grammar, Notes and Glossary* (Clarendon Press: Oxford, 1974).

WALTHER, CHRISTOPH (1563), *Bericht von vnterscheid der Deudschen Biblien vnd anderer Büchern der Ehrnwirdigen vnd seligen Herrn Doct. Martini Lutheri/ so zu Wittemberg gedruckt/ vnd an andern enden nachgedruckt werden* (Lufft: Wittenberg, 1563).

—— (1571), *Antwort Auff Sigmund Feyerabends vnd seiner Mitgesellschafft falsches angeben vnd Lügen . . .* (Lufft: Wittenberg, 1571).

WALTHER VON DER VOGELWEIDE (12th-13th cent.); ed. Friedrich Maurer, *Die Lieder Walthers von der Vogelweide*, i. *Die religiösen und politischen Lieder*, 2nd edn. (Niemeyer: Tübingen, 1960) [= ATB 43].

WATERMAN, JOHN T. (1966, 1976), *A History of the German Language* (1966; 2nd edn., University of Washington Press: Seattle and London, 1976).

WATKINS, CALVERT (1975), 'Language and Its History', in Einar Haugen and Morton Bloomfield (edd.), *Language as a Human Problem* (Lutterworth Press: Guildford and London, 1975), 85-97.

WEHRLI, MAX (1976), 'Latein und Deutsch in der Barockliteratur', in *Akten des V. Internationalen Germanisten-Kongresses, Cambridge, 1975* (Frankfurt-on-Main and Munich, 1976), i. 139-49.

WEIDENHILLER, P. EGINO (1965), *Untersuchungen zur deutschsprachigen katechetischen Literatur des späten Mittelalters* (C. H. Beck: Munich, 1965) [= Münchener Texte und Untersuchungen zur deutschen Literatur des Mittelalters, 10].

WEIFERT, L. M. (1964-5), ed. *Deutsche Mundarten*, three parts (J. F. Lehmanns Verlag: Munich, 1964-5) [with two gramophone records of the 'Wenker Sätze' in the major dialects].

WEINHOLD, KARL (1852), Über deutsche Rechtschreibung', in *Zeitschrift für die österreichischen Gymnasien* (Vienna, 1852).

—— (1881/1965) *Kleine mittelhochdeutsche Grammatik*, 14th edn., rev. Gustav Ehrismann and Hugo Moser (Braumüller: Vienna and Stuttgart, 1965).

—— (1883), *Mittelhochdeutsche Grammatik* (F. Schöningh: Paderborn, 1883; 2nd edn., repr. 1967).

WEINREICH, URIEL (1953), *Languages in Contact. Findings and Problems* (New York, 1953; 6th repr. Mouton: The Hague, 1968).

—— LABOV, WILLIAM, and HERZOG, MARVIN I. (1968), 'Empirical foundations for a theory of language change', in Lehmann and Malkiel (1968), 95-188.

WEINRICH, HARALD (1964), *Tempus: besprochene und erzählte Welt* (Kohlhammer Verlag: Stuttgart, 1964).

WEISE, CHRISTIAN (1672), *Die drei ärgsten Erznarren* . . . (Durch Catherinum Civilem: *sine loco*, 1672); ed. Wilhelm Braune (Niemeyer: Halle a/S., 1878) [= NDL 12].

—— (1676), *Schediasma curiosum de Lectione Novellarum* . . . *et Nucleo Novellarum Historico* . . . ('Sumptibus Christophori Enoch Buchta': Weissenfels, 1676) [trans. Christian Juncker, as *Curieuse Gedanken von den Nouvellen oder Zeitungen* . . . (1732)].

—— (1693), *Curiöse Gedancken von Deutschen Versen* (Leipzig, 1693).

WEISGERBER, LEO (1952), 'Die Spuren der irischen Mission in der Entwicklung der deutschen Sprache', *Rheinische Vierteljahrsblätter*, 17 (1952), 8-41.

WEITHASE, IRMGARD (1961), *Zur Geschichte der gesprochenen deutschen Sprache*, two vols. (Niemeyer: Tübingen, 1961).

WELLMANN, HANS (1972), 'Sprachgeschichtsschreibung und historische Grammatik (1968-1970)', *WW* 22 (1972), 198-220.

WELLS, CHRISTOPHER JON (1972), 'An Orthographical Approach to Early Frankish Personal Names', *TPS* (1972), 101-64.

WENKER, GEORG (1877), *Das rheinische Platt. Mit einer autographischen Karte. Den Lehrern des Rheinlandes gewidmet* (Schulte: Düsseldorf, 1877); repr. in *Deutsche Dialektgeographie*, viii (1915).

WENSKUS, REINHARD (1961), *Stammesbildung und Verfassung. Das Werden der frühmittelalterlichen gentes* (Böhlau: Cologne and Graz, 1961).

WENTZLAFF-EGGEBERT, FRIEDRICH-WILHELM, and ERIKA (1971), *Deutsche Literatur im späten Mittelalter 1250-1450*, three vols. (rde 350-8; Rowohlt: Reinbek and Hamburg, 1971).

WERBOW, STANLEY N. (1963), 'Die gemeine teutsch, Ausdruck und Begriff', *ZfdPh* 82 (1963), 44-63.

WERNER, OTMAR (1965), 'Vom Formalismus zum Strukturalismus in der historischen Morphologie', *ZfdPh* 84 (1965), 100-27.

WERNHER DER GARTENÆRE (13th cent.), *Meier Helmbrecht*; ed. Charles E. Gough (Blackwell: Oxford, 1942; repr. 1957).

WEYDT, GÜNTHER (1971), *Hans Jacob Christoffel von Grimmelshausen* (Sammlung Metzler, M 99; Metzler: Stuttgart, 1971).

WIELAND, CHRISTOPH MARTIN (1782a) [under pseud. Philomusos], 'Über die Frage: Was ist Hochteutsch? und einige damit verwandten Gegenstände. An den Herausgeber des *T.M.*', in *Der Teutsche Merkur*, 4th quarter (Weimar, 1782), 145–70; repr. in *Wielands Werke*, xxii. *Kleine Schriften, II* (*1778–1782*), ed. Wilhelm Kurrelmeyer (Akademie-Verlag: Berlin, 1954), 399–411.

—— (1782b) [under pseud. Musophilus], 'Beschluß des Versuchs über die Frage: Was ist Hochteutsch? An den Herausgeber des *T.M.*', ibid. 193–216; repr. ed. cit., 411–22.

—— (1783) [under pseud. Musophilus], 'Musophili Nachtrag zu seinem Versuche über die Frage: was ist Hochteutsch? An den Herausgeber des *T.M.*', ibid., 2nd quarter (Weimar, 1783), 307–20, with observations by the editor (i.e. Wieland), pp. 3–18, 19–30; repr. ed. cit., 423–8.

WIESINGER, PETER (1970), *Phonetisch-phonologische Untersuchungen zur Vokalentwicklung in den deutschen Dialekten*, two vols., with maps (de Gruyter: Berlin and New York, 1970) [= Studia Linguistica Germanica, 2].

—— (1973), 'Die deutschen Sprachinseln in Mitteleuropa', in *LGL* (1973), 367–77 (2nd edn., 'Deutsche Sprachinseln', *LGL* (1980), 491–500).

WILHELM, FRIEDRICH (1920), *Zur Geschichte des Schrifttums in Deutschland bis zum Ausgang des 13. Jahrhunderts*, two parts (Callwey: Munich, 1920).

—— (1932–63), *Corpus der altdeutschen Originalurkunden bis zum Jahr 1300*, five vols. (Moritz Schauenburg Verlag: Lahr, 1932–63) [i, *1200–1282* [Nos. 1–564] (1932); ii, continued by Richard Newald, *1283–1292* [Nos. 565–1657] (1943); iii, edd. H. de Boor and Dieter Haacke, *1293–1296* [Nos. 1658–2559] (1957); iv, edd. Helmut de Boor and Dieter Haacke, *1297–[Ende 13. Jahrhundert]* [Nos. 2560–3598] (1963); v, *Regesten zu den Bänden I–IV* (1963); see also Ulrich Goebel (ed.), *Wortindex zum 1. Band des Corpus der Altdeutschen Originalurkunden* (Olms: Hildesheim and New York, 1974)].

WINCKLER, LUTZ (1970), *Studie zur gesellschaftlichen Funktion faschistischer Sprache* (Suhrkamp, 417; Suhrkamp Verlag: Frankfurt-on-Main, 1970).

WINDFUHR, MANFRED (1969), ed. Hofmann von Hofmannswaldau (17th cent.) [q.v.].

Wohlgemeinte Vorschläge Zu einer Allgemeinen und Regelmäßigen Einrichtung und Verbesserung Der Teutschen Sprache In dem Ober-Sächsischen und Nieder-Sächsischen Kreise (1732) (Halberstadt, 1732).

WOLF, HERBERT (1971), 'Zur Periodisierung der deutschen Sprachgeschichte', *GRM* 52 [NF 21] (1971), 78–105.

—— (1980), *Martin Luther* (Sammlung Metzler, M 193; Metzler: Stuttgart, 1980).

—— (1984), 'Beiträge der Korrektoren zum Sprachausgleich Luthers', *Sprachwissenschaft*, 9 (1984), 108–25.

WOLF, NORBERT RICHARD (1975), *Regionale und überregionale Norm im späten Mittelalter* (Innsbruck, 1975) [= Innsbrucker Beiträge zur Kulturwissenschaft. Germanistische Reihe, 3].

—— (1981), *Althochdeutsch-Mittelhochdeutsch* (Uni-Taschenbücher, 1139;

Quelle & Meyer: Heidelberg, 1981) [= first vol. of Moser, Wellman, and Wolf].

WOLF, SIEGMUND A. (1956), *Wörterbuch des Rotwelschen* (Bibliographisches Institut: Mannheim, 1956).

WOLFF, LUDWIG (1973), 'Überlegungen zur sprachlichen Gestalt der *Eneide* Heinrichs von Veldeke', in Rainer Schönhaar (ed.), *Dialog . . . Festgabe für Josef Kunz* (Erich Schmidt Verlag: Berlin, 1973), 11–21.

WOLFRAM VON ESCHENBACH (12th–13th cent.), *Gesamtwerk*; ed. K. Lachmann (1833; 6th edn., de Gruyter: Berlin and Leipzig, 1926; repr. 1962).

WOLKE, CHRISTIAN HEINRICH (1812), *Anleitung zur deutschen Gesamtsprache oder zur Erkennung und Berichtigung einiger (zuwenigst 20) tausend Sprachfehler in der hochdeutschen Mundart; nebst dem Mittel die zahllosen — in jedem Jahre den Deutschschreibenden 10000 Jahre Arbeit oder die Unkosten von 50000 verursachenden — Schreibfehler zu vermeiden und zu ersparen* (Reclam: Leipzig, 1812).

WORSTBROCK, FRANZ JOSEPH (1976), *Deutsche Antikerezeption 1450–1550, i. Verzeichnis der deutschen Übersetzungen mit einer Bibliographie der Übersetzer* (Harald Boldt Verlag: Boppard, 1976).

—— (1978), 'Thiutisce', *PBB* (T) 100 (1978), 205–12.

Wörterbuch der deutschen Aussprache (1964), edd. Hans Krech *et al.* (VEB Bibliographisches Institut: Leipzig, 1964; repr. Hueber: Munich, 1969).

WRIGHT, JOSEPH (1907), *Historical German Grammar* (Clarendon Press: Oxford, 1907).

—— (1925), *Old English Grammar* (Clarendon Press: Oxford, 1925).

WULF, J. (1963), *Aus dem Lexikon der Mörder. 'Sonderbehandlung' und verwandte Worte in nationalsozialistischen Dokumenten* (S. Mohn: Gütersloh, 1963).

—— (1963–6), *Literatur und Dichtung im Dritten Reich* (rororo, 809–11; Sigbert Mohn: Gütersloh, and Rowohlt: Hamburg, 1963–6).

—— (1964–6), *Presse und Funk im Dritten Reich* (rororo, 185–17; Rowohlt: Hamburg, 1964–6).

WUNDERLICH, HERMANN (1892), *Der deutsche Satzbau* (Cottas Nachfolger: Stuttgart, 1892; 3rd edn., rev. H. Reis, Stuttgart, 1924).

—— (1894), *Unsere Umgangsprache in der Eigenart ihrer Satzfügung* (Emil Felber: Weimar and Berlin, 1894).

WURZEL, WOLFGANG ULRICH (1979), *Konrad Duden* (VEB Bibliographisches Institut: Leipzig, 1979).

WUSTMANN, GUSTAV (1890), *Allerhand Sprachdummheiten. Kleine Grammatik des Zweifelhaften, des Falschen und des Häßlichen* (Leipzig, 1890; 10th edn., de Gruyter: Leipzig, 1935).

WYLE, NICLAS VON (15th cent.), *Translationen*; ed. Adalbert Keller (Stuttgart, 1861; repr. Hildesheim, 1967) [= BLVS 57].

ZEDLER, JOHANN HEINRICH (1732–50), *Grosses Vollständiges UNIVERSAL-LEXICON Aller Wissenschafften und Künste . . .*, sixty-four vols. (Halle a/S. and Leipzig, 1732–50), with four supplements (1754).

Zeitschrift des Allgemeinen Deutschen Sprachvereins (1885–) [= ZADS; renamed *Muttersprache*].

Zeitschrift für Orthographie (1880–3), originally ed. Wilhelm Vietor (Wiesbaden, 1880–3).

ZEMAN, ZBYNÉK A. B. (1964), *Nazi Propaganda* (Clarendon Press: Oxford, 1964; repr. 1973).

ZENTNER, WILHELM (1939), ed. Hebel (18th–19th cent.) [q.v.].

ZESEN, PHILIPP VON (1645), *Die Adriatische Rosemund* (Amsterdam, 1645); ed. Max Hermann Jellinek, *Ritterholds von Blauen Adriatische Rosemund* (Niemeyer: Halle a/S., 1899) [= NDL 160–3].

INDEX OF NAMES

THIS lists all personal names mentioned in the text and in the endnotes, but not those given in the Select Bibliographies or in the General Bibliography.

GENERAL INDEX

T H I S index lists the main topics, geographical and place-names, and keywords. References to German and to English are too numerous to make it practical to include them.

morphs:
　allomorphs 147
　bound 146: quotation of: ch. IV n. 7;
　　rarely borrowed 273–4
　discontinuous 146–7
　free 146
　homonymous 149–50, 156, 168–9;
　　adverbial/prepositional 232; MHG
　　daz and functions 255
　inflexional 150–1, 155, 251
　lexical 147, 150–1, 155
　non-segmentable 148
　portmanteau 146–7
　segmentable 148: aspectual 238
　stem 150–1
　zero 147, 149; ch. IV n. 12
morph types 145–9
Moscherosch:
　A la Mode Kehraus 282; ch. VII n. 47
　Fruchtbringende Gesellschaft and 286
　Soldatenleben: ch. VII nn. 47, 80
Moselle 55
Moselle Frankish 109, 356, 427–8
movements, literary 389
Mundart
　ambiguity of in 18th cent. 314; ch. VIII
　　nn. 23, 32
　koloniale 136
　Mundartdichtung vs. *Volkspoesie*:
　　ch. IX n. 51
　vs. *Dialekt* (Groth and) ch. VIII n. 11
Munich 346, 352, 370
Murbach 431
Murbach Hymns 58, 62
Muret–Sanders (dictionary) 365, 382
Muspilli 51, 432; ch. VI n. 57
mutation 433; ch. I n. 16
　see also umlaut
Muttersprache 400
mysticism 60, 108, 130–3

names:
　hypocoristic 426
　officially fixed: ch. III n. 19
　17th-cent. residences and 267
　structural shift in: ch. III n. 17
naming 393
Nantes, Edict of 268
Napoleonic occupation 290
Napoleonic Wars 345, 396
nasals:
　labial (*Mampflaut*) 331
　palatal in loan-words 273

nation, German language as defining
　component of 396
nationalism 6, 290, 400–1
　and German dialectology 419–20
　and German linguistic history 419–20
　and language 397
National Socialism 28, 343, 348, 389–90,
　393, 400, 406
　Hitler-Gruß: ch. X n. 74
　institutions, names of 408–9
　language of 407–19: abbreviation and
　　408; affective terminology 408;
　　archaism 408, 417 (Germanicizing
　　412; pseudo-mystical/mythological
　　414, 416–17); biological/medical
　　terms 403, 414, 416–17; colloquial
　　and 413; dynamic/martial/heroici-
　　zing terms 414–15; euphemism
　　409, 418; foreign expressions
　　414, 418; pathological imagery
　　409; pronunciation and 355; pur-
　　ism 418; ch. X nn. 3, 32 (ADS and:
　　ch. X n. 3); religious terms 414–16;
　　sporting imagery 414; studies on
　　407–9; technological vocabulary
　　414–15
　persistent effects of: ch. X n. 80
　political style 396, 409–10, 412–14, 418
　propaganda, totalitarian 409–12
　racialism 414–18
　roman type and: ch. IX n. 17
　swastika emblem: ch. X n. 74
national unification 340
Naturalism 347, 362–3, 370–1
　speech and: ch. IX nn. 66, 80
　trivial writers and 371
needs, communicative 420
negation:
　double 205, 261
　multiple: ch. VI n. 108
　mysticism and: 132–3
　particles and 141, 185
Neogrammarians (*Junggrammatiker*) 6,
　8, 10, 71–5, 82, 87, 176
neologism 145, 281, 293, 297, 299, 315,
　327–8, 339, 382, 394, 398
　and paradigms 145
　and verbs 168
Netherlandish 138, 160, 219, 273, 294
　dialects 20, 42
　see also Dutch
Netherlands 99, 128, 222, 292, 356
Neuhochdeutsch 22